BURLINGTON WEST

AMERICAN PROGRESS.

From *Crofutt's New Overland Tourist and Pacific Coast Guide*, 1883.

BURLINGTON WEST
*A Colonization History of
The Burlington Railroad*

BY

RICHARD C. OVERTON

NEW YORK / RUSSELL & RUSSELL

This edition dedicated to the memory of

Ralph Budd

ACKNOWLEDGEMENTS

WITHOUT INVALUABLE ASSISTANCE from many sides this book could never have been written. The specific subject treated was suggested during the winter of 1934–35 by Professors Merk and Cunningham of Harvard. In 1936, the railroad company deposited all its land department records in the Baker Library of the Harvard Graduate School of Business Administration, where they were made available to the writer. At that library, Dr. Arthur H. Cole and his assistants, Mrs. Grace P. Bowser and Mr. Donald T. Clark, as well as many members of the staff, provided at all times every accommodation, while the Jones Library at Amherst, Massachusetts, offered its study facilities for two summers. In 1938–39, Harvard University granted the writer a year's fellowship which made it possible to complete the first draft of this work. During the last revision, the entire book was immeasurably enriched by letters of Charles E. Perkins which were made accessible through the kindness of his daughter, Mrs. Edward Cunningham of Boston.

Mr. Charles I. Sturgis of Chicago, Dr. Paul W. Gates of Cornell University, Dr. Arthur H. Cole, and Professor William J. Cunningham of the Harvard Business School, the late Dr. Henry Greenleaf Pearson, biographer of John Murray Forbes, Dr. James B. Hedges of Brown University, Mr. B. E. Young of Washington, Mr. Charles E. Fisher, president of the Railway and Locomotive Historical Society, Mrs. Edward Cunningham of Boston, Mr. Charles E. Perkins, Jr., of Santa Barbara, and several officials of the railroad company read all or part of the manuscript in its various stages; their suggestions were of the greatest assistance. The statistical charts in Chapters XIII–XV were prepared with the indispensable collaboration of Miss Ruth Crandall, research assistant over a number of years to Professors Cole and Burbank of Harvard. Graphs based on these statistics, together with many of the illustrations, were drawn by or under the supervision of Mr. L. F. Hanke of Chicago. In preparing the manuscript for the press, Miss Thelma Book and Mr. David W. Sargent, Jr., of Chicago labored industriously and efficiently. At Cambridge, the entire staff of the Harvard University Press coöperated in every way possible.

Throughout the last seven years, I have been under constant obligation to Dr. Frederick Merk of the History Department of Harvard University, whose friendly interest and scholarly counsel have provided an unfailing source of guidance and inspiration. Finally, to my wife, who has helped with every phase of producing this book, I owe the greatest debt of all.

R. C. O.

CONTENTS

APPENDICES

ILLUSTRATIONS

MAPS

GENERAL

Density of Population maps are from the United States *Census.* Railway Network maps were specially prepared for this book under the direction of L. F. Hanke.

RELATING TO THE BURLINGTON SYSTEM

Prepared by E. E. Ferris, 1940; Decorative border by L. F. Hanke, 1941 (Engineering Dept. C. B. & Q. R. R.).

Prepared by E. E. Ferris for A. W. Newton, 1938, for use in his manuscript history of the C. B. & Q. in Illinois.

Prepared by L. F. Hanke, 1940.

Prepared by L. F. Hanke, 1938.

From the original prepared by W. T. Steiger in Washington, 1861; now in the B. & M. Land Department Papers, Baker Library, Harvard Business School.

From a woodcut in *The Hannibal and St. Joseph Railroad Company Have Received . . . over 600,000 Acres. . . .* (Hannibal, 1859).

Showing the threat to the Burlington from the Keokuk-Des Moines line. From the B. & M. (Iowa) *Annual Report* for 1863.

GRAPHS

[*Statistics underlying these graphs are in the tables listed on page xi under Appendix F.*]

NOTE ON DOCUMENTATION

For the sake of simplicity, certain sources have been abbreviated in the footnotes as follows:

AB — Aurora Branch Railroad.

BMI — Burlington and Missouri River Railroad (the Iowa company).

BMN — Burlington and Missouri River Railroad in Nebraska.

BMR — Burlington and Missouri River Railroads. (This was not a corporate title, but is used in this work to refer to both the Iowa and Nebraska companies.)

Cap — Newspapers filed in the State Capitol at Lincoln, Nebraska. (For a description of this material, see bibliography, p. 547.)

CBP — Colonization Bureau papers.

CBQ — Chicago, Burlington & Quincy Railroad Company.

CNB — Notebooks belonging to Mrs. Edward Cunningham, Boston. (See bibliography, pp. 541–542.)

CR — Corporate records of Chicago, Burlington & Quincy R. R. Co. (See bibliography, p. 541.)

DRB — Duplicate Record Book (of company indicated).

ELA — Eastern Land Association.

HBS — Harvard Business School.

HSJ — Hannibal and St. Joseph Railroad.

HSR — H. S. Russell (Land Associates).

ILA — Iowa Land Association.

LDP — Land Department Papers of the C. B. & Q. and the B. & M. R. Railroads, Boston. (See bibliography, p. 541.)

LL — Lincoln Land Company.

MC — Michigan Central Railroad Company.

n.d. — No date for the item cited.

NL — Nebraska Land Company.

n.p. — No page number for the item cited.

NSB — Nebraska Scrap Books in the Nebraska State Historical Society Library in Lincoln, Nebraska. (See bibliography, p. 547.)

ORB — Original Record Book (of company indicated).

SPL — South Platte Land Company.

USDI — Records in the United States Department of the Interior, Washington. (See bibliography, p. 546, Under General Land Office.)

USNA — Records in the National Archives of the United States, Washington. (See bibliography, p. 546.)

WL — Widener Library, Harvard University.

BURLINGTON WEST

INTRODUCTION

Deep in a vault of the Burlington's Chicago office are half a dozen sheets of figures bound together with a clip and dated "1905." They constitute the final report of the company's land department, and on the outside is a memorandum in pencil by W. W. Baldwin addressed to Charles E. Perkins. At different times, both men had served as land commissioners for the road.

Jan. 8, 1906

Mr. Perkins:
  This closes quite a chapter in the history of the West.
  I wish I had time to write a history of the two Burlington Land Grants, and discuss them from the standpoint of the public good, as compared with probable conditions if the lands had been subject to homestead entry and private sale.
  It is a large subject, and one on which there is much general misinformation.

W. W. B.[1]

Directly beneath is the answer:

W. W. B:
  You ought to write a history of it sure — even if only a brief one.

C. E. P.[2]

Unfortunately, neither of these men lived to see a history started, but behind them, scattered in station attics and cellars from Lake Michigan to the Platte River, they left tons of records telling of their company's land and colonization work for the half century from 1856 to 1906. Chiefly from that material, this present history is written.

To most Americans of today, the building of the transcontinental lines is a familiar historical fact; so is the story of the homesteaders and the advance of the farming frontier in the lusty days after the Civil War. But there is one essential phase of western development in this period that is little known and less understood: the part played by the railroads in creating and establishing permanent communities. During the period 1850–71, Congress granted an area more than three

---

[1] W. W. Baldwin to Charles E. Perkins, January 8, 1906 (LDP).
[2] Notation by Perkins on Baldwin to Perkins, January 8, 1906 (LDP).

times as large as New England to various railroads in the South and
West so that these companies might sell the land to actual settlers and
thus make enough money to build their lines through the relatively
undeveloped portions of the country.

Yet, up to the present time, the story of individual roads has been
fully told in but two instances: by Paul W. Gates in his book *The
Illinois Central Railroad and Its Colonization Work*,[3] and by James B.
Hedges in *Building the Canadian West; the Land and Colonization
Work of the Canadian Pacific Railway*.[4] These admirable accounts of
the earliest and of the most recent rail colonizing ventures are veritable
storehouses of social and economic history. Aside, however, from several short articles such as Hedges' brief surveys of the Northern Pacific,[5]
the story for the vast empire west of the Mississippi and south of the
Forty-Ninth parallel remains untold. This present history seeks to fill,
in part, this gap.

In 1856, a portion of the Burlington system in Iowa that had been
organized four years previously received a small grant to aid in construction of its line between the Mississippi and Missouri rivers. Eight
years later this grant was increased, and at the same time a much
larger area was offered by Congress as an inducement for extending
the main line from the Missouri River approximately 200 miles westward to a junction with the main line of the Union Pacific. Aided by
the cash and credit derived from about 2,720,000 acres thus received,
the Burlington and Missouri River Railroad built its line from Burlington, Iowa, to Kearney, Nebraska, between 1852 and 1872. To some
extent in Iowa, but to a much larger degree in Nebraska, the rails
were laid in sparsely settled, undeveloped territory; in order to subsist
and to grow, the railroad company literally had to create and nourish
an entire community of farms and towns. In the case of the Burlington, the bulk of this colonization work was carried on between 1852

[3] Paul W. Gates, *The Illinois Central Railroad and Its Colonization Work*
(Cambridge, 1934).

[4] James B. Hedges, *Building the Canadian West; the Land and Colonization
Work of the Canadian Pacific Railway* (New York, 1939).

[5] Hedges, "The Colonization Work of the Northern Pacific Railroad," *Mississippi Valley Historical Review*, vol. XIII (December, 1926), pp. 311–342; and
the same author's "Promotion of Immigration to the Pacific Northwest by the
Railroad," *Mississippi Valley Historical Review*, vol. XV (September, 1928), pp.
183–203.

and 1882. Although many policies then inaugurated are still actively pursued, this book is built around the activities of those 30 years.

The most important source of primary material for this book is the collection of land department records of the Burlington and Missouri River Railroad which is in the Baker Library of the Harvard Business School in Boston. This collection is unusually complete. The essential record books, for example, have been preserved, together with all the 32,326 individual land contracts for Iowa and Nebraska, and something more than 600,000 letters. This source has been supplemented by contemporary newspapers and letters, notably those of Charles E. Perkins, by government manuscripts and printed documents, corporate records, and secondary works. Because of the existence of such an overwhelming mass of material, this book is neither a complete nor an exhaustive account of all the Burlington's varied colonizing activities. It is rather a sampling and summary of the company's policies and an analysis of the results obtained in terms of permanent community development. For example, from 1852 to 1865 there was serious doubt whether the Burlington, even with the help of a land grant and the coöperation of the community, could complete its road across Iowa. Yet it was of prime importance to southern Iowa and a prerequisite to any development of the company lands that the line should be built. Thus the joint efforts of the railroad and the community to assure construction in that particular period have received extended attention. On the other hand, when building began in Nebraska, sufficient capital was available practically to guarantee completion of the original line to Kearney Junction; thus, but passing notice has been given to construction in that state. Similarly, considerable emphasis has been placed on the land department's activities in 1866–73, when its credit and advertising policies were first fully developed and carried into effect, while events preceding and following those years have been summarized. For statistical purposes, the decade of the 'seventies has been chosen for minute analysis not only because most of the company's lands were settled then, but also because other colonizing activities such as agricultural promotion were in full swing. Finally, certain geographical regions and particular individuals have been selected for more detailed treatment than others, either because of their relative importance or because more complete information is available about them.

Naturally, there are many subjects suggested or summarized in this book which richly deserve elaboration. For example, much more might be said of construction, motive power, operations, traffic, and finance. These matters, however, properly belong in a general history of the railroad; they are mentioned here simply to provide the necessary setting for the story of colonization. Secondly, no attempt has been made to describe systematically the colonization work of the Hannibal and St. Joseph in Missouri, even though that company was the first part of the present system to receive a grant, and its activities served as a model for the work in Iowa and Nebraska. The reason for this is that although the "St. Jo" was controlled in its early years by the same men who built the C. B. & Q., it did not become part of the Burlington until 1883; until then it was separately managed and followed an independent program rather than one designed with the entire system in mind. Furthermore, its records form an entity in themselves and are of sufficient quantity and quality to justify an independent study later on. Likewise, separate economic or sociological monographs might well be written about specific towns or counties, about one or more of the racial or religious colonies brought in by the railroad, about the Homeseekers Excursions and agricultural experiments of the twentieth century, and on many other topics. They are mentioned here simply to illustrate the central question under discussion, namely, the nature and significance of the colonization induced by the Burlington.

In the popular mind, the land-grant policy has had an unenviable reputation, to say the least. As early as 1871, it was characterized in Congress as "a swindling system by which the public lands of the government had been given away to corporations regardless of the public interest." [6] By 1878, a movement was already under way at Washington to force all land-grant roads to return to the public domain all lands that they had not actually earned by complying with the terms of their several grants. It was then pointed out that such an order would affect over two-thirds of the area originally given to the roads. Indeed, the specific grants investigated then and thereafter by the Department of the Interior revealed many cases of fraud and deceit,

---

[6] Lewis H. Haney, *A Congressional History of Railroads in the United States, 1850–1887* (Madison, 1910), vol. II, p. 21; David Maldwyn Ellis, *The Forfeiture of Railroad Land Grants* (MS, Thesis, Cornell University, Ithaca, 1939).

and the misuse of a semi-public trust. It was alleged that some railways sold their tracts to speculators at prices of five and ten cents an
acre; others neglected their construction, or built tracks that were incapable of supporting trains, and still claimed their grants.[7] Still other
roads indulged in extravagant construction,[8] or concentrated their land
holdings into huge tracts, that were unavailable to the small farmer.[9]
Finally, in 1885, Secretary of the Interior Sparks, under the direction
of President Cleveland, suspended all grants for investigation;[10] as a
result, various companies were forced to return their unearned sections
to the public domain.[11] Haney, in his *A Congressional History of
Railroads in the United States*, asserts that by the late 'eighties, " 'steals'
and 'grabs' came normally to be associated with land grants."[12] Since
1900, and despite stricter government control, the status and use of
certain railroad lands have been the subject of federal investigation.[13]
These unsavory facts have been publicized.[14]

Ever since the land-grant period itself, however, there has been
some recognition of the fact that the West's social development resulting from railroad colonization was a most significant aspect of the
land-grant policy. As early as 1872, *Poor's Manual* declared: "If we
were to compare the advantage accruing from these grants, we should
say that the government as representative of the whole nation, was
most largely benefited by them; that the farmer and pioneer came next
in order; and that the railroad companies, the direct beneficiaries, the
last. No policy ever adopted by this or any other government was
more beneficial in its results or has tended so powerfully to the development of our resources by the conversion of vast wastes to all the
uses of civilized life."[15] Whether or not this development was pre-

---

[7] Haney, *op. cit.*, pp. 25-28.

[8] Edward C. Kirkland, *History of American Economic Life* (New York,
1934), p. 391.

[9] Benjamin H. Hibbard, *A History of the Public Land Policies* (New York,
1924), p. 262.

[10] Allan Nevins, *Grover Cleveland* (New York, 1932), p. 225 *et seq.*

[11] Haney, *op. cit.*, p. 28.

[12] Haney, *op. cit.*, p. 29; cf. Frederick Merk, *Economic History of Wisconsin
during the Civil War Decade* (Madison, 1916).

[13] Bureau of Corporations, *Report on the Lumber Industry* (Washington,
1911), pp. 3-34.

[14] E.g., Kirkland, Hibbard, *op. cit.*

[15] Henry V. Poor, *Manual of the Railroads of the United States* (New York,
1871-72), p. 417.

mature is a moot point, and one that is beyond the scope of this book.[16]

Up to 1940, the railroads endeavored, individually and collectively, to point out that, at least in so far as the federal government was concerned, their grants were anything but outright gifts.[17] Only alternate sections of the public domain had been patented to the companies, and the minimum price of the remaining sections had been doubled. Furthermore, the beneficiary roads were obligated to carry mails, troops, and government property at rates fixed by Congress.[18] These rates were consistently below the prevailing commercial level. In 1940 amendments to the Interstate Commerce Act made it possible for land-grant railroads to charge the published commercial rates, providing they released all claim to portions of their grants still in their possession, with certain exceptions, the principal one being that the commercial rates shall not apply "to the transportation of military or naval property of the United States moving for military or naval and not for commercial use." [19] The railroads affected by this legislation have made the necessary release.

Clearly, final judgment concerning the disposition of railroad grants as a whole must await the careful examination of the land and colonization records of a substantial number of railroad companies. Such an examination in the case of the Burlington reveals a story that by no means conforms to the popular view of land-grant roads. Therefore, either the work of the Burlington was exceptional, or the general concept of railroad land disposal needs considerable revision. Only further research can determine which alternative is true.

[16] E.g., Kirkland, *op. cit., passim.*; Ray Harold Mattison, *Burlington Railroad Land Grant and the Tax Controversy in Boone County* (MS., Thesis, University of Nebraska, Lincoln, 1936).

[17] E.g., W. W. Baldwin, "Mail Pay on the Burlington" (Chicago, 1922?); Transportation Association of America, "A National Transportation Program" (Chicago, 1938), supplement no. 2.

[18] See below, p. 81.

[19] Transportation Act of 1940, approved September 18, 1940.

CHAPTER I

Origins of the Burlington System

I. RAILROADS AND POPULATION, 1830–1845

WHEN steam railroads first appeared in the United States, about 1830, most of the people in America lived along the Atlantic seaboard from Bangor, Maine, down to Savannah, Georgia.[1] For 200 miles west of the coastline lay a belt of well-tilled farms and busy trading and manufacturing towns, and from this region of humming activity two great tongues of secondary settlement stretched westward. The older of the two, which had been in evidence before the Revolution, extended south and west through the valley of the Shenandoah, across the western portion of North Carolina, South Carolina, and finally into Georgia. Already the extremely fertile black lands of Alabama were occupied, and beyond them was the concentration of river folk between Vicksburg and New Orleans. The second tongue of settlement, which got under way after the War of 1812, closely followed the famous Erie Canal to Buffalo, continued along the shore of Lake Erie, and then dipped southward through western Pennsylvania and Ohio, and thence along the Ohio River as far as the Wabash. One wing of this advance spread far across Kentucky and Tennessee, and on to Memphis and the Mississippi River; another wing skipped lightly across central Indiana and Illinois, along the route of the National Road, and ended in a mild concentration bounded by St. Louis and Springfield on the east and by St. Joseph and Kansas City on the west.[2]

Within this entire region both old and new, cities had sprung up, according to an almost fixed formula, where two forms of transportation met, and wherever it was necessary to transfer goods and passengers. The most obvious examples of this phenomenon were the great ocean ports, particularly those with natural harbors, where goods had long been transferred between wagon and barge on the one hand

[1] *Census* of 1850, p. 9.
[2] Frederick J. Turner, *The Frontier in American History* (New York, 1910), ch. iii. Cf. Homer C. Hockett, *Political and Social Growth of the American People* (New York, 1940), pp. 466–473, and *Census* of 1830, 1840, 1850, 1860.

and seagoing vessels on the other. Boston, New York, Philadelphia,
Wilmington, Savannah, and New Orleans all owed their beginnings
to this type of trade. Other cities, such as Hartford, Albany, and Rich-
mond, had sprung up at the head of river navigation at the so-called
falls line, where another transfer of goods and passengers was necessary. More recently, Pittsburgh and St. Louis had been established
at the confluence of large rivers; Kansas City and Detroit were growing at the junction of trail and waterway.

Quite naturally, trade followed the lines of least resistance. The
greatest activity was along the coast where ocean transportation was
cheap and plentiful. Nevertheless, the Erie Canal, the availability of
the Great Lakes, and the rapidly growing canal system in Ohio and
other states were contributing to a boom in inland commerce. Travel
by highway was still painfully slow. In 1830 it was generally true that
trade moved principally by water, no matter how circuitous the route,
and that regions inaccessible to water, regardless of their other natural
advantages, lay relatively undeveloped. There were indeed many
opportunities awaiting the Iron Horse.

The financial situation was even more promising for railroads. The
decades of peace since the War of 1812 had witnessed a growth in
foreign commerce that had led to the accumulation of considerable
capital in Boston, New York, Philadelphia, and Baltimore, and bank-
ing connections had been established with Europe.[3] Furthermore, local
communities, particularly those dependent on the halting land transportation of the day, might well offer cash or pledge their credit.
West of the Alleghanies, where railroads alone could open the rich
prairies and bring in the nourishing stream of commerce, it seemed
reasonable that state aid might be obtained.

Such, very briefly, was the geographic and economic pattern that
confronted the railroad promoters of the 'thirties. With both the population and available capital concentrated in the East, it was natural
that most new projects should begin there. Their precise location,
within this section, was a matter of marginal utility guided by local
circumstances. Even in this first decade of railroading, however, the

---

[3] E. L. Bogart and C. M. Thompson, *Readings in the Economic History of
the United States* (New York, 1929), pp. 512–515; J. B. McMaster, *History of
the People of the United States* (New York, 1883–1913), vol. V, p. 123; vol. VI,
pp. 339–340; Isaac Lippincott, *Economic Development of the United States* (New
York, 1933), p. 166; Kirkland, *op. cit.*, pp. 234–235.

builders inclined to achieve one or more specific objectives — objectives
that became more and more conventional as time went on:

1. To provide overland short-cuts between established markets
   hitherto connected by circuitous or slow routes;

2. To extend central markets by networks radiating from important trade centers;

3. To tap the vast potential trade of the Mississippi River basin,
   and

4. To open for settlement and commerce inland regions hitherto
   inaccessible.

The first objective was undoubtedly the most common, and it was
pursued vigorously in all sections of the country. The Camden &
Amboy, for example, was built between New York and Philadelphia,
cities which had ample but slow means of communication both by
water and by land. The South Carolina Railroad, the longest in the
country when it was finished in 1833, connected Charleston directly
with the headwaters of the Savannah River, thus eliminating a lengthy
haul by water. In Michigan, the Detroit & St. Joseph was chartered
in 1836 to provide a short-cut between Lakes Erie and Michigan.[4]

Meanwhile, Boston, New York, and Philadelphia had become the
hubs of very considerable systems serving their respective hinterlands.
This was a phenomenon that was naturally limited at the time to the
East where population was densest, and where trading centers were
well established. It served nevertheless as a model for the West.

The desire to tap western trade was shared by nearly every ambitious
city on the seaboard. Baltimore and Philadelphia led this movement,
partly because they were geographically nearest to the most settled
trans-Alleghany regions, but more because they wanted to overcome
the initial advantage held by New York since 1825 with its Hudson
River–Erie Canal route.[5] For its part, New York itself was far from
idle; during the 'thirties it took a keen interest in the New York Central that was being built in sections west of Albany, and in the Erie
which followed almost an air line towards Dunkirk on Lake Erie.[6]

[4] Slason Thompson, *A Short History of American Railways* (New York,
1925), pp. 49, 53, 72.

[5] Edward Hungerford, *The Story of the Baltimore & Ohio Railroad, 1827–
1927* (New York, 1928), vol. I, p. 5.

[6] Frank W. Stevens, *The Beginnings of the New York Central Railroad* (New
York, 1926), chs. i–xv; Thompson, *op. cit.*, p. 192.

1840

RAILWAYS IN THE UNITED STATES, 1840.

DENSITY OF POPULATION IN THE EASTERN HALF OF THE UNITED STATES, 1840.

Even Boston strove to take its share of western trade; by 1840 a line was nearly completed across Massachusetts to Albany.[7] In the South, Charleston and Savannah pushed competing lines back towards the mountains.

The hope of using the railroad to open up vast "land-locked" areas was naturally strongest in the West. That hope, together with the disappointments attending it, was exemplified by the experience of Illinois during the 'thirties. In 1837, the Legislature of that state authorized a network of no less than 1,341 miles of state-owned roads, extending into all parts of Illinois except the northeast, which was to be served by the Illinois-Michigan Canal then under construction. The backbone of the system was to be the Illinois Central from Cairo to Galena; five cross-state routes would provide for east-west traffic. This tremendous project was to be financed by borrowing money, and the state pledged its credit to the extent of at least $20,000,000, representing a debt of $268 for every family in Illinois at the time. As might have been expected, this impossible undertaking collapsed, leaving behind only 24 miles of completed road between Jacksonville and Meredosia.[8] To make matters worse, the first locomotive shipped from the East for this railroad was lost in transit, and no one ever found a trace of it. The engine that finally did arrive broke down so often that mule power was substituted for it, and the line was eventually sold at auction for $21,500.[9] In Michigan, the story was similar, if less disastrous. There the two private companies that had undertaken construction westward to connect Lake Erie with Lake Michigan failed in the Panic of 1837. These the state took over, and by 1840 some 50 miles had been built in all; not a very outstanding achievement.[10]

In these experiences, as well as in the more successful results in the East, lay many a lesson for the builder and investor in western railroads of the 'forties. In the first place, it was apparent that rail-

---

[7] George W. Baker, *The Formation of the New England Railroad Systems* (Cambridge, 1937), p. 7; Agnes C. Laut, *The Romance of the Rails* (New York, 1929), pp. 86–89.

[8] Gates, *op. cit.*, pp. 21–23; Carlton J. Corliss, *Trails to Rails: A Story of Transportation Progress in Illinois* (Chicago, 1934), pp. 17–18; Earnest Elmo Calkins, "Genesis of a Railroad," reprinted from Illinois State Historical Society, *Transactions for the Year 1935* (Chicago? 1935?), p. 4.

[9] Corliss, *op. cit.*, pp. 18–19; Calkins, *loc. cit.*, p. 4.

[10] Thompson, *op. cit.*, p. 72.

ILLINOIS
COUNTY MAP
SHOWING
RAILROADS AUTHORIZED
UNDER
THE INTERNAL IMPROVEMENT ACT
OF 1837

roads followed population, and prospered very nearly in proportion to its density. So far as building in the sparsely settled West was concerned, therefore, it was clear that nothing could be attempted on a very large scale unless and until some outside source, presumably eastern capital or the federal government or both, would risk financial aid. Secondly, railways were proving themselves most in demand and most useful when they could connect existing centers or channels of trade, particularly when they could effect a substantial saving of time or expense over the then existing means of transportation. It was consequently logical to suppose that the shortest overland routes would eventually support railways, and that junctions or transfer points on them would become increasingly important. Finally, it was obvious that there was and would be vigorous competition on the part of rival eastern cities for western trade. Therefore, those western regions that could offer local rail connections, actual or projected, with rich productive or market areas, might well expect eastern support and a surge of rapid development.

With the arrival of the 'forties and better times generally, railroads continued to expand along the lines laid out in the preceding decade. In the East, networks radiating from the larger cities were filled in and extended; even the names of the roads, such as the Boston & Lowell, Boston & Worcester, and Boston & Providence, confirmed their purpose. Similar networks reached out from New Haven, New York, Philadelphia, and Baltimore. Meanwhile, water-routes and circuitous rail lines were replaced by direct roads; in the East through service was available from Maine to South Carolina.[11] The systems based on the seaboard stretching westward continued their progress at increased tempo. This activity in the East was inevitably reflected, on a smaller scale, beyond the Alleghanies.

The West of the early 'forties was still recovering from the speculative orgy that had ended so ingloriously in 1837. Yet the future for railroads was anything but dark. The area of profitable promotion was growing daily, and for the men with vision it was principally a question of deciding upon the most strategic route and securing financial backing. Projects were legion; by 1845 more and more of them centered about the growing city of Chicago.

[11] Baker, *op. cit.* Cf. Hockett, *op. cit.*, p. 607.

II. CHICAGO AND THE AURORA BRANCH RAILROAD TO 1850

The emergence of Chicago as a transportation center, one of the most dramatic episodes in all American history, was inevitable, for it was located not only at a crossing of routes, but at a point of trans-shipment as well. Of the native Indian trails by far the most important was the "Portage Path" which bridged the gap between the Chicago and Illinois rivers, and made possible a through route between Mississippi points and Lake Michigan. The portage varied from a few miles at high water to a trek from 50 to 100 miles through the bogs of Mud Lake at other times. This was the path used by Père Marquette, Joliet, La Salle, and the first French settlers at Kaskaskia, Kahokia, and St. Louis. It was the favorite route of priests, traders, and trappers. A second route of importance was the "Great Sauk Trail" from Rock Island along the Rock and Fox rivers around the southern tip of Lake Michigan to Malden, Canada, not far from Detroit, where Indian tribes used to collect their annuities from the British Government. Still a third trail was "Green Bay Road" connecting eastern Wisconsin with the territory east of Chicago.[12]

The importance of Chicago as a crossroads for these trails was early recognized by Great Britain as well as by the United States. At the time of the Revolution, the fur trade that originated along the Upper Mississippi and followed the Portage Path on its way to the huge fur depot on Mackinac Island was worth at least £180,000 a year to Great Britain. Thus, despite the Treaty of 1783, by which the site of Chicago fell well within the United States, the House of Lords was petitioned by British traders to establish an English fort on the site. At the time American authority in the region was shadowy at best, and it was not until Anthony Wayne whipped the pro-English Indians at the Battle of Fallen Timber in 1794 that he was able to demand and obtain from them, through the Greenville Treaty of 1795, the specific cession of an area at the mouth of the Chicago River on which to build a fort for protecting the valuable fur trade. This right was confirmed by the Jay Treaty with England in the same year, and in 1803 the United States Army finally erected Fort Dearborn.[13]

[12] Corliss, op. cit., pp. 2-3.
[13] W. E. Stevens, *The Northwest Fur Trade, 1763–1800* (University of Illinois, 1928), p. 65; D. E. Clark, *The West in American History* (New York, 1937), p. 208.

Transportation to the fort was precarious to say the least. The nearest post office was at Fort Wayne, 150 miles away, and for several years mail was brought in on foot only once a month. Until 1823, the northern part of Illinois was an unbroken wilderness, but in that year a youthful agent of the American Fur Company established a trading post at the present site of Danville, and laid out a trail from that point to Fort Dearborn, a distance of 125 miles. This was the first trail established by white men to the site of the future city, yet it was only six years before the first wagon load of lead made the journey, in eleven days, from Galena to Lake Michigan. Between Dixon's Ferry and Chicago, the driver had been forced to use the old native trail; a wagon road was not built over the route until 1832. The cost of shipping freight overland in Illinois in that period was at the rate of $10 per ton for each 20 miles, a tariff which checked agricultural and industrial growth in the interior of the state, and likewise the prospects for Chicago.[14] Despite the establishment of several stage lines during the 'thirties, Chicago needed a more efficient form of transportation to lift it from its relatively muddy obscurity.

At first, it seemed that the answer to the problem lay in the canal boat and the steamboat. As the 'thirties opened, St. Louis, Peoria, Galena, and Alton were enjoying a fast-growing river steamboat traffic on regular schedule; even the little village of Beardstown on the Illinois River counted 450 steamers arriving or departing in 1836. During the decade Adams County, which contained Quincy, had the largest increase of population of any county in the state. Neighboring Hancock County also grew rapidly, and there were big increases in Fulton, Pike, Scott, Peoria, and La Salle counties on the Illinois River.[15] Chicago, of course, had the easiest access to the East by virtue of its position on Lake Michigan, but this advantage could hardly be utilized until the lake was connected with the Mississippi. To accomplish this end the state legislature granted the right of way in 1822 for the Illinois-Michigan Canal, and five years later Congress gave the company a grant of every alternate section of land within five miles on either side of the canal. Even this donation was insufficient to interest private capital in the project. In 1833, the year of the city's incorporation, Chicago's prospects were still seriously threatened by both Michigan City and Mil-

[14] Corliss, op. cit., pp. 6–15.
[15] Gates, op. cit., pp. 14–15; cf. Census of 1870, vol. I, p. 23.

waukee, towns which had considerably less mud and much better harbors. But in 1833 Congress allotted $25,000 for cleaning out Chicago's harbor.[16] In 1836 the state of Illinois pledged its credit for completing the canal, and despite the Panic of 1837, the project was finally put under way.[17] Although the prospect of this improvement favored the growth of Chicago, its first effects were dispersed over a much wider area. In 1843 there were only 7,580 people in Chicago although there were 70,000 within 60 miles of the city, most of them within 15 miles of the canal that would not be finished until 1848.[18] As a matter of fact, so far as transit time was concerned, New Orleans was closer to more Illinois towns than was Chicago, and it was thought that Galena was the future metropolis of the state.[19] The tri-weekly stages that were running between Chicago and Galena in 1846 and the daily line in operation between Chicago and Peoria accounted for only a small fraction of the potential business. Arrivals and departures in that year numbered but eight daily, with an average of 15 passengers to the coach. Although plank roads had been agitated as early as 1840, the first one, 16 miles in length, would not be ready for traffic until 1850.[20] In the middle 'forties, it was clear that Chicago needed railroads if it were to take advantage of its unique location.

Indeed, there were by then many groups agitating for the Iron Horse. The merchants and distributors of Chicago realized that they could not adequately supply the interior without a more efficient and reliable form of transportation. The city of Galena wanted to market its lead in the East through the Chicago gateway, and towns like Peoria, Galesburg, Alton, Quincy, Rock Island, and others were zealously striving for eastern outlets. Finally, land owners and speculators eagerly awaited the rise in realty values that would inevitably accom-

[16] B. L. Pierce, *History of Chicago* (New York, 1937), vol. I, p. 92.

[17] Gates, *op. cit.*, p. 17. Cf. *Laws of Illinois*, 1835-36, p. 145; James W. Putnam, "The Illinois and Michigan Canal; A Study in Economic History," Chicago Historical Society *Collections*, vol. X (Chicago, 1918), p. 34.

[18] Gates, *op. cit.*, pp. 17, 19. Cf. Chicago Board of Trade, *Annual Report*, 1865, p. 12; Putnam, *loc. cit.*, p. 106.

[19] As late as 1842 the commercial trade of Galena surpassed that of Chicago. Galena was the scene of the first American mining rush in the 1820's and attracted a large mining population. (Corliss, *op. cit.*, p. 14; cf. A. C. Boggess, "The Settlement of Illinois, 1778-1830," Chicago Historical Society *Collections*, vol. V, Chicago, 1908).

[20] Corliss, *op. cit.*, pp. 20, 22; Gates, *op. cit.*, p. 15.

pany the building of a railway network in Illinois. It was the joint ambition of Galena and Chicago that led to the first actual construction from the latter. The Galena & Chicago Union Railroad Company, which had been incorporated in 1838, finally completed its line from Chicago to Maywood in October, 1848. On the tenth of that month Chicago's first locomotive, the *Pioneer*, arrived in the brig *Buffalo*. It had but a single pair of driving wheels, weighed only ten tons, and was second-hand.[21] Nevertheless, when it went into service on October 24, it opened a new chapter in Chicago's history. By the middle of December, 1848, the little railroad boasted ten completed miles of track and six freight cars. Its plans called for building on westward to the Fox River, thence northwesterly to Elgin and Freeport.[22]

Those settlements on the projected route of this Galena Road looked forward eagerly to the day when through traffic could be opened with the metropolis of Chicago. For the ambitious town of Aurora, however, the new line was a challenge rather than a promise, for at their nearest point (West Chicago) the rails would still be 12 miles north of the village. Of course, hauling produce or riding by stage over this distance and then using the railroad was much better than having to use the old highway for the entire 38 miles into Chicago, but even so Aurora could hardly hope to compete with those fortunate towns which had direct rail connections. What should be done? In the light of the town's early history, there was but one answer.

Aurora's first permanent settlers had been the McCartys, energetic millwrights who arrived from Elmira, New York, in 1834. They had immediately begun construction of cabins, a dam, and two mills, and by winter 15 persons were living in the vicinity. In 1835 Samuel McCarty platted the village then known as McCarty's Mills, and work soon started on two highways, one north and south along the Fox River, the other east and west from Naperville through the Mills to Big Rock. Thus the future city of Aurora created her own crossroads, although Samuel McCarty realized this was not enough; if his settlement were to prosper it would have to be on a main artery of commerce. At the time, the through coaches carrying mail and pas-

[21] C. & N. W. Ry., "Historical Background of the Chicago and Northwestern Railway" (MS. memorandum, Chicago, 1936?), p. 5; *Chicago Daily Journal*, October 9, 1848.   [22] C. & N. W. Ry., *loc. cit.*, p. 1.

sengers from Chicago to Galena followed the old road from Naperville west by way of Montgomery, three miles south of the new town.
Consequently, McCarty made an offer to the owners of the stage coach
line: if they would change their route to the new road from Naperville through the Mills, he would keep their drivers and horses free
of charge for a month. The company accepted this proposition, with
the result that McCarty's Mills not only gained the mail stage but
likewise attracted a great stream of prairie schooners laden with immigrants. Many of these travelers, recognizing the natural advantages
of the bustling community, became permanent settlers.[23] In 1837 a
post office was established and the village was officially named Aurora
at the suggestion of an early settler from the town of that name in
New York State.[24]

Located thus on a crossroads and through route, Aurora grew
steadily, and before long it was apparent that dirt highways were inadequate for the traffic of the vicinity. Plank roads were seriously considered, and several companies were actually formed, but none of them
could raise the necessary capital to begin construction. This was the
situation as the strap-iron rails of the Galena & Chicago Union reached
the Fox River at West Chicago and turned away northward. To a
community whose population had grown from nothing to 1,200 in
15 years chiefly because it had consistently recognized the value of
good transportation, the only course open was to build a railroad of
its own. On February 12, 1849, Lorenzo D. Brady, member of the
Illinois legislature from Kendall County, obtained a charter creating
the Aurora Branch Railroad and authorizing it to construct a line
from Aurora 12 miles northwards to a connection with the Galena &
Chicago Union.[25] A. C. Gibson, Benjamin Hackney, and Charles
Hoyt, all from Aurora, and Stephen F. Gale of Chicago were named
commissioners to receive stock subscriptions; capitalization was placed
at $100,000.[26]

The first meeting of the new company was held on February 21.
Gale was elected president, and the books opened for subscriptions;

[23] Carl Frederick Carlson, *Aurora, Illinois: A Study in Sequent Land Use*
(Chicago, 1940), p. 10 *et seq.*

[24] Charles P. Burton to A. W. Newton, December 30, 1938.

[25] CBQ, *Documentary History*, vol. I (Chicago, 1928–29), p. 11.

[26] A. W. Newton, *Early History of the Chicago, Burlington & Quincy in
Illinois* (MS, Chicago, 1939), p. 1.

THE GALENA AND CHICAGO UNION RAILROAD'S "PIONEER" WHICH ON SEPTEMBER 2, 1850 HAULED THE FIRST TRAIN OPERATED ON ANY PART OF THE BURLINGTON SYSTEM. THIS TRAIN RAN FROM BATAVIA TO TURNER JUNCTION OVER THE AURORA BRANCH AND THENCE TO CHICAGO OVER THE GALENA AND CHICAGO UNION.

within 24 hours $25,000 in stock was taken.[27] Encouraged, the directors immediately appointed John L. Hanchette chief engineer, with instructions to survey a line starting at Turner Junction, on the Galena Road, southward along the east bank of the Fox River through Batavia and on to Aurora.[28] Ten months later he had finished his task, and on December 20, 1849, contracts were let for grading and masonry.[29]

As in so many new enterprises, however, there were many unforeseen obstacles. By February, 1850, less than $50,000 of the company's stock had been sold,[30] although Engineer Hanchette estimated that it would cost no less than $93,237 to complete the line, exclusive of rolling stock.[31] Consequently, on March 26, 1850, the directors authorized the president to make "such a temporary loan as may be required for the construction of this road"; after prolonged discussion, five-year bonds totaling $45,000 were issued to the public.[32] The stock of the Aurora Branch, largely owned by the directors, was "irrevocably pledged," along with the company's property, for payment of these bonds. This virtually amounted to a personal guarantee of the bonds by the directors.

In March actual construction commenced, and the board, apparently undeterred by their financial problems, recorded their desire to extend their road "to the most feasible point on the Illinois River, as soon as possible." [33] Even before the completion of the original project, the builders were thinking of the future. During the spring and summer of 1850 construction proceeded apace, but because of limited means the company was forced to economize in every way possible. Some three years previously the legislature of New York State had required its railroads to replace all strap rail (a strip of iron attached to a wooden stringer) by iron T-rail. Consequently, much

[27] AB ORB, p. 2.

[28] *Ibid.*, p. 6; cf. Newton, *op. cit.*, p. 2.

[29] AB ORB, p. 6.

[30] Newton, *op. cit.*, p. 3.

[31] J. L. Hanchette, "Chief Engineer's Report, February 21, 1850," in *Aurora Beacon*, February 28, 1850. In the Burton Historical collection, Detroit, Mr. A. W. Newton discovered a statement placing the final cost of the Aurora Branch at $125,868.77. (Newton, *op. cit.*, p. 3.)

[32] AB ORB, p. 10; Lorenzo D. Brady, *Lorenzo D. Brady, His History Written by Himself* (MS, Chicago? 1877?). The latter is in the possession of Brady's granddaughter, Mrs. Olive Beaupré Miller of Chicago.

[33] AB ORB, p. 10.

of this second-hand strap was readily available at low prices in 1850, and this the Aurora Branch (as well as the Galena road) purchased; it was laid upon six-inch square longitudinal rails of Norway or yellow pine that were, in turn, braced by triangular wooden blocks and firmly spiked to the ties.[34] On August 27, 1850, six miles thus built were ready for use between Turner Junction and Batavia, and the Chicago

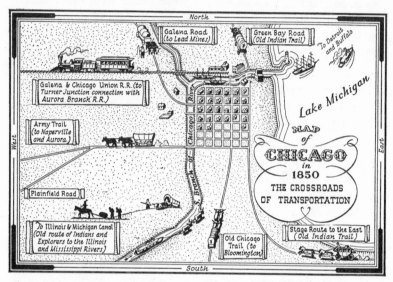

Galena Road
(to Lead Mines)

Green Bay Road
(Old Indian Trail)

To Detroit
and Buffalo

Galena & Chicago Union R.R. (to
Turner Junction connection with
Aurora Branch R.R.)

Lake Michigan

Army Trail
(to Naperville
and Aurora)

MAP
of
CHICAGO
in
1850
THE CROSSROADS
OF TRANSPORTATION

Plainfield Road

To Illinois & Michigan Canal
(Old route of Indians and
Explorers to the Illinois
and Mississippi Rivers)

Old Chicago
Trail (to
Bloomington)

Stage Route to the East
(Old Indian Trail)

papers announced that this second line to serve the city would commence its operations six days later.[35] As yet, however, the new company had not received the engine and cars it had bought in the East,[36] so it was necessary to hire the little *Pioneer* and a single coach for the occasion. This was the train that puffed out of Batavia for Chicago at six-thirty o'clock on the morning of September 2, 1850, to inaugurate service on the Aurora Branch and the Burlington system.[37]

Events now moved rapidly. On October 7, the company's own first locomotive arrived in Chicago on the brig *Patrick Henry*.[38] This

[34] Newton, *op. cit.*, pp. 4–6.

[35] *Chicago Daily Democrat*, August 31, 1850.

[36] Gale and Hackney went East in the spring of 1850 "to negotiate for locomotives and cars." (*Aurora Beacon*, May 9, 1850.)

[37] CBQ, *Corporate History* (Chicago, 1921), p. 7; Charles S. Battle, *Centennial Historical and Biographical Record of Aurora, Illinois for 100 Years, and of the C. B. & Q. R. R. for 86 Years* (Aurora? 1937?), p. 21.

[38] *Chicago Daily Journal*, October 8, 1850.

was the Norris-built *Whittlesey*, a 12-ton engine with four drivers, purchased from the Buffalo & Niagara Falls Railway. Shortly thereafter, the 14-ton *Pigeon*, with only two drivers, was added to the roster; it too was second-hand, having been built by Baldwin in 1837 for the Michigan Central.[39] Meanwhile, on October 4 the rails reached Aurora,[40] and on October 21, 1850, regular service began from that city according to the following schedule:

Leave Aurora	7 a.m. and 3 p.m.	Leave Chicago	8 a.m. and 3 p.m.
Arrive Chicago	11 a.m. and 6 p.m.	Arrive Aurora	10 a.m. and 6 p.m.

Once more the people of Aurora had brought within its limits the best available form of transportation. The results of their enterprise extended far beyond the Fox River Valley.

The completion of the Aurora Branch enabled Chicago, in 1850 a city of 29,963 persons,[41] to boast of two railroads and look forward to the creation of a network radiating from the metropolis. In the fall of that same year another event took place in faraway Washington that was of prime importance for the future, not only of Chicago, but of the entire West.

Ever since 1827 Congress had aided certain transportation enterprises in the more sparsely settled portions of the country by offering them lands from the public domain as an inducement to build the desired facilities. Usually alternate sections (640 acres) were granted for a limited number of miles on each side of the projected improvement, the United States retaining and doubling the fixed government price of $1.25 per acre upon the remaining alternate sections within the lateral limits of the grant. By 1850, some 3,500,000 acres had been given thus to highways, and a similar amount to canals.[42] As railroads proved their value it was logical that the policy of federal land grants should be extended to them also, and indeed such action had

---

[39] Railway & Locomotive Historical Society, *Locomotives of the Chicago, Burlington & Quincy Railroad, 1855–1904* (1937), pt. 2, p. 14.

[40] After much investigation, Mr. A. W. Newton has concluded that the first station, a temporary structure used only in the winter of 1850–51, was located north of Indian Creek, at or near Pearce Street. (Newton, "Aurora Branch Railroad Company: First Depot and Its Successors," MS. memorandum, Chicago, 1940.)

[41] *Census* of 1850, p. 705.

[42] Thomas Donaldson, *The Public Domain* (Washington, 1884), pp. 258, 1261; Transportation Association of America, *loc. cit.*, p. 8.

1850

RAILWAYS IN THE UNITED STATES, 1850.

DENSITY OF POPULATION IN THE EASTERN HALF OF THE UNITED STATES, 1850.

been repeatedly urged in Congress,[43] but it was not until September
20, 1850, that the first railroad bill, introduced by Stephen A. Douglas,
was passed. By this act more than 2,000,000 acres were set aside for a
company, to be chartered by the State of Illinois, that would complete
on the most favorable terms the old project for a central road from
Cairo to Galena, with a "branch" from Centralia to Chicago. United
States troops, mail, and property were to be carried at prices fixed by
Congress.[44] Enactment of this legislation opened up untold possibilities for the state of Illinois and confirmed the future of the bustling
city at the foot of Lake Michigan.

III. THE RACE FROM LAKE ERIE TO CHICAGO, 1850–1852

The unbelievably rapid growth of Chicago between 1843 and 1850,
together with the actual and projected construction of her railroads,
by no means escaped national attention. Nevertheless, by 1850 there
was still no through rail connection with the East despite the fact that
the existing systems based on the seaboard were steadily reaching out
westward for new markets. If only one of these could be developed
into a through route to Chicago, a great new artery of trade would
spring into existence. As early as 1845, a young Detroit lawyer thought
he knew how to realize this possibility.

As a result of the Panic of 1837, there were hundreds of miles of
rusting rails in the middle 'forties, sprawling aimlessly in the western
wilderness.[45] Among such lines were the old Detroit & St. Joseph,
now the Michigan Central, stretching 145 miles from Detroit to Kala-
mazoo, and the Michigan Southern extending 75 miles westward from
Toledo. Together these roads had cost the State of Michigan $3,500,000,
but as they stood they were practically worthless and the state, unable
to complete them, put the half-built and dilapidated properties up for
sale.[46]

An opportunity such as this could appeal only to youth. James

[43] John Bell Sanborn, *Congressional Grants of Land in Aid of Railways*
(Madison, 1899), ch. i.

[44] Gates, *op. cit.*, ch. ii; Corliss, *op. cit.*, pp. 24–25.

[45] Cf. Gates, *op. cit.*, p. 22; Caroline MacGill, *A History of Transportation in
the United States before 1860* (Washington, 1917), pp. 503–505; Slason Thompson, *op. cit.*, p. 118.

[46] Henry Greenleaf Pearson, *An American Railroad Builder — John Murray
Forbes* (Boston, 1911), pp. 21–24.

Frederick Joy, New Hampshire-born and a graduate of Dartmouth College and Harvard Law School, had come to Detroit in 1836. There he had observed at close range the varying fortunes of the Michigan Central; by 1845 he had become convinced that it offered a rare opportunity for private capital, and was among those who urged its sale by the state.[47] His enthusiasm was shared by John W. Brooks, a twenty-six-year-old youngster who had already served as superintendent of the Auburn and Rochester. They believed that if the line were completed to Lake Michigan it would not only open up the rich farming territory of the state, but provide a link in the shortest line from the seaboard to Chicago and the Mississippi Valley. Full of hope, young Brooks turned eastward in the winter of 1845 to seek financial backing. Some kindly fate led him to the Boston offices of John Murray Forbes.[48]

Forbes at this time was barely thirty-two, yet he was well established in Boston as a merchant of means, energy, and prudence. Born in 1813 into a family already well known in maritime commerce, he had been lucky enough to obtain a thorough secondary school education before the untimely death of one of his brothers had hurried him, at the age of seventeen, into a responsible position in faraway Canton. There his remarkable gift of winning the confidence of even the cautious Chinese mandarins, combined with his natural skill as a trader, led to his rapid rise. By the time he returned home in 1836, he seemed destined for a remarkable future.[49]

When Brooks approached Forbes, the young capitalist was looking for a position for his elder brother Bennet, and "drawn on partly by this fraternal motive and partly by the fascination of the enterprise

[47] William J. Petersen, "The Burlington Comes," *Palimpsest*, vol. XIV, no. 11 (November, 1933), pp. 381–382.

[48] *Ibid.* Also Pearson, *op. cit.*, pp. 24–25. Petersen says Brooks was a former superintendent of the Auburn and Rochester; Pearson describes him as simply "superintendent." There is no mention of Brooks in Frank W. Stevens' chapter on the A. and R. in his *The Beginnings of the New York Central Railroad* (New York, 1926), although the omission is not strange in an account as general as Stevens'. Brooks became president of the B. & M. in Iowa for the first time on September 7, 1864 (BMI ORB, p. 153). See below, p. 172.

[49] Pearson, *op. cit.*, ch. i, *passim.* In 1833–34 Forbes had made a brief visit to America during which he had married Sarah Hathaway of New Bedford. After his return from China, the couple established their home on Milton Hill, and some years later acquired also the island of Naushon in Buzzard's Bay. Forbes divided his time between these two residences, never owning a house in the city. He had six children. (*Ibid.*, pp. 12–13.)

itself," he undertook to finance the adventure. Daniel Webster was employed to draft a new charter for the road, and Brooks was sent back to Michigan to secure its passage through the legislature.[50] Meanwhile, Forbes set about raising the necessary $2,000,000 in cash and credit within the six months allotted him by the state. It was a difficult job, but one that he carried through successfully; on September 23, 1846, the new Michigan Central Railroad took possession of its property with Forbes as its first president, and Brooks as superintendent. At once they began re-conditioning and extending the old line, and thanks to Brooks' ingenuity in overcoming technical obstacles, and Forbes' persistence in raising $6,000,000 more capital, the rails reached the shores of Lake Michigan at Michigan City in the spring of 1849. From this point a ferry was available to Chicago; at the other end of the line, the company's new steamship *Mayflower* provided rapid service between Detroit and Buffalo. Business, as Joy had foreseen, began to boom.[51]

Under such circumstances, it was inevitable that rivals should appear in the field, anxious to share in the rich profits that lay in the growing carrying trade from Chicago and the West. Snapping up for a song an Indiana railroad charter that the Michigan Central had unaccountably let slip through its fingers, a group of New York financiers took over the old Michigan Southern in 1850 and began its extension through to Chicago.[52] The situation was critical for the Forbes interests, for unless they forestalled or matched their southern competitors, they would have to exchange their cherished position as part of a through route for that of a limited local line. It would no longer be sufficient merely to reach Lake Michigan and provide ferry service to Chicago. That city was rapidly becoming a hub of transportation in its own right, and only a direct connection with it would permit participation in its business. The directors of the Michigan Central met the challenge by delegating unlimited powers to their officers, and the race was on.[53]

---

[50] Pearson, *op. cit.*, p. 26. Petersen depicts Forbes as "fascinated by the prospect of sponsoring a railroad through the Michigan wilderness" and omits the other possible cause. (Petersen, *loc. cit.*, p. 382.) It is evident throughout, however, that Petersen has condensed his account from Pearson.

[51] Pearson, *op. cit.*, pp. 26–42; Petersen, *loc. cit.*, pp. 382–383.

[52] Pearson, *op. cit.*, pp. 42–47.

[53] Petersen, *loc. cit.*, pp. 383–384. Speaking in Chicago in July, 1920, Mr. W. W. Baldwin, then vice-president of the Burlington, declared: "It is a correct

To match the Southern's advantage in Indiana, the Central forces obtained control of the New Albany and Salem road, a local 35-mile line in the southern part of the state. This line had a charter so conveniently vague that it might properly authorize the construction at once of a "branch" around Lake Michigan miles from the main line, particularly when supported by the eastern capital that Forbes had been energetically recruiting. Thereupon the Southern men obtained an injunction against such a procedure from an inferior state court. The Michigan Central promptly appealed for a dismissal, and while the case was on its way to the Supreme Court of the United States, contracts were let for construction south and west of Michigan City.[54] Before this work had gone far, however, new and apparently insurmountable barriers presented themselves in Illinois.[55]

In order to carry their line into Chicago, the Michigan Southern backers had obtained an old Illinois plank road charter which, they alleged, included the right to build a railroad.[56] The Central, however, had no charter of any kind, and was therefore forced to devise ways and means of building across the state and entering the city. There seemed to be, in the spring of 1851, three distinct possibilities:

1. The Legislature of Illinois was about to award the charter and land grant for the Illinois Central to some qualified group. If the Michigan Central or its friends could obtain this, the Illinois Central could easily build a branch or deflect its main line to the Indiana border and thus provide the desired connection.
2. It might be possible for the Michigan Central to obtain a specific right of way for its own line into the city.
3. The legislature might allow certain existing short lines in northern Illinois to amend their charters so as to make a physical connection with the Michigan Central, and carry its trains into Chicago.

---

historical statement to say that the idea and development of the Burlington grew out of the purchase and extension of the Michigan Central to Chicago by Forbes and his associates." (W. W. Baldwin, "The Making of the Burlington," Chicago, 1920.)

[54] Frank F. Hargrave, *A Pioneer Indiana Railroad: The Origin and Development of the Monon* (Indianapolis, 1932), pp. 107–109. A permanent injunction was eventually denied. (*Ibid.*, p. 109.)

[55] Pearson, *op. cit.*, pp. 46–47.

[56] *Ibid.*, p. 49.

These propositions were not mutually exclusive, for although any one of them might provide access to Chicago, they all possessed additional features that made them desirable for the Michigan Central on their own account. Control of the Illinois Central would insure a source of off-line, or "foreign," traffic, and place the Forbes interests in a strong position in Chicago.[57] A special right of way would afford the quickest means of reaching the city, for it might take time for other roads, however friendly, to come to terms. Finally, control of already existing companies in the north of the state might be a first step in piecing together a strong western outlet. To the extent that these objectives were attained, the threat from the Michigan Southern would diminish. Therefore the agents sent to Springfield early in 1851 were instructed to work for all three goals; James F. Joy was in charge of this delicate task.[58]

As might be expected, the struggle for the Illinois Central charter held the spotlight during the session. Eventually the group including Forbes emerged with the prize, but only over the determined opposition of several rival groups, aided by the Michigan Southern men who, although they were not themselves interested in the Illinois Central, were naturally anxious to retard their competitors. The Michigan Central's backers did not, however, obtain a charter in their own right to build in the northern part of the state.[59] To make matters worse, the Southern's directors obtained a new charter for the Rock Island and LaSalle Railroad, which they had just bought, authorizing that line to proceed eastward to Chicago, and changing its name to the Chicago and Rock Island Railroad.[60] Thus at one stroke they not only assured themselves of a western outlet, but gained control of an alternate if round-about way of entering Chicago should their plank-road charter prove insufficient.[61]

In the light of these events, the triumph of the Forbes interests in

[57] *Ibid.*, p. 73.

[58] Gates, *op. cit.*, pp. 44–45.

[59] There is no doubt about the Michigan Southern opposition on all three points, but it is not certain that their opposition was the decisive factor in defeating two of the Central's plans. (*Ibid.*, pp. 55–57, 68.) Gates asserts that the Forbes interests had already purchased control of the Aurora Branch (*ibid.*, p. 45), but it has been impossible to verify his statement.

[60] F. J. Nevins, *Seventy Years of Service* (Chicago, 1922), p. 7.

[61] Michigan Southern & Northern Indiana Railroad, *Annual Report* for 1853 (New York, 1853), pp. 18–19, 22. Cf. Gates, *op. cit.*, pp. 45–46.

securing the Illinois Central charter appeared at best a Pyrrhic victory. But it soon proved otherwise. Early in 1851 a secret agreement was signed with the "friendly" Illinois Central which provided that the Michigan road should carry $2,000,000 of the former's bonds for two years, and in return receive permission to use the Illinois Central tracks from a junction of the two roads into the city of Chicago.[62] The money involved was to be used in the immediate construction of the necessary tracks which, according to the first plans, were to be deflected far enough eastward to touch the Indiana border and the Michigan Central's railhead. The moment this agreement became known, however, the people of Chicago voiced their vehement disapproval, for they feared that the main line of traffic might veer southwestward, thus leaving the ambitious city stranded. Sentiment came to a head in two railroad conventions held in July, 1851. The citizens wished above all things that each line should make an independent entry into their city. Plans of the Michigan Southern to utilize its own plank-road charter were smiled upon, but the Illinois Central and Michigan Central, for proposing to enter together, were in disfavor. As a result of this sentiment, the Illinois Central dared deflect its tracks only slightly, and the Forbes men were left to cover a six and a half-mile gap in Illinois as best they could.[63]

Brooks and Joy advised putting the line through without legislative authority, but John Murray Forbes demurred. The Southern men, he argued, would build highways over the track; furthermore, in principle it was as bad to cross a quarter-section as an entire continent without permission. Nevertheless, it seemed to be the only way out, for both lines were pushing across Indiana at top speed, and the Michigan Central men would not be outdone. Swallowing their scruples, they built without a charter, and triumphantly rode into the city of Chicago on May 21, 1852, one short day before their Southern rivals opened through service. Two months later, probably to the vast relief of Forbes' New England conscience, the Illinois legislature officially confirmed the unauthorized construction.[64]

Thus breathlessly, and without permission, did the Michigan Central

---

[62] Gates, *op. cit.*, p. 68 and footnotes. Pearson, *op. cit.*, p. 47.

[63] Pearson, *op. cit.*, pp. 47–50.

[64] *Ibid.* In his report to the stockholders in June, 1852, Forbes laconically observed that "we have succeeded, in spite of many obstacles, in completing our

JOHN MURRAY FORBES, 1813–1898.

arrive at its western terminus. But there was no time to lose in fruit-less rejoicing; if one skirmish had ended, it had merely signalized the beginning of another, — the race for the Mississippi, and here the Southern forces had obtained a long lead. Armed with their charter of 1851 for the Rock Island, they had actually begun construction on October 1, 1851, and indeed had brought their first trains into the city on May 22, 1852, over the lines of their Rock Island subsidiary.[65] Meanwhile Forbes and his associates were struggling to piece together a western outlet.[66]

IV. THE ORIGIN OF THE C. B. & Q., 1849-1856

Forbes' desire to find a western connection beyond Chicago was not new. In 1851 he had written one of his business associates, then in London, of "the prospects of railroad building in Illinois." [67] In the fall of 1851, however, when this desire had become an absolute neces-sity, the Michigan Central was still looking for an available connection. By a process of elimination, and because of its own successful though brief record, the Aurora Branch offered the logical solution of the Easterners' problem.

From the commencement of its operations the little road had proved prosperous and its early disposition to expand [68] was strengthened by the election of Elisha J. Wadsworth, one of the early directors, as president on February 21, 1851.[69] Wadsworth was already a success-ful merchant in Chicago. Like many businessmen of the time, he knew little of the problems of financing and building railroads, but he had a profound faith in their necessity and eventual success. Above all, he realized the importance of interesting outside capital in his company, if, as its backers hoped, it were to be extended westward.[70]

---

connection with Chicago, a city destined to become the converging point of passengers from the whole northwest, and from a large portion of the west. . . ." (MC, *Annual Report* for 1852, Boston, 1852, p. 6.)

[65] F. J. Nevins, *op. cit.*, p. 11.

[66] Pearson, *op. cit.*, p. 74. Cf. also MC, *Annual Report* for 1852 (Boston, 1852), p. 6.

[67] Pearson, *op. cit.*, p. 45.

[68] See above, p. 21.

[69] AB ORB, p. 21.

[70] Newton, "Chronology of Events Leading up to the Advent of Eastern Capi-tal into the Aurora Branch Railroad. . . ." (MS. memorandum, Chicago, May, 1939), p. 2.

It was not long before he was called upon to put his ideas into action, for the stockholders of the Aurora road, at their meeting on February 21, had requested their directors to take "such immediate measures" as would insure the extension of their line west to the Galena Branch of the Illinois Central.[71] The directors complied without delay. Subject to the approval of the board, Wadsworth and Gale were authorized to enter into any sort of agreement they deemed best, either with the Galena and Chicago Union "or any other company or companies," for the purpose of consolidating with them, or of concluding "any arrangement" for the future operation and extension of the Aurora Branch.[72] Under the circumstances, this was a necessary step, for the Galena and Chicago Union possessed a charter right to extend its line in a "lateral" direction west or southwest, and was thus in a position to delay or compete with the ambitions of the Aurora Branch.[73] Fortunately, a consolidation of the two companies did not materialize; if it had, the Burlington might never have emerged as an independent system. Instead, while an agreement with the G. & C. U. was pending, the stockholders of the Aurora company, on July 15, 1851, increased their capital stock from $100,000 to $600,000, thus providing a means for introducing outside capital and constructing their own line to a junction with the Illinois Central.[74] Finally, on January 13, 1852, they acquired, by lease from the Galena and Chicago Union, the *right* to extend their line to Mendota; the way was now cleared to put this project into effect.

Meanwhile, the increasing revenues of the Aurora Branch made it an ever more attractive investment. Shortly after the close of the first year's operation, the directors declared "a dividend of 10 per cent out of the nett [*sic*] earnings of the road, ending October 31, 1851." This dividend was paid in stock of the company, leaving the cash available for the payment of debts.[75] Small wonder that Michigan Central dollars, probably during the winter of 1851–52, began taking up securities of the Aurora road. The result was evident in the election of J. W. Brooks to the directorate on February 21, 1852. This event, which was

[71] AB ORB, p. 20.

[72] *Ibid.*, p. 21.

[73] Charter of the Galena and Chicago Union Railroad (January 16, 1836), cited in Newton, *Early History of the C. B. & Q. in Illinois, op. cit.*, p. 15.

[74] AB ORB, p. 22.

[75] *Ibid.*, p. 32.

of the greatest significance, signalized the entrance of the Forbes interests into the future Burlington system. At the same time, it provided the Michigan Central with a toehold west of Chicago. Even so, this was but a very short step towards securing a western outlet worthy of the name. With all its advantages, the Aurora Branch was only a 12-mile line, running north and south, with trackage rights over 30 miles more. Forbes and his friends could not afford to rest on their laurels.

Fortunately, northern Illinois was a fertile field for railroad building in the early 'fifties. Isolated hamlets that had maintained a precarious existence on the broad prairies suddenly began dreaming of direct rail connections with eastern markets or with the Mississippi River and the new state of Iowa beyond. If such towns were not fortunate enough to be directly on the great central railroad route or along the line of the projected Rock Island, they might at least construct short feeders to these systems. That, for example, was the situation in Galesburg and Peoria, Knoxville and Burlington, just at the time that Forbes and his associates were turning their eyes westward.[76]

For a dozen years and more these towns had watched the steady march of the Iron Horse. They had witnessed to their dismay the failure of Illinois' grandiose plan of 1837 that had left only the near-by Jacksonville-Meredosia line as its one accomplishment. Not until 1849 did it seem probable that a real railroad would bind them together. On February 12 of that year, the same day that the Aurora Branch was authorized, the Peoria and Oquawka received its charter for a line to run between the Illinois and Mississippi rivers to connect the towns for which it was named. Meetings were promptly called to raise the necessary funds. Large gatherings in Knoxville in September, and in Galesburg two months later, pledged support to the project, and on December 20 a rousing convention, called at the request of the Peorians, convened once more at Knoxville. Here it was resolved

[76] Galesburg was first settled in June, 1836. It had been conceived some two years before by one George Washington Gale, a graduate of Union College and Princeton Theological Seminary, as a colony and college town. Following the usual procedure, Gale issued a circular setting forth his plans, and within a year collected $21,000. In the fall of 1835, his group, then formally organized, purchased 17 sections in Knox County, and at a meeting on January 7, 1836, named the projected settlement Galesburg. Settlers arrived the following June. (Chas. Chapman & Co., *History of Knox County, Illinois*, Chicago, 1878, p. 665; Arthur W. Dunn, *An Analysis of the Social Structure of a Western Town*, Chicago, 1896, *passim*.)

to open subscription books, a procedure ratified by citizens' meetings all along the route.[77]

Meanwhile, a contest developed as to the route and principal western terminus of the proposed railroad. By an amendment to the P. & O. charter effective February 10, 1851, the location of that line was fixed through Farmington, Knoxville, and Monmouth, but excluding Galesburg. By another amendment on the same date, the company was authorized "to build a branch . . . to commence at or west of Monmouth; from thence [*sic*] to the Mississippi River at or about Shokokon. . . ."[78] Burlington, across the Mississippi almost opposite Shokokon, insisted that the newly authorized portion of the railroad should be the main line, while Oquawka maintained that nothing more than a branch should serve the ambitious Iowa town.[79] The first actual grading of the P. & O., however, probably commenced on the river bank opposite Burlington late in 1851, and extended to a point near the present village of Kirkwood.[80] At about the same time, work also began at Peoria, but soon ceased because the subscribers to stock could not raise the percentage of cash required by the charter as a prerequisite to construction. Thus, two lines were begun, but as 1852 opened there was not enough money in sight to complete them, and neither Galesburg nor Knoxville was assured of rail connections.[81]

In the meantime, on February 1, 1851, the old Northern Cross charter under which the pioneer Jacksonville-Meredosia line had been built emerged from the Illinois legislature with an amendment permitting the company to build northward through the Central Military Tract to a point at or near the western end of the Illinois-Michigan Canal *providing* such line should not be built east of Knoxville.[82] Thus, although Burlington, Knoxville, and Monmouth were provided, at least on paper, with some railroad, Galesburg had no prospects of any line at all.[83] The energetic citizens of that town, most of them Yankees and York Staters, were thoroughly aroused by these

[77] Chapman, *op. cit.*, pp. 217–218.
[78] CBQ, *Documentary History*, vol. I, pp. 53–54.
[79] Calkins, *loc. cit.*, pp. 9–10.
[80] CBQ, *Documentary History*, vol. I, pp. 46–47; Calkins, *loc. cit.*, pp. 9–10.
[81] Calkins, *loc. cit.*, p. 9.
[82] CBQ, *Documentary History*, vol. I, p. 573.
[83] See map, p. 224.

developments and promptly met to consider the parlous state of affairs.

Among the local leaders particularly disturbed by the turn of events was Chauncey S. Colton, who had erected the town's first permanent building for his store in 1837 and had since become the leading merchant of the community.[84] He well knew that Galesburg would be doomed to oblivion unless it shared in the blessings of the Iron Horse. Consequently, with a friend named Silas Willard, he hastened to offer the Peoria and Oquawka a $20,000 stock subscription if that company would build through the town. This effort was of no avail. Thereupon, a prompt application was made to the legislature for a mandatory change in the charter to accomplish the same result, but unfortunately both Knoxville and Monmouth had members in the House, and the senator representing Galesburg lived even south of Knoxville. Quite naturally these gentlemen declined to take action, and the situation remained as black as ever. The result was that the people of Galesburg accepted the only remaining alternative. If they could not be on anyone else's railroad, they would build their own. On February 15, only five days after the P. & O. had dealt them such a cruel blow, they obtained a charter to construct a line

commencing at Galesburg, in the County of Knox, and running from thence in a northeasterly direction on the most direct and eligible route to, and to connect with the Rock Island and LaSalle Railroad, at such point in the County of Henry or Bureau as the said company hereby incorporated may designate. . . .[85]

Their enterprise was called the Central Military Tract.[86]

For more than a year, matters moved with discouraging slowness. A preliminary survey was made, but subscriptions for the new enterprise were small, and in a meeting of the stockholders Colton definitely opposed commencing operations without more funds. When asked what he proposed to do, he replied that he would first find men

[84] Chapman, *op. cit.*, p. 665.
[85] CBQ, *Corporate History*, p. 10; *Documentary History*, vol. I, p. 37.
[86] Colton MS (WL), see Appendix C, below. The "Military Tract" was all that land between the Illinois and Michigan rivers south of the center of Bureau and Henry counties. It was so called because much of it had been patented in quarter sections to soldiers of the War of 1812. Actually few soldiers occupied it, so that squatters settled there, improved it, and often made good their right to occupancy. (Chapman, *op. cit.*, p. 107.)

who had the money and then try to convince them that it would be a good thing to back the Galesburg company. Sometime afterwards, he therefore approached the Rock Island and proposed a connection with that line at Sheffield, to be followed by a consolidation of the companies. Fortunately for the Forbes interests, this suggestion was refused.[87]

Thus matters stood in the spring of 1852 when Colton left for his regular buying trip to New York. Once there he endeavored to interest businessmen in the Military Tract, "but soon found out that they were not the class of men to build railroads."[88] Not until he reached Boston was there a glimmer of hope. Then all at once the entire prospect changed. Colton found as his companions at the American House[89] James W. Grimes of Burlington, a director of the Peoria and Oquawka,[90] and Elisha Wadsworth, president of the Aurora Branch.[91] To the chance meeting of these men after dinner, the Burlington system probably owes its existence.

According to his own testimony, it was Colton who made the significant suggestions.[92] Pointing out the painful fact that none of the lines they represented had any value separately, he proposed that

[87] Colton MS, see Appendix C. Colton says that the Rock Island was completed when he made his overtures (between the springs of 1851 and 1852). As a matter of fact, the line was not built to Sheffield until October 12, 1853 (F. J. Nevins, *op. cit.*, p. 15), and to Rock Island until February 28, 1854 (*ibid.*). Colton goes on to say that "afterwards Mr. Farnham (of C. & R. I. RR.), and Mr. Judd of Chicago came to Galesburg and proposed to build our road under certain conditions, which I refused." (Colton MS, *loc. cit.*) There is no date given for this second interview, although it was probably before Colton had the C. M. T. charter changed so as to meet the Chicago & Aurora (June 22, 1852, see below, p. 38), and certainly before the fall of 1852 when the Rock Island began surveying their line south from Bureau to Peoria (Nevins, *op. cit.*, p. 14). Cf. Dunn, *op. cit.*, p. 31.

[88] Colton MS, *loc. cit.*

[89] Baldwin, "The Making of the Burlington," *loc. cit.*, p. 11.

[90] Colton MS, *loc. cit.*

[91] Chapman, *op. cit.*, p. 221.

[92] Colton MS, *loc. cit.* Because of contradictory evidence it is uncertain just who suggested linking together the various segments that eventually made up the main stem of the C. B. & Q. from Chicago through Aurora, Mendota, Galesburg, and Burlington. According to Gates, Forbes and Joy were promoting the Central Military Tract as early as June, 1851, and were anxious to extend the Aurora Branch to meet it at that time. (Gates, *op. cit.*, pp. 44–46.) In view of the Michigan Central's great anxiety to reach Chicago and its natural desire to find western outlets, it is logical to suppose that Joy would be on the lookout

by uniting all our influences we could together build a railroad from *Burlington to Chicago*, via Galesburg: Further, that we should endeavor to engage the Michigan Central RR Co., which was composed of wealthy people, in our united project. . . .

He added that there was to be a special session of the Illinois legislature in June, 1852, and that he would undertake to have the Central Military Tract charter so amended as to allow a northern connection with *any* railroad leading to Chicago; meanwhile Wadsworth should have the Aurora Branch charter altered so as to connect with any road from the south.[93] Wadsworth and Grimes gave their hearty consent to the idea, and thereupon the three men put their heads together to work out a plan of campaign.[94]

The next day, according to agreement, Grimes returned to New York with the scheme and obtained the approval of John C. Green [95] and George Griswold,[96] both stockholders of the Michigan Central.

---

for such lines as the Central Military Tract. It has been impossible, however, to verify Gates' statements either from the sources cited or from the original records of the Aurora Branch and Central Military Tract. Furthermore, neither of these Illinois roads is mentioned in the Michigan Central *Annual Report* for 1852 although the report does speak of the potential traffic outlet over the Illinois Central (on p. 24). In a letter written in 1886 (see Appendix C, Part 1), Joy himself claimed credit for suggesting consolidation of the Aurora Branch and Central Military Tract, but the chronology on which he based his claim is open to question. The most complete and convincing account of the matter so far available is Chauncey M. Colton's 25-page manuscript (WL), written by him probably about 1878. It is reproduced in full in Appendix C, Part 2, below. The text accepts his account although the entire question is open to further research.

[93] Cf. esp. Joy's version, Appendix C.

[94] Although Grimes was personally enthusiastic, he requested that his name be kept secret from the public. This was obviously the better part of valor, for Mr. Grimes well knew that the construction of the proposed road would take all business from Galesburg and points west (including his home town, Burlington) to Chicago rather than to Peoria. Colton points out in his account that because of this enforced secrecy, "Senator Grimes has never received the credit due to his far-sighted vision in forming a combination which, in the future, should redound so greatly to the development & welfare of his own State, and to the great State of Illinois, whose interests were so intimately connected, and are today so indissolubly united to Iowa by the consummation of this great railroad enterprise." (Colton MS, *loc. cit.*)

[95] Cf. Forbes to Green, June 30, 1858. Quoted in Pearson, *op. cit.*, pp. 90–92.

[96] Griswold was not only an important stockholder of the Michigan Central, but "probably had the largest single investment in the Illinois Central." (Gates, *op. cit.*, pp. 40, 77.)

These men gave him a letter of approval to John W. Brooks at Detroit,[97] who added his blessing to the proposal providing the two charters could be amended as suggested. Meanwhile, Colton returned to Galesburg to revise the Military Tract charter. He used the Illinois Central instrument for a model, except for the land-grant clauses. The route was changed so as to allow the company to build to a point on or near the Rock Island "or on or near the line of any other railroad or railroads connecting with or extending to the . . . city of Chicago." [98] When the stockholders had approved of these changes, he set off for Springfield to put through the deal.[99] As might have been expected, he found serious opposition from the Peoria and Oquawka,[100] but in due course the charter was granted as written on June 19, 1852. The Military Tract was thus given permission to build northeastward to "a" Chicago connection, and three days later the Aurora Branch was authorized to change its name to Chicago and Aurora Railroad Company and to build southwestward to a junction with the Military Tract.[101] Meanwhile, Colton was endeavoring to secure the active aid of James F. Joy, whom he had met at Springfield for the first time. Joy was thoroughly in favor of the scheme prepared by Colton, Grimes, and Wadsworth, but declared there was one great obstacle, — the presence of the Northern Cross paralleling the Military Tract within five miles. Thereupon Colton prevailed upon the Northern Cross people to terminate their line at Galesburg; the legislature approved this change, and Joy agreed to raise eastern capital for his future western connections.[102]

Immediately new difficulties arose. Joy did indeed raise stock subscriptions for the Military Tract among his seaboard friends, but these were to be paid only if $300,000 were pledged locally. This was an enormous sum for a new, rural district to supply. Colton and his friends were still $50,000 short of their goal when Brooks and Joy appeared in Galesburg with the ultimatum that unless the entire local quota were forthcoming, eastern aid would be canceled. Once more

---

[97] Brooks was then superintendent and engineer of the Michigan Central. (MC, *Annual Report* for 1852, Boston, 1852, p. 3.)

[98] CBQ, *Documentary History*, vol. I, p. 38.

[99] Colton MS, see Appendix C, below.

[100] *Ibid.*

[101] CBQ, *Corporate History*, pp. 8, 10.

[102] Colton MS, *loc. cit.*

JOHN W. BROOKS
1818–1881

CHAUNCEY S. COLTON
1800–1885

stepping into the breach, Colton consulted his friend, Silas Willard, and between them they put up the required amount. Their action assured completion of the project.[103] On October 14, 1852, John Brooks was elected president of the rejuvenated company, Colton and Willard were among the 13 directors, and the stock issue was increased from $100,000 to $600,000.[104] At the same time, John M. Forbes and his colleague, William Amory, agreed to float a bond issue of $800,000. Thus was a through route assured from Chicago to Galesburg.[105]

There was but one missing link in the program as originally hatched in Boston, — the line between Burlington and Galesburg. To secure this outlet, the Peoria and Oquawka had to be persuaded to build through Galesburg. Colton undertook to provide the incentive. Through his friend, Grimes, he arranged to have the P. & O. directors meet in Monmouth in October on the afternoon of the same day that the directors of the Military Tract met in Galesburg. When Brooks and Joy had finished their business at the morning session, Colton piloted them, somewhat against their will, to Monmouth. The result was an agreement whereby the Galesburg group was to pay cash for 50 $1,000 P. & O. bonds, in return for which that line would build through the subscribing city.[106] As 1852 drew to a close, then, the western outlet for the Michigan Central was approaching reality, not only on paper, but on the ground. The Chicago and Aurora had started construction southwestward from Aurora, the Military Tract had let contracts for the building from Mendota to Galesburg, and the Peoria and Oquawka had agreed to build through Galesburg to East Burlington.

At first, affairs progressed smoothly enough. By October, 1853, through trains from Chicago were running on the C. & A. to Mendota,[107] and on December 7, 1854, they reached Galesburg over the completed Central Military Tract.[108] In the south and west, however, trouble was brewing. After completing some 19 miles east from the Mississippi River, the Peoria and Oquawka ran out of funds, and the Military Tract was forced to finance construction between the distressed company's railhead and Galesburg. There was no way to collect this debt except to buy the road, but the contractors, Moss, Harding &

[103] *Ibid.*
[104] Chapman, *op. cit.*, p. 224.
[105] See map, p. 40.
[106] Colton MS, see Appendix C, below.
[107] CBQ, *Corporate History*, p. 8.
[108] *Ibid.*, p. 11.

Co., had been promised a first lien and were unwilling to sell their claim at a figure acceptable to Forbes. Colton finally prevailed upon the stubborn General Harding and the equally adamant Forbes to split the difference between their figures. With the contractor's claim out of the way, the Military Tract bought the P. & O. outright, to the

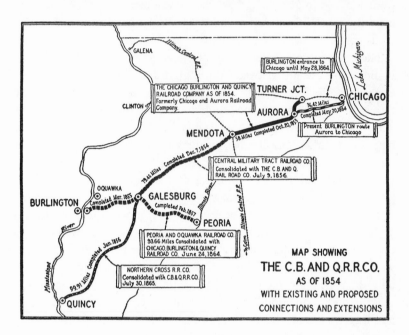

chagrin of the Peorians, who saw their hopes for a great New York-Peoria-Missouri River through route disappear into thin air.[109] Somehow, during the course of these negotiations the contractors continued their work, and on March 17, 1855, the line from East Burlington to Galesburg was opened, thus providing through service between Chicago and the Mississippi River.[110]

The importance of this through route to the towns it served was incalculable. Just before the final spike was driven, for example, the *Monmouth Atlas* exclaimed:

The Whistle of the Engine is becoming familiar to everyone and gives an impetus to business generally. Iron and ties are being brought forward,

[109] Colton MS, see Appendix C, below.
[110] CBQ, *Corporate History*, p. 11.

and the gap in the road will soon be completed, when the passenger cars will start running. We predict a heavy Spring's business — a great influx of strangers and a "tall time" generally. The boys and girls (especially the newly married ones) will want to see how the "critter" runs so fast without "bursting," and of course they will have to take a trip down east, or perhaps pay a flying visit to Burlington and take a peep at the "Hawkeyes" just across the Father of Waters. And the old folks, who "never saw the like before" will have to take a ride, just to look after the boys and girls, for fear they might not return safely, and so forth and so on. So, that, between the "old folks and young folks" and the young folks and the *girls*, we may expect a rush for the cars, so soon as they make their appearance and go through. The time has long been looked for, and when it comes, we hope there will be a "good time" generally, both with those who ride upon a rail, and those who *rail* (if there be any such), because they can't ride at all.[111]

There was no mistaking the earnest feeling behind this editorial, despite its rollicking tone. A week later, when the last rail had been laid, the same journal solemnly declared that communication had now been opened "with the universal Yankee nation, all Christendom and the balance of mankind." A new era, particularly in business relations, was officially proclaimed; indeed, was it not possible now to ship out the bountiful produce of the region, and "to visit the great commercial marts upon the Atlantic within the remarkably short space of time of from 48 to 60 hours . . . ?"[112] The people of Monmouth were about to participate in the lusty growth of a new nation, but they were surprised themselves at the speed of their own progress. Within three weeks the *Atlas* could present a list of particulars; on March 30 it reported:

The Railroad is putting new life and activity into everybody. Business is going ahead rapidly. Pork buyers and pork sellers are on the alert — wheat and other kinds of grain is coming in from the country, and as rapidly going out — hogs are taken off alive, by the hundred, to Chicago, where they are butchered and packed for the French soldiers in the Crimea; lumber and goods are arriving from abroad; strangers are on the lookout for new homes, and there seems to be a "good time" generally among business men of all classes. All kinds of produce can now be turned into cash at high prices, and if farmers do not get rich it will certainly be their own fault. With frugality and industry they can now make comfortable homes, educate their children, ride upon the railroad, and enjoy some of

[111] *Monmouth Atlas*, March 2, 1855.
[112] *Ibid.*, March 9, 1855.

the comforts in anticipation of which they have looked forward with
anxious and yearning hearts. The "good time" which has been so long on
its way, may with truth be said to have come. Let those who can do so
enjoy it, as best they may.[113]

Less than a year after this account was written, the Northern Cross
was completed between Quincy and Galesburg,[114] and the Chicago,
Burlington and Quincy existed in fact. From the date of their completion, both the Peoria and Oquawka and Northern Cross were operated as part of the Burlington system, although the companies were
not formally consolidated with the C. B. & Q. until 1864 and 1865,
respectively.[115]

This growth of the system, as well as its increasing eastern backing,
was reflected by the changes in title and in the personnel of the directorate. As early as February 14, 1855, the Chicago and Aurora renamed
itself The Chicago, Burlington and Quincy Railroad Company; [116]
and the title was retained unchanged except for replacing "Railroad"
by "Rail Road" when the Central Military Tract was formally consolidated with it on July 9, 1856.[117] Consummation of this merger
brought easterners and westerners together on the company's board.
In addition to Joy, Brooks, and five other easterners, Chauncey S.
Colton, two of the Gale family (including the founder of Galesburg),
Silas Willard, and James Bunce were elected directors.[118] A year later
the balance swung back again heavily to the East, presumably denoting
the increased financial stake of the Boston group. Of the local westerners, only Chauncey Colton remained in office (as he did until
1876),[119] and for the first time the board included John Murray Forbes,
his brother R. Bennet Forbes,[120] Edward L. Baker,[121] and Nathaniel
Thayer,[122] Boston capitalists already interested in western railroads,
and Erastus Corning[123] of the New York Central. The complexion

[113] *Ibid.,* March 30, 1855.
[114] The Northern Cross was completed on January 31, 1856. (CBQ, *Corporate History,* p. 29.)
[115] CBQ, *Corporate History,* pp. 16, 30.
[116] *Ibid.,* p. 9.
[117] *Ibid.,* p. 10.   [118] CBQ ORB, p. 89.
[119] *Poor's Manual for 1875-76,* p. 504; *Poor's Manual for 1876-77,* p. 290.
[120] CBQ, *Annual Report* for 1857 (Chicago, 1857), p. 3.
[121] *Ibid.*
[122] *Ibid.* Thayer was also interested in the Hannibal and St. Joseph. (HSJ, *Annual Report* for 1856, Hannibal, 1856, p. 3.)
[123] Frank W. Stevens, *op. cit.,* pp. 401–402. Corning was interested, along with

of the directorate remained essentially the same for the next dozen years.[124] On June 24, 1864, when the C. B. & Q. formally absorbed the successor of the Peoria and Oquawka, the present corporation, the Chicago, Burlington & Quincy Railroad Company, came into existence.[125]

V. THE PROBLEM OF EXPANSION INTO IOWA

In view of the history of those hectic years from 1845 to 1856, it would seem that the Burlington system originated chiefly from the coincidence of two circumstances: (1) the determination of several vigorous Illinois communities to bring a through railroad line within their limits, and (2) the rivalry between two active eastern groups over the potential traffic between the seaboard and the Mississippi basin. Once the Michigan Central accepted the Michigan Southern's gage of battle and began the race for Chicago and the territory beyond, it was obvious that construction would continue until one or both of the contestants reached their goal. Thus it is probable that some sort of a system would have been built to provide the Michigan Central with a western outlet, but the fact that the independent Burlington came into being along its present route was due to the vision and energy of the men from Aurora and Galesburg, combined with the ability and power of Forbes, Brooks, and Joy. John Murray Forbes originally embarked in a Michigan railroad enterprise that was supposed to end with decorum and profit when the rails reached the lake. But he found himself projected into a rough-and-tumble fight to reach Chicago ahead of his rivals, and it was only by abandoning his predilections for conventional procedure that he was able — with the stalwart help of Joy and Brooks — to win that battle. Once arrived in Chicago, there was nothing to do but keep on, for the Rock Islanders had already begun their swift race for the Mississippi. There was a trace of classical symmetry when the problem of where to expand was solved by other men who had turned promoters. Until 1850, for example, both Elisha Wadsworth and Chauncey Colton were known primarily as dry goods merchants, perfectly content to ride on other people's railroads. But when these men and their colleagues found

---

Forbes, in the Hannibal and St. Joseph as early as 1854. (See Edward B. Talcott, *Report upon the Hannibal and St. Joseph Railroad . . . and the Land*, Boston, 1854, p. 3.)

[124] CBQ, *Annual Reports* for 1858–1870 (Chicago, Boston, 1858–1870), *passim*.

[125] CBQ, *Corporate History*, p. 17.

their towns in danger of being stranded by more active competitors, they gathered up their resources and met the challenge. A benevolent fate threw these various groups together; fortunately they possessed among them the skill, imagination, and money to translate a dare into a profitable enterprise.

In view of their record, then, it was altogether logical to find them, by 1856, already interested in the rich lands and markets of Iowa just across the Mississippi from their western terminus. Constructing a railroad in a relatively undeveloped region, however, was at best a risky and difficult venture. The years since 1830 had abundantly proven that fact. During their first quarter century of existence, railroads in America were generally built from or between existing centers of population. This was entirely logical, for roads so located, if properly managed, could hardly fail to prosper, and private capital was readily available to build them. The farther west the rails pushed, however, the sparser became the population, and it was progressively harder for promoters, no matter how enthusiastic, to coax eastern dollars to their aid. For lack of outside support, the grandiose Illinois plan of 1837 had collapsed, and for the same reason the two roads across the base of Michigan had languished until the rise of Chicago guaranteed their success. When it came to building the C. B. & Q. across Illinois, even Forbes and Joy, at the insistence of their eastern connections, had demanded and obtained substantial local aid before they had underwritten the proposition. In some cases, even such a guarantee of local aid was not enough to secure outside capital. The Illinois Central, for example, had been projected some 14 years before construction had begun. Likewise, the Hannibal and St. Joseph, designed to connect the Mississippi and Missouri rivers, had waited from 1847, when it was incorporated, until 1853 before building was undertaken. The decisive factor in both these projects had been a grant of land from the federal government.

Consequently, the problem of when to expand westward through Iowa depended on whether enough aid from the community or from the federal government or both could be secured. That a railroad would someday span Iowa from the Mississippi to the Missouri was inevitable. But when was it safe to start such a project? That was the question in the minds of Forbes and his associates while they were forging their system in Illinois.

CHAPTER II

Southern Iowa Plans Its Railroad, 1852–1856

Iowa afforded a broad stage for the drama of railroad building and colonization. Stretching more than 300 miles between the Mississippi and Missouri rivers and about 200 miles north and south, the state embraced an area a fifth again as large as New York State, most of it level or only gently rolling.[1] Wet springs, warm summers, long growing seasons, and favorable winds offered a happy combination for the farmer. An average annual rainfall ranging between 26 and 36 inches and coming principally during the growing season dispelled fear of drought, although destructive blizzards, unchecked by the trees and settlements of a later day, were the nemesis of many an early pioneer. Soil for the most part was rich, windblown limestone, with areas of sandstone and gravel reminiscent of the glaciers. Constant erosion was a menace, then as now, and the periodic overflow of the muddy rivers created the occasional swamplands which developed into a political as well as an agricultural problem. On the whole, however, Iowa was as near to a farmer's paradise as could be found in America; it has been estimated that at least a quarter of all the Grade I agricultural land in the country lies within its borders.

On his famous western voyage of 1673, Père Marquette visited this favored region, but probably the first permanent white settler was his countryman, Julien Dubuque, who arrived in 1788. This young French Canadian became so friendly with the Fox Indians that they ceded him about 150,000 acres surrounding their lead mines, and he began the various operations that flourished until his death in 1810. Not only were the mines actively exploited, but farms were cleared, a furnace and mill erected, and a store set up for exchanging goods with the Indians. Twice each year boats floated down to St. Louis with ore, furs, and hides, returning with supplies, and Dubuque became one of the most important Upper Mississippi traders.[2] When he died, how-

---

[1] This and the remarks immediately following on the natural features of the state are from the Federal Writers, *Iowa* (New York, 1938), *passim*.

[2] Cardinal Goodwin, "The American Occupation of Iowa, 1833 to 1860," *Iowa*

ever, the Indians drove away his white companions and undertook to operate the mines themselves, but their days were numbered by the international events that had recently taken place.[3] Thanks to Napoleonic diplomacy and some shrewd Yankee horse-trading, the vast Louisiana Territory had fallen from the feeble hands of Spain into the lap of the United States. It was not long after Dubuque's death that the hardy trappers of J. J. Astor's American Fur Company began to erect their crude posts up and down the land; Keokuk, Muscatine, Council Bluffs, and Sioux City sprang into turbulent existence.[4] And, as the 1820's wore on, miners in northern Illinois and southwestern Wisconsin turned covetous eyes towards the old lead diggings west of the river. Some, in fact, crossed the stream and squatted on Indian land, and it required federal troops to oust them in 1831.[5] But the swelling westward tide of immigration could not be held back indefinitely, and merely awaited sufficient provocation to spill over. An excuse was not long in coming. In April, 1832, a band of Sac Indians crossed to the east bank of the Mississippi in violation of a treaty that had been forced upon them, and were slaughtered by federal troops in what has become known as the Black Hawk War.[6] The treaty terminating hostilities provided that the Indians should sell a strip of territory about 50 miles wide along the western bank of the Mississippi extending northward from the Missouri boundary to the approximate parallel of Prairie du Chien.[7] By this Black Hawk Purchase, the door to Iowa was at last thrown wide open, and settlers swarmed across the Father of Waters to their new home.

It is probable that within two weeks thereafter claims had been

---

Journal of History and Politics, vol. XVII, no. 1 (January, 1919), pp. 84–86; M. M. Ham, "The First White Man in Iowa," *Annals of Iowa*, third series, vol. II, no. 5 (April, 1896), pp. 329–344; Charles Negus, "The Early History of Iowa," *Annals of Iowa*, first series, vol. V, no. 3 (July, 1867), p. 877. In addition to Dubuque, two French farmers obtained titles in the 1790's from the Spanish authorities to land in what is now Lee and Clayton counties. (Goodwin, *loc. cit.*, pp. 84–86.)

[3] Ham, *loc. cit.*, pp. 331–332, 337.

[4] Federal Writers, *op. cit.*, *passim*.   [5] Goodwin, *loc. cit.*, p. 87.

[6] Augustine M. Antrobus, *History of Des Moines County, Iowa* (Chicago, 1915), pp. 20–21.

[7] Antrobus, *op. cit.*, pp. 22–25; Goodwin, *loc. cit.*, p. 87. See map, p. 283. Cf. Charles C. Royce, "Indian Land Cessions in the United States," *Eighteenth Annual Report of the Bureau of American Ethnology* (1896–97), pt. 2, pp. 766 *et seq.*

entered on land within the present city of Burlington, although the Purchase was not incorporated into the public domain until June 1, 1833; early the following year the Vermonter, John B. Gray, landed at the bustling outpost and named it for the town of Burlington in his own state.[8] Meanwhile, Sandusky, Fort Madison, and Keokuk were founded, and by 1836 it was estimated that 10,531 people occupied the new district attached, for the moment, to Michigan. Two years later this figure had more than doubled, and after a brief period under Wisconsin jurisdiction, Iowa was given territorial status in its own name. Expansion never halted. Iowa City was laid out in 1839 as the new capital, and when the federal census takers arrived during the next year, there were over 43,000 people in the territory. Eastern newspapers sang the praises of this huge productive garden, and it was apparent that a new state would soon be clamoring for admission to the Union.[9]

In 1843, this population was predominantly from the South or of southern antecedents. Many of the settlers came from the lower counties of Ohio, Indiana, and Illinois, where they had paused on their trek from Tennessee, Kentucky, or Virginia. They demanded from the government little more than the protection of life, liberty, and property; popular education, care of the insane and aged, and encouragement to business were deemed beyond the scope of state authority.[10] Furthermore, being devoted followers of Andrew Jackson, they were particularly suspicious of devices like banks of issue and extensive private corporations.[11] In contrast to these people, a constantly growing minority was arriving from the northland. First comers were mainly from New England, followed by bands from New York and Pennsylvania, then northern Indiana and Ohio. Many of them came for the express purpose of founding schools and churches; the college that was forerunner of Grinnell, established in 1843 in Lee County, was an example of their work. By 1850 they had set up no less than 50 academies, universities, and colleges; meanwhile, they began building up sentiment in favor of increased education, a more

[8] Antrobus, *op. cit.*, pp. 95–102.

[9] Goodwin, *loc. cit.*, pp. 87–90.

[10] F. I. Herriott, "The Transfusion of Political Ideas and Institutions in Iowa," *Annals of Iowa*, third series, vol. VI, no. 1 (April, 1903), pp. 50–54.

[11] Cyrenus Cole, *A History of the People of Iowa* (Cedar Rapids, 1921), ch. xxxiv.

liberal attitude towards business, and a sterner stand against slavery.[12]

The first convention which met to draw up a state constitution at Iowa City in 1844 reflected the social and political complexion of the day. Of the 72 present, 41 were farmers, ten were lawyers, and only four were merchants. The rest were millers, miners, mechanics, and other non-white-collar men. In the same group of 72, 44 were technically natives of northern states (though many came from the pro-South portions of Ohio, Indiana, and Illinois), 25 from the southern states, and only three were of foreign birth. Nearly all were under fifty years of age, comparatively innocent of history, but bred in the ways of the frontier and possessed of much common sense. Over howls of the Whig minority, they framed a simple constitution expressly prohibiting banks of issue and restricting corporations. As it happened, a dispute over boundaries with Congress led to the rejection of this first effort, but the constitution that was finally accepted and approved on December 28, 1846, exhibited the same suspicion of business.[13]

As in every community on the outskirts of economic life, transportation from the first was of vital importance to the people of Iowa. When in 1833 settlers began taking up land in the Black Hawk Purchase, they followed the conventional line of least resistance and built their roads along the old Indian trails. Before long the territorial legislature took an official hand and on January 25, 1839, appointed three surveyors to locate a highway from Burlington westward to the Indian country. As one writer has pointed out, this was, in a sense, the actual beginning of the "Burlington Route" to the West.[14] Mount Pleasant and New London were already in existence, and as the 'forties wore on, the rapidly increasing influx of immigrants through Burlington taxed the prairie highroad to the limit. Complaints regarding travel conditions were frequent, and newspapers began advocating an all-weather plank road. Some radicals, indeed, held that it would be better to invest the money in a railroad, but the expense of such an enterprise and the lack of eastern connections seemed at the time to be insurmountable obstacles. During the fall and winter of 1847, local

[12] Herriott, *loc. cit.*

[13] Cyrenus Cole, *op. cit.*, ch. xxxiv.

[14] Ben Hur Wilson, "Burlington Westward," *Palimpsest*, vol. XVI, no. 10 (November, 1935), p. 306. Cf. Antrobus, *op. cit.*, pp. 348–351. See map, p. 242.

meetings were held to discuss the problem, and on February 8, 1848, the Burlington and Mount Pleasant Plank Road Company was formed by prominent citizens. Surveys were made immediately, and the stock sold so successfully that the officers sought legislative authority for their enterprise. This they received on January 15, 1849, when the General Assembly granted to William F. Coolbaugh and others permission to build a highway, obtain land by condemnation, and charge tolls. It was now up to the promoters to translate their ideas into reality.

There were the usual difficulties to face: surveys had to be corrected and remade, and condemnation proceedings were complicated even when not acrimonious. For a while during the winter of 1850 money was slow coming in, but supporters of the project redoubled their efforts.[15] In February, 1851, James W. Grimes, who had industriously promoted the charter among members of the Assembly, wrote his father in New Hampshire:

We have a great railroad and plank-road fever here now. We have nearly completed a plank-road thirty miles west of this place. I am the president of the company, have had the entire responsibility and management of the work, and I think it will pay well. I have four thousand dollars of stock in it.[16]

Finally, in December, 1851, the last planks of white oak were pounded into place, and the 28-mile highway opened for business over its entire length. Toll gates every four miles took care of the business aspects of the enterprise, while even more numerous taverns catered to the human needs of the patrons.[17]

The completion of this road naturally called for a celebration which was duly held on December 18, when citizens of Mount Pleasant, Burlington, Brighton, New London, Trenton, Deedsville, "and other points interested" gathered at Mount Pleasant. As usual, they passed resolutions and congratulated themselves upon the successful outcome of their project, pointing out that they now possessed an "easy

[15] Wilson, *loc. cit.*, and "Planked from Burlington," *Palimpsest*, vol. XVI, no. 10 (November, 1935), pp. 309-323.

[16] J. W. Grimes to his father, February 15, 1851 (CNB, n.p.); cf. William Salter, *Life of James W. Grimes* (New York, 1876), pp. 18, 30.

[17] Wilson, *loc. cit.*, and "From Planks to Rails," *Palimpsest*, vol. XVI, no. 10 (November, 1935), p. 324.

and convenient transit" for their produce and supplies, not only to the Mississippi, but to the Peoria and Burlington Railway [18] and thence to the Atlantic cities. These people well realized the necessity of adequate transportation to and from the country's central markets. They expressed the hope that their new highway eventually would be but one of a chain that would develop the agricultural and mineral resources of the entire state and advance "the general personal and moral interests" of the people.[19]

This was not all. It was logical enough to praise a job well done and to indulge the hope that more highways would be built, but already a new form of transportation was proving its superiority. The next resolution made that plain:

. . . while we regard our plank roads as emphatically the farmer's highways to market and prosperity [it declared], yet we ardently look for the time when the Mississippi shall be connected with the Missouri by railway, thus facilitating communication between remote points and constituting a part of the railroad to the Pacific Ocean through southern Iowa. . . .[20]

Tracks built westward from Burlington, continued another resolution, would cross the most populous section of the state as well as form a logical extension of the Peoria and Burlington. Finally, it was resolved to memorialize Congress for a grant of public lands to aid in the construction of such a line. At the very moment it discarded dirt for planks, the "Burlington Route" was already dreaming of rails.

Railroads were not a new idea in Iowa, even in 1851. There had been talk of a pretentious double-tracked line from Belmont to Dubuque as early as 1836, and two years later in the first territorial legislature James W. Grimes had secured the passage of a memorial to Congress for a land grant to aid a line from Burlington to Mount Pleasant.[21] Obviously these notions were premature, but a scheme for a road from Dubuque westward to Iowa City and thence south to Keokuk had survived from that period until in 1849 an engineer's survey culminated in another memorial to Congress for land. Two years later, when this same project was awarded a right of way by the

---

[18] There was no railroad at this time with this corporate title. It was rather a colloquial name for the projected Peoria and Oquawka (CBQ, *Corporate History*, p. 14).

[19] *Burlington Daily Telegraph*, December 22, 1851.

[20] *Ibid.*

[21] Cyrenus Cole, *op. cit.*, ch. xlvii; Salter, *op. cit.*, p. 18.

assembly, the newly organized Davenport and Iowa City had already surveyed its route and was preparing to build.[22] It seemed inevitable that an east-west system would be constructed through Iowa City, probably connecting with the Rock Island that was already hurrying westward across Illinois.[23] Faced with this competitive situation, the citizens of southeastern Iowa had every reason to turn their thoughts and energies to a railroad of their own, nor was there apparently any hesitation in doing so because of the money already spent on the new plank road. In fact, many of those who had invested in the highway now turned eagerly to the newer project.[24] Within three weeks words at Mount Pleasant became action at Burlington.

As the new year 1852 opened, prospects were indeed bright. In a little more than a decade Iowa had increased her population fivefold until it exceeded 200,000. From Washington the correspondent of the *Burlington Daily Telegraph* wrote that the state might "safely calculate" upon drawing one-fourth of the nation's annual foreign immigration of 400,000 if only eastward rail connections were better established and if the citizens would unite in obtaining railroad land grants so that the interior of Iowa would become "more easy of access and consequently more tempting to the emigrant." [25] These conditions were coming closer to fulfillment every day. Although only a few miles of indifferent track straggled west from Chicago as 1852 opened, the success of the Iron Horse in the East was established, and men with reasonable vision realized it was merely a question of time before direct rail connection would be possible with the East. As to federal aid, Congress had already yielded to the increasing pressure for railroad grants and at any time might embark on a broad policy of aid in this respect. True, there had been no donations since that of 1850 to the Illinois Central and its southern connections, but the Hannibal and St. Joseph interests in neighboring Missouri were laboring in Congress, and if they succeeded, the chances for a subsequent grant across Iowa would definitely enter the realm of probability.[26] Of more specific encouragement in this respect was further news from Wash-

[22] Cyrenus Cole, *op. cit.*, ch. xlvii.
[23] See above, p. 31.
[24] Wilson, "From Planks to Rails," *loc. cit.*, p. 329.
[25] *Burlington Daily Telegraph*, January 13, 1852; cf. *ibid.*, January 1, 5, 6, 1852.
[26] *Cong. Globe*, 32nd Cong., 1st Sess. (1851–52), pp. 11, 22, 55, 308.

ington that Representative Mace of Indiana would shortly introduce in the House a bill making a grant for a railroad from the Wabash to the Missouri River. The projected line would start at Lafayette, Indiana, and run via Peoria, Burlington, Keosauqua, and Bloomfield; between Peoria and Burlington it would include the projected road linking those points. "Now," read the dispatch from the capital, "is the accepted time" to procure grants of land for railroad purposes.[27]

This same source, however, added a number of pertinent observations as to just how these donations would be made. The correspondent pointed out that there was a "decided opposition" on Capitol Hill to handing over any lands directly to companies or corporations, or defining routes too definitely. The general feeling was in favor of giving the lands in gross to the states who would then assume the responsibility of appropriating them to specific railroads.[28] He suggested also that all sections of Iowa should end their rivalries, join forces in their appeal to Congress, and ask for three lines directly across the state.

These propositions [he reasoned] would be sustained by the whole East . . . as completing the various chains of connection from the Atlantic to the Great Valley. They would be supported by all the southern states bordering upon the Mississippi as contributing from the teeming fields of our prairies so much more to the commerce of our river and the great markets of the South, whereas routes commencing and terminating within their own borders can command only the votes of our own delegation. . . .[29]

In the light of subsequent events, this was a significant prophecy.[30]

Fortified with such information, citizens of Burlington met in the council chamber on January 7, 1852, and heard James W. Grimes read a letter from General J. M. Morgan of Washington outlining the methods of obtaining such a grant. Five days later, another "large and enthusiastic" gathering resolved that the early construction of a transcontinental railroad was a work of the highest national importance and that "the aid of the General Government should to the utmost verge of political propriety be extended to works in that direction reaching through the states. . . ." A committee of five was appointed

[27] Burlington Daily Telegraph, January 6, 13, 1852.
[28] Ibid., January 1, 1852.
[29] Ibid., January 5, 1852.
[30] See below, ch. iii.

to prepare articles of incorporation for the Burlington and Missouri River Railroad.[31]

The men who were charged with forming this company represented the best business and legal talent the region could offer.[32] Judge Charles Mason, after graduating at the head of the class of 1829 at West Point, had turned to law and served as Chief Justice of Iowa during its entire territorial existence. In 1852 he had just finished his labors as chief commissioner delegated to revise the law code of the state.[33] His younger colleague, David Rorer, had come to Burlington in 1836 as a youthful lawyer and built the first brick house in Iowa. Since then his practice had grown steadily until he had become known as one of the state's leading attorneys.[34] Jonathan C. Hall was another rising lawyer who had moved west from New York by way of Ohio.[35] The most active of all, however, was William F. Coolbaugh, who had already shown his interest in transportation problems by appearing as chief incorporator of the plank road to Mount Pleasant. His earlier life was typical of many of the leading spirits of the West. Nine years before, as a young man of twenty-one, Coolbaugh had arrived in Burlington from Pennsylvania. Equipped chiefly with ideas, energy, and a rare gift for raising money, he had immediately opened a general store and bank.[36] When the first state assembly met, the legislators, accustomed to the paternalistic territorial government of Uncle Sam, were at a loss how to fill their empty treasury. As one of them later wrote: "We were in the condition of the man on a sinking ship who asked his fellow if he could pray, assuring him that 'something must be done, and that very quick.' So, waiving all other business, we sent for the Hon. W. F. Coolbaugh of Burlington, to act as our agent in borrowing seventy-five thousand dollars to set the wheels of

[31] *Burlington Daily Telegraph*, January 14, 1852.

[32] Antrobus, *op. cit.*, p. 353.

[33] Judge Wright, "The Yewall Portrait of Charles Mason," *Annals of Iowa*, third series, vol. II, nos. 2–3 (July–October, 1895), pp. 161–173.

[34] George Frazee, "An Iowa Fugitive Slave Case," *Annals of Iowa*, third series, vol. VI, no. 1 (April, 1903), pp. 29–30. Rorer became one of the B. & M.'s first attorneys, and held the position continuously until his death in 1884. Cf. Antrobus, *op. cit.*, pp. 398–400.

[35] Frazee, *loc. cit.*, p. 21. Hall was president of the B. & M. in 1855 and was particularly active in pushing through its construction to Ottumwa.

[36] J. T. Remey, "William F. Coolbaugh," *Annals of Iowa*, third series, vol. VII, no. 6 (July, 1906), pp. 401–412.

Government in motion and keep them so for a session at least. Mr. Coolbaugh acted promptly and successfully." [37] Three years later he had taken up his work with the plank road; it was logical now that he should be vitally interested in the railroad project.[38]

Another moving spirit of the enterprise, although not officially connected with it, was, of course, James W. Grimes. He was born in Deering, New Hampshire, on October 20, 1816. Like so many of his neighbors, he attended Dartmouth where, by coincidence, he drew James F. Joy as his tutor. His college career ended in his junior year, and after a few months in an eastern law office, he left for the West, arriving in the Black Hawk Purchase in May, 1835. There he entered into partnership with H. W. Starr, and at the age of twenty-two was sent to the first territorial legislature. His interest in railroads was already keen even though somewhat premature, for it will be recalled that at that early date he introduced a petition to Congress for a land grant for a railroad westward from Burlington. Twelve years later, after he had returned to private life, he again appeared in Iowa City in the interests of the Mount Pleasant Plank Road and subsequently took the part noted in the enterprise.[39] While the B. & M. was being organized, Grimes was in constant touch with the promoters, since his partner was one of the incorporators.[40]

The articles drawn up by these men and their associates on January 15, 1852, adopted the purposeful name of Burlington and Missouri River Rail Road Company, fixed the life of the company at fifty years, and the capitalization at $3,000,000. "The object of this incorporation," declared Article 10, "is to construct and use a railroad extending from Burlington to the most eligible point on the Missouri River; and along the most eligible routes." [41] By necessity, the western terminus and route were left vague, for there had been no detailed survey of the region, and topographical conditions were not sufficiently well known to warrant definite commitment in advance. Furthermore, this indefi-

---

[37] Alfred Hebard, "Recollections of Early Territorial Days," *Annals of Iowa*, third series, vol. II, nos 2–3 (July–October, 1895), pp. 219–220. Hebard made the first survey of the B. & M. See below, pp. 62–63.

[38] On August 2, 1852, Wm. F. Coolbaugh and two others took a mortgage of $500,000 on the Peoria and Oquawka. (CBQ, *Documentary History*, vol. I, p. 81.)

[39] Salter, *op. cit.*, ch. i. See above, p. 49.

[40] CBQ, *Documentary History*, vol. II, p. 4.   [41] *Ibid.*, pp. 4–7.

niteness would work strongly to the company's advantage in quite a different way, for it meant the line would be built where the people of southern Iowa most desired it. Their preferences, of course, would be judged by the size of their stock subscriptions.[42]

Article 12 hopefully provided for the acceptance of a federal land grant. The directors were authorized to make "any arrangements which is [sic] suitable and proper with the State of Iowa, for the purpose of securing the benefit of any lands which may be given to the State for the construction of the road herein contemplated." [43] It will be noted that the incorporators heeded the report from Washington that their grant would come, if at all, through the agency of the state rather than directly to the corporation. Article 15 provided that the directors might issue calls for installments upon stock subscriptions up to 25 per cent in any one year.[44]

Armed with these articles, the incorporators met on January 17 and elected nine directors who, in turn, proceeded to choose William F. Coolbaugh as president.[45] Their next action was significant: a committee was instructed to notify James W. Grimes of his appointment to go to Washington and use his influence to secure an appropriation of lands from Congress. Since there were as yet no funds in the company's till, the committee was further instructed to ask the Burlington City Council for a subsidy of $500 to cover the cost of Grimes' journey.[46] In due course, the city voted the sum requested, thereby providing an early and tangible example of the mutual interest between railroad and community. The fact that the donation was in city scrip worth but 80 cents on the dollar made the gift none the less significant.[47]

The reports that reached Burlington from Washington during the first months of 1852 alternately raised and dashed hopes of obtaining a land grant for the B. & M. Consideration of a bill for that purpose was resumed in the Senate in February, but its chances of passage

---

[42] See below, pp. 63–67.

[43] CBQ, *Documentary History*, vol. II, pp. 4–7.

[44] *Ibid.*, p. 7.

[45] Article 4 provided that the incorporators should elect the first board of directors. As soon as $50,000 in stock were taken, however, the incorporators were to call a meeting of stockholders at Burlington which would then, and annually thereafter, elect their own directors. (*Ibid.*, p. 5.)

[46] BMI ORB, p. 4.   [47] BMI ORB, p. 5.

were compromised by the known differences of opinion among the citizens of Iowa as to the respective merits of the Dubuque and Keokuk on the one hand and the Burlington road on the other. Although the Iowa delegates were apparently in favor of aid to both, opponents of any grant seized upon the divided local sentiment as a reason for defeating the measure.[48] Eventually, it passed the Senate, but it was generally understood there that the bill would fail in the House.[49] There was good reason for this belief, for the representatives of the old states in the lower chamber were insisting on some provision for their own constituents, such as equivalent donations of land in the territories. Furthermore, some of the eastern representatives declared they infinitely preferred aid to actual settlers rather than to railroads. The *Burlington Daily Telegraph* was inclined to fall in line with this preference, for a measure of this nature would at least mean that Iowa would soon be thronged with immigrants. "Give us but these," concluded the paper, "and we need not ask the general government for further aid."[50] Apparently that journal did not feel the railroad needed lands to finance its building. Indeed, ten days later the editor remarked that although he would "patiently await" the House's action on the bill, "the B. & M. westward is to be constructed grant or no grant."[51]

If this were a glib generalization, there was at least some excuse for it. On February 5 the subscribers to stock, anxious for work to begin, had held their first meeting. They requested the company's directors to procure the right of way for the first 30 miles "at the earliest practicable period."[52] At the same time ten stockholders were named to represent the company at the Ottumwa convention to be held on behalf of the road the following week.[53]

It seems [commented the *Des Moines Courier*] that we shall have a railroad whether Congress grants us any land or not. And that is the right spirit. For if we stick in the mud and do not try to get out, Hercules will not help us. Our citizens too seem to evince a disposition to subscribe liberally. And we verily [sic] believe that the road can be built from

[48] *Burlington Daily Telegraph*, March 10, 1852.
[49] *Ibid.*, March 29, 1852.
[50] *Ibid.*, March 19, 1852.
[51] *Ibid.*, March 29, 1852.
[52] BMI ORB, p. 5; cf. *Burlington Daily Telegraph*, February 7, 1852.
[53] BMI ORB, p. 5.

Burlington to this place [by means of a connecting line from Ottumwa] without the aid of a grant.[54]

From Burlington to Ottumwa railroad meetings were held. In the latter city the convention was so largely attended that it had to meet in the biggest available building, which happened to be the Congregational Church. Delegations from 14 counties were present, the most prominent citizens spoke, and letters were read from Judge Mason and his colleagues. According to a contemporary, the feasibility of the route was "fully demonstrated" and a string of resolutions, all expressing reasons why the road should be built, were unanimously adopted.[55] Specifically, it was resolved that since the B. & M. was "essential to the early and successful settlement of the vast public domain in the interior of the State," [56] it was entitled to the aid of the federal government; therefore, the Iowa members of Congress should be requested to secure the passage of a land grant. Furthermore, it was resolved that even though the projected line could not secure a connection with Indianapolis by way of Lafayette, "we regard the B. & M. as indispensable to the best populated and fertile portion of our state, as it will afford the only outlet for our products to the Mississippi River and connect us by way of the Burlington & Peoria, and Central Illinois, and Military Tract roads, with the lakes of the north and the railroads terminating in New York and Boston." [57] Those present pledged that even if they could not obtain a federal grant they would complete the line by their own efforts and resources at the earliest possible day.

Amid all this enthusiasm, however, there was a word of caution. The Hon. William Thompson of Mount Pleasant declared that he was in favor of land grants to railroads, but he was utterly opposed to the usual policy of raising the minimum price of the alternate sections reserved by the government to $2.50 an acre because doing so had "a manifest tendency" to retard settlement and cultivation of these tracts and operated as a "wanton hardship" to those seeking permanent

[54] *Burlington Daily Telegraph*, February 2, 1852, reprinted from *Des Moines Courier*.

[55] G. D. R. Boyd, "Sketches of History and Incidents connected with the Settlement of Wapello County, from 1843 to 1859, inclusive," *Annals of Iowa*, first series, vol. VI, no. 3 (July, 1868), pp. 185-187.

[56] *Burlington Daily Telegraph*, February 17, 1852.

[57] *Ibid.*

homes.[58] Although Thompson's point of view did not eventually prevail, it was a challenge to the B. & M. to prove its ability as a colonizer, if and when it should receive a grant.

In Washington the scene remained confused. On the theory that only an omnibus land measure might pass,[59] it was proposed to submit a bill making grants to every state in the Union except Texas, which had retained its own public domain when it joined the United States in 1845.[60] Such wholesale donations and the resulting glut of the land market would obviously overshadow if not obliterate the appeal that railroad lands would otherwise have for prospective purchasers. There was not much possibility, however, that a bill of this sort could become law.[61]

More practical competitors for congressional favor were the various homestead proposals; one such was under consideration in May of 1852, and there were those who feared its passage would render any railroad lands valueless. This the *Burlington Daily Telegraph* denied, adding: "if the question were submitted to our citizens as to which of the two they would prefer, free farms for the landless or grants for internal improvement purposes, we doubt not they would say with an almost unanimous voice, 'give us the Homestead Law and the worthy people whom it will bring among us. Give us the people, and we will build our own roads and make our own improvements.' " [62] But congressmen, even from Iowa, were moving in the opposite direction. A bill for granting land to a Wabash and Missouri River Railroad, which would include the B. & M. within its length, was accepted by the Senate; [63] meanwhile, in the House, Representative Henn spoke in behalf of three Iowa grants: from Burlington to the Missouri, from Davenport to Council Bluffs, and from Keokuk to Dubuque.[64] Not until June, however, did both Senate and House concur on any railway bill, and then not for the benefit of Iowa. Instead, they authorized a grant of over 600,000 acres to the Hannibal and St. Joseph in northern Missouri,[65] and nearly twice as

[58] *Burlington Daily Telegraph*, February 20, 1852. Cf. Gates, *op. cit.*, p. 42.
[59] *Burlington Daily Telegraph*, March 19, 1852.
[60] *Ibid.* For the position of the Texas senators regarding the Iowa grant of 1856, see below, p. 79.
[61] *Burlington Daily Telegraph*, March 19, 1852.   [62] *Ibid.*, May 19, 1852.
[63] *Ibid.*, May 24, 1852.   [64] *Ibid.*, May 14, 1852.
[65] See map, p. 117. Cf. *Cong. Globe*, 32nd Cong., 1st Sess. (1851–52), pp. 773. 782, 1504–1507.

much to the "Southwestern Branch" of the Pacific Railroad in the same state. The news of this grant aroused even the lukewarm *Telegraph* which opined that Congress would no doubt be in a similarly favorable state of mind "when they come to vote upon a bill for a road passing through the very heart of the great grain-growing region of the northwest, and piercing the frontier at a point whence the great overland emigration takes its departure for the Pacific coast. . . . We already look upon the Wabash and Missouri River bill as good as passed." [66] Unfortunately for Burlington, this optimism was unwarranted. Two months later the B. & M. bill was still languishing in Congress, and the Washington correspondent of the *Iowa State Gazette* was of the opinion that the majority of the House had decided to give all pending railroad bills the "go-by" for that session. He explained that eastern members were determined to make any grants for railroads dependent upon some *quid pro quo* in the form of an increased tariff or a division of the public domain among all states. No rise in the tariff, he predicted, could take place so long as the Mississippi Valley remained "true to the principles of Jeffersonian democracy." [67] The situation for the time being, then, was a stalemate, and Congress adjourned on August 31 without further action. [68]

This was indeed a blow to the people of southeastern Iowa, and the question arose as to what to do next. Part of the answer was found in the election of James W. Grimes as representative from Des Moines County to the fourth General Assembly that was to meet in the winter of 1852–53. [69] No one in the vicinity had had a greater interest in transportation; perhaps now he could crystallize state sentiment so that Iowa might present a united front, particularly to Congress. Within a few weeks he fulfilled these hopes. Before the session had gone far, he secured the adoption of two important measures: a general law for granting right of ways to railroads and a new memorial to Congress praying for a grant to the B. & M. The latter passed the Iowa House by the encouraging vote of 41 to 21, which prompted the editor of the *Burlington Weekly Telegraph* to write that "this demonstration on the part of two-thirds of the people's representatives will, we trust, settle forever . . . the clamors

[66] *Burlington Daily Telegraph*, June 3, 1852.
[67] *Iowa State Gazette* (Burlington), August 25, 1852.
[68] *Ibid.*, September 15, 1852.
[69] Antrobus, *op. cit.*, p. 92.

of certain papers and . . . persons against what they had hitherto decried as a local and unpopular measure." [70] On December 18, Grimes wrote his wife with understandable pride: "I have succeeded in the principal object for which I came here, viz., upon the subject of railroads. . . . We had a fierce struggle for four days, but won the battle triumphantly." [71]

In all, Iowa was now requesting aid for four east–west lines,[72] and the state's leaders at Washington, Representative Henn and Senator

[70] *Burlington Weekly Telegraph*, December 25, 1852.

[71] Grimes to his wife, December 18, 1852 (CNB, n.p.).

[72] Salter, *op. cit.*, ch. i. Cf. Peter A. Dey, "Railroad Legislation in Iowa," *Iowa Historical Record*, vol. IX, no. 4 (October, 1893), pp. 540–655. Dey cites the following memorials made by the state assembly to Congress for land grants in aid of railroads:

January	22, 1848:	Dubuque to Keokuk
January	24, 1848:	Davenport to Iowa City and Council Bluffs
December	30, 1852:	Davenport to Muscatine and Council Bluffs
January	5, 1853:	Burlington and Keokuk to a junction east of the Des Moines River, thence to Council Bluffs
January	5, 1853:	McGregor to mouth of the Big Sioux (on Missouri R.)
January	5, 1853:	Dubuque to Des Moines and the Missouri River

In his "Comment by the Editor" in *Palimpsest*, vol. XVI, no. 10 (October, 1935), p. 336, John Ely Briggs reviews Grimes' interest in the plank road and Peoria and Oquawka and reached the conclusion that: "Improvements in transportation are not created by wishing, nor is causation revealed in legal records and statistical information. The personal factor is the vital element. He who would appraise the rise of Burlington will find a master key in the career of James W. Grimes." Whether or not this praise is too sweeping, it is true that as legislator and governor, Grimes consistently upheld business interests. (See below, pp. 69, 83.) Charles Aldrich, editor of the *Annals of Iowa* in third series, vol. II, no. 5 (April, 1896), reproduced on pp. 400–401 the following letter from Grimes to General A. C. Dodge, then senator for Iowa:

"House of Reps. Iowa City
Dec. 24 '52

Dear Sir: —

I have supposed that you might desire some information in relation to the present condition of railroad matters in this city. You may obtain information from other sources, and if so you will pardon me for troubling you. The project of a road from Dubuque to Keokuk is entirely dead. It has only twenty-one friends in the House to forty-two against it, and the disproportion is about the same in the Senate. Memorials are passed in the House for three roads:

1st. A road from Burlington to the Missouri River, at or near the mouth of Platte.

2nd. A road from Davenport *via* Muscatine to Kanesville (Council Bluffs).

3rd. A road from Dubuque to Fort Des Moines.

No other memorials will pass this winter, and the above may be regarded as

Jones, worked valiantly for this program. Despite their efforts, the Congresses of 1851–52 and 1852–53 failed to take the desired action,[73] although four large grants, totaling nearly 2,000,000 acres, were made to Arkansas and Missouri in February, 1853. In a way, this was encouraging, since it constituted a fresh recognition of the land-grant principle by Congress.[74] On the other hand, the delay in granting Iowa's specific request worked heavily against the B. & M., for time was at a premium.

Ever since October, 1851, the Rock Island forces had been pushing their tracks westward from Chicago; they had reached Joliet in a year and were already considering an Iowa extension.[75] On September 4, 1852, President Jervis and other officials were sumptuously dined by the citizens of Davenport who entertained serious hopes of participating in this new project. Tentative plans were made then, and the following February the Mississippi and Missouri Railroad Company was formally incorporated with power to construct a line from Davenport to Council Bluffs. Relations with the parent line were close. Among the directors of the M. & M. were Messrs. Farnam and Sheffield, builders of the Rock Island, Ebenezer Cook, a director of the latter, and William B. Ogden, first mayor of Chicago. Azariah Flagg served as treasurer for both companies. On January 17, 1853, the Illinois legislature granted a subsidiary of the two roads permission to construct a bridge across the Mississippi between Rock Island and Davenport.[76] The B. & M. had no time to lose.

---

the settled policy of the State. I will endeavor to have the memorials forwarded to you as soon as they shall be enrolled.

Yours truly, etc.

James W. Grimes"

Aldrich states that "the principal object for which Mr. Grimes became a member of the legislature was to start a movement in behalf of building railroads, and in this he succeeded admirably. He introduced the memorial for a grant of land by Congress to aid in the construction of the Burlington and Missouri railroad, and without doubt was friendly to the other lines mentioned, which were endorsed by the legislature." (*Ibid.*, p. 401.) Grimes was wrong in saying no more memorials would pass that session. The McGregor-Big Sioux petition went through with two of those cited by Dey under January 5, 1853. (See Dey, *loc. cit.*)

[73] *Cong. Globe*, 32nd Cong., 1st Sess. (1851–52), pp. 29, 332–334, 348–352, 390, 761–769, 950–951, 967, 1508–1510, 1511–1512. The Iowa land grant was not discussed during 1852–53, in the Second Session of the Thirty-Second Congress.

[74] Donaldson, *op. cit.*, p. 269.

[75] F. J. Nevins, *op. cit.*, pp. 10–11.   [76] *Ibid.*, pp. 8–9.

At this critical juncture, aid came from a new and welcome source. James F. Joy and John W. Brooks, acting on behalf of the Michigan Central Railroad Company, informed the B. & M. directors that they would consider favorably extending financial backing to the Iowa line.[77] The effect of this offer was electrifying. On March 9, 1853, the directors resolved that "inasmuch as influential citizens of the East proffer to assist us with abundant means to secure completion of the road, . . . we are proceeding with all energy, means, and resources in our power. . . . The prosperous condition of the affairs of this company," they continued, "requires that immediate steps be taken to consider a reconnaissance and location of the road from Burlington to the Missouri River . . . and to put the first two sections of the 50 miles of said road under contract at the earliest possible day."[78] At the same time it was resolved that subscription books should be opened in all counties along the line of the road. "We have come to the conclusion," commented the *Burlington Weekly Telegraph*, "that there is no use in longer wasting time by waiting on the slow and uncertain action of Congress."[79]

The final location of the route as far as the Des Moines River was immediately undertaken by Henry Thielsen, chief engineer. At the same time, Albert Hebard, a graduate in civil engineering from Yale, was put in charge of a party with no special instructions other than to explore and hunt out the "most feasible route" for a line from Ottumwa to Council Bluffs. On their first trip westward, the party relied mainly on common sense:

We did not plant an instrument or stretch a chain [wrote Hebard of that occasion], using our eyes for a careful reconnaissance and keeping notes of all we saw. The eye is the best surveying instrument ever made, especially on preliminary work. Mathematical instruments are of course

[77] Up to the present time, it has been impossible to locate the letters specifically offering this aid. It is possible that Grimes or Colton had mentioned the B. & M. when they were conferring with Joy and Brooks on behalf of the Central Military Tract and Peoria & Oquawka. Or it is possible that Grimes because of his long acquaintanceship with Joy wrote direct to the latter. The precise answer to these questions may probably be found in the Joy letters that form part of the Burton Historical Collection in Detroit. The evidence from the B. & M. directors' minutes for 1853, however, makes it certain that Joy and Brooks were the men who made the offer of assistance at that time. (BMI ORB, p. 6.)

[78] BMI ORB, p. 6.

[79] *Burlington Weekly Telegraph*, March 12, 1853.

necessary for the final adjustment of a determined line . . . but much time is often spent and expense incurred in railroad surveys, by measuring obstacles that are apparent at a glance. . . .[80]

Even such a superficial examination convinced the party that they would have to abandon the original hope of limiting grades to 40 feet per mile, for the broad valleys were usually separated by rather high and abrupt divides. At the Bluffs, Hebard spent several days poring over the government surveys and then returned slowly eastward, carefully leveling and measuring the entire route. In subsequent years, entire seasons were consumed in more detailed reconnaissance, but the road was finally located on this original survey with the exception of a slight change near Villisca.[81] Perhaps the practiced eye was the keenest judge after all.

Nearer home the company secured a more specific location. On August 4, 1853, the mayor of Burlington was directed by ordinance to survey the "accretions" along the Mississippi River which Congress had turned over to the city's disposition. He was also authorized to lease this extensive plat to the B. & M. for the yearly sum of $1 per year providing the company would erect thereon its depot, machine shops, and other buildings. The lease was approved by the voters, 901 to 54, and the railroad acquired a strategic site of great importance.[82] At the time, however, the accretions were under water and would require expensive reclamation.

Meanwhile, the directors redoubled their drive for funds. On March 16, the people of Henry County gathered at Fairfield and requested their county judge to submit to the voters the question of taking $100,000 worth of stock in the B. & M. A preliminary convention for the purpose was called for April 20.[83] The next week a similar gathering was held in Mount Pleasant, and the citizens of the county again resolved "to stand ready with their capital and credit to do more than their share in the construction of the road."[84] On April 20, the rail-

[80] Alfred Hebard, "The Original Survey of the C. B. & Q. R.R. Line," *Annals of Iowa*, third series, vol. VI, no. 3 (October, 1903), pp. 216–219.
[81] *Ibid.* It will be noted that Hebard's account was written by him 50 years after the events described. Contemporary evidence, if and when found, may or may not confirm his recollection.
[82] Antrobus, *op. cit.*, pp. 147–148.
[83] *Fairfield Ledger*, March 28? 1853.
[84] *Burlington Weekly Telegraph*, April 2, 1853.

road convention at Fairfield opened with citizens present not only from Henry but also from Des Moines, Jefferson, Wapello, Decatur, and Marion counties. After rehearsing the need of the country for the B. & M., they resolved that they would furnish abundant security in the form of stock subscriptions to the "capitalists who will furnish money to build the road." They also requested the governor to call a special session of the legislature in June for the purpose of authorizing counties to subscribe to stock in such companies.[85]

The governor refused to heed this appeal. As a result, many counties which in their official capacity wished to aid the road had no alternative but to subscribe for the stock on their own responsibility. They assumed that if their action were overruled by the Iowa Supreme Court, such a decision would be obtained before any stock should have been issued.[86] Proceeding on this basis, certain citizens of Des Moines County petitioned their judge to ask the electors whether they would subscribe $150,000 and issue bonds of the county to the company for a like sum in payment for the stock issue. Meetings were held throughout the county to whip up enthusiasm, and the *Burlington Weekly Telegraph* reported on July 29 that "there appears to be no other feeling than that they [the people] are in favor of the loan." [87] The proposition passed, 1617 to 236.[88] At the same time Wapello County was swinging into action. Following a preliminary meeting in Agency City in March,[89] its citizens gathered in Ottumwa on August 23 and voted that the county should become a stockholder to the extent of $100,000, said stock to be paid for by an issue of county bonds redeemable in 20 years and bearing not more than eight per cent interest. The bonds were not to be issued, however, until construction was actually under contract, and installments were not to exceed five per cent of the total per month. On behalf of this plan, "the county was thoroughly canvassed by gentlemen favorable to the proposition." As a result, when the vote was taken on September 24, it passed by a majority of 651. Subsequently, the company asked that private individuals in the county subscribe for $40,000 additional stock; by December 15, this too was accomplished.[90]

[85] *Burlington Weekly Telegraph*, April 30, 1853.
[86] *Ibid.*, June 4, 1853.
[87] *Ibid.*, July 29, 1853.
[88] Antrobus, *op. cit.*, pp. 353–354.
[89] *Burlington Weekly Telegraph*, April 2, 1853. [90] Boyd, *loc. cit.*, p. 187.

The need for raising cash led to an amendment in the company's articles of incorporation in November, 1853. Originally only 25 per cent of subscriptions could be called in one year; under the new arrangement this was raised to 60 per cent, equally divided on a monthly basis.[91] An entirely new article permitted the directors to receive subscriptions from any counties or municipal incorporations "upon such terms and conditions as may be agreed upon by them — such counties or municipal incorporations being entitled to all the rights and privileges of individual stockholders."[92] From the beginning the B. & M. was to be a coöperative neighborhood venture, inextricably bound up with the future of the region it served. Affairs were moving briskly.

As these developments were taking place, the directors of the B. & M. and their friends in the East were preparing for closer collaboration. Early in June, 1853, R. B. Forbes, brother of John Murray Forbes, arrived in Burlington and with Messrs. Warren and Tallant, the latter a director of the B. & M.,[93] drove out to Mount Pleasant and back. The easterner was vastly impressed by the countryside:

> It is *very fine* farming land [he wrote his wife], all settled and culti-vated, and if I had been dropped down there blindfolded, I should have imagined myself to be within a few miles of some of our great cities. I expected something wild, but I found it much more thickly settled than on the road of one hundred and twenty miles from Dubuque to Muscatine. We saw where the [B. & M.] road was being graded; seemed to be several feet thick of black loam, at least four feet, and the newly graded road looks just like a fine garden-bed prepared to plant strawberries, or other delicate plants. Nothing seems more necessary but to put in the crops — no stones or stumps. . . .[94]

This information he repeated in a letter to J. F. Burch, Esq., of Chi-cago, with the request that it be sent on to Joy and Forbes.[95]

[91] CBQ, *Documentary History*, vol. II, p. 7.
[92] *Ibid.*
[93] Warren became a director on October 26, 1853 (BMI ORB, p. 10); neither he nor Tallant was reëlected on March 29, 1854 (BMI ORB, p. 14).
[94] R. B. Forbes to his wife, June 10, 1853 (CNB, n.p.). Forbes was "so much pleased with the country" that he bought three farms with two houses on them, totaling 380 acres. (*Ibid.*)
[95] Forbes to Burch, June 10, 1853 (CNB, n.p.). Although there is no specific statement that one purpose of R. B. Forbes' trip was to investigate the B. & M., circumstantial evidence makes it almost certain that this was so. As noted in the

About the first of July, Joy in company with J. W. Brooks "as representatives of the Michigan Central Railroad Company" came west to Galesburg to confer with Coolbaugh and Tallant, who had been appointed by the B. & M. directors to secure the coöperation of the easterners in constructing the line from Burlington to the Missouri River. The precise nature and extent of the aid actually given has not been determined; it is probable that Brooks and Joy took either a considerable block of B. & M. stock or county bonds held by the railroad.[96] In any event, three days later the B. & M. directors elected their benefactors to two vacancies on the board and unanimously named Brooks as president of the company.[97] By the latter part of September, Thielsen had finished his task of locating the line as far as the Des Moines River at Ottumwa; he was immediately sent east in company with Coolbaugh for another conference with Brooks and Joy. Thus the enterprise was no longer a purely local matter. For richer or poorer, East and West were joined together in a common undertaking.

This effective collaboration came none too soon, for competition from the north showed no sign of slackening. On September 1, 1853, at Davenport, amidst blaring bands and profuse oratory, the first earth was turned for the Mississippi bridge. By the end of the following February, the Rock Island rails reached the eastern bank of the river, and on June 29, 1855, the first railroad spike was driven at Davenport as the Mississippi and Missouri began its race westward. As soon as the bridge builders could finish their task, through traffic would be established between central Iowa and the East.[98]

The B. & M. strained every nerve to meet this challenge. Momentarily, in the winter of 1853, hope rose again for federal aid. "The signs are favorable that a grant will be made in aid of the completion of the B. & M. . . . ," wrote the *Burlington Weekly Telegraph* in December, "provided the road shall be put under contract at an early

---

text, he asked to have this report forwarded to Messrs. Joy and J. M. Forbes. Pearson states that the latter "had seen the value to the Michigan road of this route across Iowa . . . *as far back as the summer of 1853*" (Pearson, *op. cit.*, p. 85; italics supplied); it is probable that J. M. Forbes sent his brother in order to obtain a firsthand account of the region. R. B. Forbes later became a director of the road. (BMI, *Annual Report* for 1858, Boston, 1858.)

[96] BMI, *Annual Report* for 1855–56 (Burlington, 1856), p. 15.

[97] BMI ORB, p. 8.   [98] F. J. Nevins, *op. cit.*, pp. 15, 19–20.

day." [99] In April, 1854, however, news from Washington was again discouraging. The adverse fate of Wisconsin and Minnesota railroad grants boded no good for the projects in Iowa.[100]

Nevertheless, late in March Thielsen's location to Ottumwa was officially adopted,[101] and in May contracts were made for building bridges, furnishing ties, and grading the line to Ottumwa. This last function, clearing and grading, was parceled out among no less than 18 different contractors, many of them local farmers who undertook to prepare the roadbed for a few miles near their home.[102] Meanwhile, the stockholders, meeting on March 29, took a new oath of allegiance. "As 'in union there is strength,'" they resolved, "the stockholders in said company hereby pledge themselves, individually and collectively to use their influence in every fair and honorable way to promote the success of said road in preference to any and every other project, and to abstain from furnishing any aid either individually or collectively to any other similar project until the success and construction of the B. & M. R. R. R. are rendered certain." [103] This declaration might imply that some stockholders had indulged in divided loyalty; henceforth none but hundred-per-centers would be welcome.[104]

[99] *Burlington Weekly Telegraph*, December 3, 1853. "The grant is sure to come," added the paper, "if by our own action we shall put the road upon such a basis as to claim the attention of Congress." (*Ibid.*)

[100] *Iowa Capital Reporter* (Iowa City), April 5, 1854.

[101] On March 22 from the western boundary of Burlington to Agency City; on March 29 from Agency City to Ottumwa. (BMI ORB, pp. 12–13.)

[102] The following awards were made on May 3, 1854: To Alfred Hebard, the building of the bridges on the entire first section of 75 miles, with the exception of the bridges over Skunk River and Big Creek; to Charles H. Snelson, the furnishing of the ties for Sections 1–20; to Sandon Mullen, the furnishing of ties for Sections 21–75.

The following further awards were made on May 4, 1854: To Patrick Ryan, the clearing and grading of Sections 2, 27, 56; to J. B. Neenan, *do.*, 3–5; to A. G. Nye, *do.*, 6, 9; to Eggley Handson & Co., *do.*, 7–8; to Michael Leary, *do.*, 10–12; to Herman Mathews, *do.*, 13–15; to Patrick Quinn, *do.*, 16–18; to Michael Connell, *do.*, 20, 26, 31–32; to Lewis Kramer, *do.*, 23–25; to P. M. Guthrie, *do.*, 33–34; to Golden & Sill, *do.*, 35–36, 42–45; to Johnson & Bennett, *do.*, 19, 21–22, 70–72; to Prentiss & Saxton, *do.*, 28–30, 46–48, 51–53, 73–75; to Eggers & Bunnell, *do.*, 37–39, 57–61; to W. Pratt, *do.*, 40–41, 64–69; to Alexander Fulton, *do.*, 54–55; to Emerson Penwell & Co., *do.*, 49–50; to M. O. Shaughnessey, *do.*, 62–63. (BMI ORB, p. 19; cf. Wilson, "From Planks to Rails," *loc. cit.*, pp. 330–331.)

[103] BMI ORB, p. 14.

[104] On the same date (March 29) the directors voted "that all stock subscribed

During the spring and early summer of 1854, the work on the line proceeded with "considerable energy."[105] In June, George Sumner of Boston was employed as subscription agent for the eastern states; in addition to his traveling expenses he was to receive one per cent of his sales, *providing* he disposed of not less than $1,200,000 in capital stock.[106] There was little prospect of the new agent reaching this quota, however, for the financial stringency that had begun in the winter of 1853–54 was becoming more acute daily. On July 5, the directors reluctantly ordered Thielsen to reduce construction to the point where he could pay all contractors from installments actually due on private subscriptions along the line. At the same time the directors agreed, in consideration of an offer by J. M. Forbes and others, to advance $25,000 on the hypothecation of Des Moines County bonds and to become individually liable for the raising of a like sum by similar means.[107] But even these heroic measures were in vain. By the end of the summer, lack of funds forced suspension of all work except on some scattered sections between Burlington and Mount Pleasant.[108] A crowning blow came in December when the president of the United States in his annual message to Congress expressed grave doubts as to the wisdom of further grants to railroads.

It is not enough [he declared] that the value of a particular locality may be enhanced; . . . [one must] look beyond present result to the ultimate effect. Even admitting the right of Congress to be unquestionable, is it quite clear that the proposed grants would be productive of good and not of evil? The reasons assigned for the grants show that it is proposed to put the work speedily in construction. When we reflect that only 17,000 miles were completed . . . in a quarter of a century; when we see the crippled condition of many works commenced . . . on sound principles; when we contemplate the enormous absorption of the capital withdrawn from the ordinary channels of business, the extravagant rates of interest paid to continue operations, the bankruptcies . . . can it be doubted that the tendency is to run to excess in this matter?
Is it not better to leave all those works to private enterprise, regulated and when expedient, aided by the cooperations of the state? . . . If to

to the B. & M. R. R.R. conditioned to be paid upon any other route than the one adopted by the board of directors, be excluded from voting." (BMI ORB, p. 13.)

[105] BMI, *Annual Report* for 1855–56 (Burlington, 1856), p. 8.
[106] BMI ORB, p. 21.
[107] *Ibid.*, p. 22.
[108] BMI, *Annual Report* for 1855–56 (Burlington, 1856), p. 8.

enable these companies to execute their proposed works, it is necessary that the aid of the general government be given, the policy will present a problem . . . so important to our political and social well being as to claim the severest analysis.[109]

Luckily for the morale of the stockholders, a silver lining promptly appeared at several places around the dark cloud.

Since the very beginning of its separate political existence, Iowa had been dominated by the conservative, Democratic, anti-business elements of the state. Their political ideas had been embodied in the constitution of 1846,[110] and their candidate for governor in 1854, Curtis Bates, stood squarely on these traditional principles. But the opposition had been growing steadily. From New England particularly came pioneers with a passion for education, free business enterprise, internal improvements, and humanitarian reform.[111] Thus, when the two Democratic senators of the state, Dodge and Jones, failed to judge accurately the strength of this group and voted in favor of the Kansas-Nebraska Act in May, 1854, a political revolution burst over Iowa that swept the old leadership into permanent oblivion. James W. Grimes, campaigning for the corporation vote and roundly denouncing squatter sovereignty, defeated Bates for the governorship in November; James Harlan, almost an abolitionist in belief, took Dodge's Senate seat, and the Whigs secured a working majority in the lower house of the Iowa legislature. Only the state senate offered a problem, for there the Democrats held a majority of one. Grimes, impatient to go forward with progressive legislation and an ultimate revision of the constitution, saw his plans shattered by the narrowest of margins. William F. Coolbaugh solved the riddle. Nominally a Democratic senator, he had ample reason to believe in the business policies of the new governor even if he did not agree with his political views.[112] Placing business before politics and, as one historian put it, "the state above his party," [113] he made Governor Grimes' program possible. Hereafter the railroads of Iowa, and particularly the B. & M., might expect complete coöperation from the state authorities.

Another favorable event of immense importance to the B. & M.

[109] *Messages and Papers of the Presidents* (New York, 1897–1917), vol. VI, p. 2823.

[110] See above, p. 48.

[111] Herriott, *loc. cit.*, p. 54.

[112] Cyrenus Cole, *op. cit.*, chs. xl, xliv–xlvi, *passim.*   [113] *Ibid.*, p. 273.

took place on March 17, 1855, when the Forbes-Joy interests finally opened their through line from Chicago to East Burlington, just across the river from Burlington, Iowa.[114] To signalize this achievement in suitable fashion, a mammoth celebration was held in Burlington on May 31 at which the "beauty and fashion, chivalry and power" of Ottumwa, Mount Pleasant, Burlington, and way points mingled with the "selected elegance" of the East. Lewis Cass, Stephen A. Douglas,

RAIL ROAD CELEBRATION.

Burlington, Iowa, May, 1855.

Dear Sir: With pleasure we announce to you that we are directed by the City Council to invite you to be present and participate in the Celebration of the

Opening of the Chicago and Burlington Rail Road,

which will take place in this City on Wednesday, May 30th, instant.

We trust that no ordinary event will be allowed to deprive us of the pleasure of your attendance on this occasion.

Very Truly Yours,

SILAS A. HUDSON, Mayor.

JOHN G. FOOTE,
A. W. CARPENTER, } Committee of Arrangements.
J. F. TALLANT.

INVITATION TO CELEBRATE COMPLETION OF THE C. B. & Q.
TO THE MISSISSIPPI, 1855.

the mayor of Chicago, and other luminaries arrived in a "superb" ten-car train and were received by a committee headed by Governor Grimes. Music, dancing, speeches, and feasting lasted far into the night.[115]

Encouraged, the B. & M. directors renewed their drive for funds and authorized President J. C. Hall to invite proposals for building the entire line to Ottumwa.[116] By June 21, 1855, several bids had been received, and Hall was ordered to go to Chicago and discuss the

---

[114] See above, p. 40; cf. CBQ, *Corporate History*, map and chart opposite p. 7.
[115] Petersen, *loc. cit.*, pp. 393-394.   [116] BMI ORB, p. 30.

proposition with James F. Joy.[117] None of these proved satisfactory to the directors, but on August 4, the firm of Clarke & Hendrie offered to construct "a single-track railroad from Boundary Street, Burlington, to the east bank of the Skunk River in Henry County" for $24,500 a mile. They promised to finish the job by June, 1857. This proposal the directors accepted, providing the builders would reduce their price per mile to $22,500.[118] Clarke & Hendrie agreed, and the contract was signed on August 16.[119] "Our friends at Mt. Pleasant," jubilated the *Weekly Hawk-Eye & Telegraph*, "may begin to look for the locomotive. It is coming this time sure."[120]

Work was put under way immediately, and on New Year's Day, 1856, the first locomotive, a wood-burning, brass-trimmed engine with funnel stack, chuffed out of Burlington a few miles and returned.[121] Here at last was a dream fulfilled. The next day the chief engineer was requested by the directors to report upon the practicability and cost of building a bridge across the Mississippi at Burlington. The future was beginning to look brighter, nor was it a moment too soon; on January 4, the rival M. & M. ran its first train through from Davenport to Iowa City, a distance of 67 miles.[122] The B. & M. could look forward to plenty of competition.

As the track layers pushed westward in 1856, the surrounding countryside buzzed with activity. As early as January the *Mt. Pleasant Observer* noted that 200 homes had been constructed that season, and that there were still not half enough to supply the demand.[123] On April 30, 1856, the first B. & M. passenger train made its appearance. "We may therefore," observed the *Weekly Hawk-Eye & Telegraph*, "take an affectionate leave of that time-honored institution, the stage coach."[124] By May the rails reached Danville,[125] and on June 17 the

[117] *Ibid.*, p. 33. [118] *Ibid.*, p. 39.

[119] BMI ORB, p. 41. At the time, the firm of Clarke & Hendrie was composed of: Walter P. Clarke, Walter P. Clarke, Jr., S. G. Clarke, F. B. Clarke, Charles Hendrie, Fitz Henry Warren, William Henry Starr, William H. Postlewait, David Remick, and J. F. Tallant. (*Ibid.*)

[120] *Weekly Hawk-Eye & Telegraph* (Burlington, Iowa), August 8, 1855.

[121] Wilson, "From Planks to Rails," *loc. cit.*, pp. 331–332.

[122] F. J. Nevins, *op. cit.*, pp. 22–23.

[123] *Weekly Hawk-Eye & Telegraph*, January 9, 1856, reprinted from *Mt. Pleasant Observer*.

[124] *Weekly Hawk-Eye & Telegraph*, April 30, 1856.

[125] Wilson, "From Planks to Rails," *loc. cit.*, *passim.*

cars ran to New London for the first time; [126] the next month they went through to Mount Pleasant.[127] In 1854, that town had had a population of 1,300; when rail service was opened in 1856, it had already grown to 3,245 and expected 1,000 more people before the end of the year. Sixty new buildings, costing from $1,000 to $30,000, were under construction, and it was said that 100 dwellings and business houses would find tenants in one day "at heavy rents" if they were to be had.[128] Even in Ottumwa, still beyond the railhead, the demand for lots was so great that two new additions to the town were laid out.[129] In Mills County, almost on the Missouri River, the citizens gathered to discuss ways and means of helping the B. & M.[130]

[126] *Weekly Hawk-Eye & Telegraph*, June 18, 1856.
[127] Wilson, "From Planks to Rails," *loc. cit.*, *passim*.
[128] *Weekly Hawk-Eye & Telegraph*, July 16, 1856.
[129] *Ibid.*, May 21, 1856.
[130] *Ibid.*, February 27, 1856.

CHAPTER III

CONGRESS, SECTIONALISM, AND THE LAND GRANT, 1856

I. SECURING THE GRANT

IN THE spring of 1856, the long struggle of the Burlington and Missouri River Railroad for federal aid came to a successful conclusion. Finally heeding the persistent importunities of the Iowa delegation, the House of Representatives on May 8, 1856, agreed to a magnificent land grant for four Iowa railroads, including both B. & M. and M. & M. On the following day, the measure arrived in the Senate, the arena of sectional conflict. Up to that time, passage of Iowa land-grant bills in the upper house had been a mere gesture, for the lower chamber had been consistently opposed. Now, however, the tables were turned. Since the House on the previous day had finally passed a four-road grant,[1] it was obvious that the Senate's action would be decisive, and therein lay the danger. No grants had been made for over three years. Could it be done now without precipitating an explosion?

Faced with this responsibility the members give rapid thought to their sectional interests, for Senator Jones of Iowa is already on his feet, pleading for immediate consideration of the bill.[2] His argument is eminently logical:

This bill is the very same as four or five others previously passed, except that there is now less land for distribution. In fact, holders of military bounties have been rapidly absorbing the best Iowa land, thus depriving the Treasury of the revenue it would ordinarily receive through normal sales.[3] In the 24 hours that have elapsed since the House passed its resolution, it is said that over $40,000 worth of warrants have been rushed into Iowa for location along the projected routes. Thus, is it not essential that the bill be taken up at once for

---

[1] *Cong. Globe*, 34th Cong., 1st Sess. (1855–56), pt. 1, p. 1146. Under Thornborough's guidance, the House passed the resolution (H. R. No. 56) by 79–59 on Thursday, May 8. There was no debate in House. (*Ibid.*, p. 1161.)

[2] *Ibid.*, pp. 1166–67.

[3] *Ibid.*, p. 1167.

debate? Senator Foot of Vermont objects. Why, he demands, should there be four routes in Iowa from the Mississippi to the Missouri? Certainly such a measure should be referred to the Committee on Public Lands so that "other parties" may be heard. Jones scents trouble, but he has his answer ready. The only "other interests" involved are a group of speculators, self-styled as the Philadelphia, Fort Wayne and Platte Valley Air Line Railroad Company, who wish to build a fifth road across the state. Their scheme has found no favor with the Iowa Assembly, although three legislatures have memorialized Congress for the bill as it stands, providing for four lines starting from the Mississippi, with the upper two joining at 42 degrees 30 minutes and proceeding thence to Sioux City. Do not the honorable gentlemen understand that passage of this grant will aid the federal treasury, the state, and accomplish the building of an important artery of trade? [4]

Biggs of North Carolina takes the floor. He asks for reference to the Committee; there should be time to examine the extent and location of the grant. Patiently, Jones replies that this has already been done, and the Committee's approval received for identical grants. Yulee of Florida comes to his support: if the principle of aid to railroads has been established, and if the details of this act are satisfactory to the Iowa delegation, why should the Senate hesitate? The "Little Giant" from Illinois agrees. This bill merely involves the basic principle of congressional grants to the roads, declares Douglas, and "if there be any roads in America that come fairly within this principle which we have recognized heretofore as proper, they are those embraced in the present bill." [5] But Foot has no intention of yielding so easily; he changes his tactics for the moment: will the Senate vote for reference so that one or two roads may be cut out of the bill? The Vermonter is trying to avoid attacking the principle by offering specific objections; Adams of Mississippi brings him back to the point. "We are acting," he says, "on the principle that the increased value of the public domain, in consequence of the construction of such a road, will be a full equivalent for the land granted. In that view, it is wholly immaterial what the number of acres may be." And, he

---

[4] *Cong. Globe*, p. 1167.

[5] *Ibid.*, p. 1168. Douglas brought out the fact also that bills similar to this had previously passed the Senate.

adds, gratuitously but very much to the point, this is *not* a plot to rob the older states.[6] At last the curtain is raised on the sectional conflict and the champions take the cue.

Lewis Cass of Michigan jumps to his feet. If Illinois, Missouri, Arkansas, and Indiana have received bountiful land grants from the federal government, why should Iowa be denied or, for that matter, Michigan and Wisconsin?[7] With an air of resignation Kentucky's Crittenden attempts an answer. He bewails the fact that the old states derive no benefit from the vast public domain although in glorious times past they "acquired it, fought for it, bought it." Nevertheless, he is reconciled to its loss and merely pleads for the privilege of supervising its disposal. What parts of the Union, for example, will be connected by the roads in question? Senator Jones answers in great detail. There will come a time, he says, when the Pacific Railway will pass through Iowa; through routes from Davenport and Burlington will some day reach South Pass, there to meet other through lines from Hannibal and St. Louis and proceed on to the coast. Furthermore, — he turns to his western colleagues — he has always supported grants to other states, and surely Iowa's generosity should find its reward. Crittenden smiles.

"I discover," he says paternally, "that these gentlemen have been very generous with each other. Let them treat us in the same spirit. We, the representatives of the old States, look on good naturedly and allow the younger States to have their frolic in their own way."

"Do it once more?" Jones flashes back. The Senators laugh.

"I expect to do it, but in due season," replies the Kentuckian, his dignity gravely imperiled.[8]

Still Senator Foot remains unappeased. As chairman of the Committee on Public Lands, he offers to hold a special meeting the following day, a Saturday, and report back Monday morning. That will mean three more days' delay, with probably no change in the eventual outcome. It sounds like outright obstructionism, and Jones asks bluntly what is to be gained by such reference.[9] Wilson of Massachusetts comes to the rescue with an argument of compelling force. He too represents an old commonwealth, he says, and 20 years ago

6 *Ibid.*, p. 1169.
7 *Ibid.*
8 *Ibid.*, p. 1170.

9 *Ibid.*

Massachusetts supported Mr. Clay's scheme of distribution. But that policy failed and should not be revived.

"We of Massachusetts," he continues, "we of the Atlantic Coast, who are engaged in manufactures and commerce, all have a direct interest in the settlement and development, growth and prosperity of the new states of the interior." [10]

Solidly he plumps for the new Iowa grants, and thus encouraged, Stuart of Michigan rises to answer more specifically Crittenden's earlier fears. Kentucky, says Stuart, has gained enormously by the Missouri and Arkansas grants. Furthermore, is it not true that the old states at least had the privilege of disposing of their own lands in times past, whereas the new members of the Union have had to sit by while Congress parceled out their public domain to Indians, veterans, and the old states as bounty? Is it not just that Congress now redress the balance by making railroad grants that will inure to the benefit of these new states? Wherein, he asks, lies the logic of "old state generosity"?

Senator Seward of New York is becoming impatient at such bickering. Unfortunately, he comments aciduously, Iowa has too much land and the Senate has too much time. Reference would gain precisely nothing. Any railroads built today are national, and "no railroad can be made in the State of Iowa, or in any other state in any direction which will not increase the trade that is to be poured into the city of New York." [11]

The motion to refer is defeated, and the bill moves to a third reading, one step nearer passage.

Crittenden rises again. He is genuinely interested in the present grant, but likewise concerned to make it fair. He offers an amendment to the bill that would direct the governor of Iowa to sell all the granted lands and divide the proceeds equally between the four roads, an amendment, incidentally, that would completely eliminate any colonization work by an individual railroad. Once more Jones has his answer ready. That scheme, he replies, was discussed in the Illinois Central case six years previously and discarded. In the present instance, furthermore, the southernmost road [the Burlington and Missouri River] runs through the most thickly settled and richest part of the state; its owners, he alleges, can almost construct the line with-

---

[10] *Cong. Globe*, p. 1171.   [11] *Ibid.*, pp. 1171–1172.

out government aid. Thus, is it any hardship that because of prior settlement that company will receive the smallest grant? Or would it be fair to have the northernmost road, which needs more support, share the proceeds of its larger grant with the B. & M.? Moreover, adds Senator Geyer, since no land passes to a railroad under the grant until 20 miles have been actually constructed, aid to one road would be dependent on the fortunes of another if the Kentuckian's suggestion were adopted. Crittenden withdraws his amendment. The Senate prepares to vote on the major question.[12]

The distribution of that vote was a model of sectional loyalty. From the course of the debate, it was apparent that two areas would lend earnest support to the grant: the manufacturing East, and western states with public domain that could hope for similar bounties. Adjoining regions might be expected to give less vigorous approval or divide their vote. On the other hand, the old South and one-time western states whose public lands were exhausted had nothing to gain and possibly something to lose by handing out what they regarded as the common treasure of the nation. Consequently, their opposition was written off in advance. As it turned out, individual votes conformed to this pattern with amazing fidelity.

SENATE VOTE ON THE IOWA RAILROAD GRANTS, MAY 9, 1856

Region	Pro	Con	Not Voting
New England			
Me-NH-Vt-Mass-RI-Conn	6	0	6
Middle Atlantic			
NY-NJ-Pa-Md-Del	4	1	5
Old South			
Va-NC-SC-Ga	0	5	3
New South			
Fla-Miss-Ala-La-Ark	7	0	3
New West			
Ind-Ill-Mich-Wis-Iowa-			
Mo-Tex-Cal	11	0	5*
Old West			
Ky-Tenn-Ohio	3	3	0
	31	9	22

* One vacancy each in California, Indiana, Missouri.

[12] *Ibid.*

The six New Englanders who registered an opinion supported the grant, and all but one of them came from the lower three states where manufacturing was concentrated; the sixth was Hale of New Hampshire, representing a commonwealth already partly industrialized. The other half of the New England delegation refrained from voting, and it is significant that this group included both Senators from Maine and Vermont and one from New Hampshire, the regions least likely to share in mill and rail prosperity. The result in the Middle Atlantic States was almost exactly the same: four members voted for the bill, five remained silent, and one, Brodhead of Pennsylvania, cast his ballot in the negative. This lone exception, running counter to the purely sectional tide, represented a genuine conviction fortified by several years of study; in fact Brodhead's single speech on this occasion was to refer back to his full exposition four years earlier.[13]

At that time he had objected on four grounds to the whole principle of land grants. First, it was an unconstitutional form of internal improvement. Here was the spirit of Jackson's Maysville veto, parallel to the southerner's suspicion of national works but even more indigenous as a westerner's opposition to remote control. Second, such grants were not only "local and partial" in character, but they would bring "numerous applications in years to come."[14] No more prophetic words were ever spoken; in the two decades following their utterance, Congress parceled out nearly 150,000,000 acres for railroad grants, aside from the scores of applications that were turned down. Third, Brodhead had continued, the effect of the grants in practice was to allow the United States to make substantial improvements in the fortunate regions where public lands still remained, and not elsewhere. This, he maintained (as did many of his colleagues), was grossly unfair to the old states. And finally, he asserted, the policy would inevitably lead to rail monopolies. This point, advanced in 1852, entitled its originator to some claim of prescience. In a day when communities were employing every expedient to lure the iron gift horse to their gates, there were few men indeed who were looking into his mouth.

Brodhead, however, was not merely destructive. The public lands, he had said, should be graduated in price (as was done in 1854), and proceeds should be divided among all the states. Here was a combination of Benton's championship of the actual settler and Clay's

[13] *Ibid.*, p. 1171. His earlier remarks are in *Cong. Globe*, 32nd Cong., 1st Sess. (1851–52), pp. 280–281.   [14] *Ibid.*

endeavor to compensate states like Kentucky and the East. Railroad construction should be left to private or state hands. Such a policy, Brodhead had concluded, would serve several purposes: it would provide cheap lands, promote good feeling among the states, remove constitutional objections, abate a tendency to centralization, and prevent monopolies. When the roll was taken in 1856, Brodhead saw no reason for changing his position of 1852.

As usual the Old South presented an unbroken front against the Iowa grants. With no public lands, no opportunity to share in a commercial boom, and a deep mistrust of the North's increasing power, this area cast five votes in the negative, while three men withheld their opinion. In the particular case of this bill there was doubtless another more specific reason for the southern attitude. Ever since 1850, Douglas, aided by the North, had been endeavoring to put through a federally subsidized transcontinental rail line, as well as to organize the Platte country through which he hoped it would pass.[15] The South was not opposed to a railroad project *per se*, but would agree to it only if at least one line were built on the southernmost of the five 1853 surveys.[16] Since there was no economic justification at the time for more than one road, however, it was apparent that the middle route, extending west from Iowa, would be the logical one. Thus the grant under discussion possessed an additional disqualification in southern eyes.

In contrast to this solid opposition, unanimous approval came from the newer regions of the South and West. Florida, Mississippi, Alabama, Louisiana, and Arkansas still possessed huge tracts of public domain; all of them had received, or were hoping to receive, grants similar to the Iowa donation.[17] This situation was even more true of the Northwest Territory states (except Ohio) and the trans-Mississippi region. These two areas gave 18 votes for the bill; eight senators were unrecorded, including the two from Texas where there was no public land. There was not a single dissenting vote.

Midway between the antagonistic South and the enthusiastic West lay Kentucky, Tennessee, and Ohio. Opinion here was sharply

---

[15] George F. Milton, *The Eve of Conflict* (Boston, 1934), pp. 90–107, 150–154.
[16] *Ibid*. Cf. also: Hibbard, *op. cit.*, pp. 247–248; Frederick L. Paxson, *History of the American Frontier, 1763–1893* (Boston, 1924), pp. 429–431, 434; Theodore Clarke Smith, *Parties and Slavery* (New York, 1906), p. 240; George M. Stephenson, *The Political History of the Public Lands* (Boston, 1917), pp. 125–126.
[17] Donaldson, *op. cit.*, pp. 764–765, 812–815.

divided. Certainly the objections to the grant cited by Brodhead and Crittenden applied in full measure, yet Stuart's contention that these states would gain by the through traffic to be created and Wilson's enumeration of the industrial benefits were likewise in point, particularly for Ohio. Still, that state cast both its votes in the negative and was joined by Thompson of Kentucky. On the other hand, Crittenden and the two Tennessee senators gave their approval, thus evenly dividing the section's vote. Although there was no public land in Tennessee, it would seem that that state had more in common with Alabama and Mississippi than with its eastern neighbors who opposed the grant.

At the last moment the victory thus handily won was almost snatched away. When the Senate convened again on Monday morning, May 12, Crittenden and Foot endeavored to force reconsideration of its previous action on the ground that a projected fifth line in Iowa would be irreparably hurt by the measure as passed.[18] The argument was far-fetched to say the least, for the alleged object of this belated solicitation was nothing more than the visionary Philadelphia, Fort Wayne and Platte River Air Line. Its promoter had apparently waged a clever campaign in Washington as his petitions show,[19] but Senator Jones aptly pointed out that if he were determined to build railroads in Iowa, he should join one of the lines already started.[20] Nevertheless, the vote for reconsideration was perilously close. By a count of 15–19, the Crittenden-Foot move was blocked;[21] it is significant that all but one of the affirmative votes came from the East and South, and all but three of the negative ballots from the New South or New West. Plainly the frontier wanted its railroads.[22]

[18] *Cong. Globe*, 34th Cong., 1st Sess. (1855–56), pt. 1, p. 1213.
[19] *Ibid.*
[20] *Ibid.*, p. 1218.
[21] *Ibid.*, p. 1220.
[22] The vote for reconsideration, on May 12, was as follows:

Region	Pro	Con	Not Voting
New England	5	1	6
Middle Atlantic	3	1	6
Old South	2	0	7
New South	0	8	2
New West	1	8	7
Old West	4	1	1
	—	—	—
	15	19	29 (*Ibid.*)

The land-grant act that was thus pushed through Congress and signed by President Pierce on May 15 provided for aid to four roads to be located along the following general lines: [23]

1. Burlington to a point on the Missouri River near the mouth of the Platte River,
2. Davenport via Iowa City and Des Moines to Council Bluffs,
3. Lyons City northwest to Maquoketa, thence due west as nearly as possible on the 42 parallel to the Missouri River, and
4. Dubuque to a point on the Missouri River near Sioux City. [24]

The act followed the Illinois Central model [25] in several respects: it granted the land directly to the State of Iowa for eventual transfer to the corporations, and it limited the donation to a maximum of all alternate sections (square miles) for six miles on both sides of the line. If, when the routes were "definitely fixed," [26] this quota could not be filled within these limits because of prior disposal of the land by the federal government, the railroads were empowered to select up to the full amount of the deficit from the alternate sections within 15 miles of the track. Title to the lands thus selected would not pass from the state to any railroad, however, until the track was built and accepted by the state. Then as each 20 miles was so accepted, the company in question would receive up to 120 sections (76,800 acres) embraced within the length of its newly completed rails. Proceeds from land sales were to be applied solely to construction. In addition, Congress amply protected the federal government by doubling the price on the ungranted alternate sections within the six-mile limits, stipulating that the roads "shall be and remain public highways for the use of the government of the United States, free from toll or other charge upon the transportation of any property or troops of the United States," [27] and by reserving to Congress the right to fix the price for carrying mails. If the roads should not be completed in ten years, unsold lands were to revert to the United States.

[23] *Statutes-at-Large*, vol. XI, p. 9. See also, CBQ *Documentary History*, vol. II, pp. 11-13.

[24] See map, p. 82.

[25] *Statutes-at-Large*, vol. IX, pp. 466-467. For a summary of its provisions, see Gates, *op. cit.*, pp. 41-42.

[26] *Statutes-at-Large*, vol. XI, p. 9, sec. 1.

[27] *Ibid.*, sec. 3.

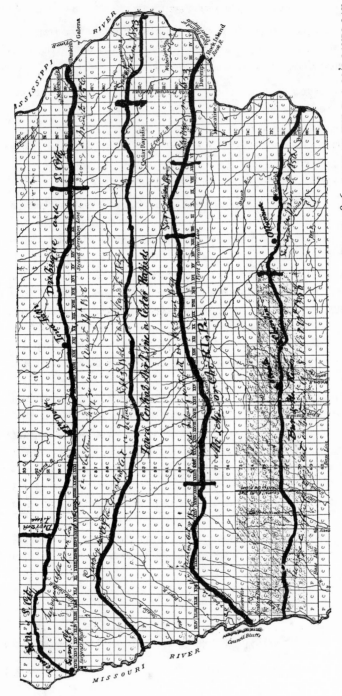

ROUTES OF THE FOUR IOWA RAILROADS WHICH RECEIVED FEDERAL LAND GRANTS ON MAY 15, 1856. MOST OF THE B. & M.'S LANDS LAY WITHIN THE FAINTLY SHADED AREA.

It will be noted that by the terms of this act, the railroads could not select their lands, thus withdrawing them from private entry, until their routes were "definitely fixed." Except where exact surveys were already available, however, it would take time for the companies to comply with this provision, and in the meanwhile speculators and settlers could establish private claims upon lands that might otherwise fall to the railroads. To prevent such an eventuality, Senator Jones had gone to Thomas A. Hendricks, commissioner of the General Land Office, the moment the Iowa bill passed the House of Representatives (May 8) and had asked him to telegraph the several offices in Iowa to withdraw "all lands from sale and location within the probable limits of the grant." [28] The commissioner complied on May 10, and these instructions were repeated by mail to the various offices on the fifteenth.[29] Four days later Hendricks wrote Governor Grimes at length, instructing him what duties devolved upon the state under the premises. Since the grant had been made to Iowa, the state was to appoint agents to select lands which would accrue to the railroads. To make these selections possible, the various companies should immediately locate their lines, and maps showing these routes should be certified by the state and transmitted to the General Land Office as well as to the local offices in Iowa. Hendricks pointed out that under the terms of the act, title to the granted sections did not vest in the state until these maps of location were properly filed; thus speed was desirable. Furthermore, definite land selections would enable the commissioner to restore to the market ungranted tracts closed to private entry by his dispatches of May 10 and 15.[30]

The governor lost no time.[31] The Assembly of Iowa was called into special session in July, 1856, and proceeded to pass an act "to accept the grant and carry into execution the trust conferred upon the State of Iowa . . . upon the terms, conditions, and restrictions contained in . . . the act of Congress. . . ." [32] By this instrument, the

[28] Thomas A. Hendricks to James W. Grimes, May 19, 1856 (LDP).

[29] The failure of some of these messages to arrive and later countermanding instructions caused serious complications. See below, pp. 89–90.

[30] Hendricks to Grimes, May 19, 1856 (LDP).

[31] William Larrabee in *The Railroad Question* (Chicago, 1893), pp. 321–322, notes that the Mississippi & Missouri directors asked the governor to convene the assembly in extra session on June 2, 1856.

[32] CBQ, *Documentary History*, vol. II, pp. 13–16. Preamble and sec. 1 of the Iowa Act, approved July 14, 1856.

four grants, from south to north, were conferred upon the Burlington and Missouri River Railroad, the Mississippi and Missouri, the Iowa Central Air Line, and the Dubuque and Pacific.[33] Section 6 heeded Commissioner Hendricks' warning and provided that:

the lines and routes of the several roads above described shall be definitely fixed and located on or before the first day of April next [1857] and maps or plats showing such lines or routes shall be filed in the office of the governor. . . . It shall be the duty of the governor, after affixing his official signature to file such map in the department having the control of the public land at Washington; such location being considered final only in so far as to fix the limit and boundary within which such lands may be selected. . . .[34]

If the railroads could not find their quota within these limits, the governor's agents were empowered to select others according to the federal act. The roads were required to have completed and equipped 75 miles by December 1, 1859, 30 miles in addition every five years thereafter, and the entire line by December 1, 1865. Failure in this respect would lead to forfeiture of the grant.[35] Thus the Iowa act particularized Congress' injunction to finish the lines in ten years; as a matter of fact, extensions had to be granted to all companies.[36]

Section 9 was an illuminating commentary on western railroad conditions of the day, revealing the hopes and fears of a people who on occasion had suffered from the clashes between rival roads. It provided that the gauge of all roads should be four feet, eight and one-half inches; there should be no Erie War or narrow-gauge substitute in the promised land.[37] Iron in the track was to be of approved quality and pattern, probably meaning it was to be imported from England, "and the roads shall be completed and finished in a style and of a quality equal to the average of other first-class western roads." This was a rather vague criterion. The final injunction was highly practical: it required the beneficiary roads to interchange facilities, equipment, freight, and passengers with any road that might intersect them "and at such rates as shall not in any case exceed the regular tariff of charges on such road or roads." [38] Anxious as the people of Iowa were

[33] Iowa Act of 1856, secs. 2–3, inclusive.
[34] Ibid., sec. 6.
[35] Ibid., sec. 8.
[36] See below, p. 172.
[37] Cf. MacGill, op. cit., pp. 366 et seq.; Thompson, op. cit., p. 118.
[38] Iowa Act of 1856, sec 9.

to have their lines built, they had no intention of creating monopolies that might restrict railway growth or penalize the community by dictatorial tactics. Some of the legislators and probably the governor himself must have been familiar with problems which had arisen in the East.[39]

The next three sections made provision for settlers who had *bona fide* claims to lands granted to the railroad: such persons were to prove their claim valid before a judge, receive a certificate, and, unless the interested railroad could disprove their contention, obtain the privilege of purchasing 160 acres at $2.50 per acre from the company. Sections 13-16 technically placed the companies under complete control of the state legislature; within 90 days the several companies were to assent to the law. "Said railroad companies accepting the provisions of this act shall at all times be subject to such rules and regulations as may, from time to time, be enacted and provided for by the general assembly of Iowa, not inconsistent with the provisions of this act, and the act of Congress making the grant." [40] A more sweeping statement could hardly be imagined. Furthermore, beneficiary companies were to make annual reports of their meetings and submit "a detailed statement, as far as practicable, of the amount of their expenditures, liabilities, &c." Finally, no company should in any event have "any claim or recourse whatever upon the State of Iowa, for a misapplication of said grant, incumbrances or conditions in this act imposed." [41] Governor Grimes signed the act on July 14, 1856.

The roads immediately took steps to confirm and protect their grants; their first move was in common. Ten days after approval of the Iowa act, officials of all the beneficiaries except the Iowa Central met at Davenport. Colonel Williams and Henry Thielsen — the latter chief engineer and later land surveyor — represented the Burlington and Missouri River. Platt Smith, president of the Dubuque and Pacific, was appointed chairman, and Ebenezer Cook, a director of the M. & M. and the Rock Island, secretary. Unanimously, Bernhart Henn of Fairfield (on the B. & M.) was appointed agent of the companies present and directed to proceed to Washington, there to "make such arrangements in relation to the grant of land to these

[39] Cf. Charles Francis Adams, *Chapters of Erie* (Boston, 1871).
[40] Iowa Act of 1856, sec. 14.
[41] *Ibid.*

companies as in his opinion shall be most for their advantage." He was authorized to engage such assistants as seemed desirable and to incur such expenses "as he may deem necessary in the prosecution of the Business." [42] At the same time, Colonel Mason of the Dubuque line and Mr. Judd, a director of the M. & M., were appointed to confer with Hon. John Wilson, commissioner of the General Land Office, upon the subject of rendering services to their companies "with power to make such arrangements with him as they may deem proper." [43] The companies agreed to share expenses equally for these undertakings and to invite the Iowa Central Air Line Railroad to coöperate. The meeting was then adjourned *sine die*.

On September 3, 1856, the Burlington and Missouri's board of directors formally adopted a unanimous resolution accepting the Iowa assembly's act regranting them the lands, and "assenting to all the provisions of the same." [44] At the same moment, plans for expansion were adopted. The chief engineer was ordered to make a survey from Ottumwa through the southern tier of counties to a point on the Missouri River near Nebraska City. And, lest his work be in vain, Thomas Newman and N. Lathrop were appointed a committee to visit all counties and towns on the line of the road from Ottumwa to the Missouri River "and receive for this company any donations of land, town lots, or other property that may be made to the company, and make such provisions with responsible persons along the line of said road, that will as far as possible secure to the company the free right of way from Ottumwa to the Missouri River." [45]

These activities marked the opening of a new chapter in the Burlington's land history. They hinted also at a new era for southern Iowa. Indeed, the metamorphosis of the region had already begun.

II. THE DISPUTE OVER WITHDRAWAL

During 1854–56, while the company was so busy laying its first rails and securing its heritage of land, Iowa was rapidly becoming a scene of unprecedented activity. This was partly due to a barrage of spontaneous publicity that spread the news of this prairie paradise through-

[42] Minutes of the Meeting, July 24, 1856 (LDP).
[43] *Ibid.*
[44] Resolution of Directors, September 3, 1856 (LDP).
[45] BMI ORB, p. 85.

out the East. Guidebooks and letters from pioneers rehearsed Iowa's virtues with enthusiasm and picturesque pride, and "the folks back home" were strenuously urged to come west. As if to emphasize this propaganda, a severe cholera epidemic in the Middle States and drought along the Ohio Valley during 1854 prompted family after family to leave for a more hospitable spot. They came to Iowa in droves, their wagons laden down with household effects, their cattle crowding the muddy, inadequate roads; during the fall and early winter of 1854, some 20,000 people crossed the Burlington ferry in one month. On June 30, 1855, the land office reported that over 3,250,000 acres of Iowa public lands had been occupied during the preceding twelvemonth. By the end of 1856, this two-year wave of immigration had borne 190,000 persons into the state and almost doubled its population.[46] Burlington itself had increased at least 100 per cent, thanks chiefly to the railroad from Chicago that had reached the opposite bank of the Mississippi during the period. The city now boasted no less than 13 houses of worship; two large schoolhouses costing $4,000 each; two daily and weekly newspapers; three foundries; two engine and machine manufactories; planing mills; steam flouring mills; woodworking establishments; steam-driven factories turning out wagons, plows, brushes, candles, matches, and starch; pork-packing plants; banking houses; hotels; and, as one guidebook put it, "almost everything else found in any city." [47]

These guidebooks, however, did not always limit themselves to prosaic statistics. Their lyrical passages described Iowa as a land of Olympian perfection:

From the hilltops the intervening valleys wear the aspect of cultivated meadows and rich pasture-grounds, irrigated by frequent rivulets, that wend their way through fields of wild hay, fringed with flourishing willows. On the summit level spreads the wild prairie, decked with flowers of the gayest hue, its long undulating waves stretching away till sky and meadow mingle in the wavy blue.

Here, now, where less than twenty years ago the red man fought his battles with his sanguinary foe, and chased the bison and the elk, monarch

[46] Goodwin, loc. cit., pp. 96–99. This article relies heavily for this period on D. E. Clark's "The Westward Movement in the Upper Mississippi Valley during the Fifties" in Proceedings of the Mississippi Valley Historical Association, vol. VII (1913–14), p. 212.

[47] Nathan H. Parker, The Iowa Handbook for 1856 (Boston, 1856), pp. 85–86.

of all this glorious scene, are the prairie farms and prairie homes of Iowa. Rich with teeming wealth of soil, and waving in the breeze, stands the grain in these fair fields, while Art and Nature combine to render beautiful the homes of her noble sons of toil. As the traveler advances, he meets with lots of heavy timber skirting all the numerous streams that find their way to the rivers that intersect this beautiful State. Not alone on the water-courses does the timber lie, for frequent groves dot the extended landscape on every hand, like islands in this sea of green. Art, Science and Manufactures gather their busy multitudes here, and take possession of these sylvan scenes. . . .[48]

Is it small wonder that easterners left their rocky, tilted farms for such a paradise? Is it strange that the railroads were optimistic about their future? Yet in the face of these natural advantages and the apparently endless stream of immigrants, the B. & M. had serious difficulties to overcome before it could place its lands on the market and launch its colonization program. Most of these difficulties arose from the fierce competition for Iowa's land.

There was nothing unusual about land hunger on the frontier. It had stirred Thomas Hooker to move his flock from Cambridge to the beckoning Connecticut River Valley over two centuries before; it had dislodged men and communities from their older homes down through the years until the stupendous influx into Iowa during the middle 'fifties was regarded as a perfectly logical climax to a recognized and well-nigh universal urge. The difficulties arose when this hunger produced conflicts betwen different claimants for the same plot of ground. Unfortunately, the land laws of the United States were often drawn in terms so vague or administered so inconsistently that even honest men made mistakes. Two officials with the best of motives might interpret differently a clause in the law or a ruling from the Secretary of the Interior. Settlers with every intention of obeying requirements might file their claim incorrectly, or unwittingly improve sections already reserved for other purposes.[49] The mere necessity of copying endless lists of almost similar figures and of carrying out all clerical details by longhand inevitably caused complications. But the whole matter was confused beyond all hope of simple solution by the fact that often there was carelessness, inefficiency, and doubtful practice on the part of officials and settlers alike. At Washington, overburdened clerks went

[48] Parker, *op. cit.*, pp. 22–23.
[49] See below, ch. viii.

through their motions with agonizing lethargy and questionable accuracy.[50] The higher-ups had their constituents to consider and were frequently ill-informed or ill-advised about technical details.[51] When, as in the case of the railroad grants in Iowa, United States lands were given first to the state, transactions had to pass through the inexpert hands of an additional official hierarchy. The nadir of confusion in this respect occurred when Iowa turned over the administration of her swamplands to county officers.[52] On the other hand, dishonest applicants for land, particularly under the preëmption law, injured the interest of their law-abiding fellows and were the nemesis of conscientious officials. Claims of *bona fide* settlement were filed without the slightest basis in fact, and some witnesses swore to anything that might provide their friends with a tenable title, for land was the passport to wealth in Iowa and the West.[53] Under such circumstances the B. & M. received its grant. Trouble had begun even before President Pierce had a chance to sign the congressional act.

It will be recalled that, at the request of Senator Jones, the commissioner of the General Land Office had telegraphed the local Iowa offices on May 10, 1856, to withdraw all lands from private entry that might fall within the limits of the grants to any beneficiary road.[54] Five days later, when the Land Act passed the Senate and was signed by the president, these telegraphic instructions were confirmed by mail.[55] In due course these various dispatches reached the land offices at Des Moines, Sioux City, and Chariton but never arrived where they were

[50] See below, pp. 146, 304.
[51] See below, pp. 136, 149.
[52] See below, ch. v.
[53] See below, pp. 126–127.
[54] See above, p. 83. Hendricks to Grimes, May 19, 1856 (LDP). See also memorandum, probably written by C. A. Van Allen, attorney for the company in the preëmption cases in 1861 (LDP); also Henn to C. R. Lowell, December 6, 1859 (LDP). Before the passage of the land grant through either house of Congress, the Iowa delegation had endeavored to get the president to withdraw the lands along the line of the roads from market, it having been represented to them that large quantities were being entered for speculation. During the previous session of 1854–55, the president had withdrawn large tracts for similar reasons, but in 1855–56 the administration changed its policy, and refused to make any withdrawals until a given grant should pass the House of Representatives. Thus the withdrawal in Iowa was delayed until May 10, the day after the House had acted. (*Ibid.*)
[55] Hendricks to Grimes, May 19, 1856 (LDP); Van Allen memorandum, 1861? (LDP); Henn to Lowell, December 6, 1859 (LDP).

most needed, — at the Council Bluffs office in whose district almost all the Burlington lands lay.[56] What happened to them no one ever found out for sure, but the company was convinced that they had been intercepted by speculators at Ft. Des Moines.[57] After several months of quiet investigation, the B. & M.'s agent at Council Bluffs wrote Henn that "all parties" there felt satisfied that fraud had been practiced; where or how was still a mystery.

We only know [he reported] that the word came by the passengers that the RRd Grant had passed & that the Ft. Des Moines & this office had been telegraphed to, to close & that the Ft Des Moines & Sioux City office closed & this office did not, the R & R [register and receiver] never received either dispatch [by wire] or letter, but closed on their own responsibility and that the houses here who had connections at the Fort were urged every mail to locate all the warrants they had, not to stop for good selections, but to take all they could get. . . .[58]

Even a post office investigation failed to produce any evidence.[59]

Whatever the cause of this affair, passage of the B. & M. grant galvanized land agents and speculators into action. They were seized with the conviction that the last opportunity for securing land in the Council Bluffs district at anywhere near the minimum price had arrived. Crowding into the registrar's office they bid against each other to secure land that ordinarily sold for $1.25 an acre. "Every acre of land was entered," reported the local newspaper, "without reference to its quality and even then the demands were not half supplied." [60] Although this was an exaggeration, the news of the railroad grant did precipitate a real boom. Public land sales in the Council Bluffs district during the first three months of 1856 amounted to 8,086.49 acres; [61] in the succeeding three months the figure rose to 20,072.40 acres.[62] It was only after this boom had taken place that the Council Bluffs officers

[56] Henn to Lowell, December 6, 1859 (LDP); cf. H. S. Hooton to Henn, July 20, 1857 (LDP).

[57] Hooton to Henn, July 20, 1857 (LDP); Henn to Lowell, December 6, 1859 (LDP).

[58] Hooton to Henn, July 20, 1857 (LDP).

[59] Henn requested a post office inquiry in his letter to the commissioner of the General Land Office, August 4, 1857 (LDP). Two years later he commented on the failure of that investigation (Henn to Lowell, December 6, 1859, LDP).

[60] Weekly Hawk-Eye & Telegraph, June 18, 1856.

[61] General Land Office, Receiver's Accounts (1856), vol. XXIV, p. 557.

[62] Ibid. (1856), vol. XXV, p. 329.

closed their doors and withdrew from entry what probable railroad lands were left.

This logical action, on May 31, might have limited the loss to the railroad had not the General Land Office introduced a new complication. During the spring numerous congressmen who were anticipating railroad grants for their states had requested the Department of the Interior to withdraw from market the lands that were to be granted. The department complied with these requests *except* that it exempted from withdrawal all entries under the Preëmption Act of 1841 (whereby a settler could occupy and improve from 40 to 160 acres of public domain and thus secure the right to purchase his tract at the end of a specified number of months for $1.25 per acre). To make this exception uniform for all states with railroad land grants, the General Land Office sent additional special instructions to the Iowa offices on June 19, 1856, to the effect that the "absolute withdrawals" ordered on May 10 and 15 in that state *were not intended to include preëmptions.* Thereupon the lands reserved for the B. & M. were again thrown open for this type of entry, and preëmptioners continued to file claims without let or hindrance.[63]

Obviously, these developments were depriving the railroad of some of the best acres along the road. From the company's point of view, of course, the influx of *bona fide* settlers into its territory eventually would prove a great asset, for although they would deprive the railroad of revenue from land sales, they would become shippers and travelers over the line. But many claimants had no intention of remaining on their sections, and if their claims were held valid, they could hold land off the market for a speculative profit and thus retard the very settlement they might have promoted. Furthermore, in view of its slender financial resources and to assure its construction, the company was forced to safeguard its chances of receiving some substantial return from its lands. There were two possible remedies available, and both were applied.

First, Henn gathered proof that many of the preëmption entries made under the order of June 19 were fraudulent. This material was

---

[63] Henn to Lowell, December 6, 1859 (LDP). Henn does not cite the definite date in June countermanding the first withdrawal, but this is supplied in Van Allen's memorandum of 1861 (LDP), and the answering argument of J. R. Morledge on August 17, 1861 (LDP).

sent to Commissioner Hendricks on October 9, accompanied by a plea
to reissue the withdrawal order. On October 18, Hendricks complied,
and two days later confirmed his action by telegraphic dispatches to
the Iowa offices. By this order the absolute withdrawal of lands from
preëmption entry became effective on October 20.[64]

The second possible remedy lay in having the line of the B. & M.
"definitely fixed" as soon as possible. Under the terms of the federal
grant, this action would automatically withdraw lands from any sort
of private entry, including preëmption, by making them liable for
selection by the railroad.[65] But just what did the law mean by "definitely fixed"?

In his letter of May 19, 1856, to Governor Grimes, Commissioner
Hendricks of the General Land Office provided a clue when he wrote
that the title of the state would vest in the alternate sections within
six miles of the road and in the "lieu" lands within 15 miles "from
the date of filing the maps of location at the local land offices." [66]
These instructions seemed explicit enough, but Section 6 of the regranting act of the Iowa legislature obscured the requirements by
providing that maps should be filed *not* in the local land offices, as
Hendricks had suggested, but with the governor and secretary of state
of Iowa. The former was to affix his signature and forward them to
the General Land Office in Washington.[67] This change in procedure,
so trivial on the surface, meant that news of the railroad selections
would be delayed in reaching the local offices, causing prolonged uncertainty and more possibility of conflict with private land claimants.

But even this defect was not as serious as the provision of the Iowa
act which said that a route when "definitely fixed" was to be "considered final only in so far as to fix the limit and boundary within
which lands may be selected." [68] The obvious import of this wording
was that the all-important location of the route need be only a tenta-

[64] Steiger to Edmunds, November 26, 1861 (LDP).
[65] Section 1 read, in part: ". . . in case it shall appear that the United States
have, *when the lines or routes of said roads are definitely fixed*, sold any parts
thereof as aforesaid, or that the right of preëmption has attached to the same,
then it shall be lawful for any agent or agents, to be appointed by the Governor
of Said State, to select . . . lieu lands outside the six but within the fifteen-mile
limit. . . ." (*Statutes-at-Large*, vol. XI, p. 9. Italics supplied.)
[66] Hendricks to Grimes, May 19, 1856 (LDP).
[67] CBQ, *Documentary History*, vol. II, p. 14.
[68] *Ibid.*

tive one susceptible to changes. The General Land Office had immediately objected to this phraseology. On August 20, 1856, Acting Commissioner Joseph Wilson wrote to Iowa's secretary of state saying that this clause apparently conflicted directly with the act of Congress requiring the routes to be definitely fixed. "A route merely for fixing the limits of the grant," he declared, "will not be acted upon here, it must be something real and fixed; the grant cannot be in one place and the actual route in another." "Although," he added, "slight variations of the line, such as are unavoidable in the progress of construction of such works would be admissible, any material changes of route would be considered as acting in bad faith with the United States and cannot be tolerated. . . ."[69] Secretary McCleary's answer was what might have been expected. The disputed wording, he said, was merely to allow for these minor changes rendered absolutely necessary for construction purposes.[70]

While government officials were thus arguing over the theoretical meaning of "definitely fixing" the route, the directors hastened to comply with the requirements as they interpreted them. On July 25, 1856, with Coolbaugh in the chair, they resolved that, in compliance with the sixth section of the Iowa act,

this Board hereby adopts the line marked out in the map this day submitted by their Chief Engineer . . . extending from Burlington to a point on the Missouri River designated on said map, as the line definitely fixed for this road, and that said line is hereby adopted, established and located as the line of said road for the purpose designated in said act.[71]

If a formal declaration were all that was necessary to "definitely fix" a location, this resolution was adequate. It was, however, nothing more than a formal declaration. There is no evidence that any actual survey on the ground had been made since Hebard's preliminary one three years before, and indeed at the same meeting it was resolved that

the Chief Engineer be, and is hereby instructed to make without delay the necessary surveys for the extension and construction of the Burlington and Missouri River Railroad from Ottumwa west to the Missouri River.[72]

It was clear that the company felt a verbal or declaratory fixing of the route was all that was necessary for selecting lands. The wording

---

[69] Joseph S. Wilson to George W. McCleary, August 20, 1856 (LDP).

[70] McCleary to Wilson, August 29, 1856 (LDP).

[71] BMI ORB, p. 84. [72] Ibid.

of the Iowa act might easily lead them to this conclusion, and the governor was of the same mind, for on August 5, he certified that this declaratory map had been filed in his office in compliance with the Iowa law and forwarded both map and certificate to Washington.[73] Acting Commissioner John Hood acknowledged their receipt on August 20, but not without objection.

He perceived that the governor's certificate did not state the route was "definitely fixed." Rather than return it, however, he held both map and certificate and respectfully requested a "supplemental certificate under the seal of the State . . . to be annexed to the map, setting forth the fact that the map exhibits the route of the road as 'definitely fixed' in compliance with the Act of Congress." [74] Apparently Grimes never sent this amended certificate.[75] Neither the state nor the railroad companies admitted any inadequacy in the certificate; they based the location of their lands *within six miles* of the track on the route selected in August, 1856. On the basis of this same declaratory selection, Henn on September 4 also forwarded to the General Land Office a claim for all odd sections *between the six- and 15-mile limits*; these were known as the "lieu lands." [76] Thus, by mid-September, 1856, a map had been filed and the lands selected.

In view of the uncertainties in the situation, however, the company turned to the practical matter of laying the actual survey on the ground. In the Council Bluffs district, where the bulk of the Burlington lands lay, work was commenced on September 29 and completed on October 13, 1856.[77] As it turned out, this action was both wise and important, for in response to a query by the Department of the Interior, the attorney-general ruled on December 19, 1856, that the company's title to lands *did not attach to any particular parcel of the public domain* "until the necessary determinative lines shall have been fixed

[73] Copy of certificate (LDP), and copy of letter John Hood to James W. Grimes, August 20, 1856 (LDP).

[74] Hood to Grimes, August 20, 1856 (LDP).

[75] *Ibid.*, penciled annotation by Steiger added on April 10, 1865 (LDP).

[76] Henn to Wilson, September 22, 1855 (LDP). This letter, containing the lieu land claim, reached Washington on September 10. (Steiger to Edmunds, November 21, 1861, LDP.)

[77] Argument of J. R. Morledge, August 17, 1861 (LDP); Steiger to Edmunds, November 26, 1861 (LDP). See also dates cited in numerous railroad-preemptioner cases, e.g., Synopsis of Proof submitted in letter of Henn to Steiger, August 4, 1857 (LDP).

on the face of the earth." [78] In view of this ruling that the "declaratory map" filed on August 20 was insufficient, at least in the attorney-general's estimation, to withdraw lands selected by the railroad from private entry, the railroad's representatives endeavored to establish beyond question the various dates on which the actual survey was completed. This was obviously a complicated task, for it meant proving just when the field party finished its labors in each particular range and township. On January 16, 1857, Henn wrote Commissioner Hendricks calling attention to the Black opinion, requesting suspension of all private entries made under any pretext *after* the railroad's route was fixed "on the face of the earth" and assuring the commissioner that all steps were being taken to procure authenticated evidence of the dates of progress of each field survey.[79] Even this was not enough to make sure of the company's title. On February 16, 1857, the attorney-general issued another opinion which held that although "surveying and marking the lines on the ground" gave an "equitable or inchoate title" to the state (on behalf of the railroad), "the State perfects its title by filing the plats in the land office." [80] Consequently, on March 24, 1857, the officers of the company formally certified the definite map of actual survey. Three days later the Iowa secretary of state confirmed receipt of this certified map [81] and forwarded it to the General Land Office at Washington where it arrived on April 7.[82]

[78] *Opinions of the Attorney-General* (December 19, 1856), vol. VIII, pp. 244–247.

[79] Henn to Hendricks, January 16, 1857 (LDP). The copy of this letter includes also a copy of the Dubuque & Pacific survey sent to the commissioner as an example of the type of map to be filed showing dates of actual survey by means of red flags.

[80] *Opinions of the Attorney-General* (February 16, 1857), vol. VIII, p. 395.

[81] Secretary of State's certificate, March 27, 1857 (LDP).

[82] Chronology of B. & M. Iowa Land Grant (LDP). This was compiled by Steiger and sent to A. E. Touzalin on January 17, 1879 (LDP). In the settlement of preëmption claims, the date of actual survey in the field was used to determine when the company's title attached. (Legal Record, LDP.) Nevertheless, in 9 Wallace 89 (1869) the United States Supreme Court decided that "the location of the railroad was not made on the ground and adopted by the company until March 24th, 1857" and as a result, the B. & M. title was listed in the report of the General Land Office as taking effect on that date (Commissioner G.L.O., *Annual Report*, 1881, p. 179). In 1887, the same source indicated that the B. & M. maps were filed on April 7, 1857, thus making this the official date on which the title attached (*ibid.*, 1887, p. 324). This was the date when the map and certificate of the Iowa secretary of state reached the General Land

Unquestionably, the route of the B. & M. was now "definitely fixed," although the tangled skein of events had paved the way for many possible controversies.[83] It was probable, for example, that preëmptioners would endeavor to establish May 31, 1856, as the effective date of withdrawal at Council Bluffs rather than May 23 when Hendricks' written orders should have arrived, and equally probable that the railroad would question the validity of the instructions of June 19, temporarily permitting preëmptioners to claim land within the grant. Furthermore, the date when the final withdrawal went into force might be advanced if it could be proved that the actual survey, equivalent to an order of withdrawal, preceded October 20 opposite the specific tracts in dispute. These matters, however, were destined to wait until 1861 when the Department of the Interior reopened the entire conflict between preëmption and railroad claims.

At first glance it would seem that these events exhibited exceptional inefficiency, but this conclusion is not necessarily true. Land hunger in the West was not an intangible characteristic, but an active, ever present force that impelled men to resort to strong measures in quest of land and more land. As a result of it, the state, the railroad, and individual settlers were in outright competition. It is true that the company realized that its welfare would be promoted by a thickly settled region, and was thus in a sense favorable to settlement on any basis. But the Burlington and Missouri River Railroad was in sore need of funds; it had to establish its land title and make profitable sales if it were to lay its rails. Consequently, the officers found themselves in the uncomfortable position of having to compete with persons whose friendship they wished to retain as future shippers and travelers. Preëmptioners had less to lose by pressing their claims; the friendship of the railroad at that time was a dubious asset. Therefore, many continued to file their claims on the merest suspicion of adequate proof for title. The state was anxious for new citizens and naturally opposed to anything that would retard settlement. In Washington the Land Office was deluged with business, staffed by inadequate help in

---

Office (Chronology of B. & M. Iowa Land Grant, LDP). Despite these complications, the actual date of survey was apparently the only one used in litigation over title.

[83] A chronological table of the events referring to withdrawal and survey will be found in Appendix A, below.

the subordinate positions, and directed by transient political officers at the top. Even the most efficient executives would have had their hands full untangling the conflicting interpretations of the congressional and state acts. The entire situation was probably typical of the period rather than exceptional.

Under these conditions the railroad could do little more than submit its map, register its complaints, and pray for the best. By 1857, the Department of the Interior had accepted the actual surveys as completed on October 13, 1856, as determining the location of the road and had issued a binding order withdrawing lands within the railway grant limits. It was now up to the General Land Office to make out official lists of sections accruing to the railroad. Until that were done, the company's land-selling program could not begin.

CHAPTER IV

ORGANIZING THE RAILROAD LAND DEPARTMENT, 1856–1859

As THE memorable year 1857 opened, there was indeed nothing un-usually impressive in the 30 miles or so of track that crept west from Burlington. Clarke & Hendrie were faithfully fulfilling their contract, and it seemed likely that they would reach their goal of Skunk River by the specified date of June 1, but even that accomplishment would be of doubtful value from a traffic standpoint. Unless the road could reach the Des Moines River at Ottumwa, some 30 miles further on, it could hardly hope to participate in the growing stream of trade from the interior of the state southeastward to the Missouri River and St. Louis. A year previous the fulfillment of that goal would have seemed incredibly remote, but with 1857 came a burst of hope and optimism. At last the Iowa company could offer something besides enthusiasm and wishful thinking; its land grant might be a source of wealth to whoever could afford to develop it.

James F. Joy, then president of the Chicago, Burlington and Quincy, was hardly the man to let such an opportunity slip by. Since March, 1855, his line had touched the Mississippi opposite the B. & M.'s start-ing point at Burlington; the western road was a natural outlet now made doubly attractive by its potential wealth.[1] Joy hastened east to confer with Brooks and Forbes, each of whom had already helped the B. & M. financially.[2] The former was now president of the Michigan Central, and the latter retained his interests in both C. B. & Q. and M. C. Both men promised Joy renewed support in the form of stock subscriptions. It is more than probable that Forbes had long realized that the unexpected race westward between the Michigan Central and the Michigan Southern interests could end only at the Missouri River. He saw that the time had now come to push through the Iowa part of the system; his only hesitation sprang from the increasingly dark clouds that were appearing in the nation's financial skies.[3] Still, this

[1] See above, p. 81, and map, p. 224.
[2] See above, pp. 62–68.
[3] Pearson, *op. cit.*, p. 85.

was no ordinary opportunity, and it most certainly would not bear postponement. Forbes assured Joy that $1,500,000 could be raised for new stock. Then he set about making good his word. His letter to Erastus Corning on May 11, 1857, made the case clear:

> . . . I had vowed a vow to touch nothing new; but the Iowa Road with its rich and populous country, and its 300,000 acres of *Free Soil* seems to me so very important an extension of our lines that I cannot help taking rather more than my share there. . . .
>
> *Personally* I should not be sorry to see it dropped; as it may lead to some care and thought, . . . but it would be as bad a mistake for the companies to let it go to the enemy as it was for us . . . to let the road round the foot of Lake Michigan go to warm the Southerners into life! — as bad a mistake as it *would* have been to let the Military Tract and Aurora become tributaries to the Rock Island, which we barely escaped making under similar circumstances. . . .[4]

These analogies were pertinent, and it was both fortunate and significant for the future of the system that Forbes and Brooks recognized the need for prompt action in Iowa. If they and their eastern colleagues were to assume new risks, however, it was necessary for them to have closer control of the road's policies. Consequently, at the meeting of the board of directors held in Burlington on May 18, Edward L. Baker of New Bedford was elected president and given authority to call subsequent meetings whenever and wherever he and three directors felt it necessary. Actually, this meant that the directors would gather thereafter in Boston; in anticipation of the fact a local secretary and local treasurer were appointed to care for financial matters in Burlington.[5]

The drive for stock subscriptions began immediately. While Forbes was recommending the securities to his friends in New York and New England, Brooks collaborated with Joy in issuing a joint circular to the Michigan Central stockholders, urging them to invest in the Iowa line. By the end of 1857, he reported that the response to this appeal had been prompt and complete,

> especially by that portion of our stockholders most acquainted with the locality and prospects of that road. . . . This doubtless offers one of the

[4] *Ibid.*, p. 86.
[5] BMI ORB, p. 98. The first meeting of the board in Boston was held on June 9, 1857. (BMI ORB, p. 99.)

best investments to be found in the West considered for its own merits alone, [and] its extension will open a very productive feeder to our own road.[6]

Meanwhile, Forbes had raised the $1,500,000 he had promised.[7]

It was now clear that the small Iowa line was definitely regarded in the East as a vital link in an expanding system. In so far as this fact virtually guaranteed continued financial support it was an asset of incalculable value. But this very assumption of responsibility by absentee backers inevitably made certain local groups feel that their support was no longer so essential. Nothing could have been farther from the truth. Unless individuals, towns, and counties along the line of the route continued their efforts, progress would be delayed if not altogether stopped. As it was, construction during 1857 was slow indeed, even though service was opened to the Skunk River in June. There it stopped, and by autumn the prospects for further progress became even more remote when the financial crisis in the East resulted in a paralysis in iron production.[8] The directors recognized on October 1 that what little work was under way would have to be wholly or partially suspended. The winter of 1857 and first few months of 1858 were dark indeed.

Under the circumstances, James F. Joy organized a public meeting at Burlington on behalf of the railroad in April, 1858; his appeal for help was emphatic and precise. The city, he urged, should free the company from the burden of first mortgage bonds on the second division of the road, between the Skunk River and Ottumwa, by purchasing $75,000 in stock to be repaid when the division should be finished. Secondly, Joy asked the city to substitute a deed in fee simple for the lease of the river accretions as soon as the company should spend $20,000 improving these accretions and upon completion of the line to Ottumwa. The easterner made it clear that the success of the road depended upon the favorable consideration of his proposition. Otherwise immediate construction would not only be doubtful but hopeless; delay, he concluded, would be ruinous. When questioned as to what guarantee the city would have if it supplied the funds, Joy pointed to the money already spent by the company and to the fear of

[6] MC, *Annual Report* for 1857 (Boston, 1857), p. 7.
[7] Pearson, *op. cit.*, p. 86.
[8] BMI, *Annual Report* for 1858 (Boston, 1858), p. 3.

losing the land grant unless Ottumwa were reached by December, 1859.[9]

Editorial comment on Joy's appeal was favorable. After two weeks the *Burlington Weekly Hawk-Eye* declared they had heard no good reason why the accretions should not be given to the road. The tract was then under water, they pointed out, and of no possible use; the railroad would reclaim it, build permanent structures, and employ many local persons, "thus adding to the population and business of the town and enhancing the value of real estate."[10] As to the stock subscription, the editor minced no words. It was perfectly evident, he said, that the land grant alone was not sufficient to assure construction. Yet the local citizens who had money were refusing to support the road on the theory that the Michigan Central and C. B. & Q. needed the line anyway as a feeder. "This," concluded the editor, "is not our idea. We are in favor of backing our friends."[11]

One contributor to the same paper, signing himself "Justice," disagreed. Why, he asked, should the city donate accretions and city credit "for the purpose of filling the pockets of a few individuals who make it a practice (warrior-like) of demanding tribute money every time they visit us, and threaten us if we do not comply with their request, with total annihilation?" The company, "Justice" continued, could not need any deed to the accretions to help reach Ottumwa, for they had offered not to accept the deed until *after* that town was reached. "I understand," he concluded, "the company is interested in land lying adjacent to all the depots between here and the Missouri River, . . . there being . . . a chance for speculation. . . ."[12]

Some of these charges brought a prompt response in adjacent columns. The B. & M., it was pointed out, was not rich, for its grant was still a potential rather than an actual asset. Furthermore, a very small percentage of the stock subscriptions voted locally had been paid; the company's largest item of means was $300,000 in cash voted "by her Eastern friends."[13] This defense was sound and truthful, yet there were other grounds for "Justice's" feeling. Suspicion of absentee owners had characterized "back-country" thinking in America ever since Bacon's Rebellion nearly 200 years before.[14] And it did seem

[9] *Burlington Weekly Hawk-Eye*, April 27, 1858.
[10] *Ibid.*, May 11, 1858.   [11] *Ibid.*   [12] *Ibid.*   [13] *Ibid.*
[14] T. J. Wertenbaker, *Virginia Under the Stuarts* (Princeton, 1914), *passim*.

that Joy's visits to Burlington coincided with appeals for funds; it is possible, too, that his impatience with local conservatism made his requests appear to be "warrior-like" demands.

Even so, "Justice's" charge that the company was interested in land near depots for purposes of speculation was not literally justified. It was indeed true that as early as June, 1853, when R. B. Forbes made an inspection trip to Mount Pleasant and back with Messrs. Warren and Tallant, he purchased for his own account three farms totaling 380 acres. One of these he specifically cited as "near the railroad and near to a proposed station." [15] At the time neither he nor Warren had become directors of the B. & M. although Tallant was on the board.[16] Later, in September, 1857, six of the B. & M.'s nine directors, with other associates, formed the Missouri Land Company to buy and sell tracts along the Hannibal and St. Joseph R. R., which they also controlled.[17] No similar organization was set up at that time for Iowa,[18] and as a matter of fact the Missouri Land Company was operated by men acting in their own behalf rather than as directors of a railroad. Nevertheless, the man on the street or on the farm was not aware of such distinctions. Therefore, the B. & M. found itself the object of criticism because of the individual ventures of its officials. In the spring of 1858, however, antagonism to the company in Burlington must have been negligible, for the city provided the $75,000 cash for stock "demanded" by Joy and on June 22, 1858, agreed to execute a deed for the accretions whenever the B. & M. should reach Ottumwa, and provided the company spent $20,000 improving the reclaimed area.[19] These actions, reported President Baker, might "justly be viewed as an indication of . . . continued confidence in the company, and an appreciation of the benefits of the road to the city." [20]

[15] R. B. Forbes to his wife, June 10, 1853 (CNB, n.p.).

[16] BMI, *Annual Report* for 1858 (Boston, 1858), pp. 2, 19.

[17] Articles of Agreement, Missouri Land Company, dated September 1, 1857 (LDP). The six B. & M. directors were: Edward L. Baker (also president of the company), John W. Brooks, Erastus Corning, John M. Forbes, R. B. Forbes, and Nathaniel Thayer. Another signer of the agreement was H. H. Hunnewell, after whom the present town is named.

[18] See below, pp. 182–185.

[19] CBQ, Deed of 1866, referring to Conditional Deed of June 22, 1858 (LDP). For fulfillment of the conditions stipulated in the deed of 1858, see below, p. 218.

[20] BMI, *Annual Report* for 1858 (Boston, 1858), pp. 4–9.

Meanwhile, on May 19, the directors ordered the president "to push the road through as fast as its finances will warrant." [21] By August 1 the rails were laid into Fairfield, nearly 16 miles beyond the Skunk River.[22] The opening of the line to traffic shortly thereafter was the signal for a monster celebration. Over 900 persons clambered into a special train at Burlington, and many others joined the party at Middle-

NOTICE OF OPENING OF SERVICE BY THE B. & M. TO FAIRFIELD, IOWA, 1858.

town, New London, Mount Pleasant, and Rome. At Fairfield a repast was spread upon a table 986 feet long, and there, after the banquet, toasts were in order, — "to IRON, the metal which transcends in value the finest gold; its magic tissues make distant nations neighbors, . . . to the IRON HORSE, . . . to AGRICULTURE, the basis of all real prosperity; without it the Iron Horse would starve, . . . to GOVERNOR LOWE for his intelligent support of the Railroad system of Iowa," and finally, ". . . to the Burlington & Missouri River Railroad: with untiring energy and zeal in a time of great financial embarrassment and depression of railroad securities, and during the most un-

[21] BMI ORB, p. 108.   [22] CBQ, *Corporate History*, p. 129.

favorable of seasons, they have prosecuted their work and extended their road further West than any other Iowa road . . . !" [23] Here at last was the reward for community and railroad alike; both joined in the celebration with equal zest.

It was but a few days later, while local enthusiasm was still high, that Vice-President J. G. Read at Burlington received from Bernhart Henn the summary of the road's future possibilities that he had requested some time before; a statement of this sort would be of great use to the eastern backers and among prospective investors. The author, now back at his law practice at Fairfield, was a busy man, but no task could have been more congenial to him than the preparation of this report. He was singing the praises of his own beloved Iowa, and his letter was a masterpiece of salesmanship and tact. Starting with the incontrovertible assumption that the great westward stream of migration would seek and follow the easiest, most direct route, he proceeded to show why, in his estimation, Iowa was the natural channel for such a movement, and why, also, it would attract permanent settlers.[24]

If an observer would look at a map of the nation, he began, he would at once observe

that Southern Iowa and Northern Missouri are as central in location in the United States as the "bull's eye" to a shooting target — that the delta formed by the two great rivers of the World — the Mississippi and the Missouri — has a more prominant [sic] position than any other portion of the map — therefore, *the line* of *inland communication* between the people residing on the Atlantic coast and those on the Pacific coast — other things being equal — must cross this delta — and although there will, no doubt, in time, be many routes of Rail Road across the Continent — some one will be the *great thoroughfare* — it to be determined by *population* — *quickness of transit* — *certainty* of *arrivals* and cost of construction — all of which again depend, in a great measure on Climate & Soil — and these, I feel free to say, are not only equal to, but *better* than any other portion of the United States. . . . So far, *population* as it has flowed West from Plymouth Rock keeps along between the 40th and 43rd parallels — concentrating as it leaves the Eastern States more towards the 41st. *Commerce* on the Atlantic board has for a long time concentrated towards the 41st parallel and the line of the B. & M. R. road is in this very latitude. . . .[25]

[23] *Burlington Weekly Hawk-Eye*, September 7, 1858.
[24] Henn to Read, September 6, 1858 (LDP). The letter is reproduced in full in Appendix B, below.   [25] *Ibid.*

Thus, continued Henn, southern Iowa was certain to become a channel of trade. In fact, the residents had found, particularly in the 1850's, a ready sale and high price for their surplus. Of course, the lure of California, the government bounties for settling Oregon,[26] the religious enthusiasm stirred up by Brigham Young and the "later political movements[27] and speculations in Kansas & Nebraska" had lured many Iowans further westward, and while this state of things had been detrimental to Iowa, it proved that it was "the very locality for a profitable Rail Road." Now, in addition to possessing these advantages as a thoroughfare, the state was being recognized as one of the most favorable spots for permanent agricultural settlement. For this, he went on to explain, there were indeed many good reasons.

Throughout Iowa, rainfall was adequate; the soil was rich black loam, well drained by the natural slope of the terrain. Timber was abundant along the line of the projected railroad; in fact, there was more than there had been 20 years previously since cultivation had reduced the danger from fires. Rock, admittedly, was scarce, but bricks were easy to make from readily accessible material. The greatest natural resource of all was coal. Particularly around Ottumwa were rich deposits "which, when properly developed will alone pay the running expenses of the entire road, besides affording a cheap and convenient fuel for operating the road and keeping in motion the factories, shops, and mills which must grow up and make another class of freightage."[28] Unquestionably, Henn continued, the country could support a railroad. Unlike the East, there was no waste land whatever along the route, no mountains, marshes, or "barren knobs" unsuitable for cultivation. Of equal importance for the future, there were very few non-resident property owners, particularly along the first 100 miles of line west of Burlington.[29] Further west perhaps a fifth of the

[26] Between 1850 and 1855 the United States gave approximately 2,500,000 acres to settlers in Oregon as an inducement to take up residence there. (Donaldson, *op. cit.*, p. 296.)

[27] Henn to Read, *ibid.* This obviously referred to the feud between the northern and southern elements in Kansas between 1855 and 1858. (Smith, *op. cit.*, chs. ix, xv.)

[28] Henn to Read, *ibid.* Over 6,000 tons of coal were carried eastward from the Ottumwa region in 1866 (BMI, *Annual Report* for 1866, Boston, 1866). See p. 178.

[29] Absentee landowners who failed to improve their property were the curse of many western states. For a specific example, see Merk, *op. cit.*, pp. 238–271.

land was held by absentees, but "the late monetary crisis [of 1857]
. . . has had a very beneficial effect in stopping speculation & further
purchases by non-residents. . . ."[30]

In view of these circumstances, Henn felt confident that even when
the line reached Ottumwa, it would pay dividends of ten per cent, for
it would then tap the rich Des Moines Valley. Before railroads had
been built in the state, all trade had run southeasterly along the rivers
to St. Louis, but Henn pointed out that "your road has changed that
trade town by town as it has approached it, and will continue so to
change the trade, until it shall absorb all within say thirty miles of
its track, — unless headed off by some rival road."[31] Nevertheless, it
would not be enough merely to reach the Des Moines River. Other
roads would most certainly be built clear across the state, and unless
the B. & M. wished to become a mere branch of the C. B. & Q., it
would have to meet this challenge. "If . . . it is pushed through
to the Missouri, the trade of three embryo cities of importance
on that river, Nebraska City, Omaha & Council Bluffs, will throw
their trade into this channel and will open up a career of prosperity. . . . As soon as time will permit," concluded Henn, "I will
give you such statistical information as will show the truth of my
predictions. . . ." Meanwhile, Read and his superiors could contemplate the rosy future outlined for them by their enthusiastic cham-
pion.

There were indeed good reasons why the Boston office should be
interested in the prospects of Iowa. In the B. & M. Report for 1858,
Henn, as "Agent of the Company," had estimated that there were
256,095 acres within 15 miles of the track to which the B. & M. was
clearly entitled, and 55,930 more claimed by the state as swampland.
The latter, he said, were really arable and thus subject to claim by the
company; they would boost the total grant to well over 300,000 acres.[32]
There was no doubt of the wealth inherent in this land, but even
Henn hesitated to put a specific value on it, since that depended on the
development of the country. Settlement, however, should certainly be

[30] Henn to Read, *ibid.*

[31] *Ibid.* The B. & M. was actually threatened by a rival road in 1863. (See
below, p. 166.) The arguments then employed by the officers of the company to
induce support from the stockholders followed Henn's reasoning.

[32] BMI, *Annual Report* for 1858 (Boston, 1858), p. 6. For the swamplands
dispute, see below, ch. v.

rapid, he declared, "as nature has done everything to make it attractive and inviting." [33]

Another reason why Forbes should be more than ever interested in Iowa was the fact that he was just completing his first major financing for the B. & M. Receipts from his earlier drive for stock had enabled the company to struggle through the winter and resume building in early 1858, but nearly $1,000,000 more was necessary to carry the rails to Ottumwa.[34] He undertook to provide the bulk of this through flotation of new bonds. Already there were two mortgages totaling $625,000 and paying eight per cent against the first 35 miles of line. Consequently, the new $1,000,000 eight per cent loan to be dated October 1, 1858, became a third lien on that part of the property, a first charge against the additional 40 miles being constructed to Ottumwa, and a prior claim on the entire land grant. Because of this last feature, it was known as the "Land Mortgage." Under its terms the trustees were to receive all proceeds from land sales, but prospective purchasers would be amply protected, for when they should complete full payment on their land, they were to receive a title in fee simple "absolutely and forever released from any lien on account of said bonds." [35] John Murray Forbes, H. P. Kidder, and John N. A. Griswold were the trustees; all three had already taken part in western railroad financing, and their support now came as an endorsement of the road's future.[36] The proceeds of this new issue did not, of course, reach the full par value; the company actually received only $833,000 in cash.[37] But it was enough to insure completion to Ottumwa. Boston capital would put Bernhart Henn's prophecy to the test.

With such a stake in the future of the B. & M., Forbes was naturally interested in the individuals who were to be in charge. In the summer of 1858, the ranking official in Burlington was John G. Read, vice-president and superintendent, concerned wholly with engineering and

[33] BMI, *Annual Report* for 1858 (Boston, 1858), p. 6.

[34] *Ibid.*, p. 4. The company estimated it would need $925,000 to finish the line to Ottumwa.

[35] CBQ, *Documentary History*, vol. II, pp. 81–82.

[36] For Forbes' activity, see above, ch. i, and Pearson, *op. cit.*, *passim*. Kidder had appeared, for example, as trustee of the Hannibal and St. Joseph (*Documentary History*, vol. II, pp. 858–868); Griswold, son of one of the heaviest investors in the Illinois Central, had been president of that line during 1855. (Gates, *op. cit.*, p. 77.)

[37] BMI, *Annual Report* for 1859 (Boston, 1859), p. 4.

operating problems.[38] President Baker and Secretary-Treasurer Denison were both in Boston; [39] it would be well for Forbes to have a more direct link with the financial affairs on the spot, and he looked around for a suitable man. Typically enough — for Forbes was always a great believer in youth [40] — his choice fell upon Charles Russell Lowell, twenty-three year old nephew of the poet and diplomat.[41] The appointment of this young man was a piece of great good fortune for the road; his qualifications were without doubt unique.

Lowell had been graduated three years before from Harvard at the head of his class; his brilliant record and even more brilliant prospects won him Forbes' interest and a position as clerk in the Bostonian's office. After six months of absorbing bookkeeping and business methods, Lowell entered the iron industry at Chicopee and went from there to Trenton, New Jersey, into the rolling mills. It was a work he loved, and thus it was a keen disappointment when his health broke and he was forced to spend two years traveling throughout Europe, riding, reading, writing, and studying as he regained his strength.[42] Throughout this period Forbes kept up his lively interest in the lad, and when Lowell returned to America in the spring of 1858, Forbes picked him as the ideal person for the job in hand and promptly had him appointed assistant treasurer of the B. & M., with headquarters in Burlington.[43] Sometime during the sultry days of August the young man arrived at his new post. As he wrote his mother, the little river city "had a half-fledged look, the pinfeathers being very apparent," [44] but he finally admitted that "as a sojourning place, it is not to be sneezed at." [45]

It was not long before he was fully engrossed in the business at

[38] BMI, *Annual Report* for 1858 (Boston, 1858), p. 2; for the nature of Read's work, see BMI, *Annual Report* for 1860 (Boston, 1860), pp. 14–17.

[39] BMI, *Annual Report* for 1858 (Boston, 1858), p. 2.

[40] Pearson, *op. cit.*, pp. 96–106.

[41] *Ibid.*, p. 103.

[42] Edward W. Emerson, *Life and Letters of Charles Russell Lowell* (Boston, 1907), pp. 4–17.

[43] Emerson, *op. cit.*, p. 17; Pearson, *op. cit.*, p. 103; BMI, *Annual Report* for 1859 (Boston, 1859), p. 2.

[44] Lowell to his mother, September 13, 1858 (Emerson, *op. cit.*, pp. 169–170). Lowell's letters throw a penetrating, good-humored, and informative light on Burlington as it was in 1858–60.

[45] Lowell to C. E. Perkins, June 28, 1859 (CNB, ch. iv, pp. 13–15).

hand. Construction during the latter part of 1858 had been slower than usual, and toward the end of November a local newspaper published a communication attacking the whole principle of railroad grants as they applied to Iowa. The writer pointed out that in 1856 the state was prosperous, increasing in population, and possessed land assessed at some $40,000,000. Enactment of the four grants in that year, however, resulted in withdrawal of public land from private entry and an immediate cessation of immigration. The price of land, it was said, dropped abruptly, town lots were a drug on the market, and the produce "raised by the toiling thousands" did not pay the expense of hauling it to market. It was suggested that Iowa needed only an eastern and a western outlet, and that thereafter railroads to carry off surplus grain and stock would be constructed as demanded.[46]

The editor of the *Burlington Weekly Hawk-Eye,* commenting on the same subject a week later, was somewhat more moderate in his statements and incidentally offered young Lowell some sage advice. He admitted that railroads unquestionably increased the value of property but pointed out that that did not mean an increase in the number of inhabitants. After the closing of the land offices in June, 1856, he said, Iowa had been overrun by land speculators, so that persons desiring to become settlers could not secure homes except at exorbitant prices; the result had been a diversion of population to the cheap government lands of Missouri, Kansas, and Nebraska. "The first and greatest want of immigrants is cheap lands and not railroads," he continued, and undertook to prove his statement by citing the experience of the Illinois Central Railroad. That company, he explained, had settled its territory by "a sort of hot-bed forcing system." They had sold their lands at high prices but with long credit and low interest. The result had proved disastrous because many of the lands had reverted to the company. "The lesson is," he concluded, that "no matter what may be its proximity to a railroad, no man can afford to pay fabulous prices for land to be used for agriculture." Nevertheless, the future was not entirely black. Although the depression had ruined many persons, the editor noted that it had swept away speculators, town lots, and farms, and would again bring cheap lands into the market. It would, he prophesied, do what the railroad could not do, namely, bring them new citizens. Finally, it would show railroad

---

[46] *Burlington Weekly Hawk-Eye,* November 23, 1858.

companies "that *people* along their line will be of vastly greater value to them than land," and that it would be "infinitely better to sell their lands at moderate prices to active, thrifty farmers than . . . to sell at larger prices to men who only pay in promises." [47]

This was indeed sound advice, and it was based on experience. It was true that the Illinois Central, in its eagerness to create a populous community, had made terms so attractive that buyers were tempted to over-purchase. When times grew difficult, these settlers were often unable to meet their installments and many contracts had to be canceled. Frequently, these cancellations were carried out by mutual consent so that the original purchaser could exchange his old contract for one embracing a much smaller amount of land.[48] Nevertheless, this experience, together with the *Hawk-Eye's* comment, constituted a timely and pertinent piece of advice for Lowell and the B. & M.

Meanwhile, stimulated by eastern financial support, the road continued construction in 1859 even though the year began under highly discouraging conditions. Late in February, for example, the people of Wapello County resolved that they were not in honor bound to meet their stock subscriptions to the B. & M. Why, they argued, should they contract a debt for their children to pay in order to sustain "a monopoly among us, which while it benefits a small portion of the county, operates oppressively upon the rest"? The local editor took issue with this conclusion although he concurred with the reasons for it. The county, he said, had no reason to repudiate its debt even though it might have been a foolish bargain. From now on, he agreed, railroads should be on a pay-as-you-go basis, for he was convinced that the absentee eastern owners were interested only in the profits that would come from the state.[49] Local opinion of this sort was only one obstacle before the road. Excessive rains [50] and the unparalleled dullness of business arising from generally short crops made the year difficult for all western railroads. "Hope deferred has made the hearts of many sick," reported President Baker in April. The B. & M. was not making profits, and its securities were constantly decreasing in market value. But even then the prospect was brightening. Growing crops

[47] *Burlington Weekly Hawk-Eye*, November 30, 1858.
[48] Gates, *op. cit.*, pp. 269–279.
[49] *Burlington Weekly Hawk-Eye*, March 1, 1859.
[50] Lowell to his mother, April 15, 1859 (Emerson, *op. cit.*, pp. 174–175).

promised an abundant harvest, and the increased demand for western products was encouraging.[51] The editor of the Burlington newspaper commented on another cause for optimism. He pointed out that needy speculators, land-poor farmers, railroads, the state, and the general government all had so many acres for sale that the land market was glutted; therefore, it was an extremely favorable time to buy. "Iowa," he concluded, "is now in a transition state. She is getting rid of the early settlers who are leaving the eastern and central part and in their stead the state is filling up with good, skillful, thrifty farmers." [52]

For Lowell this situation brought extra responsibility; in the summer of 1859, Forbes placed the organization of a land department on his shoulders. Until this time, Bernhart Henn of Fairfield and his Washington assistant, William T. Steiger, had been handling the complicated business of obtaining from the General Land Office correct lists of the lands which would eventually be certified in fee simple to the railroad when the tracks were laid.[53] On March 23, 1859, the Secretary of the Interior had finally certified 187,297.44 acres in the Council Bluffs land district as falling to the road within the 6- and 15-mile limits,[54] and three days later Commissioner Hendricks forwarded the long-awaited lists to Henn.[55] Shortly thereafter, 43,426.34 acres more were certified in the Chariton (subsequently Des Moines) land district, bringing the total reserved for the B. & M. to 230,723.78 acres.[56] Organization of a railroad land department could be delayed no longer. Lands had to be surveyed, title established, and a sales program adopted that would turn the huge undeveloped area into a vigorous community and provide ready cash for the railroad.

The task before Lowell was beyond the powers of one man. Forbes himself recognized this fact and recommended to Lowell another young man, this time but eighteen years old, who could serve as clerk and assistant.[57] The boy was Charles Elliott Perkins, a cousin

[51] BMI, *Annual Report* for 1859 (Boston, 1859), p. 3.
[52] *Burlington Weekly Hawk-Eye*, April 26, 1859.
[53] Henn to Boston office, February 1, 1859 (LDP).
[54] Hendricks to Henn, March 26, 1859 (LDP). See map on p. 242. Date confirmed in BMI Legal Record, vol. I, p. 5; also in the 1922 Valuation Docket Lists (LDP).
[55] Hendricks to Henn, March 26, 1859 (LDP).
[56] Memorandum by Perkins, November 1, 1863 (LDP).
[57] Thomas Hedge, *Charles Elliott Perkins* (Boston?, 1931), pp. 13–18.

of Forbes,[58] at whose house Lowell had met him. He was the eldest son of a God-fearing New England couple of modest circumstances who had settled in Cincinnati, and at the moment he was working for a wholesale fruit concern in that city as an apprentice without pay.[59] At Forbes' suggestion, Lowell sent Perkins a frank and cordial invitation to accept the position at Burlington. The road was but a small one, Lowell pointed out, and there would be much drudgery, yet there would be many pleasant features as well, and the opportunities for learning all phases of railroading were excellent.[60] At the same time Forbes himself wrote his young cousin:

> If I continue so unfortunate as to be concerned in railroads, I can help you on better in that direction than any other, and if you can fit yourself to manage such matters well, you can be more useful in that line than any other. There is a great want of good, trustworthy business men for the management of our railroads, and I therefore incline to have you try to get into that business when you change. You know Lowell — the B. & M. Railroad is under the direction of myself and my friends a good deal, and if you can make yourself useful there, you would certainly stand a good chance of having your services recognized by pay and promotion when the proper opening comes. So unless you can get some satisfactory place in Cincinnati, I incline to advise you to write Mr. Lowell that you will come, or else to go and look for yourself and talk with him about it.[61]

Fascinated with the prospects, Perkins accepted, not knowing that one day he would succeed to the presidency of the entire system.[62] When he arrived in Burlington early in August, he was glad enough to work for $30 a month and to accept Lowell's kind invitation to share his own cottage, along with a young Bohemian named Leo Carper, the company's general freight and ticket agent. Life for these youngsters was strenuous; hours were long, they worked many Sundays and often toiled at night with sperm-oil lamp and candles. The social life of the day was practically non-existent. During the free evenings, Lowell would occupy himself with the *Philosophy of Im-*

---

[58] Perkins' grandfather and Forbes' mother were brother and sister (Edith Perkins Cunningham, *Owls Nest*, Boston, 1907, p. 20 and chart opposite p. 24).

[59] CNB, ch. iv, pp. 1-2; cf. Cunningham, *op. cit., passim* and esp. pp. 173-174, 238-239.

[60] Lowell to Perkins, June 28, 1859 (CNB, ch. iv, pp. 13-15).

[61] CNB, ch. iv, pp. 10-12.

[62] On September 29, 1881 (Hedge, *op. cit.*, p. 29). On September 22, 1864, he married the daughter of Robert Bennett Forbes. (*Ibid.*, p. 23.)

manuel Kant or recently published works of Darwin, providing he was not going over statements and figures with Perkins and Carper.[63]

Although Lowell's title in 1859 was assistant treasurer and land agent and Perkins was merely a clerk, the road was such a small one that they were in close touch with all its affairs. Lowell was a particularly good friend of Vice-President and Superintendent John G. Read, and the latter consulted him freely and frequently. At the end of June, the local paper had commented on the satisfying progress of the road towards Ottumwa and cited the great amount of work done on reclaiming the river accretions, concluding that "the history of the road thus far under the administration of Mr. Read has been one of success and its past good fortune augurs well for its future prosperity." [64] The citizens of Ottumwa apparently shared this opinion, for a month later they granted the company a right of way, grounds for a station, and three additional acres "in order that business from as large an extent of country as possible may be attracted and drawn to [Ottumwa]." On its part the company agreed to use these grounds for railroad purposes only, to build there whatever shops might be necessary in Wapello County, and to complete its road to Ottumwa before October 1, 1859.[65]

Within a fortnight of Perkins' arrival in Burlington, however, the absentee directors of the property, along with this same J. G. Read who seemed so popular, became the objects of a vigorous attack. John G. Foote had originally been the treasurer of the B. & M., but when his office was taken over by Denison in Boston, he had been dismissed and he now took up the cudgels against absentee control. In an open letter to the publisher of the *Burlington Weekly Hawk-Eye*, dated August 13, 1859, he insisted that the B. & M. should be managed so as "to promote . . . the interests of the State and of the City and not entirely the interests of a few non-resident stockholders and directors." Disclaiming any personal jealousy, he pleaded for more local representatives on the board of directors and advocated a legislative provision for periodical examination of all Iowa railroad companies. The

[63] Perkins to Edward W. Emerson, August 20, 1906. (CNB, n.p.) Cf. Pearson, *op. cit.*, pp. 103–105. When Lowell was killed in Sheridan's charge at Cedar Creek in October, 1864, Forbes wrote that he left the "memory of a genius departed." (*Ibid.*)

[64] *Burlington Weekly Hawk-Eye*, June 28, 1859.

[65] BMI ORB, pp. 118–121.

B. & M., he suggested, should be investigated particularly to determine whether the directors of the railroad had any private interest in the accretions, in any land adjacent to the railroad, or in construction contracts.[66] Although such an investigation was never made, the situation was not what Foote probably imagined. By the terms of the lease of the accretions, the reclaimed land could be used only for railroad purposes and therefore not for any personal benefit.[67] This restriction did not, however, apply to other land along the railroad which was available to the public, and it is possible that individual directors had purchased acreage along the route. As yet they had formed no townsite company.[68] As to construction profits, no B. & M. director had been an associate of Clarke & Hendrie when the contract had been signed for building the entire line to Ottumwa.[69] That contract remained in force until the job was completed, and apparently no action was ever taken on Foote's suggestions.

Read was attacked from another quarter. A petition signed by a group of local businessmen was addressed to stockholders and directors of the road, specifically asking for his removal. A week later President Baker came to his support. He wrote that he appreciated how difficult it was to find men without faults to manage the company's affairs, and how often the company would probably fail before it won public confidence and "before all shall realize that our interests and those of the community are the same — that our aims must be to develop and bring out the resources of the country [in order] that we may swell the business of our road. . . ." He urged that the community reserve its judgment until the company had had a chance to prove its worth.[70]

The most effective support for his plea was the opening of the road to Ottumwa on September 1, 1859. The day was set apart for celebration, and nearly all the cars and locomotives on the road were gathered

[66] John G. Foote to C. Dunham, in *Burlington Weekly Hawk-Eye*, August 13, 1859.

[67] Original lease, June 16, 1856 (CR).

[68] See above, p. 102.

[69] J. F. Tallant and Fitz Henry Warren, members of Clarke & Hendrie, had once been B. & M. directors. They both failed of reëlection, however, on March 29, 1854. (BMI ORB, p. 14.) The contract with their firm was not signed until August of that year. (See above, p. 71.)

[70] W. F. Coolbaugh to C. Dunham, and E. L. Baker to certain petitioners (*Burlington Weekly Hawk-Eye*, August 20, 1859).

at Burlington. At seven-thirty in the morning an excursion train half a mile long started on its way westward loaded to capacity. On the cars were the first battalion of Iowa Volunteers, members of the local fire department, an artillery company with its cannon, three bands, "an immense number of citizens and their ladies, and quite a number of invited guests from the East, including reporters from the Chicago Press. . . ." At every station more cars were added and finally a third locomotive. When the train arrived in Ottumwa at noon, between 2,000 and 2,500 people emerged from it "to the great astonishment of the good people then and there assembled." Mayor Gillaspie of Ottumwa uttered a speech of welcome to which Mayor White of Burlington responded. Thereupon a procession was formed, and to the music of the bands the crowds marched to a grove east of the depot grounds. A monster picnic followed during which appropriate resolutions were adopted and countless speeches made. Few persons, however, were interested in oratory; they were bent on enjoying themselves. At four-thirty the excursion train left the scene of festivity with all the guests except those who, like Carper and Perkins, danced all night and ran into debt buying champagne for their young ladies *"and their mothers."* [71]

The editor of the *Burlington Weekly Hawk-Eye* took the occasion of this excursion to compliment the road on its achievements. He noted, with a trace of agreeable surprise, that not a single accident had occurred during the day either on the cars or at Ottumwa, and he asserted that much credit was due Superintendent Read for carrying so many people safely and on time. He complimented the road upon its ballast and track, its depots and water stations, and particularly upon its handsome fences which he suggested would not only prevent the killing of stock with its incident litigation and hard feeling but also many accidents. [72] There was more he might have added. By reaching the banks of the Des Moines River at Ottumwa the Burlington and Missouri River now tapped a main artery of interior traffic and could look forward to a steady and profitable increase of freight business. Furthermore, a traveler could leave Ottumwa at four o'clock in the morning and reach Chicago, 280 miles away, shortly after seven

[71] *Burlington Weekly Hawk-Eye,* September 3, 1859; Charles E. Perkins to his wife, September 3, 1873 (CNB, ch. x, pp. 23–24).

[72] *Burlington Weekly Hawk-Eye,* September 3, 1859.

o'clock the same evening.[73] With its own trains running 75 miles between two important terminals, the B. & M. thus grew from sprawling adolescence to vigorous young manhood. If this growth continued, it would not be long before the rails would reach the land-grant area and active colonization could begin.

It was under these circumstances that Charles Lowell, the cultivated scholar from Beacon Hill, aided by his young clerk from Cincinnati, delved promptly into the mysteries of administering the company's vast estate. The multifarious problems before the young men ranged from serious matters of public policy to the most minute detail of office routine. Obviously, their first major undertaking would be to find out where and what the company lands were; only then could they be priced, advertised, and sold to actual settlers. This task would require trained experts in the field, and a central office where standard practices of accounting and recording would insure smooth and efficient operation. Thus Lowell found himself compelled to master and to organize a mass of detail before he could approach the major problems. Logically enough he turned to the companies who had had experience in disposing of a federal land grant.

Fortunately, these concerns were as favorably disposed as Henn to do all they could in the way of advice. In fact, Lowell had already availed himself of their coöperation. At Detroit he had pored over the books of the St. Mary's Ship Canal Company, and at Chicago he had inspected the Illinois Central's land department. The latter's system impressed him as being unusually complete but far too cumbersome for a small concern, and he inclined toward the simpler procedure of the Canal Company.[74] This opinion was confirmed when, on the cordial invitation of the Hannibal and St. Joseph officials,[75] he visited the newly organized land office of that company in Hannibal. They, too, had started off with the Illinois Central system but had quickly abandoned it in favor of a simpler one.[76] Lowell determined to follow

[73] *Burlington Weekly Hawk-Eye*, October 15, 1859.

[74] Lowell to G. S. Frost (of St. Mary's Ship Canal Company, Detroit), August 17, 1859 (LDP). The Canal Company had received a grant of 750,000 acres on August 26, 1852. (Donaldson, *op. cit.*, p. 259.)

[75] J. L. Lathrop (treasurer of H. & St. J., Hannibal) to Lowell, August 13, 1859 (LDP).

[76] Lowell to Frost, September 22, 1859 (LDP).

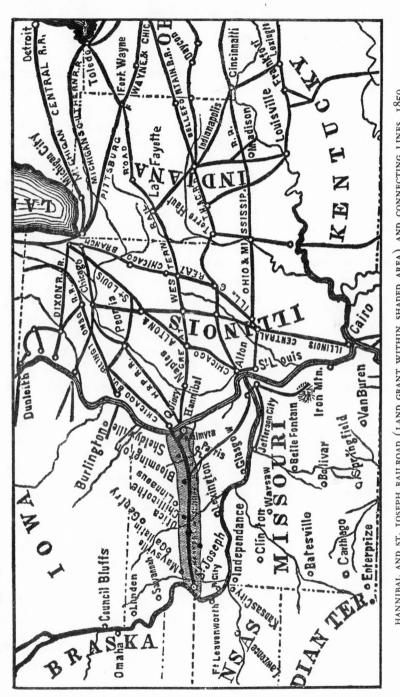

HANNIBAL AND ST. JOSEPH RAILROAD (LAND GRANT WITHIN SHADED AREA) AND CONNECTING LINES, 1859.

the Missouri road, but throughout his tenure relied heavily on both of his good-natured neighbors for advice.[77]

The friendly interdependence of these three early land departments is worthy of comment, both from a general and specific standpoint. Competition between them was vigorous to say the least; as early as 1859 the Hannibal and St. Joseph was advertising in Illinois Central territory,[78] and as time went on, the rivalry grew increasingly keen.[79] Yet there seemed to be no cessation of correspondence and apparently no hard feelings due to the wholesale copying of technique.[80] In fact, the industrial genealogist can trace with ease the parentage and relationship of more than one land-selling idea. The Illinois Central was, of course, the originator of most of the basic procedure, — office organization, survey, advertising, sales, and public relations. Many of the later and smaller lines looked to this pioneer for their ideas,[81] but the Hannibal and St. Joseph was by far the most assiduous and important imitator.[82] Since this line was controlled, in 1859, by the Forbes interests, it was but natural that relations between it and the B. & M. should be close. Both lines successively stood out among their contemporaries in the land-selling field; without stretching the analogy too far, they could be considered the son and grandson of a noble progenitor.

But a long road lay ahead before Lowell could claim the distinction of this relationship. Even though he knew something of the workings of other departments, there were new problems for the Burlington and Missouri River to meet. Thus, as soon as the office forms were returned with approval from Boston, Lowell turned particularly to the one man who had been intimately connected with the company's land matters from the beginning, Bernhart Henn. This gentleman had resigned his position as agent of the four Iowa roads in Washington and had turned over his work there to William Steiger, but he was "on call" in the near-by town of Fairfield and had offered to give what

---

[77] See below, pp. 161–162.

[78] Gates, *op. cit.*, p. 184, and the same author's "The Railroads of Missouri, 1850–1870," *Missouri Historical Review*, vol. XXVI (January, 1932), pp. 130 *et seq.*

[79] Gates, *op. cit.*, pp. 308–313. See also below, p. 161.

[80] See below, pp. 193–194.

[81] Gates, *op. cit.*, pp. 184, 308.

[82] Gates, *op. cit.*, p. 184.

advice he could in organizing the new department at Burlington.[83] Lowell invited him to come down late in September, and the two men laid out before them the crowded docket.[84]

The simple matter of land survey presented no visible complications; the experience of the government and other land-grant companies was readily available, as were also many of the men who had done that type of work. But the inevitable conflict with preëmptioners and swampland claimants settled on railroad land promised to be long and difficult of solution. Some mention has already been made of the former in connection with the withdrawal of lands in 1856, but their troubles, centering about priority of location, formed but one phase of the preëmption dispute.[85] The basic difficulties were over the matter of alleged fraud.

Ever since the Preëmption Act of September 4, 1841, settlers had been allowed to occupy from 40 to 160 acres of public domain and secure, by registration of their claim at the district land office and by paying a small fee, the right to purchase their tract at the end of a specified number of months for $1.25 an acre. To qualify for this privilege, the settler was required actually to enter upon the land in person, erect a dwelling, and improve the tract by cultivation. Unless he did so, he could not legally receive his final patent or title from the government.[86] Yet it was a notorious fact that exaggerated claims were entered and patents applied for by speculators who had no real intention of residing on or improving the land. To prevent validation of these fraudulent claims, the company had succeeded, in 1856, in obtaining the suspension of all doubtful entries within the Iowa grant limits.[87] Some 16,000 acres were thus tied up, and it would be part

[83] Henn to Read, August 16, 1859 (LDP). Henn continued to give aid to the company (e.g., Perkins to Henn, July 24, 1861, LDP, and August 20, 1862, LDP); in a very practical sense, he was one of the "founding fathers" of the Iowa lines.

[84] Lowell to Henn, September 22, 1859 (LDP). As a matter of fact, Lowell's first recorded departmental letter had been an inquiry to Henn. (Lowell to Henn, August 15, 1859, LDP.) Lowell wanted to know whether it would not be a good idea to have the governor, R. P. Lowe, certify the lists showing company lands as listed at Washington. This was designed as a safeguard in case of future disputes, although it was apparently never used as such by the company. Lowe complied with Lowell's request. (Lowell to Henn, November 21, 1859, LDP.)

[85] See above, pp. 89–96.

[86] Donaldson, *op. cit.*, pp. 214–215.

[87] See above, p. 92.

of the examiners' task not only to verify the date of each preëmptioner's entry but also to discover whether the requirements of the act had been followed in good faith. Only then could the company's claims be dropped or pressed, and the land awarded to the rightful owner.

Unfortunately, the swampland tangle was infinitely more complicated. The Swamp Act, approved on September 28, 1850, was designed to enable any state in the Union containing public lands that were swampy or overflowed to construct the necessary levees and drains to reclaim the useless tracts. To achieve this purpose, all sections "the greater part of which [were] . . . 'wet and unfit for cultivation'" were granted to the states in which they lay, subject to disposal by their legislatures, "provided, however, that the proceeds of said lands, whether from sale or direct appropriation in kind, [should] . . . be applied, exclusively, as far as necessary, to the purpose of reclaiming said lands by means of the levees and drains aforesaid. . . ." [88] It will be noted that in contrast to the federally administered preëmption lands, swamplands were under the control of the states. In the case of Iowa, matters were further complicated by entrusting the selection and use of such lands to county authorities. As a result, the Iowa counties, including those within the B. & M.'s grant, were given a vested interest in having as much acreage as possible classified as swampy. Lands so designated were, of course, "appropriated" and thus unavailable to the railroad under the terms of its grant.

Between 1856 and 1859 this situation had led to prolonged correspondence and negotiations between company, state, and General Land Office. The B. & M. endeavored (1) to establish its definite location and consequent right to its lands prior to county selection of swamp tracts, or failing in that, (2) to dispute the swampy character of lands so classified. The state, on behalf of the counties, opposed these efforts, and the Washington authorities, under the handicap of distance and overwork, tried their best to harmonize the conflicting interests. By August, 1859, the most the company had obtained was a promise by Acting Commissioner Wilson that certain swamp selections would not be approved unless and until the B. & M. could present its case.[89] It was up to the railroad, therefore, to secure evidence on which to base its claims.

[88] *Statutes-at-Large,* vol. IX, p. 519.
[89] For the details of the swamplands imbroglio, see next chapter.

Thus, when Lowell began his active administration of the land department in the late summer of 1859, a three-fold task lay before him: to survey the vacant lands within the grant, to examine preëmption claims, and to investigate lands selected by counties as swampy. Of the 307,200 acres claimed by the company in return for building 80 miles, it had received some 230,000 acres. The rest was disputed as follows:[90]

Land Districts	Swamp Claims	Preëmption Claims	Totals
Council Bluffs	47,763.80	14,989.03	62,752.83
Chariton (Des Moines)*	12,050.87	1,357.81	13,408.68
Totals	59,814.67	16,346.84	76,161.51

* Extending westward to the eastern boundary of Range 34, near Albia.

The fact that so much of the company's grant was under conflict was not peculiar to the B. & M. In 1860, the Commissioner of the General Land Office reported that eight states, including Iowa, had received grants in 1856 and 1857 to aid in the construction of 45 railroads. "Much difficulty," he said, "has been experienced in the adjustment of these grants, owing to the numerous conflicts which have arisen. Antagonistic interests, presenting questions of law and fact, are constantly coming before the department for examination and decision, often involving interests to a large amount, and requiring much care in their adjudication."[91] Obviously, Lowell had his work cut out for him, and it was not materially lightened by the fact that others shared his predicament. Of all his problems, that presented by the swamplands was most vexing.

[90] Steiger to Lowell, November 25, 1859 (LDP).
[91] Commissioner of the General Land Office, *Annual Report*, 1860, p. 27.

CHAPTER V

The Swamplands Imbroglio, 1850–1859

There is admittedly an air of mustiness hovering about the long-forgotten story of the swamplands dispute. Episodes that once brought forth the resounding oratory and amazing ingenuity of western lawyers and excited the blunt passions of land-seeking settlers now lie buried in endless bundles of close-written reports, yet they are as typically western as the cow pony or sod house. Nothing could provide a better commentary on the haphazard, free-and-easy methods of government and administration at the time, particularly in respect to the public domain. The fact that the swamplands dispute assumed such importance recalls the intensity of the land-hunger of those days, and its very complexity reflects the curious frontier genius for clothing essentially unlawful acts in apparently legal circumlocution.

The Swamp Act of September 28, 1850 had been specific as to its extent and purpose. It gave to the beneficiary states only those 160-acre tracts that were more than half wet and unfit for cultivation. Proceeds from the sale of these lands were to be applied exclusively, so far as necessary, to their reclamation.[1] There was no question as to the intention of Congress, but it seemed that much of the West believed in a government of men, not of laws.

It was originally believed, when the swamplands project was first suggested, that information in the General Land Office afforded sufficient evidence for the equitable selection of the swampy lands contemplated in the law. Therefore the bill passed by the Senate in September, 1850, granted only such lands as were designated on the plats of that office as swampy. A letter from Hon. R. W. Johnson, congressman from Arkansas, however, brought Congress' attention to the fact that the plats on file did not include the required evidence. Consequently, the House Committee on Public Lands revised the Senate's bill so as to grant "all those swamp and overflowed lands rendered thereby unfit for cultivation" without any restriction as to the source

---

[1] *Statutes-at-Large*, vol. IX, p. 519.

from whence this information would proceed.[2] Thus it was left to the commissioner of the General Land Office to set up the criteria he would accept for determining which lands were really swampy, an elastic grant of discretion, the exercise of which would be not only intrinsically difficult but almost certain to provoke criticism. Commissioner Butterfield issued the first explanatory circular to all registers and receivers, dated November 21, 1850.[3]

Butterfield cited the act as it stood and proceeded to expound it according to his own views. In addition to swampy land, he said, the act pertained to all lands which, though dry part of the year, were subject to inundation at the planting, growing, or harvesting season, so as to destroy the crop and therefore be unfit for cultivation. As a rule of determination, he suggested "taking the average of the seasons, for a reasonable number of years" — probably a well-intended formula, but certainly vague enough to open the door wide for anyone looking for loopholes. Receivers were requested to make out lists of all lands "thus granted" to the state, and they were reminded that the "only reliable data" for so doing were the field notes of the surveys.[4] Then came Butterfield's bland observation:

If the authorities of the State are willing to adopt these field notes as the basis of those lists, you will so regard them. *If not, and those authorities furnish you satisfactory evidence* that any lands are of the character embraced by the grant, you will so report them. . . . The affidavits of the county surveyors and *other responsible persons* that they understand and have examined the lands . . . should be sufficient.[5]

In other words, after specifically designating what the "only reliable data" were, the commissioner authorized receivers to accept also affidavits of presumably "responsible persons." Lands thus selected were to be reserved from further sale or disposal by the United States. The effect of this notice was to give the states the choice of accepting

[2] Hendricks to McClelland (Secretary of the Interior), May 12, 1856 in *Senate Executive Document No. 86*, 34th Cong., 1st Sess. (1855–56), p. 3. Cf. *Cong. Globe*, 31st Cong., 1st Sess. (1850), p. 1999, and Commissioner of the General Land Office, *Annual Report*, 1851, p. 18.

[3] *Senate Executive Document No. 86*, 34th Cong., 1st Sess. (1855–56), p. 3.

[4] Commissioner of the General Land Office, *Circular*, November 21, 1850. Reprinted in *Senate Executive Document No. 86*, 34th Cong., 1st Sess. (1855–56), pp. 7–8.

[5] *Ibid.* Italics supplied.

United States field notes, or the word of their own agents for the character of the land. Naturally, they chose the latter course.[6]

The next move was up to the states involved, and in the following February, Iowa passed a law authorizing the commissioner of the state land office to take such steps as might be necessary to secure the grant. This meant (1) selecting the parcels of ground that were swampy, (2) listing them in the local land office, and (3) eventually receiving from Washington final patents or deeds proving outright ownership on the part of the state. It is important to bear these three separate steps in mind, for there was often delay and dispute involved before all three were accomplished. Once the patents should be received from Washington, the commissioner was authorized to dispose of the lands, and proceeds of such sales, after defraying costs of selection and reclamation, were to revert to the state treasury. County surveyors were given the authority to contract for levees and drains subject to the governor's approval.[7] Apparently Iowa, at least, was prepared to act in the spirit of the original swamplands grant.

Events of the next five years, however, belied this intention. Perhaps the enormous increase in population between 1850 and 1855 and the resulting pressure for lands proved too strong a temptation for the custodians of this vast area. At any rate, during these years, whatever high-mindedness may have existed in state councils was seriously compromised. The first wayward step was apparently an innocent one: by an act of January 13, 1853, Iowa granted all her swamplands to the counties wherein they lay, and provided for their selection by agents

[6] Prior to April 21, 1854, it was the practice in one district land office at least to compare state selections with the notes on file, and to reject lists obviously at variance with the actual survey. Such conscientiousness on the part of federal officials brought on a storm of protest from the state's agents. It was contended that descriptions of soil contained in the original field notes were too vague and indefinite, and written with too great carelessness to permit accurate discrimination between wet and dry land; that, in addition, many of the surveys were executed in time of drought. Consequently, it was earnestly requested that the reliable citizens on the spot be trusted fully. The pressure was too strong upon the commissioner, and he directed the troublesome office to accept local testimony. Under this decision hundreds of thousands of acres were certified that had previously been rejected on the evidence of field notes. (Jno. Loughborough, Surveyor-General at St. Louis, to Thomas A. Hendricks, Commissioner of the General Land Office, July 30, 1857, reprinted in *Senate Executive Document No. 249*, 50th Cong., 1st Sess. (1888), p. 9.

[7] Iowa *Laws*, 3rd Sess., ch. lxix. Reprinted in Iowa Register of the State Land Office, *Annual Report* for 1863 (Des Moines, 1863), p. 43.

to be appointed by the county court. As before, sale and reclamation were contemplated, although responsibility for administration was placed in county hands.[8] The effect of this transfer was of vital importance, for in that day the county organizations varied greatly in personnel and efficiency. Apparently in the more remote northern and western sections the county officers constituted the bulk of the population;[9] it is even recorded that the lone inhabitant of one county held every office.[10] Two years later, on January 25, 1855, counties organized even in this way were allowed to use proceeds from the sale of "irreclaimable" swamplands for the erection of public buildings if such a course were approved by the "people" of the county. This state law, if not flatly contradictory to the letter of the basic Swamp Act, was certainly contrary to the spirit, since it made no provision whatever for the drainage contemplated by Congress.[11]

[8] Iowa *Acts* of 1853, p. 29. Summarized in Iowa Register of the State Land Office, *Annual Report* for 1863 (Des Moines, 1863), pp. 43–44. Illinois and Missouri also turned over their swamplands to the counties. Cf. *Senate Executive Document No. 249*, 50th Cong., 1st Sess. (1888), p. 2.

[9] Cyrenus Cole (*op. cit.*, ch. 1, *passim*) paints a colorful but unconfirmed picture of some of the more fantastic county governments. His most sweeping description applied to the northwest portion of the state is as follows: ". . . But other men in those days who stole thousands instead of horses, and who robbed the future instead of log stables fared better. They were men who plundered whole counties. When the Third General Assembly in 1851 divided the rest of the state into counties, many of them were without residents. It did not take schemers long to see the opportunity that was afforded them. A few men would acquire so-called residences in one of the unsettled counties. They built a few shacks, or even one would do. Then they proceeded to set up a county organization on paper. They pretended to elect county officers. They were willing to hold two or even three offices each, if there were not enough men to go around. Of course they kept all their records in legal form for they were educated scoundrels. Then they passed resolutions to build bridges and court houses and to drain swamps. They let contracts for such *quasi* improvements, issued warrants in payment or issued bonds which were sold to "innocent" purchasers. They had certain processes of make-believe to give validity to their work. A ditching machine dragged across a swamp left the trace of the performance of a contract, even if it did not carry off the surplus waters. A few polings driven by the sides of a stream with a brush fire over them left the remnants of a bridge that had not been built, and charred foundations of a cabin were the visible evidences of a court house that had once stood there. All cases were not so flagrant, but all were bad enough. . . ." (*Ibid.*, pp. 306–307.)

[10] Charles Aldrich, "The County Judge System," *Annals of Iowa*, third series, vol. X, no. 1 (April, 1911), pp. 42–48.

[11] Iowa *Acts* of 1855, p. 261. Summarized in Iowa Register of the State Land Office, *Annual Report* for 1863 (Des Moines, 1863), p. 44.

The opportunities for fraud and maladministration under such a regime were legion. The vagueness of the original act of Congress had been bad enough, but entrusting its administration to county agents whose actions subsequently brought on federal investigation ensured trouble. Obviously, only lands rendered actually unfit for cultivation were supposed to be included within the scope of the law, yet some agents listed sections that had been profitably farmed year after year, and whose only drawback was occasional excessive moisture or overflow once or twice a decade. Sometimes the lands had been dry within the memory of the oldest inhabitant.[12] The fact that these county selections had to be accompanied by sworn affidavits of the agent, corroborated by residents familiar with the land and trained in surveying, and finally certified under the county seal apparently added not one whit to their credibility. The complaint of the harassed surveyor-general at St. Louis referring to the early 'fifties was typical:

. . . although many tracts were reported that I felt positive could not possibly be swamp land, yet *any proof which I might require that it was so would be cheerfully and readily furnished.* Every form of affidavit, no matter how stringent, that I sent to the agent was adhered to strictly by them in making their returns. Nearly a million acres of land have thus

[12] Hibbard, *op. cit.,* p. 274. For specific instances in Iowa, see below, pp. 154–155. An inquiry by the Senate in 1888 into the "improper and unlawful selections" under the Swamp Act brought out the fact that fraud had been rampant, especially in those states where administration of the act had been placed in county hands. The surveyor-general for Arkansas wrote the General Land Office in 1852 that settlers were actually allowing their improved land to be classed as swamp so that they could purchase it from the state at a price under the $1.25 United States minimum; three years later the same officer reported that although the granted lands "are in many instances subject to occasional inundation . . . that they are thereby rendered unfit for cultivation I cannot admit to be true. . . . There are thousands of acres of land confirmed to the State under this grant . . . comprising lands unsurpassed in intrinsic value, fertility and productiveness by any others in the State. . . ." (*Senate Executive Document No. 249,* 50th Cong., 1st Sess., 1888, p. 3.) In January, 1854, the surveyor-general for Illinois observed that the counties of that state were using the grant to enrich themselves "for the very simple reason that the act is itself not generally considered as disreputable." (*Ibid.*) In a letter written April 4, 1856, Commissioner Hendricks stated that 3,250,000 acres had been reported as swamp in Missouri; upon further inquiry, most of these were rejected as being some of the best lands in the state. (*Ibid.*) Commenting on this evidence, Commissioner Stockslager, in 1888, added that "this applies to Illinois and Iowa as well as Missouri." (*Ibid.,* p. 4.)

been reported here, examined and certified . . . , out of which I feel sure that there are not 10,000 acres that are really swamp.[13]

When, in 1853, the state of Iowa granted permission to use proceeds from swampland sales for erection of public buildings, a quasi-legal basis was afforded for further fraud, for it required only a mild stretch of the imagination to regard areas as "irreclaimable" if by doing so the healthy land hunger of actual settlers could be converted into cash for public improvements.[14] To cap the climax, county agents were paid in proportion to the number of acres they picked out as swamp, usually 10 or 15 cents per acre and sometimes as much as one-fourth of the land selected.[15] Under such circumstances the administration of the Swamp Act proceeded in Iowa. Luckily, final patents confirming selections were issued sparingly by the General Land Office, for, to its credit, title was withheld whenever there was a dispute pending.[16]

As might be expected, the chief sufferers from such an execrable system were the *bona fide* settlers under preëmption and other laws on whom often fell the burden of proving, at great expense, the obviously dry character of their land in order to prevent its being confirmed as swamp.[17] By 1855, Congress was forced by the complaints over this situation to grant some measure of relief and, on March 2, passed an act which confirmed all individual (or corporate) entries even though such purchase or location was made *after* selection by the swamp agents but *before* swampland patents had actually been issued by the General Land Office to the states. In other words, those settlers who had successfully resisted the unwarranted selections of county agents up to that time were rewarded by a final title.[18] Section 2 of this act provided that if the states could subsequently prove that any of the lands thus confirmed to settlers had actually been

---

[13] Loughborough to Hendricks, July 30, 1857, reprinted in *Senate Executive Document No. 249*, 50th Cong., 1st Sess. (1888), p. 10. Italics supplied.

[14] Cf. Hibbard, *op. cit.*, p. 285. ". . . not only was open fraud practiced in the selection, but the counties bartered . . . the lands for all sorts of considerations such as public buildings, bridges and the like, purposes foreign to the intent of the United States acts granting the land." (*Ibid.*)

[15] Loughborough to Hendricks, July 30, 1857, *loc. cit.*

[16] Hendricks to McClelland, May 12, 1856. Reprinted in *Senate Executive Document No. 86*, 34th Cong., 1st Sess. (1856), p. 4.

[17] *Senate Executive Document No. 249*, 50th Cong., 1st Sess. (1888), p. 2.

[18] *Statutes-at-Large*, vol. X, p. 634.

swampy on September 28, 1850, they would be entitled to lieu lands elsewhere in the public domain or to a cash indemnity.[19] Thus, the burden of proof was shifted to the states, where it belonged, and the implication plainly made that the original selections were not reliable.[20] The defects in this legislation were (1) its failure to reach the fundamental evils in state administration, and (2) its lack of any provision for the future. Since the county agents failed to mend their ways, new settlers on hitherto unselected lands found themselves in the same position as their predecessors. In fact, by the end of 1855, some 700,000 acres in all were disputed, and the commissioner of the General Land Office euphemistically reported to the Secretary of the Interior that these cases were becoming "onerous and burdensome."[21] The pressing need for further adjustment led the commissioner to issue a public notice on December 21, 1855.[22]

The purpose of this declaration, as stated in its opening words, was to settle once and for all the swamplands imbroglio and to afford individual owners of areas selected as swamp but actually dry an opportunity to submit evidence to that effect. To insure speedy action, the commissioner stated that unless such evidence were filed under oath with the register and receiver of the proper local land office within six months, the swamp selection would be confirmed, and patents issued to the state. Excepted from this regulation were lands already patented to the states or approved to individuals under the Act of March 2, 1855. Six weeks later, on February 11, 1856, the land office issued a supplementary circular containing instructions for carrying out the December ruling. The prescribed course of action was discouragingly complicated. All individual affidavits were to be forwarded to the General Land Office within a month of their receipt; when the six months' period should end (June 21, 1856), the Washington office would return to the local registers a list of all contested lands within their districts, and a calendar of hearings should be posted. Set questions were prescribed for these hearings, and the completed written testimony was to be sent again to the General Land

---

[19] *Statutes-at-Large*, vol. X, p. 634. Lieu lands were given the state in exchange for areas located under the preëmption law or with scrip; cash indemnity was paid for land actually purchased by settlers.

[20] *Senate Executive Document No. 249*, 50th Cong., 1st Sess. (1888), p. 4.

[21] *Senate Executive Document No. 86*, 34th Cong., 1st Sess. (1856), p. 5.

[22] *Ibid.* Original copy in LDP.

Office. The case would be closed and the title finally established only when a decision issued from this source.[23] Perhaps this was the only way in which justice could be obtained, but it meant that titles would be delayed for an indefinite period. Between December and May, some 150,000 acres in Iowa alone were involved in cases under this ruling. On May 7, the Senate, seeking a short cut, passed a resolution calling for information as to what new legislation was needed.[24]

Commissioner Hendricks must have had an inkling of what sort of law Congress had in mind, for on April 4 he had written the Secretary of the Interior that any sweeping confirmation of swamplands to the states would work a gross injustice on innocent settlers, who were then proceeding under the instructions just outlined of December, 1855, and February, 1856, governing the settlement of disputes.[25] Now, in reply to the Senate's request, Hendricks reiterated this cardinal point: any law validating selections would indeed simplify the work of the land office, but it would hardly settle any matter of principle, although Congress could insist upon this sort of solution to the problem if it wished to do so. Commenting on what evils he thought might properly be corrected by a new law, Hendricks pointed out that the 1850 act had imposed no time limit within which a state was required to make its selections; as a result, no state had completed the process, and settlers were still haunted by the fear of having their lands turned in as swampy. He suggested that a 12- or 18-month limit be imposed after survey of the township within which selections should be made. Passing to the heart of the problem, the commissioner walked with more cautious tread and gingerly dropped the real difficulty into the broad lap of Congress:

It might be left to the judgment of Congress [he wrote] to determine the propriety of enacting that where any party shall knowingly swear or affirm falsely in any case involving the right of the States to hold lands selected under the act of September 28, 1850, such party shall, *upon conviction thereof*, suffer as for wilful and corrupt perjury. *A law of this tenor would prevent further fraudulent selections, drive from the field all who are not well assured of their ability to sustain their cases, and be an impassable barrier in the way of all who seek, by frivolous pretenses, to*

[23] *Ibid.*
[24] *Senate Executive Document No. 86*, 34th Cong., 1st Sess. (1856), *passim.*
[25] *Senate Executive Document No. 249*, 50th Cong., 1st Sess. (1888), p. 5.

delay the adjustment of the grant, to the manifest injury of the States, and the federal government. . . .[26]

But Congress paid little attention to the recommendations of its experienced adviser. On March 3, 1857, it acted in vigorous and peremptory fashion.

According to the law passed on that date, *all* selections of swampy and overflowed lands granted to the several states and theretofore made and reported to the commissioner of the General Land Office, "so far as the same shall remain vacant and *unappropriated*, and not interfered with by actual settlement under any existing law of the United States," were confirmed, and patents would be forthcoming. Nothing in the new act, however, was to interfere with the law of March 2, 1855 (validating individual entries on selected but unpatented swamplands), and the provisions of that law were brought up to the present date. The net effect of this new legislation, then, was to confirm all swamp selections on vacant land no matter how the selecting was done, and to award areas then under dispute to the individual (or corporate) claimants, reserving to the state the right to lieu lands or cash indemnity if it could prove such sections actually were swampy on September 28, 1850.[27]

In practice, this act multiplied the difficulties of settlers, railroad, and land office alike. Farmers often occupied land some time before entering the formal claim required under the Preëmption Act, and during this period their sections were technically "unappropriated." The Act of March 3, 1857, was passed without warning to such persons, and when, after that date, they endeavored to record their claim, they frequently found their land irrevocably patented as swampy. They were then forced to come to terms with the county or state administrators of the swamplands, paying whatever those agents were allowed to charge.[28] This situation constituted a serious threat for land-grant railroads as well as for individuals, for unless the companies could prove that their lands were "appropriated" on March

[26] Hendricks to McClelland, May 12, 1856, in *Senate Executive Document No. 86*, 34th Cong., 1st Sess. (1856). Italics supplied.

[27] *Statutes-at-Large*, vol. XI, p. 251. Italics supplied.

[28] S. M. Stockslager (Commissioner of the General Land Office) to J. S. Vilas (Secretary of the Interior), August 16, 1888, reprinted in *Senate Executive Document No. 249*, 50th Cong., 1st Sess. (1888), p. 5.

3, 1857, they also were liable to find their acres certified to the counties, and consequently of no use in providing funds for construction of their lines. This would not only deprive them of funds for construction but, of more importance, prevent their carrying out a consistent colonization policy designed to attract permanent settlers.

Nevertheless, had the state and county selecting agents limited themselves to areas that were actually wet, the confusion caused by this sweeping act of confirmation might have been limited. Immediately after its passage, however, additional lists of selections poured in, containing, for some counties, virtually every acre that had been unappropriated prior to March 3, 1857, without regard to the true character of the area and in the hope of obtaining lieu lands or cash indemnity.[29]

Lately I have received a list of lands [wrote one surveyor-general in July, 1857] situated amongst and embracing portions of the Ozark Mountains, which are sworn to as swamp. Tracts are reported which by the field notes are shown to be "too mountainous and hilly for cultivation." [30]

Unfortunately, the legislators at Des Moines did nothing to prevent such malpractice in their state. In fact, their legislation, either by accident or design, definitely encouraged it. Early in 1858, they authorized agents to complete selections in the unorganized counties and on March 22 of the same year stretched the original Swamp Act even further than before by permitting the counties to use proceeds from swampland sales not only for constructing educational buildings, but also for roads, railroads, and bridges.[31] The result of this legislation was inevitable: it gave the counties an increased stake in the outcome of the swamplands dispute and made it certain that they would not give up an acre without a lively struggle.

Thus, by 1858, the Iowa land-grant railroads were confronted with a situation that would certainly require delicate handling. If they were to attract future shippers and travelers, they would have to keep in the good graces of the communities along their line. On the other hand, unless they wished to lose a considerable portion of their granted lands by uncontested swamp claims, they would have to oppose these same communities, probably in the courts. The dilemma was an

[29] *Ibid.*
[30] Loughborough to Hendricks, July 30, 1857, reprinted in *Senate Executive Document No. 249*, 50th Cong., 1st Sess. (1888), p. 10.
[31] Iowa *Acts* of 1858, *loc. cit.*

uncomfortable one, and particularly embarrassing for the Burlington and Missouri River, since the western part of its grant, especially in Mills County, embraced thousands of acres which on rare occasions were overflowed.[32] The vagueness and conflict of the various state and federal acts which, by 1858, pertained to these lands made it certain that it would be extremely difficult for either the railroad or the counties to establish their title. During 1858 and 1859, however, a series of rulings by the Attorney-General of the United States and the Secretary of the Interior clarified the situation.

When the B. & M. had received its grant on May 15, 1856, the lands subsequently disputed had already been selected as swamp but not yet confirmed to the state by patent from the General Land Office.[33] The question arose, therefore, whether the mere act of selection had vested title in the state, or whether the lands were still free and thus subject to the railroad grant. Since there was no ruling on the point at the time, the lands had been placed in suspension. On November 10, 1858, an opinion by Attorney-General Black sought to dispose of the question.

The particular case before Mr. Black referred to a dispute in Missouri and Arkansas, but it was analogous to the B. & M. situation as far as it went. The swamplands in this instance had been selected *but not patented* when, on February 9, 1853, Congress included them within the limits of certain railroad grants. To whom did they belong?[34] The states maintained that the act of selection by their agents was sufficient to establish title and render the lands ineligible for regranting. The railroads, on the other hand, held that the act of selection had no legal effect, that the lands were subject to the more specific railroad grant, and that they were in fact "appropriated" for that purpose. In his opinion, however, the Attorney-General not only upheld but extended the claims of the state. He said in effect that

[32] There were 47,763.80 acres in the Council Bluffs district alone that were within the railroad grant, but currently held in suspension because of swamp claims.

[33] Iowa Register of the State Land Office, *Annual Report* for 1863 (Des Moines, 1863), p. 54. It will be recalled that the United States dealt only with the state governments, to whom the grant was made by the Act of 1850. In Iowa, however, the counties had actually received the lands under the state law of January 13, 1853, and consequently the conflict was between the railroad and the individuals who had purchased swamplands from the county agents.

[34] *Ibid.*

swamplands were incapable of moving, and therefore the Swamp Act of 1850 had been a grant *in presenti,* immediately attaching to all lands falling within the definition of swamp. Selection was necessary simply so that the tracts in question could be properly described in the final patents, and as soon as such selection was made, title definitely vested in the state.[35] In answer to the railroads' argument, Mr. Black denied that their grants were the more specific; unlike the swamp grants, they were not *in presenti* but *in place,* and did not become fixed until the actual line was staked out on ground.[36] In the case before him, the states had made their selections long before the railroads were surveyed, and were thus entitled to the disputed tracts.

Since the Iowa swamp selections within the Burlington's grant had all preceded the survey on September and October, 1856, it was clear from this ruling that the B. & M. could not hope to secure the disputed lands on the basis of priority or of a more specific claim. Fortunately for the company, there was another possible approach. Would state selections still serve to establish title if they had been fraudulently made and embraced lands that really were not swampy? The Burlington already strongly suspected the existence of extensive fraud within its grant limits, and was gathering as much information as it could on this point.[37] There was, however, one serious defect in the company's case: the Act of March 3, 1857, had sweepingly confirmed all swamp selections that were "unappropriated" on that date, apparently regardless of whether or not they had been fraudulently made, and as yet there had been no ruling on what constituted an act of appropriation. The B. & M., of course, felt that it had "appropriated" its lands by the survey in the fall of 1856, but the directors did not formally adopt this survey until March 24, 1857.[38] If it should be decided by the Secretary of the Interior or by the courts that this later adoption was a prerequisite to appropriation, then the company might well find its claims of fraud automatically cut off by the Act of March 3, 1857. Commissioner Hendricks was aware of these complications. Consequently, when Attorney-General Black's opinion of

---

[35] This confirmed the earlier opinion of Attorney-General Stuart of December 23, 1851, that the Act of 1850 was *in presenti.* (*Opinions of the Attorney-General,* vol. IX, 1858, pp. 253–256.)

[36] This confirmed his opinion of December 19, 1856. See above, pp. 94–95.

[37] Steiger to Thielsen, October 30, 1857 (LDP).

[38] See above, p. 95.

November, 1858, failed to throw any light on them, he immediately wrote to the Secretary of the Interior, outlining the situation and giving his own views on the subject.[39]

The commissioner presented his case by citing a specific example. He pointed out that there were certain Arkansas railroads whose routes had been fixed *after* the swamp selections within their grants, but *before* these selections had been confirmed either by specific action of the General Land Office or by the Act of March 3, 1857. According to Mr. Black's opinion, the mere selection was sufficient to vest title in the state. The railroads, however, suspected fraud had been practiced in making these selections, and under the terms of the public notice of December 21, 1855, were gathering evidence to support their contentions.[40] The question now arose (1) whether these selections, if fraudulent, vested title in the state and (2) whether the disputed lands, being unconfirmed to either the railroad or the state on March 3, 1857, automatically inured to the latter under the act of that date. Hendricks felt that both these points should be answered in the negative

for the reason that the grant of 1850 was by description "Swamp and Overflowed" and that *no title vested in the State under it except for lands of that description,* — that the [Arkansas] railroad grant of 1853 is of lands (not disposed of) in place, and that it took hold of all *dry land not subject to overflow,* falling within the granted boundaries, and that they thereby became appropriated, notwithstanding the State may have wrongfully selected and reported them as Swamp . . . prior to the location of the roads, . . . and such lands became disposed of . . . and are not confirmed by the Act of 3rd. March, 1857. . . .[41]

In other words, the existence of fraud was sufficient to invalidate a swamplands title secured to the state by the simple act of selection, or by the confirming Act of March 3, 1857.

There was one aspect of this Arkansas case, however, that might not hold in Iowa. The commissioner reminded Secretary Thompson that the Arkansas railroads had fixed their routes before March 3, 1857. Suppose they had not done so? This, Hendricks said, might be the case in Iowa; he concluded that in such an event all pending

[39] Hendricks to Thompson, December 2, 1858 (LDP).
[40] See above, p. 133.
[41] Hendricks to Thompson, December 2, 1858 (LDP). First italics supplied; second in original.

swamp contests would be automatically cut off, and the land, however fraudulently selected, would fall to the state as swamp.[42] In his reply of December 10, 1858, the Secretary of the Interior agreed with the commissioner's conclusions on all these points.[43]

In summary, then, the rulings by which the Land Office would be guided were as follows:

(1) Where there was no fraud involved, the mere prior selection by a state of swampland was sufficient to establish the state's title, and to render the land ineligible for subsequent granting to a railroad.

(2) Where fraud was involved, neither prior selection by the state nor the Act of March 3, 1857, vested title in the state *providing* the railroad in question had definitely fixed its route prior to March 3, 1857.

(3) If, however, the railroad had not definitely fixed its route by March 3, 1857, then the prior swamp selections by the state, even though fraudulent, were confirmed by the act of that date.

Since fraud was involved, the sections disputed by the Burlington and Missouri River Railroad obviously fell into either the second or third category depending on whether (1) the survey of September-October, 1856, or (2) the adoption of that survey on March 24, 1857, constituted "definitely fixing" the route and thus "appropriating" the land. Unfortunately for the railroad, counties, and land purchasers, this final question remained unanswered for a decade.[44] In the meantime, the railroad could strengthen its position by securing as much evidence as possible concerning fraudulent selections.

Even this precaution, however, was likely to be of no avail. The circulars of December 21, 1855, and of February 11, 1856, had indeed provided railroads with a means of contesting swamp selections,[45] but would these circulars apply to companies whose lines had not been fixed by March 3, 1857? In other words, would affidavits indi-

[42] *Ibid.*
[43] Thompson to Hendricks, December 10, 1858 (LDP).
[44] The matter was finally settled by the Supreme Court of the United States in 1869. It was then held that no route was finally fixed until adopted by the directors. See below, p. 267.
[45] See above, pp. 128–129.

cating the dry nature of so-called swamplands be sufficient to reopen cases presumably closed by the 1857 act? Upon this point, Secretary Thompson and Commissioner Hendricks exchanged correspondence throughout the early part of 1859, the former manifesting increasing impatience with the prolongation of the dispute, and the latter becoming more and more impressed with the fraudulent nature of the county selections and consequent justice of the railroad claims.[46] It was the Secretary, however, who had the final word on July 23; it boded no good for the Burlington and Missouri River: the state, he pointed out, was entitled to all these tracts under one or the other of the two grants. (This, of course, was technically true, but actually false, for by 1859 the railroad grant had been turned over to the company and the swamplands to the counties.) Therefore, the Secretary continued, the only interest of the United States was faithfully to administer the laws, and

this we shall not accomplish by delay. . . . Should the adjustment be delayed, for investigations to be made, we *could only expect thereby to avoid a few mistakes, which if made we may assume would not seriously injure any one,* and to the State and the United States, the delay would be a greater detriment than any number of errors that can occur. . . .[47]

This observation on the part of the Secretary indicated that he did not understand the actual posture of the dispute and the rights of the parties most intimately affected by it. On the easy assumption that

[46] On April 5, 1859, Hendricks wrote Thompson calling his attention to the fact that railroads were still submitting proof of fraudulent swamp entries under the procedure of the Public Notice of December 21, 1855, and the Circular of February 11, 1856. The secretary had objected to the continuation of this policy, but instructed Hendricks that "if the certification of any such tracts as swamplands inuring to a State under the Act of September 28th, 1850 is contested by the production of any proof of information sufficient to create a doubt as to the actual character of the tract or tracts, you will be under the necessity of obtaining such authentic evidence or official reports as will enable you to decide." (Thompson to Hendricks, April 15, 1859, referred to in LDP.) Thus while denying the practice of the earlier circulars, Thompson upheld their principle. The commissioner immediately replied that the affidavits submitted showed that the tracts in question were "specifically . . . dry lands" and added: "It is respectfully submitted whether these affidavits may not be sufficient to 'create a doubt' as to the character of the lands and bring the premises under the terms of your orders. . . ." (Hendricks to Thompson, July 15, 1859, LDP.) The secretary answered this communication on July 23 as indicated in the text above.

[47] Thompson to Hendricks, July 23, 1859 (LDP). Italics supplied.

immediate adjustment "would not seriously injure any one," he directed:

(1) that all swamp selections regularly reported and on file in the General Land Office on March 3, 1857, should be confirmed "so far as the lands remained vacant and unappropriated" on that date;

(2) that lands would be regarded as unappropriated unless the railroad title had already vested in them;

(3) that if railroad title had vested prior to March 3, 1857, lands should not be confirmed as swamp unless they were in fact so on September 28, 1850, and that the true nature of such tracts should be determined from records, papers, and affidavits "now on file." [48]

The implications of these instructions were important: they tacitly admitted that even fraudulent selections would be confirmed unless a railroad had obtained its title before March 3, 1857, and they restricted the investigations of the commissioner to records then on file, thus cutting off any evidence that might be supplied later, even though it might refer to the actual character of the lands at the time the Swamp Act was originally passed.

Quite naturally, Steiger, the company's Washington agent, was alarmed at this turn of events and sought to forestall any irrevocable action on the part of the General Land Office.[49] On August 15, 1859, Acting-Commissioner Wilson assured him that no approvals of swamp selections would take place "until the extent of the cases to be investigated as contemplated in the Secretary's letter shall be ascertained. You will be fully advised of the course to be pursued in these cases, when they shall be taken up. . . ." [50] This information Steiger probably sent on to Treasurer Denison in Boston, for the latter wrote Lowell a month later, informing him that although the Secretary of the Interior was apparently willing to consider only such documentary proof concerning swamplands then on file, Steiger would press his

[48] Ibid.

[49] Steiger wrote to Chief Engineer Thielsen on June 30, 1859, that "we . . . have a hard fight on hand to prevent the indiscriminate approval of swamp selections interfering with the Railroad selections at present suspended, thus reversing all the former decisions and actions. . . ." (LDP).

[50] Ibid.

claim for the admission of new evidence. Steiger also suggested that the company get sworn statements "from reliable men who *know* about the lands" as soon as possible, and forward them to Washington. "If you have engaged any man for your western examination," he concluded, "such an one might take up the matter first. If not, better see Henn about it." [51] Thus it came about that the men hired by Lowell in the fall of 1859 were to investigate lands claimed both by the railroad as part of its grant and by the counties as swamp.

[51] Denison to Lowell, September 15, 1859 (LDP).

CHAPTER VI

Early Problems of the Railroad Colonizers, 1859–1860

I. THE SURVEY

To GUIDE him in the details of surveying, Lowell already had before him a memorandum that Henn had thoughtfully prepared in April, 1859, a fortnight after the Secretary of the Interior had certified the first large parcel of lands to the B. & M.[1] This memorandum, concise and penetrating, formed the basis of all subsequent examinations:

Examiners

As soon as a "clear list" of the grant is obtained from the General Land Office, a copy, by Districts, will be furnished to the Company, when one or more *Examiners* should be appointed. They should be surveyors, good judges of land, should be able to write a legible hand, and should be good business men generally. Each examiner should be supplied with sufficient blank books to cover the field of his operations, of a form similar to the accompanying sample marked "B," to contain 100 pages each. These examiners should be instructed as follows:

Examiners instructions:

Examine minutely each 40 acre tract described in the list — taking them in numerical order as respects, Townships, Ranges and Sections, making note in your blank book of *each 40 separately*, giving the *quantity* each of *prairie* and *timber* — the *quality* and *component parts* of the *soil* — the *slope* of *surface* — the *growth* of *vegetation* — the *average diameter* and *heighth* [sic] of *timber* — the *kind* of *trees.* — Note all the *streams, sloughs, bayous, ponds, lakes* & *springs* of *pure* and *mineral* water — giving their *flow* and *duration.* Note all *Rocks, ledges* and *quarries* of *limestone, Sandstone, granite, marble, Slate,* &c. Note all evidences of *coal, gypsom* [sic], *iron ore, lead, water-lime, grindstone rock, zinc, copper,* and other *mineral deposites* [sic]. — *Take specimens* of *all minerals* and of all important quarries of building rock and label each specimen with the Description of the tract of land on which it is found, thus: *"Found on N. W. 74 of S. E. 74 sect. 15, T. 75, R. 16 W."* Note the *quantity* and *thickness* of any *mineral* or *stone deposite* [sic]. *Mark on the map* in your blank book the locality of all *streams, bluffs, prairie, timber, groves, minerals, ledges, elevations, depressions* and *topographical data,* and write your notes on the opposite page *as fast as you examine each 40 acre tract.*

[1] See above, p. 111.

Note all important *magnetic variations*, and the precise spot of such variation. Note all farms or other improvements on land belonging to the R. R. Company or on land adjoining thereto, with the full name and Post Office Address of the owner of such farm or improvement. Note the distance of each 40 from the R. R. and from the nearest station — also its distance from the nearest mills town or Post Office. Make enquiry and note the value of land in each neighborhood — also the average yield of Corn, Wheat Oats, potatoes, barley, rye, &c. Whenever you find any extraordinary peculiarity in the appearance or in the yield of the soil, take a specimen of about one pound weight and label it. Take, also, specimens of grain, Stalks of grain and other Agricultural products — labelling all with a description of the tract of land on which it was raised. Make depots for depositing your specimens as often as you may find it necessary, and pack them so as they will be easily transported on your return trips, when you will bring them to the head office, or if you have opportunity, send them there, from time to time, with catalogues of each package sent.

Note the *depth* of *Wells* and the *quality* of *Water* in each neighborhood, and if you can, preserve a bottle of water from *each* important mineral spring, tightly corked and labeld [*sic*] showing *situation* and *flow* of spring.

Note the names and the residence of every farmer who lives immediately near the Rail Road, and the name and residence of each housekeeper with whom you stop. Note, too, the exact locality of all X roads, taverns, stores, school houses, Mills, churches, towns, &c, which lie in the region of your operations.

Whenever you find improvements on any land belonging to the Company, note the name of the owner, the locality of his residence, the time he or she has occupied them — and when the improvements were made.[2]

In regard to the general problems of surveying, this memorandum offered complete directions. There were several additional details, however, on which Lowell needed information, and for this he turned to Josiah Hunt, land agent of the Hannibal and St. Joseph. How much would an examination cost? Was it safe to turn over the entire examination to one man by contract? Could Hunt forward a copy of the instruction book given to each examiner? Whom would he recommend as an examiner? How long would it take to explore the grant, and how thoroughly should it be done?[3] These questions were more than mere trivialities. The earlier lines had had to learn the hard way, by experience, and that had taken two things the B. & M.

[2] Henn Memorandum, April, 1859 (LDP).
[3] Lowell to Hunt, August 9, 1859 (no copy found, but referred to in LDP); also Lowell to Hunt, August 23, 1859 (LDP).

did not currently possess, time and money. A careless examiner would mean faulty valuation; a few cents change in price per acre meant precious dollars; meticulous notes now might save expensive litigation later on. Yet the new company was anxious to move as fast as possible, for it would have to be ready when the customers should arrive.[4]

Hunt replied in detail to the various inquiries. He had paid one examiner $120 a month. From that amount the man had purchased his equipment and horse.[5] But it would be impossible to estimate how much it had cost to examine the whole Hannibal and St. Joseph grant, for it was done along with other work under four administrations. Generally, however, two good men in a party could cover a township in a day if chaining were unnecessary and the topography easy. In timberland, it would take longer.[6] On the whole, it was better not to turn over the work to one man by contract, for "the temptation to slight the work is too much for poor human nature." Hunt was forwarding a complete set of printed instructions which, he noted, were very much like the Illinois Central forms but somewhat "simplified." [7] He recommended John Mills of Quincy as a reliable surveyor, and finally urged Lowell to have the examination very thoroughly done "even if the outlay therefor be considerable. In the short time we have been selling, I have found the advantages of what we do know, and felt the want of further information." [8]

Lowell summarized and relayed this information to Treasurer Denison. He was convinced of the wisdom of a thorough survey, and recommended that each tract be examined by two independent parties.[9] Meanwhile, John Mills of Quincy replied to Lowell's inquiries by offering to undertake the survey for $150 a month, assuming that the country was sufficiently like northern Missouri so that he could locate section corners and "find farm houses where we could be kept overnight." The last point was important, for if camping were necessary, it would cost more and take longer to finish the job.[10] From Fairfield,

---

[4] Lowell was anxious to put the lands on the market as soon as possible. See below, p. 146.
[5] Hunt to Lowell, August 26, 1859 (LDP).
[6] Hunt to Lowell, August 13, 1859 (LDP).
[7] Hunt to Lowell, August 26, 1859 (LDP).
[8] Hunt to Lowell, August 13, 1859 (LDP).
[9] Lowell to Denison, August 23, 1859 (LDP).
[10] Mills to Lowell, August 27, 1859 (LDP).

Henn added some fine points to the data Lowell had already obtained,[11] and Mills wrote again, now declining Lowell's return offer
of $120 a month but adding an illuminating summary of his earlier
work for the Hannibal and St. Joseph. The examination, he said, had
been made by two men, starting at a known section corner. One of
the two would walk a mile east or west; then each would start north
parallel to the other, observing the territory for a half-mile on each
side.

We kept our step by a pocket compas [sic] & measured the distance by
counting the steps of the horse, checking out whenever we came to a farm,
witness tree, or any other way by which we could determine our position.
. . . I don't know but you might think this not a very acurate [sic] way
of examining, but with a good horse and some little practice a man can
run a line very correct — full enough for the examination you wish. . . .[12]

Fortunately for the company, Lowell did not agree to any such
haphazard technique. Examiners were provided with odometers, con-
sisting of a wheel pushed along the ground on the end of a stick and
equipped with a clock-like measuring device.[13] Furthermore, the land
department issued printed instructions meticulously covering every
phase of the work; they were based on Hannibal and St. Joseph
practice although that line had never reduced its technique to writing.[14]
By early October, 1859, the first party, under Engineer Thielsen, was
ready to take the field,[15] and Lowell wrote his final words of advice:

After all is said and written on the subject, much must still be left to
your own judgment. Bear in mind that the final object of the examination
is to get data for the correct *valuation of each 40*. With this idea always
present, work as fast or as slow as you think best. . . .[16]

[11] Henn to Lowell, September 27, 1859 (LDP). Henn said most section corners were easily found since a post was sunk in a mound at each one. Later
searching proved this to be incorrect in many instances. (See below, p. 144.)
He wrote that each examiner would need a large pocket compass, light Jacob-
staff and chain.

[12] Mills to Lowell, October 7, 1859 (LDP).

[13] Thielsen to Lowell, October 10, 1859 (LDP). On rough ground the clock-
work used to cause considerable trouble. Knight wrote at one point that he had
discontinued the use of the "patent wheelbarrow until I find less brush." (Knight
to Lowell, January 29, 1860, LDP.)

[14] Lowell to Thielsen, October 6, 1859 (LDP).

[15] Lowell to Henn, September 22, 1859 (LDP).

[16] Lowell to Thielsen, October 6, 1859 (LDP).

There would be no compromising with quality if Lowell could prevent it. Samples should be taken of all types of soil, "each sample labelled and numbered, so that reference can be made to it by *number* in future reports." Examiners were instructed also to keep their eyes peeled for town sites and for any land worth reserving to the company for ties, timber, or fuel. Nor was that all:

> In examining *disputed tracts* — whether swamp or preemption — great care should be taken to avoid giving offense. Actual settlers should be advised to make application at once to this office, describing tract and naming *their* price; in no case will they suffer injustice — they will have the land at our lowest valuation. . . .[17]

To live at all the railroad would have to be a good neighbor. The final touch was characteristic:

> Make your examinations as thorough & your reports as full as if on each 40 you were writing to your ladylove & describing the Paradise where you hoped to pass with her a blissful middleage [*sic*]![18]

Thielsen had his orders.

He had not been in the field a week before complications arose. There were cases where preëmptors had obviously complied with the requirements of their act, but had settled within railroad limits under a misapprehension. In such instances, it seemed unnecessary to Thielsen to make a particular examination of the land; it might alarm the occupants who had settled and made their improvements in good faith. Would it not be sufficient to make a very general survey of such tracts?[19] Lowell replied with an emphatic yes: collect simply the skeleton information,

> pat the children on the head, swear they are the image of their father, and leave all in a good humor. However valid our claim, and however valuable the land, I fancy it will always be our policy to charge *bona fide* residents only our minimum rates. Therefore by all means save time and avoid offense. . . .[20]

Thus was the good neighbor policy confirmed.

Meanwhile, Lowell hired John W. Ames of Mendota to come down

[17] *Ibid.*
[18] *Ibid.*
[19] Thielsen to Lowell, October 15, 1859 (LDP).
[20] Lowell to Thielsen, October 21, 1859 (LDP).

and take charge of a second examining party,[21] and by the end of October this group, working in Henry County, reported it was "getting along fine, fine horse, fine weather, fine country, all right but the land." [22] As winter set in, however, the going became difficult; on November 21, Thielsen sent in the first full report of progress and conditions. In a little more than a month, he had been able to examine 453 "forties" (18,120 acres), averaging 13 to 14 a day. This figured out as costing about one and a third cents per acre for actual surveying, or between that figure and two cents, including time spent in the stage and writing reports.[23]

This progress fell short of the Hannibal and St. Joseph rate of a township a day, but Thielsen defended the record on several grounds. For one thing, it required considerable time and much chaining to ascertain the exact location of water fit for livestock. Secondly, and more important, it was especially difficult to find government markers, since the surveyors, instead of making mounds and pits and driving stakes in the mounds, merely dropped the stakes on the ground where the mounds should have been made. At least it was supposed they so left them, for Thielsen occasionally found a half-consumed or decayed one somewhere near the proper spot. Local residents explained this haphazard procedure by saying that the ground was frozen at the time of the survey. At any rate, the railroad examiners were compelled to ride until they found timber with marked witness trees indicating section lines. From these they ran a line across the prairies to the next clump; it was slow work, but the only method of making an accurate map. Thielsen advised Lowell to inform the surveyor-general about the situation, for he realized full well that it would be a "source of litigation for a long time to come." [24]

[21] Lowell to Ames, September 29, 1859 (LDP). In this letter which first offered the position, Lowell explained that the entire survey would cover about 200,000 acres, and that it would merely be necessary to "find corners, & sketch off the distribution of bluffs, woods and water." Ames accepted promptly (Ames to Lowell, October 1, 1859, LDP), whereupon Lowell invited him to "come down and stay under my rafters & spy out the land. I am keeping house so you will cause me no sort of trouble! There is no wife or anything of that sort — no troublesome creature about so come down at once. . . ." (October 5, 1859, LDP.)

[22] Ames to Lowell, October 26, 1859 (LDP).

[23] Thielsen to Lowell, November 21, 1859 (LDP).

[24] Ibid.

As the winter wore on, two more examining parties, under J. M. King[25] and S. G. Knight,[26] joined those of Thielsen and Ames in the field, and J. S. McClary took charge of a special swamplands investigation in the western end of the grant.[27] Traveling and living conditions as reported by these five groups were enough to discourage anyone but the hardiest product of the frontier. Winter rain, snow, and squalls alternated in dreary succession.[28] A heavy fall one night would provide a foot of thick slush the next day, bad enough on the open prairie but a "serious inconvenience" in the numerous brush-covered areas where hazel, plum, prickly ash, and "shoemake" were bound together with thorny vines into a barrier sometimes ten feet high.[29] The greatest inconvenience was the scarcity of farmhouses. When the day's work was done, it was often necessary to wander four or five miles to find the nearest dwelling,[30] and then, as Thielsen wrote, its accommodations were likely to be of a sort "that would be too nauseous to stand if we were not usually too hungry or tired to care much about it."[31] Most settlers had only one bed to spare and usually the weary examiners had hours of paper work to do before they could occupy even that. Abbreviated notes, written in the field with gloves on from the back of a moving horse and often blotted by rain or snow, had to be carefully transcribed,[32] and a brief résumé sent to Lowell. Sometimes conditions made even this clerical work impossible. Thielsen found the only warm room in one house so filled with stage drivers, movers, and workmen that there was no space for writing.[33] A report arrived from Knight written in pencil because his ink had frozen solid and he could not wait for a thaw,[34] and King once explained that he had failed to write at one point because the only light available had come from an open fire; when he moved near enough to write, his clothes were in danger of burn-

[25] King to Lowell, January 8, 1860 (LDP).

[26] Knight to Lowell, January 29, 1860 (LDP).

[27] McClary to Lowell, January 11, 1860 (LDP).

[28] Knight to Lowell, February 26, 1860 (LDP).

[29] Knight to Lowell, January 29, 1860 (LDP).

[30] Thielsen to Lowell, November 21, 1859 (LDP); Knight to Lowell, February 26, 1860 (LDP).

[31] Thielsen to Lowell, November 21, 1859 (LDP).

[32] Ibid.

[33] Thielsen to Lowell, November 17, 1859 (LDP).

[34] Knight to Lowell, February 12, 1860 (LDP).

ing, and at any greater distance, he was likely to freeze. In fact, he added, it was "necessary to keep [a] constant rotary motion, thawing & warming one side while we cooled & froze the other."[35] It would seem that he had a legitimate excuse for his silence. Nevertheless, it apparently occurred to none of the surveyors to postpone his travels until spring. Immigration into Iowa in the fall of 1859 had been heavier than at any time since 1856,[36] and Lowell was eager to have the examination completed so as to put the lands on the market at the very earliest moment.[37] The parties in the field were making that possible, despite bad weather, rough country, and sparse settlement.

Lowell was wise enough to appreciate fully the difficulties facing his men; he wrote that he was entirely satisfied with their progress:

If we are spending a percentage more per acre than the Hannibal & St. Jo or Illinois Central Railroads, we are spending it in the right place — I will try to save it elsewhere. The aggregate is trifling compared with the advantage we may reap from knowing exactly what we are selling. . . .[38]

He urged continued thoroughness, and the lesson was not lost on young Perkins.[39] Meanwhile the special problems raised by the preemption and swamp conflicts called for special treatment.

II. THE PREËMPTION AND SWAMP CLAIMS

Both these matters had inherent defects from the point of view of administration, for it was not enough merely to settle the actual conflicts in the field. The ultimate disposition of any given case rested with the Land Office in Washington, and might have to pass through the local registers and receivers as well.[40] To add to the confusion, all lists were copied by longhand, and the slightest clerical error was sufficient to stall an entire negotiation.[41] Even Steiger and Lowell, men of experience and intelligence, found themselves occasionally working

[35] King to Lowell, January 8, 1860 (LDP).

[36] Lowell to ?, November 6?, 1859 (LDP). This increase in 1859 was natural in view of the recovery from the Panic of 1857; it probably included persons from the East who had lost heavily in that depression.

[37] *Ibid.*

[38] Lowell to Thielsen, December 8, 1859 (LDP).

[39] See below, p. 163.

[40] E.g., Thielsen to Lowell, November 21, 1859 (LDP).

[41] E.g., Steiger to Lowell, November 25, 1859 (LDP), and November 28, 1859 (LDP).

at cross-purposes, although the latter, situated as he was between his field men and Washington, had to bear the brunt of most misunderstandings.[42]

The preëmption problem in particular reappeared in an acute form late in 1859. In October, Steiger placed in the hands of the commissioner of the General Land Office all the documentary proof Henn had been able to gather in 1857, and wrote Lowell that he had in his possession all the facts necessary to procure cancellation of all invalid preëmptions on railroad land "except in fraudulent cases."[43] In other words, Steiger was prepared to dispute the claims of preëmptioners who had mistakenly settled on railroad land and improved it, but he had no information about those who had entered claims on company sections and then deliberately failed to comply with the settlement and improvement requirements of the Preëmption Act. Thus it was up to Lowell to procure information concerning persons in this latter category. Lowell wrote at once to Henn, posing several questions that had been forming in his mind.[44] Was there, in the first place, "any royal road to the discovery of fraud"? Were there, so far as Henn knew, any claimants who had entered preëmption claims at $2.50 an acre, as specified by the Iowa Act of July 14, 1856, for the even sections within the lateral limits of the railroad grant? And if any of these claimants had, under a misapprehension, settled on the odd sections belonging to the company, would it not be a good policy to sell them their tracts at the $2.50 price rather than at the market price that the railroad would charge when construction of the road increased realty values? Finally, what constituted proof of railroad title; were the certified lists recently received from Washington sufficient, or would a more formal patent be forthcoming? To obtain further information on this last point, Lowell sent an inquiry to Hunt of the Hannibal and St. Joseph; what form of title did that road consider necessary?[45]

Hunt's reply arrived first. His company had no other documentary title to its lands than the certified lists, but in order to give individual purchasers something more substantial, the railroad had persuaded

[42] E.g., Steiger to Lowell, November 4, 1859 (LDP).
[43] Steiger to Lowell, October 25, 1859 (LDP).
[44] Lowell to Henn, November 2, 1859 (LDP).
[45] Lowell to Hunt, November 21, 1859 (LDP).

the Missouri legislature to pass an act requiring the company to file in the recorder's office of each county a list of lands owned therein. The law added that such a list should be taken in all legal proceedings as *prima facie* evidence of title. This law had proved a great convenience to the Hannibal and St. Joseph in matters of litigation, for it saved them from taking the original books all over the state.[46] Lowell, however, took no immediate steps to follow suit. A talk with Governor Lowe had shown the executive willing to add his certification to the lists already received, and in fact he did so late in December.[47]

Meanwhile, Lowell's concern over the complexity and importance of preëmption disputes was justified by a letter from Thielsen written from the field. Apparently numerous preëmption claimants on odd sections, particularly near the 15-mile limits, had been allowed by the register and receiver at Council Bluffs to pay for their lands in cash or military bounty warrants even though the railroad had already been "actually located" on the ground and the tracts in question were notoriously company property. The reason in these particular cases was not hard to find. It seemed that an officer in the land office was also agent (at a 40 per cent commission) for some company dealing in land warrants. From another source came information that the register himself had assured settlers they would be allowed to prove up their claims (under the Preëmption Act); yet when they had attempted to do so a year later, a new register informed them that their duplicate certificates of entry were without value. Thielsen was worried about the effect of this unscrupulous policy. What, he asked, was to be done in cases where deluded settlers had made their applications weeks and months after the road's location (September 28, 1856), or worse still, "where the land was only obtained for speculation instead of actual settlement, and the letter of the law only satisfied enough to hold the land, the preëmptor selling [at] the first opportunity"?[48]

Furthermore, there were political involvements which would have

[46] Hunt to Lowell, November 29, 1859 (LDP).
[47] The original suggestion of having the governor certify the lists apparently came from Lowell; he mentioned the idea in a letter to Henn on November 2, 1859 (LDP). On November 21, Lowell reported having had a satisfactory talk with the governor (LDP). Eight days later the lists for Chariton and Council Bluffs were sent to the executive (LDP), and on December 27 they were returned with a certificate of their correctness (LDP).
[48] Thielsen to Lowell, November 21, 1859 (LDP).

to be carefully handled. Among the settlers who had been allowed to enter preëmption claims on railroad lands in the Council Bluffs district was a one-time lawyer and close friend of both Senators Jones and Harlan. When his claim was declared invalid by the new register, he quite naturally appealed to his friends at Washington.[49] Jones had championed the grants in 1856,[50] and Harlan believed in encouraging the development of business in the newly settled territory.[51] Yet it was an elementary political axiom that no western congressman could afford to overlook the attitude of his constituent towards the right to own the land he occupied. The claim, they wrote, was by all means valid *if the railroad had not complied with the conditions of its grant,* and in any event, they sympathized very deeply with the settler. Thus fortified with good words, the latter was contemplating a petition to Congress to validate his claim or procure lieu lands elsewhere. Thielsen, anxious to forestall such action and to placate community feeling, tactfully informed him that *bona fide* settlers and preëmptors would probably not be charged any more for their claims by the railroad company than by the government. Then he wrote Lowell that "this matter ought to be settled as soon as possible." Thielsen was by no means an alarmist, but his position was sound. He had found that the people of western Iowa, compelled to send their goods 105 miles by road to the nearest market at St. Joseph, were anxious to have a railroad and were disposed to support it. But even a cursory examination by the company of land held under preëmption claim was causing uneasiness.[52]

More than ever, Lowell was now convinced of the necessity of keeping on good terms with actual settlers who, for one reason or another, found themselves without title on railroad lands. "Avoid giving unnecessary trouble and offense," he urged Ames, "and let the farmers understand that the railroad will treat them fairly, but that we must have the facts before we can judge what is fair."[53] To Thielsen he was even more explicit. Complete information was, of course, essential, not only in dealing with the various government agencies (federal and state), but to expedite settlement and "to quiet

---

[49] *Ibid.*

[50] See above, pp. 73 *et seq.*

[51] Cyrenus Cole, *op. cit.*, chs. li–lxi.

[52] Thielsen to Lowell, November 21, 1859 (LDP).

[53] Lowell to Ames, December 14, 1859 (LDP).

all uncomfortable feeling" [54] on the part of residents should the lands eventually be awarded to the railroad. Furthermore, Lowell was particularly anxious to learn whether the settlers themselves thought their claims were tenable; "this *ought*, perhaps, to make a little difference in our adjustments, though it will be a variable element difficult to calculate." [55] His final word trenchantly summarized the company's attitude:

Keep it constantly before the farmers that we are a *railroad* company & not a *land* company — that settlers are more important to us than a high price for our land — & that no claims will be used as an engine of injustice; it would be a miserable policy. . . .[56]

The B. & M.'s attitude in the case of fraudulent entries was naturally of another sort. The contest there was not with *bona fide* settlers, but with speculators who were attempting to secure lands to which they had no right and with a government that failed to stop such injustice. The Preëmption Act of 1841 specified that after filing a preëmption claim, the individual should erect a habitable dwelling, reside on and improve his plot for a year before receiving his final patent.[57] Reports from Thielsen revealed how often these requirements were flagrantly evaded by claimants and overlooked by land officers.[58] At the time of the examination these lands were "in suspension," which meant that no further action was possible towards issuing a patent until investigation was made by the government. The company's evidence was designed to convince the Department of the Interior that many tracts were in fact vacant and should inure to the railroad, or at least be held in suspension pending further investigation.

The facts in these cases were strikingly similar. Most plots had anywhere from a few square yards to six or eight acres broken, but seldom improved. On one, Thielsen found a trench dug one shovel deep and one shovel wide forming a rectangle about 12 by 20 feet, with a small stake driven in the middle; another boasted the base logs and ridgepole of a cabin, and part of one acre broken. The most frequent comment, however, was "no trace or appearances of any im-

[54] Lowell to Thielsen, December 8, 1859 (LDP).
[55] *Ibid.*
[56] *Ibid.*
[57] Donaldson, *op. cit.*, pp. 214–216.
[58] See below, pp. 187–188.

provement whatever." [59] This testimony Lowell forwarded to Steiger, who handed it to the commissioner of the General Land Office with a request for further postponement of confirmation. Lowell gave it as his opinion in regard to all these disputed tracts that "in scarcely one of them has the spirit of the preëmption act been complied with, though in some few the letter of the law may have been fulfilled." [60] An afterthought prompted him to clarify his position by another letter on the same day; it was important that Steiger should not have any misapprehensions. The company had no intention of wresting lands from actual settlers even if they had no title; "we may have to make a case in each class in order to decide the principle, and whether we lose or win, shall have a ground for relief from Congress." [61] It was only the *fraudulently entered and actually vacant* tracts that the railroad wished to recover.

The commissioner was uncoöperative.[62] He demurred at further suspension, and seemed annoyed that the company had waited for over three years from the date of the grant to enter its complaint. Lowell was indignant but patiently wrote directly to the Land Office. The company's agents had been present in July and August, 1857, when the original year-old preëmption claims were being proved up, but further action would have been mere "tilting against windmills" until the government-certified lists arrived. This had occurred late in 1859; they then had to be sent to Des Moines for comparison and additional certification, and had been in Lowell's hands only a fortnight.[63] Thus a delay of six months more in the final determination of the disputed tracts was hardly an unreasonable request. Confronted with this information, the commissioner agreed, and the matter was postponed indefinitely until full investigation could be made.[64] There, for the moment, the preëmption matter rested. Meanwhile, the B. & M. land department was endeavoring to reduce the swamp imbroglio to manageable proportions.

On March 3, 1857, Congress had passed an act which confirmed all

[59] Affidavits from Thielsen, January 3, 1860 (LDP).
[60] Lowell to Steiger, January 12, 1860 (LDP).
[61] *Ibid.*
[62] *Ibid.*
[63] Lowell to Joseph S. Wilson (Acting Commissioner), January 13, 1860 (LDP).
[64] See below, p. 191.

disputed swamp selections to the states unless the contested tracts lay within the grant limits of a railroad whose line was already "definitely fixed." Since it was still undecided whether or not the B. & M. had established its definite location prior to that date, it was doubtful whether the company could gain anything by gathering additional testimony disputing swamp selections, particularly since the Secretary of the Interior on July 23, 1859, declared that he would interpret the law strictly, and further that he would consider protesting affidavits only if they had been filed prior to March 3, 1857.[65] But Steiger was sure that the Department would relent. On November 4, 1859, he wrote Lowell that the company had been "repeatedly promised" that *every* interfering swamp selection would be fully investigated.[66] Acting Commissioner Wilson had renewed this pledge, in part, in August, 1859, and Steiger did not intend to let the promise lapse.[67] Consequently, it was up to Lowell to gather all possible testimony and have it ready for immediate use if and when a full investigation should be ordered.

Lowell explained this situation to the various examining parties,[68] and shortly after the first of the year sent them affidavits to be filled out by the local residents respecting the character of disputed lands. These questionnaires were drawn with the care of a contract and were designed to establish firmly the points that were most vulnerable in the original selections, namely, the actual status of the tract under consideration and the qualifications of the selecting agents. Seven of the fifteen questions inquired into the productive capacity of the plot: what could be grown there, which portions if any were subject to overflow, and for how long? The remaining queries concerned the witness himself. For example, how near did he live to the tract? Was he there in September, 1850? Was he familiar with the terms and technique of public surveying? Was he making his statement from personal knowledge or from the representation of others? Was he directly or indirectly interested in the determination of the controversy? [69]

[65] See above, p. 136.   [66] Steiger to Lowell, November 4, 1859 (LDP).
[67] See above, p. 137.
[68] Lowell to McClary, January 4, 1860 (LDP); Lowell to Ames, January 9, 1860 (LDP).
[69] Land department interrogation, January 4, 1860 (LDP); supplemental questions quoted in Lowell to McClary, January 9, 1860 (LDP).

Lowell impressed upon his men the necessity of obtaining the most respectable witnesses to fill out these declarations, and as a double check upon their probity, he suggested that the county judge or sheriff be asked to certify to their credibility.[70] "Of course," he added, "these questions need not be asked unless you think the answer will be such as is desired." [71] The company was interested only in proving that evasion of the Swamp Act existed.

Most of the swamplands lay in the extreme western part of the grant along the Missouri River bottoms, and reports sent from that section by McClary made it clear from the start that it was going to be extremely difficult to collect testimony there that would be favorable to the railroad. The chief obstacle was the widespread sentiment in favor of the St. Joseph and Council Bluffs Railroad. This projected line when built would presumably bring even more business into the existing channel of trade north and south, so that the people along its route were naturally inclined to support it as against a competing line whose completion appeared doubtful to say the least. The fact that the Burlington was claiming lands already occupied made its position even more trying and difficult. Proponents of the north-south line quite understandably sought to capitalize on both these factors; when McClary arrived he found one of them canvassing Mills County and making speeches with the dual purpose of securing an appropriation for the St. Joseph road and fighting the B. & M. claims. Under the circumstances, he asked Lowell whether it would not be wise to hold up the affidavits for the time being, and to hire a local lawyer who was thoroughly acquainted with the lands in question and the people holding them.[72] A situation of this sort gave point to the suggestion received from Henn about the same time that it might be wise for the company to propose a compromise with each county judge, allowing the county one-third or one-half of the disputed tracts, rather than to contest the entire lot. "This would," he wisely observed, "save time, cost and individual excitement on the part of the claimants." [73]

Time hardly improved the situation, although McClary's consistently

[70] Lowell to McClary, January 4, 1860 (LDP); Lowell to Ames, January 9, 1860 (LDP).
[71] Lowell to McClary, January 9, 1860 (LDP).
[72] McClary to Lowell, January 11, 1860 (LDP).
[73] Henn to Lowell, January 16, 1860 (LDP).

acidulous comments could be attributed in part to the fact that he had contracted bilious fever from eating the only available staple of diet, fat pork.

> I must say [he lamented], this is the toughest country I ever got in both in living and inhabitants. The game appears to be *Dog eat Dog*, but I think I will get acclimated in a short time. . . . There is the greatest set of sharpers in this town that I have ever met before. . . . I have not yet found a man that appears to be on a friendly feeling with us in regard to the Swamp lands; they all appear to think that the Co. has not the least right to them and it goes hard to have no friends in a strange land, but I think I shall bring some of them over in time.[74]

Still, there was much to be said from the standpoint of the people. Most of them held deeds and duplicates from the county judge, issued on the basis of the original "swamp" selections. They told McClary they had paid for their land once, and demanded to know just what the company intended to do if it established its title. From Knight in Page County came similar news. The farmers there were convinced that the Burlington, if it obtained their lands, would sell to the highest bidder, or at least ask more than the $1.25 they had paid to the county. Furthermore, they had been told in St. Joseph that the north-south line was soon to be built, whereas the B. & M. would never cross Iowa. According to the story, the latter had mortgaged all its lands, spent its money, consolidated with another company, and was planning to turn northwestward up the Des Moines Valley from Ottumwa.[75] Clearly, in the face of such rumors, the company had a hard row to hoe. For the time being, all it could do was to offer the emphatic assurance that no injustice would be done to any *bona fide* settler.

The affidavits that were procured in February, 1860, confirmed the opinion of the road that at least many of the original swamp selections were unjustified. Two statements will suffice as typical illustrations:

> James M. Harper of Appanoose County swears that he is familiar with the tract in question, that it is on the highest part of the prairie divide between the Des Moines and Chariton Rivers, and is overflowed by no river or stream, no swamp or bog or any part of it; can be cultivated in ordinary crops without Drainage and that land adjacent and similar in soil, situation and character is and has been successfully cultivated for

[74] McClary to Lowell, January 23, 1860 (LDP).
[75] Knight to Lowell, February 12, 1860 (LDP).

several years past without Dykes, Drains or Levees, and that he is not interested in the controversy.[76]

The evidence was none the less compelling in cases where occasional overflow occurred:

Jesse W. Buck of Appanoose County swears he is now and has been a resident of said county for the last 18 years, that he was familiar with the following tracts . . . in Sept. 1850 and had been ever since . . . and that all the . . . tracts of land . . . are situated wholly or in part upon the low medow [sic] bottom land near the Chariton River and are subject to the overflow of said River during seasons of very high floods and freshets and that the said tracts of land have been under water either wholly or in part from such overflow five or six times during the sixteen years he has been familiar with them, and he further states that at all other times and seasons said tracts of lands are dry good medow lands and contain no marsh bog or swamp upon them excepting a small patch of wet land containing less than five acres . . . and he further says that the aforesaid tracts of land may be successfully cultivated in grain and other staple produce without Drains or Dykes except during the seasons of the overflow of the Chariton River, and that he is not interested in the controversy. . . .[77]

Such evidence, as it came to Lowell, was forwarded to Steiger and made ready for presentation to the commissioner of the General Land Office as soon as it would be admissable.

III. MISCELLANEOUS CLAIMS

During these negotiations, Judge Rorer, legal adviser to the road, had been studying both the federal and state granting acts of 1856 to see whether the company was receiving all the land to which he felt it was legally entitled. In December, 1859, he placed his conclusions in Lowell's hands, and the latter promptly summarized and forwarded them to President Baker. According to Rorer, Congress in 1856 had fully intended that the railroad should receive the *equivalent* of *every* odd section within 6 miles, even if it had to go beyond the 15-mile lieu-land limit to do so. This outer limit, he explained, could not, like the 6-mile limit, "be considered a measure of *quantity*, — the quantity required is already otherwise determined, but it is a convenient, familiar boundary within which the Government assumes that we shall find that quantity." [78] Because of this assumption, the

[76] Affidavit, February 18, 1860 (LDP).
[77] Affidavit, February 25, 1860 (LDP).
[78] Lowell to Baker, December 17, 1859 (LDP).

federal bill made no provision for obtaining lands beyond 15 miles, but the State Legislature, in its act of acceptance, appears to have foreseen the case, providing in Section 6 how "agents shall from time to time be appointed to make such selections as *may be* (not have been) authorized or granted by Congress" — evidently anticipating further legislation as to the *manner* of making up the quantum granted.[79]

Lowell was impressed with this reasoning. If, he wrote, it was an accurate appraisal of the company's rights as understood by the state legislature, the B. & M. was in a strong position to demand relief from Congress, particularly since the grant was not a gratuity in the first place because of the "very substantial *quid pro quo* being reserved in Sect. 3 of the federal act, providing for free transportation of government material." [80]

> Indeed [he continued], if we become a link in the Pacific Road, and Democratic administrations continue to indulge in Utah demonstrations and British boundary disputes, it may be found that even with the most liberal construction of the grant, the Government has not been so "munificent" as sharp.[81]

In any event, the matter should be looked into if Mr. Joy agreed. The company had built 80 miles and was thus entitled to 480 sections or 307,200 acres; actually it had at the time received some 230,000 acres, and might acquire some of the disputed swamp and preëmption lands that made up part of the difference, but that was all. "It is high time," Lowell concluded, "that we got a Bill introduced 'For the Relief of the B. & M. R.R.'"

The case thus presented by Rorer and seconded by Lowell hinged on two points of particular interest in the light of subsequent events: first, the assumption that both Congress and the Iowa legislature had contemplated giving the company the maximum acreage under the grant even if it meant exceeding the 15-mile limits, and, secondly, the contention that the grant itself was not a gratuity but an exchange for value received. In regard to the first point it will be recalled that when the 1856 grant was being considered in the Senate, Crittenden of Kentucky had noticed that the four beneficiary companies would

[79] Lowell to Baker, December 17, 1859 (LDP).

[80] *Ibid.* The act is reproduced in full in CBQ, *Documentary History*, vol. II, pp. 11–13.

[81] Lowell to Baker, December 17, 1859 (LDP).

receive widely varying amounts of land. He had therefore proposed an amendment to the bill authorizing the governor of Iowa to sell all the granted lands and to divide the proceeds equally among the beneficiary roads. Jones had objected to this suggestion. The land grants, he had pointed out, were designed to subsidize roads built through sparsely settled areas where there was not enough traffic to support them otherwise. The southernmost road in Iowa (the B. & M.) ran through the part of the state then most thickly settled. Therefore, he concluded, it was only fair that, *because of this prior settlement*, this company should have the smallest grant.[82] From this remark it would seem clear that the Senate at least realized that the Burlington would not obtain its maximum quantity of land, or as much as it would if its line ran through vacant territory. Furthermore, the wording of the act as finally passed did not sound as though the 15-mile limit were of no effect: "the land," it read, "shall in no case be further than 15 miles from the lines of said roads."[83] There appears little doubt of what Congress had in mind.

The attitude of the Iowa legislators is more difficult to determine. They had indeed provided that

if it shall appear that the lands that have been donated by the act of Congress . . . cannot be obtained by said companies within the limits and along any part of the line aforesaid, the governor shall from time to time appoint agents to make such selections as may be authorized or granted by congress for the lines aforesaid. . . .[84]

This, however, was the only provision for the selecting agents, and clearly Congress had already authorized them to select lieu lands only within 15 miles. Thus the phrase "as may be authorized" must have meant "as are already authorized." Furthermore, it would seem somewhat inconsistent to have a state legislature that was so mindful of swampland and preëmption claimants leaning over backwards to obtain additional lands for the railroad.

At the time that Rorer and Lowell presented these ideas to Baker, no "Relief" bill for the B. & M. was forthcoming. But the belief that

[82] See above, p. 77. Cf. *Cong. Globe*, 34th Cong., 1st Sess. (1855–56), pt. 1, p. 1172.

[83] *Statutes-at-Large*, vol. XI, p. 9.

[84] Iowa Act of July 14, 1856, conveying the U. S. land grant to the B. & M. See CBQ, *Documentary History*, vol. II, p. 14.

the company had not received its share of lands may have had its effect in producing the later grant of 1864, which added nearly 100,000 acres to the original grant in Iowa.[85] Rorer and Lowell's second contention, that the B. & M.'s grant was no gift, was indeed destined for a long career; other land-grant roads made similar claims, all of which were eventually recognized by federal legislation long after the Burlington had sold its grant.[86]

While Rorer was thus investigating the railroad's rights, Steiger in Washington had likewise been busy exploring another possibility of obtaining more land for the company. His first thought was to claim the islands in the Mississippi and Missouri rivers opposite the ends of the grant, but the best he could obtain was a suspension of this land from private entry.[87] His next idea was to claim a semi-circular region in Nebraska within a 15-mile radius of the end of the tract at Council Bluffs, or wherever the terminus should be located. The commissioner promptly and properly quashed this notion, but Steiger was unconvinced and persisted in viewing the matter as still open.[88]

IV. PREPARING AN ADVERTISING PROGRAM

While the extent of its grant was being thus determined, the Burlington land department was laying the foundations for what would ultimately become its most important work, the advertising and sale of its lands. Early in October, President Baker in Boston thought the time had come for preparing a pamphlet of some 10 to 20 pages "cracking up Iowa." He suggested to Lowell something like those already issued by the Illinois Central and Hannibal and St. Joseph, only on a smaller scale, with particular emphasis on the possibilities of grape growing and wine making in the prairie vineyard. Such information, he said, might be printed in German and French and distributed abroad.[89]

---

[85] See below, p. 170.

[86] Transportation Act of 1940, approved September 18, 1940.

[87] Steiger to Lowell, December 14, 1859 (LDP).

[88] Memorandum by Steiger (LDP). The question was automatically settled in 1864 when the company received its Nebraska grant. See below, pp. 170–171.

[89] J. G. Forster (of the Boston office) to Lowell, October 8, 1859 (LDP). It is possible that Baker's particular emphasis on grapes as a crop and on Germans, Swiss, and French as possible customers came from Colonel Louis Schade, a lawyer in Burlington who had applied to the Hannibal and St. Joseph for a commission to distribute German pamphlets in that country "in such a way as

Lowell picked up the cue with alacrity, and dispatched several inquiries to farmers and friends in the state.

We are beginning to find [he wrote to Hon. Charles Mason] that he who buildeth a railroad west of the Mississippi must also find a population and build up business. We wish to blow as loud a trumpet as the merits of our position warrant. To the European, corn and cattle offer no special attractions, but if we can promise tenfold of the crops with which he is familiar, — grapes, rye, barley, wheat, etc., then we stir him. . . .[90]

Mason's reply was enthusiastic. For over 15 years he had cultivated Isabella and Catawba grapes, with never a failure; he already had from 6,000 to 8,000 vines and was convinced that the Iowa soil was equal to any in Germany. Vines could be obtained for less than $25 per thousand; it cost less than $200 an acre to trench the land and set them out, and one man could thereafter tend six or eight acres. At the moment, the yield was anywhere from 200 to 500 gallons of wine per acre, which sold at prices ranging from $1.25 to $2.00 a gallon. Grapes brought 10 to 20 cents a pound. With a typical allusion to the broader benefits of wine making, Mason concluded:

I hope to see the day when the limestone bluffs which skirt our rivers will be lined with vineyards contributing not only to our national wealth, but to our public morals and general prosperity.[91]

Quite obviously the temperance movement that was currently absorbing the restless consciences of New England had not reached the uninhibited West.[92]

Lowell's inquiry to Henn brought out less enthusiastic but even more valuable information. No wine, as yet, had been manufactured in Henry County, for although grapes thrived there, the banks of the Des Moines were better suited to their cultivation. Sorghum, however, was a great success, and no less than 1,000 barrels of molasses were

---

greatly to benefit the company for a modest compensation." J. M. Brooks (President of the Hannibal and St. Joseph) wrote Lowell about this offer on September 2, 1859, and asked the latter to check up on Schade's qualifications. (LDP.) Since Brooks and Baker were in the same office, the episode may well have prompted Baker's action. If so, it illustrates another link between the Missouri and Iowa roads.

[90] Lowell to Mason, October 20, 1859 (LDP).

[91] Mason to Lowell, November 3, 1859 (LDP).

[92] Cf. Arthur C. Cole, *The Irrepressible Conflict* (New York, 1934), pp. 160–164.

produced that very fall. Broom corn, sugar beet, and hops, all of them familiar to Europeans, were likewise easy to grow. Henn added an illuminating commentary. "In speaking of the character of the country in a circular for foreign circulation," he wrote, "I think the idea could best be conveyed by instancing Hungary as a country of similar appearance and as bearing similar crops." [93]

To George Griffin of Albia, in Monroe County, Lowell addressed an inquiry about sheep raising. His approach was a model of tact.

I understand [he began] that you are raising sheep on your farm. Our Company are getting their lands into the market & are anxious to collect information as to all those branches of farming which are likely to be most profitable in this tier of counties. For this we must rely upon those farmers who have had the enterprise to try something besides corn & hogs. I should be very much obliged if you would take the time to answer the following questions. . . .[94]

When did he start sheep raising? How large a flock did he begin with? Where did he buy the sheep, in the state or out, and for how much? How large was his flock now and what was the usual percentage of increase? Was the climate or country in any respects unfavorable, and were there any fatal diseases? How many sheep would one acre support in summer? How many months in the year did they need to be fed, and what did they eat? Was there any trouble in selling wool on the spot, and what price did it fetch? Was wool growing on the whole profitable and would he recommend others to enter it? Finally, did he have any general suggestions as to sheep raising or other types of agricultural pursuits? Apparently Lowell would be satisfied with nothing less than complete information.

It must not be concluded from these letters that the Burlington was solely interested in crops and stock raising that were out of the ordinary or that would appeal only to Europeans. To Captain Daniel Rider of Fairfield, Lowell explained that although the company wanted to attract "a good class of foreign immigrant" by tempting him with familiar crops, it did not mean that the railroad would overlook prospective settlers from this country. A strong appeal would be made to eastern farmers, "and to these, the great staples corn, wheat, hogs

[93] Henn to Lowell, October 25, 1859 (LDP).

[94] Lowell to Griffin, December 14, 1859 (LDP). Griffin's reply is not in the incoming files.

and cattle are always the tests of a state's capabilities." Consequently, perhaps Rider could provide some statistics showing what could be accomplished in these fields by five or ten years' hard labor; also, any suggestions as to manner and cost of breaking, fencing, and preparing a farm, and the probable returns for the first year or two. Such information would be extremely useful to the newcomer, and, Lowell concluded,

it is by giving a wide circulation to facts & suggestions of this sort that the Illinois Central R. R. has turned so much of the emigration to that state; we wish to trumpet the prairies of Southern Iowa, & we think we have as great or greater advantages & inducements to offer, but we must have our facts from the old settlers. . . .[95]

These were sound observations on Lowell's part, and his opinion of the B. & M.'s lands was not confined to himself, for the Illinois Central land department, recognizing the superior appeal of Iowa's virgin soil, cut its land prices to meet this new competition.[96]

Meanwhile, in northern Missouri, the Hannibal and St. Joseph was putting into effect precisely the type of advertising and sales policy that Lowell had in mind. Late in 1859 there appeared a 60-page booklet, booming that company's 600,000 acres and including every sort of information that would be useful for the immigrant. A full-page map showed the country's main trunk lines, and a smaller map of northern Missouri indicated the location of the land grant. There followed a full description of prices and terms of credit, several paragraphs each on the natural and commercial resources of the region, and finally a number of letters giving statistical information and actual examples to endorse the company's claims. The pamphlet was enlivened by half a dozen lithographs depicting a Missouri farmer's home, typical landscapes, and the cities of Hannibal and St. Joseph.[97] The general format of the entire publication was obviously copied from that of the Illinois Central; Lowell was anxious to emulate and improve upon these successful pioneers.[98] The success of the Missouri road's campaign was another inducement; the Hannibal land office, opened July 12, 1859, already had sold 14,131.09 acres by November

[95] Lowell to Rider, November 2, 1859 (LDP).

[96] Gates, op. cit., pp. 308–318.

[97] HSJ, "The Hannibal and St. Joseph Railroad Company Have Received . . . over 600,000 acres. . . ." (Hannibal, 1859).

[98] Gates, op. cit., ch. ix.

for an average price of $10.24 an acre.[99] A system that could produce these results was certainly worth considering.

There was, indeed, plenty that Iowa could afford to advertise. During the decade 1850–60, there had been a four- to sevenfold increase in improved land and in the value of farms and implements. The gain in livestock, both in numbers and value, was nearly in the same proportion. Cereals, animal products, tobacco, potatoes, hay, sugar, and molasses advanced in still larger ratio. The produce of orchards and market gardens increased 15 times.[100] More important to both state and railroad was the revival of immigration into Iowa. Despite the depression of 1857, the census in 1860 revealed that population had leaped from 192,214 to 674,913 in a decade.[101] Doubtless encouraged by this fact, the State of Iowa itself inaugurated a publicity policy in 1860 that promised to help the B. & M. In that year the governor was authorized to appoint a commissioner of emigration to be located in New York City whose duty would be to turn the tide of immigration toward Iowa in so far as possible. Ex-Lieutenant-Governor Rusch was chosen for the position, and left at once for the East.[102] There was every reason to believe that his mission would be successful. As fall approached, it appeared that the B. & M. might share in a modest but substantial prosperity.

It was while matters were in this comparatively promising state that Charles Lowell resigned from the company. His letter to Treasurer Denison, dated October 25, 1860, was self-explanatory:

> I know I may assume without vanity that you will be sorry to hear I have resigned my place on the B. & M. — I know it because I am sorry myself to tell you so, although I am changing to a business which has always had the strongest attractions for me. I have never got over the "iron fever," and when a place was offered me at Mt. Savage [Maryland], though the pecuniary prospect was no better than at Burlington, the chance to become an iron-master was too good to be refused. . . .[103]

The loss to the road was indeed serious, for aside from his business ability, Lowell had brought a degree of culture and tact into his work

[99] HSJ, *Annual Report* for 1859 (Boston, 1859), p. 32.

[100] Commissioner of the General Land Office, *Annual Report*, 1867, pp. 26–27.

[101] *Census* of 1900, vol. I, p. 18.

[102] F. C. D. McKay (Secretary of the American Emigrant Co.) to Perkins, March 16, 1865 (LDP).

[103] Lowell to Denison, October 25, 1860, in Emerson, *op. cit.*, p. 191.

that had smoothed the path of the infant railroad in a relatively rough and suspicious community. Fortunately for the company, however, Lowell had broken in an assistant whose alert aggressiveness combined with natural ability and sound judgment more than replaced whatever he lacked in formal education. To Forbes he wrote: "Perkins is an exceedingly smart man and is by far the best clerk in this office. He is very correct, careful, and a hard worker, although I would suggest that he would command respect in almost any position, for his judgment is excellent." [104] To Denison, Lowell added: "No endorsement [of Perkins] is needed from me, but I offer my guaranty that both personally and B.-M.-ically you will be glad you have got him." [105] Read shared this opinion, and at his suggestion the board of directors on November 9 appointed Perkins, who was not yet twenty years old, to Lowell's position of assistant treasurer and land agent; his combined salary was raised to $800 a year.[106] The years that lay directly before him were to put his ability and ingenuity to a severe test.

[104] Lowell to Forbes, October? 1860 (CNB, ch. iv, p. 31).
[105] Lowell to Denison, October? 1860 (CNB, ch. iv, pp. 38–40).
[106] BMI ORB, p. 128.

CHAPTER VII

THE B. & M. MARKS TIME, 1860–1866

IN NOVEMBER, 1860, when Perkins took the helm of the land department, Lincoln had just been elected by the combined votes of the North and West, and sectional antagonism was near the bursting point. In December, South Carolina, carried away by her radicals, dissolved all connection with the Union, and the administration at Washington seemed unable to cope with the situation. By April, 1861, armed conflict had begun; for four years the nation's economy was geared to the exigencies of wartime.

Behind the lines, society in the different sections of the country was variously affected by the war.[1] In the South, an artificial though picturesque world crashed to the ground; in the North an unsophisticated community of small businessmen and farmers was transformed overnight by the rise of a vigorous industrial class with little idealism but with definite and practical ideas about making money. The technical revolution that had been taking place in the Northeast was speeded up immeasurably by the demands of the conflict, and the crude outlines of big business were sketched out to accommodate the new economy. In the West, a process of social consolidation was taking place. Fed until 1861 by the most energetic elements of both North and South, this newer region was necessarily left somewhat to its own devices during the war, for both internal and foreign immigration fell off abruptly. At the same time, it shared in the industrial advance of the North, particularly in the fields of transportation and agricultural machinery.[2]

In the opening months of the conflict, however, the role of the West was not so obvious as it later became.

What is to be our fortune in the future — whether to fall back, or to come up again to last year, and go beyond it, we cannot foresee [wrote President Baker to the B. & M. stockholders in May, 1861]. Our prosperity

---

[1] Cf. Arthur C. Cole, *op. cit., passim.*

[2] Emerson D. Fite, *Social and Industrial Conditions in the North during the Civil War* (New York, 1910), *passim.*

depends, we suppose, very much upon the success of the Government in putting down rebellion, and restoring peace and confidence. We can only promise the utmost vigilance in promoting the interest of the Company, and the strictest economy in the management of its affairs. . . .[3]

Even the political complexion of Iowa was uncertain. From Council Bluffs, Van Allen wrote to Perkins that "the feeling among the people grows stronger every day in favor of secesh since the Battle of Bulls [*sic*] Run. At least they are more open in their sympathy with them than before. Still, on the other hand, there is a strong patriotic feeling. . . ."[4]

Almost at once the company was intimately reminded of the conflict. On July 15, 1861, John G. Read, Vice-President and Superintendent, resigned his position to enter the army, his place being taken by Henry Thielsen, Chief Engineer.[5] Nor was dislocation of personnel the only problem that resulted from war conditions. Money, at that time, consisted of the notes of various banks scattered all over the country and of Burlington city scrip, which was accepted locally. The value of bank notes, particularly those coming from the South, changed every day so that the officials of the railroad never knew, when they received a remittance, whether the company's bank would accept the bills or not.[6]

Although any further construction during 1861–62 was out of the question, business on the road was not so poor as the officials feared; net operating income fell only $8,859.92, from $118,420.16 at the end of the 1861 fiscal year to $109,560.24 for the year ending April 30, 1862. The embargo on the Mississippi which closed the southern market for Iowa corn still continued, but the capture of New Orleans by Union troops and the steady progress of gunboats up the river gave promise that this important artery of commerce would soon reopen. The directors felt it was "reasonable to hope that our Iowa products will soon be in better demand, and command prices which will pay transportation. . . ."[7] Nevertheless, it was impossible to raise enough money to pay interest on the land mortgage in October, 1861, and the company was forced to issue income bonds, maturing in four years,

[3] BMI, *Annual Report* for 1861 (Boston, 1861), p. 3.
[4] Van Allen to Perkins, August 3, 1861 (LDP).
[5] BMI ORB, p. 135; *Burlington Weekly Hawk-Eye*, August 10, 1861.
[6] C. E. Perkins to ?, 1861 (CNB, pp. 50–51).
[7] BMI, *Annual Report* for 1862 (Boston, 1862), p. 3.

for the amount owed. Four months later, in February, 1862, when interest became due on the first and second mortgage, a one-year extension was necessary. Fortunately, the bondholders of all classes were agreeable, and the company did not have to face reorganization. There were troubles enough without that, however, for the Iowa legislature passed a bill taxing one per cent of the railroad's gross earnings. This, President Baker wrote, was an "exhaustive policy," for by delaying

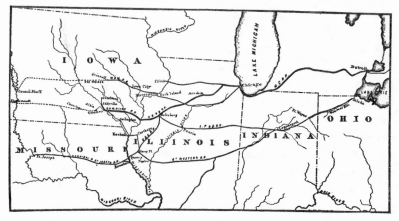

COMPETITIVE POSITION OF C. B. & Q.—B. & M. LINES, 1863.

construction of the railroads it would certainly discourage immigration and the influx of capital into the state.[8]

A year later, in June, 1863, the most serious threat to the company's well-being came from a different quarter. Business, as shown by net receipts, was excellent; net operating income for the year rose to $141,-675.88.[9] The drawback to this gratifying situation was the opening of a direct railroad line from Toledo through Indiana and Illinois to Keokuk, where it connected with the B. & M.'s rival, the Keokuk and Fort Des Moines Railroad. Already this latter company had built northwestward from its terminus on the Mississippi River, across the Burlington road at Ottumwa and on to Eddyville, not far south of the capital. Thus the lucrative trade of the Des Moines Valley was being diverted, and there was a real danger that the B. & M., at the moment it had begun to fulfil the predictions of its friends, would

[8] BMI, *Annual Report* for 1862 (Boston, 1862), pp. 4–5.
[9] BMI, *Annual Report* for 1863 (Boston, 1863), p. 3.

lose much of its business. The obvious remedy was immediate construction westward along the line of the original surveys. As Baker
pointed out,

we need only to cross the Des Moines River and proceed on our surveyed
route to regain in a little distance the lost equality, and to secure as we
go on a perpetual advantage over all competitors for the business of Southwestern Iowa, a vast extent of productive country, with no road but ours
even projected for its accommodation.[10]

But the lagging payments on stock subscription, the inability of the
road to meet interest on its mortgages, and the general unwillingness
of capital to undertake a venture in wartime through sparsely settled
lands were enough to render any construction at the time unthinkable.
Baker was well aware of this, yet he urged the stockholders to "unite
upon some plan to make their security good again, and their property
available. It is gratifying to find," he added, "that after a cessation
of nearly five years, the tide of emigration is beginning to set again
into Iowa." [11] Not the least of the road's assets was its president's
optimism.

Baker's warning did not go unheeded. Several of the largest of the
company's bondholders united in presenting a comprehensive plan for
saving the road.[12] Their reason for demanding immediate action was
irrefutable, and Baker bluntly stated it in an explanatory circular:

If they [the bondholders] wait the course of events, and do nothing to
promote the needed extension of the Road, there is great reason to fear
that the legal remedy of foreclosure will, in the peculiar relation of the
Road to the business on which it depends, prove unavailing to save them
from serious loss. . . .[13]

In other words, with the Keokuk line cutting off the B. & M.'s chief
existing source of traffic, immediate action by the bondholders was
imperative. Under the circumstances, it was proposed to issue a new
seven per cent mortgage of approximately $6,000,000, sufficiently large
not only to furnish bonds in substitution of all those then outstanding (including bonds on deferred interest), but also to provide
$18,000 per mile for extension of the road to the Missouri River. The

[10] *Ibid.*, p. 4.
[11] *Ibid.*, p. 5.
[12] BMI, *Annual Report* for 1864 (Boston, 1864), p. 3.
[13] BMI, Circular to Bondholders, October 7, 1863 (LDP).

old bondholders were to exchange their eight per cent securities in part for this new issue, and in part for seven per cent preferred stock, according to the following ratios:

First Mortgage holders to receive 85 per cent in new bonds, 15 per cent in stock
Second   "   "   "   "   70 "   "   "   "   "   30 "   "   "   "
Land   "   "   "   "   75 "   "   "   "   "   25 "   "   "   "

As in the case of the mortgages it supplanted, the new indenture would name as security all of the line and rolling stock, and all lands previously granted or that might be received in the future from the United States or from the State of Iowa. The actual management of the railroad and of the lands, however, would be left in the hands of the existing company, and the purchasers of B. & M. lands would receive their tracts "in fee simple, absolutely and forever released from any lien on account of said bonds" upon full payment of the contract price.[14]

In presenting this plan, President Baker urged the road's bondholders to realize that at the moment their old bonds were unsaleable and in danger of losing all their value. Acceptance of the plan to lighten the burden of fixed charges would not only make the new issue attractive to purchasers, but also give the stockholders an added motive for paying their subscriptions promptly, thus providing more cash for the extension of the road.[15] Further encouragement was given to stock subscribers by the action of the board of directors on December 11, 1863. The board pointed out that most of those who had subscribed in 1857 and were then, in 1863, behind in their payments were railroad employees of the connecting lines of the road "who were induced by personal feeling to subscribe for the extension of the line, and did faithfully undertake to fulfil their engagements until their means were cut off by the revulsion of that period, which especially affected railroad interests and men."[16] Under the circumstances, the directors resolved that if these delinquents returned their partially receipted certificates of subscription, they would receive in return fully paid stock for the amount of money they had actually sent in.

While this proposition lay before the bondholders, two events of the greatest significance for the future of the B. & M. were taking

[14] CBQ, *Documentary History*, vol. II, pp. 88–90.
[15] BMI, Circular to Bondholders, October 7, 1863, *loc. cit.*
[16] BMI ORB, pp. 146–147.

place. On April 30, 1864, a committee was appointed by the directors of The Chicago, Burlington and Quincy Rail Road Company to propose a plan to secure the business of the B. & M. and the country tributary thereto by offering aid in extending the Iowa line towards the Missouri River. Two months later, this committee pointed out that unless the B. & M. was extended, the C. B. & Q. would not only lose most of the business it was receiving from that road, but would forfeit the opportunity to share in the business resulting from the further development of that important territory. Fortunately, a logical solution was readily available. Each line originated a great deal of traffic destined for the other and collected the full tariff for the entire haul. Since the B. & M., however, was only about one-third as long as the C. B. & Q., the latter was entitled to the greater share of the total amount taken in by the former. Up to this time the B. & M. had balanced the account by regular cash payments. The C. B. & Q. committee now proposed that their line should receive half of whatever was owed by the B. & M. "in such of the preferred stock or bonds to be issued for the extension of said Burlington and Missouri River Railroad as in the opinion of the Directors may be necessary to secure the construction of about fifty-six miles of the same. . . ."[17] At their annual meeting on June 24, 1864, the stockholders of the Chicago road accepted this proposal. In commenting upon it, President Van Nortwick emphasized the potential value of the Iowa line to his company and declared that "the requisite aid may be provided with but slight inconvenience to this Company. . . ."[18] Thus the plan would apparently benefit all concerned: if the B. & M. accepted the proffered aid, it could use for construction cash that would otherwise be paid to the C. B. & Q. for joint traffic, while the latter line would be increasing its interest and control in a valuable feeder without any serious inconvenience to itself. The entire proposition, however, depended on whether the Iowa bondholders would agree to the new seven per cent bond issue that would make extension possible. While they were making up their minds, their company fell heir to another grant from the United States.

Various officials of the B. & M., particularly Perkins, Rorer, and Steiger, had long felt that because of the interference of the swamp

[17] CBQ ORB, p. 249.
[18] CBQ, *Annual Report* for 1864 (Boston, 1864), p. 6.

and preëmption claims [19] and because of the delay over absolute withdrawal in 1856,[20] the company would be deprived of lands which Congress really intended it to have. As early as 1859, Lowell had declared that there should be an act for the relief of the B. & M.; [21] just such a law, amending the original grant of 1856, was signed by President Lincoln on June 2, 1864.[22] By its terms, the company was entitled to receive "as the road progresses" an amount of land equal to that mentioned in the original act; selections might be made anywhere within 20 miles of the track.[23] This meant that all vacant even sections within 15 miles (the old limits) and all vacant *odd and even* sections between 15 and 20 miles could now be claimed by the Burlington and Missouri River providing there was no existing *bona fide* title or improvement. The new act would add over 100,000 acres to the railroad's holding,[24] providing final location were made, and 20 miles built west of Ottumwa by July 1, 1865.[25] Thus another potent reason was presented to the road's owners for continuing construction at the earliest possible moment.

Another and even more compelling inducement appeared just one month later. One of the most enthusiastic officials of the B. & M. was Henry Thielsen; he not only shared Perkins' hope that the line would soon be pushed to the Missouri River, but looked forward to the day when it would bridge that stream and continue on across Nebraska. His hopes were shared by James F. Wilson, a resident of Fairfield, and in 1864 a member of the national House of Representatives. Possibly at Thielsen's instigation, Wilson introduced an amendment to a bill that was then pending before Congress to increase federal aid to the Pacific railroad and to provide certain branches for that line.[26] Wilson's amendment, which became a part of the law approved July 2, 1864, authorized the B. & M. to

extend its road through the Territory of Nebraska from the point where it strikes the Missouri River south of the mouth of the Platte River, to some point not further west than the one hundredth meridian of west

[19] See above, pp. 122–138; 146–155.
[20] See above, pp. 89–92.
[21] See above, p. 156.
[22] *Statutes-at-Large*, vol. XIII, p. 96.
[23] CBQ, *Documentary History*, vol. II, pp. 16–17.
[24] Baldwin to Mitchell, March 18, 1922 (LDP).
[25] *Statutes-at-Large*, vol. XIII, p. 345.
[26] Memorandum by Perkins, November 5, 1901 (CNB, n.p.).

longitude, so as to connect, by the most practicable route, with the main trunk of the Union Pacific Railroad. . . .[27]

In order to aid in the construction of the B. & M., Congress granted "every alternate section of public land . . . designated by the odd numbers, *to the amount of ten alternate sections per mile* on each side of said road . . . not sold, reserved or otherwise disposed of by the United States, and to which a preëmption or homestead claim may not have attached at the time the line of said road is definitely fixed." [28] There followed the customary provisions for filing a map and accepting the grant within one year of the passage of the act, for examination by federal commissioners of each 20-mile stretch when completed, and for completing the whole within ten years' time. This law, unlike either of the grants in Iowa,[29] donated an *amount* equal to 20 square miles for each mile of line built; there were no lateral limits designated, so that the company supposed it could go anywhere in Nebraska opposite its line to find the necessary acreage. Assuming the road would be 185 miles long, the railroad would receive 2,368,000 acres, over six times as much as it owned in Iowa. With this added inducement to reach the Missouri River and beyond, almost all of the first and third (land) mortgage bondholders accepted the company's refinancing scheme during 1864, and the new consolidated mortgage was put into effect for them during that year.[30]

This encouraging action had its coincidental counterparts on the line itself. In November, 1864, the B. & M. added a regular train to its schedule to accommodate the rapidly increasing stock business. "The hog market is quite lively," reported the *Burlington Daily Hawk-Eye* on November 15; "there are quite a number of parties buying and shipping East." [31] As 1865 came, however, many of the second mortgage bondholders of the B. & M., unlike their fellow investors, still refused to turn in their old securities in exchange for the new seven per cent mortgage and preferred stock. As a result, the refunding process was incomplete, the company felt unable to accept the C. B. & Q.'s proposal, and further construction in Iowa was delayed.[32]

[27] *Statutes-at-Large*, vol. XIII, p. 356.
[28] *Ibid.* (Italics supplied.)
[29] See above, pp. 81, 170.
[30] CBQ, *Documentary History*, vol. II, pp. 93–94.
[31] *Burlington Daily Hawk-Eye*, November 15, 1864.
[32] BMI, *Annual Report* for 1865 (Boston, 1865), p. 4.

In despair, Perkins wrote to J. M. Forbes on February 12. He feared the company would lose its second Iowa grant of 1864 entirely unless Congress allowed more time for completing the next 20 miles. Furthermore, competing railroads would "no doubt" exert pressure in Congress to defeat any remedial legislation. "Whatever we do about extension of time," he concluded, "must be done quickly. . . ." [33] Less than a month later the crisis was past; on March 3 the B. & M. was given an extra year of grace, and thus was not obligated to complete its next 20 miles until July 1, 1866. [34] This relief came none too soon. On March 27, Perkins reported to Forbes that chiefly because of B. & M.'s failure to build, the people were talking of constructing "a perfect network of [competing] railroads in southern Iowa." [35]

The coöperation of Congress, however, failed to impress those obdurate B. & M. bondholders who had not yet exchanged their securities under the plan of October, 1863. In his report to the stockholders in May, 1865, President Brooks indicated his plans for overcoming the impasse. These second mortgage holders, he explained, felt aggrieved because they were to receive a smaller proportion of new bonds than either the first or third (land) mortgage holders, even though their lien came ahead of the last named. There was, however, a perfectly valid reason for this apparent partiality: the second mortgage would mature in 1869, whereas the other two issues would not come due until 1876 and 1883, respectively. Under the circumstances, the company did not feel warranted in altering the ratio of exchange and, with a view to speeding matters, had consulted counsel who had found that there were enough legal imperfections in the terms of the second mortgage to render it incapable of enforcement. The company, Brooks declared, had no disposition to disown its acts or repudiate its obligations, but if certain bondholders persisted in their disagreement, "there will be no alternative for the Company but to take the decisions of the courts for the guide of their future actions, even though it should result in a total loss to those who have not exchanged their bonds." [36] This indeed would be strong action, but such was needed under the circumstances. The Keokuk-Des Moines line was constantly increasing

[33] Perkins to Forbes, February 12, 1865 (CNB, n.p.).

[34] *Statutes-at-Large*, vol. XIII, p. 573.

[35] Perkins to Forbes, March 27, 1865 (CNB, n.p.).

[36] BMI, *Annual Report* for 1865 (Boston, 1865), p. 4.

its power to the west and north of the B. & M. terminus at Ottumwa, and the M. & M. was threatening to build a spur southward to Fairfield, which would drain away even more traffic. Furthermore, the offer of the C. B. & Q. might be withdrawn, although officials of the B. & M. realized that their greatest hope of success and prosperity lay through a connection, physical and financial, with the Chicago road. Finally, as Brooks pointed out, "the opening of our road across the State of Iowa will of itself furnish business for the Nebraska extension, and make it an object to construct this link, by which we shall be connected with the Pacific Trunk road. . . ." [37]

In order to satisfy themselves at first hand as to the prospects of the Iowa road, no less than seven of the B. & M.'s eastern bondholders visited Iowa in May.[38] Of even more importance than their visits, however, were the three trips made by James F. Joy through B. & M. territory during the spring and summer of 1865. Joy was not only president and director of the C. B. & Q., but likewise a director of the Iowa company. The object of his first excursion was "to see the people and see if any money could be raised for the extension of our road." [39] It was obvious that if there was a strong showing of local support, the bondholders, particularly the owners of the second mortgage, might be more disposed to accede to the plan suggested in 1863 and so vigorously encouraged in 1865. The events of the first trip were typical.

With Perkins and Thielsen as guides and companions, Joy started out from Burlington at six-thirty o'clock on Thursday morning, May 18. Traveling by rail through Ottumwa to Eddyville, the three men there climbed into a covered wagon and drove 16 miles to Albia, where they arrived at seven o'clock in the evening. After supper Joy invited some of the town's leaders to meet at the city clerk's office. The B. & M., he said, would probably be pushed ahead if there were sufficient local aid; arrangements were made forthwith to hold a public meeting the following Saturday, and the railroaders turned in. "Of course," wrote Perkins, "we were the observed [sic] of all the town and made a sensation." [40] The following morning the little party left for Chariton,

[37] Ibid., p. 5.
[38] Denison to Perkins, May 15, 1865 (CNB, n.p.).
[39] Perkins to his wife, May 21, 1865 (CNB, ch. vi).
[40] Ibid.

31 miles farther west. The rolling prairies were particularly beautiful on that spring day and occasionally the travelers got out and walked beside the wagon. By way of diversion, they discussed Darwin's theory of the origin of species, although they interrupted their conversation long enough to inquire about the prices of farm land whenever they had the opportunity. Covering the last mile on foot from necessity rather than choice as the result of a broken axletree, they reached the principal hotel in time for dinner and again Perkins reported that "many of the citizens came to see the elephant." [41] A visit from the president of the C. B. & Q. was indeed a portent of action.

After the meal, Joy held his usual meeting, this time in the local court house. He stated unequivocally that if the people of Chariton wanted the railroad they would have to raise $50,000. This they thought they could do, but they reminded the promoters that local payments would be dependent on the actual construction of the line. Speeches, of course, were made, although Perkins noted that he "only looked on and talked aside to the farmers occasionally." [42] After the meeting he walked about town with Joy and picked out some good property to buy.

The next day Thielsen took the stage for Nebraska to continue his surveying, while Joy and Perkins started out for their appointed meeting in Albia. When they reached the court house at the appointed hour, however, they found that a trial was in progress and that the railroad meeting would have to wait. Finally, at four o'clock in the afternoon, Joy addressed the gathering that had come to hear him. It was not an enthusiastic meeting, and Perkins thought the people showed much less spirit than at Chariton. By five-thirty the two were on their way back to Ottumwa, covering the last 16 miles of their journey on a hand car in one hour and fifteen minutes. Despite the doubtful reception at Albia, Perkins returned from this trip full of encouragement. He felt that Joy had been pleased with his progress and had little doubt but that the road would be built.[43] A

---

[41] Perkins to his wife, May 15, 1865 (CNB, ch. vi).

[42] Ibid.

[43] Perkins was not only enthusiastic about the road but about his own prospects as well. "Our road is going ahead, I know," he wrote, "there is indeed hardly the least doubt of it — and in conversation yesterday, speaking of pay, etc. (not *my* pay), Mr. Joy said, 'You are a young man, and if this Road goes on you are on the way to a fortune,' showing that he thinks there are chances

fortnight later he reported that the company was earning "lots of money," [44] and in June plans were completed for a bridge across the Skunk River and large new buildings at Mount Pleasant. [45] There was one qualification to his optimism. "Our western people don't show the disposition they ought in the building of a railroad," he wrote Forbes on June 17. "Mr. Joy is coming out again in July, as I suppose you know." [46]

Meanwhile, most of the second mortgage bondholders consented to exchange their securities, and on June 15, 1865, the board of directors met in Boston. In an optimistic frame of mind, undoubtedly because of the recent return of peace to the nation, they listened favorably to Joy's report of the prospects in the West, and on motion of Mr. Forbes, voted to issue $600,000 worth of income bonds for the purpose of extending the road. At the same time the president of the company was authorized to enter into the agreement previously proposed by the C. B. & Q., whereby that company would accept such securities as those just authorized in lieu of cash balances due on account of joint traffic. Having made this provision for partially financing further construction, the directors voted for an extension of 56 miles to Chariton and authorized the president to sell common or preferred stock to bring the funds available up to the required amount. [47] Since the C. B. & Q. was already committed to carry out its agreement with the B. & M., the only remaining prerequisite to further extension was this continued local sale of stock. Forbes summarized the situation when he wrote Perkins that the road was "sure to go" if Mr. Joy succeeded in getting his $100,000 in Iowa. [48]

Joy was not a man to waste time; on Friday, June 23, he and Perkins were off on their second trip westward in search of money. This time they drove by covered wagon from Ottumwa to Albia,

---

to make money here — and I begin to see them very clearly. This Road is to be an immense thing to manage. I am to be the Chief Manager, if I hang on and prove myself equal to it — to do this latter will require immense labor and patience. It is a very useful place, a 'wide field of opportunity' — and will shortly become a profitable place." (*Ibid.*)

[44] Perkins to his wife, May 29, 1865 (CNB, ch. vi).
[45] Perkins to his wife, June 12, 1865 (CNB, ch. vi).
[46] Perkins to Forbes, June 17, 1865 (CNB, ch. vi).
[47] BMI DRB, n.p.
[48] Perkins to his wife, June 20, 1865 (CNB, ch. vi).

and on June 24 held a three-hour meeting there on behalf of their railroad.[49] The next day the pair reached Chariton, but since it was Sunday, they confined their activities to attending a Methodist prayer meeting. Not until Monday morning, therefore, was business resumed and then it was under rather unexpected conditions. By ten-thirty Joy was well launched on his usual speech when the blare of a circus band filled the room, — Yankee Robinson's Big Show had come to town! Quite naturally, every listener in the hall promptly left to hear the music, and philosophically enough, Mr. Joy sat down and waited till they came back. This they did when the music had stopped,[50] and soon afterwards these same people, with their neighbors in Albia, gave definite assurance that they would provide $100,000, including the right of way, at the rate of 19 per cent a month as the road should progress. "They understand," wrote Perkins, "that extension may depend on their efforts and will work for it." [51]

Two months later Joy made another trip to Burlington, but on this occasion traveled south by steamboat to Fort Madison and thence by rail to Keokuk. Primarily, his visit was to arrange certain traffic facilities over the Keokuk-Ottumwa line in connection with the construction of the B. & M. west of the latter point.[52] On the way, however, he undoubtedly turned over in his mind the possibility of a railway between Burlington and Fort Madison. Later in the fall there was considerable newspaper comment concerning such a line. One contributor strongly urged that such a road be independently built,

[49] That evening Joy and Perkins were invited to a supper which consisted of coffee, oysters and canned strawberries and peaches. Perkins was understandably amazed by the discovery of oysters in June, fully 1,300 miles from the sea. "Of course Mr. J. and I did not touch them," he wrote his wife, "but the Albians ate them as if it was probable they would never get another chance (!), which I thought quite probable — and am not at all sure yet that the select few are not all dead from the effects. Those country people do live fearfully. How they can do it and *continue to live*, I don't understand. After the supper a collection was taken up to pay for it, but Mr. Joy and I were not called on! It cost $12, so I learned next day. . . ." (Perkins to his wife, June 28, 1865, CNB, ch. vi.)

[50] Perkins to his wife, June 28, 1865 (CNB, ch. vi).

[51] Perkins to Forbes, June 29, 1865 (CNB, ch. vi).

[52] Perkins to his wife, September 1, 1865 (CNB, ch. vi). Apparently the Keokuk line was not particularly coöperative. On September 5, Perkins wrote that he was about to have a little fight over the connections at Ottumwa and that "railroading would be rather dull work if we had no enemies." (Perkins to his wife, September 5, 1865, CNB, ch. vi.)

JAMES FREDERICK JOY, 1810–1896.

rather than attached "to the C. B. & Q. kite." He went on to criticize roundly James F. Joy and other "prominent gentlemen connected with the C. B. & Q. . . . [who] rarely accomplish anything but swallow up the labor and industry of others." [53] Indeed, there was no doubt about Joy's unpopularity in certain quarters. Perkins was well aware of it, and reported one comment that Joy would any day rather accomplish his purpose by a fight than by persuasion. Nevertheless, Joy's powers of persuasion had unquestionably been a vital factor in enabling the B. & M. to prosper and expand. In September, the road was earning about $50,000 a month and spending most of it by building the new bridge at Skunk River and a new depot at Mount Pleasant.[54] During the same month John S. Wolf & Co. was given the contract to construct the line to Albia.[55]

In the spring and summer of 1866 construction proceeded at a moderate pace although there were various annoying delays. One hot July morning, for example, Perkins reached his office to find a long dispatch from Wolf & Co. saying that the joints for fastening the new rails west of Ottumwa were complete failures. Alarmed lest work might be indefinitely delayed, he left at once for the railhead, six and one-half miles west of Ottumwa. There he found all work stopped because of the heat and the engineers behaving "very stupidly" about the new rail fastening. But in half an hour Perkins had shown them how to install the new joint, and by the time he left he was satisfied that construction would continue without interruption.[56]

Such minor inconveniences were to be expected in any major undertaking. Of more importance was the necessity of retaining the vigorous coöperation of the road's eastern backers, particularly James F. Joy, who, in addition to being president of the C. B. & Q., had accepted the same position with the B. & M. in May, 1866, when J. W. Brooks resigned on account of illness.[57] Joy was reëlected for the full term of one year on July 18.[58] Meanwhile, in June, Joy reported to the C. B. & Q. stockholders that, with the construction then

[53] *Burlington Daily Hawk-Eye*, November 28, 1865.
[54] Perkins to his wife, September 5, 1865 (CNB, ch. vi).
[55] Perkins to his wife, September 8, 1865 (CNB, ch. vi).
[56] Perkins to his wife, July 28, 1866 (CNB, ch. vii).
[57] BMI ORB, p. 170.
[58] BMI DRB, n.p. At the same time, Brooks, Forbes, and Joy were placed on the Executive Committee.

COMPARATIVE STATEMENT

Of Increase and Decrease of Articles carried for the year ending April 30th, 1866, and the season since May 1st, 1865, compared with the corresponding time last year.

EAST.

DESCRIPTION OF ARTICLES.		Year 1866.	Year 1865.	Increase.	Decrease.
Horses and Mules,	No.	101	125	.	24
Cattle, ...	"	32,841	34,650	.	1,809
Hogs, ...	"	98,135	141,790	.	43,655
Sheep, ...	"	16,594	10,753	5,841	.
Live Game, Poultry, &c.	lbs.	2,164	460	1,704	.
Butter, Eggs, Dressed Game, &c. . .	"	52,678	2,060	50,618	.
Dressed Hogs, . .	"	326,051	819,303	.	493,252
Pork, ...	"	850,118	2,866.772	.	2,016,294
Lard, ...	"	429,812	608,437	.	178,625
Beef, ...	"	1,070,375	547,576	522,799	.
Tallow, ...	"	253,925	145,686	108,239	.
Hides, ...	"	581,673	558,062	23,611	.
Wool, ...	"	605,344	216,360	388,984	.
Wheat, ...	"	935,943	1,082,878	.	146,935
Corn, ...	"	337,170	3,031,814	.	2,694,644
Other Grains, . .	"	1,680,585	3,500,422	.	1,819,837
Flour, Meal, Millstuffs, &c.,	"	253,597	169,995	83,602	.
Beans, Peas, Hops, &c.,	"	1,970	113,553	.	111,583
Flax, Hemp, &c. . .	"	102,843	281,460	.	178,617
Grass and other Seeds, .	"	302,373	750,635	.	448,262
Green Fruit, . .	"	54,750	130.812	.	76,062
Roots and Bulbs, . .	"	26,335	43,228	.	16,893
Hay, ...	"	.	101,976	.	101,976
Broom Corn, . .	"	.	4,199	.	4,199
Lumber and Timber,	ft. b. m	140,700	236,055	.	95,355
Staves and Hoop Poles,	cords,	268	347½	.	79½
Lathes, ...	M	.	.	.	.
Shingles, . . .	"	.	.	.	.
Empty Barrels, &c., .	lbs.	140,758	188,848	.	48,090
Wood for Fuel, . .	cords.	.	.	.	.
Coal, ...	lbs.	13,849,930	12,060,420	1,789,510	.
Lime and Cement, .	"	.	.	.	.
Brick, ...	No.	.	.	.	.
Building and other Stones,	lbs.	12,288	66,388	.	54,100
Salt, ...	"	1,390	100,000	.	98,610
Dry Goods, . . .	"	61.023	52,901	8,122	.
Drugs, Medicines, Paints, &c.	"	16,590	15,115	1,475	.
Liquors and Wines, .	"	61.634	253,635	.	192,001
General Groceries, .	"	91,223	79,655	11,568	.
Leather, Boots, Shoes, Saddlery, . .	"	13,367	11,531	1,836	.
Hatters' Goods, . .	"	562	3,033	.	2,471
Books and Stationery. .	"	66,194	43,787	22,407	.
Crockery and Glassware,	"	3,713	11,263	.	7,550
Furnishing Goods, Gas Fixtures, &c. . .	"	46,558	14.649	31,909	.
Hardware, Iron, Steel, &c.	"	159,018	172,614	.	13,596
Stoves and Turner's Ware,	"	31,033	12,349	18,684	.
Agricultural and other Machinery, . . .	"	301,124	151,751	149,373	.
Furniture and House- hold Goods, . .	"	486,739	452,981	33,758	.
Other manufactured Ar- ticles not enumerated,	"	125,036	157,236	.	32,200
Sundries, . . .	"	169,528	696,011	.	526,483
Total of all Articles in lbs.		80,988,314	97,026,620	.	16,038,306

COMPARATIVE STATEMENT

Of Increase and Decrease of Articles carried for the year ending April 30th, 1866, and the season since May 1st, 1865, compared with the corresponding time last year.

WEST.

DESCRIPTION OF ARTICLES.		Year 1866.	Year 1865.	Increase.	Decrease.
Horses and Mules, .	No.	244	556	.	312
Cattle, ...	"	34	43	.	9
Hogs, ...	"	626	2,604	.	1,978
Sheep, ...	"	5,766	37,962	.	32,196
Live Game, Poultry, &c.	lbs.	.	.	.	.
Butter, Eggs, Dressed Game, &c. . .	"	25,450	9,605	15,845	.
Dressed Hogs, . .	"	330	143	187	.
Pork, ...	"	24,457	7,075	17,382	.
Lard and Tallow, . .	"	1,175	953	222	.
Beef, ...	"	1,485	1,665	.	180
Tallow, ...	"	.	.	.	.
Hides, ...	"	422	1,557	.	1,135
Wool, ...	"	3,470	.	3,470	.
Wheat, ...	"	313,436	261,795	51,641	.
Corn, ...	"	76,492	39,000	37,492	.
Other Grains, . .	"	258,048	1,283,775	.	1,025,727
Flour, Meal, Millstuffs, &c.	4,840,651	3,725,977	1,114,674	.
Beans, Peas, Hops, &c..	"	91,432	29,501	61,931	.
Flax, Hemp, &c.. .	"	167,080	9,390	157,690	.
Grass and other Seed, .	"	61,064	51,335	9,729	.
Green Fruit, . .	"	184,068	351,222	.	167,154
Roots and Bulbs, . .	"	74,754	315,463	.	240,709
Hay, ...	"	.	.	.	.
Broom Corn, . . .	"	.	.	.	.
Lumber and Timber,	Ft. B. M.	9,268,836½	2,981,216	6,287,620½	.
Stave and Hoop Poles, .	cords.	5	21½	.	16½
Lathes, ...	M.	46½	86½	.	40
Shingles, . . .	"	6,358½	3,691¼	2,667¼	.
Empty Barrels, &c. .	lbs.	189,150	350,265	.	161,115
Wood for Fuel, . .	cords.	.	.	.	.
Coal, ...	lbs.	287,700	131.770	155,930	.
Lime and Cement, .	"	200,594	122,253	78,341	.
Brick, ...	No.	1,000	.	1,000	.
Building and other Stones,	lbs.	480,830	525,623	.	44,793
Salt, ...	"	7,001,920	8,286,770	.	1,284,850
Dry Goods, . . .	"	2,289,025	1,790,428	498,597	.
Drugs, Medicines, Paints, &c.	"	1,768,010	1,073,077	694,933	.
Liquors and Wines, .	"	636,216	340,559	.	204,343
General Groceries, .	"	7,049,272	5,500,661	1,548,611	.
Leather, Boots, Shoes, Saddlery, . . .	"	1,063,898	814,252	249,646	.
Hatter's Goods, . .	"	70,077	87,395	.	17,318
Books and Stationery, .	"	206,601	117,562	89,039	.
Crockery and Glassware,	"	912,875	637,873	275,002	.
Furnishing Goods, Gas Fixtures, &c. . .	"	80,125	90,517	.	10,392
Hardware, Iron, Steel, &c.	"	4,212,546	2,456,700	1,755,846	.
Stoves and Turner's Ware,	"	978,636	1,235,930	.	257,294
Agricultural and other Machinery, . .	"	3,148,315	2,586,406	561,909	.
Furniture and Household Goods, . .	"	1,978,401	2,100,812	.	122,411
Other Manufactured Articles not enumerated,	"	1,716.703	2,813,074	.	1,096,371
Sundries, . . .	"	691,336	1,266,534	.	575,198
Total of all Articles in lbs.		72,652,403	58,374,040	14,278,363	

under way, the Iowa line would extend 132 miles west of Burlington (i.e., to Chariton), thus securing to the Illinois company "a very valuable business."[59] A month later, he wrote Perkins that it was probable the road would be pushed right through to the Missouri and that he was contemplating another inspection trip across the state.[60] This tour, the fourth that Joy and Perkins made together, took place between August 8 and 18.[61] During its course Perkins noted that many of the local people were not very "enterprizing" on the railroad question, although he thought construction of the line was precisely what the undeveloped country west of Osceola needed.[62] Perkins watched Joy anxiously to see what his decision would be towards further extension. The pair returned east by way of Kansas City and St. Joseph, and the younger man noted that Joy was extremely interested in the possibility of a road northward from Kansas City along the Missouri River. Nevertheless, at the conclusion of the journey, Perkins apparently had no doubts of the outcome so far as the B. & M. was concerned. "The trip," he wrote, "has been a very interesting one and very profitable one to me. As a result of it Mr. Joy will recommend another 50 miles of road [i.e., to Afton] at once for us and if he can make arrangements with the Pacific R. R. for a bridge over the Missouri so as to get us a connection with that road he will recommend that we go right through."[63]

[59] CBQ, *Annual Report* for 1866 (Chicago, 1866), p. 12.
[60] Perkins to his wife, July 25, 1866 (CNB, ch. vii).
[61] See Appendix D, below, for Perkins' letters describing this journey.
[62] Perkins to his wife, August 9 and 10, 1866 (CNB, ch. vii).
[63] Perkins to his wife, August 19, 1866 (CNB, ch. vii). These words were written the day after the conclusion of the trip. In referring to them, however, Mrs. Edward Cunningham, daughter of C. E. Perkins, has said: "My father at this time was over-optimistic as to Mr. Joy's views about western Iowa. As a matter of fact, Mr. Joy was not nearly so enthusiastic about extending the B. & M. as my father hoped or supposed he was, and it was not long before he became interested in projecting railroads into Missouri rather than into western Iowa and Nebraska." (CNB, ch. vii, n.p.) Her conclusion finds support in the following letter written by Perkins to Lafayette Young, editor of the *Des Moines Capital*, on May 30, 1904: "After the war," he wrote, "our Boston people were persuaded to undertake an extension of the Burlington & Missouri River Railroad to Chariton, fifty-six miles from Ottumwa, and in August, 1866, I made my second trip across the State with James F. Joy, of Detroit, then President of the Company. The end of track was a few miles west of Chillicothe, say ten miles beyond Ottumwa, where we left the railroad and took a carriage and pair. . . . After six or seven days, stopping briefly at the county seats, we landed at Platts-

On September 11, 1866, the directors of the C. B. & Q. noted in their minutes that the B. & M. would soon open its road to Chariton and that it was "evident" that an additional extension would benefit the Illinois company. They resolved to call a special meeting of the stockholders at Chicago on October 4 to consider the propriety of giving further aid to construct the Iowa line another 60 miles.[64] At this meeting, James F. Joy was appointed chairman, and after due deliberation a preamble was unanimously adopted that again rehearsed the importance of the B. & M. to the C. B. & Q. "The advantages of the extension of that road," it concluded, "are not only permanent, but become each year of still larger proportions by reason of the rapid settlement and development of the resources of the section through

mouth. *The result of this expedition was that Mr. Joy definitely decided against an extension to the Missouri River, and he doubted the wisdom of going even as far as Chariton. He told me he did not believe a road through the counties of Clarke, Union, Adams, Montgomery, and Mills, could be made to pay in thirty years, and that he should advise his eastern friends not to take the risk of building. He acted on this conviction, and a year or so later resigned the presidency, because his view did not prevail.* Mr. Joy's wide experience as a successful railroad pioneer in Michigan, and in Illinois, necessarily gave great weight to his opinion, but fortunately, as it turned out, John M. Forbes and John W. Brooks, of Boston, and James W. Grimes, of Iowa, did not agree with him, and the road was built in spite of very hard sledding, financially, — and with serious doubt about the result for several years." (Perkins to Young, May 30, 1904, CNB, n.p. Italics supplied.) This letter was published in the *Des Moines Capital*, and in 1906 was republished in W. W. Merritt's *A History of the County of Montgomery* (Red Oak, Iowa, 1906, p. 66). It was quoted again by W. W. Baldwin, Vice-President of the Burlington, in an address before the company's engineering department at Chicago on July 2, 1920 (*Professional Engineer's Magazine*, September, 1920, p. 17). Mr. Baldwin's remarks were subsequently reprinted in a separate pamphlet entitled "The Making of the Burlington" (Chicago, 1920; the letter appears on pp. 15-16), which was widely distributed. On its face, the letter of 1904 seems inconsistent with the contemporary letter of 1866. Mrs. Cunningham suggests, however, that her father was not only undoubtedly swayed by his own enthusiasm when he wrote in 1866, but also that he was definitely endeavoring to present the situation to his wife in the most encouraging terms possible. Furthermore, she feels that the passage of time and course of events between 1866 and 1904, together with Mr. Joy's known interest in the Hannibal and St. Joseph and the Council Bluffs and St. Joseph roads in 1867 and thereafter (see text, pp. 220–222), led Mr. Perkins, in 1904, to ascribe more pessimism to Mr. Joy in 1866 than Mr. Joy felt at that time. Mrs. Cunningham and the present writer agree, therefore, that the two letters are not so inconsistent as they first appear, and that Mr. Joy's actual attitude in 1866 lay somewhere between the two extremes described.

[64] CBQ ORB, pp. 308–309.

which it runs." It was therefore resolved that the agreements signed on June 24, 1864, by which the C. B. & Q. was receiving its division of joint tariff earnings in securities of the Iowa road, be extended so as to guarantee extension of about 60 additional miles *beyond* Chariton.[65] Furthermore, on October 10, 1866, the C. B. & Q. directors voted that construction should be commenced on a bridge across the Mississippi River at Burlington with the purpose of finishing the structure "by the time the Burlington and Missouri River Railroad should be done to Chariton." [66]

As was inevitable, the construction or projected construction of the B. & M. through Iowa, and subsequently Nebraska,[67] created opportunities for those with capital to buy land along the line that either might be developed into a town or sold for farming purposes. It was logical that the men most active in such matters should be those connected with the railroad itself, because they were on the spot, were familiar with the projected route, and were able to secure the necessary capital.[68]

These men sought to make money through the rise in realty values. A prerequisite to their success was the construction and increasing activity of the railroad. This, of course, had originally been made possible by the stockholders. On the other hand, the traffic of the railroad could not grow unless the community it served was stable and prosperous. Therefore, like the company's land department itself, those interested in land, either as individuals or in groups, endeavored to encourage those elements that would form the nucleus of a permanent settlement. The donation of lots for a mill, a store, or a church by a townsite company often sufficed to establish a new shipping and receiving center which would provide more business for the railroad.[69] Thus, while the promoters were given a chance to profit by the construction of the railroad, they in turn risked their private capital to create towns that would contribute to the prosperity of the B. & M. and of the community at large.

Whether the new towns and farming areas which these companies fostered could have been developed without speculative capital, or whether their development was premature, are moot points. It seems

[65] CBQ ORB, pp. 310–311.
[66] *Ibid.*, p. 312.
[67] See below, pp. 285–289, 411–412.
[68] Cf. Gates, *op. cit.*, chs. vi & vii.
[69] See below, pp. 234–236.

beyond question, however, that the promoters of these individual ventures were bent upon establishing permanent settlements. Early in 1865, when an agent was commissioned to draw up a bond to be executed when selling tracts, "especially . . . for town lots," he asked Judge Rorer to draft a clause that would require the purchaser to make improvements.[70] The judge suggested the following:

But this sale is upon express condition that improvements by the purchaser or his assigns shall be made on the premises so sold, to the value of _____ within _____ months from this date; and unless so made, the contract to become void. The amount already before then paid thereon to be forfeited to the vendor & possession of the premises to be redelivered to the vendor with all that is thereon — and these conditions & said time are of the essence of the contract.[71]

The substance, and possibly the exact wording, of this clause was made a part of subsequent land association contracts.[72]

From the records available, it is not entirely clear when the first systematic buying of lands near the B. & M. in Iowa began; possibly it was before the rails reached Ottumwa. There is, for example, an abstract of title to some 80 acres in Jefferson County bought on behalf of Denison, Baker, and Brooks on November 5, 1858.[73] That these men were already associated with each other and had an agent acting for them suggests that they had either already made regular purchases, or were contemplating doing so. Certain it is, however, that by 1864, Denison and one or probably more of his colleagues had organized the Iowa Land Association for the specific purpose of buying and selling town lots in the city of Burlington, along the line as far as Chillicothe, 82 miles west, and in Monroe and Adams Counties.[74] For the modest sum of $100 a year, Perkins was persuaded to "look after" these investments;[75] his work consisted of managing personally the property in Burlington, examining outlying farmlands or future townsites, checking the reports of the association's local agents, and keeping his superiors in Boston informed of progress.

In February, 1864, for example, Perkins wrote from Burlington that

[70] Perkins to Rorer, January 9, 1865 (LDP).
[71] Memorandum by Rorer, January, 1865 (LDP).
[72] HSR, Receipt for Bond, October 24, 1868 (LDP).
[73] Abstract of Title to land in Jefferson County, 1849–65 (LDP).
[74] ILA, Trial Balance, January 1, 1867 (LDP).
[75] Perkins to his wife, April 22, 1864 (CNB, ch. v).

he had a five-acre lot to rent and was taking the day "to see the man and agree upon price, etc." [76] Much of the time Perkins devoted to the association, however, was along the undeveloped territory of the road. In March he spent a day at Coalport which, he wrote, consisted of "two houses, one of which is a 'hotel,' and a store. The store is also the squire's office and post office, one man attending to all; with the help of his sister." [77] There the association owned 160 acres, and Perkins made his trip in an unsuccessful effort to rent them to a group of miners; on his way home, he stopped off four miles west of Burlington to look at a five-acre lot he rented to an Irishman for $40. [78] During April and May, accompanied by Thielsen and traveling by hand car, Perkins was off again, on these occasions to Batavia, Whitfield, and Agency City, where there were "towns" to look after. "*Towns* they are on paper," he observed; "meadows or timber land, with here and there a house, in reality." [79]

By the next year, however, Batavia was advancing. During the spring of 1865, as agent for the association, Perkins donated $75 to aid construction of a church, [80] and a lot was transferred to the Methodist-Episcopalians for a consideration of $1.00. [81] Between May and November the local agent in the village disposed of 40 lots and 5 acres of farmland to 29 purchasers for $2,945. [82] In July, 1866, with the war over and construction again under way, the association decided to promote the new town of Frederic, 16 miles west of Ottumwa.

I shall have two or three more towns to name very soon [wrote Perkins]. . . . They should be short and easily pronounced. Frederic, I think is a very good name. It is now literally a cornfield, so I cannot have it surveyed, but yesterday a man came to arrange to put a hotel there. This is a great country for hotels. [83]

On October 6, 1866, Perkins paid William H. Moss $7 for "laying out Town of Frederic." [84] Civilization was on the way.

[76] Perkins to his wife, February 21, 1864 (CNB, ch. v).
[77] Perkins to his wife, March 5, 1864 (CNB, ch. v).
[78] *Ibid.*
[79] Perkins to his wife, April 18, 1864 (CNB, ch. v); cf. letters to same, April 22, 1864, May 1, 1864 (CNB, ch. v).
[80] ILA, Receipt, June 20, 1865 (LDP).
[81] ILA, Memoranda of land sales at Batavia, May–November, 1865 (LDP).
[82] *Ibid.*   [83] Perkins to his wife, July 22, 1866 (CNB, ch. vii).
[84] ILA, Receipt, October 6, 1866 (LDP).

Meanwhile, Forbes had commissioned Perkins to buy land for him and Thayer,[85] and in June, 1864, Perkins was offered an opportunity to participate as a partner in the enterprise.[86] The chief object was to buy and develop property west of Ottumwa; during the next two years, however, while the B. & M. was being constructed, most of the group's operations concerned property in Burlington.[87] In the meantime, Perkins not only acquired several plots there adjoining his home, but also contemplated purchasing lots facing on the public squares of Albia and Chariton on his own account. Together with Thielsen and Peasley, he proposed buying 80 acres just west of Des Moines.[88] The reason for these investments was not far to seek. "Twenty years hence," he wrote in 1864, "you will not recognize the Illinois and Iowa of today." [89]

By the fall of 1866, the future of the B. & M. seemed promising indeed. Since the opening of the Civil War in 1861, the Iowa company had shown its ability to survive under the most difficult circumstances and to enlist sufficient financial support to resume construction. Relations between it and the Chicago, Burlington & Quincy were closer than ever in respect to operation and finance; more and more the separate lines were assuming the aspect of a major rail system. Finally, Congress had added to the B. & M.'s holdings in Iowa, and promised a huge grant in Nebraska when construction should warrant it.

It was during these busy years of 1860 through 1866 that Perkins guided the growth of the B. & M. land department at Burlington. It was his responsibility not only to establish the company's title to its various grants and settle the troublesome disputes over swampland and preëmption claims, but also to pave the way for the sale and settlement of its vast properties. He had turned to his task, in the fall of 1860, with vigor and determination.

[85] Perkins to his wife, June 14, 1864 (CNB, ch. v).
[86] Perkins to his wife, June 20, 1864 (CNB, ch. v).
[87] HSR, Trial Balance, April 1, 1868 (LDP).
[88] Perkins to Forbes, June 17, 1865 (CNB, n.p.).
[89] Perkins to his wife, June 20, 1864 (CNB, ch. v).

CHAPTER VIII

Charles E. Perkins Watches the Company Lands, 1860–1866

Before Perkins had been in office two months, the board of directors formally selected the lands to which they were entitled under the original Iowa grant of 1856 by virtue of actual construction.[1] According to this act, the company was to receive 120 sections (square miles) for each 20 miles of line finished; thus for the 80 miles to Ottumwa, it could choose 480 sections, or 307,200 acres. Along the whole line, however, from Burlington to Council Bluffs, and in both land districts, there were but 306,994.95 acres potentially available, even including the 75,000-odd acres disputed by swampland or preëmption claimants. Thus the first selection was the only one made in Iowa, and because almost none of the public domain east of Ottumwa had been available in 1856, it brought lands to the railroad that lay beyond the railhead and extended west to the Missouri River.[2]

As if to offset the calamity of war and the uncertain state of business, Steiger sent encouraging news from Washington. On March 18, 1861, the commissioner of the General Land Office had finally consented to reopen the preëmption contests in the Council Bluffs district. Hearings were to be held before the local officers, and Steiger warned Perkins that the claimants would use every effort to discredit the information so laboriously collected by the company.[3] Perkins immediately endeavored to meet this situation by sending C. A. Van Allen, a lawyer, into the western counties to present the railroad's viewpoint and forestall popular opposition. By June 24, this goodwill ambassador reported that "things are working more pleasant and harmonious [sic] between myself, the [local land] officers & preëmptors everyday, — the old hostile suspicious jealous feeling against the Co. is nearly gone. . . ."[4] Whether or not this was so, when the cases came up for hearing in August, the attorneys for the preëmptioners marshaled every possible argument on behalf of their clients.

[1] On November 26, 1860 (BMI ORB, p. 129).
[2] Perkins to Denison, September 20, 1861 (LDP). See map, p. 242.
[3] Steiger to Perkins, March 18, 1861 (LDP).
[4] Van Allen to Perkins, June 24, 1861 (LDP).

The preëmptioners' first point was a long recitation of the withdrawal dispute designed to prove that no railroad location was valid within the six-mile limit of the track prior to the actual location of the line on the ground, nor between the 6- and 15-mile limits until the location was filed in the land offices (spring, 1857).[5] Following the various rulings of the Department of the Interior, the company answered that the preëmption withdrawal was binding in May and June, 1856 (i.e., between the first withdrawal and its countermanding order), and that no private entries at all were tenable after the road's survey in September and October of that year.[6] Secondly, the preëmptioners asserted that no railroad title of any kind was valid until the line of the road was actually staked out upon the ground. They also held that even in 1861 no one knew exactly where the company would build, "and we think, and very much fear, they never will have a Railroad there." Thus, the attorneys urged, the company's claims were far less tenable than those of the preëmptioners.[7] This contention, however, had no legal weight, for the filing of the company's survey in the land offices, even though subject to minor changes, was sufficient definitely to fix the route. Third, the road's opponents resorted to *de facto* argument. "We have *some* title," they urged, "whether we have fulfilled the exact letter and spirit of the preëmption law or not; we have bought the land and paid the Government full price for it, and we have possession of the lands, while neither the Railroad companies nor the State have paid anything for the land, made no Rail Road, and in fact have no claim either in equity or in law to one foot of the land in the Council Bluffs District." There was no denying the first part of this statement, even though it was an admission of weakness and beside the point. Occupants of the land did indeed have whatever weight attached to possession, and they had paid $1.25 an acre for their holdings, whether or not, as they suggested, they had complied with the spirit and letter of the law. The fact that the railroad and state had not given cash for their lands while the preëmptioners had paid for theirs was inapropos; the federal government expected a *quid pro quo* in other forms from both state and

[5] Argument of J. R. Morledge & Co. (counsel for the preëmptors, Council Bluffs), August 17, 1861 (LDP).
[6] See above, p. 94.
[7] Argument of J. R. Morledge & Co., August 17, 1861 (LDP).

railroads. Thus the conclusion that the company had "no claim" was hardly justified. Finally, the preëmptioners sought to dispose of the railroad's proof of fraud by asserting that since the latter had no tenable claim to land outside the six-mile limits, it possessed no corresponding right to inquire into preëmptions in that locality. Furthermore, they said, the word of local land officers concerning improvements should be accepted, "and such improvements are in fact a substantial fulfillment of the law . . . by which the sole object of the law has been in all the above cases obtained, viz. giving the land to *actual settlers*, in preference to the wealthy speculator, Rail Road Companies, or other *soul-less corporations & monopolies*." Even if the arguments of the preëmptioners could be and were disproved, the force of such sentiment might well remain. It was a factor the railroad did well to recognize in its relations with the community.

The week after the hearings at Council Bluffs, Perkins wrote Steiger that all but three of the preëmption cases had been argued. The company's lawyer, Van Allen, had obtained as full a transcript as possible of the evidence, but this had been difficult because the local register and receiver refused to let him copy the official record although the privilege had been granted the attorneys for the other side. This boded no good for the company. Perkins feared that the Council Bluffs officers might send certain selected cases to Washington at once for decisions, hoping that the railroad would not be prepared. Therefore, he urged Steiger to keep an eye on the General Land Office so that any papers submitted by the register and receiver might not be skimmed over and too readily endorsed by headquarters.[8] For the next year and a half, the fate of these preëmption lands rested in Washington; it was up to Perkins to keep the road's neighbors as happy as possible and to make what new friends he could. To help him, N. P. Woods was appointed as field worker in the western counties whence in time a local attorney wrote that

his style suits our people very well indeed. Quite a feeling exists here against you, and he has been able to *soften* it considerably by his manner and ability to please the farmers and convince them that you have a *soul*. . . .[9]

Intangible as it was, this accomplishment was of vital importance.

[8] Perkins to Steiger, August 23, 1861 (LDP).
[9] Wm. Hale (of Glenwood) to Perkins, November 24, 1862 (LDP). Hale

Meanwhile, settlers along the line began applying for various tracts from the railroad; on June 15, 1861, for example, applications for B. & M. R.R. lands received up to that time were classified as follows:

Prices offered	Acres in Des Moines District	Council Bluffs District
(none specified)	874	2,528
$1.25	120	40
1.50	—	40
2.00	128	40
2.40	40	—
2.50	200	985
2.75	40	—
3.00	—	370
4.00	—	40
	1,402 acres	4,043 acres

In other words, definite applications had been made for 5,445 acres.[10] To these various requests, Perkins would invariably send a personal reply explaining that no lands were on sale yet, but that the applicant's name would be placed on file and notice given when the tract was placed on the market.[11] Aside from the fact that the war had slowed both immigration and construction of the B. & M., however, it would have been unwise for the company to sell or even to advertise its lands so long as some 16,000 acres were disputed under the preëmption law[12] and nearly 60,000 acres involved in swamp claims.[13] In the fall of 1861, however, the situation in respect to the swamplands was suddenly clarified.

On October 25, 1861, the General Land Office approved 2,082.38 of the 47,193.86 acres of disputed swamplands in the Council Bluffs district to the state.[14] All the rest, 45,111.48 acres, was certified to the

later acted as agent and attorney for Mills County in adjusting the swampland dispute.

[10] CNB, n.p.

[11] There are hundreds of letters of this type in the books for 1861–63. See, for example, Perkins to Samuel Hindman (of Albia), October 18, 1861 (LDP).

[12] Of the 16,346.84 acres disputed, 14,989.03 were in the Council Bluffs district. (Steiger to Lowell, November 25, 1859, LDP.)

[13] Of the 59,244.73 acres disputed, 47,193.86 were in the Council Bluffs district; there were 12,050.87 acres contested in the Chariton (Des Moines) district. (*Ibid.*)

[14] Memorandum, October 25, 1861 (LDP).

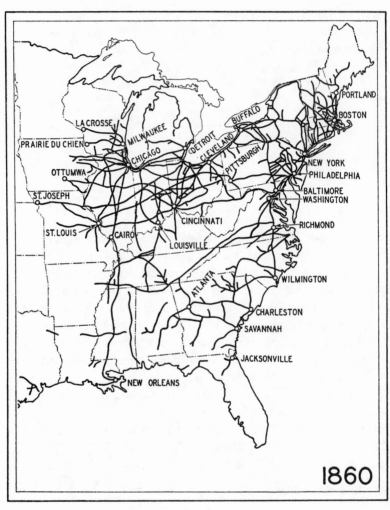

1860

RAILWAYS IN THE UNITED STATES, 1860.

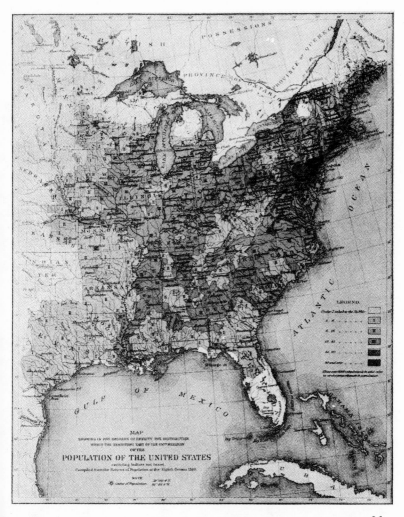

DENSITY OF POPULATION IN THE EASTERN HALF OF THE UNITED STATES, 1860.

railroad on March 21, 1862.[15] At the same time, something over 4,000 acres involved in preëmption suits were awarded to the company,[16] and finally, on April 7, 1863, approximately 7,000 more were certified from the same source so that only 3,867.81 of the original 14,989.03 acres claimed by preëmptioners remained in contest. There were, to be sure, some 12,000 acres of swamplands still contested in the Des Moines district, and a handful of undecided preëmption cases at Council Bluffs, but the total "suspended" list had been cut from over 75,000 to under 20,000 acres.[17]

As a result of these decisions, the B. & M. was at last able to consider the disposal and colonization of its granted lands with some degree of certainty. In so far as the preëmption disputes were concerned, the rulings of the Department of the Interior seemed particularly conclusive, for these cases could not be reopened unless the individuals involved were willing to sustain the trouble and expense of instituting court action.[18] Unfortunately for the railroad, however, the swampland decisions gave less promise of permanence because they affected adversely not only certain individuals but the State of Iowa as well, and the officials at Des Moines were in no mood to sit idly by. In a letter to Denison in May, 1862, Steiger summarized the situation. In the course of his investigations at Washington, he had satisfied himself that lands had been approved to the state as swampy

than which there are no better . . . for cultivation within her limits, and I have little doubt that of upwards of 3 millions acres approved to her as swamp up to this time, 2/3 of it would be found of the same character if sifted out by the rules applied in our case. I mention this fact to show you the deep interest which the state has at stake in the stability of the decisions and approval of the Department . . . since she actually holds two-thirds, certainly more than half her approved swamp lands on this tenure. . . .[19]

It seemed to Steiger that in view of their precarious title, the state officials would do well not to fight over the few thousand acres awarded to the railroad, but in case they should, he urged Denison

[15] Memorandum, March 21, 1862 (LDP).

[16] Memorandum by Perkins, November 1, 1863 (LDP).

[17] Ibid. See also Steiger to Lowell, November 25, 1859 (LDP).

[18] There were several cases that later arose in the courts to test various preëmption land decisions. See below, p. 405.

[19] Steiger to Denison, May 29, 1862 (LDP).

to appeal as directly as possible to the United States Supreme Court, "for I can well imagine the difficulties and prejudices which we should encounter [in the state courts] . . . and do not believe that the Railroad Company could get fair play, however just their claims." Nor was there any question in Steiger's mind but that the B. & M.'s position had been thoroughly examined and vindicated. "I am free to say," he concluded, "that in all my experience in land matters, I know of no case subjected to a more rigid scrutiny before approval of the lands to the railroad grant."[20] Ironically enough, however, the Supreme Court itself was ultimately to find a hole in the railroad's case.[21] Meanwhile, the Secretary of the Interior dispatched a precautionary note to the governor of Iowa:

In view of the numerous cases presented to this office of parties claiming lands as purchased from the state under the swamp law of Sept. 28, 1850 *which have not been patented to the State*, I have the honor to say, that this office has uniformly held that this class of lands should not be disposed of by the State or other authority [i.e., counties] *until by the terms of the law the title has become vested by the issue of the patents*. A contrary course brings embarrassments on the state, and retards the proper execution of the law by the Department *which alone determines all the interests arising under the grant* and the subsequent amendatory enactments.[22]

Even though the Burlington's position was thus confirmed and its land titles put on a firmer basis, conditions in the summer of 1863 hardly warranted inauguration of a colonization program. Immigration, so promising in 1859, had virtually come to a standstill, both from foreign and domestic sources. Eastern capital was being absorbed by the demands of the conflict, and the individuals most able to help the Burlington, notably John Murray Forbes and the friendly officials of the Hannibal and St. Joseph, were completely occupied either in government service or in keeping their immediate businesses operating under war conditions.[23] Construction beyond Ottumwa was,

---

[20] Steiger to Denison, May 29, 1862 (LDP).

[21] In 1869. See below, pp. 266–267.

[22] Edmonds to the governor of Iowa, June 3, 1862 (LDP).

[23] Forbes was serving in the Quartermaster's department in charge of providing vessels for supply of Union troops on the southern seaboard (Pearson, *op. cit.*, pp. 115–116). The Hannibal and St. Joseph, which had started sale of lands in 1859, was completely disrupted by the war. Its line changed from Union to Confederate to Union hands, and at times operations were stopped. The complete land department records of this company, part of the Burlington collection, pro-

therefore, out of the question for the time being, and until the line could be extended through the granted lands, thus giving them a reasonable value, it would obviously be unwise for the company to embark on a systematic disposal of its property. Upon this point, officials of the company were fully agreed.[24]

To this general rule, however, there was an important exception. With the railroad's title to the disputed preëmption and swamplands clearly established at last, the company was free to pursue a prompt and generous policy with *bona fide* settlers who found themselves without title on these tracts.[25] Three years before, Lowell had emphatically assured such individuals that they need have no fears.[26] As the probable outcome of the disputes had become known late in 1862, however, anxious queries reached the B. & M. One farmer, for example, finding his supposed preëmption title invalid, explained that he had made over $500 worth of improvements on his plot and had paid his taxes faithfully. The local agent to whom he wrote assured him that the B. & M. was an honorable company, and forwarded the correspondence to Perkins.

My own opinion [the latter replied] is that in cases of this kind, the Co. should give title to the holder of the property for very little if any more than the Govt price; if more, give time. Any other course, [despite] . . . the company's undoubted legal right, would work more harm than good. . . .[27]

Perkins wished to treat purchasers of county swamplands that had fallen to the company in the same way by allowing them to rebuy their tracts at the county price of $1.25 an acre, and then to collect their original purchase money from the counties. Early in January, 1863, he wrote Hunt, outlining his projected policy and asking him how the Hannibal and St. Joseph had dealt with preëmptioners and swamp claimants on company land.[28] Hunt replied that in the act

---

vide an illuminating sidelight on the war in the West. (HSJ, Land Department Letter Books.)

[24] Perkins to Denison, August 12, 1864 (LDP).

[25] Decisions of the department could, of course, be litigated in the federal courts. This was actually done in Fremont and Mills counties. See below, p. 264.

[26] See above, p. 143.

[27] Postscript by Perkins on letter from Hendershot & Burton to Rorer, August 12, 1862 (LDP).

[28] Perkins to Hunt, January 9, 1863 (LDP).

regranting the United States lands to the railroad, the State of Missouri had allowed preëmption claimants four months to prove their settlement and to buy at $2.50 per acre (the government "double minimum," twice what Perkins contemplated charging). If they did not do so, the company allowed them to stay on their tracts, providing they signed an acknowledgment of tenancy-at-will until some other buyer offered the full railroad market price. The Hannibal and St. Joseph had been less lenient with persons who had bought so-called swamplands from the counties. These people had acted knowing there was a shadow on their titles, and unless they paid the full railroad figure (collecting their original purchase money from the counties if they could), they were ejected. But, concluded Hunt, "as you are situated, I should think the liberal course you propose to be your best policy."[29] Perkins acted in accord with this advice. In August, 1863, the company made it known that holders of invalidated swamp titles on railroad land would have an opportunity to buy, for a limited period, at the rate of $1.25 an acre; it was left up to them to recover their original purchase money from the county land offices.[30] In the early fall, Perkins sent notices to this effect to as many such settlers as he could reach, announcing dates on which sales would begin in the five Iowa counties containing the bulk of disputed lands,[31] and promising that the offer would remain open for three months thereafter. The proposition was renewed in the winter of 1863–64.[32] In November, 1863, preëmption claimants were notified of a similar offer and given two months to comply with the company's terms.

Outright squatters under no title at all presented more of a problem, and Perkins was puzzled as to what course to follow. In Iowa, the law gave possession to anyone who had squatted for ten years unchallenged, but since there was no way of ascertaining the number

---

[29] Hunt to Perkins, January 26, 1863 (LDP).

[30] Perkins to J. F. Tracy (of Des Moines), February 29, 1864 (LDP).

[31] Perkins to N. P. Woods, September 15, 1863 (LDP). The places and dates of sale were as follows:

Quincy (Adams County)	October 19–20
Frankfort (Montgomery County) ...	October 22
Glenwood (Mills County)	October 24, 27
Sidney (Fremont County)	October 29–30
Clarinda (Page County)	November 2–3

[32] Perkins to J. F. Tracy, February 29, 1864 (LDP).

of such individuals except by sending a man over each 40 acres, he decided it was better to risk losing scattered parcels of land than to incur this expense. As a partial remedy, however, and to check up on the 1859–60 survey, one township in each of the original examiner's territory was rechecked.[33] Thus the most pressing and annoying problems before the land department were put on the way to solution.

The company realized, of course, that selling any lands at $1.25 was a sacrifice from a financial point of view, but Perkins explained that they did so "because we are interested in keeping people in the Country, and in having the good will of the Counties. This alone," he added, "ought to convince our friends that we hope someday to have a road to the Missouri."[34] The plan of payment offered these $1.25 purchasers was generous. They were allowed to pay cash, as over half of them did, or to give notes for one, two, or three years.[35] As might be expected, the contracts worked out for these credit sales followed the Illinois Central and Hannibal and St. Joseph models without material changes save that they were more liberal in not requiring any down payment of principal.[36] Interest only, at ten per cent, was required when the contract was signed; thereafter, the principal, with interest on the unpaid portion, was paid off in equal annual installments.[37] The parcels of ground involved were predominantly 40-acre tracts; during 1863 and 1864, the company made 60 sales, all of them in the Council Bluffs district. In June, 1865, Perkins authorized King to make one last effort to locate (1) holders of county swampland certificates, and (2) preëmption claimants on railroad land. The former were to be given three months to purchase at $1.25 an acre; the latter could buy at prices based on the merits of the land

---

[33] Memorandum by Perkins, November 1, 1863 (LDP). "When I came to write instructions for the Land Examiners," Perkins wrote later, "I copied Lowell's old ones word for word, and could not improve in any way." (Perkins to his wife, May 9, 1865, CNB, ch. vi, n.p.)

[34] Perkins to J. F. Tracy, February 29, 1864 (LDP).

[35] BMI, Contract Ledger No. 1 (LDP).

[36] For a comparison of the Illinois Central, Hannibal and St. Joseph, B. & M. (Iowa) and B. & M. (Nebraska) contracts, see below, pp. 295–296. On short credit sales, the Illinois Central required a down payment of 25 per cent of the principal, with the balance in three equal annual installments (Gates, *op. cit.*, pp. 159–164); the Hannibal and St. Joseph required one-third of the principal when the contract was signed, and the rest in two equal annual installments (LDP).

[37] BMI, Contract Ledger No. 1 (LDP).

minus improvements. The results of this offer, however, were negligible. Only two small plots were sold in 1865 and one early in 1866.[38] Consequently, by the spring of 1866, Perkins reported that all swampland claimants had been accommodated [39] and that no more preëmption cases would be reopened.[40] The books showed that by its 63 sales the railroad had disposed of 5,065.14 acres for $6,331.46.[41]

		STATISTICS OF SALES 1863–1866									
		Number of Plots Sold					Number of Sales			Acres	Value
		(Size by Acres)									
	40	40–80	80	80–160	160	160–320	Cash	Credit	Total		
1863	13	1	8	7	2	0	16	15	31	2,367.22	$2,959.02
1864	9	3	7	8	1	1	18	11	29	2,420.56	3,025.74
1865	1	0	1	0	0	0	2	0	2	120.00	150.00
1866	0	0	0	1	0	0	1	0	1	157.36	196.70
	23	4	16	16	3	1	37	26	63	5,065.14	$6,331.46

In the light of subsequent events this was not a large transaction, — less than two per cent of a single month's sales in 1870, — but it brought results vastly more important than the acres and dollars involved. In the first place these sales at a nominal figure were evidence of the railroad's desire to accommodate members of the community who were put in an embarrassing position through no fault of their own. Secondly, the experience of working out contracts, setting up books, and dealing directly with customers afforded the land department certain preliminary training in the technical aspects of land selling, even though the sales were of a special nature and at a uniform price. Since in every case the company was dealing with established settlers, there were extremely few instances of delinquencies in payment or cancellations of contract, but in the latter part of 1865, a case arose involving both which suggested what the railroad's policy would be later on. In October, 1863, Noah Biggs had purchased 120

[38] Perkins to King, June 30, 1865 (LDP); Perkins to Mansfield & Ball, July 12, 1865 (LDP); BMI, Sales Book "A." (LDP).

[39] Perkins to Denison, February 16, 1866 (LDP).

[40] "We have stopped all sale on old claims that were not applied for within the time specified. . . ." (Perkins to W. T. Ewing, May 11, 1866, LDP.)

[41] BMI, Sales Book "A." Also land department, Trial Balance of May 24, 1866 (LDP). The latter source shows that the lands approved to the road had increased 811.77 acres from 286,296.88 to 287,108.65. These minor adjustments took place throughout the history of the grant as clerical errors and overlooked tracts were discovered. The Valuation Docket Report of the C. B. & Q. RR., made in 1922, lists 18 separate approvals for Iowa of 1,000 acres or less. (LDP.)

acres at the prevailing $1.25 price, paying $48.75 down, and giving notes for the balance to be paid in three equal installments.[42] During the following year, Biggs died. His widow failed to meet the payment due in October, 1864, and, according to the terms of the contract, technically forfeited the land as well as the down payment. Perkins, however, was unwilling to take advantage of this circumstance. "The railroad," he wrote Mrs. Biggs, ". . . is willing to deal with you considerately, understanding that you are a Widow & in indigent circumstances." Consequently, he made her two propositions: either she might pay $1.25 (making a total of $50 paid in), obtain a deed for 40 acres, and relinquish the rest of the land; or the company would refund her husband's cash payment and take a release from the entire contract.[43] As a matter of fact, the lady made use of both offers. In August she accepted the first alternative [44] but changed her mind two months later, whereupon the railroad refunded her the $50 in full.[45]

While these preliminary sales of 1863–66 were being made, the perennial swampland bugaboo continued to dog the land department. As early as November, 1863, J. A. Harvey, register of the state land office, served notice in his biennial report that Iowa had no intention of submitting quietly to the Department of the Interior's decisions regarding the swamplands.[46] Devoting more than half of his 100-page pamphlet to the matter, he absolved the state from maladministration, took sharp issue with the actions of the federal officials, and pictured the land-grant railroads as illegal recipients of lands to which they were not entitled.[47]

Harvey's chief grievance was the fact that the General Land Office

[42] BMI, Contract Ledger No. 1, Contract No. 6 (LDP).

[43] Perkins to Biggs, July 21, 1865 (LDP).

[44] Perkins to Biggs, August 5, 1865 (LDP).

[45] Perkins to Biggs, October 6, 1865 (LDP).

[46] Iowa Register of the State Land Office, *Annual Report* for 1863 (Des Moines, 1863).

[47] "The difficulty," the state register declared, "cannot be attributed . . . to anything done by the State in the premises. It is found in the course pursued by the Land Department [i.e., General Land Office and Department of the Interior] at Washington, ... It seems to be the special design of the Department . . . to thwart her [Iowa's] efforts, and by every pretext to delay . . . [the swamp act's] administration, and to curtail the advantages the State is entitled to receive therefrom. . . . The Commissioner has certified thousands of acres to the State for Railroad purposes that come fully and completely within the Swamp Land Grant. . . ." (*Ibid.*, pp. 53–61.)

suspected Iowa of bad faith in selecting as swampy large amounts of dry lands, and in turning the administration of the act over to the counties "to avoid difficulty with the General Government." [48] His defense of this action was illuminating:

Whilst I do not claim that *all* the lands selected are swamp land within the meaning of the Grant, I do say that neither the State nor the counties designed any fraud upon the Government; and that the amount of dry land selected is not sufficient in quantity to warrant any such opinion, or justify even a suspicion of unfairness. Many of these lands were selected in the years 1854 and 1855, immediately after several remarkably wet seasons, and it is not strange that the Agents then did select some as swamp and overflowed land which would not appear as such after a few succeeding dry seasons. And it is equally easy to account for the dry land (if any there be) in the later selections, consistently with good faith. . . .[49]

Therefore, the General Land Office, according to Harvey, was not justified in allowing these selections to be called in question before the local land officers. Speculators, he said, had used this privilege to "wrest from the counties a large amount of swamp lands," basing their claims on the testimony of "irresponsible and reckless men . . . who, for a few dollars for each affidavit, would testify to the character of land that they never saw." It was to save the state from this "ruinous policy" that the Iowa delegates in Congress had sponsored the law of March 3, 1857, which fully confirmed the state's selections. And now the commissioner of the General Land Office had held this law was only a qualified confirmation, and "certified thousands of acres to the State for Railroad purposes that come fully and completely within the Swamp Land grant." [50]

The railroads, Harvey continued, were claiming "all Swamp lands in odd numbered Sections within the limits of their several roads," on

---

[48] Iowa Register of the State Land Office, *Annual Report* for 1863, p. 57.

[49] *Ibid.*, p. 58. What this "equally easy" accounting was, Harvey never revealed. In his entire report, the only action of the state which he allowed could be "reasonably construed" as supporting the federal government's "false impression" was the Iowa law of April 8, 1862, allowing each county to appoint an agent for presenting its claims at Washington. Harvey admitted that "in some instances parties who, for a mere private speculation, have purchased the interest of counties, get themselves appointed special agents and go to Washington to press their claims before the Commissioner," thus riveting upon that official's mind "the erroneous impression previously received." Such agents, he suggested, should be replaced by a single state representative. (*Ibid.*, pp. 58–59.)

[50] *Ibid.*, pp. 59–61.

the grounds (1) that the state's swamp title did not attach until the final patent was issued from Washington, (2) that the selections were open to contest because of their fraudulent nature, and (3) that the railroad rights to their grant attached before the confirmatory act of March 3, 1857. The register undertook to answer these points in order. If the swamp grant was *in presenti*, then the first point fell to the ground. As to the second, the Secretary of the Interior's order of February 8, 1860, requiring the use of the original field notes to determine the status of contested swampland was a "great error" because of "the very loose and careless manner in which the public lands of the West have been surveyed." Therefore the testimony of the state's agents, who acted under oath "with a *direct* reference to the character of the land," should be preferred to such evidence. Finally, these swamplands awarded to the railroads had been selected "long before the Act of May 15, 1856," [51] and were consequently not available to the roads. Therefore,

if any legislation can be devised by the General Assembly that will meet the case and compel the Railroad Companies to relinquish their claim to these lands, it ought to be immediately done. At all events, these lands should not be certified or transferred by the State to the Railroad Companies. So that if the several Counties are compelled to resort to the Courts to avert the impending damage and establish their rights, they may not have to contend against the Executive sanction of the State to the erroneous course and acts of the Land Department at Washington. . . .[52]

This presentation by Harvey was not altogether logical. Even though all the wrongful state selections had been the result of honest misapprehension, that fact was poor reason for objecting to contests arising from these mistakes. Furthermore, all contests were finally decided in Washington and not at the local land offices,[53] so that the testimony of "irresponsible" and "reckless" men could easily be checked against the field notes which, although admittedly rough, gave some clue as to the arability and wetness of the tracts in question. The most vulnerable points of Harvey's argument, however, were his flat statements that erroneous selections had been honest mistakes, that such mistakes were "not sufficient in quantity" to "justify even a sus-

[51] *Ibid.*, pp. 60–62.
[52] *Ibid.*, pp. 62–63.
[53] See above, p. 129.

picion of unfairness," and that the railroads claimed "all Swamp lands in odd numbered Sections within the limits of their several roads."

In his *Annual Report* for 1865 the commissioner of the General Land Office noted that as of September 30 of that year, 58,650,242.71 acres had been selected by 13 states as swampy; in addition, 366,674.11 acres and $513,826.84 had been given these states as indemnity for swamplands sold as arable or located with bounty warrants. These "enormous concessions," he continued, suggested the "necessity" for a new law which would prescribe exactly the method of filing swamp claims, define precisely what was and was not swampy, limit the period of selection, and specify whether or not patents could be granted to states without a definite showing that the "condition of the grant — namely, constructing of levees and drains . . ." had been fulfilled. "Charges of fraud," concluded the commissioner, "in the mode of making swamp selections not yet patented, and of false representations as to the character of lands on which indemnity is sought, have induced the appointment, under the secretary's orders, of a special agent to make field examinations, and from personal investigation and by collection of credible testimony to make report with the view to definitive departmental action on claims following in this category. His work is not yet completed, but the reports already made fully justify the precautionary measures heretofore adopted in this matter. These reports indicate that while the mere form of proof for indemnity may be complied with, the premises on which indemnity is sought are, in many instances, among the most desirable farming lands." [54] Indeed, in Iowa alone, no less than 553,293.33 acres, selected by the state agents as swampy, had by 1863 been rejected as such by the Department of the Interior and certified to the railroads. Despite Harvey's assertions to the contrary, it would seem that this constituted a "sufficient" quantity of land to "justify the suspicions" of even the most charitably minded federal officers. [55] Years later another complete investigation by the United States proved conclusively that some of the best farm lands in Iowa had been selected as swampy. [56] It is difficult to escape the conclusion that, as in the case of other bene-

[54] Commissioner of the General Land Office, *Annual Report*, 1865, pp. 17–20.

[55] Iowa Register of the State Land Office, *Annual Report* for 1863 (Des Moines, 1863), p. 61.

[56] *Senate Executive Document No. 249*, 50th Cong., 1st Sess. (1888), p. 3.

ficiaries of the Swamp Act, fraud did creep into the Iowa selections, and the "suspicions" of the federal officers were warranted. Finally, Harvey's statement that the railroads were claiming "all Swamp lands in odd numbered Sections within the limits of their several grants" was untrue. The companies were claiming only those sections that were actually dry; [57] the bases on which they claimed them, however, were as Harvey had reported.

The register's final recommendation that the state should compel the railroad companies to relinquish the swamplands awarded them boded no good for the future. Yet in March, 1864, the authorities at Des Moines made a conciliatory gesture by suggesting that the B. & M. accept state-owned lands "equally valuable" within 30 miles of the track in place of the contested sections. The company was amenable to this proposition,[58] and it was apparently still being considered in November of that year when Steiger wrote Perkins that although he could not advise him as to the practicability of the contemplated exchange (since the county accounts were confused), peace was to be preferred if reasonable terms were offered.[59] There is no record, however, of any such compromise, and in March, 1865, Perkins invited President St. John of the Rock Island [60] and President Platt Smith of the Dubuque & Sioux City [61] to coöperate with the B. & M. in protecting the railroads' interests in respect to swamplands. Representatives of the companies met in July, and Smith was appointed head of a committee to suggest desirable legislation.[62] By this time, however, the legal status of contested swamplands was on the way to determination as the result of local lawsuits in the western part of the grant.

In October, 1863, the month when the very first contracts were signed, various individuals in Mills County who had bought swampland and now found their tracts awarded to the railroad refused to consider the company's offer to sell, and started suit to test the decisions of the Department of the Interior. In response, Perkins withdrew

[57] See above, ch. v.

[58] Perkins to R. L. B. Clark (of Des Moines), March 14, 1864 (LDP).

[59] Steiger to Perkins, November 25, 1864 (LDP).

[60] Perkins to St. John, March 12, 1865 (LDP); St. John to Perkins, March 29, 1865 (LDP).

[61] Perkins to Smith, March 27, 1865 (LDP); Smith to Perkins, March 30, 1865 (LDP).

[62] Smith to Rorer, July 22, 1865 (LDP).

his offer from those who were known participants in the litigation [63] but continued to encourage sales to those who disassociated themselves from the proceedings. In an effort to publicize the generous terms of these sales, he wrote on February 29, 1864, to a member of the Iowa House of Representatives, outlining the B. & M.'s policy.[64] Apparently the information arrived at a psychological time, for the member from Mills County had been doing what he could to swing opinion against the B. & M. by stating that honest farmers were being forced from their well-tilled farms by a soulless corporation.[65] Indeed, the entire legislature was seriously considering the possibility of revoking the federal grants that had been given the railroads through the medium of the state. One proponent of this policy explained his position in a letter to the *Burlington Daily Hawk-Eye*:

Des Moines   Feb. 12, 1864

Dear Sir: . . .

Those who favor the resumption of the RR grants, ask only . . . that that step be taken solely to enable the State to protect the rights and interest of the people in the re-bestowment or further disposition of these lands. They are willing that the RRs should have all that they can fairly ask, but not license to disregard all their obligations and the rights of all other persons and parties. By resuming its legal rights, the State will be in a position to enforce its proper demands upon those who are not always overscrupulous in their exactions. . . . It is to the interest of the State to foster Railroad enterprise, but not to build up exacting monopolies. . . .[66]

Six weeks later word came from Des Moines that nearly an entire week had been spent by the House in discussing the "Resumption Question." The railroads, warned the correspondent, "cannot afford to have it re-opened much oftener. They lose strength with every airing it receives." [67] Despite the fact that nothing came of this agita-

[63] Perkins to Peasley (a subordinate in the land department), October 15, 1863 (LDP). Two residents of the county, Kingsbury and Hickman, had already accepted the company's $1.25 offer when a suit was started in their name against the railroad. Perkins promptly withdrew the offer to sell, but when the men said the action had been begun without their knowledge, he authorized the sale to proceed providing the men would dismiss the suit and pay all costs. (*Ibid.*) Perkins thought that speculators were responsible for this and other suits. (Perkins to Tracy, February 29, 1864, LDP.)

[64] Perkins to Tracy, February 29, 1864 (LDP).

[65] Tracy to Perkins, March 3, 1864 (LDP).

[66] *Burlington Daily Hawk-Eye*, February 16, 1864.

[67] *Ibid.*, April 10, 1864.

tion, the B. & M. continued to have trouble on account of the swamp-lands. During the spring and summer of 1864, some 1,200 acres had been disposed of in Mills County when, in August, 1864, the board of supervisors there started suit in the state district court against the B. & M. on behalf of all holders of county swampland certificates, thus incorporating the individual cases already instituted into one action.[68] Thereupon the railroad stopped all sales in the county but with evident reluctance, for, as Ames wrote an applicant from the region, "our wish has been to close up all these cases. . . . We offered what we thought liberal terms, . . . and have been willing to settle for less than one-fourth (in most cases) the real value of the land. . . ."[69] The railroad's policy of stopping sales in this region inevitably caused some hard feelings. Just as it was being put into effect, H. C. Watkins wrote from Glenwood offering to repurchase from the B. & M. land he had once bought from Mills County as swamp; he added that he was expecting to join the army, and it seemed necessary "that sub-lunary affairs should be settled where a wife and babies are to re-main."[70] Perkins in responding explained why no sale could be made,[71] but Watkins replied:

I can only say in answer that I was actuated in making application by the common right every man has to *buy his peace*, and only asked for the same right that has not yet to my knowledge been refused to you by any one.[72] In reference to the suit [of Mills County against the railroad] I can only say that I have been a private citizen for nearly two years, and cannot assume that I have any influence that would operate upon the Officials either in prosecuting or quitting the suit. . . . I am refused a privilege which by general rule has been accorded to all. If I am to be selected as a target for persecution, "*nuf ced*" — though poor in purse, I hope to survive it. . . .[73]

It was just this sort of feeling on the part of the people that the company wished to prevent, but with title to all its Mills County lands under the shadow of litigation, there was no alternative but to stop

[68] BMI, Legal Record, p. 8; Transfer Record, p. 289 (LDP).

[69] Ames to W. H. Taft, August 23, 1864 (LDP).

[70] Watkins to Perkins, August 18, 1864 (LDP).

[71] Perkins to Watkins, August 23, 1864 (LDP).

[72] The policy had just been put into effect, and it was possible that Watkins had not heard of its general application. (Watkins to Perkins, August 31, 1864, LDP.)

[73] *Ibid.*

sales. For the time being, then, the matter rested in the hands of the court.

Meanwhile, however, Perkins was far from idle. Like Judge Rorer, he was convinced that Congress had intended, in 1856, to give the company the equivalent of six sections per mile in the western, unsettled part of its grant.[74] The second donation of 1864 had seemed to confirm this intention,[75] yet if the swamplands were lost by a court decision, there would not be enough land even within 20 miles of the track to make up the amount contemplated by the first grant of 1856. Furthermore, Perkins, like Steiger, was convinced that the counties had claimed as swampy lands that could not possibly fall within that classification. Nevertheless, because of the vague and conflicting interpretations as to when the swamp and railroad grants attached and as to what constituted a final patent, it was not unlikely that through some technicality the courts might reverse the decisions of the Secretary of the Interior. Consequently, Perkins was moved to take measures which would protect what he believed to be the just interests of the company. He explained his plans in a letter to John Murray Forbes on February 10, 1865.[76]

In July, 1864, Congress passed an act allowing the B. & M. to change its route providing a map of the change were filed by July 1, 1865. Perkins was already contemplating his objection to this time limit because final location could be best decided only as the track progressed, "but," he now told Forbes, "the topography of the country is not the only consideration. . . . For instance, if the people of Mills County continue to be inimical, it may be policy to change our line out that way, but we do not want to do it now." [77] According to the original survey, the B. & M. would pass directly through Glenwood,

---

[74] It will be recalled that Rorer's plea was for lands along the western eighty miles of the line; the company officials, as well as the sponsors of the 1856 grant in Congress, realized that the B. & M. would never secure their full quota along the eastern and well-settled portion of their line. See Jones' argument in the Senate, summarized above, pp. 76–77.

[75] Particularly these words: "the Burlington and Missouri River Railroad Company . . . shall be entitled to receive . . . an amount of land per mile equal to that mentioned in the act of 1856 to which this act is an amendment, *as intended to aid in the construction of said road. . . .*" (CBQ, *Documentary History*, vol. II, p. 17. Italics supplied.)

[76] Perkins to Forbes, February 10, 1865 (LDP).

[77] *Ibid.*

the Mills County seat and by far the most important town in the section. As Perkins well knew, to leave this settlement off the road would blast its dreams of becoming a thriving main-line community; consequently, his weapon was a powerful one. As it happened, events moved rapidly. Early in March, 1865, J. M. King organized a party to run the new survey,[78] and by midsummer a line had been located ten miles south of Glenwood.[79] Subsequently, another route was laid out ten miles to the north of the town.[80] Meanwhile, Fremont County, directly to the south, instituted a court action similar to the Mills County case; [81] as 1865 drew to a close the lines of battle were tightly drawn.

The next move came from Mills County. In July, 1866, William Hale, as agent and attorney for the county, approached the railroad with a compromise plan. If the company would build through Glenwood, the board of supervisors would relinquish their claim to unsold swamplands, assign any long-term contracts then pending, and reimburse the company in cash for money already collected on account of the lands.[82] For some undisclosed reason, — possibly because Mills County did not withdraw its suit from the district court or because Fremont County refused to join the compromise,[83] — Perkins rejected the offer. For the moment, at least, the railroad preferred to await court action.

Another less controversial result of the company's sales of 1863–66 was to draw forth applications from persons who, although they held no special claim, wished to buy B. & M. land. Perkins reported to Treasurer Denison in 1864 that there were at least three separate

[78] King to N. B. Hazen, March 9, 1865 (LDP). King offered a job on the new surveying party to a friend of Hazen's who had just graduated from college. The pay was $45 a month and expenses. (*Ibid.*)

[79] Perkins to Joy, July 26, 1866 (LDP).

[80] BMI, Transfer Record (LDP).

[81] Perkins to Joy, July 26, 1866 (LDP).

[82] BMI, Transfer Record (LDP).

[83] Perkins to Joy, July 26, 1866 (LDP). Apparently the Mills County officials made their offer on the grounds that they wished to ease the minds of the holders of county swampland certificates, but Perkins was skeptical of this explanation. "However much Mr. Hale and the Board of Supervisors may say about quieting the apprehensions of purchasers," he wrote, ". . . the true reason for their making this proposal is the running of a line (a year or more ago) by our engineers ten miles south of Glenwood. I had that line run with some such result in view. . . ." (*Ibid.*)

groups of this sort.[84] First were those who owned adjoining tracts and wanted to enlarge their farms. Perkins was against accommodating such people until they were willing to pay the higher price that could reasonably be asked when the railroad construction improved realty values. "They select the best pieces in their neighborhood," he explained, "and I don't think either our own interest or justice to them required we should sell." The second class included those who had no special claim but gave evidence of becoming permanent settlers. Perkins doubted whether these could pay what the railroad hoped to receive, and at the moment they comprised a very small group. The final category was made up of squatters without title, who had occupied and improved the land, sometimes over a period of years, in hopes that they could eventually buy or establish a claim. Perkins advised selling to such people at a reasonable and current price, for he felt it worked against the Burlington to have any proven settler move away who was disposed to make a fair arrangement. He would not lay down a general price scale, for the grant as a whole was definitely not in the market, and in cases where squatting was evidently done to secure the land cheaply for speculative purposes, he would make the price prohibitive. But to established farmers, he would sell the several hundred acres involved at a figure that seemed equitable in each individual instance. He asked the board's opinion on this policy.

A letter written from the field by J. M. King a year later pointed out the hazards of selling land to any squatters at all. King found that people were pouring into Mills County and squatting on railroad land with the hope and expectation that the company would "deal fairly" with them. By this, they meant they would have a chance ultimately to buy the land at the prices current when they moved in. The situation placed the road in an uncomfortable position. If squatters were driven off or prevented from settling, the community at large, and particularly the county taxing authorities, could accuse the road of retarding settlement. Yet, if they were allowed to occupy and improve the land, it would be well-nigh impossible to evict them or secure the price that would be justified after completion of the road.[85] Perkins, realizing the gravity of the situation, immediately

[84] Perkins to Denison, August 12, 1864 (LDP).
[85] King to Perkins, July 3, 1865 (LDP).

solicited Joy's advice. The counties of Iowa, he explained, were desirous of attracting immigrants and so, of course, was the railroad, "but not $2,000,000 worth. We can better wait and sell lands at $10 [an acre] than sell now at $5, which would be double the average price." [86] Perkins was decidedly opposed to attracting people by promises of fairness; perhaps the company could not sell much anyhow, but it would certainly lose the choicest lands by any premature development. Joy's reply expressed succinctly the entire philosophy behind the federal land-grant policy as he understood it:

> As to allowing parties to settle on your lands with any idea that they are to have more favorable terms than any other purchasers, it should not be thought of for a moment. All the world should know that this cannot be. If you publish a notice, which will be proper, it should state that these lands are given as a fund to construct this road — that sold at present prices they would produce nothing for such purpose, that it is only by realizing their prospective value, that they will be of service in the aiding of construction & this can only be by mortgage on time & then when the lands have been made valuable by the road's being built, selling them at their then value to repay the money. The community should understand that we are struggling to build the road & need all the credit we can get from all sources in deeding these lands & that therefore we cannot waste or sell them at present prices & must realize all the value the road will give them.[87]

Later on Perkins made the same inquiry of Peter Daggy, for years chief of the Illinois Central's vast land department, concerning treatment of squatters.[88] His answer, while not so comprehensive as Joy's, was more informative from a technical point of view. The Illinois Central's charter had allowed preëmptioners on railroad land to acquire their plots for $2.50 an acre. This privilege had been abused by squatters and had caused the company considerable loss. It was almost impossible to oust them, and in some instances, written leases were arranged for one, two, or three years at a nominal rent. At the end of that time, most of the squatters left peaceably, but the system caused more vexation than it was worth. Consequently, the company thereafter uniformly refused permission to occupy lands until they were actually purchased, for settlement inevitably meant improvement, and

[86] Perkins to Joy, July 8, 1865 (LDP).
[87] Joy to Perkins, July 10, 1865 (LDP).
[88] Cf. Gates, *op. cit.*, pp. 156–157.

when a *bona fide* purchaser arrived, he would find the land occupied by another. Lawsuits would ensue, and unless the railroad paid all costs and perhaps damages, it would gain a bad reputation and the ill will of both parties and their friends.

If you could rely upon the settler purchasing the land himself [he concluded], it might do, but not one in fifty will do so, and on the contrary will sell out his improvements, and the first thing you know, some stranger has possession, and your lessee gone to parts unknown. We prefer letting improved farms lie idle to giving possession to anyone. . . .[89]

This was good advice, born of sad experience. Whether or not it was the determining factor in Perkins' mind, the Burlington followed it in fact. To the countless applications for purchase that came in at an increasing rate after 1864, the land department made the same reply: that the application would be filed, and the applicant duly notified when the lands were placed on the market. "Until that time, it would be better for all concerned that *no improvements* should be made upon the land, so as to avoid all chance for hard feelings on the score of misunderstanding, and difference of opinion. . . ."[90] *Bona fide* settlers, however, who had already made improvements had nothing to fear: "The Railroad Company," wrote King, "will not seek to take advantage of one who may have improvements on its land but will sell the land to the owner of the improvements at the same figures as if unimproved land of the same quality and location. . . ."[91] Thus on the one hand the land department sought to discourage newcomers from occupying company land, and on the other to retain real settlers by a promise of equitable treatment. Meanwhile, actual sales were rigorously limited to swampland or preëmption claimants on company land.

Since the sales were conducted under special conditions and because of the war, no formal attempt was made to advertise the B. & M. lands. Nevertheless, Perkins continued to obtain what information he could about Iowa's resources and concerning publicity methods. In November, 1861, for example, he learned from a resident of Fairfield that coal was plentiful and in fact "inexhaustible" in that vicinity. About half a dozen mines were operating and selling their

[89] Daggy to Perkins, November 30, 1865 (LDP).
[90] Perkins to Joshua Fearell, August 14, 1866 (LDP).
[91] King to George Hovey, June 21, 1866 (LDP).

output at the surface for four and six cents a bushel.[92] During the next year with the southern cotton supply restricted, the Department of Agriculture forwarded several bushels of upland cotton seed to the company with the request that it be tried in Iowa soil. Perkins found several persons willing to try it, particularly the Icarian community in Adams County.[93] Later on he requested more complete instructions concerning cotton culture, but presumably the experiment was a failure.[94]

Throughout this period, the company did not launch any publicity of its own but supported projects that would advertise the state as a whole. One such enterprise in 1864 drew forth from Perkins a revealing expression of policy. William Duane Wilson, a state official, wrote that he was planning to issue a guide to Iowa in which the amount of text devoted to each railroad would be in proportion to the amount of paid advertising each company inserted. This scheme put Perkins in an uncomfortable position. He extricated himself as best he could. His response began by praising unreservedly the general idea but, he cautioned Wilson, "your book purports to be for the benefit of the immigrant as well as for the benefit of the state, and such it should be *in fact.* . . . As a state officer you will be thought to view the whole ground impartially, and so you should. . . . Otherwise [the book] would soon be known to be unreliable." Therefore, the idea of apportioning editorial comment according to the amount of monetary support by the railroads was "wrong"; the guide should say all that was necessary about each company. Furthermore, the wisdom of outright advertising by the roads was a moot point. Would it not be better to print a map showing all lines within the state? On this basis Perkins would gladly subscribe for 100 copies at 60 cents each, but feeling as he did, would do no more, except to match the subscriptions of the other railroads. "Do not understand me," he con-

[92] N. A. Hitchcock to Perkins, November 16, 1861 (LDP).

[93] The Icarians were socialists and followers of Etienne Cabet, French Revolutionist of 1830. They had started their experimental community in 1853 after purchasing 3,000 acres of government land. (Benjamin F. Gue, *History of Iowa*, New York, 1903, vol. III, p. 292; Harold Underwood Faulkner, *American Political and Social History*, New York, 1937, pp. 269–270.)

[94] Perkins to J. H. Barrett (Commissioner of U. S. Patent Office), December 29, 1862 (LDP); J. F. Grinnell (Acting-Chief Clerk of the Department of Agriculture) to Perkins, January 13, 1863 (LDP); John Bixby (of Adams County) to Perkins, March 10, 1863 (LDP); Perkins to Icarians, March 24, 1863 (LDP).

cluded, "as questioning at all the intention to make the book true and reliable, but it should not only be true as far as it goes, but should cover all the ground." He would, he added, be glad to obtain publication estimates from Boston.[95] Apparently Wilson profited by this candid criticism, for two months later Perkins sent him a list of the company's lands for inclusion in the publication.[96] More important, the company had gone on record as to the type of advertising it would authorize.

Meanwhile, the agency most active in advertising the state was the American Emigrant Company. It will be recalled that during 1860 and 1861, Iowa had supported a State Board of Emigration with an agent named Rusch at New York City. In his final report, Rusch had warmly commended the work of this private company, and since that time it had expanded its publicity work until it had practically taken over the functions of the defunct state board. By 1865, it had agents in Sweden, Germany, England, and Scotland, and in that year it also hired Owen Bromley of the Iowa state legislature as its representative in Wales.[97]

Such was the situation as the war drew to a close and Perkins began gathering data for an advertising campaign. A letter from McKay of the American Emigrant Company brought forth a recital of that organization's efforts to date. He also enclosed copies of his company's circular advertising its 500,000 acres in Iowa, and of its *American Reporter*, a monthly paper distributed gratis in England and in Germany.[98] An inquiry to Peter Daggy of the Illinois Central had a result of more interest to the present day than to contemporaries. Daggy apparently showed Perkins' letter to his corresponding clerk, and that gentleman, Augustus Dickens by name, promptly applied to the B. & M. for a position. He had, it seems, been a resident in Illinois for nine years and was thoroughly familiar with the workings of a land department. A further claim to consideration was unique:

As a brother of Charles Dickens, the English Author [he modestly wrote], I have picked up a smattering of literary "ability" that might be

[95] Perkins to Wilson, August 22, 1864 (LDP).
[96] Perkins to Wilson, October 13, 1864 (LDP).
[97] F. C. D. McKay (General Agent of the American Emigrant Company) to Perkins, March 16, 1865 (LDP).
[98] *Ibid.*

Illinois Central Rail Road Co.

Chicago, March 22d 1865

Personal

C E Perkins Esq
Supt
B & M R R Co,- Burlington, Iowa,

Dear Sir,-

In conversation with Mr. Dazey, my personal & intimate friend, & Secretary of this Department, with whom I have been officially connected the past five years, he alluded to your letter to him of 20th inst,-

As corresponding clerk of this Office I have had many opportunities of becoming perfectly familiar with land matters, & after a nine years residence in this Country, I know something about the routine of business as established in America, of which I am a Citizen

As a brother of Charles Dickens, the English Author, I have picked up a smattering of literary "ability" that might be useful in getting up land pamphlets &c, and I might be able to "guild the frame without spoiling the picture",-

But as I am now in receipt of $1400 a year, and the last three years have had a present of from $250 to $350 each Christmas, your proposed terms would hardly meet my requirements,-

CHARLES DICKENS' BROTHER APPLIES FOR A JOB WITH THE BURLINGTON

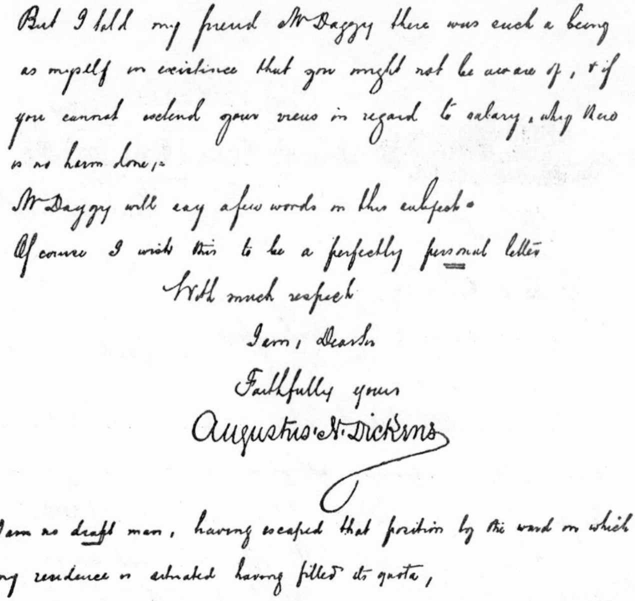

[handwritten letter]

But I told my friend Mr Daggy there was such a being
as myself in existence that you might not be aware of, + if
you cannot extend your views in regard to salary, why then
it no harm done;—

Mr Daggy will say a few words on this subject.

Of course I wish this to be a perfectly personal letter

With much respect

I am, dear sir

Faithfully yours

Augustus N. Dickens

I am no draft man, having escaped that position by the word on which
my residence or estate had having filled its quota,

CHARLES DICKENS' BROTHER APPLIES FOR A JOB WITH THE BURLINGTON

useful in getting up land pamphlets etc. and I might be able to "guild [sic] the frame, without spoiling the picture." [99]

Unfortunately for the literary reputation of the Burlington, Mr. Dickens was not employed. This fact, however, was no reflection on the applicant's ability, for even though the uncertainties of wartime were passing, the company again decided not to launch a full-fledged advertising campaign until completion of the line through the richest lands lying between Ottumwa and the Missouri River had enhanced their value.[100]

The taxability of railroad lands in the various counties presented a final annoying and delicate problem during 1863–66, chiefly because there was no clear legal rule on the subject. Under a state law of Iowa, the property of railroad companies up to and including 1862 could be taxed only through the shares of the stockholders. Therefore, taxing company lands before that date was laying a double tax and hence illegal. Since 1862, in respect to lands certified to the company,

[99] Dickens to Perkins, March 22, 1865 (LDP).
[100] CBQ, *Annual Report* for 1866 (Chicago, 1866), p. 4.

the question had remained open. The railroad claimed that they were not subject to tax because the B. & M. title was conditional upon finishing the road; until that time, they belonged to the United States. Furthermore, the grant of lands was to assist in building the line, and the imposition of state taxes would obviously make this more difficult. The courts of such states as Illinois and Missouri had upheld this position. Nevertheless, the highest court of Iowa decided that any lands held in fee simple were subject to tax, and many counties, particularly Union and those in the western part of the state, had uniformly assessed the railroad's property ever since 1856, including on their lists tracts not granted until 1864, uncertified areas, and lands held while the stockholders were taxed prior to 1863.[101] In 1865, when certain counties took steps to sell B. & M. lands for unpaid taxes, Perkins promptly notified the treasurers of all counties that the railroad would redeem the tracts under protest.[102] Eventually, however, the matter would have to be regulated on a more permanent basis.

Meanwhile, the resumption question reappeared at Des Moines. In March, 1866, the representative from Henry County introduced a bill which provided for resuming all grants of companies whose roads were not completed and equipped within the time originally specified by the state. These lands, the bill further provided, should be then reconveyed to the companies with this further proviso: "That the General Assembly of the State of Iowa expressly reserves the right to regulate and prescribe rates and tolls upon said Rail Roads when, in its opinion, they are exorbitant or unjustly oppressive to the people, & that no lands shall be certified to . . . said companies till they have accepted in writing the terms, conditions and limitations herein made."[103] Commenting upon this proposal, the *Mt. Pleasant Home Journal* declared that this was precisely the sort of bill that was needed.[104] It was not passed, but it was a serious reminder of the close connection between the progress of railroad construction, land department policy, and relations with the community.

On May 24, 1866, Perkins summarized for Denison the work of the

---

[101] Ames to Beymer (of Union County), August 2, 1867 (LDP), contains a good summary of the entire situation up to that date.

[102] Perkins to Joy, October 23, 1865 (LDP); Perkins to treasurers of Iowa counties, October, 1865 (LDP).

[103] *Mt. Pleasant Home Journal*, March 23, 1866 (LDP).

[104] *Ibid.*

land department up to that time. The newly granted lands of 1864 had not yet been certified, but the company's examination of them was nearly completed, and Perkins hoped to classify and evaluate each parcel of 40 acres during the next few months. The most serious problems yet to be settled were the swamp and tax matters. As to the former, both Fremont and Mills counties had won their cases in the state district courts, but the railroad was appealing the decisions. The tax situation was little better. Wapello County had held railroad lands taxable, and a careful survey by the company revealed that about 26,000 acres of railroad land had been sold by various counties at tax sales. These, however, could be redeemed within three years, and Perkins advised that this should be done.[105] For the time being, company sales were discontinued, and the first chapter of the land department's existence as an active selling agency came to a close.

Meanwhile, the B. & M. was taking the steps necessary to establish title to its grant in Nebraska. According to the granting act of July 2, 1864, the company had to accept its gift and file a map of location within one year. Under the circumstances, this was not an easy task, for the Indians along the westernmost portion of the projected line persisted in making trouble during November and December, 1864.[106] Nevertheless, by mid-December, Thielsen had run a line as far as Fort Kearney, some 50 miles east of the 100th Meridian.[107] The directors of the B. & M., therefore, formally accepted the Nebraska grant on January 16, 1865,[108] and on June 15 officially adopted the survey as far as Fort Kearney.[109] It was probable that the B. & M. road would be automatically terminated by effecting a junction with the Union Pacific at this point, but since the latter line had not been definitely located as yet, Engineer Thielsen continued his survey up the Platte River to the 100th Meridian,[110] filing his map of this last portion on March 8, 1866.[111]

Meanwhile, Perkins was attempting to have the government lands

[105] Perkins to Denison, May 24, 1866 (LDP).
[106] Commissioner of the General Land Office, *Annual Report*, 1864, p. 8.
[107] Perkins to Forbes, December 13, 1864 (CNB, n.p.).
[108] Perkins to Steiger, January 5, 1866 (LDP).
[109] BMI ORB, p. 158.
[110] Perkins to Grimes, January 29, 1866 (LDP).
[111] T. M. Marquett, Brief submitted to the Secretary of the Interior, 1887 (HBS).

THIELSEN'S SURVEYING PARTY IN NEBRASKA, NOVEMBER, 1864.

within the probable limits of the B. & M.'s Nebraska grant withdrawn from private entry so as to avoid any such embarrassing confusion as had taken place in Iowa nine years before.[112] His task, however, was extremely difficult, for it was not at all clear just where his company's lands would be. Both the B. & M. and the Union Pacific had been granted ten alternate sections on each side of their tracks, and the latter was required to make its selections within lateral limits of 20 miles.[113] Presumably the B. & M. also would wish to choose its sections within 20 miles of its road if possible, although it was not specifically required to do so by Congress.[114] Since the Burlington left the Missouri River at a point well within 40 miles of the Union Pacific, and since it would join that line at or near Fort Kearney, it was obvious that the two land grants would overlap to a considerable degree. Furthermore, since the U. P. had the older grant and thus held the prior claim, it was clear that the Burlington could secure its full quota only by establishing its right to the *equivalent* of 20 sections for each mile constructed, and even then a great deal of its acreage would be more than 20 miles from its line of railroad. Perkins perceived these difficulties at once and guided his actions accordingly.

On October 27, 1865, he warned Treasurer Denison of the Union Pacific's determination to stand on its rights and "swallow up" the conflicting B. & M. grant.[115] A week later he wrote Steiger at Washington to urge the Secretary of the Interior to delay any final decision as to the extent of the Burlington grant until President Joy and Senator Grimes could present the company's case personally.[116] Steiger secured the desired postponement, and while doing so showed Secretary Harlan that the B. & M. stood to lose approximately 1,500,000 acres unless the road were permitted to select lands further than 20 miles away from its track. Meanwhile, Perkins was pressing for the withdrawal of government lands from private sale, at least along the line of the B. & M. where there was no question of conflict with the Union Pacific.[117] On January 20, 1866, he addressed a direct appeal to Grimes asking the senator to take up the matter with the Secretary

[112] See above, pp. 89 *et seq.*
[113] *Statutes-at-Large*, vol. XII, p. 492; vol. XIII, p. 358.
[114] See above, p. 171.
[115] Perkins to Denison, October 27, 1865 (LDP).
[116] Perkins to Steiger, November 2, 1865 (LDP).
[117] Perkins to Steiger, January 20, 1866 (LDP).

of the Interior.[118] As a result of this vigorous action, Secretary Harlan, on January 30, 1866, withdrew from sale ten alternate sections on each side of the B. & M. line *whether or not* they were within 20 miles of the track. The effect of this decision was to reserve 2,382,208 acres in all for the company, that amount being the equivalent of 20 sections per mile for the 186.11 miles from Plattsmouth to Fort Kearney.[119] Final certification of these lands would, of course, have to await construction of the road and its acceptance as satisfactory by the United States. By April the company had received a map showing the limits of its grant from the commissioner of the General Land Office,[120] and at the end of June, 1866, J. M. King was appointed the company's official agent to select the actual tracts.[121] For the time being, this was all that the B. & M. contemplated doing in respect to its lands west of the Missouri River. Its president reported at the time, "We have too much on our hands in Iowa, just now, to do more than the preliminary work in Nebraska for the present." [122]

Indeed, for Perkins the burden of work was continually increasing, for in addition to his various duties as land agent for the company, he was the ranking operating officer at Burlington. The revival of construction west of Ottumwa meant more responsibility and further demands on his time.[123] Aware of this situation, Perkins addressed a letter in April, 1865, to Dr. Nicholas E. Soule, who had been his teacher at Cincinnati years before:

Tomorrow I start Henry [Thielsen] out West with a young Englishman to look over some of our lands. . . . We have some 400,000 acres of these lands. They are now all in my hands — no Commissioner has been appointed and no Land Department thoroughly organized. We can't sell much until we get more railroad built.

If it could be arranged, how should you like to take the management of the Company's lands? It is a very interesting business — devising ways

[118] Perkins to Grimes, January 20, 1866 (LDP).

[119] T. M. Marquett, Brief of 1887, *loc. cit.*, pp. 2, 12.

[120] Perkins to Steiger, April 9, 1866 (LDP).

[121] Perkins to Joy, May 11, 1866 (LDP); Perkins to King, June 26, 1866 (LDP).

[122] BMI, *Annual Report* for 1866 (Boston, 1866), p. 4.

[123] Perkins to Forbes, December 13, 1864 (CNB, n.p.). Perkins had joined the Union Army in December, 1863, but recurrence of an old eye affliction requiring two operations left him, much to his regret, ineligible for service. He returned, therefore, to his old position at Burlington, which had not yet been filled. (CNB, ch. iv, pp. 74–75, 81–84.)

and means to settle them with good people, publishing pamphlets, circular letters, etc., in English and German, and sending an agent perhaps to Europe. . . . I want it to go into the hands of somebody who will manage it creditably, and I know *of course* that the Company would be devilish fortunate to secure the services of yourself. . . .

This Road must extend — I hope, of course, to continue in charge of it for some years to come, and as the Road grows I must cut loose from some of my other duties — labor must be divided more. It is perhaps not necessary for me to tell you that it is no easy matter to get good, honest, public-spirited men in these parts. This country needs such. *You* could do much good out here. You and I together, I know, could accomplish something. . . . If I could see you and talk over this land matter I should like to. Your literary experience and knowledge would be of great value to us. . . .[124]

Although Dr. Soule felt that he himself could not undertake the work, he replied enthusiastically about the task that lay ahead:

I was very much interested in your sketch of the work of the prospective founder of Iowa cities. What a glorious future lies before some creative and administrative genius, better than Oglethorpe's work, better than Lord Baltimore's! I think that your comprehensive view of his duties is very fine, and it certainly is very exciting and exhilarating.[125]

Eventually, in the latter part of 1866, Perkins turned over the direction of the land department to Colonel J. W. Ames,[126] a man who had first been employed as an examiner of lands in the winter of 1859–60 [127] and who had had ample opportunity to acquaint himself with every detail of the department's work. Whether or not he could equal Perkins' record remained to be seen. During the war years of economic uncertainty, and despite the difficulties of the swampland and preëmption disputes, Perkins had completed the organization of his department, worked out and applied a sales program, and done what he could to keep his road in the good graces of the community. His efficiency was now recognized by his superiors, for they retained him as chief officer of the expanding Iowa railroad.[128]

[124] Perkins to Dr. Soule, April 25, 1865 (CNB, ch. vi).
[125] Dr. Soule to Perkins, April 30, 1865 (CNB, ch. vi).
[126] The first letter signed by Ames as land agent was dated December 4, 1866 (LDP).
[127] See above, pp. 143–144.
[128] Although he had been in actual charge of the B. & M. since the departure of Vice-President Read to the war in 1861, he was not appointed superintendent until 1865. (CNB, n.p.)

CHAPTER IX

RAILS FOR IOWA AND A PROJECT FOR NEBRASKA, 1866–1869

I. IOWA

IN JUNE, 1858, the city of Burlington had agreed that it would execute a final deed for the Mississippi River accretions when the railroad should have extended its tracks to Ottumwa and providing the company spent $20,000 improving the partially submerged land in question.[1] By 1866 these conditions had been fulfilled, and on December 5, Mayor Corse promptly carried out the city's part of the bargain by signing a final conveyance. This deed, however, contained further stipulations that assured a continuing identity of interest between city and company. Not only were the former accretions limited strictly to railroad purposes as before, but it was provided that the B. & M. should place its shops either upon the reclaimed land, or in any event within the limits of Burlington. Otherwise, the conveyance should be null and void.[2]

On June 5, 1867, Perkins dispatched a report to Joy on the state of the B. & M. Work had begun on the Mississippi River bridge in January,[3] and Perkins now pointed out that besides increasing business in general between southern Iowa and the East, the bridge would specifically enable the B. & M. to "hold its own" in the Des Moines Valley against the Rock Island from Davenport, and to carry grain direct to Chicago instead of to St. Louis via Keokuk and the river.[4] This latter change would, of course, mean much additional business for the C. B. & Q. As to construction, Perkins reported that during the preceding 12 months, 47 miles of road had been added to the original 75, thus bringing the line to a point just 9 miles east of Chariton. Earnings had increased to the rate of $600,000 per annum and might exceed that figure if, as Perkins hoped, another 35 miles

[1] See above, p. 102.
[2] CBQ, Deed of December 5, 1866 (LDP).
[3] CBQ, *Corporate History*, p. 437.
[4] Perkins to Joy, June 5, 1867 (CBQ, *Annual Report* for 1867, Chicago, 1867, pp. 56–58).

could be put into operation before winter. He did not anticipate a proportionate rise in expenses as the road progressed, and therefore estimated that upon reaching Afton, 180 miles from Burlington, the railroad would earn more than enough to pay the interest on its entire debt. From Afton it was but 100 miles to the river. "There can be no reasonable doubt," he concluded with a shrewd eye on his audience, "that after the completion of our road to the Missouri River, the improvement of both the road and the country through which it passes, will resemble the improvement of the C. B. & Q. Road, and the country tributary to it during the last ten or twelve years." [5] Joy was delighted with this account. "It is well done," he wrote Perkins in a personal note, "and will create a good impression both of the road and of yourself. It is wholly business-like and all just as it should be." [6] Indeed, Joy was so impressed that he not only reproduced Perkins' communication in full in his annual report to the C. B. & Q. stockholders a few days later, but called their especial attention to it.[7] He himself used many of Perkins' estimates in commenting on the future importance of the B. & M. to his own line.

Joy reminded his stockholders that the arrangement whereby the Chicago road could purchase up to $60,000 worth of the B. & M.'s preferred stock every six months had been in effect for nearly two years,[8] and that the maximum amount of securities had been taken up at every opportunity.[9] He explained that under the terms of the B. & M. consolidated mortgage of 1863, $18,000 per mile could be obtained from the sale of bonds for the sole purpose of construction,[10] but that this money would become available only when the difference between that amount and the actual construction cost of $25,000 a mile was made up by the sale of stock such as that being purchased by the C. B. & Q. If, Joy continued, the full $18,000 worth of bonds for each of the 181 miles yet to be built (from east of Chariton to Council Bluffs) were taken up, a debt of $3,258,000 would be created with

[5] Ibid.

[6] Joy to Perkins, June, 1867, quoted in letter of Perkins to his wife, June, 1867 (CNB, n.p.).

[7] CBQ, Annual Report for 1867 (Chicago, 1867), pp. 15, 53–58.

[8] See above, p. 175.

[9] In three installments, the C. B. & Q. had paid $180,023.22 for B. & M. preferred stock. (CBQ, Annual Report for 1867, Chicago, 1867, p. 22.)

[10] See above, p. 167.

interest payable of $288,060 annually. During the fiscal year 1865-66, however, the B. & M. had cleared $473,999.46 over expenses with only 88 miles in operation, and at the moment (June, 1867), it was earning at the rate of $600,000 per annum, more than enough to pay the mortgage debt and stock dividends as well. Therefore, concluded Joy, there could hardly be

a possibility of doubt of the value of all these securities when there shall be a further section of fifty miles added to the road. Nor to those who consider the rapid development of the West, and the ease with which its prairies are subdued and brought under cultivation and the fact that at least nineteen-twentieths of the country along the line of the road yet remains unimproved, and yet to be settled and made to contribute to the revenues of the road, would there seem to remain any question either of the entire safety of the investment in the additions of business it will bring to the C. B. & Q. Railroad.[11]

During the summer of 1867, Perkins and Joy continued their collaboration. The former felt that certain southwestern Iowa counties were hindering progress of the B. & M. by laying too heavy taxes on the company's lands and by making local aid conditional on locating the line along certain specified routes. Consequently, he composed a letter to the citizens of the region, setting forth the railroad's case.[12] Thinking it best to have such a communication come from a high source, Perkins sent it on to Joy with the suggestion that the latter sign it as president. This he did without alteration, and ordered a general distribution made in the disaffected territory.[13]

In Boston, however, Treasurer Denison was reaching the startling conclusion that Joy was losing interest in the Iowa road. In a letter to Forbes on August 9 he reported that Thayer had declared that the Council Bluffs & St. Joseph was at the moment the most important link to be pushed so far as the C. B. & Q. was concerned. When Denison had pointed out that the completion of the B. & M. across Iowa and to Kearney, Nebraska, would give the C. B. & Q. a much more direct connection with the Pacific road than the Council Bluffs and H. & St. J. roads, Thayer had replied: "Joy says B. & M. only brought C. B. & Q. $300,000 business last year, while H. & St. J.

[11] CBQ, *Annual Report* for 1867 (Chicago, 1867), p. 16.
[12] See below, p. 246.
[13] CNB, ch. vii, p. 62.

brought $500,000." "So," observed Denison, "B. & M. is to have the
kicks and the C. B. & Q. and . . . St. J. is to have all the coppers." [14]

Thayer's implication to Denison was that Joy was displeased with
the B. & M. because of its failure to match the H. & St. J. showing.
Yet this conclusion was hardly warranted. The new and uncompleted
B. & M. never had equaled the established H. & St. J. as a source of
traffic, nor could it be expected to do so as yet. Joy's reports to the
C. B. & Q. stockholders had certainly reflected no displeasure at this
fact but rather agreeable surprise that the Iowa line was doing as well
as it was. Denison was well aware of this and indicated it by his
next paragraph. In fact, he not only revealed Thayer's motives for
disparaging the B. & M., but offered a plausible reason for any possible
lack of enthusiasm on Joy's part:

Mr. Joy is friendly to B. & M. [continued Denison to Forbes] but he
got Thayer into the River Road and he is doing his utmost to get him
into the road from Kansas City south, which has no end. Unless Mr.
Brooks will take Mr. Joy's place and enlist our people in the enterprise, I
do not see but it must stop again. The river road will no doubt be a good
thing for H. & St. J. and so it will for B. & M., when it is done; but to
choke off B. & M. and build a road to carry off its western business, to
make H. & St. J. prosperous, is rather rough on B. & M. It is not only
unfair to B. & M. but it is wrong to C. B. & Q., whose interests are suffer-
ing by loss of prestige in western Iowa, & loss of influence with the Union
Pacific, whose managers begin to doubt whether they have not overesti-
mated its power and loss of business, which is and will be more and more
as B. & M. lags along, or stays dead fixed in the middle of Iowa.

The western Iowa people, when asked to help B. & M., say they have
no faith in its completion. . . .

Unless we rally our forces, and put the B. & M. through at once, we
shall irretrievably lose the grand opportunity which we now have to make
its success complete, and establish it and the C. B. & Q. as the great line. [15]

If the situation was indeed as Denison thus described it, it was apparently Thayer rather than Joy who was chiefly interested in pushing
the Council Bluffs & St. Joseph at the expense of the Iowa line. On
the other hand, if Joy had, as Denison said, encouraged Thayer to
invest in the "River Road," a reason existed for him to exchange his
earlier aggressiveness on behalf of the B. & M. for passive acquiescence.
Yet the record of Joy's official actions both before and after Denison

[14] Denison to Forbes, August 9, 1867 (CNB, ch. vii, pp. 62–65).
[15] Ibid.

wrote to Forbes indicated no pause in his enthusiasm,[16] although it is possible, of course, that Joy's votes and statements as president of both B. & M. and C. B. & Q. did not at all times reflect his personal preferences. However this may have been, there was no denying Denison's statement that the people of western Iowa were growing increasingly skeptical of the B. & M.'s ability to reach the river; Perkins' reports from the region emphasized the need for action.[17]

On August 21, 1867, the B. & M. directors met at Boston and "Mr. Joy having declined a reëlection to the presidency for the purpose of reinstating Mr. Brooks," the latter was unanimously elected. Forbes, Joy, and Brooks were named for the executive committee.[18] At once Perkins wrote his wife, who was visiting in the East, that he wanted very much to have Forbes and Brooks, particularly the latter, come to Iowa in October. "You might urge him if you get a chance," he suggested. "I am fully satisfied that the B. & M. ought to go ahead and now is the time. . . . I feel in my bones that it must go ahead."[19]

Brooks, however, probably because of his poor health, did not accept the presidency of the road, and on September 18 Joy was reëlected to his old post. On his motion the directors immediately resolved to offer the remainder of the unsold land mortgage bonds to the public, and on Thayer's suggestion the company's treasurer was instructed to issue these bonds specifically "for the extension of the road to Afton."[20] Exactly three months later, the directors took three more significant steps. First, they authorized the executive committee to order a full survey of the country between Afton and the Missouri River and to adopt the best route. Next, they voted to submit two alternate plans to the Union Pacific for a bridge over the Missouri River: (1) if the U. P. would build at Bellevue, the B. & M. would complete its road and make a connection "as soon as possible," or (2) if the U. P. built one bridge at Omaha and a second some 35 miles south, the B. & M. would bring its line to this latter point with all possible speed. Finally, the directors unanimously voted to double the capitalization of the B. & M. to $6,000,000.[21] There was no question but that the board wanted action.

---

[16] See above, pp. 219–220, and below, pp. 223–224.

[17] See above, p. 187, and below, pp. 247–248.

[18] BMI ORB, p. 180.

[19] Perkins to his wife, September 4, 1867 (CNB, ch. vii, n.p.).

[20] BMI DRB, n.p.   [21] Ibid.

Meanwhile, the tracks pushed steadily, if slowly, westward; by the end of 1867, they reached Woodburn, almost exactly half way between the Mississippi and the Missouri. The following July, Joy reported to his C. B. & Q. stockholders that arrangements were complete for pushing forward the B. & M. "with all possible vigor to the Missouri," either opposite Plattsmouth or Omaha.

> In either case [Joy continued] it will have a connection with the . . . Union Pacific quite as good as that of any road connecting with it from the east, and will be enabled from its [own] connections east, as well as by its own favorable route, to command a fair share of business . . . with that road while controlling all the local business of the country for a distance of 300 miles, through which it runs. . . . [This] country . . . is of great fertility and will be rapidly developed, . . . and with the road opened through, . . . the time cannot be far distant when its contributions to the business of our [C. B. & Q.] road must be doubled and trebled beyond what they now are.[22]

Joy then reported that, by authority of its stockholders, the C. B. & Q. during the foregoing year had supplied another $1,200,000 to the B. & M. through the purchase of securities. He explained that the support thus given had enabled the Iowa company to dispose of all its remaining land mortgage bonds and thus secure enough money to reach the Missouri River. By such aid, he concluded, the C. B. & Q. would become the majority stockholder in what was actually an extension of its own main line.[23] Joy declined reëlection as president of the B. & M. on July 13, 1868, and was succeeded by Brooks.[24]

On August 13, 1868, the bridge across the Mississippi at Burlington was opened for traffic.[25] The structure was of iron, 2,237 feet long, 26 feet deep, and 15 feet 9 inches wide, carrying a single track;[26] it cost $1,227,044.81, including the approaches at both ends.[27] This physical link between the two roads was of incalculable importance from the standpoint of service and put the Burlington system in a much stronger competitive position, particularly in respect to the Rock Island, whose bridge at Davenport had been completed since 1856.[28]

---

[22] CBQ, *Annual Report* for 1868 (Chicago, 1868), pp. 15–17.
[23] *Ibid.*
[24] BMI ORB, p. 190.
[25] CBQ, *Corporate History*, p. 437.
[26] CBQ, *Annual Report* for 1868 (Chicago, 1868), p. 41.
[27] CBQ, *Annual Report* for 1869 (Chicago, 1869), p. 17.
[28] F. J. Nevins, *op. cit.*, p. 17.

By June 1, 1869, the B. & M. had reached Cromwell,[29] and as it became evident that the rails would certainly reach their goal, B. & M. securities rose to par on the market.[30] In the meantime the Council Bluffs and St. Joseph Rail Road had opened its line from Council

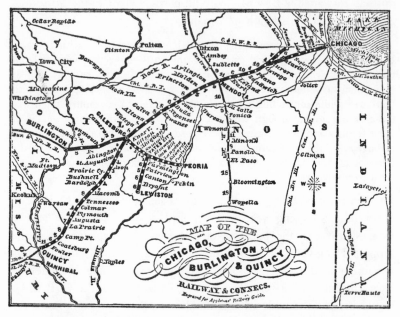

THE C. B. & Q. IN 1869, ILLUSTRATING THE ORIGIN OF ITS TITLE.

Bluffs southward to the Missouri state line, crossing the B. & M. right of way at what later became Pacific Junction.[31] Thus, when the B. & M. should reach that point, it would be possible to gain access to Council

[29] CBQ, *Corporate History*, p. 129.

[30] Joy reported these facts to the C. B. & Q. stockholders as follows: ". . . The Burlington & Missouri to Omaha is fast approaching completion, opening a route as eligible and direct as any other between Chicago and the Pacific Road. Both this Road and the easy and unbroken connection with the Kansas roads, promise large increase to the traffic of this Company. It may be added, and will, perhaps, remove any lingering doubt in the mind of any stockholder as to the safety and propriety of the aid extended to the Burlington & Missouri River Company, that as that Road approaches completion its stock has risen to par in the market, and with a prospect therefore in the future, of a return to the Company of full value for the full amount of the aid rendered, in addition to the increased volume of business which it will furnish to us, and which was the real object of the aid given. . . ." (CBQ, *Annual Report* for 1869, Chicago, 1869, p. 13.)

[31] CBQ, *Corporate History*, p. 243.

Bluffs over connecting tracks. Six miles beyond the Junction lay East Plattsmouth, the final goal of the B. & M., and directly opposite the point where Thielsen's survey for a Nebraska extension began. With their rails hurrying across Iowa, the directors of the B. & M. turned their attention to the vast country beyond the Missouri River.

II. NEBRASKA

That portion of Nebraska through which the new B. & M. would run presented a sharp contrast in many respects to the territory east of the Missouri. From a physiographic standpoint, however, the two regions had much in common. The whole state of Nebraska was a gently rolling plain descending gradually from an elevation of 4,662 feet at Scottsbluff, near the Wyoming border, to 2,136 feet at Kearney and only 984 at Plattsmouth. Timber was limited mostly to the neighborhood of the occasional streams such as the Republican and the various branches of the Blue and Loup rivers. A topography of this sort presented practically no difficulties to construction [32] and was admirably suited for immediate conversion to productive farming. In the matter of soil, the company was equally fortunate, since the entire railway zone lay within the fertile loess area. One of the most important features of this deposit was its high degree of natural drainage. Thus, despite floods or heavy falls of rain, water percolated downward and was retained for a substantial period as in a sponge, rather than running off and carrying much of the soil with it. On the other hand, in times of drought moisture was brought to the surface by capillary attraction, so that vegetation was protected, except under extreme conditions, against the vagaries of the climate. Such soil, because of its cohesiveness, made excellent roads and supplied the material for the sod huts associated with Nebraska's earlier history. For the farmer, its fine texture assured ease of plowing, whereas its speed in drying meant that he missed a minimum amount of time from the fields during rainstorms. Finally, its chemical properties, added to its mechanical advantages, guaranteed a high degree of fertility.

As to climate, rainfall was uncertain for much of the state, but the entire railway grant lay within the 24-inch line.[33] Tornadoes, hail-

---

[32] BMI, *Annual Report* for 1865 (Boston, 1865), p. 5.
[33] Nebraska rainfall apparently comes in cycles of uncertain duration. During

storms, blizzards, and prairie fires occasionally did severe local damage, but in time, suitable precautions lessened the danger from these sources.[34]

The first permanent white settlement in Nebraska had been made by the American Fur Company in 1810, but during the four decades that followed, the government jealously guarded this area for its Indian charges, and as late as 1853 only a handful of permits had been granted white men for entering. In the next year, however, when the agitation for the organization of the Nebraska territory became acute, squatters began pouring across the river. By March the Indian titles had been quieted, and on July 22, 1854, the first public land office was opened at Omaha.[35] At first, it would seem that but little attention was given to agriculture.

The air [wrote one historian] was full of speculation, and the early activities of the settlers were directed mainly to the advancement of their civic interest or, in other words, to the sale of corner lots.[36]

The newcomers looked upon themselves for the most part as transients who would move back to their eastern homes once they had made their fortune. Furthermore, there was a general feeling that the land was hardly adapted to farming. Even by 1860, only 3,982 out of 28,841 persons in the territory were reported as engaged in farming.[37] At first, settlement was considerably hindered by the presence of the ubiquitous speculator, so that much of the land was left unimproved, but the development of claims clubs and coöperative action on the part of actual settlers tended to minimize this evil.

As was entirely normal in the absence of roads and railways, early

---

the 1870's, precipitation was steadily rising, and since the scanty record then available failed to produce the other phase of the cycle, it was believed that the increase would be permanent. This led to the naive theory of Professor Aughey that "Rain follows the Plow." (Cf. Samuel Aughey, *Sketches of the Physical Geography and Geology of Nebraska*, Omaha, 1880, ch. iv.)

[34] The above information on soil, topography, and climate is from H. E. Bradford and H. A. Spidel, *Nebraska, Its Geography and Agriculture* (New York, 1931), p. 69.

[35] Donaldson, *op. cit.*, p. 175.

[36] Arthur F. Bentley, "The Conditions of the Western Farmer as Illustrated by the Economic History of a Nebraska Township," *Johns Hopkins University Studies* (Baltimore, 1893), vol. XI, p. 12.

[37] *Ibid.*

settlement followed the rivers, chiefly the Missouri and the Platte. The latter provided a natural route for the Pacific railroad, which was begun in 1864. By 1867, when Nebraska was admitted as a state, the Union Pacific had penetrated 305 miles west from Omaha. In the same year the Indian menace was considerably reduced by the federal government's adoption of the reservation policy which, though imperfect, offered more security than before to the pioneer farmer.[38] Thus, if the B. & M. were to share in the development of the state and qualify for its grant, it was time to take action.

At first, however, Brooks was decidedly skeptical. Writing to Forbes in April, 1868, he said that to make the Nebraska road "good for anything," they would need (1) money from Congress "nearly or quite enough to build the road," (2) at least 1,500,000 acres of "*good* land *decently watered*," and (3) a fair supply of fuel, a large part of which should be wood for fencing. He then proceeded to list what appeared to him obvious disadvantages. Coal, he said, would cost so much that settlers could not be attracted "as rapidly as required either to make the road pay, or sell the land to this generation." Furthermore, about half of the projected line would be so near the Union Pacific "as to ruin the business on that half," and keep the B. & M. on bad terms with a line upon which it would depend for "fair treatment" in respect to through traffic. Finally, he did not see how, in the long run, "cereals" could be brought "across both the Missouri and Mississippi Rivers in such quantities as to make it pay." In closing, however, Brooks frankly stated that he had "hardly any knowledge upon which to found an opinion." [39] Brooks' objections, therefore, were more valuable from a theoretical than a practical standpoint. Clearly, more authentic information was necessary.

To secure this, Perkins and Henry Strong went to Plattsmouth, Nebraska, in December, 1868. There they met the "leading people," including J. Sterling Morton, and from them obtained a much more favorable report. "We are of the opinion, from all we can gather on the subject," Perkins and Strong wrote Brooks, "that the South Platte country as far west as 75 or 100 miles from the Missouri River is,

---

[38] Paxson, *op. cit.*, pp. 505 *et seq.*

[39] Brooks to Forbes, April 2, 1868 (CNB, n.p.). Brooks added: "I have had such a toothache for the last 24 hours that my opinion is not worth much anyhow." (*Ibid.*)

contrary to what we had supposed, almost as rich in climate and soil as any part of Iowa. . . ." For the region beyond 100 miles they had not been able to obtain definite information, although residents of the section claimed all the territory as far west as Grand Island was equally good.

With this view [they concluded], the land question of Nebraska becomes one worthy of attention. We believe that the country south of the Platte River in Nebraska will in a short time be able to support several railroads and that the business from southern Nebraska is worth an effort on the part of the B. & M. to get it.[40]

The result of this report was that Perkins and Strong were called to Boston to consider the immediate organization of a separate subsidiary for building west of the Missouri River. It was felt that the existing B. & M., to which the Nebraska land grant had been given, had neither the organization nor personnel at hand for the task. Consequently, in order to "get in new blood on a broader basis," Forbes proposed to form an entirely new corporation to which the land grant could be transferred; [41] to this the directors of the B. & M. agreed on February 5, 1869.[42] Such action, however, made it necessary to secure the assent of Congress, and Perkins and Strong were forthwith sent to Washington for that purpose. Neither Senator Grimes, to whom Perkins explained the entire situation, nor Senator Harlan, chairman of the Committee on Pacific Railroads, saw any objection to the plan, and the latter sponsored a joint resolution authorizing the B. & M. to transfer its grant to a new company to be called the "Burlington and Missouri River Railroad Company in Nebraska." [43] The resolution went through both houses without difficulty, and on April 10, 1869, was approved by President Grant.[44] On May 12, the new company was formally organized.[45] Its first board of directors, elected by the stockholders on October 28, 1869, was composed of Sidney Bartlett, Nathaniel Thayer, John M. Forbes, John W. Brooks, John A. Burnham, Cyrus Woodman, and Charles E. Perkins, four of

[40] Perkins and Strong to Brooks, December 18, 1868, quoted in Memorandum from CEP n.d. (CNB, ch. vii, pp. 71–75).
[41] Memorandum from CEP n.d. (CNB, ch. vii, pp. 71–75).
[42] BMI ORB, p. 192.
[43] Memorandum from CEP n.d. (CNB, ch. vii, pp. 71–75).
[44] Statutes-at-Large, vol. XVI, p. 54.
[45] CBQ, Documentary History, vol. III, p. 3.

whom were directors of the B. & M. of Iowa.[46] At their first meeting on November 15, Brooks was named president of the Nebraska company,[47] Cyrus Woodman became vice-president,[48] while Thomas Doane of Massachusetts, a man "who had had no experience in building poor roads," was made engineer.[49] On June 23, 1869, the stockholders of the Iowa B. & M. voted to turn over their rights and privileges in Nebraska, including the land grant, to this new organization on condition that an agreement should be made concerning their "connecting and business arrangements."[50] While this formality was pending, the Nebraska company gave the first tangible evidence of its existence. On July 4, 1869, to the accompaniment of a brass band and a parade,[51] ground for the new road was broken at Plattsmouth.[52] Once more the Burlington system was on its way west.

III. IOWA AND NEBRASKA

For Perkins, whose hands were already full directing the construction of the B. & M. across Iowa, the new enterprise in Nebraska meant added responsibilities. In July, 1869, he and Woodman opened the stock subscription books for the new company in Plattsmouth, and on behalf of themselves and the other directors subscribed for all of the $7,500,000 issue that was not taken up at once by local parties.[53] The *Nebraska Herald* reported that the entire transaction had been completed in 15 minutes.[54] Perkins was constantly on the move.

We left Omaha at nine this morning [he wrote on July 24], and came by cars sixteen miles to Pacific City, thence drove over to Glenwood, four

[46] BMN DRB, p. 7. The directors on the Iowa board also were Brooks, Forbes, Burnham, and Thayer. (BMI DRB, n.p.)

[47] CBQ, *Documentary History*, vol. III, p. 3. For Forbes' opinion of the character of the men in charge of the new system, see *Letters and Recollections of John Murray Forbes*, edited by Sarah Forbes Hughes (Boston, 1899), vol. I, pp. 160–164.

[48] BMN DRB, p. 9.

[49] BMN, *Annual Report* for 1873 (Boston, 1874), pp. 5–6. When Doane left Nebraska to help construct the Hoosac Tunnel, it was said that he had given the men of the West "an example of their own push and energy." (J. Sterling Morton, *Illustrated History of Nebraska*, Lincoln, 1905–1906, vol. II, p. 497.) For Doane's contribution to colonizing activities, see below, pp. 373–376.

[50] BMI ORB, p. 195; BMN DRB, pp. 18–20.

[51] Handbill, July 4, 1869 (LDP).   [52] CBQ, *Corporate History*, p. 319.

[53] Memorandum from CEP, n.d. (CNB, ch. vii, pp. 71–75).

[54] *Burlington Daily Hawk-Eye*, August 4, 1869, reprinted from *Nebraska Herald*.

miles, to dinner, then back to Pacific to meet Hopkins of the Council Bluffs & St. Joseph Road, then over to the Missouri, six miles, through mud and water, and across the River by ferry to Plattsmouth. . . . On the ferry boat, coming over about dusk, the captain said he understood I was looking for work on the Railroad! I did not enlighten him much; he saw me talking to some wild Irishmen who *were* coming over to get work, hence perhaps his conclusions. . . .[55]

The next day Perkins drove as far as Weeping Water, but there his wagon came to grief in a mud hole, so he and his companion, Mallory, spent the night with an accommodating miller. They were off at four the following morning, reached Lincoln for lunch, and drove 30 miles back along the Salt Valley to Ashland for the night. "I never saw such land for farming in my life," Perkins reported enthusiastically, "and I consider our railroad enterprise an assured success." [56] Returning to Iowa, he passed through Glenwood and east of that town inspected a force that was busy grading the Iowa road. Twenty miles beyond Red Oak he lunched with another superintendent of construction in his tent and reached Corning on July 29, the day the rails were laid into the town. "This is some day — say in 30 years — going to be a great country, and all of these little one-horse towns will be thriving and pretty places then. . . . This state and Nebraska are going to make perhaps the richest agricultural communities in the world." [57]

Before that happy day should arrive, however, hard work lay ahead of the railroad builders, and of Perkins in particular. "There is a great deal to be done to finish the B. & M. by January 1st," he wrote. "I don't *fear failure*, but there is considerable wear and tear about the change from a little road to a big one, a great many new men needed and some of them sure to be failures, and a great deal of detail to be looked after. . . ." [58] A fortnight later, writing from Corning, he confessed he was "realizing some of Grant's military difficulties in operating a long way from a 'base.'"

We are laying track and building telegraph from the Missouri River eastward, as well as westward towards that stream, and everything we use has to go 300 miles around over other railroads. So it takes good organizing and close watching to make things move placidly. Then the Nebraska

[55] Perkins to his wife, July 24, 1869 (CNB, ch. vii, pp. 77–78).
[56] Perkins to his wife, July 26, 1869 (CNB, ch. vii, pp. 78–79).
[57] Perkins to his wife, July 27, 1869 (CNB, ch. vii, pp. 79–81).
[58] Perkins to his wife, August 1, 1869 (CNB, ch. vii, pp. 81–84).

CHARLES ELLIOTT PERKINS, 1840–1907.

road people call on me for everything, so I have enough to keep me busy. It is, . . . however, . . . a pleasant kind of "busy." [59]

By September, the road was completed to Villisca, and on November 26, at Glenwood, Perkins made a single laconic entry in his notebook: "Last rail laid and spiked at noon today. Went through with special train to Plattsmouth." [60] The *Burlington Daily Hawk-Eye* of the next day carried a special dispatch:

The last rail [it read] was laid . . . at Glenwood in the presence of the officers of the companies [*sic*] and a large assembly of visitors. . . . No formal ceremonies were observed; everybody was satisfied to accept the situation without the customary buncombe. . . . The officers of the road, the contractors and the capitalists who have aided in this undertaking are alike entitled to congratulations for the business-like energy and liberality which has prosecuted this work to such an early and happy completion. All hail to Plattsmouth! [61]

Thus, without fanfare did the Burlington and Missouri River Railroad, organized more than 17 years before, live up to its name.

Service over the new road to East Plattsmouth was begun on January 1, 1870, and two days later was extended to Council Bluffs, by way of Pacific Junction. [62] Both the Chicago & Northwestern and the Rock Island had reached the Bluffs before the B. & M., however, and their service was already well established. Perkins hit upon a plan he hoped would overcome this disadvantage. At the time there were no Pullman dining cars operating west of Chicago, but the Pullman Company owned two combination sleeper-diners, the "Cosmopolitan" and the "Brevoort," available for such use. [63] One of these went west on a trial run from Chicago on January 15. On the following day this car returned on the first through train between Council Bluffs and Chicago over the B. & M. — C. B. & Q. [64] Regular service westward began January 17, and in addition to a diner and sleeper,

[59] Perkins to his wife, August 17, 1869 (CNB, ch. vii, pp. 88–89).

[60] Memorandum by CEP, November 26, 1869 (CNB, ch. vii, pp. 91–92).

[61] *Burlington Daily Hawk-Eye*, November 27, 1869.

[62] CBQ, *Corporate History*, p. 243.

[63] Memorandum by CEP, n.d. (CNB, ch. vii, pp. 91–92).

[64] Memorandum by CEP, January 15, 1870 (CNB, ch. vii, p. 94). On the westbound trip of this car, Perkins, in company with Peasley, Ladd, and Beckwith of the Burlington office, took his first meal on the B. & M. between Burlington and Ottumwa. (*Ibid.*)

the train that night carried the special car "Omaha," equipped with
an organ and laden with railroad and newspaper men. "The idea,"
explained Perkins, "is to get the Chicago papers to give us a 'blow.'[65]
Things," he added in his notebook, "will begin to get into their regular
channels this week."[66]

The establishment of regular through freight and passenger service
over the B. & M. marked the dawn of a new era for the whole southern
section of Iowa, and particularly for those towns on the road. Indeed,
the new artery of commerce had already had a stimulating effect on
the community it served. Montgomery County, which had shown a
substantial growth of 39.5 per cent in population during the two years
1867–68, doubled its numbers in the succeeding 12 months.[67] Its principal township of Red Oak, containing 820 souls in 1869, boasted
2,222 a year later,[68] as well as a new town government to handle its
affairs.[69] The change in the more populous and longer-settled Mills
County was equally significant. There had been an actual decline of
.8 per cent in that county during 1867–68, but the succeeding year
witnessed an upturn of over 25 per cent.[70] Glenwood increased from
1,659 to 2,133 in the same period,[71] while the fortunes of such towns
as Quincy in Adams County, or Frankfort in Montgomery, declined
as the railroad passed them by. Once again it was clear that the
destinies of company and community were inseparably linked.

During the busy years when the B. & M. was pushing westward
from Ottumwa to the Missouri River, Perkins continued to participate
in or act as agent for the several groups who were promoting town
lots or farm lands along the road. He himself was a partner of Forbes
and Thayer in one such enterprise whose business was transacted in
the name of H. S. Russell, trustee.[72] In addition to buying and selling
scattered tracts in Union, Adams, and Lucas counties, the three associates concentrated their efforts in developing such towns as Russell,
Lucas, Woodburn, Murray, and Elliot. All but the last, which was

[65] Perkins to his wife, January 12, 1870 (CNB, ch. vii, p. 93).
[66] Memorandum by CEP, January 17, 1870 (CNB, ch. vii, p. 94).
[67] Iowa, *Census* for 1880 (Des Moines, 1883), p. 199.
[68] *Ibid.*, p. 550.
[69] Merritt, *op. cit.*, p. 283.
[70] Iowa, *Census* for 1880, *loc. cit.*
[71] *Ibid.*, p. 542.
[72] Perkins to William Irving, May 17, 1867 (LDP).

just north of Red Oak, were on the main line of the B. & M., projected or built, between Albia and Creston.[73]

The operations of these "Russell Associates" were varied. In February and March, 1867, for example, their agent, H. C. Sigler, who was on the lookout for new opportunities of investment, wrote Perkins from Osceola:

> I write you now about a piece of land owned by a gentleman here lying in Union County . . . 10 miles west of Afton at the end . . . of your R. Road in same section. Says it is *first-class*. . . . Your engineers who have been out can tell you something of it & you can see from R.R. survey just where it lies — if it suits you what is the most you will give for it? There is 87½ acres in the piece. I will see that taxes are paid and clear.
>
> If an opportunity shall offer & many will — what is the most you will give per acre for 1st class prairie? A gentleman from Illinois writes me he wants to sell 160 acres which is good No. 1 — I would like to know what you would price it at, 6 or 8 mi. from town. . . .[74]
>
> When will you locate Depot grounds? . . . There is an effort being made to get Mr. Thielsen when he comes up to locate Depot west of Town, which is not the best place for it. . . .[75]

From another agent at the same place, D. N. Smith, came the information that the best purchases could be made from absentee owners, for residents held out for higher prices. Thus, concluded Smith, "my judgment is that you had better secure the next point west of Afton before non-residents catch the mania of Union County."

> My idea [he added] is that nothing will be lost in paying a good price for small pieces of land precisely where you want a station, provided we can buy the land adjoining so that the whole purchase will be bought at low figures & make a round profit on the whole when you sell. . . .[76]

Fortified with such information and having before him a map of the railroad survey, local crossroads, and existing settlements, Perkins determined which purchases should be made from time to time, and at what figure.[77] Stations, of course, had to be located at fairly regular intervals and near existing roads, but even under these conditions

---

[73] HSR, Trial Balance, April 1, 1868 (LDP); cf. HSR, plat showing the lands purchased for this association, n.d. (LDP).

[74] HSR, Sigler to Perkins, February 28, 1867 (LDP).

[75] HSR, Sigler to Perkins, March 15, 1867 (LDP).

[76] HSR, Smith to Perkins, March 2, 1867 (LDP); cf. HSR, Smith to Perkins, May 28, 1867 (LDP).

[77] E.g., HSR, Perkins to Smith, May 20, 1867 (LDP).

there was enough leeway in the precise sites so that sometimes they could be placed on or near tracts owned by the associates.[78]

At the site of Russell, secured in the spring of 1867,[79] the associates immediately started construction of a "snug" warehouse and dwelling. The warehouse, Smith reported in May, would be ready when the rails reached the spot. "We will have a good reliable man there," he added, "with his family such as you can trust to sell lots & do other business for you."[80] When the rails did arrive, Perkins authorized the new agent, N. B. Douglass, to offer two lots and a cash subscription to the first denomination that would build a church in the town. By August the Episcopalians accepted this offer; eventually the association gave them three lots, sold them a fourth for $25,[81] and made a subscription of $50 for the new edifice.[82] Even before this transaction was completed, the Presbyterians, hearing of the matter, offered to put a building under way immediately in exchange for two lots and a cash donation. Douglass wrote for instructions. "I think," he observed, "the two churches would be a great benefit to the growth of the town."[83] Asked for more details by Perkins, Douglass reaffirmed his belief that "two churches would flourish here." The Episcopalians, he explained, had then only a few members, but they were "all of a wealthy aristocratic class."[84] They already had six loads of timber on the spot and planned a structure 30 by 60 feet, with a tower and steeple in front.[85] The Presbyterians, with a large and active membership, expected other denominations to help build their church in return for using it a portion of the time.[86] Perkins thereupon authorized the second donation. As it turned out, the Presbyterians were unable to put up their church that fall, but their leader wrote Perkins that work would surely begin in the spring. "I am also making an effort," he added, "to get some one to come there [Russell] & when the roads are opened & the slews [sic] bridged, I think the

[78] HSR, Memoranda of possible locations for stations west of Chariton and Osceola, 1867 (LDP).
[79] HSR, Smith to Perkins, April 17, 1867 (LDP).
[80] HSR, Smith to Perkins, May 4, 1867 (LDP).
[81] HSR, Douglass to Perkins, August 21, 1867 (LDP).
[82] HSR, Receipt, September 25, 1867 (LDP).
[83] HSR, Douglass to Perkins, September 3, 1867 (LDP).
[84] HSR, Douglass to Perkins, September 12, 1867 (LDP).
[85] HSR, Douglass to Perkins, September 16, 1867 (LDP).
[86] HSR, Douglass to Perkins, September 12, 1867 (LDP).

station will commence going forward." [87] Already the prospective pastor was taking an interest in his parish.

Meanwhile, Douglass was busy with new buyers. By November he had sold eleven lots and a five-acre tract for $325. Five of these parcels were to be paid for in cash upon delivery of the deed, the rest on six months'.to a year's credit at ten per cent interest. Included among the purchasers was William Fulkerson, who planned to build a stockyard on the railroad, and a Dr. F. M. Sanderson, lately of Ohio, who proposed to put in a vineyard and fruit garden as soon as possible. "It requires a great deal of effort," reported Douglass, "and considerable of humoring to get a town started to build up, but by *continued* effort I hope to succeed." [88]

Russell was not the only scene of activity. From Lucas, in March, 1868, came an offer from W. S. Hughes, an old settler. He said he knew of a Chariton merchant, W. W. Baker, and a blacksmith who wanted to settle in the village. Would Perkins appoint him agent for the associates? The latter replied in the affirmative and said that he had written Baker direct offering to deed him a lot free for his shop. "We propose," he added, "to give away ten or 15 scattering lots to parties who will improve [them]. . . ." [89]

At the same time, the affairs of the Iowa Land Association [90] were progressing along similar lines. In the middle of 1867, the group valued its properties as follows: [91]

Location	Amount	Value
Burlington	4½ lots	$3,893.21
"	5 acres	661.88
Batavia	Town Hall	100.00
"	?	895.72
Agency City	6 acres	583.00
Coalport	?	1,656.35
Fairfield	?	2,392.08
Whitfield	?	4,386.05
Frederic	?	1,649.35
Chillicothe	?	2,568.70
Adams County	?	1,412.82
Monroe "	160 acres	1,983.92

[87] HSR, Rev. W. C. Hollyday to Perkins, October 22, 1867 (LDP).
[88] HSR, Douglass to Perkins, November 5, 1867 (LDP).
[89] HSR, Hughes to Perkins, March 13, 1868, with penciled draft of reply on back (LDP).   [90] See above, pp. 183–184.
[91] ILA, Trial Balance, June 30, 1867 (LDP).

At Frederic in particular the usual activity incident to founding a new town was in evidence.

> Miss Beard is here with Rev. Lee of Rome [reported Agent Fraser in 1869]; good prospect of getting up a nice little church which I am anxious to see and other buildings will naturally follow. . . .[92]

As at Russell, a lot was donated for the purpose,[93] and the railroad brought in free the necessary lumber for construction.[94] Meanwhile, Fraser himself, with a partner, planned construction of a grist mill. When it was time to lay the foundations, however, $1,500 cash was still needed, and Fraser wrote Perkins' assistant that he thought, under the circumstances, that the I. L. A. should lend him the amount. "Without mills and other places of business," he reasoned, "the real estate owned by them would be worth much less." [95] The argument was convincing, and the loan arranged.[96] By 1870, more than $30,000 was invested by the Association, most of it in town lots and farm lands.[97]

Although the Russell Associates and the Iowa Land Association were apparently the most active enterprises dealing in real estate along the route of the B. & M., they were not the only ones in which some of the individual railroaders participated. In November, 1868, for example, D. N. Smith at Chariton forwarded to Perkins deeds representing transactions of $10,598 for a B[urlington?] Land Association and of $9,176.90 on account of E. W. Emerson, trustee.[98] It is possible that these operations were connected with the I. L. A., but they may have been independent. Whatever their technical status, their function was identical: to earn returns upon funds invested and to build up a permanent community along the line of the railroad. Meanwhile, the land department of the B. & M. was slowly crystallizing its own program.

[92] ILA, Memorandum by A. N. Fraser, 1869 (LDP).
[93] ILA, Receipt for Lot #110, Frederic, November 23, 1869 (LDP).
[94] ILA, Fraser to Irving, September 28, 1869 (LDP).
[95] ILA, Fraser to Irving, September 2, 1869 (LDP).
[96] ILA, Fraser to Perkins, September 4, 1869 (LDP).
[97] ILA, Trial Balance, January 31, 1870 (LDP).
[98] Smith to Perkins, November 16, 1868 (LDP); cf. Perkins, Memorandum, July 17, 1868; also cf. Beymer to Perkins, November 24, 1868 (LDP).

CHAPTER X

Colonel Ames Sells Ten Thousand Acres, 1866–1869

THE welcome arrival of peace in the spring of 1865 had marked the beginning of a new era in the United States.[1] The foreign immigration that had reached a new peak just before the conflict revived almost immediately to its former level and, so far as the West was concerned, was augmented by thousands of former soldiers and eastern farmers who turned for a livelihood to the vast region beyond the Mississippi. This internal migration was encouraged by the Homestead Act, passed during the war, which offered 160 acres of the public domain free to every single person or head of a family who would settle upon and improve his tract over a period of five years. A rapidly growing transportation system, backed by the capital of the North, speeded the westward movement, and improved agricultural machinery facilitated cultivation of the raw but fertile prairies.[2] Western Iowa and eastern Nebraska, with their vast tracts of fertile, unoccupied lands, were in a peculiarly advantageous position to benefit by these circumstances, for they lay directly at the end of the westernmost railway lines and across the path of migration to the Pacific.

I. IOWA

During the three years from the fall of 1866 through the fall of 1869, Colonel Ames presided over the land department, and to the best of his ability prepared for the moment when the company's lands would be placed on general sale. With the annoying swampland and preëmption cases apparently out of the way, the new agent thought he could see a clear track ahead by the end of 1866. The partial reëxamination and sale of lands in 1863–66 provided some clue as to a proper price level and selling technique.[3] Meanwhile, the extension of the track steadily westward automatically enhanced the value of adjacent railroad lands. Late in January, 1867, Ames was reporting

[1] Faulkner, *op. cit.*, pp. 371 *et seq.*
[2] Paxson, *op. cit.*, pp. 505 *et seq.*
[3] See above, p. 195.

enthusiastically to Denison that he was busy arranging the lands in classes according to their intrinsic value as reported by the examiners. After that he proposed to prepare schedules of prices, terms, "and then, upon approval by the Company, shall be ready to begin sales. All of which I hope may be accomplished early in the coming spring. . . ." [4]

Ames, however, was doomed to disappointment. When he wrote, the railhead was still in Monroe County, 75 miles away from the Council Bluffs district which contained the company's most valuable lands.[5] Consequently, no authorization was forthcoming from the board of directors to begin sales, and Ames had the thankless task of turning away eager applicants and discouraging would-be squatters. To individual settlers he wrote that filing an application to buy carried no right of occupancy, and that farmers wishing to acquire land immediately should purchase from private parties.[6] This warning was repeated to local land-selling agencies, and the injunction added that such agencies must make it plain that the B. & M. charged no fees for answering inquiries; the right of examination and inquiry must remain free for all.[7] In spite of the increasing pressure to sell, the company likewise reiterated its determination not to throw the bulk of its grant on the market:

> We do not wish to offer the lands in the Council Bluffs District for sale [wrote Ames] until we can advertize largely and bring in settlement from outside the state, and we cannot do this until we can offer to land purchasers transportation to neighborhood of the lands. We feel pretty confident that we can induce an emigration — judging from experience of other Land Grant roads — that will authorize higher rates on lands in our counties, both ours and all others, than are now the rule. . . .[8]

Meanwhile, he began working out in his own mind a pricing and credit policy for use when the grant should finally be put on the market.

The experience of the older roads as well as the B. & M.'s earliest practice afforded ample and readily available precedents for this

[4] Ames to Denison, January 31, 1867 (LDP).

[5] See map, p. 242.

[6] Ames to Ritchey, May 25, 1867 (LDP); Ames to Handayside, July 1, 1867 (LDP).

[7] Ames to Ritchey, May 25, 1867 (LDP); Ames to Hale & Stone, December 21, 1867 (LDP).   [8] *Ibid.*

undertaking. Both the Hannibal and St. Joseph and the Illinois Central had worked out long-time credit schemes which had enabled them to attract *bona fide* settlers.[9] Furthermore, Perkins had already hinted that the B. & M. would offer an installment plan;[10] the question before Ames was simply at what level prices could be fixed and how liberally credit should be offered. His first ideas appeared in response to an inquiry from a resident of Mills County. It was doubtful, he wrote, whether any land would be sold as low as $2.50 an acre; prices would be fixed with reference to the enhanced value of the land resulting from the construction of the road. A term of years — five or more — would be given in which to make payments at a fair rate of interest. Relatively high prices, he pointed out, would discourage speculators, but work no hardship on real settlers, for the generous time allowance would permit payment out of proceeds from crops. "Of course," he concluded, "it is a vital point with the Company to secure actual settlement, with regard to the future interest of the road."[11]

During 1867 these vague ideas took more definite form. Ames was kept busy answering numerous requests from would-be purchasers, and as his correspondence continued, various details became crystallized. Eventually, he favored a plan of payment over a period of ten years,[12] in equal installments, with interest at seven per cent.[13] He contemplated prices that would range from $2.50 to $3 an acre on the rougher and more remote tracts to $10 an acre "for best farm lands within 4 or 5 miles of a station or county seat."[14] Presumably, the price would be even higher at the center of settlements.[15]

We raise the price [explained Ames] to ensure sale to actual settlers, our object being to settle the country and create RR business, rather than to raise money at once by low sales [i.e., low prices], which would tempt mere speculators to buy for a rise, thus excluding settlement. . . .[16]

[9] For the Illinois Central, see Gates, *op. cit.*, pp. 254–279; for the Hannibal and St. Joseph, see their pamphlet of 1859 and *Annual Reports* for 1861, 1864, 1871.   [10] Memorandum by Perkins, August 12, 1862 (LDP).
[11] This letter was actually written by J. M. King during Ames' temporary absence, King to Hale (of Glenwood), December 29, 1866 (LDP).
[12] Ames to Usher, March 6, 1867 (LDP); Ames to Kempton, July 12, 1867 (LDP).
[13] *Ibid.* Also Ames to Handayside, July 1, 1867 (LDP).
[14] Ames to Howard, August 15, 1867 (LDP).
[15] Ames to Usher, March 6, 1867 (LDP).
[16] Ames to Kempton, July 12, 1867 (LDP).

In other words, as Lowell had said, the Burlington was a railroad, not a land company.

As 1868 opened, the progress of the road across Iowa still did not warrant a general sale,[17] although there were numerous scattered tracts along the fringes of the grant in the old Chariton land district that Ames decided to sell.[18] The road had already been built past them, and they had presumably attained their full value as unimproved tracts. Furthermore, their sale would test out the newly formulated pricing policy and bring a certain amount of ready cash into the treasury. In the latter part of January, therefore, Ames notified 20 individual applicants that he would sell them the parcels they wished to buy, either on credit for 10 years at 7 per cent interest, or for cash at a 20 per cent discount.[19] Discouragingly enough, only three of these particular farmers responded, and all of them purchased for cash.[20] Meanwhile, although he continued to deal with individuals, Ames turned to various land agencies in the eastern counties. To Miller, Fee & Vermillion, for example, at Centerville in Appanoose County, he wrote on February 1, 1868, offering the same plans of sale and adding a third scheme whereby the purchaser could buy at the cash price by paying one-third of the principal down, and the rest in equal parts in the next two years with interest at ten per cent. The agents were offered one per cent of the gross amount of a long-term sale, and three per cent of the principal on cash or two-year sales.[21] This system, as worked out by Ames, appeared as shown on page 241. The arrangement was strictly experimental; Ames wrote that he would be willing to make whatever changes seemed wise. He also made it clear that the lands were not to be advertised as belonging to the company, as he did not consider it honorable or fair to attract immigration until the main body of B. & M. lands was on sale, nor, he added, did he want to make other counties jealous. Ten days later, the agency for Keokuk County was offered to S. A. James of Sigourney on the same basis,[22] and Ames undertook to explain the low commis-

[17] The line was approaching Osceola. (CBQ, *Corporate History*, opposite p. 129.)   [18] Ames to Take (of Chicago, Illinois), January 9, 1868 (LDP).
[19] Ames to various applicants, January 21–24, 1868 (LDP).
[20] BMI, Sales Book "A" (LDP).
[21] Ames to Miller, Fee & Vermillion, February 1, 1868 (LDP).
[22] Ames to James, February 10, 1868 (LDP). The firm name was McCoy & James.

sion rates by pointing out that agents would certainly profit in the
future by the Burlington's "national" advertising. As to prices he was

---

PLANS OF SALE FOR B. & M. LANDS IN APPANOOSE COUNTY [23]

Example of sale of a forty-acre tract at $10.00 per acre on ten years' time —
at 7 per cent interest. At date of purchase a year's interest
only to be paid to bind the contract, — the payments
will fall due with interest as follows:

		Interest	Amount
Feb. 1, 1868 — (Date of Purchase) — 7 int. on $400		$28.00	$28.00
" 1869 — 1st. payment of $40 — 7 int. on balance		25.20	65.20
Feb. 1, 1870 — 2nd. payment of $40 — 7 int. on balance		22.40	62.40
" 1871 — 3rd. " 40 — "		19.60	59.60
" 1872 — 4th. " 40 — "		16.80	56.80
" 1873 — 5th. " 40 — "		14.00	54.00
" 1874 — 6th. " 40 — "		11.20	51.20
" 1875 — 7th. " 40 — "		8.40	48.40
" 1876 — 8th. " 40 — "		5.60	45.60
" 1877 — 9th. " 40 — "		2.80	42.80
" 1878 — 10th. " 40 — "		—	40.00

Principal $400   Interest $154.00 $554.00

For same land, deduct 20 per cent for cash, making cash price $8.00 per
acre, — or will sell on cash terms and 10 per cent
interest on two years time:

		Interest	Amount
Feb. 1, 1868 1/3 of principal in cash	$106.67	—	$106.67
Feb. 1, 1869 " " "	106.67	$21.34	128.01
Feb. 1, 1870 " " "	106.66	10.66	117.32

Principal $320.00 $32.00 $352.00

Agent's fees on ten-year sale, 1 per cent of gross amount to be
paid on date of contract $5.54
Agent's fees on cash sale, 3 per cent of sales 9.60
Agent's fees on two-year sale, 3 per cent of principal 9.60

---

candid about his ignorance: "I cannot judge of the prices very well
not being familiar with your selling rates [for similar land]. . . .
Please let me know if you think [those offered are] too high. . . ." [24]
Within a fortnight, Ames was already altering the arrangements

[23] Memorandum by Ames included in letter to Miller, Fee & Vermillion, February 1, 1868 (LDP).   [24] Ames to James, February 17, 1868 (LDP).

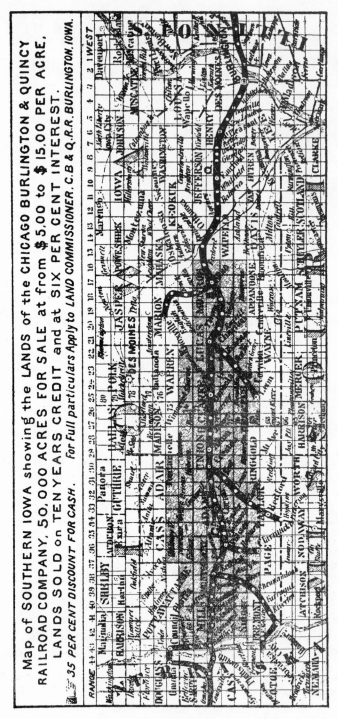

Map of SOUTHERN IOWA showing the LANDS of the CHICAGO BURLINGTON & QUINCY RAILROAD COMPANY, 50,000 ACRES FOR SALE at from $5.00 to $15.00 PER ACRE. LANDS SOLD on TEN YEARS CREDIT and at SIX PER CENT INTEREST. For full particulars Apply to LAND COMMISSIONER. C.B & Q. R.R. BURLINGTON. IOWA. 35 PER CENT DISCOUNT FOR CASH.

AREA IN SOUTHWESTERN IOWA (SHADED) WITHIN WHICH MOST OF THE B. & M. LANDS IN THAT STATE WERE LOCATED.

with Miller, Fee & Vermillion. He was uncertain about the prices he had suggested for the plots in question, and suggested that the disappearance of timber might have altered their value. Also, he agreed to allow a three-year payment plan, similar to the two-year scheme except that the payment of one-third principal was at the end rather than the beginning of the first year.[25] By the end of March, there had been no sales in Appanoose County and only five scattered ones elsewhere;[26] Ames wrote his agents again. He suggested that since the ten-year credit prices were high and nobody seemed interested in them, it might be well to restrict sales to a cash or three-year basis; this would at once lower prices 20 per cent. Furthermore, in view of the fact that the company was doing no advertising, he was willing to offer a five per cent selling commission. Prices, he admitted, were based on examinations of 1859–60, and therefore he urged his correspondents to use their judgment in altering them, although he wished to be asked about any reductions.[27] Meanwhile, having heard from McCoy & James that the company's lands in Keokuk County were among the worst there,[28] he authorized them to slash $7 rates to $5, and $4 prices to $3.[29] A few weeks later the firm of Trimble & Carruthers was offered the agency for Davis County. Ames fixed the prices on each tract in the county but asked to be informed if they proved either too high or too low. In the former case, he offered to pay the agents 50 per cent of the added amount, but he enjoined them not to let purchasers understand that the rates were variable nor, on the other hand, to drive away actual settlers.[30] In December he instructed James in Keokuk County to cut prices once more, as much as 50 per cent with a minimum of $2.50,[31] and in June of the next year he gave Hartman, the agent for Warren County, authority to raise prices at his discretion and to lower them to 20 per cent of the original figure, with a $4 minimum, if he thought it wise.[32]

[25] Ames to Miller, Fee & Vermillion, February 20, 1868 (LDP). This letter crossed one from the agents suggesting that the company's prices were too low. (Miller, Fee & Vermillion to Ames, February 20, 1868, LDP.)
[26] BMI, Sales Book "A" (LDP).
[27] Ames to Miller, Fee & Vermillion, April 16, 1868 (LDP).
[28] McCoy & James to Ames, February 22, 1868 (LDP).
[29] Ames to James, February 26, 1868 (LDP).
[30] Ames to Trimble & Carruthers, April 24, 1868 (LDP).
[31] Ames to McCoy & James, December 23, 1868 (LDP).
[32] Ames to Hartman, June 8, 1869 (LDP).

Meanwhile Ames himself dealt directly with countless individual applicants.[33] Those who applied for land west of Union County or for the lands granted in 1864 were, of course, turned away, the former because of the company's decision to wait until its line was completed in the Council Bluffs district,[34] and the latter because certification of the second grant had not yet arrived from Washington.[35] Whenever the plots applied for were salable, however, Ames would laboriously outline his plans of credit and arrange a price to suit the individual circumstance. Frequently a deal was consummated; occasionally the applicant was stubborn, such as a Mr. Ruch who offered $150 cash for a 40-acre tract. The local agent, acting under instruction, informed him that this was below Ames' minimum, and the would-be buyer replied "he would be d—d if he would pay a cent more & would only pay that to keep some d—d fool from getting it." [36] This time Ames stuck to his guns. "We will not consent," he informed the agent. "He can go without it as he seems so willing to." [37] Six months later another farmer bought the tract for $224.[38] On the whole, prices were fixed differently for each individual plot.[39]

There was obviously little system about Ames' policy. He was, to be sure, handicapped by the fact that the lands he was selling were scattered in communities where realty values differed because of local conditions unknown to him. Furthermore, the 1859–60 appraisals were least useful where settlement had progressed fastest since those years. Yet he apparently made no attempt to classify and inspect the tracts he sold, or to work out a uniform plan of payment. Even the notes which were received under the two- and three-year plans were printed for five years, adding to the existing confusion.[40] During 1868 the company disposed of only 1,352.78 acres in 30 transactions, the plots averaging slightly over 45 acres each. Book receipts amounted to

[33] BMI, Letter Books No. 4 and No. 5 (LDP), passim.
[34] E.g., Ames to White, December 5, 1868 (LDP).
[35] Ames to Steiger, October 22, 1867 (LDP).
[36] McClanahan to Ames, September 12, 1868 (LDP).
[37] Ames to McClanahan, September 16, 1868 (LDP).
[38] BMI, Sales Book "A" (LDP).
[39] E.g., Ames to Hogeland, February 5, 1868 (LDP). Ames turned down Hogeland's first offer of $5 per acre on long credit or $4 cash, but accepted $4.25 in three annual installments. (BMI, Sales Book "A," LDP, Sale No. 70.)
[40] Ames to Miller, Fee & Vermillion, February 20, 1868 (LDP), and April 16, 1868 (LDP).

$6,984.92, but only a fifth of this was in actual cash. The average price paid was $5.16 an acre,[41] considerably more than the government price, but far below what Ames had hoped to secure.

Meanwhile, many of the old and several new problems arose before the department. Individuals and agents alike had to be warned against allowing settlement without purchase on company land.[42]

> Squatters have come to Iowa [wrote Ames] with ideas of fabulous cheapness of land, and I do not want any to settle on our lands if our prices, when revealed, are going to spread dissatisfaction & ill feeling. We expect to get something above the present average of land values and prefer to hold them untouched till ready to sell. . . .[43]

Timber depredations in the same vicinity had always been troublesome [44] and were now becoming acute. In November, 1868, Ames had urged King to put men in the field immediately to report and prosecute thieves on a systematic basis; [45] a month later he reported that King was about to "start a force of cavalry to guard the premises." By dint of much time and labor, the company succeeded in apprehending numerous culprits,[46] but at best it was ticklish business, for the sensibilities of the inhabitants, particularly in the western part of the grant, were easily irritated.[47]

At the same time, the uncertainty of the status of railroad lands as to taxes made it obvious that some permanent basis should be worked out.[48] In January, 1867, Steiger requested Ames for a complete summary of the practice of each county and the status of lands therein. Ames was apparently somewhat flabbergasted by the request; it would, he said, take an examiner a very long time to examine the records of each county and involve considerable expense.[49] For the moment, Steiger let the matter drop, and a few months later James

[41] BMI, Sales Book "A" (LDP).

[42] Ames to Wilson, May 9, 1868 (LDP); Ames to Simon & Breson, June 1, 1868 (LDP).

[43] Ames to White, December 5, 1868 (LDP).

[44] E.g., Smith to Read, January 16, 1868 (LDP); Knight to Lowell, February 12, 1860 (LDP).

[45] Ames to King, November 28, 1868 (LDP).

[46] Ames to White, December 5, 1868 (LDP).

[47] E.g., King to Ames, March 15, 1868 (LDP). King was expecting a "warm time" with certain known timber thieves.

[48] See above, pp. 212–213.

[49] Ames to Steiger, January 11, 1867 (LDP).

F. Joy wrote the various western counties asking them to follow their own interests, as well as the railroad's, by striking the railroad lands off their lists.[50] At the same time, the company started a test suit in Madison County, where the lands held were few, and where an unfavorable decision would not entail a serious loss.[51]

Fremont County responded to Joy's overtures by flatly refusing to strike railroad lands from the tax lists.[52] Thereupon, Ames wrote to Steiger to find out whether the company could press its point that until final certification, title rested with the United States. He was anxious that the county supervisors should realize that title had not yet been certified to the railroad and was conditionally retained by the United States until the company should fulfill its part of the compact.[53] The Supreme Court of Iowa blasted Ames' plans in this respect. The railroad, it decided, became liable for taxes on adjacent lands when each 20-mile stretch of track was completed; subsequent United States certification was simply evidence of title already existing.[54] By November, 1867, Ames could give Steiger a fairly accurate if unfavorable picture of the company's position:

> In tax matters just now we are depending more upon the good will of the Counties than upon legal weight. They see that to tax our lands impedes value of our land bonds, upon which we largely depend for building road. They want the road more than the taxes. This, of course, is not the case with all, but with several of the more important. . . .[55]

During 1868 many of the counties reached a decision as to their position. Monroe County near the eastern end of the grant,[56] Decatur in the center,[57] and Montgomery at the west[58] struck railroad lands from their lists. Mills made a compromise, rescinding back taxes, and offering to grant two more years of exemption if the tracks were

---

[50] Ames to Beymer, August 2, 1867 (LDP).

[51] The injunction preventing Madison County from selling railroad lands for delinquent taxes was reported in the *Burlington Daily Hawk-Eye* for September 4, 1867. Ames sent it to King the next day. (LDP.)

[52] Ames to Stockton, October 22, 1867 (LDP).

[53] Ames to Steiger, October 22, 1867 (LDP).

[54] Ames to King, October 28, 1867 (LDP).

[55] Ames to Steiger, November 29, 1867 (LDP).

[56] Ames to Perry & Townshend, October 1, 1868 (LDP).

[57] Ames to J. W. Penny, January 13, 1868 (LDP).

[58] Ames to Wayne Sterrett, September 25, 1868 (LDP).

located through Glenwood, the county seat.[59] This offer was part of the delayed swampland settlement; the railroad accepted it with alacrity.[60] Madison County refused to remit taxes but allowed delinquents to settle for the full amount plus 20 per cent.[61] Adams County was adamant. The company had diverted its track from the county seat of Quincy and, as Ames wrote, the railroad was consequently "not in very good repute there." [62] As the year closed, other counties were still to be heard from.

Meanwhile, the question of state resumption of the railroad land grants again came to the fore in Des Moines. In his message to the legislature in January, 1868, Governor Stone advocated a moderate policy. Admitting that some of the roads had failed "even substantially" to comply with the conditions of their grants, he nevertheless reached the conclusion that

in view of the many difficulties which have confronted their efforts heretofore, and the assurances now given of a vigorous prosecution of the respective enterprises, we shall, in my judgment, be fully justified in the exercise of still further leniency toward them. It is the part of wisdom to encourage . . . by liberal measures the prosecution of these needed enterprises. . . . Any system of legislation therefore tending to their discouragement should be avoided unless clearly demanded by considerations promotive of the public good. . . .[63]

Upon this last point, there was considerable difference of opinion among his listeners. A special correspondent of the *Chicago Tribune* assigned to cover the situation at Des Moines reported "a sort of undefined hostility to the railroads generally on the part of the body politic." He was convinced that one ground of this feeling arose from "the jealousy of corporate power created by the great land grants in favor of these corporations." [64] If the four roads that had been given grants in 1856 had completed their lines, he pointed out, some 1,300 miles would have been built; actually, they had then laid something less than 800 miles of track. Thus, he observed, "some considerable amount of hostility is to be palliated, if not excused. If the people

[59] Ames to King, September 21, 1868 (LDP).
[60] See above, p. 205.
[61] Ames to King, October 7, 1868 (LDP).
[62] Ames to King, September 21, 1868 (LDP).
[63] *Daily Gazette & Argus* (Burlington), January 15, 1868.
[64] *Chicago Tribune*, January 28, 1868.

'have their mad up,' it must be confessed it is not altogether without reason." The situation, he continued, was being canvassed "very freely and fully" by members of the legislature, although in the case of several railroads, including the B. & M., the failure to complete construction on the date originally set was excused "by not a few who have given the subject the most careful attention." [65]

Clearly there were too many conflicting opinions to warrant a general act of resumption applicable to all roads. The determining consideration in each individual case seemed to be whether or not the line was actually being built, and in this respect the B. & M. found itself in an increasingly favorable position. In March, 1868, for example, a citizen of Montgomery County wrote that engineers were busy preparing the way for contractors from Afton to the Missouri River. Consequently, he felt that "those who seek to take away their grants, or *resume*, are not with us, . . . [but are] against one of the greatest and honestly prosecuted works of Iowa." [66] The writer, however, claimed to speak only for the B. & M., and admitted he knew nothing about railroad grants in other parts of the state. Once again it was obvious that the best insurance for the Burlington's lands and its future colonization work lay in its ability to complete its line.

Although 1869 opened full of promise for the Burlington and Missouri River Railroad as a whole,[67] the year merely brought to the land department important and sometimes vexing problems. In March a letter arrived from Herman Roos of Chicago, agent of the then potent Inman Line and editor of the *Svenska Amerikanaren*, which claimed to be the only political Swedish paper in the United States. Roos himself had lived in Page County, Iowa, for 16 years, and he now offered to direct both Swedish and German immigrants to the Burlington's lands if a satisfactory commission arrangement could be made.[68] Ames' reply was vague. After explaining that sales were authorized only so far as the line was actually built, he mentioned that at the very moment the Swedish Lutheran pastor at Burlington, the Reverend Mr. Halland, was on the spot looking over Page and Montgomery counties, although Ames presumed "his scheme would be in

[65] *Chicago Tribune*, January 28, 1868.
[66] *Daily Gazette & Argus*, March 17, 1868.
[67] See above, p. 224.   [68] Roos to Perkins, March 24, 1869 (LDP).

harmony with your own object." [69] As a matter of fact, Halland selected the unapplied-for tracts in four townships in those counties, and Ames agreed to reserve them for a year from April, 1869.[70] Nevertheless, Roos sent his traveling agent, one Soderberg, to southern Iowa and upon his return made a definite offer to Ames. Would the B. & M. give Roos the agency to sell to Scandinavians, paying him 2 per cent on long-term contracts, and $3\frac{1}{2}$ per cent on cash and short-term sales? Would the company allow settlement, under written contract, prior to placing the lands on sale, and would they pay for Scandinavian advertisements and circulars? Finally, could Roos, who was not Lutheran, promote settlement in the four townships selected by Mr. Halland "without consideration to religious opinions"? Roos explained the inclusion of the last point by enclosing a copy of the Scandinavian Lutheran newspaper wherein Halland declared that "no person, devoted to vices or belonging to other religious denominations will, under any circumstances, be received on the selected lands. . . ." [71] Here was a new problem to be met, and its urgency was apparent three days later when L. D. McGlashon of Red Oak reported that a certain Wiklund who had made inquiries about purchasing tracts in the Scandinavian townships had been referred to Halland. McGlashon was extremely skeptical of the results because Wiklund, he said, represented Baptists and Methodists,[72] and would therefore probably receive a chilly reception from the Lutheran pastor. Clearly, it was up to the land department to make its position known in the matter of sectarian discrimination; for the moment, questions of terms and commissions were of secondary importance.

In answering McGlashon, Ames assured him that Wiklund need not be alarmed about the religious aspect of Halland's settlement, — "there is room eno' for all — the B. & M. do not propose to favor one sect more than the rest. . . ." [73] To Roos, Ames was even more emphatic. He assured him that although Halland might be agent, the company was the owner of the lands "and will admit no sectarian qualifications as necessary in any purchasers. I mean to have such

[69] Ames to Roos, March 29, 1869 (LDP).

[70] Ames to Hospers, April 17, 1869 (LDP). George Harris later honored this agreement. See below, p. 306.

[71] Roos to Ames, April 26, 1869 (LDP).

[72] McGlashon to Ames, April 29, 1869 (LDP).

[73] Ames to McGlashon, May 4, 1869 (LDP).

lands open to all Swedish emigrants without limitation."[74] Thus, once and for all, was the religious issue settled. From time to time, colonies organized by different sects were located on company land, but there is no evidence that any prospective purchaser was ever turned down either by the company or by its agents on account of his beliefs.

As Ames was enunciating this obviously sound policy, his efforts to attract purchasers received a vigorous boost from another department of the company. From the very beginning of its existence, the Burlington and Missouri River Railroad had realized that its success in a new country would be predicated upon the number of people that could be induced to settle in its own territory, whether or not they happened to purchase railroad land. Unlike the eastern railroads, the B. & M. followed no long-established channel of trade, nor did it connect populous manufacturing centers. Consequently, it had to create as well as to nourish the community it served. In this respect, the position of the railroad was identical with that of the state; as a matter of pride and business, the officials at Iowa City and, later, Des Moines continually looked forward to a rapid increase in population.[75] Yet little had ever been done in an organized fashion by either the state or the land department of the B. & M. to induce the necessary immigration. There were, of course, reasons in each case. The one formal attempt of the state in 1860–61 had failed through no particular fault of its own, and since that time the activities of the American Emigrant Agency had doubtless dulled the official sense of responsibility in the matter.[76] At any rate, when the Citizen's National Association of New York City, interested in westward colonization, wrote Governor Merrill late in 1868 requesting circulars and a contact with the State Board of Emigration, the Governor had to reply that no literature or board existed. His own eloquent letter, however, drew a vivid picture of the state at the time.[77]

---

[74] Ames to Roos, July 9, 1869 (LDP). Unfortunately there is no record of what Ames said to Halland, since the latter lived in Burlington and was doubtless visited personally.

[75] E.g., Iowa Register of the State Land Office, *Annual Report* for 1861 and 1863 (Des Moines, 1861, 1863).

[76] See above, p. 210.

[77] Samuel Merrill to Peter Cooper, November 28, 1868, in *Annals of Iowa*, vol. VII, no. 1, pp. 98–104.

The silence of the railroad was based on different considerations. Both Lowell and Perkins had made extended inquiries with a view towards publishing a pamphlet similar to the Illinois Central's or the Hannibal and St. Joseph's, but first the war and then the decision to postpone a general sales campaign had stopped further action. The latter consideration still held good in the spring of 1869 and placed Ames in an uncomfortable position. He was certainly anxious to sell lands in the eastern part of the grant, but he was averse to launching a drive that would apply to only a small part of the grant and would have to be completely revised as soon as the rest of the lands were put on sale. Furthermore, he feared that if it were generally known that the company was selling its tracts, he would be deluged with correspondence and accused of partiality for selling in one sector and not in another.[78] The Burlington's passenger and freight agents, however, suffered from no such handicaps or inhibitions. They needed shippers and travelers year in and year out and were not particular whose land such customers might purchase. Thus, since both state and land department officials were inactive, it was logical that A. E. Touzalin, General Ticket Agent at Burlington, should sponsor the company's first large-scale advertising.

The Southern Iowa Land and Railroad Gazette appeared at Burlington in April, 1869, and in its first column contained a statement of purpose that was both logical and disarmingly candid:

The great and numerous advantages offered by Southern Iowa to eastern settlers of every kind and degree are but little known beyond the borders of our own State. The State, herself, uses but poor and slight, if indeed any means, to call attention to her vast resources, and thus attract people to her thriving cities and towns, and her fertile plains. It therefore behooves those who are greatly interested in her advancement to bestir themselves.

There is certainly no individual, or corporation of individuals, more directly and deeply interested in the welfare, and advancement of Southern Iowa, than is the Burlington and Missouri River Railroad Company. *They are aware that that which conduces to the benefit of the State, will necessarily redound to their own especial advantage.* They believe that the great advantages of Southern Iowa, have only to be fairly and fully understood to be eagerly grasped by thousands desirous of finding homes in the West. They have therefore formed a combination with the land interest of this portion of the State, and will hereafter publish this bi-monthly journal,

[78] Ames to Miller, Fee & Vermillion, February 1, 1868 (LDP).

which will endeavor to give correct views of all subjects connected with the general interests of this portion of the State. . . .[79]

Such a statement left little to the imagination. No one could deny the B. & M.'s obvious stake in the welfare of southern Iowa, and the company's confession of faith in the region's future sounded plausible and sincere. Furthermore, two phrases were particularly noteworthy. The first was the company's frank avowal of its profit motive; the second was the unashamed announcement that the "interests" had formed a "combination" to exploit their favored region.

At the top of its front page, the *Gazette* featured a map showing the region from Toledo to Omaha and indicating in detail the four southern tiers of Iowa counties. Principal railroad lines were accurately enough drawn — including the rival Rock Island — but, comprehensibly enough, only the Council Bluffs district lands of the B. & M. were shaded. The ten columns of text and six of advertising not only revealed the source of the *Gazette's* inspiration but provided a clue to the type of immigrants desired by the "interests" of southern Iowa. From the point of view of propaganda technique, the make-up of the paper was cleverly arranged to lead the reader's attention from the general aspects of Iowa to the particular features in the B. & M. region that would appeal to the desired client. The first page illustrated this procedure; directly under the map was an introductory article on Iowa, followed by a more detailed description of southern Iowa. Next came an account of the common school system of the state and finally a summary of the livestock industry. These last two articles were probably for the benefit of people in New York and New England. The former itemized every detail of the permanent school fund of over $4,000,000 and indicated an expenditure of nearly half that amount during 1867 alone. The latter, in the form of a letter from ex-Congressman Grinnell, very significantly compared the state's livestock conditions to those in New England, New York, Indiana, Illinois, Michigan, and Wisconsin. Immigrants were invited to settle in southern Iowa "near school[s], churches and railways." It would seem that this appeal was directed to the book-loving, God-fearing, and thrifty folk of the rural North. The rest of the *Gazette's*

[79] Original copy, addressed to Dr. L. J. Williams, 1 Mt. Vernon Street, Boston, Massachusetts (HBS). So far as has been ascertained, only this first number was ever issued. (Italics supplied.)

text included short notes on eight Iowa counties, either directly on the company's line or containing some railroad land,[80] a long article on the B. & M.'s history and progress,[81] and a statistical summary of livestock shipments over Iowa roads showing the Burlington as the principal carrier in proportion to its mileage.[82]

Four of the six columns of advertising were filled with 24 notices from as many land agents in different counties; every county through which the B. & M. ran was represented, and all the rest save Polk were adjacent to the line. Of the firms listed, just a third had some indirect connection with the company. Four of them were or became the exclusive land-selling agents in their region,[83] three were in charge of obtaining the rights of way,[84] and one was handling legal work for the road.[85] But all of them, if successful as land agents, would bring potential shippers and travelers within the Burlington's reach. The two remaining columns of advertising were devoted exclusively to the road. The first exhibited a woodcut of the "Magnificent Iron Railroad Bridge" just finished over the Mississippi and proclaimed that three daily trains left Chicago for Burlington without change. There passengers could make close connections for B. & M. points as far west as Afton, whence they could proceed by the Western Stage

[80] The counties described were Adams, Clarke, Jefferson, and Mills on the main line; Cass, Taylor, and Ringgold with company lands, and Polk, included because of the state capital.

[81] The article outlined the formation and construction of the road, and promised completion to Omaha by December, 1869; it likewise exhibited receipts from freight and passengers through 1868, showing an increase for every year.

[82] The figures were based on the report of Iowa railroads to the secretary of the State Agricultural Society in 1868; they referred to the Northwestern, the Rock Island, and the B. & M.

[83] The four agents were: Ith. S. Beall of Ringgold County, who applied for an agency about the time the *Gazette* was issued and opened an active one when the lands in his county were put on sale (Ames to Beall, April 7, 1869, LDP); B. F. Elbert of Monroe County (Ames to Elbert, October 30, 1868, LDP); E. W. Hartman of Warren County, who applied on April 16, 1869, to Touzalin for an agency, and later completed negotiations with Ames (Ames to Hartman, May 3, 1869, LDP); E. F. Riley of Clarke County (Ames to Riley, August 1, 1868, LDP).

[84] These were: John Bixby of Adams County (Ames to Bixby, September 14, 1868, LDP); J. B. Packard of Montgomery County (Ames to Packard, August 21, 1868, LDP); J. D. Wright of Lucas County (Ames to Wright, June 2, 1869, LDP).

[85] H. A. Copeland of Mills County (Perkins to Copeland, February 11, 1869, LDP).

Company to Council Bluffs and Omaha. The final column was devoted to the Burlington's land grant.

It was obviously necessary to tread warily in booming lands that were not yet on sale, and the column over Ames' signature was a masterpiece of restraint. The Burlington, he explained, had received 375,000 acres of land, of which 300,000 were in the eight southwestern counties of Adams, Montgomery, Mills, Cass, Pottawattamie, Taylor, Page, and Fremont on the "Missouri Slope." In boldface type it was emphasized that this region was less injured by drought or heat than any "similar" lands in Illinois or Iowa, "and also less injured by the occurrence of Flood, High Water, and long Rainy Seasons." After describing the need for population in the region, the article explained that "on the opening of the line to traffic" these 300,000 acres would be offered for sale to "actual" settlers only, on the "long credit principle" giving ten years for payment so that installments could be met out of each year's current receipts from crops. No further details were given as to the plan of payment or interest. The final paragraphs frankly stated the land department's situation:

> Though these lands are not yet for sale, it is deemed important to call attention to them at once, that all proposing to visit Iowa during the coming season with a view to choice of place of future settlement, can have plenty of time to make selections. Circulars and descriptive catalogues, maps, &c, &c, will ultimately be issued, and may then be had, with any further information desired, of J. W. Ames, Land Agent, Burlington, Iowa.

The effect of this forthright publication, distributed to approximately 15,000 persons, was prompt and gratifying. The local agent of Hartford's Phoenix Insurance Company wrote that in looking over the *Gazette* he was "reminded that everything is moving and soon your RR lands will be in market. . . ."[86] More significant were inquiries from prospective heads of colonies. One of the most important came from the Hollanders of the Pella Settlement in Marion County, just east of Des Moines. These people were precisely the type the railroad wished to attract. They had come to Iowa in a body in 1847, and by their orderly and industrious habits had prospered and won the respect of their neighbors.[87] During the optimistic days of the Des Moines

[86] R. W. Crampton to Ames, April 26, 1869 (LDP).
[87] Cyrenus Cole, *op. cit.*, pp. 228–230; cf. Gue, *op. cit.*, vol. III, p. 384.

River project they had even founded a "port" on the projected water thoroughfare only to have their hopes crushed when the enterprise failed.[88] Since then the gradual rise of surrounding realty values had made it progressively harder for them to expand, and they were now looking about for more space at a price within their range.[89] Within a fortnight of the *Gazette's* publication, two of their leading citizens wrote the company for additional information on railroad lands.[90] Could they obtain 50,000 to 70,000 acres? Who owned the non-railroad sections? What was the quality of the land and how much timber was left? On what basis would the company sell? [91]

Ames replied that the company had several contiguous townships in Montgomery, Adams, Page, and Fremont counties where the B. & M. owned about half the land. The soil was excellent, he said, sufficiently timbered for the present population and with indications of coal although no shafts had been sunk. Conditions of purchase were that actual settlement should take place, only necessary timber could be cut before full payment was made, and the purchase price would be from $7 to $12 an acre, payable over ten years at 7 per cent interest. Ames explained that no sale could be made until the line was built and that there were already some 900 applications for this land filed in Burlington, but, he averred hopefully, probably half of these would not materialize into regular offers when the time came to sell. "Allow me to add," he concluded graciously, "that we appreciate the industry

[88] In 1846 Congress had granted Iowa alternate sections of public lands for five miles on either side of part of the Des Moines River. The purpose was to improve the river for navigation. Although the state spent considerable money on the project, it never reached completion. (Cyrenus Cole, *op. cit.*, ch. xxxvi.)

[89] N. J. Gesman (of the *Weekly Pella Blade*) to Ames, April 17, 1869 (LDP). Gesman attributed the rapid development of Jasper County chiefly to the "steady industry and frugal habits" of the Hollanders; he referred to them as "emphatically a people suited to bring out the resources of a country and to build up a prosperity not transient but enduring." Recently, however, further immigration from Holland, the influx of Americans, and the exemplary prosperity of the region was boosting land prices and making expansion difficult. The Dutch, he explained, "do not possess that Metropolitan trait of character which characterized the American nation. It is consequently necessary for them, when they do move, to go in the capacity of a colony. . . ." They would, he said, send out investigating committees in the very near future, and in the meantime would appreciate whatever prepared information Ames could send them.

[90] Gesman to Ames, April 17, 1869 (LDP), and Henry Hospers (Mayor of Pella) to Ames, April 13, 1869 (LDP).

[91] Hospers to Ames, April 13, 1869 (LDP).

and character of such settlers as those at Pella, and from self-interest also should be glad to have them on our line." [92] There were further letters back and forth on the subject, but nothing more for the time being.[93]

In January, 1868, the Burlington and Missouri River had placed on sale approximately 75,000 acres of land in the Des Moines district east of range 34. By May, 1869, Ames had succeeded in disposing of only about 8,500 acres at prices roughly averaging $6 an acre.[94] How much of this was his own fault is not easy to determine. He had, of course, been unable to advertise on a large scale. Headquarters at Boston had not issued very complete or definite instructions; it appears that they rather relied on the technical advice and suggestions of the men on the spot. Yet Ames' attitude had been distinctly one of a subordinate rather than the head of an autonomous department whose duty, among other things, was to make suggestions. On May 14, 1869, however, he dispatched an eight-page letter to Perkins, obviously to be forwarded to the East, with a thoroughgoing critique of his own department and concrete suggestions for its improvement.[95]

Ames came to the point of his letter and offered his excuses all in the first sentence. "There are certain things that I think ought to be done at once in the Land Department," he wrote, "but which I cannot feel that I am authorized to do, because I do not really quite understand the extent of my authority as Land Agent." There was something naive about this statement. Ames had held his position for over two and a half years, and the problems he proceeded to enumerate — taxes, bookkeeping procedure, and sales — had all been present during this time. That, nevertheless, was his excuse, and having made it, he went on to expound the intricacies of the tax situation.

The land tax, he declared, was "the most pressing matter" before the department, and it should be settled immediately by compromise in all counties west of the existing terminus. The policy then in effect of staving off the Madison County test case from term to term was accomplishing nothing, for there was only the "rather wild hope" of inducing the supervisors to reduce their assessments because of the

[92] Ames to Hospers, April 17, 1869 (LDP).

[93] Hospers to Ames, April 20, 1869 (LDP); Ames to Hospers, April 27, 1869 (LDP).

[94] BMI, Sales Book "A" (LDP); Ames to Beall, October 25, 1869 (LDP).

[95] Ames to Perkins, May 14, 1869 (LDP).

possibility of the court's deciding against them. If, eventually, the railroad should lose the case, it would then be necessary to pay not only all back taxes but penalties as well. Thus it would be much wiser to compromise all assessments; there was reason to believe that this could be done by paying about half the amounts due. The company should put an "attorney of influence" conversant with the law before each board of supervisors in the counties west of Afton, and press for a solution of the matter before it passed the point of negotiation. The situation was somewhat better in the counties east of Afton where, in many cases, the company lands had not been listed until 1868. Ames suggested that the amounts outstanding be paid up before the June meetings of the various boards. If all this were done, he felt that sales should begin in the current year, perhaps in the fall "when land hunters are prosperous." But to get ready for this, there was a great deal to be done.

Much land of the second Iowa grant (sections within 20 miles) was as yet unexamined, and Ames might have added that the original lands had not been appraised since 1859–60 save for occasional re-examinations to check the thoroughness of the first work. Since timber depredations were at their lowest ebb in spring and summer — "the thieves being busy with honest industry" — Ames suggested that the corps of timber guardians be enlisted as examiners; did he have authority to order this? Then, if sales were to occur in the fall, the department should be advertising at once with maps and circulars, "and this is a job wherein I do not know my authority, as it involves large expense and requires office help." In addition to advertising, the second grant would have to be priced, and Ames advised that an entirely new method of accounting be adopted: all payments should be made direct to the treasurer in Boston, and no accounts at all should be kept in the land office. "Won't this lessen the responsibility & the circumlocution and the men necessary to carry on the Land Dept.?" he asked. All blanks and books should be changed to conform with this; the system of the Hannibal and St. Joseph might well be investigated with a view to adoption. There, if Ames understood rightly, the trustees of the land mortgage in Boston assumed all authority, priced all lands, got up plans of sales and accounts, and simply placed their instructions in the hands of the resident land agent, "all of which makes a difference in the position of the Land Agent and the amount of office labor, and especially responsibility of the local Land Dept. Here, there seems to be no organized head outside this office, and this office must do all the work at the risk of going wrong. . . ." What, for example, was Ames' authority in settling homestead and preëmption disputes, to advance or lower the scale of prices, to permit prepayment of land contracts, to fix agents' commissions, to issue land exploring tickets?

It was strange that Ames was so mystified about these points on each of which he had already exercised his discretion. Nevertheless, he now pointed to his lack of authority and the necessity of his doing all the work "at the risk of going wrong." There were, he reported, over 1,000 applications for land now in the office; these had come before the *Gazette* had appeared, and since that time several large offers had arrived. The mere labor of answering these communications was beyond the power of one man. Furthermore, in addition to his land department work, Ames was in charge of the right of way business and handled many of the road's purchases of rails and equipment. At least it could be said on his behalf that he was busy.

Ames now came to the concrete suggestions in his mind: (1) he himself should be sent to Hannibal to investigate from top to bottom the Hannibal and St. Joseph system, and particularly to get George Harris to recommend and spare a man from his office who would not only be capable of helping in platting lands, recording taxes, answering applications, making lists, changing the books, and getting up advertisements, but also be familiar with the Hannibal and St. Joseph experience. For this work, a first-rate man should be attracted; otherwise the policy would be fruitless. (2) Ames should meet D. N. Smith at Glenwood and arrange with him to put attorneys before all western county tax boards with authority to effect compromises. (3) Ames should next go through the eastern counties paying up all accumulated bills and establishing agencies for the sale of B. & M. lands there. "I think," he concluded, "this whole programme is important, and of *immediate importance,* — whether I continue to be Land Agent or am superseded. I do not want to be superseded, and do not believe it necessary or advisable. However, all the above are apart from this question entirely."

Ames' letter brought prompt action. On May 19, Perkins wrote to J. W. Brooks in Boston, apparently endorsing fully Ames' suggestions.

The urgency of the situation was not lost on Brooks. He telegraphed immediately to Perkins: "You are authorized to act your judgment on the whole tax matter. Lands should all be examined and valued as rapidly as possible." [96] His letter of May 24 confirmed and expanded these instructions. It was important, he said, that the *whole* grant be examined so that "the [Burlington?] office" could readily turn to the information and keep it up to date. It would indeed save much time if the entire Hannibal and St. Joseph system of books, blanks, and forms were adopted. Sales, however, should not be begun at the moment "because it seems to us as if it would be better to get the road through first, unless there are acres where a very full price would be paid. We ought to get equal to an average of full $10 per acre, and interest for them." The suggestion of Ames to import a competent man from Hannibal was emphatically endorsed, but the proposal to hire agents in the various counties was vetoed: "The Illinois Central began that way but soon gave it up as working bad [*sic*] from some reason which I don't recollect." [97] Of course, agents for showing lands would have to be kept, but not necessarily for selling them.

This letter was significant for more than one reason. At last it authorized the first steps of an active colonization program; the days of marking time were definitely numbered. Secondly, it revealed that the eastern directors had abundant confidence in the local management at Burlington. This was of incalculable value, for it meant that the land department could act positively and without hesitation. In the hustling, impatient, highly competitive West, speed was often the essential ingredient of success. Finally, Brooks' letter furnished fresh evidence of the extent to which the B. & M. could profit by the experiences of the older land-grant railroads. The time and money that could thus be saved was, of course, unlimited. At the very least, it enabled the Iowa road to start its large-scale colonization work with matured and well-tried policies rather than with prolonged and costly experiments. In the case of the books and accounting forms, for example, those used in Hannibal had originally been based on the Illinois Central models but had been modified to conform with the Missouri conditions which so nearly approximated those in Iowa.

[96] Brooks to Perkins, May 24, 1869 (LDP). The letter quoted the telegram, apparently despatched on May 19 or 20.
[97] *Ibid.*

Thus, when the Burlington adopted these various practices, they had been doubly tested. The Illinois road's experience with agents was equally apropos, particularly since Ames had already employed several in the eastern counties and might have extended the practice. During

BURLINGTON ABOUT 1872. C. B. & Q. BRIDGE IN THE FOREGROUND.

1854, David Neal, Land Commissioner of the Illinois Central, had appointed nine local agents, paid on a commission basis. Within a year, however, this policy had been abandoned because, in the opinion of the road's directors, these agents were being paid far more than their services were worth, they were not bonded, and there was reason to believe that they were selling the best lands first without particular regard to obtaining the full market price for them.[98] Perhaps the Burlington would have been more fortunate with its agents, but the scheme was hardly worth trying after what had happened to the Illinois Central. Brooks' letter, based on experience, was thus not only a signal to go ahead but a chart of where to go. Armed with it, Ames spent the busiest summer and fall of his entire career, for he seemed determined to carry out in the shortest possible time the strenuous program he himself had suggested.

As the *Gazette* spread eastward from Burlington, inquiries increased. H. A. Burger, agent of the Cunard Line in Chicago and of the Swedish Commercial Company, offered to direct immigrants to B. & M. land for a suitable commission, and requested maps and circulars.[99]

[98] Gates, *op. cit.*, pp. 160–165.
[99] Burger to Ames, July 16, 1869 (LDP).

From Portland, Maine, H. M. True informed Ames that parties were gathering for the westward trek and would like more information.[100] To both men Ames had to reply that no further pamphlets were available; in brief terms he outlined what the company's policy of sales would be when the line was completed.[101] In August a searching letter arrived from the Reverend Robert Thomas, a Pennsylvania Welshman, who had been appointed to seek out land for a colony of some 200 families, "mostly farmers, labourers, mechanics — some miners — and all good, honest & religious Christians. . . ."[102] Equipped with a B. & M. exploring ticket, sold at a special rate to prospective land buyers, he had ridden to the railhead at Cromwell, and from there had gone by stage to Glenwood.[103] He intended to go on to Kansas and northern Missouri but was so impressed by Montgomery County that he was hopeful that the "Directors of the Railroad" would authorize a special low price for such a desirable group of settlers, particularly since they would take from 25,000 to 50,000 acres. Their purpose, he explained, was to build homes, schoolhouses, churches, and storehouses in a central spot, and surround them with farms. If the company would make "reasonable" terms, he could assure from 100 to 200 Welsh families the first two years, and others later. A great many, he predicted, would come from New York, Pennsylvania, and Ohio, "and thousands more will follow them from Wales during the next five years." Of course, Thomas concluded, if the price were too high, he would reluctantly have to advise his countrymen to buy at the government price in Nebraska or Kansas.

Ames' reply was careful, patient, unencouraging.[104] Unfortunately, he said, the directors of the B. & M. lived in Boston, and the process of getting them together in special meeting was too lengthy and serious a task to be thought of except in dire emergency. Furthermore, when they met, they would have to rely for the information about Iowa on the reports from their own land department. "In other words, the schedule [of prices] now in preparation would not be changed."

[100] True to Ames, July 7, 1869 (LDP).

[101] Ames to Burger, July 19, 1869 (LDP); Ames to True, July 12, 1869 (LDP).

[102] Thomas to Ames, August 16, 1869 (LDP).

[103] Thomas thanked Ames for the exploring ticket, and then rather painfully noted that the stage had charged him $8.50 for the ride from Cromwell to Glenwood (*ibid.*). The present rail fare for the 73 miles is about $1.50.

[104] Ames to Thomas, August 20, 1869 (LDP).

Nevertheless, it was proper to say that the first price list would be made out lower than subsequent ones, thus favoring first comers. For colonies, however, it would be impossible to give a special rate, for that would be giving one man an advantage over another simply because he happened to be in a large group, and "it would hardly be for our interest to create ill feeling against us throughout the greater part of the people, for the great part of the settlement here will be by isolated emigrants as it has been most everywhere else. Special privileges to any people or class for any reasons whatever we shall [have] to guard against carefully." Prices on farming land would be fixed according to topography and distance from stations. They would probably range from $4.50 an acre for "the most remote and poorest pieces" to $15 for fertile tracts near the road, a substantial advance over prices on the company's easternmost tracts and not particularly encouraging for thrifty applicants. Nevertheless, Ames concluded, "I shall be glad to have the largest possible Welsh settlement on our line, feeling sure that no class of emigrants make better citizens."

This letter, like others Ames had written, settled several important points and drew attention to a number of other matters. The decision not to accord special rates to colonies was probably a wise one for the very practical reason indicated. The fact that Ames could take this stand, together with the rather high range of indicated prices, suggested that he had increasing confidence in the company's ability to dispose of the grant on favorable terms. There was indeed direct evidence of this optimism. Writing to Hospers late in April, Ames offered him commissions of only two per cent on long-time, and three and a half per cent on short-time and cash sales, in contrast to the five per cent offered in 1868.[105] "The applications for our land are now so numerous," he explained, "and the offers for agencies at percentage rates also so plenty that we feel no doubt of our being able to sell all our land without incurring any expense above the percentage named. . . ."[106] Perhaps the steady progress of the line across the state was generating courage in the land department.[107] There was certainly little ground for rejoicing on the basis of sales statistics

[105] See above, p. 243.

[106] Ames to Hospers, April 27, 1869 (LDP).

[107] In August the rails had reached Corning in the center of Adams County. (CBQ, *Corporate History*, p. 129.)

themselves; despite the *Gazette* and Ames' lengthy correspondence, there were but 28 sales in the first six months of 1869.[108]

The reply to Mr. Thomas was noteworthy for other reasons also. Ames apparently had no objections to referring to the B. & M.'s absentee ownership; it is doubtful whether he would have done so had there been any considerable public sentiment against it at the time. There was one aspect of Boston control, however, that was causing some embarrassment and required frequent explanation. The so-called "Land Mortgage" of 1858, under which the entire grant became collateral for a loan, specified that no deeds could be issued to purchasers of railroad lands except by the trustees in Boston upon receipt of the purchase money in cash or land bonds themselves.[109] This inevitably meant considerable delay, and Ames spent much time prompting the busy trustees in the East or soothing impatient settlers in the West. Sending a deed for signature on one occasion to Treasurer Denison, Ames explained that the buyer was an emigrant Swede "and of course ignorant enough to be very suspicious of delay. I should like therefore, to return his deed very soon, that other Swedish emigrants may be encouraged to buy our lands." [110] To the buyers, Ames carefully explained the requirements of the mortgage, always adding that the deed, when given, was a full release and that the land was not subject to seizure if the loan were defaulted.[111] This situation also made it impossible for purchasers to offer railroad stock as part payment for their land, because the trustees, John M. Forbes, J. N. A. Griswold, and Henry Kidder, were acting in capacities outside the company, and therefore could not convert the stock into cash except at market prices. When, in June, 1868, a purchaser had offered B. & M. stock, Ames had explained that at the moment it was selling for about ten cents on the dollar and that the trustees would look to him for the balance.[112] Only 12 months later the same stock was approaching

---

[108] BMI, Sales Book "A" (LDP).

[109] CBQ, *Documentary History*, vol. II, p. 77.

[110] Ames to Denison, May 12, 1869 (LDP). Denison did his best to secure the necessary signatures to deeds as quickly as possible, but Griswold lived in New York, Forbes was frequently absent, and Kidder occasionally so. "I agree," he once wrote Ames, "that deeds ought to be furnished promptly to purchasers of our lands, but am afraid it will never be in our power to do it without a change in our trustees." (Denison to Ames, May 13, 1869, LDP.)

[111] Ames to T. J. Anderson, September 7, 1869 (LDP).

[112] Ames to Allen White, June 8, 1868 (LDP).

par,[113] but there is no record of its ever having been received in payment of land.

Meanwhile the swampland dispute was progressing along its tortuous way. In December, 1866, the district court of Iowa had rendered decisions in favor of Fremont and Mills counties, and the highest court of the state had affirmed its action the following spring. As planned, the railroad appealed to the Supreme Court of the United States,[114] and there the matter was resting when, on July 13, 1868, a committee, appointed by Mills County for the purpose, approached the railroad with a new compromise.[115] There were, in all, 23,000 acres in dispute in the county. Of these, 9,080 had never been disposed of to private parties, and the committee offered to quitclaim them to the company outright, together with 4,550 acres subject to squatter and preëmption claims. According to the county authorities, half of these claims were invalid so that, in summary, the B. & M. would receive 13,630 acres of which approximately 2,275 might eventually be lost to individuals.[116] In return for 9,000-odd acres for which Mills County had issued swampland certificates and collected payment, the committee offered $10,000 cash plus $3,000 in installments due on long-term contracts, a total of $13,000.[117] In summary, then, this part of the county offer was as follows:

Offered to B. & M.

1.   9,080 acres   For 9,080 acres still free and unsold.
2.   4,550 acres   For 4,550 acres unsold but approximately half subject to valid preëmption and squatter claims.
3. $13,000   For approximately 9,370 acres sold.

These swamp lands [Ames explained to Denison] are undoubtedly the finest part of the grant, and the part of their proposition offering to settle this point ought not to be accepted if our chance is good before the U. S. courts. But this is not necessarily connected with the rest of their offer, which is really their bid for the Glenwood line. . . .[118]

The "rest of the offer" was the "virtual promise" of the committee to obtain a right of way through the county. They were not empowered

[113] CBQ, *Annual Report* for 1869 (Chicago, 1869), p. 13.
[114] BMI, Transfer Record No. 1, p. 289 (LDP); Ames to King, June 3, 1867 (LDP).   [115] BMI, Transfer Record No. 1, p. 289 (LDP).
[116] Ames to Denison, August 3, 1868 (LDP).
[117] Ames to Denison, July 13, 1868 (LDP).
[118] Ames to Denison, August 3, 1868 (LDP).

to do this but were willing as individuals to sign bonds for its accomplishment. Furthermore, they assured the railroad of future exemption from land taxation *providing* the company built on the original survey. This was the proposition submitted to induce the B. & M. to build by way of Glenwood, and the county committee asked particularly that it be brought before the directors when they fixed the final route.

Of course [cautioned Ames] as soon as the decision of the Directors is known, no promises or terms can be obtained, and the Committee cannot obtain any names on a Right of Way bond. Let any decision be kept secret until we obtain such promises and terms in writing. I write at the instance of Mr. Perkins. . . .[119]

The railroad was taking no chances. Finally, the county offered to continue the suit pending in the United States Supreme Court from term to term until the compromise was fully carried out; thereupon it would be dismissed, and each party would pay their own costs.[120] The committee gave the railroad two months to accept their offer.[121]

Naturally this proposition appealed to the officers of the B. & M., particularly when Mills County formally rescinded all back taxes on railroad lands and exempted them for the next two years, providing the line were run through Glenwood. By the middle of September, 1868, the directors had decided to accept the compromise in respect to the lands and cash payment,[122] but they asked and obtained from the county an extension of the entire offer until November 1 to consider further where the line should be located.[123] Meanwhile, the greatest secrecy was observed, probably for the reasons suggested by Ames. Finally, on October 31, 1868, a formal acceptance was given by the railroad to the committee, and nine days later the board of supervisors unanimously confirmed and ratified the agreement.[124] William Hale [125] and H. C. Watkins [126] were appointed county agents to superin-

---

[119] Ames to Denison, July 13, 1868 (LDP).

[120] BMI, Transfer Record No. 1, p. 289 (LDP).

[121] Ames to Smith, September 16, 1868 (LDP).

[122] Ames to King, September 21, 1868 (LDP).

[123] Ames to Smith, September 16, 1868 (LDP); Ames to King, September 21, 1868 (LDP).

[124] BMI, Transfer Record No. 1, p. 289 (LDP).

[125] William Hale was known to Perkins, and had had friendly feelings toward the railroad. In 1862 he had commended the company on the tact and methods of its preëmption agent, N. P. Woods. See above, p. 188.

[126] H. C. Watkins had endeavored, in 1864, to purchase some disputed swamp-

tend execution of the contract, and D. N. Smith and H. A. Copeland were named to serve for the company in a similar capacity. At last the railroad felt that the thorny swampland tangle, at least in Mills County, was on the way to solution.[127]

Both sides immediately began to carry out their part of the agreement, and during the next twelve months put most of the various provisions into effect:[128]

(1) the railroad at once placed its line under contract via Glenwood,

(2) the county quitclaimed to the B. & M. 9,340 acres (instead of the 9,080 originally listed), the total acreage free and unsold,[129]

(3) claimants of swamplands under county preëmption certificates (involving the 4,550 acres subject to private claims) were notified through the newspapers to appear before the county and railroad agents to prove up their claims; if they were successful, they were allowed to take up their land by paying $1.25 to the company; fraudulent claims, however, were rejected and the land deeded outright to the B. & M., and

(4) the county agreed to pay $10,000 to the railroad in cash in return for swamplands already sold,[130] and assigned to the railroad all unpaid installments; sales recently made on time where nothing had been paid in were cancelled, and the land deeded to the company.

Thus, by the fall of 1869, it seemed that an amicable settlement had finally been reached; it was just at that moment, however, that a bombshell blasted the carefully laid plans.

When Mills County made the original offer for a compromise in 1866, the Fremont County authorities had refused to consider any agreement with the railroad and had pinned their hopes on a favorable judicial decision.[131] Along with Mills, they had been successful in the state courts and now, in the December, 1869, term of the United States Supreme Court, they won a complete and final victory.[132] Over

---

land from the company, but had been turned down because of the pending lawsuit. See above, p. 203.

[127] "Probably this will solve all Mills County matters. . . ." (Ames to King, September 21, 1868, LDP.)

[128] BMI, Transfer Record No. 1, p. 289 (LDP).

[129] The quitclaim was submitted to Ames and sent by him to Denison on October 6, 1869 (LDP).

[130] The money, however, was not actually paid and was later the subject of further controversy. Legal Records, *passim* (LDP).   [131] See above, p. 205.

[132] *Fremont County v. B. & M.*, 9 Wallace 89 (1869).

12,000 acres,[133] originally selected as swamp but certified to the B. & M. by the Secretary of the Interior in March, 1862,[134] was returned to the county. As Perkins had feared, the decision turned on a small but all-important point:

> The location of the road [held the Court] was not made on the ground and *adopted by the company till the 24th, March 1857, which was after the confirmatory* act [of March 3] of that year. This [act] confirmed all [swamp] selections made at the time, and . . . as the railroad company at this time, for the reasons above stated, had not perfected their grant so as to become invested with the title to any of the selections . . . they can set up no appropriation of any of these lands under their grant, which leaves them [i.e., the lands] subject to the confirming act of 1857. . . .[135]

In other words, the Court followed the original interpretation of Secretary Thompson in 1858 that if the railroad had not "definitely fixed" its route when the confirming Act of March 3, 1857, was passed, then that act confirmed swamp selections to the state no matter how fraudulent these selections may have been.[136] What the Court now made clear for the first time was that the formal adoption of the survey by the road's directors was a necessary part of fixing the route. Thus, because of its inexplicable delay in adopting the line that was run in the fall of 1856,[137] the B. & M. found itself without any defensible claim at all to the thousands of acres of swamplands in dispute.

The result of this decision would have been serious enough had it been limited to the lands lost in Fremont County and to the precedent it afforded for other counties and individuals claiming swamplands held by the railroad. The greatest blow to the company was the unexpected effect of the Court's ruling on the Mills County situation. According to the terms of the compromise, the case pending between the B. & M. and Mills County was to be continued from term to term until each party to the agreement had carried out the various stipulations. For some reason, however, the clerk of the Supreme Court was never notified of this arrangement,[138] with the result that on the

---

[133] The exact amount was 12,642.53 acres. (BMI, Legal Record No. 1, p. 7, LDP.)

[134] See above, pp. 189–190.

[135] *Fremont County v. B. & M.*, 9 Wallace 89 (1869). Italics supplied.

[136] See above, p. 135.

[137] See above, p. 95.

[138] BMI, Transfer Record No. 1, p. 289 (LDP).

day of the Fremont decision and in accordance with the opinion therein, the Mills County suit was tried and a decree entered in favor of the county.[139] All this took place while the compromise was being carried out in good faith by both parties. Thus, as 1869 closed, the swamp imbroglio that had already caused so much confusion entered another period of uncertainty. Would every holder of county swampland certificates try to recover his land on the basis of the Fremont case? Would Mills County abide by the unfulfilled parts of the compromise, such as paying the $10,000 previously received from her swampland purchasers? Time alone would answer these questions, but the railroad could be certain that there was trouble ahead.

During this period the matter of taxes continued to be troublesome. There was still no definite ruling on the part of the courts as to whether or when lands granted by the United States became company property subject to state tax. Unfortunately it was a matter of sufficient monetary importance to be of real concern. In Warren County, for example, in 1869, the company had to pay $2,631.80 in accumulated taxes, as well as $74.20 to redeem lands sold for delinquency.[140] But the most annoying aspect of the situation was its uncertainty; the B. & M. was unable to calculate its liabilities at any given time. A trip by Ames to western Iowa, however, put the machinery in motion for compromising the assessments, and through correspondence and visits he sought to satisfy the various boards of supervisors in the eastern counties. Meanwhile, he traveled over the Nebraska lands[141] and wrote Harris at Hannibal about securing an able assistant.[142] Land sales in 1869, which were still confined to the Des Moines district of Iowa, showed some slight upturn. There were nearly twice as many sales in July–August–September as in the preceding three months, and this record was exceeded slightly by the last quarter.[143] All told, the company disposed of 4,310.99 acres in 1869 for $27,195.41, bringing its totals to 10,728.91 acres and $40,511.79 for the period since the first sale in October, 1863.[144]

---

[139] BMI, Transfer Record No. 1, p. 289 (LDP). There is no record of this decision in Wallace's reports.

[140] Hartman & Swan to Ames, July 27, 1869 (LDP).

[141] Ames to various persons, July, 1869 et seq. (LDP).

[142] Ames to Harris, July 13, 1869 (LDP).

[143] The sales by quarters in 1869 were as follows: 13–15–26–30, total, 84. (BMI, Sales Book "A," LDP).   [144] BMI, Sales Book "A" (LDP).

II. NEBRASKA

Although Ames' activities were primarily centered in Iowa during 1866–69, he was responsible for his company's land matters in Nebraska as well. At the very beginning of his administration, affairs in that state had run into a snag.

In January, 1866, Secretary of the Interior Harlan had withdrawn from private entry ten alternate sections on each side of the projected line of the B. & M. with no restriction as to lateral limits.[145] During 1866 Harlan was succeeded by O. H. Browning. To this new incumbent, J. Sterling Morton, a leading citizen of Nebraska, addressed a fervent plea to the effect that the withdrawal ordered in January would injure the territory by excluding homesteaders from an unnecessarily large portion of the public domain.[146] Browning was apparently convinced by this argument, and on December 17, 1866, indicated that he intended to restore to market all odd sections farther than 20 miles from the route of the B. & M.[147] Since the company knew it could not find the full quota of its grant within such limits because of existing settlements, its officials were naturally alarmed.

No pains should be spared [wrote Ames to Steiger] to change the Secretary's decision . . . The Company has proceeded to examine and survey the lands under Secretary Harlan's decision, and of course has expended considerable sums thereon; the title thus given to the Company ought not to be lightly disturbed . . . Would it be out of place also to notice the *tone*, — the unprovoked abuse of an established and progressive RR — of Mr. Morton's letter? . . .[148]

At Washington, Steiger endeavored to show, among other things, that it was the originators of the Pacific Railroad bills and not the Burlington and Missouri River who had drawn up the terms of the grant. Ames agreed with this reasoning and went even further:

the "injury" complaint [he declared flatly] is bosh, — with the even sections open to Homesteads, no settler need be turned away for forty years to come. Indeed, nobody is injured but the Land Speculator who wishes to *enter* the land & then let it lie idle. Any law which operate[s] against them is necessarily a benefit to the Ter[ritory]. Nobody is more interested in its genuine & early settlement than the RR Co. . . .[149]

[145] See above, p. 216.   [146] Ames to Steiger, January 25, 1867 (LDP).
[147] T. M. Marquett, Brief of 1887, *loc. cit.*, p. 2.
[148] Ames to Steiger, December 28, 1866 (LDP).
[149] Ames to Steiger, January 25, 1867 (LDP).

Unfortunately for the company, neither Steiger's arguments nor Ames' letters changed the Secretary's mind. On March 1, 1867, he restored all lands to public market in Nebraska that Harlan had withdrawn on behalf of the B. & M. except for the odd sections within twenty miles of the track.[150] Until the company's land examinations could be completed within these limits, it was impossible to ascertain exactly how much land might be lost if this decision should be upheld by subsequent secretaries or by the courts, but the B. & M. realized that it stood to lose more than half of the 2,400,000 acres it had hoped to receive.[151] By the fall of 1869, when construction of the B. & M. had begun in Nebraska and the company was thinking about beginning its land sales, the matter still remained unsettled.

Late in January, 1869, Ames had sent King across the icebound Missouri to spy out the region. The going at that time of year was difficult; travel over the rough and rutted dirt roads was exclusively by stage coach or on horseback.[152] The country itself was still a remote, inaccessible prairie, but it lay south of the Platte River in a rich sector of the state, and even in its unimproved condition gave promise of a great future.[153] As yet Ames was not prepared to authorize anything more than King's cursory examination, but it was apparent to Nebraska residents, as well as to the company, that it would soon be worth while to build the Burlington through the area and to sell lands along the line. Consequently, during the spring of 1869, numerous persons wrote to Ames to find out when this activity would begin and, particularly, whether settlers could occupy and improve the tracts before they were put on the market.[154] To one such inquiry late in April, Ames replied that it was difficult to give a definite answer, for he did not yet know whether or not Nebraska affairs would be in the hands of a separate company. If they should be, the Iowa organization did not wish to make any commitments for the future which might prove embarrassing to a new company. Therefore, in justice to the settler, it was best to say simply that (1) actual settlers had better not occupy railroad land until they could be sure

[150] T. M. Marquett, Brief of 1887, *loc. cit.*, p. 2.
[151] *U. S. v. B. & M. R. RR*, 98 US 334 (337), (1878).
[152] King to Ames, February 9, 1869 (LDP).
[153] See full description, above, pp. 225–227.
[154] Vifquoin to Ames, March 9, 1869 (LDP); Peet to Ames, April 15, 1869 (LDP).

of terms, prices, and conditions; (2) no restriction would eventually be placed on the number of acres that could be bought, provided a certain proportion was cultivated annually; (3) prices would vary according to the quality of the land, proximity to towns and stations, and so forth; (4) if the Iowa company disposed of the lands, they would do so on the basis of ten-year credit at seven per cent interest. "In the present uncertainty," however, Ames advised his correspondent to buy of other parties. "I have only given you an outline of the *probable* policy in case this Company continues to hold the grant." [155] Clearly Ames was uninformed by the main office what plans were in store, and he was forced to resort to the familiar tactics of stalling and, at the same time, keeping the residents in good humor. While he was thus engaged, the directors of the B. & M. reached the conclusion that new management was needed in their land department.

In November, 1869, Colonel Ames resigned his position, and George S. Harris, chief of the Hannibal and St. Joseph's land department, took his place. [156]

No move could have symbolized more strikingly the transition from the preliminary to the active stage of the Burlington's colonization work. During the three difficult years from 1866 through 1869, Ames had personified the inactive policy of the B. & M.'s land department. Conscientious, courteous, unimaginative, he had felt that his most important task was to preserve and build up the goodwill that was so vital to the company in its contacts with the community. Whether dealing with state officials, large colonizers, or the humblest preëmptioner, he had endeavored to make them feel that the railroad was genuinely interested in their particular problem and was willing to treat everyone fairly in the premises. The confidence born of this policy was, of course, invaluable. On the other hand, his haphazard pricing policy and his lack of initiative would have been serious handicaps when the time came for the company to sell the bulk of its grant. Thus, as that day approached, a change was made. The task before Harris was indeed enough to challenge the most ambitious man.

[155] Ames to Peet, April 28, 1869 (LDP).
[156] The last letter signed by Ames was dated November 17, 1869 (LDP); the first signed by Bacon for Harris was dated November 24, 1869 (LDP).

CHAPTER XI

CONSOLIDATION AND CONSTRUCTION, 1870–1873

WITH the close of the Civil War the United States had entered a period of unparalleled expansion. Protective tariffs, the demands of the conflict, and inflation had attracted men with capital into new manufacturing and commercial enterprises. Stimulated by increasing demands of the West, the return of a southern market, and freedom from government interference, the output of American mills and shops more than doubled from 1860 to 1870 and was destined to increase threefold by 1880. As part of this enormous growth, railway mileage grew from 30,626 in 1860 to 52,922 ten years later; it reached 93,267 in 1880. Socially, a widespread movement to the cities was on foot, while in the field of politics, the doctrine of *laissez faire* was approaching the height of its influence.[1]

Coincident with this industrialization and partly responsible for it was the tremendous extension of the agricultural West which resulted to some extent from economic dislocation in the East and in Europe, but more particularly from the liberal land policy of the United States government, by which 155,504,994 acres were granted to various railways by 1880 and over 55,000,000 acres to individual homesteaders.[2] During the 'seventies a region equal in extent to the British Isles and Sweden was brought under cultivation, and while the production of wheat increased 45 per cent, that of corn doubled. The adoption of labor-saving machinery together with a new interest in scientific farming stimulated this growth, and led to an overproduction that was largely responsible for the Granger movement of the middle 'seventies and the subsequent decrease in farm produce during the 'eighties. Meanwhile the best lands of the Middle West had been put to the plow.[3]

[1] For the general aspects of post-war expansion, see, for example: Louis M. Hacker and Benjamin B. Kendrick, *The United States Since 1865* (New York, 1939), chs. vii–xvi; Kirkland, *op. cit.*, chs. x–xiii. Statistics of manufacturing output and railway mileage are from the *Census* of 1880.

[2] Donaldson, *op. cit.*, pp. 261–268; 331–335.

[3] Solon J. Buck, *The Agrarian Crusade* (New Haven, 1920), chs. ii–v. Statistics of cultivated land are from the *Census* of 1880.

The financial history of the country reflected this prodigious growth. Bank loans rose to new heights in the early 'seventies, and the fever of speculation was rampant. But such expansion was not without severe growing pains. The disastrous panic precipitated by Cooke's failure in the fall of 1873 brought a day of reckoning that lengthened into five years before business and agricultural activity resumed their former tempo. Meanwhile some million persons were thrown out of work, and western farmers were unable to meet their mortgage payments.[4]

One important result of this economic metamorphosis was a social upheaval of far-reaching consequence. The lure of the cities added to the thought of free land produced an exodus from the older rural districts of alarming proportions. Meantime the European stream of immigration increased steadily, for in addition to the "pull" of free land and unbounded industrial opportunity in the western world was added the "push" of conditions at home. Despite the Civil War, nearly 2,500,000 foreigners arrived in the 'sixties, and during the next decade, 2,812,191 entered the country. In the latter period, Great Britain contributed approximately a third, followed by Germany, Sweden, and Norway.[5] The decade of the 'seventies was a period of contrasts for the Burlington, of high hopes and rapid accomplishment followed by trying times and eventual success. In particular, the years 1870 through 1873 witnessed a consolidation of the system and great physical expansion.

I. IOWA

Ever since Forbes, Joy, Brooks, and Baker had crossed the Mississippi in 1857 to lend their capital and energy to the B. & M., it had been obvious that the Iowa line had become, in fact, a part of the C. B. & Q. and, in a lesser degree, of the Michigan Central. On this premise, Joy and Forbes had successfully appealed from time to time to the stockholders of the older companies for aid to the B. & M., and for this reason the bridge had been built at the sole expense of the

---

[4] Buck, *op. cit.* Statistics of bank loans are from F. W. Hewes and Henry Gannett, *Scribner's Statistical Atlas for 1880* (New York, 1883), plate 89.

[5] Arthur M. Schlesinger, *The Rise of the City, 1878–1898* (New York, 1933), *passim*; United States, *Compendium of the Tenth Census* (Washington, 1883), p. 8. Statistics of immigration are from Treasury Department, *Statistical Abstract*, vols. I, III (Washington, 1879, 1881), *passim*.

"Q" across the Mississippi. Furthermore, by converting its traffic balances into B. & M. stock, the C. B. & Q. had acquired virtual control of the Iowa line. It was entirely logical, therefore, that this close relationship should be recognized by formal corporate action.

On February 23, 1871, the directors of the B. & M. of Iowa, meeting in Boston, appointed a committee at the suggestion of Forbes to meet with representatives of the C. B. & Q. Its members were instructed to consider the relations between the two roads and to see whether a plan could be devised "for their mutual permanent advantage." [6] On June 5 the C. B. & Q. board, likewise on the motion of Forbes, appointed a similar committee for the same purpose.[7] The outcome of these joint deliberations was a foregone conclusion, since six of the C. B. & Q.'s twelve directors served on the B. & M.'s smaller board of nine. On October 3, 1872, the Iowa company committee's recommendation that their road be leased to the C. B. & Q. with authority to sell was adopted, and a meeting of the stockholders was called for December 24 at Burlington to consider and act upon the report.[8]

The *Burlington Daily Hawk-Eye* thereupon devoted a long editorial to the approaching change. "To observing persons," it remarked, "this consummation has long been regarded only as a question of time." What would the effect be on the city of Burlington? There were those, the editor declared, who were "fearful" that the business and growth of the city would be retarded, but would this necessarily be true? The change of management would, of course, displace some of the young men then employed in the general office, but however desirable their retention might be, the contrary could not be regarded as an extremely "serious matter." There would still be required a large number of officers and employees to handle the growing business centering in Burlington, so that the change in this respect would be "hardly noticed." As to the shops, the prospects pointed to more rather than less work.

"The main cause of anxiety, however," the editor continued, was the question of freight rates to the West, and the fear of "unfavorable discrimination against our wholesale trade, lumber business, and manu-

---

[6] BMI ORB, p. 213.   [7] CBQ ORB, p. 359.
[8] BMI ORB, pp. 238–242. Those directors on both boards were: John W. Brooks, John A. Burnham, John M. Forbes, James F. Joy, Nathaniel Thayer, Robert S. Watson. (BMI ORB, p. 242.)

facturing interests." On this point, the journalist did not contemplate trouble. "We do not think," he said, "it has ever been the policy of the C. B. & Q. Company to discourage the growth of towns and cities along their line." There were, he recalled, some persons who thought the bridging of the Mississippi would be ruinous to the city and particularly to the wholesale trade, but, in fact, it proved to be the "very reverse."

We believe [concluded the editor] that the interests of our city and those of the consolidated company so far as they concern us, are in a great measure identical, and that what is good policy for one will be advantageous to the other. A generous treatment of the railroad companies on the part of the city, will insure just and generous treatment in return, and the prosperity of all will follow.[9]

Charles Beardsley, who wrote this editorial, forwarded it to Joy, and on October 21, the latter replied from Detroit that "the considerations alluded to in that article are so well founded that I have hardly any additional suggestions to make. . . . The business of your city, of all kinds," Joy assured him, "is too important to be in any degree neglected or injured by the company." Indeed, it would be distinctly to the interests of the company "to use all possible means to build up its trade and multiply its population."[10] How this could be done under the consolidated regime Joy particularized at great length.

Thus, at the threshold of its greatest period of expansion, the company reaffirmed its interest in as well as its dependence upon the community it served. The confidence expressed by the *Hawk-Eye's* editor was naturally gratifying to the railroad, even though his sentiments, as yet, were apparently not universally shared. In a letter to Forbes written two days later, Perkins remarked that consolidation did not please the Burlington people but he did not see how it could "set the town back any."[11]

At the meeting of the B. & M. stockholders, the agreement between the two roads was approved, whereupon the *Burlington Daily Telegraph*, whose attitude toward the railroad was consistently restrained, cautiously remarked: "In so far as railroads tend to aid and develop the prosperity and future success of Burlington, we wish them all

[9] *Burlington Daily Hawk-Eye*, October 17, 1872.
[10] Joy to Beardsley, October 21, 1872 (CNB, n.p.).
[11] Perkins to Forbes, October 23, 1872 (CNB, ch. x, pp. 11-12).

unlimited success." [12] On December 31, 1872, the C. B. & Q. signed a perpetual lease of the Iowa property with the understanding that outright consolidation should take place as soon as the exchange of stock could be effected.[13] As a result, the railroad from Chicago to the Missouri River became one in name as well as in fact. Meanwhile, the intimate connection between this combined system and the Nebraska road was signalized by a significant change in official responsibility.

In September, 1872, Brooks had written Forbes that a strong man was urgently needed in Nebraska to take control of and look after the interests of the system there. He pointed out that although Thomas Doane was a good engineer and had many other excellent qualities, he was not primarily an operating man or particularly well fitted to deal with the public. Perkins on the other hand had proved his ability in these respects, and Brooks hoped that Forbes would persuade him to take the vice-presidency of the B. & M. in Nebraska.[14] This Forbes was able to do, and late in October Perkins formally accepted his new appointment.[15] His comments to Forbes on the policy he thought should be followed west of the Missouri were not only significant in view of subsequent developments, but also revealed something of Perkins' knowledge of human nature. "The problem in Nebraska," he wrote, "needs a consolidation of that interest with C. B. & Q. to solve it satisfactorily! But, as I wrote Mr. Brooks today, I suppose a suggestion of that kind now would frighten some of the C. B. & Q. stockholders as much as Iowa consolidation did a few

[12] *Burlington Daily Telegraph*, December 27, 1872.

[13] CBQ, *Corporate History*, p. 131; CBQ, *Annual Report* for 1872 (Chicago, 1873), p. 19.

[14] Brooks to Forbes, September 14, 1872 (CNB, ch. x, pp. 8–9); cf. Brooks to Doane, October 8, 1872 (CNB, ch. x, p. 10).

[15] BMN, *Annual Report* for 1873 (Boston, 1874). Brooks felt Perkins should move to Omaha. "With a continued residence at Burlington," he wrote Forbes, "we could not well get rid of the feeling in Nebraska that this was too much of an Iowa road, and besides what we want is to have the control of our affairs there in the hands of a man on the spot who is looked upon as one of the people. A Nebraska man managing a Nebraska enterprise. This would bring untold relief to me and make us all feel safe as to our property there while his position in the State could not be otherwise than of the most satisfactory character. I hope you will be able to persuade him to go there." (Brooks to Forbes, September 14, 1872, CNB, ch. x, pp. 8–9.) Perkins' hesitation in accepting the Nebraska post was due to his reluctance to leave Burlington. As a matter of fact, he did not have to do so. (CNB, ch. x, pp. 17–18.)

years ago! The only fear I have for the C. B. & Q. is the want of a far-reaching and consistent policy. If the whole C. B. & Q. and Nebraska interest could be united under one able management it would make a great railroad, and I believe it is the true policy to bring this about." [16]

During the early years of the 'seventies, J. W. Ames, relieved of his position in the land department, served as assistant treasurer at Burlington,[17] and although Perkins continued, now for $200 a year, as agent of the Iowa Land Association, Ames took over much of the detailed work for this enterprise. New projects were few, however, and it was chiefly a matter of supervising the lease and sale of property already acquired.[18] The Emerson Land Association likewise continued its operations, but in 1873, Perkins reported: "It doesn't look very brilliant. Land has been very dull." [19]

II. NEBRASKA

In 1870, southern Nebraska presented a striking contrast to the railroad builders. As far west as Lincoln population density varied between 6 and 18 per square mile, but beyond that point there were few settlers; the territory surrounding the western half of the B. & M.'s projected route was a veritable wilderness, and even Woodman doubted whether it would be wise to build beyond Hastings. Nevertheless, the junction point with the Union Pacific was fixed at Fort Kearney.[20] At the time this was indeed an outpost of civilization. In the spring of 1870, for example, while the route was being relocated west of Denton, it was necessary to keep the engineering parties fully armed, and on one occasion, earthworks were thrown up against roaming Indians.[21] When, in July, Doane traveled from Fort Kearney to the Republican River, he first secured a military escort composed of Major Gustave von Blucher and five men. "We saw," he reported,

[16] Perkins to Forbes, October 23, 1872 (CNB, ch. x, pp. 11–12).

[17] Perkins to Forbes, February 8, 1873 (CNB, n.p.).

[18] ILA, Packet of Correspondence, 1871–1874. See esp. Receipt for Salary, December 19, 1874 (LDP).

[19] Perkins to Thielsen, January 31, 1873 (CNB, n.p.).

[20] T. E. Calvert (former General Superintendent) to C. F. Manderson, May 22, 1898 (LDP). Calvert recalled that "the fact that it [Fort Kearney] was the only point west of the Big Blue River having a name and being shown on the maps in that vicinity, had probably much to do with its selection." (*Ibid.*)

[21] BMN, *Annual Report* for 1873 (Boston, 1874), pp. 6–7.

"tens of thousands of buffalo. No Indians were in sight. Saw a few white men on the Republican who the Major said were horse thieves."[22]

At the eastern end of the state, however, matters were progressing rapidly. The arrival of the B. & M.'s rails from the East at the banks of the Missouri late in 1869 meant that the new company in Nebraska could be supplied directly by its parent road. Although the lack of a bridge at Plattsmouth required reliance on a ferry, with all the consequent delay and annoyance, construction moved ahead rapidly in 1870. A preliminary report by federal officials, in February, described the first ten miles completed, "the best constructed road in the West," and expressed surprise at finding it "so substantial, smooth and perfect."[23] By the middle of that month, 18 miles were open to Louisville, and almost simultaneously A. E. Touzalin arrived in Plattsmouth to open a ticket office.[24] "He is ever on the alert, and is bound to draw traffic over the B. & M.," commented a local paper a few weeks later.[25]

On July 4 the rails were within a mile of Lincoln, and the company celebrated the occasion by offering a free round trip from Plattsmouth to Lincoln for all who wished to go. Not enough passenger coaches were yet available for such a train, however, so the excursionists used flat cars equipped with benches. Overhead, slats had been fastened to uprights, and across them were nailed freshly cut cottonwood branches as protection against wind and smoke. The affair was a rousing success and doubtless unique in the experiences both of the participants and the railroad.[26] On July 26, 1870, service was opened to the city of Lincoln, and by the end of the year, 60 miles of the road west from Plattsmouth were in operation; for 25 miles beyond, the grading was completed.[27] Oak ties and 57-pound rail were used for the first 63 miles, and all but 6 miles of the line had masonry abutments; the entire road was kept under a maximum grade of 22 feet per mile.

---

[22] Memorandum by Doane, July, 1870, quoted in Calvert to Manderson, May 22, 1898 (LDP).

[23] *Nebraska Herald* (Plattsmouth), February 10, 1870 (NSB).

[24] *Ibid.*, February 17, 1870 (NSB).

[25] *Ibid.*, March 31, 1870 (NSB).

[26] Colonel Bion J. Arnold (a passenger on the train) to Charles E. Fisher, December 14, 1935. (Used with special permission of Colonel Arnold.)

[27] *Ashland Times*, January 20, 1871 (NSB).

Meanwhile, various connecting roads were being built or projected into the Burlington's land-grant area. When Nebraska had been admitted as a state in 1867, commissioners had been designated to select a capital city. They had chosen a point on the projected route of the B. & M. in Nebraska, originally known as Lancaster, and renamed Lincoln in honor of the President. Immediately thereafter the Omaha and South Western Railroad was organized by private interests to build from Omaha to the new capital and beyond, in a southwesterly direction. No construction was undertaken, however, until work had begun on the B. & M. at Plattsmouth. Twenty miles were then built from Omaha to the Platte River at Oreapolis, where a connection was made by ferry with the B. & M.[28] Since this connecting line afforded a potential entrance into the fast-growing city of Omaha, the B. & M. in 1870 promptly concluded with it a temporary traffic arrangement.[29] At the same time, the Midland Pacific built westward from Nebraska City on the Missouri River, and in June, 1871, reached Lincoln.[30] Rumors of more roads were everywhere. Hall County officially offered the B. & M. $100,000 in subscriptions to its securities if the company would join the Union Pacific at Grand Island instead of at Kearney.[31] The citizens of Fremont on the Platte River sought to interest the people of Ashland, on the B. & M., in a new north-south road by declaring that "one road is no road"; there must be competition.[32] Still another line was projected from Ashland to Columbus.[33]

The B. & M. did not stand passively by in the face of this competition, actual or threatened. During the winter of 1870–71, engineers were sent out to survey lines from Ashland northwest to Wahoo and north to Fremont, whereupon the company was accused of mere stalling to defeat their rivals' flotation of bonds.[34] Other citizens of Ashland defended the "enterprise and zeal" of the B. & M.,[35] however, and when in May, 1871, the company cut the running time from

[28] BMN DRB, p. 45; see map, p. 402.

[29] CBQ, *Corporate History*, p. 360.

[30] *Ibid.*, p. 343; see as part of Nebraska Railway, map, p. 402.

[31] *Ashland Times*, August 12, 1870 (NSB).

[32] *Ashland Times*, December 9, 1870 (NSB), reprinted from *Fremont Tribune* (Fremont, Nebraska); *Ashland Times*, December 23, 1870 (NSB).

[33] *Ashland Times*, December 23, 1870 (NSB).

[34] *Ibid.*, and March 24, 1871 (NSB).

[35] *Ashland Times*, March 3, 1871 (NSB), reprinted from *Carlisle Herald* (Carlisle, Pennsylvania), January 26, 1871.

Ashland to Plattsmouth down to an hour and a half for the 30 miles, the editor of the local paper proclaimed that "this road knows how to run a railroad and accommodate the public." [36] Next month the *Nebraska Herald* reported that the B. & M.'s business was increasing so rapidly that there were insufficient cars and locomotives. [37]

Encouraged by this state of affairs, the board of directors on July 25, 1871, issued a circular to the stockholders. Therein they pointed out that when the road was commenced, it had been impossible, because of the newness of the venture and the uncertainties of the future, to make any definite plan for its completion. The business on the 55 miles to Lincoln, however, made it seem certain that the entire line to Fort Kearney could more than earn its interest on the necessary investment. In addition, the flood of immigration pouring into the South Platte country, and the public land sales under the preëmption and homestead laws convinced the directors that it was their "duty and . . . interest to furnish railroad facilities as quick as possible." [38] Consequently, they voted that $1,500,000 in bonds and $2,250,000 in stock be offered for sale to the stockholders. The response to this proposal was completely favorable, and the company determined to complete the entire road in 1871 if possible. Early in the fall, however, this plan received a setback from an unexpected quarter.

Under the terms of the grant of 1864, it was provided that each 20-mile strip of track as completed should be inspected by commissioners of the federal government. If their report to the General Land Office indicated proper construction, the railroad would then be entitled to receive patents for its granted lands. During September, 1871, the first 80 miles of the B. & M. west of Plattsmouth were duly examined, and on September 18 the commissioners completed their report. [39] It was favorable, but they pointed out that for the first 63 miles they had found rail weighing 57 pounds a yard, whereas for the last 17 miles, 48-pound rail had been used. These facts they reported to the Secretary of the Interior, Columbus Delano, who in turn wrote to President Brooks for an explanation. The latter's reply was

[36] *Ashland Times*, May 5, 1871 (NSB).
[37] *Ashland Times*, June 16, 1871 (NSB), reprinted from *Nebraska Herald*.
[38] BMN DRB, pp. 41–43.
[39] Delano to Grant, September 29, 1871 (USDI).

B. & M. IN NEBRASKA NO. 7, THE "WAHOO," BUILT AT MANCHESTER, N. H., 1870.

an illuminating summary of the engineering problems facing the new road.

Just before undertaking this road in Nebraska, he explained, the company had completed the Burlington and Missouri River Railroad across Iowa. The grades upon every working division of that road had a maximum in both directions of 68 6/10 feet per mile. Since such grades required "a large class of locomotives to move the traffic over them," a rail weighing 57 pounds per yard had been laid over the entire route. Likewise, the preliminary surveys for Nebraska indicated that there would be grades of upwards of 50 feet to the mile. Since much time would have been necessary to make a final location for the whole line and thus determine the exact grades which would be required, the work of construction at the east end of the road had been undertaken at once, and rails had been ordered of a weight suitable for large locomotives. While the eastern portion of the line was being built, Brooks continued, thorough examinations had been made of the country along the rest of the route, and it was found that a little to the southward, the line could be located with a maximum grade of 21 12/100 feet to the mile. The advantages to the company and the public of reducing the grades from about 50 feet to 21 feet were so great that Congress was petitioned, and passed an act approved May 6, 1870, allowing the necessary change and relocation of the line west of Denton. Therefore, said Brooks, the company had bought 48-pound rails for the rest of the line, and these had already been laid as far as Mile Post 140.[40]

On November 10, Delano replied that the 48-pound rail already laid would be acceptable, but that beyond Mile Post 140, 56-pound rail should be used. Four days later Brooks wrote he would comply with these instructions.[41] As a result of this delay, the railhead was still 50 miles short of Kearney at the end of 1871.

Meanwhile, on July 19, 1871, the B. & M. made its first and in some ways most important acquisition in Nebraska when it leased the Omaha and South Western for 999 years. Work began immediately on a bridge across the Platte River to connect the two lines, and at the north end of the leased road the tracks were extended a mile and one-half northwesterly in the city of Omaha to obtain better terminal

[40] Brooks to Delano, October 2, 1871 (USNA).
[41] Brooks to Delano, November 14, 1871 (USNA).

facilities. In the fall of 1871, the newly leased company, supported by a local bond issue, constructed a road southward from Crete to Beatrice, a distance of 31 miles.[42] During the next summer the main line of the B. & M. was completed, and on September 18, 1872, the final connection was made with the Union Pacific at Kearney Junction.

There was, to be sure, some difference of opinion as to the smoothness of the track. The Reverend Darius Jones, an enthusiastic booster and occasional employe of the company, declared that he was "surprised at the excellence of the road bed," [43] but a fellow divine, likewise a consistent supporter of the B. & M., bluntly remarked that "the track was so rough the bell rang of its own accord." [44] Whoever was right, it could not be denied that in less than two years the company had built a main line of 191 miles from Plattsmouth to Kearney and had acquired complete control of approximately 50 miles more by its lease of the Omaha and South Western.[45] The B. & M. thus obtained direct rail connection with Omaha and the five roads converging there, provided an alternate route for transcontinental traffic, and by means of the Plattsmouth ferry formed part of a separate through line to Chicago.

According to a circular issued by the directors to the stockholders January 22, 1873, the construction account, including interest, for the combined B. & M. and O. & S. W. lines of 241 miles amounted to $6,577,183.70, as of November 30, 1872. Receipts from the sale of bonds and stock had amounted to $6,416,655.00. Earnings of $225,829.01 in 1871 and $466,495.75 in 1872, less operating expenses, had been applied to interest payments. Between November 30, 1872, and the date of the circular, however, the directors had been called upon to pay the amounts necessary for completing the extreme western portion of the line, for the bridges across the Platte River near Kearney Junction and at Oreapolis, and for the maturing interest on the Omaha and South Western bonds due December 1, 1872, and on B. & M. bonds due January 1, 1873. These demands exceeded the means derived from all sources by about $500,000 which, as the circular pointed out, was "a very small deficiency in so large an undertaking, so creditably done

[42] CBQ, *Corporate History*, pp. 360–361.
[43] *Burlington Daily? Hawk-Eye*, November?, 1871 (LDP).
[44] Motier A. Bullock, *Congregational Nebraska* (Lincoln, 1905), p. 155.
[45] CBQ, *Corporate History*, p. 321.

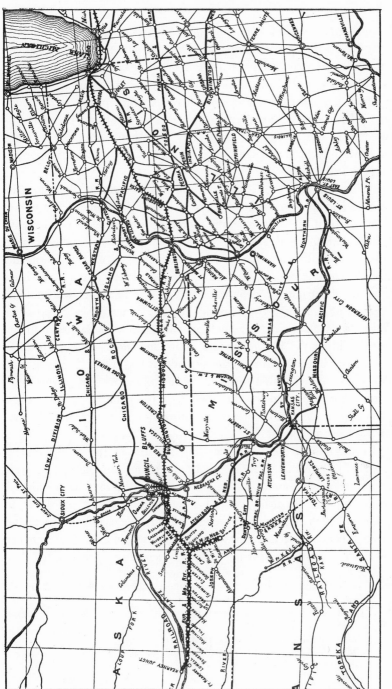

THE B. & M. IN NEBRASKA AS PART OF THE THROUGH ROUTE TO AND FROM CHICAGO VIA THE B. & M. (OF IOWA) AND THE C. B. & Q., 1873.

as to elicit the special commendation of the Government examiners, and the unvarying encomiums of all who have been over the road." [46] As the directors believed that the road could pay its expenses and interest with some assistance from the land department during 1873 and without any aid from that source thereafter, they proposed financing the balance due for construction by bonds to be offered to the stockholders in the amount of $600,000.[47] In other words, the original B. & M. in Nebraska together with the O. & S. W. would cost approximately $7,000,000.

At the time there was some feeling that Woodman, the officer in charge, had spent too much money in building the line.[48] He wrote, however, that "there is generally more danger of building a road too poorly than too well, and my council [*sic*] is to err if at all on what I think to be the safe side of true economy." [49] With this sentiment, the directors agreed. "While considerable money might have been saved in the original cost by constructing [the line] . . . less substantially, and still more by adopting heavier grades," they reported in 1874, "we shall avoid the annoyance and expense of half reconstructing it during the first few years of its operation, — a fate that has proved so disastrous to many new roads in the West." [50] There was, however, another reason for solid construction; "in view of our large land grant," observed the directors, ". . . the public . . . had a right to expect a well-built, first class railroad; . . . we have fully met the[se] just demands." [51]

By the end of 1873, the operating statistics of the new company revealed a growing business and bright prospects. During the year, 3,390 carloads of grain, compared with 1,224 in 1872, were shipped from points on the main line to Chicago and the East.[52] At the same time, although net railway revenue fell off imperceptibly, due to the high expenses of a new line, gross earnings doubled.[53] "We do not like to make estimates for the future," observed the directors, but they

---

[46] BMN, Circular to the Stockholders, January 22, 1873 (BMN DRB, p. 55).
[47] *Ibid.*
[48] Quoted in Calvert to Manderson, May 22, 1898 (LDP); Perkins to Forbes, September 8, 1873 (CNB, n.p.).
[49] Calvert to Manderson, May 22, 1898 (LDP).
[50] BMN, *Annual Report* for 1873 (Boston, 1874), p. 6.
[51] *Ibid.*
[52] *Ibid.*, p. 19.   [53] *Ibid.*, p. 20.

hinted at another doubling of gross, accompanied by only a slight rise in expenses.[54] "We trust," they concluded, "we may be allowed to congratulate the stockholders upon the results, thus far, of the undertaking, and still more upon the outlook for the future." [55]

Within four years, a well-integrated "system" of some 240 miles had thus been constructed on what was virtually an unoccupied prairie. This would have been "impracticable," as the directors frankly stated, without the "liberal grant of land" from the federal government; specifically, funds derived from mortgages upon the land had helped pay for ties and rails, rolling stock and buildings. The growing traffic, however, that had nourished the road in its first three years and that constituted the promise of an even greater future, was derived from the farmers and townspeople in B. & M. territory. Yet in 1870, that territory, particularly west of Lincoln, had been hardly civilized. How, in the short space of four years, had a whole community sprung into being? Why, at the end of 1873, was the company so optimistic about the growth of its business?

There were two principal reasons. One obviously was the construction of the railroad itself, which made all lands, whether owned by the company or not, accessible and attractive for settlement. The other was the tremendous colonization effort already put forth and planned for the future by the land department of the B. & M.

To a far greater degree than was true in Iowa, the directors of the company were called upon to create in Nebraska their own source of traffic; unlike the Union Pacific, their lines were not nourished during the 'seventies by through business. The B. & M. was dependent upon the products and needs of the territory it served; consequently, its imperative interests lay first in establishing a sound agricultural community, and secondly in encouraging the growth of shipping and receiving centers. The former objective was clearly by far the more important, and its attainment was consistently the principal concern of the B. & M. land department.[56] The creation of towns presented a more complex problem and this called for the organization of separate townsite companies; for even more compelling reasons than obtained in Iowa, these were undertaken throughout the 'seventies in Nebraska

[54] *Ibid.*, p. 13.
[55] *Ibid.*, p. 17.
[56] See chs. xii–xv below.

particularly by men who were individually connected with the railroad.

In the first place, the future of towns strategically situated on the main line of the B. & M. was practically guaranteed and presented an attractive opportunity for speculation. Because, as in Iowa, they had access to some capital and because they knew the route and the approximate locations of stations, the officers of the road were in a favorable position to take advantage of this opportunity. The fact that they did so naturally provoked hostility from time to time not only against themselves, but against the railroad as well, for their connection with the corporation and their access to "inside" information was well known. On the other hand, where the lack of development encouraged over-speculation, it was clearly not in the interests of either the community at large or the railroad that real estate promotion should be in the hands of irresponsible persons, or that town sites should be sold at exorbitant boom prices. Rather, the objective of citizens and company alike was the orderly and permanent development of the region.

During the early 'seventies, the most active of these companies was the Eastern Land Association, organized in September, 1870. Its founders were J. W. Brooks, J. M. Forbes, J. N. Denison, Henry Strong, J. W. Ames, C. E. Perkins, A. M. Ghost, Thomas Doane, George S. Harris, A. E. Touzalin, and W. B. Strong; its purpose was to buy and sell lands in the state of Nebraska and "principally upon the line of the Burlington & Missouri River Railroad." Each subscriber was to pay in $10,000, or as much thereof as was required by the trustees, namely Forbes, Brooks, and Denison, in whose names all lands were to be bought and sold for the benefit of all parties. Since the actual transactions were to be carried out by an agent, the trustees did not receive any fee for their services. Furthermore, they were to make all purchases in cash and keep books open to the inspection of all subscribers at any time. Profits, if any, were to be distributed from time to time, and the life of the association was fixed at ten years unless it was unanimously agreed to extend it.[57]

From available records it is not clear when this group began operations or where their first activities were concentrated. It is probable, however, that soon after their organization they began buying lands in and around all main line towns, including the "alphabetical sta-

[57] ELA, Articles of Agreement, September, 1870 (LDP).

"B. & M. F:MILY PHOTOGRAPH," AT BURLINGTON, JANUARY 14, 1873.

Standing, Left to Right: D. Dorman (Tie Agent); W. Irving (Purchasing Agent); R. S. Skinner (Agent); G. F. Chalender (Master Mechanic); T. E. Vaughn (Clerk); G. O. Manchester (Assistant in Land Department); J. W. Ames (Assistant Treasurer, former Land Commissioner); T. S. Potter (Superintendent); E. C. Brown (?); C. H. Smith (?); S. H. Mallory (Contractor); C. E. Yates (Superintendent of Telegraph).

Seated, Left to Right: F. E. Fayerweather (Auditor); W. B. Strong (General Manager); C. E. Perkins (General Superintendent, former Land Commissioner); A. E. Touzalin (General Passenger Agent); G. S. Harris (Land Commissioner); Captain W. Beckwith (Contractor).

tions" west of Lincoln which the railroad had named:[58] Crete, Dorchester, Exeter, Fairmont, Grafton, Harvard, Inland, Juniata, Kenesaw, and Lowell.[59] In the summer of 1871, the *Saline County Post* reported that in Crete, "town lots are mainly held by a company of B. & M. men, and are worth from $50 to $500. . . ."[60] A year later, the same association was credited with donating 52 of these lots to the Congregational College that had meanwhile been founded there.[61]

Some clue as to the methods of this group was revealed by the *Beatrice Express* early in 1872. On February 10 it reported that

D. N. Smith, Esq. of Burlington, who is at the head of the Town Company, an organization under the auspices of the B & M, and who occupies himself in spying out and purchasing town sites, arrived [in Beatrice] last week, and preached Sunday evening in the M. E. church. His business here was to aid in making selections of land. . . .[62]

Three months after this preliminary trip, Smith returned in a special train, accompanied by Touzalin and H. B. Scott of Burlington. Aside from selecting at the United States land office in Beatrice 320,260 acres inuring to the railroad under its grant,[63] he purchased 120 acres for the association, just south of the town already existing. The local newspaper welcomed this move and reported "general rejoicing that it has been taken," for it was felt the purchase would induce the railroad to make Beatrice a central point in their southern Nebraska system, and would justify the land department "in employing their great scheme of advertising for the town's benefit."[64] By October, 300 maps were distributed showing both Beatrice and South Beatrice, the latter divided into 473 lots, 44 by 140 feet. Appropriately enough, streets were named for Ames, Perkins, and Doane.[65]

Meanwhile, the *Beatrice Express* explained how the association conducted its operations at Lowell. The section of land constituting the

[58] These were probably named by Thomas Doane, which would explain the predominance of New England names. Cf. Calvert to Manderson, May 22, 1898 (LDP).

[59] SPL, Statement of the South Platte Land Co., 1876 (LDP). This organization succeeded the Eastern Land Association. See below, p. 288.

[60] *Saline County Post* (Crete, Nebraska), July 7, 1871 (NSB).

[61] Unidentified paper, June 9, 1872 (NSB).

[62] *Beatrice Express*, February 10, 1872 (NSB).

[63] *Ibid.*, May 4, 1872 (NSB).

[64] *Ibid.*, May 11, 1872 (Cap).

[65] *Ibid.*, October 31, 1872 (NSB).

town site was preëmpted, it reported, "by an original and comprehensive method." Four men, agents of the company, built a house in
the center of the section so that each corner would rest on a different
quarter-section. "The four enterprising pre-emptors then took up their
residence in the house, each in one of the four corners thereof," and
all of them broke a few acres in his "particular province." When they
had successfully proven up their claim, the property was handed over
to the association which, by the summer of 1872, was retailing it in
lots 22 by 140.[66] Not all towns, however, needed such rigorous
methods. At Fairmont, Dorchester, Juniata, and Kearney, for example,
development proceeded conventionally enough, although in the spring
of 1873 A. Gorham, writing from Harvard, remarked that a "feeling
of hostility . . . already exists to some extent against the Association." [67]
On the other hand, that same fall the *Beatrice Express* observed that
the townsite company had placed its property on the market "not for
the purpose of getting speculative figures for lots, but to induce settlement. They wish to develop the embryo town into a well-peopled
city . . . and stand ready to sell on very reasonable terms either for
cash or on time to suit the purchaser." [68]

On April 20, 1873, the South Platte Land Company was incorporated by the participants of the Eastern Land Association to take the
place of the older organization. The new company had as its object
"the purchase and sale of real estate and the plotting and laying out
of towns and villages" in Nebraska. Its capital stock was fixed at
$350,000 and its directors were authorized to buy the property of its
predecessor.[69] According to an inventory made some time later, this
transaction must have involved nearly $200,000, a figure suggesting
the extent of the association's purchases during the early 'seventies.[70]

[66] *Beatrice Express*, July 25, 1872 (NSB).

[67] Arthur Gorham to Perkins, April 22, 1873 (LDP).

[68] *Beatrice Express*, August 7, 1873 (NSB).

[69] SPL, Articles of Incorporation, April 20, 1873 (LDP).

[70] In a memorandum dated July, 1874, stockholders of the Eastern Land Asso-
ciation were listed as follows: J. M. Forbes, $37,882.88; Henry Strong, $15,807.09;
T. Doane, $15,331.23; J. N. Denison, $18,947.10; Denison Spl, $3,277.36; W. S.
Houghton, $17,666.66; J. W. Brooks, $18,947.10; J. W. Ames, $12,503.92; G. S.
Harris, $14,278.94; W. B. Strong, $7,179.00; C. F. Morse, $3,472.50; A. M. Ghost,
$1,254.87; Horatio Harris, $8,902.21; Hugh Montgomery, $4,451.11; Alpheus
Hardy, $3,338.33; Fisher Ames, $4,142.49; Arthur Gorham, $1,795.90; Jas. L.
Gorham, $3,881.44. The total holdings amounted to $193,060.13.

The work of this group, together with that of the smaller independent townsite companies that sprang up in such towns as Caldwell and York,[71] was not, of course, part of the railroad's formal colonization effort. Nevertheless, in so far as it contributed to the permanent settlement of B. & M. territory, it seconded the activities of the B. & M.'s land department.

[71] *Beatrice Express*, March 16, 1872 (NSB); *Blue Valley Record* (Milford), April 11, 1872 (NSB).

CHAPTER XII

George S. Harris Reorganizes the Land Department, 1869–1870

I. IOWA AND NEBRASKA

For purposes of construction, finance, and operation, the directors of the B. & M. had decided, in 1869, to have a separate organization to operate the railroad in Nebraska, particularly since the Iowa company was being absorbed by the C. B. & Q. according to a fixed plan that did not include any properties west of the Missouri River.[1] In land matters, however, much could be gained by having a consolidated department for the two companies. Even if accounts were kept separately, a single administration would eliminate competition between the two grants, substantially cut advertising and agency costs, and enable each line to benefit from the other's experience. Furthermore, first-rate land commissioners were rare, and now that one had been found, it was obviously wise to use his talents to the greatest advantage. Such considerations were doubtless in the directors' minds in giving Harris the management of the combined B. & M. land departments.[2]

When George S. Harris entered the employ of the Burlington system, he was probably the best known land-grant commissioner in the country. For nearly six years he had managed the Hannibal and St. Joseph's 600,000 acres in northern Missouri and had succeeded in selling approximately four-fifths of them to immigrants, thus adding, according to a contemporary newspaper, 100,000 people to the population of Missouri.[3] His methods were not new, for they were based almost entirely upon those of the Illinois Central,[4] but they were simplified, improved, and administered with energy and success. Thus,

[1] See above, pp. 274–276.
[2] Harris to Brooks, January 10, 1870 (LDP). In the fall of 1869, Harris retained his post as commissioner of the Hannibal and St. Joseph land department, but relinquished it on January 1, 1870, since the Iowa and Nebraska departments took all his time. (*Ibid.*)
[3] *Hannibal Courier*, June, 1870 (LDP).
[4] Gates, *op. cit.*, p. 184; Brooks to Perkins, May 24, 1869 (LDP).

in addition to his capacity for action, he brought to the Burlington confidence bred of experience.

The superb agricultural facilities of Iowa and Nebraska were now fully recognized. Furthermore, immigration was increasing daily. In both states, the influx of new citizens and the future in agriculture furnished incentives to throw the company lands on the market. As if these were not enough, there were additional compelling reasons for prompt action. Just north of the B. & M. in Iowa lay the old M. & M., now part of the Rock Island, with a land grant of some 550,000 acres ready for sale.[5] Further west the Kansas Pacific and the Union Pacific had already organized land departments.[6] By the end of 1869, the former had sold nearly 500,000 acres, and the latter reported that it was advertising in 2,539 papers and magazines with a combined circulation of 7,250,000 in the United States, Canada, England, Germany, France, Scandinavia, Wales, and Bohemia.[7] In addition, more remote roads such as the Northern Pacific and Santa Fe were pursuing active colonization work, thus producing a highly competitive atmosphere.[8] It behooved the B. & M. to swing into action without delay.[9]

At the outset, however, Harris was reminded that not everyone in Nebraska approved of the company's possession of such a heritage of land in the state. As early as December, 1869, the *Omaha Daily Herald* lamented the fact that a federal grant in Nebraska had been given a

[5] *Poor's Manual for 1871–72*, p. 223. This was an approximate figure used probably pending establishment of title. Like the B. & M., the Rock Island had obtained a second supplementary grant in 1864. After April 1, 1874, the Rock Island reported that 643,289.04 acres had been certified to it by the United States. (*Poor's Manual for 1875–76*, p. 533.)

[6] See map, p. 345. The Kansas Pacific began its colonization activities in 1868, the Union Pacific in July, 1869. (*Poor's Manual for 1870–71*, p. 229, and *Omaha Daily Herald*, 1870, LDP.) Although the St. Joseph and Denver City was geographically nearer the Burlington and Missouri, and had already received approximately 1,600,000 acres, it was not a serious competitor. (*Poor's Manual for 1870–71*, p. 81.)

[7] *Omaha Daily Herald*, n.d., 1870 (LDP).

[8] The former organized its land department in 1869. (James B. Hedges, "The Colonization Work of the Northern Pacific Railroad," *loc. cit.*, p. 320.) The latter began operations sometime during 1870. (Glenn D. Bradley, *The Story of the Santa Fe*, Boston, 1920, p. 124.)

[9] The Burlington and Missouri officials were fully aware of this competition and cited it as the chief reason for the rapid organization and liberal attitude of the land department. (BMN, *Annual Report* for 1873, Boston, 1874, p. 16.)

"foreign corporation," as it termed the B. & M. The *Nebraska Herald*, of Plattsmouth, sprang to the defense.

> How much better off would we be [it asked] with our lands in the hands of a home corporation? If a foreign corporation makes more money to hold these lands than to dispose of them soon would not a home corporation do the same thing? Are they not all made of the same kind of men? We know that it has seemed so far to be a disadvantage to the state to have so large a proportion of our lands tied up in railroad grants; but we also know that the Union Pacific have done more to advertise Nebraska than all the other advertising put together that has ever been done by home railroad companies, newspapers and every other species of advertising. We believe the *Herald* will agree with us. We further know that Mr. Harris, land agent of the Burlington and Missouri, is inaugurating a system of advertising for the disposition of their lands which will do more to advertise our state than all [previous efforts] including what the Pacific Company has done. . . . Mr. Harris has been the means of settling a large portion of Missouri. . . . The direct advertising of Nebraska lands will be of more benefit to the state than all the damage occasioned by the tying up of so large a portion of our domain.[10]

It was up to the B. & M. and its land department to justify this confidence.

The territory in which Harris was to work comprised some of the best farm land in the nation. The agricultural value of southern Iowa had been proven by two decades of experience, and now that it was at last easily accessible, it offered an unsurpassed opportunity for colonization. The population of Iowa as a whole had risen from 674,913 in 1860 to 1,194,020 in 1870, and, judging from the general influx into the West, there was every reason to suppose that this upward trend would continue.[11] Naturally, Harris was anxious to place his "400,000 acres of Iowa lands for sale before the people as soon as possible." [12] The prospects in Nebraska were even more promising. Most of the state's 122,993 inhabitants in 1870 lived in the southeastern counties near the Burlington's 2,500,000 acres.

No one realized more fully than George Harris that the success or failure of the Burlington's land department would depend in a large measure on the price and credit policies adopted by the company. And probably no one else on the system had a better insight into the many

---

[10] *Nebraska Herald*, December 16, 1869.
[11] *Census* of 1900.
[12] Harris to Butler, November 20, 1869 (LDP).

diverse factors involved in the problem. It was a tribute to Harris
that the directors gave him a virtually free hand in the administration
of his department, even when doing so involved a considerable
outlay without any prospects of immediate returns.[13] From the com-

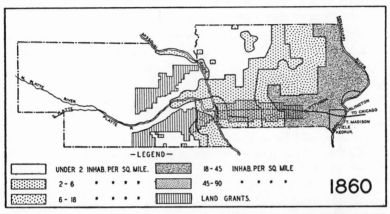

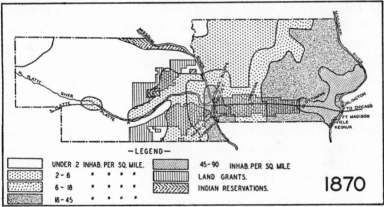

TREND OF POPULATION IN IOWA AND NEBRASKA IN RELATION TO THE B. & M.
LINES AND LAND GRANTS, 1860–1870.

pany's standpoint, the primary consideration in fixing land prices was
one that was universally shared and approved at the time: the necessity of filling up the country. Only thus could the railroad have the
indispensable clientele of shippers and travelers, and any sales policy
that restricted immigration or antagonized actual settlers for the sake
of some immediate pecuniary advantage would clearly defeat its own

[13] Harris to Brooks, January 10, 1870 (LDP).

ends. The making of money from land sales as a separate business, although highly desirable and constantly in view, was to be subordinate to the progress of colonization. This point had been clearly enunciated ten years before by Lowell,[14] and reiterated by Perkins.[15] Indeed, Harris himself had been guided by it in his highly successful administration at Hannibal.

Translated into practical terms, this meant that either the cash price for land had to be low or, if higher ultimate returns were desired, some long-term financing plan should be offered the purchaser. Of the two alternatives, Harris favored the latter.

It has always been true in Missouri [he reported to President Brooks] that we could get higher prices on our Long Credit of ten years than other land dealers could for cash, or on shorter time. . . . Besides, in view of the fact that our immigration is confined to poor men generally — for the rich do not emigrate to the frontier — success in making sales is far more certain on a long & generous credit than upon a different policy. . . .[16]

Further consideration brought forth only one reservation to this general conclusion. In respect to timber lands, the company felt it would be unwise to grant long credit, for too many settlers would be tempted to strip off the wood in the first year or two and then depart, leaving the land at a greatly reduced value. Otherwise, the policy of "generous credit" was thoroughly endorsed.

Another feature that would aid purchasers of modest means and improve the companies' cash position at the same time was the acceptance of land mortgage bonds of either company at their face value in lieu of cash. This scheme had been inaugurated by the Illinois Central as early as 1854[17] and copied by the Hannibal and St. Joseph[18] where, of course, Harris had become familiar with it. He wrote Brooks early in January, 1870, that if the plan were adopted for the B. & M. lines, it would cause a constant demand for bonds, especially if they could be bought at a "respectable discount" so as to give the land buyer a part of the benefit. Ultimately, he predicted, it would put up the market value of the securities to par. As a further help to persons of limited means, he suggested that arrangements should be made to

[14] See above, p. 150.
[15] See above, p. 193.
[16] Harris to Brooks, January 25, 1870 (LDP).
[17] Gates, op. cit., p. 160.
[18] HSJ, Land Pamphlet (Hannibal, 1860), p. 9.

allow a group of men to band together to purchase a full bond. Finally, he urged that the company should sell its bonds directly rather than through brokers; this procedure had saved the Hannibal and St. Joseph $16,000 in commissions. "Your $4,000,000 Nebraska Land Bonds can very soon be cancelled," persuasively concluded the commissioner, "with proceeds from the sale of lands. Shall it be done?"[19] The answer was in the affirmative.

Thus, in March, 1870,[20] it was announced that prairie lands would be sold on a ten-year credit basis at six per cent interest, and that both prairie and timber lands could be bought on two years' credit at ten per cent interest or for cash, a reduction of one-fifth from long-term prices. Bonds of the two companies would be acceptable at their face value for their respective properties.[21] The scheme of payment was identical with that in force on the Hannibal and St. Joseph,[22] and similar to that suggested but never used by Ames in 1868.[23] In the case of long credit, interest only would be payable at the time the contract was signed and for the first year thereafter. At the beginning of the third year, one-ninth of the principal would be due, and an equal amount annually thereafter until the obligation was liquidated ten years after the contract had been signed. If short credit were chosen, the settler would pay one-third of the principal down and the balance in two equal annual installments. This entire system was to be a standard practice for both Iowa and Nebraska land departments.[24]

Contracts offered under these arrangements not only afforded protection for the company's equity in the property, but also made provision for the permanent development of the community. Most of the conditions imposed on the buyer were copied directly from the older companies. For example, the new B. & M. contracts reserved a 200-foot right of way through each tract in case the line should be located there, and the purchaser was to pay all taxes and assessments.[25] These requirements had appeared in the Illinois Central, Hannibal and St.

---

[19] Harris to Brooks, January 10, 1870 (LDP).
[20] *Nebraska City News*, March 5, 1870 (LDP).
[21] BMR, Circular of Terms, April 25, 1870 (LDP).
[22] HSJ, *Annual Report* for 1870 (Boston, 1870).
[23] See above, p. 241.
[24] BMR, Circular of Terms, April 25, 1870 (LDP).
[25] BMN, Contract Ledger No. 1 (LDP).

Joseph,[26] and B. & M. of Iowa contracts.[27] Furthermore, the ten-year contracts stipulated that within each of the three years succeeding the date of the agreement, the purchaser or his assigns should improve by tillage or "some other course of good husbandry" at least one-tenth of the land, so that at the expiration of three years, three-tenths of the premises would be under cultivation. This clause was identical with one in the Hannibal and St. Joseph long-term contracts, and a modification of the original Illinois Central requirement that half the tract be improved over five years.[28] Like the Missouri road, the B. & M. prohibited the buyer on credit from removing timber except for fuel or building purposes, but unlike that company it excused its purchasers from the condition in certain contracts "that no spirituous liquors of any kind in quantities less than one gallon shall ever be sold upon the premises herein described." [29] Perhaps Harris felt that the injunction to cultivate the land discharged the companies' obligations as to the behavior of the community. On the whole, these requirements were not onerous. The provisions for cultivation were designed to discourage speculators and to guarantee a future source of traffic for the roads. The stipulations about timber were bred of sad experience with stripping. The *bona fide* settler would have little difficulty complying with the various terms.

Prices, of course, would be based on the valuations that were under way both in Iowa and Nebraska.[30] The factors that Harris would consider were nature of the soil, proximity to the railroad and other settlements, water supply, timber, and any particular advantages peculiar to each tract. A cardinal point in his pricing policy was the provision for frequent revaluations in the future; Harris intended to keep his schedule in line with prevailing realty values.[31] A flexible system of this sort would enable the company to retain customers by

[26] Samples of both I.C. and H.S.J. contracts are in a scrapbook kept by the BMR land department (LDP).

[27] BMI, Contract Ledger No. 1 (LDP).

[28] This strict provision was not thoroughly enforced by the Illinois Central, and was later modified. (Gates, *op. cit.*, pp. 159–160.)

[29] This curious requirement appeared only in the short-term contract.

[30] See below, pp. 305, 311–312.

[31] Harris to Brooks, November 2, 1869 (LDP); Harris to Brooks, January 25, 1870 (LDP).

lowering prices in hard times, and to share in any general prosperity by raising them in good times.[32]

Another task connected with the organization of the combined departments was the adoption of uniform record books and standard office routine. Naturally, Harris came with a predisposition in favor of the Hannibal and St. Joseph methods, but one of his first moves

OMAHA ABOUT 1872. UNION PACIFIC BRIDGE IN THE BACKGROUND.

was to write Commissioner Calhoun of the Illinois Central, requesting him to send along the forms of his tract book which Harris remembered, from a former visit, as being superior to anything at Hannibal.[33] Later he visited both the Illinois Central and Union Pacific land departments and planned to look in at the office of the Santa Fe, for, as he reported, "something is to be learned from all such visits." His final conclusion, however, was that on the whole the Hannibal and St. Joseph system excelled all others for comprehension, utility, and simplicity.[34] It was consequently adopted for both Iowa and Nebraska

[32] After the Panic of 1873, the company was forced to lower prices considerably. (See below, pp. 413–421; 429–435.)

[33] Harris to John B. Calhoun (of Chicago), October 7, 1869 (LDP).

[34] Harris to Brooks, January 25, 1870 (LDP).

land offices, and by the middle of January, books and blanks were ready for use.[35]

Even more important than prices and accounting was the matter of personnel, and in this respect Harris resembled John Murray Forbes in the stress he laid on securing able assistants.[36] He felt that a great point was gained in securing first-class employes and that too many corporations signally failed in that respect. "We had better pay too much for competent and reliable men," he told Woodman, "than to have incompetent and unreliable men for less than they are worth. . . ."[37] In October, 1869, the Illinois Central, which had already contributed much in ideas to George Harris' equipment, produced a valuable addition to the new company when Otto Synnesvedt applied for a job as examiner and appraiser. When Harris had found out from the Central's land commissioner that the applicant was not only a good judge of land but also a Scandinavian well versed in his countrymen's ways, he hired him and in the spring sent him to Lincoln as part of the permanent staff.[38] Superintendent Woodman was asked to provide the newcomer with a horse and start him out to solicit land applications, examine lands, report valuations, look after invalid homesteads and preëmptions, and get all possible data. At the same time he was to help with all Swedish advertising.[39]

An appointment of greater significance was that of Professor J. D. Butler. When he was hired by Harris, the professor was already known as a world traveler, having visited four continents, and as a lecturer, instructor, entertainer, and regular correspondent for various newspapers not only in his native Wisconsin but also in the larger American cities and in Europe.[40] Harris learned, on October 6, 1869, that Butler was homeward bound from Honolulu, and immediately telegraphed to arrange a meeting at Omaha, where the professor was to be entertained by General Alvord.[41] The results of the conference

[35] Harris to Brooks, January 10, 1870 (LDP). Plat and tract books had been ready since October, 1869. (Harris to Woodman, October 16, 1869, LDP.)

[36] Pearson, op. cit., pp. 96–106, 154–180, and above, pp. 108, 111–112.

[37] Harris to Woodman, November 29, 1869 (LDP).

[38] Harris to Synnesvedt, October 16, 1869 (LDP).

[39] Harris to Woodman, March 18, 1870 (LDP).

[40] There are many letters by Harris to his superiors outlining Butler's qualifications; e.g., Harris to Robert Harris (of Chicago), October 16, 1869 (LDP); Harris to Brooks, January 10, 1870 (LDP).

[41] Harris to Butler, October 6, 1869 (LDP).

were fruitful; Butler agreed to become "advertising correspondent" for the Iowa and Nebraska lines, and the two B. & M. companies undertook jointly to furnish a salary of $2,500 per annum. In explaining this arrangement to President Brooks, Harris said that his idea was to popularize Iowa and Nebraska lands through Butler's widely published "entertaining & practical letters," and by means of "well-concocted circulars, Posters & a judicious amount of advertising" which, he was certain, would produce "a big stampede of immigrants for these favored lands. I am going in distinctly," he revealed, "for large colonies of Yankees, Canadians, English, Welsh, Scotch, Bohemians & Scandinavians." [42] To Butler, his directions and suggestions were even more specific.

It was all well enough for the professor to do his writing in Wisconsin, but the commissioner had definite ideas as to how Butler should gather his information and how it should be presented.

I . . . deem it very important [he wrote] for you to spend enough time in Iowa (and Nebraska too by & by) to become thoroughly posted in all items of local interest by seeing the country with your own eyes & coming in personal contact with Tom, Dick & Harry & thus learning to word-paint current moving interests better than you can by reading all the books, pamphlets & papers published. . . . Besides, there will be [more] . . . freshness, originality, vigor & snap to your plain *Anglo-Saxon words* than can be possible if you quote all the finest things said or written by the best authors; my ambition is to have you excell [sic] them all, and I am confident you will. . . .[43]

There was wisdom in this advice. Harris well knew the appeal of unvarnished practical information.

I have contemplated from the start [he continued] that you would lecture here & there as you have opportunity. This will not injure but rather help your usefulness for the B. & M. RR & its Land Dept. by giving to yourself and them a profitable notoriety, as you will of course tuck in Iowa & Nebraska Lands in such a way as to advertise them, & the people not know the motives, either in lecture rooms or in the columns of the numerous periodicals to which you gain access. . . .[44]

This scheme of "oblique advertising" was dear to Harris' mind; in the same letter he suited action to words by reminding Butler that

[42] Harris to Brooks, November 2, 1869 (LDP).
[43] Harris to Butler, November 20, 1869 (LDP).
[44] *Ibid.*

the Congregational Church in Burlington had, at the moment, no regular preacher, "& if you will give me timely notice, it's very probable that I can arrange for you to preach for us. . . ."[45] Apparently there was nothing sacrilegious to Harris in this suggestion; it was merely a part of his advertising campaign.

Turning to the subject matter that Butler should present, the commissioner explained that potential settlers should be as fully informed as possible about their future homeland. For example, Butler should find out the cost of building materials, of rails for fencing, of breaking and plowing per acre. Did the Osage orange do well for hedges in Iowa, and how much would 100 shrubs cost? How soon would they afford adequate crop protection? What was wood worth a cord? Was coal abundant and at what price? For what could good horses or breeding mares be bought? How much were oxen, milch cows, sheep, stock hogs? Was there any good clay for brick? Was there enough lime and sand and building stone for the average farmer? Was there enough timber for fuel and building purposes, and sufficient water? What of the health of the country; should the settler guard against any particular diseases? Finally, how poor could a man be to set himself up and do well in Iowa and Nebraska?[46] These were the questions that Harris knew from experience homeseekers would certainly ask; the encyclopaedic Illinois Central[47] and Hannibal and St. Joseph[48] pamphlets had devoted a short paragraph to each of them. Harris planned to have the B. & M. pamphlets printed in German, Danish, and Scandinavian as well as in English, and to have them distributed through an "economical arrangement" by the ocean transportation companies. This, he pointed out, would be a wise policy, for it would fix a goal in the minds of the emigrants before they left their homes and save them for the railroad from "the army of landsharks besetting them as soon as they land in America & when they pass through Chicago."[49]

From his experience in Hannibal, Harris had acquired great faith in the efficacy of these pamphlets, and since they were to carry complete information, he saw no reason for long and involved columns of

[45] Ibid.
[46] Ibid.
[47] Gates, op. cit., ch. ix.
[48] HSJ, Land Pamphlet (Hannibal, 1860).
[49] Harris to Woodman, December 8, 1869 (LDP).

expensive newspaper advertisements such as the Illinois Central had used. He preferred rather very brief notices merely stating that the pamphlets were available to anyone interested; such squibs had brought hundreds of inquiries a day to the Hannibal and St. Joseph. This was the system Harris recommended and planned to adopt. Furthermore, he strongly urged that family and agricultural rather than urban papers be used as media; he doubted strongly whether the Illinois Central's expenditure of $6,000 in the *Boston Post, Advertiser*, and *Traveler* had sold an acre, and in corroboration cited the Central's land commissioner to that effect.[50] This observation by Harris, based on past experience, together with his stated aim for the future to attract farmers, laborers, and mechanics, was illuminating. It would seem that if the West were serving as a safety valve for the overcrowded East, it was doing so by draining off the surplus agricultural population rather than attracting city workers away from their jobs. Harris had apparently perceived this phenomenon and planned to be guided accordingly.

In addition to pamphlets, the commissioner suggested the use of bulletin boards, car posters, handbills, and particularly circulars, — all of them containing simply headline information and referring the reader to the company for further details. Finally, he recommended the issuance of 10,000 maps at once on a self-liquidating basis. They should show North America on one side and the United States on the other, the latter indicating the location of the B. & M.'s Iowa and Nebraska lands. Such maps, he estimated, could be prepared for 50 or 75 cents, and sold for slightly more all over the United States, Canada, and Europe. This plan too had been tried at Hannibal with great success.[51] By January, 1870, the commissioner was planning to order no less than 100,000 maps.[52]

Early in January, Harris corrected and returned to Butler the proof of an article entitled "The Homesteader" with the suggestion that it be published in the *Boston Journal*, the *Rutland Herald*, and "all other

---

[50] Harris to Brooks, January 10, 1870 (LDP).   [51] *Ibid.*

[52] Harris to Brooks, January 26, 1870 (LDP). Harris thought it might be wise to sell the maps at cost because of their advertising value but eventually favored adding 10 or 15 cents to the price. He consulted Brooks as to what other railroad lines to include. (*Ibid.*) Eventually the maps included, in very faint lines, the Rock Island, Northwestern, Illinois Central, Union Pacific, and Kansas Pacific, all of them rivals. (LDP.)

good papers throughout the land." The letter gave the commissioner an opportunity to digress on several subjects pertinent to future advertising. He hoped, for example, that the two B. & M. lines would some day be called the "Burlington and Fort Kearney," for at the moment, "hardly a man in the U. S. can tell where the roads are. This is a RR'd age, and such things ought not to be." The suggestion was good in theory, but hardly practical in a day when every system was building beyond its original terminals. Referring to terms of land sale, the commissioner gave some clue as to how settlers might expect to be treated. The B. & M., he said, would proceed just like the Hannibal and St. Joseph who during the past decade

have made scores & scores of poor men rich & happy with good homes with their liberal system of credit & generous disposition & treatment of their customers *if from any good cause their land buyers want indulgence to meet their payments.* This course of conduct has characterized first the "Illinois Central RR Co." & then the "old reliable Hannibal & St. Jo" and doubtless will the great "U. P." & the "Burlington & Missouri River Roads." . . . [53]

As to whether the B. & M. was sufficiently worthy of the people's confidence, Harris pointed out that the same owners and managers were operating the Michigan Central, the Hannibal and St. Joseph, the St. Joseph and Council Bluffs,[54] the Missouri River, Fort Scott and Gulf,[55] and the Great Western of Canada [56] —

one of the richest, if not *the richest* railroad association in the world. Among the Directors & prominent Stockholders of these great trunk Railroads are the solidest of the "solid men of Boston." Possessing long-tried & sterling integrity, combined with immense wealth, they must & will command as they eminently deserve, the entire confidence of all. . . .[57]

Provided with information of this sort and with the results of his own observation, Butler submitted the manuscript for a circular on Iowa by the end of January, 1870,[58] and soon after, Harris ordered 20,000 of them to be printed.[59] Meanwhile articles by the professor

---

[53] Harris to Butler, January 13, 1870 (LDP). (Italics supplied.)

[54] Now part of the Burlington Lines.

[55] Now part of the St. Louis–San Francisco Railway Company.

[56] Now part of the Michigan Central (New York Central) Lines.

[57] Harris to Butler, January 13, 1870 (LDP).

[58] Harris to Brooks, January 25, 1870 (LDP).

[59] Harris to Osborn & Snow (of Burlington), March 17, 1870 (LDP). The cost was $11 per thousand.

had appeared in such widely separated organs as the *Watchman and Reflector*, a Boston Baptist paper, and the Madison, Wisconsin, *State Journal*, which sold its "insides" to about 15 country newspapers and thus tapped a wide market in what Harris termed "one of the best states to induce immigration from." [60]

As winter gave way to spring, Harris reached a decision on the matter of agencies. Local ones would be established as the lands were put on sale, "probably as soon as the first of April," [61] but he was willing to arrange for out-of-state agencies at once. To R. Hollub of Hannibal, for example, he offered a commission of three per cent on all sales in Iowa or Nebraska; he promised to send circulars along within a month. The English edition would come first and then, when there was time, the German one.

I have so poor an opinion of the French & Italian immigrants for agriculturists [he revealed] that I shall not issue any circulars in their languages. My efforts will be most confined to Germans, Scandinavians, English, Welsh and Scotch, as they make good farmers together with all I can induce from the Northern and Eastern States & the British Provinces of America.[62]

This statement elaborated his position as outlined to Brooks some months previously; [63] in time he was to change his mind about Frenchmen.[64]

---

[60] Harris to Brooks, January 26, 1870 (LDP). A typical voucher for Butler's expenses was as follows:

Services for January (1/12 of $1,250)	$104.17
Services for February	104.16
Meals in Chicago and Galesburg at $1.50	3.00
Meals on cars	2.00
Meals at Plattsmouth	.75
Omnibus: Chicago $1.50, Madison $.50	2.00
Sleeper, five nights	10.00
Newspapers $2; postage $.50	2.50
Hotel at Burlington	1.50
	$230.08*

* This was the amount charged the Nebraska road, and presumably represented roughly half of Butler's expenses. (Voucher to J. D. Butler, March 17, 1870, LDP.)

[61] Harris to L. L. Lundy (of Oskaloosa, Iowa), March 13, 1870 (LDP).

[62] Harris to Hollub, March 5, 1870 (LDP).

[63] See above, p. 299.

[64] See below, p. 347.

II. IOWA

While these matters pertaining to the combined department were being worked out, Harris devoted special attention to the separate problems in each state. Naturally enough, he expected to be ready for business in Iowa first where, in contrast with Nebraska, there was already an existing land organization. Furthermore, now that the line was finished to the Missouri River, the entire grant in Iowa could be thrown on the market the moment the department was ready to administer it. Affairs in the Burlington office, however, were sorely in need of attention, and Harris had no illusions as to the task ahead of him. "An office is to be fitted up," he wrote, "and the whole Iowa Land Department is to be remodelled, or nearly so." [65] J. Dana Bacon, formerly one of Colonel Ames' assistants, was put in charge, and by November, 1869, Harris optimistically hoped that reorganization would be completed during the winter so that he could give most of his own time to the work in Nebraska.[66]

But there was more than optimism needed to unravel the tangled skein at Burlington. From the jumbled records on file there it was difficult to determine in many cases whether certain parcels of land belonged to the company or not. Harris uncovered numerous lists from the commissioner of the General Land Office purporting to give the railroad sections, but many of them covered the same ground, one correcting another, and in the end often conflicted with lists of preemption, homestead, swamp, or tax-sale lands. To add to the confusion were Steiger's endless reports. Steiger had laboriously attempted to bring order out of the chaotic Land Office rulings, and to obtain a favorable decision in the swamp and preëmption disputes, but there was no denying the mess at Burlington.[67]

Even the information concerning lands clearly belonging to the company was woefully inadequate. Since the original examination of the Iowa grant a decade previous there had been no comprehensive survey of the company's lands or readjustment of prices. The partial reëxamination ordered by Perkins in 1863 had been on too small a scale to serve as a general reappraisal, and in any event, the informa-

---

[65] Harris to Butler, November 20, 1869 (LDP).
[66] *Ibid.*, and Harris to Woodman, November 29, 1869 (LDP).
[67] Harris to Brooks, December 28, 1869 (LDP).

tion then gathered was now obsolete.[68] During the years 1866–69, Ames had simply sold plots for what he thought they would bring, and frequently his guesses were wide of the mark.[69] As early as November, 1869, Harris had written to Brooks that he deemed it one of his "highest duties" to be personally conversant with the value of each parcel of unsold land;[70] later he flatly declared it would be "folly" to attempt any sales in Iowa before a new survey had been made and a complete price schedule adopted.[71] Consequently, by mid-December he had 17 "capable & reliable" men at work examining every 40-acre tract in the state that belonged to the company.[72] Turning to the ministry, he hired the Reverend C. H. Pratt of Brookfield, Missouri, to set up the new lists in proper form and introduced the newcomer to Bacon with the injunction to "crowd the work along."[73] By January Harris himself had made three trips through Iowa,[74] and found the work sufficiently far along to confirm his conviction of its necessity, for it revealed that most of the Iowa lands had been grossly undervalued. He looked forward to the completion of the difficult task within a few weeks, when he planned to review the final reports with D. N. Smith, "the old and efficient land explorer of this Company."[75]

While this much needed reorganization was taking place in the Burlington office, Harris was kept busy replying to the numerous requests for land that kept pouring in from would-be purchasers. To all of them he explained that for the moment no sales were being made but that full details would be published when the lands were thrown on the market. This, he hoped, would occur about April 1, 1870,[76] and possibly sooner in Iowa.[77] With certain important colonists, Harris

[68] See above, p. 195.
[69] See above, ch. x.
[70] Harris to Brooks, November 2, 1869 (LDP).
[71] Harris to Brooks, January 10, 1870 (LDP).
[72] Harris to Brooks, January 18, 1870 (LDP).
[73] Harris to Pratt, December 2, 1869 (LDP); Harris to Bacon, December 8, 1869 (LDP).
[74] Harris to Brooks, January 1, 1870 (LDP).
[75] Harris to Brooks, January 18, 1870 (LDP). A month later Harris wrote: ". . . a sharper, shrewder man than this same *strong* ex-Methodist minister D. N. Smith I have not met in the West & I think Mr. Perkins will fully endorse this statement." (Harris to Brooks, February 15, 1870, LDP.)
[76] Harris to various persons, February, 1870 *et seq.* (LDP).
[77] Harris to Brooks, January 25, 1870 (LDP).

took particular pains. A large party of Canadians who were in search of lands in Nebraska had impressed him as exceptionally desirable immigrants, and he instructed the local agent to keep them occupied exploring until the final prices were ready.[78] "They have money," he wrote, "and are good substantial people & will draw other Canadians. . . . Please nurse & beguile them so they will tie to us. In other words, please be wise as the serpent, etc. . . ."[79] His tactics in regard to the Reverend B. M. Halland of Burlington, who had visited western Iowa in April, 1869, were somewhat different. He was anxious enough to have him and his Scandinavian flock buy their chosen tracts, but Harris thought that the prices quoted by Ames were too low and could not therefore be indefinitely offered. On March 30, 1870, he gave them 30 days in which to accept the original terms; thereafter they would be required to pay the scheduled prices and established rates of interest.[80]

At the same time, it was necessary to revise the arrangements Ames had made with various agents throughout Iowa. To Ithamar S. Beall, for example, Harris wrote in December, 1869, requesting him to return all the blank notes and contracts in his possession. He explained that sales were being suspended during reappraisal, and that when they were resumed, a different procedure would be followed. For one thing, no promissory notes would be accepted for land bought on credit.[81] This practice, inaugurated by the Illinois Central,[82] had been copied by Perkins and Ames.[83] Harris, however, was determined to follow the Hannibal and St. Joseph policy of selling either for cash or in accordance with a long-term contract,[84] the object being "to simplify the manner of doing business as much as possible. When lands are paid for," he elaborated, "we shall give a deed. When bought on time, a contract until the same is paid in full."[85] It was obviously a safer risk for the company to part with a deed only after all payments

[78] Harris to Woodman, March 1, 1870 (LDP).

[79] Harris to Woodman, March 8, 1870 (LDP).

[80] Harris to Halland, March 30, 1870 (LDP).

[81] Harris to Beall, December 18, 1869 (LDP); cf. Harris to J. W. Penny (of Leon, Iowa), January 12, 1870 (LDP).

[82] Illinois Central contract (LDP).

[83] Cf. BMI, Contract Ledger No. 1 (LDP).

[84] HSJ contract (LDP).

[85] Harris to Beall, December 18, 1869 (LDP).

had been made, and all agents would be guided accordingly in the future.

The commitments that Ames had made with private parties presented a far more serious problem. Ever since 1865 the Iowa land department had accepted applications for purchase for lands not yet on sale, and by December, 1869, some 2,000 of them had piled up in the Burlington office. Although these applications were not legally binding preëmptions on the tracts in question, they constituted a moral obligation on the company, and to disregard them would certainly cause ill feeling. There was no telling how many of the applicants would eventually become purchasers, but as Harris rightly perceived, "owing to assurances given by Genl. Ames to these applicants that they should have the first choice to buy the lands selected, the good faith of this Land Dept. requires that these promises should be fulfilled."[86] The situation was unfortunate, for Harris was convinced that irresponsible speculators had taken advantage of the policy to monopolize the best sites along the whole line in Iowa without paying a dime for the privilege. This, he felt, was all wrong, for it would clog sales to actual settlers and ultimately embarrass the department in its relations with the community.[87] On the other hand, a workable preëmption plan would be highly useful, for it was already obvious that the company would wish to sell lands in the five eastern counties of Nebraska before it had completed enough construction to obtain certification of the tracts from the United States,

the "red tape" of which is too slow to answer the practical wants of the masses who desire to emigrate to Nebraska early enough to "break prairie" & get in & reap crops in the coming autumn. . . .[88]

Consequently, Harris decided to make a prolonged visit at Burlington to devise some preëmption technique that would eliminate the speculator evil and at the same time provide a basis for future operations. "I fear it will prove a perplexing job and retard our progress," he

[86] Harris to Brooks, January 18, 1870 (LDP). The wording of the applications was, in part: "To the Land Agent, B & M RR. Sir: I am anxious to purchase the above described tract of Land at the price named, cash. If, when your lands are ready for Market, you cannot accept this figure, please write me your terms of sale. . . . The application is not to be held binding, but will receive due attention when the lands are brought into the market." (BMI, Application Books, LDP.)

[87] Harris to Brooks, December 13, 1869 (LDP).

[88] Harris to Butler, January 13, 1870 (LDP).

reported to Brooks, but "the experience will be instructive & we can act in Nebraska all the wiser for it." [89]

Two weeks of intensive investigation convinced Harris more than ever that the plan as practiced in Iowa, and also on the Union Pacific in respect to lands not yet on sale, merely encouraged irresponsible persons to obtain a virtual refusal of the land at the company's valuation. He suggested, therefore, that henceforth $20 be deposited with each application for 40 acres, said amount to be allowed in payment of the land within 30 or 60 days after the railroad had served notice that its title was complete and the lands on sale. If the preëmptor failed to exchange his certificate for a contract, he was to forfeit his deposit; if, on the other hand, the company failed to obtain final title, the deposit would be returned without interest.[90]

Brooks thought these terms were too stiff and suggested that the preëmption process should be made at least as favorable to the buyer as an actual purchase. Harris quickly agreed to this logic, "& especially so," he wrote, "as Mr. Woodman and myself contemplated securing only such preëmptors as would become actual settlers and not mere venturing speculators." [91] He consequently recommended that the company require as a deposit either one-third of the short-credit value of the land, or six per cent of the long-credit price. The latter scheme would put the preëmptor on exactly the same footing as the purchaser by contract. Nor would the company stand to lose by giving him this treatment for, as Harris pointed out, the lands would be steadily increasing in value, and if the preëmption should not result in an actual sale, the tracts could be revalued and sold to another buyer at an advanced price. Thus, the B. & M. could "well afford to adopt a liberal & popular policy in this matter." [92]

Since Perkins was anxious to place the Iowa lands on the market at the earliest possible moment, Harris set February 15, 1870, as the date for beginning sales in that state,[93] and in anticipation of the event

---

[89] Harris to Brooks, December 13, 1869 (LDP).

[90] Harris to Brooks, December 28, 1869 (LDP).

[91] Harris to Brooks, January 25, 1870 (LDP). Harris had recently received a report from Treasurer Lathrop of the Hannibal and St. Joseph indicating that the line had realized a substantial profit from the resale at an advanced price of lands forfeited through cancellation of contracts. (*Ibid.*)

[92] *Ibid.*

[93] Harris to Brooks, November 2, 1869 (LDP), and January 25, 1870 (LDP).

moved the Burlington staff into new quarters on the second floor of a new brick building almost opposite the passenger depot. Outside, a bold sign advertising "Iowa and Nebraska Lands" attracted the attention of every newcomer to the city; [94] the wheels were ready to turn as soon as price lists were made ready and the office completely organized. This, however, proved to be a longer task than anyone anticipated in the fall, and the date for beginning sales was postponed to April 1, 1870.[95] The postponement was indeed fortunate, for the final appraisals of the land examiners did not reach Burlington until March and then, to Harris' dismay, he found the suggested prices so far below what he had been used to in Missouri for similar lands that he and King started a hectic, last-minute revision. By April they had completed the new schedule for the region east of the center of Adams County and were ready to offer it for sale; the rest of the Iowa grant would have to be withheld until revaluation was complete. In the meantime, Harris was rushing to put affairs in shape west of the Missouri River. "I have never," he reported to Brooks, "worked so incessantly early & late & night & day as I have during the past winter." [96]

III. NEBRASKA

From the beginning of his administration, the commissioner gave his chief attention to the work in Nebraska. There was indeed more of a challenge in the sparsely populated, potentially rich farm lands stretching out west of the Missouri. In 1869, with the Indian menace being eliminated and a horde of anxious homeseekers pressing along the frontiers, Harris was convinced that the area needed only a railroad and intelligent publicity to spring into life; he determined to provide both with all possible speed. His faith in the future of the West and in the company's ability to exploit it was boundless; even before a foot of rail had been laid west of the river or an acre of land sold, he wrote to Brooks:

If I am as successful in carrying out my plans as I expect to be, we shall want more land within three or five years — and with this feeling I am looking with interest for some arrangement to turn up whereby your com-

[94] Harris to Brooks, November 2, 1869 (LDP).
[95] *New York Tribune*, March 4, 1870.
[96] Harris to Brooks, April 28, 1870 (LDP).

RAILWAYS IN THE UNITED STATES, 1870.

DENSITY OF POPULATION IN THE UNITED STATES, 1870.

pany will acquire more RR land on paying terms, say towards Denver and thence on through Colorado, Utah, Nevada or Arizona & California. There are enough people in the United States, British Provinces and Europe to well occupy all these patches [sic] of territory — all that is necessary to accomplish this result is to practically and wisely adopt the proper means — and I fancy that as your "Boston Ring" are now well started in this program, it will not be completed nor stop till the whistle of your own engines are heard on the coast of the Pacific. . . .[97]

Such was the dream; in the meantime it was necessary to set up an organization in the prairie state. To this work Harris turned with vigor.

The commissioner realized that for several reasons the logical location for the Nebraska land department headquarters was Lincoln. It was centrally located in respect to company lands, accessible, and, as the capital of the state, an excellent advertising center. More important, it was apparent that many prospective purchasers would be Nebraskans who held or would obtain the maximum 80 acres within the grant limits under the homestead and preëmption acts, and who would next wish to purchase adjacent railroad lands. Since the United States land office was at Lincoln, it would be to the company's advantage to have its headquarters at the same spot to facilitate such transactions. By so doing the company would also save itself the commissions it would otherwise have to pay local agents or middle men, and Harris remarked that this potential saving would be large enough to pay for a separate office building.[98] Lincoln was chosen forthwith, but for the time being the ambitious commissioner had to content himself with rented quarters.[99]

As these matters were taking shape in Lincoln, a thorough examination of the company's land, similar to the survey in Iowa, was in progress in the eastern portion of the state. Since the appraisals were being made for the first time, however, and would form the basis for

[97] Harris to Brooks, November 2, 1869 (LDP).
[98] Harris to Brooks, September 30, 1869 (LDP). Harris had his eye on a lot 25x60, next to the principal hotel, already equipped with a stone foundation, and for sale at $2,500. Other unimproved lots, 25x140, were for sale at $1,500. (Ibid.)
[99] During the summer of 1870, offices were rented in a building belonging to Mr. A. C. Tichenor. Late in August, however, the building fell down and the department was forced to take up temporary quarters elsewhere. (Harris to Tichenor, September 2, 1870, LDP, and Harris to Synnesvedt, September 2, 1870, LDP.)

the entire price schedule, their accuracy was a matter of utmost importance. Harris engaged three of the most competent men he could find for the work, but even so he was not disposed to delegate final responsibility in the matter. Thus when the field work for Cass, Otoe, Saunders, Gage, and Lancaster counties was completed in November, 1869, he prepared to make a personal examination to "verify, revise and harmonize" the whole list. Local appraisers, he felt, were too apt to be influenced by private and speculative considerations, and he regarded his own inspection as a necessary and "fixed purpose" of his program.[100]

Such an undertaking was not an easy task for a man of fifty-five in the dead of winter, especially in view of other pressing business which was continually calling him to Plattsmouth, Hannibal, and Burlington. His reports of flooded streams, snowstorms, and the cold recalled the experiences of the Iowa surveyors a decade before.[101] But in spite of these handicaps, he kept at his rounds, and by January had made eight extended trips through Nebraska in addition to three through Iowa, thus obtaining a thorough knowledge of the lands he was to sell. From the company's standpoint, at least, his exertions were worth while, for among other things he reached the conclusion that prices on railroad lands could be materially increased over the first local estimates.[102]

Meanwhile, Harris was considering ways to obtain more lands for the B. & M.,[103] and in the middle of November called at the capital in Lincoln to sound out the prospects for a state donation on behalf of the Omaha and South Western, which was already allied with the B. & M. Governor Butler was away, and Harris found Auditor Gillispie in an irritable mood owing to the fact that he had just been approached by John I. Blair of the Union Pacific. Blair had demanded, for the Sioux City branch of that road, all the choice state lands adjacent to the line, basing his claim to preference on the fact that his was the "pioneer" railroad, the first to open up the state, and the foremost in attracting immigration. These arguments had apparently served merely to convince the auditor of the railroads' grasping ways,

[100] Harris to Brooks, January 1, 1870 (LDP).
[101] See above, pp. 145–146.
[102] Harris to Brooks, January 1, 1870 (LDP).
[103] Harris to Brooks, November 2, 1869 (LDP).

and he had replied that all state lands should be classified and then every road to which grants had been made should be given a pro rata share of each class of land, good and bad, irrespective of when the road was constructed. Such a policy seemed far too conservative for Harris and, as he reported to Woodman, "I saw it was useless to attempt then to mollify Mr. G.'s tone so I dropped the matter with

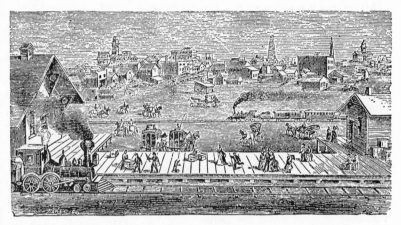

LINCOLN ABOUT 1872. B. & M. STATION IN LEFT FOREGROUND.

the conviction that Gov. Butler and Secy. Kennard are the majority & the two of the three to negotiate with." [104] Harris was right. By February, 1870, Blair had obtained the lands he sought for his Sioux City branch, and relying on this "good precedent," Harris persuaded the governor and secretary to grant 20,000 contiguous acres in northeastern Jefferson County. Moreover, the governor indicated a willingness to grant some alternate even sections of state lands in Saline County within the company's 20-mile limit, thus forming a solid block of land ideal for the formation of a colony.[105]

Harris now prepared to offer the first block of company lands to the public. About February 1 he opened a branch land office at Plattsmouth,[106] and two weeks later announced that the sale of approxi-

[104] Harris to Woodman, November 20, 1869 (LDP).

[105] Harris to Woodman, February 16, 1870 (LDP). In addition to Harris, the railroad was represented by Chief Engineer Doane, Examiner D. N. Smith, and Attorney T. M. Marquett. (*Ibid.*) The B. & M. in Nebraska eventually received 50,000 acres from the state. (BMN, *Annual Report* for 1873, Boston, 1874, p. 13.)

[106] *Nebraska Herald*, February 3, 1870 (NSB).

mately 300,000 acres would begin in the five eastern counties of Nebraska on a preëmption basis on April 1.[107] This announcement at once crystallized the situation; on February 17, only two days after it was made, an excursion train of 200 people, loaded into three box cars and a flat car, rode a few miles out on the line to explore the company's lands.[108]

Mr. Harris is doing more to advertise Nebraska and to settle it up with a good class of people than will [all] the immigration societies the Legislature can charter in the next five years [declared a Plattsmouth paper in March]. We believe in Immigration Societies, but we believe in Harris more. . . .[109]

At last the Burlington was ready to begin its colonization work on a grand scale.

IV. THE FIRST GENERAL SALES

Promptly on April 1, 1870, the land department machinery which Harris and his assistants had so laboriously constructed began to operate in both Iowa and Nebraska. By July 26, when the rails reached Lincoln, it was running at full speed.[110] In the older state, the company was able to give deeds for lands bought for cash and to complete contracts for parcels bought under the three- or ten-year credit plan.[111] In Nebraska, however, all transactions were made according to the preëmption plan which had been worked out by Harris during the winter.

Under his scheme buyers were invited to apply for a certificate of preëmption from the land department, describing the plot they wished to acquire. From the outset it was made clear that although the company intended to issue these certificates "liberally," it would reserve the right to reject any application; [112] in so far as possible, the B. & M. was determined to exclude speculators. If the application were accepted, a form was sent out, giving the price for the indicated tract and outlining the desired plan of payment. As a matter of fact, almost all the Nebraska sales came under the ten-year plan whereby only six per cent interest on the full purchase price was paid for the first two

---

[107] *Nebraska Herald*, February 17, 1870 (NSB); *Nebraska City News*, March 5, 1870 (LDP); *New York Tribune*, March 4, 1870. All notices were dated February 15.   [108] *Nebraska Herald*, February 17, 1870 (NSB).

[109] *Ibid.*, March 17, 1870 (NSB).

[110] CBQ, *Corporate History*, p. 319.   [111] See above, p. 295.

[112] BMN, Preëmption Circular, April 25, 1870 (LDP).

years.[113] The company urged the prompt remittance of this first installment, for until it was made, the agreement was not binding.[114] In respect to the future, the company promised to announce by letter and newspaper notice when the day should come for exchanging these preëmption certificates for regular contracts. If, after this notice, the buyer did not sign his contract within 60 days, he would lose his right to buy and forfeit any money paid in, as well as all his improvements upon the land. He would then have to leave his land within ten days or pay $50 a month rent to the railroad until he departed peaceably or was ejected.[115] These conditions were obviously directed against speculators; they in no way interfered with the easy payment schedule designed to aid the actual settler. As a rule, the company preferred selling its full sections in parcels of 160 acres or more and advised applicants who wished less ground to join with one or more partners in taking the larger amount. Isolated tracts of 40 and 80 acres, however, were sold as wanted.[116]

In addition to the necessary instructions, the land department undertook to point out in form letters sent to Nebraska preëmptioners the advantages of its prices and terms over those offered by other land-selling agencies. For example, in each township, the state owned two sections of school land, which were being offered in competition with the railroad sections on a ten-year installment plan at ten per cent interest. The company showed that because of its advantageous credit plan it was cheaper to buy from the railroad at $10 an acre than to purchase from the state at $7.00. Furthermore, the B. & M. in Nebraska could offer a choice of eighteen sections per township, whereas the state had but two sections for sale within the same area.[117] As to the more general aspects of their policy, the company emphasized the appealing fact that the B. & M. long-term plans enabled the industrious and enterprising farmer to use his ready cash during the first three years on his land for equipment and improvements, and that thereafter the small annual payments could be met with proceeds from crops and livestock.[118]

[113] BMN, Sales Record No. 1 (LDP).
[114] BMN, Preëmption Application Acknowledgment, 1870 (LDP).
[115] BMN, Preëmption Circular, April 25, 1870 (LDP).
[116] BMN, Preëmption Application Acknowledgment, 1870 (LDP).
[117] BMN, Preëmption Circular, April 25, 1870 (LDP).
[118] BMN, Preëmption Application Acknowledgment, 1870 (LDP).

Professor Butler, busily writing columns for newspapers throughout the country, repeated these arguments and added a good many more during June and July. Not only were the railroad terms offered in both states equivalent to a loan, said he, but the title given by the company was above suspicion. Under the circumstances, this was a telling appeal, for the only lands available within 20 miles of the B. & M. tracks were for sale either by the company or by speculators, and the titles given by the latter were hardly reliable. Furthermore, Butler suggested, the railroad would assuredly be a lenient creditor. "I can think so," he continued, "and yet not waver in my faith that railroads are 'soul-less corporations.'" [119] This was, perhaps, a left-handed endorsement, but the professor had obviously taken the measure of his audience. He used the same technique to justify the company's prices, declaring:

The truth is [that] a man may believe railroad land prices low and yet not waver in his faith that corporations have no souls. The railroad must either sell its land or fail. . . . Selfishness and benevolence alike dictate the policy it has adopted. . . . [120]

Aside from the prices and terms thus eloquently defended, the early financial policy of the company included another special inducement to prospective buyers. From the first, the B. & M. offered land exploring tickets to points in both Iowa and Nebraska. Although the full fare was charged for these, the amount collected in the state where land was bought was credited against the purchase price, providing the contract was signed within 30 days. [121]

From some quarters, public sentiment at once approved of the road's financial policies. In a letter which may have been solicited, one veteran Nebraskan commended the "generous liberality" towards settlers, and waxed sentimental as he evoked "benedictions and blessings" on the company for its attitude towards those who were homeless and landless in the world. [122] On the other hand, a citizen of Weeping Willow, Nebraska, declared there was a "general feeling of

[119] J. D. Butler, "Nebraska Ramblings," *Chronicle of Vermont*, July 9, 1870 (LDP).

[120] J. D. Butler, "Ho for Nebraska" in ?, June 22, 1870 (LDP).

[121] BMR, News Sheet, April, 1870 (WL).

[122] Moses H. Sydenham to Harris, September 9, 1870, in the *Nebraska Herald*, September, 1870 (LDP).

disgust and indignation" in regard to the course pursued by the B. & M. The writer compared the company's price policy unfavorably with that of the Union Pacific, and predicted that the state would lose settlers to Minnesota and Kansas as long as the B. & M. charged from $8 to $20 an acre. He concluded that the government should have set a maximum price of $2.50 an acre or, better still, have granted the railroad money instead of land.[123]

This attack was easy to understand. It was indeed true that the lands of the B. & M. in Nebraska were more expensive than those of the Union Pacific, since they were sold during the nine months of 1870 when they were available for an average price of $9.37 an acre [124] as compared with $4.46 an acre for the older road.[125] But the terms offered by the latter were not so liberal as the B. & M.'s since a quarter of the principal was demanded as a down payment and the balance in three equal annual installments, together with interest at six per cent.[126] Furthermore, $8 to $20 was a misleading characterization of the Burlington prices, for even during the first three months, when presumably the choicest lands were taken up,[127] the cumulative average price was only $9.82.[128] As to the feared loss of immigration, while Kansas was increasing 176 per cent and Minnesota 154 per cent during the 'seventies, Nebraska grew 310 per cent,[129] mostly in B. & M. territory.[130] The conclusions of this letter, therefore, written just 18 days after land sales began, were somewhat premature.

More sober and far more accurate appraisals appeared in the editorial columns of the local press. Two weeks after the beginning of sales, the *Nebraska Herald* noted that $40,000 worth of land had been sold and "every foot of it, so far, is for actual settlement. This is one

[123] "Weeping Willow Letter" in the *Nebraska Herald*, April, 1870 (LDP).

[124] BMN, Sales Record No. 1 (LDP). See table below, p. 323.

[125] *Poor's Manual for 1871–72*, p. 525.

[126] U. P. RR., "Guide to the Union Pacific Railroad Lines. . . ." (Omaha, 1870), *passim*.

[127] "The sales of the first three or four months after the organization of the Department were exceptionally large, because many persons had been waiting to purchase, and came in as soon as the office was opened. . . ." (BMN, *Annual Report* for 1873, Boston, 1874, p. 28.)

[128] BMN, Sales Record No. 1 (LDP). See table below, p. 323.

[129] C. D. Wilbur, *The Great Valleys and Prairies of Nebraska and the Northwest* (Omaha, 1881), p. 346.

[130] See below, p. 454.

of the great features of the land system of this company; they desire to favor the actual settler, as it not only advances the value of their unsold lands, but it gives business to their road."[131] Harris himself could not have prepared a better statement. Two months later the *Nebraska City Press* stated that the B. & M. lands were sold on such terms "as make them really better than [free] Homesteads, which can now be obtained only on the frontier."[132] As time went on, the general tenor of local newspaper comment reflected this sentiment.[133] Meanwhile, Harris was working out an agency system which would stimulate sales while avoiding the confusion and abuses of the discarded Illinois Central practice.[134]

The agents employed by the Burlington were often specialists in their knowledge of some locality or type of people. In every case they were to sell only at prices fixed by the main office and to receive a commission fixed by Harris. To M. B. Warner, for example, he offered three per cent on colonies of from 50 to 150 families, and for groups of this size he recommended Cass and Pottawattamie counties in Iowa, or the five eastern counties of Nebraska. Prices, he added, ranged between $3 and $12 an acre.[135] To the Reverend Henry M. Grant, a retired minister, he named the same commission for forming colonies in the eastern states and Canada, and suggested Pennsylvania, Ohio, New York, and "the Canadas" as especially fertile fields for proselyting.[136] With an eye to German immigrants, Harris offered M. Solkuk the usual three per cent for working among newcomers of that nationality and promised to forward him circulars in German as soon as they were ready.[137] In dealing with the Reverend B. M. Halland of Burlington, who already had a large circle of contacts, the

[131] *Nebraska Herald*, April 14, 1870 (NSB).

[132] "Nebraska" in the *Nebraska City Press*, June, 1870 (LDP). Cf. "Settlers . . . within the limits of the grant can better afford to pay $10 per acre than to have lands distant from means of transportation. . . ." (*Poor's Manual for 1871–72*, p. 417.) This was a general statement referring to all land grants.

[133] See below, pp. 339, 457, 460.

[134] See above, p. 306.

[135] Harris to Warner, April 28, 1870 (LDP).

[136] Harris to Grant, April 29, 1870 (LDP). Harris may have been influenced by the Illinois Central's land commissioner who told him personally in Chicago that he could "have all the Yankees and welcome & that he could move 20 other men to buy their lands easier than he could one Yankee!" (Harris to Brooks, January 10, 1870, LDP.)

[137] Harris to Solkuk, April 29, 1870 (LDP).

commissioner was more conservative. Until August 10, 1870, he allowed him two per cent on long-credit sales, and two and one-half per cent on short-credit or cash transactions. After that date, however, the commissions were reduced to one per cent and one and one-half per cent respectively; even so, the ambitious pastor earned $3,229.60 in nine months during 1870 by virtue of selling 19,319.38 acres in Iowa.[138]

Although the activities of agents of this sort familiarized the people with the Burlington and its colonization, the chief source of publicity was the extensive advertising campaign that spread into new fields with increased momentum as the weeks sped by. Professor Butler, in addition to continuing his columns and letters in various newspapers,[139] took an extended trip through the East during the late summer. As usual Harris had "one practical suggestion, — Don't be too classical, but popularize your style & go for the crowd and you'll get it. Be a western man out & out." [140] Butler was without doubt the most important individual advertising agent, yet his work was but one phase of a diversified program.

The small notices stating the bare facts of the land grants and offering further information upon application continued to appear in both English and foreign-language newspapers.[141] In Great Britain full-page advertisements appeared in several big newspapers by July, 1870.[142] During the summer a map of southeastern Nebraska was issued, showing the B. & M. completed as far as Lincoln and indicating very roughly the location of company lands west of the Missouri River.[143] At least two editions of single-sheet map circulars showing lands in both states came out about the same time, the first

[138] Agreement with Halland, August 12, 1870 (LDP); BMI, Sales Book "A" (LDP).

[139] E.g., J. D. Butler, "Iowa and Nebraska" in *State Journal* (Madison, Wisconsin), August 27, 1870 (LDP).

[140] Harris to Butler, August 10, 1870 (LDP). Harris almost lost the services of Butler, since there was a strong movement in the spring to appoint him chancellor of the University of Nebraska at a salary of $3,000. Harris, approached by one of the regents, had been lukewarm to the idea. "I do not feel like favoring it," he wrote Butler, "for I want to people Nebraska & then move on to the Conquest of Mexico. Still I shall consent if you desire it." (Harris to Butler, April 16, 1870, LDP.) Apparently Butler turned down the offer if it was ever formally made.

[141] Harris to Hitchcock & Walden (of Chicago), April 23, 1870 (LDP).

[142] *Nebraska Herald*, July 14, 1870 (NSB).

[143] BMN, Map of Southeastern Nebraska, 1870 (LDP).

of 10,000 copies,[144] the second of 50,000.[145] In addition to outlining the terms and plans of payment, including the requirement of cultivation, these circulars gave a list of local agents who could furnish specific directions for exploring B. & M. lands, quote prices, and consummate sales.[146] Such circulars were put to a wide variety of uses. The editor of the Corning (Iowa) *Gazette* promised to fold them in free of charge with his newspaper, so Harris sent him 300 copies.[147] But most of them went to individuals who inquired about the lands in general. From the very first Harris contemplated, and later issued, copies specifically directed towards special national groups, notably the English, Welsh, Scotch, and Scotch Irish.[148] Of a more colorful nature were the red and white or red, white, and blue posters which Harris ordered in batches of several thousand for distribution in this country at ticket offices, and for stations and docks all over the world.[149]

In addition to these formal means of publicity, there were certain ways in which the road could spread its message and build up good will that should be considered a part of the advertising program. Butler, for example, was not the only informal letter writer. Harris discovered a Scotch-Irish Episcopal rector of Plattsmouth whose father was a tenant farmer in the old country, and persuaded him to write an open letter to his homeland comparing the hardships of the Irish system with the advantages of Iowa and Nebraska.[150] Ithamar Beall, the agent at Mount Ayr, Iowa, suggested another fruitful possibility to Harris: the donation of school sites to certain communities. The commissioner agreed that this "might be advantageous to the Company in case their lands would bring larger prices. I will consider the

---

[144] On April 23, 1870, Harris asked R. P. Studley & Co. of St. Louis to quote prices on (a) a cheap lithograph map of southeastern Nebraska, (b) a sectional map of Nebraska lands, (c) 10,000 pamphlets, (d) sheet-map circulars "something like the one I issued for the H. & St. Jo RR. Co." (Harris to R. P. Studley & Co., LDP.) On June 6, Harris ordered the 10,000 circulars.

[145] Harris to Denison, July 27, 1870 (LDP); *Nebraska Herald*, October 20, 1870 (NSB).

[146] Harris to W. H. Hendrickson, August 10, 1870 (LDP).

[147] Harris to George W. Frank (of Corning), April 22, 1870 (LDP).

[148] Harris to Butler, April 16, 1870 (LDP); Harris to George B. Osborne (of Cardigan, Wales), May 5, 1870 (LDP).

[149] Harris to Matthews & Warren (of Buffalo, New York), August 10, 1870 (LDP).

[150] Harris to Butler, April 16, 1870 (LDP).

matter," he promised, "whenever cases arise and parties state when and where they wish to build."[151] Later on, he carried out his good intentions.[152] A more obvious way of making friends was granting fare reductions for special purposes. Thus only three-fifths of the regular rate was charged over the B. & M. in Nebraska to the first annual fair of the Nebraska Central Agricultural and Breeders Association, held near Ashland in October, 1870.[153]

On the whole, the community welcomed this advertising as booming the entire region, but there was an occasional snag. During the spring of 1870, the Nebraska State Board of Emigration issued three pamphlets, in English, German, and Scandinavian. Although these publications were presumably non-partisan, only the B. & M. advertisement appeared among its pages.[154] In a communication entitled "Nebraska Misrepresented," a German objected through the columns of the Omaha Republican to this partiality,[155] and about the same time, a similar objection appeared in the Nebraska Herald. The explanation and answer appeared in the latter paper in June. It was pointed out that on April 4 the State Board had invited all Nebraska railroads to advertise at the rate of $50 a page, but only the Burlington and Missouri had availed itself of the opportunity. Furthermore, the pamphlet was at least bi-partisan for its description of the North Platte region was taken wholesale from the Union Pacific's advertisements.[156] Thus the road offered an explanation, but the episode justified Perkins' earlier insistence on strict impartiality in any official publications.[157]

It was by these various types of advertising that the B. & M. spread abroad general information concerning its lands. No matter how extensive the publicity, however, there were many individual questions from potential purchasers that could be answered only by correspondence from the main office or by personal investigation. Harris was frequently called upon to indicate what the chances were for various types of employment. To carpenters in Vermont and Wisconsin, for

---

[151] Harris to Beall, April 15, 1870 (LDP).

[152] See below, p. 334, footnote 31.

[153] Ashland Times, August 19, 1870 (NSB).

[154] F. Renner in the Nebraska Herald, June 2, 1870 (NSB).

[155] "Nebraska Misrepresented" in the Omaha Republican, June 16, 1870 (LDP).

[156] F. Renner in the Nebraska Herald, June 2, 1870 (NSB).

[157] See above, pp. 209–210.

example, he wrote that pay in Iowa and Nebraska was about $2.50 to $3 a day, but that he could not guarantee work for them, since the trade was out of his line of business. Nevertheless, he added, "as I never see an idle carpenter who is willing to labor, I conclude that there is plenty of employment for all good workmen in that line." [158] His reply to a machinist from Wisconsin was of the same sort. Wages in that occupation ranged from $2.50 to $5, he said, and although he knew of no particular demand at the moment, "opportunities are continually opening to those who are on hand to improve them." [159] In other words, although Harris was naturally very anxious to paint as bright a picture as possible, he consistently refused to appear as the guarantor of work. The commissioner's caution was not wholly the result of his desire to keep out of embarrassing situations. From his experience in Missouri he knew the dangers of hasty purchase or overexpansion. Thus he urged Butler to tell eastern applicants to look before they leapt, and that it was "folly to buy too much land and thus lock up idle capital." [160] In his own correspondence, he pointed out that the company never selected land for absentee purchasers; it was better for the applicant to do his own choosing. [161]

The results of land sales in Iowa and Nebraska for the nine months of 1870 were more than satisfactory. Even during the opening weeks of operation in April, when total sales reached only 19,302.18 acres, [162] nearly as much land changed hands in each state as had been disposed of in the entire period up to 1870. [163] The next two months witnessed the height of the boom; immigrants arriving in the normal spring influx [164] joined with purchasers who had been waiting to acquire company land [165] to push sales up to 34,701.67 acres in May, and 38,523.02 in June. About 55 per cent of this acreage was sold in the

[158] Harris to Ulysses R. Beaver (of Columbus, Wisconsin), April 25, 1870 (LDP); Harris to Henry S. Chamberlain (of Factory Point, now Manchester Center, Vermont), April 26, 1870 (LDP).

[159] Harris to Henry W. Herbert (of Belmont Station, Wisconsin), April 25, 1870 (LDP).

[160] Harris to Butler, August 10, 1870 (LDP).

[161] Harris to Chamberlain, April 26, 1870 (LDP).

[162] BMI, Sales Book "A" and BMN, Sales Record No. 1 (LDP).

[163] The B. & M. (Iowa) sold 10,728.91 acres in 1863–69, inclusive.

[164] The seasonal spring increase in immigration was noticeable as a regular trend in both states in almost every year of the 1870's. See below, p. 385.

[165] See above, p. 317, footnote 127.

older, more accessible state of Iowa, although June found the two regions running almost neck and neck. Book sales of the combined departments for the first three months were just under $1,000,000, although only about $4,000 in cash was actually taken in, — all of it in Iowa. Throughout the three summer months and October, the

IOWA *

		Acres	Value	Number of Sales	Average Price	Average Size of Plots
1870 —	April	9,615.59	$ 85,444.85	105	$ 8.89	91.58
	May	20,646.23	237,474.83	226	11.50	91.36
	June	19,991.68	255,050.31	199	12.76	100.46
	July	11,760.93	153,026.97	122	13.03	96.40
	August	17,095.01	218,013.92	168	12.75	101.76
	Sept.	10,937.62	140,932.08	118	12.89	92.69
	Oct.	8,523.77	112,535.45	96	13.20	88.79
	Nov.	6,467.00	87,013.96	71	13.46	91.08
	Dec.	3,709.42	46,684.85	49	12.59	75.70
GROSS		108,747.25	$1,336,177.22	1154	$12.42	94.24
Less Cancellations		680.00	7,516.80	3		
NET		108,067.25	$1,328,660.42	1151		

NEBRASKA †

		Acres	Value	Number of Sales	Average Price	Average Size of Plots
1870 —	April	9,686.59	$ 92,205.04	117	$ 9.52	82.79
	May	14,055.44	150,237.54	80	10.69	175.69
	June	18,531.34	172,493.39	102	9.31	181.68
	July	5,266.78	42,282.19	32	8.03	164.59
	August	3,836.56	35,078.72	32	9.14	119.89
	Sept.	3,957.77	32,742.16	27	8.27	146.58
	Oct.	5,267.92	43,371.54	35	8.23	150.51
	Nov.	540.85	5,751.05	5	10.63	108.17
	Dec.	480.00	3,120.00	6	6.50	80.00
GROSS		61,623.25	$577,281.63	436	$ 9.37	141.34
Less Cancellations		240.00	1,760.00	2		
NET		61,383.25	$575,521.63	434		

* BMI Sales Book "A."
† BMN, Sales Record No. 1.

pace slackened on both sides of the Missouri, particularly to the westward, where many farmers were compelled to plow and sow their first sod crops before the cold weather set in. Throughout November and December the decline continued gradually in Iowa, and abruptly in Nebraska, where sales dropped to ten per cent of the average summer figure as only eleven persons bought preëmption certificates. Even this handful of buyers was probably composed of farmers enlarging their holdings,[166] for it was next to impossible for pioneers to build and settle on raw prairie during the howling winter months. As the year closed, then, the Iowa office reported total net [167] sales of 108,067.25 acres for $1,328,660.42, and the Nebraska office, the sale of 61,383.25 acres for $575,521.63.

The statistics of these transactions as to size of plots sold, terms chosen, and prices were revealing, not only as an indication of the different conditions in the two states, but also as a hint of what was to come. Furthermore, to some extent the figures measured the success of the Burlington's price and advertising policies, particularly when compared with the results of other roads.

One striking point of contrast lay in the size of tracts sold. In Iowa, where there were fewer large parcels and the company's land lay wedged in between occupied sections,[168] plots averaged but 94.24 acres.[169] In Nebraska, however, the average was 141.34 acres and would have been higher but for 66 40-acre sales in April (there were only 18 more transactions of this size in the eight months following).[170]

IOWA — 1870

Month	Under 40 acres	40	Between 40–80	80	Total 80 or under	Between 80–160	160	Over 160	Total over 80	Grand Total
April	1	24	8	45	78	6	18	3	27	105
May	4	61	15	81	161	25	34	6	65	226
June	3	43	19	56	121	23	43	12	78	199
July	0	37	4	35	76	11	32	3	46	122
August	2	27	6	75	110	13	35	10	58	168
Sept.	2	23	8	52	85	7	24	2	33	118
Oct.	6	22	6	35	69	6	19	2	27	96
Nov.	5	12	5	26	48	7	15	1	23	71
Dec.	1	17	7	15	40	3	5	1	9	49
TOTALS	24	266	78	420	788	101	225	40	366	1154

[166] Sales dropped abruptly from an average size of over 150 acres in October to 108.17 acres in November, and 80 acres in December. Since the company preferred to make sales in 160-acre lots, and sold only isolated pieces in smaller quantities, it is almost certain that these late fall sales were to farmers owning adjacent tracts.

[167] There were two cancellations in Nebraska, and three in Iowa during 1870. "Net" figures represent totals after cancellations.

[168] BMI, County Maps (LDP).

[169] BMI, Sales Book "A" (LDP).

[170] BMN, Sales Record No. 1 (LDP).

NEBRASKA — 1870

Month	Under 40 acres	40	Between 40–80	80	Total 80 or under	Between 80–160	160	Over 160	Total over 80	Grand Total
April	1	66	5	12	84	5	23	5	33	117
May	1	10	2	12	25	3	35	17	55	80
June	0	3	3	19	25	7	46	24	77	102
July	0	0	1	5	6	2	20	4	26	32
August	0	4	1	11	16	0	15	1	16	32
Sept.	0	1	1	10	12	0	13	2	15	27
Oct.	0	0	1	16	17	6	8	4	18	35
Nov.	0	0	1	2	3	0	2	0	2	5
Dec.	0	0	0	6	6	0	0	0	0	6
TOTALS	2	84	15	93	194	23	162	57	242	436

There were probably several reasons for this high Nebraska figure. In the first place, many purchasers were buying enough for an entirely new farm, rather than adding a small patch to what they already held.[171] Secondly, the land department was making a special effort to encourage sales in 160-acre units;[172] in fact, over a third of all pre-emptions were for that amount, and there were 57 sales for even larger amounts. Finally, the prices in the new and relatively undeveloped region west of the Missouri were lower than in Iowa. Except for the first month of operations, when the 66 high-priced 40-acre plots were sold in Nebraska, this fact was reflected in the average prices paid; for the nine months the figure was $9.37 an acre west of the Missouri River, as compared to $12.42 in Iowa.

As Harris expected, the ten-year credit terms were by far the most popular. In this respect the two states resembled each other. In Iowa, less than 1,000 acres were sold for cash during 1870, about 6,500 on short credit, and over 100,000 on long term. In Nebraska, the preference was even more pronounced: there were but three cash sales, involving 400 acres, and only ten short-credit transactions, amounting to some 2,800 acres, as compared with 423 ten-year credit sales that disposed of nearly 60,000 acres. These trends were of particular interest because they indicated what might be expected in the future. The overwhelming preference for liberal credit made it clear that the company could not expect a prompt cash return on its property. The

[171] Advertisements concerning Nebraska continually referred to the purchase of entire farm tracts; there was less emphasis on this point in Iowa advertisements (LDP).

[172] See above, p. 315.

consistently smaller plots and higher prices in Iowa as compared with Nebraska suggested a permanent differential in these respects, while the volume of sales, particularly in the older state, seemed to prove that the lands were not overvalued. It was impossible to detect any seasonal variation in the statistics of the first few months because the year's business did not begin until April, and because the early monthly returns included the very considerable backlog that had piled up before the land department commenced operations.[173] The falling off of sales in both states during the summer and the more abrupt decline during the cold months conformed to expectations.

Compared with its nearest rivals in Iowa and Nebraska, the company's showing was definitely encouraging for the future. B. & M. sales in Iowa were almost five times greater and netted $5 an acre more than those of the neighboring Rock Island.[174] Part of this disparity could be explained by the fact that many of the latter's lands were in Audubon and Shelby counties which were then at a considerable distance from any railroad.[175] It is also possible that the less liberal terms of the Rock Island discouraged some settlers; their long-credit scheme allowed only seven years to complete payments instead of ten.[176] In Nebraska, the Union Pacific had sold 292,000 acres by December, 1870, but this represented the results of 18 months of effort as compared to 9 for the B. & M., and had brought in an average return of only $4.46 an acre[177] as contrasted with $9.37 for the Burlington.

To achieve his results, Commissioner Harris had spent approximately $120,000, of which a third was used in Iowa and the rest in connection with the much larger grant west of the river. Unfortunately, the details of the Nebraska expenditures for 1870 alone are unavailable, but the Iowa statistics are illuminating.[178]

[173] See above, p. 307.

[174] *Poor's Manual for 1878*, p. 727. During the year from April 1, 1870, to March 31, 1871, the Rock Island sold 28,022 acres for $213,575 at an average price of $7.63.

[175] C. R. I. & P. RR. "Description of Six Hundred Thousand Acres of Choice Iowa Farming Lands" (Davenport, 1871).

[176] BMR, Scrap Book No. 5, p. 49 (LDP).

[177] *Poor's Manual for 1870–71*, p. 525.

[178] Figures for Iowa are in CBQ, *Annual Report* for 1874 (Chicago, 1874), p. 58. The *Annual Report* of the B. & M. RR. in Nebraska for 1873 gives only the cumulative figures through 1872. The total Nebraska expenses for 33 months were

IOWA LAND DEPARTMENT EXPENSES — 1870

Office Expenses	$ 1,461.53
Salaries	8,381.71
Travel Expenses — Postage	913.12
Examining & Appraising	7,368.38
Timber Land Patrol	519.25
Swampland Expenses	490.08
Quitclaim — Disputed Titles	590.42
Town Lot Expenses	—
Legal Expenses	1,460.98
Commissions	1,362.36
Exploring Tickets Redeemed	4,584.90
Home Agencies	6,264.35
Advertising	6,957.64
Foreign Agencies	180.00
TOTAL EXPENSES	$40,534.72
Taxes	33,911.43
EXPENSES & TAXES	$74,446.15

Commissions, home and foreign agency expenses, advertising, and the redemption of land exploring tickets totaled nearly $20,000. These comprised the direct promotional expenses as distinguished from fixed office overhead and such items as legal fees, timber land protection, and title guarantees. Thus, roughly, about half of the budget in Iowa could be considered fixed, and the rest variable in proportion to sales and advertising.

For the future, the company could hardly hope to equal this showing for Iowa, either in total receipts or in the proportionate level of expenses, for sales east of the Missouri would doubtless decline after the rush of the first few months, whereas advertising costs would mount as the publicity campaign progressed. Furthermore, although examining expenses would certainly decrease, some outlay would be necessary annually if Harris carried on his reappraisals from time to time.[179] On the other hand, expectations for Nebraska were more favorable, for whereas the combined departments had disposed of 30 per cent of the Iowa lands by the end of 1870, only 2.5 per cent of

---

$292,337.32. On a pro rata basis, a probable estimate for 1870 would be $80,000. (BMN, *Annual Report* for 1873, Boston, 1874, p. 33.)

[179] See above, p. 305.

the vast Nebraska property had been sold. Thus, the Burlington could look forward to rising sales without a proportionate increase in expenses in the newer state. Under the circumstances, as 1871 opened, the company began to devote its major efforts to the region west of the Missouri River.

CHAPTER XIII

Boom Years for the Land Department, 1871–1873

I. ESTABLISHMENT OF TITLES

During the years 1871–73, the land department of the Burlington and Missouri River roads reached the height of its activity. Of basic importance was the final establishment by both companies of their land titles. From its experience in Iowa, the original B. & M. had discovered that it was unwise to give a deed to its customers until the Department of the Interior had certified the Congressional grants.[1] Consequently, when land sales on a large scale had begun in April, 1870, deeds were given only for those Iowa sections granted in 1856 and confirmed to the company from 1859 through 1863.[2] All other lands which the Burlington felt sure of receiving, namely, those included in the second Iowa grant of 1864 and the alternate sections within 20 miles of the track in Nebraska, were sold for preëmption certificates which could be exchanged for deeds when and if the government perfected the company's title.[3] The company now bent its efforts to obtain these final certifications. In Iowa the matter did not present any serious complications; it was primarily a question of selecting the scattered available lands within 20 miles of the road and excluding those which were subject to other claims. This was completed in due course, and in 1872 the B. & M. east of the Missouri received enough additional lands free and clear to bring its total granted acreage up to 359,708.45 acres. There were in addition 20,600 acres in the state still subject to litigation, some of which the railroad could hope to receive later.[4] In Nebraska, however, the problem was greater and more difficult.

Ever since 1867 when Secretary of the Interior Browning had accepted J. Sterling Morton's reasoning that the B. & M.'s grant was

---

[1] See above, p. 306.
[2] See above, p. 314.
[3] See above, pp. 314–315.
[4] CBQ, *Annual Report* for 1873 (Chicago, 1874), p. 57. Of these, 600 were claimed by homesteaders, 6,000 by preëmptioners, and 14,000 were in suspense because of the contract concluded with Mills County. (*Ibid.*)

limited to a region within 20 miles of the track, despite the lack of such limitation in the act itself, only those odd-numbered sections available within that distance had been withdrawn and earmarked for the railroad.[5] Within this area, however, the B. & M. could find less than half of its full quota of lands because at both ends of its line, and particularly in the west, its potential claims were nullified by the prior grant to the nearby Union Pacific.[6] Thus, through its Washington agent, W. T. Steiger, the B. & M. had consistently endeavored to secure a reëxamination of its claim to the *equivalent* of 20 sections per mile of road regardless of how far the land might be from the track. By 1871 this effort met with success and the company obtained the counsel of the noted lawyer, Edward R. Hoar, of Massachusetts. Pending Hoar's final appeal, Steiger submitted to the Secretary of the Interior on November 9, 1871, a statement of fact which he declared might have an important bearing upon the question at issue.[7]

A few days previously, wrote Steiger, Hon. James F. Wilson, former member of Congress from Iowa, had been in Washington and had authorized Steiger to state that he, Wilson, had drafted and introduced the sections of the 1864 Act under consideration, "and that he *intentionally* omitted the usual clause limiting the sections [to within 20 miles of the track] because only lands and no Govt. Bonds were granted."[8] Steiger then cited the *Congressional Globe*[9] showing that Wilson had carefully explained that only land was being granted, and thus concluded that "Congress voted intelligently upon the measure."[10]

In his final argument submitted to Secretary Delano on November 13, Hoar supported and elaborated upon this point. The Act of 1864, he pointed out, providing both bonds and lands for the Union Pacific, had expressly restricted choice of the latter to a fixed distance from the railroad. Those sections of the act pertaining to the B. & M., on the other hand, omitted any specific lateral limits, merely stating they should be "on the line of the road" and "*to the amount* of ten alternate sections [on each side] per mile."[11] It was a well settled rule, said Hoar, that

[5] See above, p. 270.
[6] See map opposite p. 332.
[7] Steiger to Delano, November 9, 1871 (USDI).
[8] *Ibid.*
[9] *Cong. Globe*, 38th Cong., 1st Sess. (1863–64), pt. 5, p. 3180.
[10] Steiger to Delano, November 9, 1871 (USDI).
[11] Hoar to Delano, November 13, 1871 (USNA). (Italics are Hoar's.)

if, in the same act, there are two provisions of like character, one of them carefully limited, and the other without such limitation, it is the strongest evidence of the intention of the legislature that the limitation should not apply to the second case. It shows beyond question that the attention of the legislature was directed to the subject; and that as they expressly said it where they meant it, where they did not say it, it was because they did not mean it.[12]

Furthermore, he added, Congress knew there were interfering grants in B. & M. territory and omitted the usual lateral limits with that information in mind. He concluded by urging the Secretary to withdraw enough lands so that the railroad could select the acres necessary to fill its quota.

Two days later, Delano forwarded his decision to Willis Drummond, Commissioner of the General Land Office. After a thorough examination of the facts, wrote Delano, he found himself in agreement with his predecessor, Secretary Harlan, who had originally held the B. & M.'s grant was not restricted laterally and whose decision Browning had reversed in 1867.[13] Guided by this decision, the commissioner on December 11 ordered the withdrawal "from preëmption & homestead entry, private sale & locations . . . of all the odd numbered sections of land" in certain Nebraska districts north and south of the B. & M. tracks.[14] Thus the railroad's long-standing claim was upheld, and the scope of its colonization activities in Nebraska automatically doubled. Clearly, Delano's decision was one of utmost importance.

At once, the company began its selections north of the Union Pacific grant, but not without local objection. "What will free American citizens think," asked a Dakota City correspondent of the *Nebraska Statesman,*

of . . . a jump of 90 miles clear over the Platte River and the Union Pacific with its grant 40 miles wide, to take lands among an unoffending people who will be no more benefited by the Burlington and Missouri than by some road in China. More than that it gobbles up the very lands which might be granted in aid of railroads through their own country which *would* benefit them and give value to their lands. . . . I have seen poor

---

[12] Hoar to Delano, November 13, 1871 (USNA).

[13] Delano to Drummond, November 15, 1871 (USDI).

[14] Willis Drummond to register and receiver of the Grand Island (Nebraska) Land Office, December 11, 1871. (Reprinted in the *Grand Island Independent,* January 9, 1872, LDP.)

men make application to homestead and preëmpt these lands for *actual settlement* and they were *refused* by orders of the agent.[15]

Although the ruling of the Secretary was simply a belated recognition of the equity of the railroad's claim, there was some substance in this complaint. As in the case of similar sentiments expressed in Iowa a decade before, it placed upon the railroad the burden of showing that its grant was justified, not only as an aid to construction but also as a means of developing the community.

By June, 1872, all selections of "outside lands" had been made, and between that month and November, 2,370,433.16 acres were patented by the United States to the B. & M. in Nebraska. Of these, 1,160,198.81 acres were within 20 miles of the track and 1,210,234.35 acres beyond that limit.[16] Since the State of Nebraska had already conveyed 50,000 acres to the railroad in 1870 and 19,004.48 acres were eventually received from the Omaha and South Western, the grand total of Burlington lands in Nebraska by the end of 1872 was over 2,400,000 acres, approximately seven times the amount granted in Iowa.[17] Thus, the land department had received patents for practically all of its Iowa and Nebraska lands[18] and could guarantee a permanent title to its customers. Those who had already purchased under the preëmption plan were promptly notified to exchange their certificates for a deed or, in the case of a credit sale, for regular contracts.[19]

[15] *Nebraska Statesman* (Lincoln, Nebraska), April 20, 1872 (NSB).

[16] BMN, Journal "B," p. 4 (LDP).

[17] Baldwin to Mitchell, March 18, 1922 (LDP). Prior to its lease to the B. & M. in Nebraska, the Omaha and South Western received 40,000 acres from the State of Nebraska as an aid for constructing the line from Omaha to Oreapolis. The B. & M. never acquired any interest in these lands. (CBQ, *Documentary History*, vol. III, pp. 318, 321–322; Land Department Memo, December 11, 1882, O. S. W. File, CR.) After the lease, the Omaha and South Western received another grant from the state, originally intended to embrace 60,000 acres. Most of these lands were never obtained by the state, however, and those that were became subject to other claims. After various compromises the Omaha and South Western received 19,004.48 acres; these were "all the lands which the O. & S. W. Co., as represented by the B. & M., obtained for the road from Crete to Beatrice." (Land Department Memo, December 11, 1882, *loc. cit.*)

[18] During 1875, 3,437.61 additional acres were certified in Nebraska. (Baldwin to Mitchell, March 18, 1922, LDP.)

[19] BMR, Notice, December 20, 1872. (Reprinted in Lincoln, Plattsmouth, and Nebraska City newspapers, LDP.) BMR. Notice to Purchasers, 1873 (LDP).

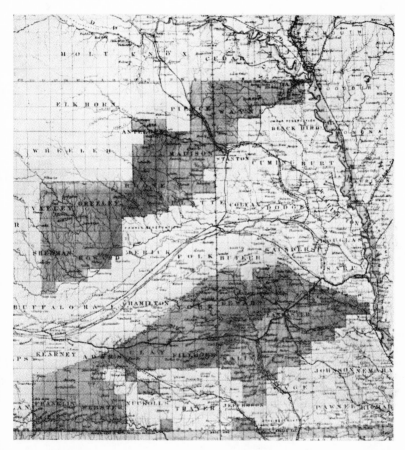

AREAS NORTH AND SOUTH OF THE PLATTE RIVER (SHADED) WITHIN WHICH
B. & M. LANDS IN NEBRASKA WERE LOCATED. THE UNION PACIFIC LANDS LAY
BETWEEN THESE TWO AREAS.

II. PRICE POLICY

During the early 'seventies and, as a matter of fact, throughout the decade, the Burlington land department remained very much as George Harris had organized it during the winter of 1869–70, although of course it expanded in personnel as business increased. All Iowa sales were consummated and recorded in the office at Burlington, and those in Nebraska were handled at Lincoln. In each of these central offices were complete maps and plats of all the company's lands, so that a customer could complete his transaction there if he wished to do so. Almost all land buyers, however, preferred to inspect personally the various tracts available, and indeed the railroad encouraged them to do so by directing them to the local agents in both states who were thoroughly familiar with the lands in their vicinity and whose job was to aid prospective customers.[20] In 1872, for example, the company had 22 men at this work in Iowa and 16 in Nebraska;[21] as time went on, this number increased.[22] In addition to their work as guides to the B. & M. lands, these agents could receive applications for any tracts that might be selected, execute the preliminary papers, and forward the documents to the proper central office. Thereafter, if his application were accepted, the purchaser dealt directly with either Burlington or Lincoln.[23]

Prices, following Harris' original plan, were fixed and recorded at the Burlington and Lincoln offices; they were based on the thorough land examinations of 1869–70 and varied for each particular tract in accordance with the soil, location, water supply, timber, proximity to a railroad station, and other advantages.[24] To avoid the embarrassment encountered by the Illinois Central, local agents were not permitted to vary these prices.[25] Once the grants were on the market, the only concessions allowed were discounts offered publicly from time to time by the central offices,[26] and the only changes in price came from the periodic revaluations made necessary by general economic conditions.[27]

[20] BMR, News Sheet, March? 1872 (LDP); BMR, Instructions and Offers to Agents, 1873? LDP).

[21] BMR, List of Local Land Agents, March? 1872 (LDP).

[22] See below, p. 445.

[23] BMR, News Sheet, March? 1872 (LDP).

[24] BMR, News Sheet, 1873 (LDP).

[25] See above, p. 260.

[26] See above, p. 318.

[27] BMR, Price Books (LDP).

A single exception to this practice occurred in eastern Nebraska when the lands there were first offered to purchasers. Immigration into that region in 1870 was exceptionally heavy, and there was not enough land available, either public or private, to satisfy the demand for it. Consequently, as the Burlington successively opened its tracts to settlement, it frequently found that there were several applicants for the same plot. In such cases it published notices specifying the time and place where such lands would be auctioned off to the bidder offering the highest advance over the fixed price.[28]

This procedure, however, was strictly the result of special conditions, and in all its advertising, the company emphasized its policy of fixed prices. Its circulars did not, of course, attempt to state specifically what these prices were, but they indicated the factors on which they were based, and gave the general range for each county. In March, 1873, for example, the figures shown on page 335 were published for the unsold lands in Iowa and the South Platte district of Nebraska.[29]

These, of course, were the "asked" rather than "bid" prices. The actual figures at which these lands passed from the company to the individual purchasers were revealed by the sales statistics at the end of each month and year. Most of these transactions were with individual purchasers. In at least two important cases, however, lands were reserved for sale to colonies. In Jefferson County, the company possessed approximately 40,000 acres of contiguous tracts that had been donated by the State of Nebraska. These were sold at the regular prices and terms, but they were handled through the agency of the Reverend Darius E. Jones of Burlington and earmarked for members of his Plymouth Colony.[30] Similarly, a like amount of land was reserved in York County for the Mayflower Colony that was being recruited principally from Earlville, Illinois.[31]

During 1871 and 1872, the Burlington saw no reason to alter the terms of payment that had been in effect since April, 1870.[32] Land

[28] BMN, Notice, December 15, 1870 (LDP).
[29] BMR, Circular, March? 1873 (LDP).
[30] *Saline County Post*, June 16, 1871 (NSB).
[31] *Blue Valley Record*, December 21, 1871 (NSB). This paper noted that 40 acres had already been set aside for educational purposes. "Instances of substantial aid from this corporation to this end," it observed, "are none the less gratifying because they are only acts of justice or business prudence." (*Ibid.*)
[32] See above, pp. 295-296.

could be bought in either state for cash, or on short or long credit, and the ten-year contracts retained the requirement that one-tenth of the area must be cultivated during each of the first three years.

IOWA

County	Acres Unsold (approx.)	Price Range per Acre *
Fremont	13,000	$10 to $18
Mills	17,000	11 " 25
Pottawattamie	9,000	7 " 16
Page	15,000	8 " 23
Montgomery	35,000	8 " 30
Taylor	12,000	7 " 17
Adams	23,000	6 " 18
Cass	11,000	7 " 20
Union	12,000	6 " 19
Clark	9,000	6 " 18
Lucas	10,000	5 " 15
Monroe	10,000	5 " 13
Madison	3,000	5 " 12
Ringgold	4,000	5 " 12
Adair	2,000	7 " 14

* The company noted that certain tracts near important railroad stations were of greater value than indicated in this table.

NEBRASKA
(South Platte only)

County	Acres Unsold (approx.)	Price Range per Acre
Lancaster	140,000	$4 to $20
Cass	37,000	8 " 20
Saline	105,000	4 " 18
Gage	20,000	5 " 9
Otoe	12,000	7 " 10
Seward	130,000	4 " 10
Jefferson	30,000	5 " 8
Saunders	28,000	3 " 8
Fillmore	117,000	5 " 10
York	140,000	4 " 10
Polk	3,000	4 " 10
Clay	90,000	4 " 10
Nuckolls	6,000	4 " 9
Adams	55,000	2 " 8
Hamilton	20,000	4 " 8
Kearney	37,000	2 " 6

Land exploring tickets were still sold to prospective customers, and a corresponding but more vague concession was offered in freight rates. The land buyer was instructed to go to the general freight agent of his local railroad and to state "distinctly" that he was bound for the

Burlington's lands with his household goods, stock, and other equipment, and that he desired the "lowest special rates through." Thereupon, he would be "accommodated in the best manner." [33]

A more unusual innovation was the establishment of two emigrant homes, at Burlington and Lincoln, where prospective land purchasers

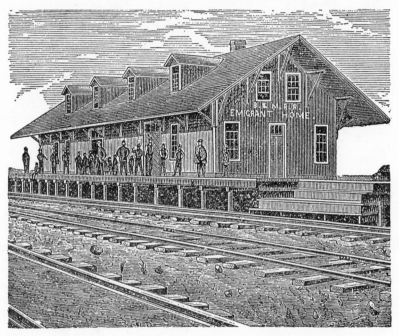

B. & M. EMIGRANT HOME AT LINCOLN, OPENED IN 1871.

could stay with their families free of charge for a reasonable length of time while they were looking for suitable tracts of land. Food was provided at cost. The Burlington home was located in the lower floor of the land department's office,[34] but at Lincoln a separate building, 100 by 24 feet, was constructed for the purpose in the spring of 1871. It included a kitchen and dining room with running water, enough sleeping quarters for ten families,[35] and was located next to the depot so passengers could be unloaded directly from trains.[36] Upon its com-

[33] BMR, News Sheet, 1872 (LDP).
[34] BMR, News Sheet, April, 1870 (WL).
[35] *Nebraska State Journal* (Lincoln, Nebraska), July 17, 1871 (NSB).
[36] *Ibid.*, April 28, 1871 (NSB).

pletion, the new home was described as "very clean and orderly"; during the year ending June 10, 1872, no less than 636 persons stayed there, including 254 men, 111 women, and 271 children.[37] The company proudly claimed to be the first railroad to use such homes [38] and continually drew attention to them,[39] although one candid English visitor remarked that "the people who use . . . [the Lincoln] building are of course expected to rough it; for no railway, however opulent, would find it politic or profitable to provide luxurious quarters under such circumstances." [40] Nevertheless, the scheme saved money for the immigrant, and, like the land exploring ticket or special freight rates, was equivalent to a concession in price.

Finally, the company formally announced a policy that Butler had hinted at in the summer of 1870: [41]

in case of unexpected reverses or disappointments, a reasonable indulgence can always be obtained by making a frank and honest statement of facts. The Railroad Company is able to wait. It is better to have such a creditor than to be in the hands of an individual who, even if disposed, may not have the ability to accommodate. . . .[42]

Later statements of a similar nature pointed out that with the company's liberal terms it would be very unlikely that accommodation would be needed.[43] As events later proved, such optimism was hardly warranted.

In a circular issued to the stockholders of the B. & M. in Nebraska on January 22, 1873, the directors summarized the company's reasons for adopting such a price policy.

In selling our lands [they explained], the policy has been to make such terms as would most favor immigration and settlement on them which

[37] Unidentified newspaper, June 10, 1872 (NSB).

[38] J. D. Butler, "Nebraska, Its Characteristics and Prospects," n.p., 1873 (LDP). These houses certainly antedated those later built by the Union Pacific, since in June, 1872, that road was just converting a former baggage and freight warehouse at Omaha, 18x80 feet and two stories high, to receive immigrants. (*Omaha Daily Herald*, June 7, 1872, LDP.)

[39] E.g., BMR, News Sheet, April, 1870 (WL); S. O. Ingham, "Lincoln, the Capital of Nebraska," in the *Peninsula Herald* (Detroit, Michigan?), 1872 (LDP); BMR, Pamphlet, 1879 (LDP).

[40] Edwin A. Curley, *Nebraska, Its Advantages, Resources, and Drawbacks* (New York, 1875), p. 224.   [41] See above, p. 316.

[42] BMR, News Sheet, March? 1872 (LDP).

[43] BMR, News Sheet, March? 1873 (LDP).

experience proves is best promoted, not by low prices so much as by easy payments, enabling settlers with very small means to meet their engagements out of the products of their land.[44]

Through its various avenues of publicity, the Burlington pointed out in detail and at great length the various special advantages of its terms and inducements. They were, first and foremost, a virtual loan which was particularly helpful to the man of moderate means who needed what cash he had to buy seed, equipment, and building material. Interest at six per cent was approximately half of the legal rate in Iowa and Nebraska; thus it was cheaper to buy of the railroad at, say, $4 an acre on ten-year credit than to borrow on the market for a similar period and purchase from the United States under the Preemption Act for $2.50, the price of the alternate sections within the grant limits. Furthermore, in the long run, buying railroad land was cheaper than renting from an established owner. A usual rent in Iowa was one-third the produce. Suppose, pointed out one B. & M. circular, a farmer leased 40 acres and raised 36 bushels an acre which, at 25 cents a bushel, sold for $360. His annual rental would amount to $120, or $1,200 over a ten-year period. On the other hand, if the same man bought 40 acres from the railroad for as high as $10 an acre, he would pay $544 in principal and interest over ten years. Adding $80 for taxes, $300 for fencing, $76 for repairs, he would still have $200 left for erecting a cabin before spending $1,200. Finally, the probable rise in land values would give the owner a chance to realize a profit in capital value that would not accrue to any tenant.[45]

As early as 1871, actual experience seemed to bear out these estimates. A letter from Dorchester, dated December 28, 1871, told of one Edward Jones who had purchased 140 acres of railroad land for $10.40 an acre early in the same year. His expenses had included $1,456 for his land, $330 for breaking 110 acres, $60 for a corn planter, and $190 for labor, a total of $2,036. At the end of the season, he sold his harvest of 6,000 bushels of corn for $1,380, and 150 tons of hay for $750, bringing him $2,130, or $94 more than his total outlay.[46] Even though this letter may have been solicited, the case was not unique; the railroad

[44] Circular to the Stockholders, January 22, 1873, as ordered by the board of directors on January 13, 1873 (BMN ORB, p. 55).

[45] BMR, News Sheet, March? 1872 (LDP).

[46] BMR, News Sheet, March? 1872 (LDP).

received frequent evidence that their customers could, with due diligence and average luck, establish themselves in a remarkably short time on the fertile lands of western Iowa and eastern Nebraska. As time went on, these miniature success stories were naturally published and spread abroad through the land department's advertising.[47]

The opportunities offered by this policy were duly noted in the public press. The *Ashland Times*, for example, remarked that these were "certainly easy terms for farmers,"[48] and a paper in neighboring Illinois characterized the various credit schemes as "acceptable to all, rich and poor."[49] At Crete, the *Saline County Post* approached the matter from a more realistic standpoint:

It is not pleasant [ran its editorial] to be in debt, but when the alternative is no farm or a debt, it is wisdom to purchase of the B. & M. Also, where the alternative is a farm paid for and no money left to work it, or a farm bought of the B. & M. company on long credit, let a man choose the latter every time. He will be better off in a few years. . . .[50]

In explaining the more general purposes of its policy to the public, the company made no attempt whatever to conceal its profit motive but did point out with emphasis that its own interests were identical with those of the community. With a candor that was almost belligerent, the land department declared in one of its news sheets of 1872 that

no road proves a good investment unless its local freight and passenger traffic is heavy. No such traffic can exist except in a well-tilled and well-settled region. Therefore the railroad men have every inducement to advance the development of the country which their line traverses. . . . It is to be expected that they will sell low to actual settlers and furnish them every facility in the way of long credit, cheap freights, etc. *It is not to be supposed that railroad corporations surpass all men in disinterested benevolence, but it is beyond question that they know their own interest, and so will take some pains to help you earn a dollar whenever they can thus make two for themselves.*[51]

[47] E.g., BMR, Pamphlet of 1878 (LDP). For a more complete indication of the development of the Burlington region, see the graphs of land in farms and improved acreage figures on pp. 458–459, below.

[48] *Ashland Times*, March 17, 1871 (NSB).

[49] *Carlinville Democrat* (Illinois), March 28, 1872 (LDP).

[50] *Saline County Post*, January? 1872 (LDP).

[51] BMR, News Sheet, March? 1872 (LDP). Italics supplied.

Such logic could hardly be disputed. With equal frankness, the *Saline County Post* of Crete, Nebraska, indicated what one portion of the community thought of the situation:

We are strongly anti-monopoly, whether railroad or any other [it announced editorially]. Still, we have no sympathy with the . . . censure of the B. & M. Company [contained in an attached communication]. Their officers we regard as honest and honorable men, and their work in Nebraska as eminently for the good of the State. . . . Without Eastern capital, it is evident that railroads in Nebraska could not have been built for years to come. But without railroads, when would the state have been settled up? . . . People may grumble at the railroad companies, but they are a necessity of the age. What should be done is, not to attempt to destroy them nor to create a prejudice against them, but to control them by law and to appreciate their worth. The truth is, that the *true* interests of both the people and the companies are *identical*, and what is needed is that all concerned should be convinced of this.[52]

The first major revision of sales policy was put into effect on January 1, 1873, and it was in the direction of further liberality, particularly in respect to Nebraska. The cash and short-credit plans of payment remained as before, but in both states the popular ten-year arrangement was made more attractive by not requiring any payment on principal until the beginning of the fifth year; then and annually thereafter, one-seventh was to be paid until the contract was liquidated at the end of ten years. Furthermore, if the long-credit purchaser wished to pay up in full at the end of one year, he would receive an 18 per cent discount from the original long-credit price; at the end of two years, 15 per cent, and at the end of three years, 10 per cent. Land exploring tickets were made cheaper: if land was bought in Iowa, free fare was offered to the actual purchaser over the C. B. & Q. all the way from Chicago to his destination; if the purchased land was in Nebraska, only half-fare was required through Illinois and Iowa, and none at all west of the Missouri River. Each member of the purchaser's family was charged but half-fare from Chicago and points west on the Burlington to destination in either state. In regard to household goods or stock shipped over the C. B. & Q.–B. & M. by actual purchasers for their own use, the companies undertook to make cash refunds of all freight paid over a certain amount according to the following schedule:[53]

[52] *Saline County Post*, December 15, 1871 (NSB).
[53] BMR, Circulars, 1873 (LDP).

All over $50 per car from C. B. & Q. points to East Plattsmouth, Iowa
All over $55 per car from C. B. & Q. points to Plattsmouth, Nebraska
All over $35 per car from Quincy, Illinois, and Burlington, Iowa, to any
point in Iowa
All over $40 per car from Quincy and Burlington to Plattsmouth
All over half the regular rates on the B. & M. RR in Nebraska

A final inducement, destined to be of prime importance and applying only to Nebraska lands bought on long credit, was the offer of a
20 per cent credit against principal providing the purchaser improved
and cultivated one-half of his lands within two years of purchase.[54]
This offer was incorporated in the contract itself and would become
effective if the buyer could produce an affidavit witnessed by two disinterested persons stating that he had complied with the requirements.[55]

In presenting these terms, the company reiterated its previously stated
purposes in unmistakable language:

No speculator [it claimed] can be so much interested as the R. R. Co.
is in the prosperity of the settlers along its line. It grows with their growth
and strengthens with their strength. Local traffic is its life. . . .[56]

And in more formal words, Harris announced that the company's
offer of such extraordinary inducements was:

to aid the new settler in beginning and extending improvements rapidly,
to increase the sale of lands, to build up a carrying trade for the Railroad,
and to enrich and develop this beautiful country as quickly as possible. . . .[57]

Without question this was true, although it was not the only reason
dictating a liberal policy. With prices stabilized at approximately $12
per acre in Iowa, and near $8 an acre in Nebraska during 1871 and
1872, sales had steadily declined in the older state and even stood still
in Nebraska in the latter year. Furthermore, west of the Missouri the
Union Pacific was still outselling the Burlington.[58] Good business
strategy demanded lower prices and easier terms.

III. DOMESTIC ADVERTISING, 1871–1873

As the Burlington's colonization work progressed, advertising assumed an increasingly important role. If the railroad were determined

[54] BMN, Circular, 1873 (LDP).
[55] BMN, Long-Term Contract, 1873 (LDP).
[56] BMR, News Sheet, March? 1873 (LDP).
[57] BMN, Circular, 1873 (LDP).
[58] See graph, p. 415.

to create a thriving community, it was necessary not only to attract numbers of immigrants to its territory but also to bring in the type of settler who, because of his character and resources, would improve his land and become a permanent citizen. For such persons, both in this country and in Europe, there was naturally vigorous competition; other railroad companies,[59] private land associations,[60] and even certain states [61] were spending vast sums to secure the best type of newcomer. Consequently, in order to hold its own, the B. & M. had to do more than merely inform the public of the advantages of Iowa and Nebraska; it had to convince people that these states, and the Burlington lands in particular, possessed unique and superior advantages. Such a task required foresight, ingenuity, and money.

In the United States, the company realized that the bulk of its customers would immigrate singly or as the head of a family; consequently its publicity was primarily an appeal to the individual. As early as 1869, however, Colonel Ames had been approached by the leaders of groups who wished to form colonies along racial or denominational lines, or according to the origin of the settlers.[62] Both Ames and Harris had been receptive to these schemes,[63] and indeed by 1871, several hundred Swedish Lutherans under the leadership of the Reverend B. N. Halland had established themselves at Stanton, Iowa, and other groups were being formed.[64] From the railroad's point of view, these colonies, if composed of the right type of individuals, speeded the entire process of colonization with a minimum of trouble, for their leaders

[59] E.g., the Chicago, Rock Island and Pacific R. R., the Union Pacific R. R., the Northern Pacific R. R., etc. General summaries and some statistics on the advertising activities of these roads may be found in *Poor's Manual* after 1869. More specific accounts are in Gates, *op. cit.*, James B. Hedges, "The Colonization Work of the Northern Pacific Railroad," *loc. cit.*, pp. 311–342, and the same author's "Promotion of Immigration to the Pacific Northwest by the Railroads," *loc. cit.*, pp. 183–203.

[60] E.g., the St. Mary's Falls Ship Canal Co.; the Lincoln Land Co., etc. There is no good comprehensive account of these companies, but see Theodore C. Blegen, "The Competition of the Northwestern States for Immigrants," *Wisconsin Magazine of History*, vol. III (September, 1919), pp. 3–29.

[61] E.g., Iowa and Nebraska (see below, pp. 359, 362), and cf. Blegen, *loc. cit.*

[62] See above, pp. 248–250; 254–256.

[63] Harris had been instrumental in forming a New England colony on the Hannibal and St. Joseph lands in northern Missouri during the Civil War. (HSJ, Land Department Records.)

[64] BMR, News Sheet, March? 1872 (LDP).

did most of the proselyting, sometimes for a commission,[65] and handled the business arrangements for the whole unit. Thus, the company sought to appeal to such groups as well as to individuals.

The chief sources of the Burlington's advertising were, of course, the central offices at Burlington and Lincoln. George Harris and Professor Butler, who were largely responsible for all formal publicity, divided their time between the two places, and as a result of their efforts, thousands of articles, maps, and circulars, together with a mountainous correspondence, put the virtues of Iowa and Nebraska before the people of this country and Europe. In addition, they arranged special excursions to bring prospective customers from other states, encouraged all forms of public relations or gratuitous publicity, and guided the campaigns of the company's agents throughout the United States and Europe. The core and yardstick of their activity, however, was the advertising copy they sent out from their main offices.

As in the opening months of operation, brief newspaper notices appeared in as widely varying media as the semi-weekly edition of the *New York Tribune* [66] and the *Moline Review*.[67] Their contents, with very minor exceptions, were identical:

IOWA AND NEBRASKA LANDS [68]
for sale by the
Burlington & Mo. River R. R. Co.
Millions of Acres
on Ten Years' Credit at 6 per cent Interest
No part of principal due for two years and thence
only one-ninth yearly till paid in full
Products will pay for land and improvements
within the limit of this generous credit.
Better terms were never offered, are not now,
and probably never will be,

[65] During 1870, Halland was paid commissions varying from two and one-half per cent to one per cent on his sales. After August 10, 1870, he received one and one-fourth per cent on cash and short-credit sales, one per cent on long-credit sales. During 1870, alone, he was responsible for the sale of 19,319.39 acres for $189,599.80, and received $3,229.60 in commissions. (BMI, Sales Record "A"; Agreement of August 12, 1870, LDP.)

[66] *New York Tribune*, March 29 through April 19, 1872.

[67] *Moline Review* (Illinois), January 13, 1872 (LDP).

[68] *New York Tribune*, March 29 through April 19, 1872; cf. *Ottawa Republican*, February 8, 1872 (LDP); *Rural New Yorker*, March 4, 1871.

CIRCULARS giving full particulars are
supplied gratis; any wishing to induce
others to emigrate or to form a colony,
are invited to ask for all they want
to distribute. Apply to:
George S. Harris, Land Commissioner
for Iowa Lands — at Burlington, Iowa
and for Nebraska Lands at Lincoln, Neb.

Supplementing these brief notices and containing approximately the same information, long narrow handbills, 8 by 36 inches, were distributed from Burlington for the use of off-line agents. In addition to their text, they contained on one side an accurate railroad map of the United States and on the other two lithographed views of southeastern Nebraska. The name of the local agent appeared at the bottom with the notice that he was prepared to issue circulars, provide more complete information, or sell land exploring tickets to either Iowa or Nebraska.[69]

The circulars to which these notices referred appeared during the earliest months of the road's activity and continued throughout the decade. Their chief virtue was their timeliness, for they not only contained the latest terms and special inducements, but afforded the company a convenient means of combatting any particular adverse criticism and of presenting any special information that happened to be important at the moment. The circular of April 25, 1870, primarily designed to set forth the preëmption terms in Nebraska, has already been mentioned.[70] The next year, a separate edition featured the new emigrant houses,[71] and in 1872, attention was drawn to the growing Plymouth Colony in Jefferson County[72] and to the terms and implications of the recently passed Soldiers' Homestead Act.[73] All of these editions gave full particulars of the B. & M. terms, some included a defense of the credit policy,[74] and the later ones gave statistics of the companies' sales.[75] As early as May, 1871, these circulars were appearing in English, German, and Bohemian, and plans were under way for

[69] BMR, Flier, 1872? (LDP).
[70] See above, p. 315.
[71] Saline County Post, May 5, 1871 (NSB).
[72] BMR, Circular of May, 1872 (LDP).
[73] BMR, Circular of April, 1872 (LDP).
[74] BMR, Circular of April, 1870 (LDP).
[75] BMR, Circular of May, 1872 (LDP).

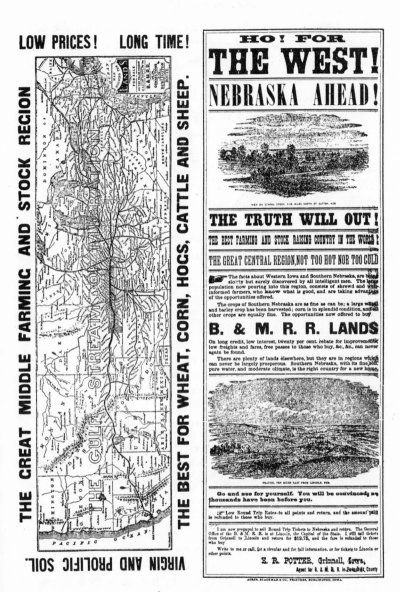

HANDBILL USED BY LOCAL AGENTS TO ADVERTISE B. & M. LANDS. MAP SHOWS LOCATION OF "THE GULF STREAM OF MIGRATION" AND (IN SHADED PORTION) APPROXIMATE LOCATION OF B. & M.'S IOWA AND SOUTH PLATTE LANDS.

duplicating them in other languages. "This," commented the *Saline County Post*, "indicates enterprise." [76]

News sheets, printed in regular newspaper form and containing a mass of information that would be useful to the immigrant, particularly if he were a foreigner, carried the circular idea a step further. After explaining the advantages of emigration and the means by which it could be effected, these sheets carefully described the exact location of company lands, illustrated the various credit schemes by which they could be obtained, and added numerous pertinent "Suggestions to Land Buyers and Others." There were also testimonials of crop yields, miscellaneous notes dealing with agricultural experiments, summaries of the Iowa and Nebraska laws concerning fences and herds, and paragraphs about the railroad's colonies and the homestead lands. The list of contents of the 1873 edition reveals the encyclopaedic nature of these sheets: [77]

These Iowa & Nebraska Lands
How is a Buyer to Select Lands?
Prices of Land
Special Inducements
Terms of Payment, — Liberal Deductions
Advantages of Long Credit
Suggestions to Land Buyers and Others
Soldiers' Homesteads
When to Come and How to Begin
Iowa and Nebraska: (Facts concerning the Region: Climate, Soil, Pine lumber, coal, stone, crops, fruit, honey, stock-raising, town and villages, education free to all, houses, prices, dressed lumber, brick, fuel, fencing, wages, waterpower, markets & communications, Taxes)
Iowa
Nebraska
Agricultural Statistics
Colonies
Ways to reach Iowa and Nebraska

Of all the advertising material issued by the Burlington during the early 'seventies, the news sheets were the most revealing as to the railroad's basic policy in regard to the type of person it wished to attract. The fact that they were published in English for distribution in the

[76] *Saline County Post*, May 5, 1871 (NSB).
[77] BMR, News Sheet, March? 1873 (LDP).

northeastern United States, Canada,[78] and the British Isles,[79] and in Scandinavian, German, French, and Bohemian for circulation among the people of those nations,[80] indicated that George Harris' previously expressed preference for the residents of northeastern America and northwestern Europe [81] had been followed by the land department. Whether or not the commissioner's predisposition for these people was affected by the fact that they already were responsible for the bulk of Iowa's and Nebraska's population [82] is difficult to determine. At any rate, the land department continued to encourage immigration in existing channels rather than to develop new sources of supply. The only variation from earlier practice was the inclusion of the French, of whom Harris had once expressed a low opinion as agriculturists,[83] and this change could probably be explained by the fact that the company's appeal was directed primarily to the families of Alsace-Lorraine, next to the German border.[84]

As to the occupation of its customers, the Burlington was naturally primarily interested in farmers, and the entire emphasis of the news sheet, as well as other forms of publicity, was on the farming possibilities of Iowa and Nebraska. Nevertheless, in its desire to develop a well-rounded community and to attract self-sufficient colonies, the railroad pointed out to certain other classes the opportunities of the growing region. Under the caption "Who Should Emigrate?," the 1872 sheet listed first "Farm Laborers." Pointing out that the opportunities of becoming self-sufficient in the West were far better than in the East, it declared: "if you go far enough [west], your country will give you a farm, or, by laboring no harder than you do now, you can soon earn one on railroad lands near to schools, churches, markets. . . ." The second class listed was "Sons of Eastern Farmers," who were told that there was not room enough for them on the old homestead. The next category was entitled "Journeymen Mechanics," which included carpenters, blacksmiths, coopers, shoemakers, machinists, and brick and stone masons. Such persons were told that no community could exist

[78] These sheets were distributed by agents, all of them located in this region.
[79] See below, pp. 359–366.
[80] See below, pp. 366–369.
[81] See above, p. 299.
[82] *Census of 1870*, vol. I, pt. I, pp. 336–342.
[83] See above, p. 303.
[84] See below, p. 366.

without them and that the wages of skilled labor rose the further west one traveled; "diversified industry is good for a State, and is good for those who diversify it." The fourth group appealed to were "All Young Men," with the admonition that "Old folks . . . monopolize the best chances and places" in the older states. Finally, "Many Young Women" were told that "The West has need of you as teachers. . . ."[85]

In presenting these opportunities, however, the railroad did not intend to guarantee employment for everyone who came into its territory, nor would it give encouragement to individuals who wanted specific assurance of work before leaving their old homes. In fact, so many persons wrote to Harris on this subject that in 1873 he had a form letter prepared that was reminiscent of Ames' personal replies four years earlier.[86]

Burlington, Iowa, ... 1873.

Dear Sir:

Numerous applications are made to this Department by persons desiring to come West to secure employment, others who wish to purchase land of the R. R. Co. and make part payment in labor, others who want to know where is the *best* place to locate as a newspaper proprietor, lawyer, physician, teacher, etc., or to trade in groceries, hardware, millinery, dry-goods, agricultural implements, etc., and others still, who wish to secure of our lands and give in exchange such property as they may have elsewhere.

These applications are so numerous that it is impossible to make written answers to each, and the following is as distinct reply as can be made to all:

The business of this Department is confined exclusively to the care and sale of the lands belonging to the Railroad Company.

We have no knowledge whatever of the requirements for labor by the Corporation or by individuals through the country, and could only obtain such by an expenditure of time which it is impossible to devote to it.

In a growing country like this, changes are frequently being made, labor of all kinds, to a certain extent, is required, and opportunities to engage in business are constantly offering; and the man who is on the spot with his eyes and ears open to watch and hunt for such opportunities for labor or business, will stand a fair chance with a multitude of others who are constantly on the look out for similar chances.

This is all that can be said in reply to any one looking for employment, for it is entirely impracticable to expect to secure a situation unless a man is on the spot to give personal attention to it.

The changes in business in the older settled towns and cities, and the

---

[85] BMR, News Sheet, March? 1872 (LDP).
[86] See above, pp. 270–271.

inevitable wants of new places, afford constantly recurring opportunities for the trades and professions in all their variety, and those who wish to improve such should come and see for themselves. This cannot be done without the expenditure of time and money, but it is the *only* safe and satisfactory course to pursue.

We do not exchange our lands for other property, and we do not receive labor in part payment for them, but our terms of sale, which are *exceedingly* liberal, are distinctly stated in my printed circular, and from those no variation can be made.

Were it in my power, I should be glad to render personal aid to all who make enquiries of the character I have alluded to, but a moment's consideration will convince any intelligent man that it is entirely impracticable for me to do so.

GEO. S. HARRIS,
Land Commissioner.[87]

Another warning which the railroad was forced to issue, and which appeared with increasing emphasis in succeeding years, was addressed to persons without any capital whatsoever. In 1872, the news sheet simply stated that the newcomer

should have a few hundred dollars to start with, — sufficient to meet the expense of putting up at first a low-cost house, to purchase a pair of horses, a wagon, cow, pigs, tools, etc., and such outfit as is needful for a beginner and his family. . . .[88]

The next year, however, found a much more strongly worded paragraph on the same subject:

Before coming to purchase lands, see to it that you have the necessary means, and make careful consideration as to their expenditure. None should come without proper forethought and needful capital; but with these the way is open and prospects bright.

It is difficult to make progress anywhere without capital, and nowhere is the need of money more keenly felt than in a new settlement.

You will require money for the expenses of transportation for yourself and family, and such household goods and stock as you may determine to bring; for the first small payment of interest on the land purchased; for buildings and other improvements; for farming tools and provisions until you can make and sell a crop.

. . . Business openings of all kinds are frequent, and labor and clerical assistance are required to a limited extent; but those coming without means and dependent entirely upon employment must take their chances. . . .[89]

[87] BMR, Form Letter, 1873 (LDP).
[88] BMR, News Sheet, March? 1872 (LDP).
[89] BMR, News Sheet, March? 1873 (LDP).

That this caution was necessary was confirmed by a communication to the *Springfield* (Massachusetts) *Republican* dated at Fremont, Nebraska, March 21, 1871, from one "R. F." who gave an appealing yet sober account of the immigrant's chances in his locality:

> If a young man has $2,000, or even $1,500, so that he can put $600 into a house and $300 into a team, and from $350 to $500 into a second-hand homestead, and then has patience, industry, calculation, docility in hearing advice, and economy, he will do well enough if his wife can be contented. There is often the greatest difficulty. Such a young man, so circumstanced, will be sure, in five years, to have a property worth $8,000 or $10,000. It is for him to judge whether he can make his $1,500 realize that amount in New England in that time. If a young man has nothing, he can earn more money at the East than at the West. The industries here are few, wages low, money is scarce. A young man coming here with nothing can do little more than make a living. If he has a family, he must economize as few eastern people do. Within ten miles of this place, there are families living in so-called houses 14 by 16 feet, built of sod, selling their corn at 15 cents per bushel, and their pork at 4 cents per pound, going without tea, coffee, sugar, and other necessities of life, unable to raise enough money to pay their taxes. They hope for better times and that hope sustains them. If those times come, and they hang on by the skin of their teeth till they do come, they will be better off than if they had remained East. But some of them won't hold on, and some will die in the struggle. More anon. R. F.[90]

In all of its news sheets, the railroad sought to take account of such conditions as these, for in the long run its own prosperity depended upon the permanence and wealth of the community through which it ran.

To accompany its written propaganda, the B. & M. issued a variety of maps, some showing the entire region between Chicago and San Francisco,[91] others simply Iowa and Nebraska.[92] So accurate were the latter, boasted Butler, that they could show the location of each eighth of a section.[93] In April, 1873, an elaborate wall map, 53 by 24 inches, was published of the region between the Missouri River and Kearney Junction. It showed not only the natural features and roads

---

[90] "Life in Nebraska, A plain, unvarnished tale of frontier life and capabilities," in the *Springfield Republican*, April? 1871 (LDP).

[91] *Cass County Democrat* (Plattsmouth, Nebraska), May 10, 1871 (NSB).

[92] *Beatrice Express*, April 6, 1872 (NSB).

[93] *Ibid.*

but the limits of the granted lands and the various B. & M. colonies as well; it sold for 30 cents.[94]

More striking than the maps was a volume of 20 Nebraska scenes that Commissioner Harris had prepared early in 1872.[95] This little booklet was distributed throughout the United States and Europe,[96] and the ubiquitous Professor Butler even succeeded in showing it to the Japanese ambassador as he rode through Nebraska on the Union Pacific. The Oriental diplomat politely obliged the company with a public statement of approval.[97] Local comment was equally prompt and enthusiastic:

Mr. H[arris] has displayed admirable tact in getting his lands before the people, but . . . the twenty views which he has had electrotyped from sketches made on the field, by an artist of taste and ability, will do more to advertise Nebraska favorably, and give correct ideas of the topography of this state than anything that could possibly be said or written. The commissioner, fertile in expedients, and generally happy in the selection and use of them, has made a golden hit in these composite representations. Thousands will be attracted by them to seek a home in South-eastern Nebraska. . . .[98]

This puff from the *Saline County Post* was matched by articles in the *Beatrice Express*,[99] the *Adams County Gazette*,[100] and the *Omaha Tribune & Republican*.[101]

The land department, however, was not the only source of B. & M. publicity. Supplementing regular formal advertisements were the picturesque columns contributed to various newspapers by a loyal corps of "unofficial spokesmen," who wrote under their own or assumed names as individuals and were thus able to praise the company's policy and motives with an air of disinterest. One such was the Reverend Darius Jones who handled the formation and establishment of colonies on

[94] BMR, Map of Nebraska (LDP).
[95] BMR, "Views and Description of Burlington and Missouri River Railroad Lands. . . ." (Omaha? 1872.)
[96] *Beatrice Express*, March 23, 1872 (NSB).
[97] *Omaha Tribune & Republican*, March, 1872 (LDP).
[98] *Saline County Post*, 1872 (LDP).
[99] "Advertising Truly an Art" in *Beatrice Express*, March 23, 1872 (NSB).
[100] *Adams County Gazette* (Juniata, Nebraska), 1872 (LDP).
[101] "We may add that the Burlington and Missouri River Road is . . . doing both itself and the State incalculable good, by showing up so clearly the advantages and latent wealth of the latter. . . ." (*Omaha Tribune & Republican*, March? 1872, LDP.)

the railroad land. To papers from Iowa to Massachusetts he sent letters on Nebraska, citing stories of successful immigrants, defending the weather, and expounding the railroad's policies.[102] By far the most untiring correspondent, however, was Professor Butler; his observations covered everything and anything connected with the Burlington. In the *Nebraska Herald*, for example, he discussed how the B. & M.'s ten-year credit scheme had originated with the Illinois Central "which in consequence now runs through a farmer's paradise" and how that system had been imitated by the Hannibal and St. Joseph.[103] To the *Janesville* (Wisconsin) *Gazette* he sent an account of a trip over the Burlington and took the occasion to praise the men in charge.[104] From Madison, Wisconsin, he dated a communication giving in detail the wages of different types of labor and the prices of land near Burlington, Iowa. Coal miners, he pointed out, received $70 a month, shop girls $6 to $12 a week, female domestic servants $2 to $2.50 a week, mechanics $1.65 to $4 a day, painters $3.25 a day, tailors $15 to $18 a week, railroad engineers $3.25 a day, and firemen $1.75. Improved farming land, he added, was worth $75 an acre, but the railroad still held 200,000 unimproved acres "adjacent" in the state to which it would transport purchasers free from Burlington. "Prices," he concluded frankly, "are no lower than those of private individuals for similar tracts, but . . . credit is longer." [105] When strikes assumed menacing proportions in England, the professor turned punster and urged the public to "strike out" for Nebraska.[106] But his rhetorical masterpiece was a description of the 400-mile belt of territory stretching across the United States and including in its center the Burlington's lands. This "Gulf Stream of Migration," as it was termed on the company's maps,[107] was, according to Butler, "so latitudinarian that it is said to be bounded on the north by the 'Aurora Borealis,' and on the south by the Day of Judgment." [108]

[102] "Our Nebraska Letter" in the *Burlington Hawk-Eye*, December 4, 1871 (LDP); "Nebraska" in the *Boston Traveler* (Massachusetts), March 21, 1872 (LDP).

[103] Letter signed "xyz" from Madison, Wisconsin, March 17, 1871, in the *Nebraska Herald*, March 23, 1871 (NSB).

[104] "From Nebraska" in the *Janesville Gazette*, November, 1871 (LDP).

[105] Letter from J. D. Butler, January 6, 1872, reprint in? (LDP).

[106] "Strikes" in the *Nebraska Independent* (Lincoln), September 5, 1872 (LDP).

[107] See map, p. 345.

[108] J. D. Butler, "Nebraska, Its Characteristics and Prospects," n.p., 1873 (LDP).

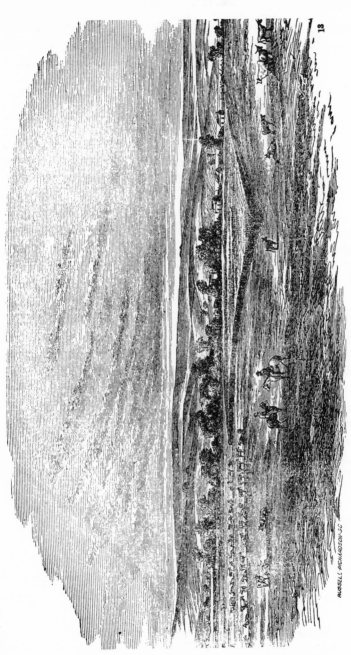

RUSSELL P. RICHARDSON · SC

PRAIRIE, EIGHT MILES EAST FROM LINCOLN, NEB.

FROM "VIEWS AND DESCRIPTION OF BURLINGTON AND MISSOURI RIVER RAILROAD LANDS . . ." — 1872.

Naturally, such literary outbursts brought some amusingly acidulous comments from the local journalists. Editorially, the *Ashland Times* readily admitted that the Burlington was "the best line in the West," but it went on to vent its opinion of Butler:

> The truth is [expostulated its editor] a certain literary deadbeat, who, like the rest of his species, is barefooted on top where his brains ought to be and wears sandstone goggles to keep him from seeing anything useful, — this peripetetic [*sic*] old sardine, one Prof. Butler, spends his time riding on the road on a free pass, and annoying the R. R. Co. and the press with effete details of his Wandering Jew Excursions. We've got a stack of his truck above 14 feet high. . . .[109]

Obviously, the ornate phraseology of the learned professor did not impress some of his neighbors. Perhaps that accounted for Harris' advice to Butler to use good old-fashioned Anglo-Saxon words.[110] Nevertheless, the information that Butler sent out was complete, important, and doubtless new to prospective immigrants who were not already in the West. At least Harris thought that he was a worth-while investment.

A similar type of publicity were the notices and letters sent out independently by the leaders of the railroad colonies. In Iowa, the Reverend B. N. Halland continued his colonization efforts throughout the early 'seventies;[111] in Nebraska, the Reverend D. E. Jones [112] and his colleague, the Reverend Henry Bates,[113] boomed their Plymouth Colony in Jefferson County, and their fellow-preacher, the Reverend C. S. Harrison, advertised his temperance Mayflower group in York County.[114]

---

[109] *Ashland Times*, April 12, 1872 (NSB).   [110] See above, p. 299.

[111] BMI, Sales Record "A":

Date	Acres Sold	For	Commission #
Apr 1–1870 to May 31	13,043.98	$110,296.38	$2,205.93
Jun 1–1870 to Dec 31	6,275.40	79,303.42	1,023.67
Jan 1–71 to Dec 31–72	1,901.60	29,533.00	295.33
Jan 1–73 to Mar 1–75	3,341.42	56,215.00	562.15
	24,562.40	$275,347.80	$4,087.08

\# 2% to August 10, 1870; 1% thereafter. See letter Harris to Halland, August 10, 1870; this altered arrangement made on May 13, 1870, whereby Harris agreed, on behalf of BMI and BMN, to pay 2% on long credit and 2½% on short or cash sales. (LDP.)

[112] BMR, News Sheet, March? 1872 (LDP). Jones also advertised in the *Boston Congregationalist*, the *New York Christian at Work*, *New York Christian Union*, *New York Independent*, *New York Missionary Herald*, and the *Chicago Advance*. (*Saline County Post*, August 19, 1872, NSB.)

[113] Henry Bates, Circular Letter, 1873 (LDP).

[114] BMR, News Sheet, March? 1872 (LDP).

The column inserted in the *Deckertown* (New Jersey) *Independent* by S. H. Sayer, who was seeking to organize a colony from that state, was typical. His group, he wrote,[115]

will consist of one hundred or more persons useful to make up an intelligent and enterprising agricultural community about as follows:

80 Farmers, 160 acres each
5 Carpenters
5 Masons
2 Merchants of General Mdse.
2 Blacksmiths
1 each of: Doctor and Drug Store Proprietor, Hardware Merchant, Harness Maker, Hotel Keeper, Lawyer, Miller, Minister, Printer, School Teacher, Undertaker and Furniture Dealer, and Watch Maker. . . .

Each member of this group was to have 160 acres regardless of profession; anyone interested was urged to communicate with Sayer at once. About the same time, the Ottawa, Illinois, newspaper noted that the Reverend H. R. Roberts, formerly Congregational pastor in the neighboring town of Peru, had returned there to organize a colony for settlement on railroad lands. "Parties desiring to go west" were urged to call upon him and obtain information about the enterprise.[116]

Letters written by new settlers to their hometown papers constituted another means of keeping the B. & M. before the public. It is more than likely that some of these were inspired by the railroad, but equally probable that others were spontaneous. In any event, they had the advantage of appealing to a selected group in their own language and usually appeared under some such enticing caption as: "A Pioneer's First Season on the Raw Prairie," [117] "An English Mechanic on the Mississippi," [118] or "Letter from a Cape Ann Boy in Nebraska." [119] Most of them contained some puff for the B. & M. One writer, for example, pointed out that immigration had been much more rapid in eastern Nebraska than elsewhere in the state and that the company had "exhibited the same resistless push . . . as they did in southern

[115] *Deckertown Independent* (New Jersey), 1872 (LDP).
[116] *Ottawa Republican*, February 8, 1872 (LDP).
[117] *New York Tribune*, February 14, 1872 (LDP).
[118] *Times* (Peterborough? England), May, 1872 (LDP).
[119] *Gloucester Advertiser* (Massachusetts), 1872? (LDP).

Iowa." [120] Another wrote early in 1872 to the *New York Tribune* that he had bought 320 acres from the railroad a year before on long credit. His total outlay for the first year of $919.70 had brought him a return of $4,104; obviously he was well on the way to prosperity.[121] A woman wrote the *Berkshire County Eagle* of Pittsfield (Massachusetts) that the B. & M. deserved high praise for the "better type" of citizen they were attracting, chiefly because of the ten-year credit plan with its six per cent interest rate. She pointed out that with the legal rate in Nebraska twelve per cent, "many a cute Yankee loans his funds for enough to cover his annual payment and leave a surplus besides." [122] Such tales must have inspired many a thrifty easterner, and the investigations of Hollingshead have revealed the efficacy of this particular type of informal advertising. Tracing the cases of 300 men who followed their brothers to Saline County and purchased railroad land between 1871 and 1883, he found that 263 of them had bought tracts directly adjacent to their brothers and that the rest were in the near vicinity. The average time lag between the arrival of two brothers was thirteen months. Of 411 persons from Illinois who settled on B. & M. lands in Seward County from 1871 through 1880, 341 of them fell into groups of three or more who had come from the same community within an average time of eleven months. Two hundred and ninety-eight of the 341 settled in the same township of Nebraska.[123]

In addition to the formal and informal publicity originating in Iowa and Nebraska, the B. & M. roads gradually increased their advertising throughout the northeastern United States and Europe. In this country, the agents generally issued their own circulars or composed columns for the local newspapers. On January 13, 1872, for example, the *Moline* (Illinois) *Review* reported that the Burlington's representative, Major Rasmussen, had sold $14,000 worth of Iowa and Nebraska lands the previous week. "He is one of the heaviest and liveliest real estate men we know of," continued the article. "He advertises a garden patch of

[120] Henry W. Williams, "Letter from Nebraska" in *New York Independent*, 1872? (LDP).

[121] *New York Tribune*, February 14, 1872 (LDP).

[122] Anna S. Dimock, "Life on the Frontier" in the *Berkshire County Eagle* (Pittsfield, Massachusetts), 1872? (LDP).

[123] August deB. Hollingshead, *Trends in Community Development; A Study in Ecological and Institutional Processes in 34 Southeastern Nebraska Communities, 1854–1934* (MS Thesis, University of Nebraska, Lincoln, 1935).

two million acres in another column, which see, read, reflect upon." [124]
The activities of C. C. Cole in Pittsburgh were on an even grander scale.
With suitable publicity he journeyed west to inspect the company's
lands in person,[125] and upon his return issued a colorful appeal particularly addressed to the young agriculturists of his region.[126] D. D.
Garland, traveling agent, journeyed incessantly north of the Ohio, dis-
tributing maps and pamphlets summarizing the railroad's policy, and
providing all kinds of pertinent information.[127] The work of these
men was duplicated and expanded during the early 'seventies throughout the northeast; by 1875, there were over 150 agents in the United
States singing the praises of Iowa and Nebraska.[128]

Meanwhile, these states were officially interesting themselves in the
matter of immigration, thus indirectly aiding the Burlington's colonization work. Although Iowa's experience with a paid commissioner
of immigration at New York City during 1860–62 had been unsuccessful,[129] that state created a new board in 1870 that immediately
showed promise of obtaining satisfactory results. Under its auspices,
a handbook entitled "Iowa: the Home for Immigrants" was published
in English, German, Dutch, Danish, and Swedish, and as a result of
its distribution, inquiries were arriving from prospective settlers at the
rate of 100 per month by 1871. By the end of 1872, 45,000 copies of the
handbook had been circulated in this country and Europe. The annual
budget supporting this laudable activity, however, was but $5,000, so
that agents could be hired only when the railroads agreed to share
expenses.[130] This the B. & M. promptly did in the case of E. T. Edginton, who left for England in the summer of 1870.[131] Late in 1872, the
original board was reorganized and its appropriation doubled by the
legislature, with the result that 15,000 German pamphlets and 7,000
each in Swedish and Norwegian were promptly distributed. In September, 1873, however, the board went out of existence entirely, and

[124] *Moline Review*, January 13, 1872 (LDP).
[125] *Pittsburgh Leader* (Pennsylvania), 1872 (LDP).
[126] *Ibid.*
[127] D. D. Garland, Circular, 1873 (LDP).
[128] See below, p. 445.
[129] See above, p. 210.
[130] Marcus L. Hansen, "Official Encouragement of Immigration to Iowa," *Iowa
Journal of History and Politics*, vol. XIX, no. 2 (April, 1921), pp. 159–195.
[131] See below, p. 359.

CIRCULAR ADVERTISING B. & M. LANDS, 1873.

thereafter until 1880, the railroads were left to publicize the state as best they could.[132]

Events in Nebraska were somewhat similar. A state board of immigration was set up in 1870, pamphlets issued, and a commissioner appointed to reside in New York City. Nevertheless, as in the case of Iowa, limited resources precluded satisfactory results, even a reorganization of the board in 1873 failed to improve its efficiency, and the state authorities seemed willing to let the railroad companies bear most of the expense of advertising. Some towns employed agents, and occasionally the steamship companies aided in publicizing Nebraska.[133] On the whole, however, the Burlington relied on its own efforts or on those of its friends.

IV. FOREIGN ADVERTISING, 1870–1873

From the day that George Harris assumed his position as land commissioner for the Burlington in the fall of 1869, he was interested in launching a European publicity campaign on behalf of the railroad.[134] He had already established an outlet for Hannibal and St. Joseph advertising material in Scotland[135] and, during October and November, discussed with Henry Wilson of Burlington the possibility of the latter's appointment as B. & M. agent in England.[136] Nothing came of these negotiations, however, and it was not until the following spring that a feasible proposition appeared. In May, 1870, Edward Edginton of Chariton, Iowa, was appointed by the state board of immigration to act as their agent in the British Isles, and late in that month he wrote Harris to suggest that he might also be useful as the railroad's representative in that territory.[137] The suggestion appealed to the commissioner, and on June 6, Edginton outlined in detail a ten-point plan of campaign; it was identical with the one approved by the state board, and he contemplated acting in the dual capacity of state and railroad agent. "I propose," he wrote,

[132] Hansen, *loc. cit.*

[133] Annadora Foss Gregory, *The History of Crete, Nebraska, 1870–88* (MS Thesis, University of Nebraska, Lincoln, 1932).

[134] See above, p. 299.

[135] James Mitchell (of Stonehouse by Hamilton, Lanarkshire, Scotland) to Harris, September 11, 1869 (LDP).

[136] Henry Wilson to Harris, November 1, 1869 (LDP).

[137] Edginton to Harris, May 27, 1870 (LDP).

1st. To devote my entire time to the circulation of documents, to the exclusion of all other business;

2nd. Establish an office in Liverpool for the purpose of furnishing emigrants with reliable information as to the advantages of this State;

3rd. To board every steam or other vessel leaving with emigrants on the day of departure, to furnish a liberal supply of documents to the most intelligent among them, for the purpose of reading during the passage;

4th. Visit every hotel and boarding house in the city frequented by emigrants, and give them all the information they may require, as to lands, climate, wages, etc. etc.;

5th. Seek out and correspond with persons employed by large bodies of individuals to make choice of locations and purchase lands for them, also with agents employed by or to form Co-operative Societies;

6th. Distribute and place in every public building, Hotel, R. Rd. Station, a map of the State showing the line of the route and lands belonging to the B. & M. R. Rd;

7th. After the close of emigration season visit large manufacturing towns and agricultural districts in England and Scotland for the purpose of circulating documents and disseminating information;

8th. Obtain names and places of residence of all parties desiring or intending to emigrate during the ensuing season, and correspond with them;

9th. Publish short articles in newspapers chiefly read by the emigrating class;

10th. Deliver short addresses to parties of emigrants on the superior advantages presented by this State. . . .[138]

Harris was impressed with this program; during July he agreed to pay Edginton $60 a month and his expenses,[139] and on August 6, the latter sailed for Liverpool on the new 4,000-ton steamer, *Italy*.[140] As a starter, he took with him 500 B. & M. maps and circulars.[141]

Edginton's first task on reaching England was to make a systematic survey of all advertising media and determine the cost of issuing posters, handbills, maps, and circulars; the small supply of the latter that he brought with him was exhausted in a week. With great precision, he listed over 50 publications in the order of their usefulness and grouped them into those solely devoted to agriculture, county newspapers primarily interested in agriculture, London weekly papers, and

[138] Edginton to Harris, June 6, 1870 (LDP).
[139] Edginton to Harris, July 30, 1870 (LDP), and October 15, 1870 (LDP).
[140] Edginton to Harris, August 6, 1870 (LDP).
[141] *Ibid.*

daily or weekly papers published in large country towns. He inquired into the cost of billboard advertising at stations and of issuing all sorts of circulars and handbills. All of these findings he sent off to Harris, so that the commissioner might fashion his instructions on the basis of complete information.[142] Even before he had received a full reply, however, Edginton was busy carrying out part of the program he had outlined the previous spring.[143] He reported the distribution of over 3,000 pamphlets to passengers on board vessels leaving for America, in boarding houses, among emigrant agents, and in railroad cars. Even more important, he talked with every person of influence that he could find.

By January, Edginton's campaign was in full swing. Under instructions from Harris, he ordered 2,000 large show cards, 10,000 two-color handbills, 10,000 large circulars with maps, 50,000 small circulars for distribution by agents at hotels and boats, and an advertisement to be inserted during alternate weeks in 20 English and Scotch newspapers.[144] In the meantime, he was busy traveling to London and elsewhere in England to talk with people who intended to leave for Iowa in April.

Most of them [he wrote] have considerable capital and intend purchasing large tracts of land in the S. W. part of Iowa, in Mills or Montgomery Counties. They intend taking with them some fine blooded Stock, Horses, Cattle, etc., etc. They are highly respectable people and will be a great acquisition to the State. I expect to go North in a few days to see some others who contemplate going. . . .[145]

Despite these reports of undoubted activity, however, Harris was already planning to organize the English campaign on a much larger scale than originally contemplated, with Edginton in a subordinate position.[146] In February he hired Cornelius Schaller as the B. & M.'s European commissioner, appointed Henry Wilson [147] as his assistant

[142] Edginton to Harris, August 27, 1870 (LDP); August 28, 1870 (LDP); August 30, 1870 (LDP); September 9, 1870 (LDP); September 16, 1870 (LDP); October 10, 1870 (LDP).

[143] Edginton to Harris, October 15, 1870 (LDP); October 25, 1870 (LDP).

[144] Edginton to Harris, January 31, 1871 (LDP).

[145] Edginton to Harris, January 26, 1871 (LDP).

[146] Schaller to Harris, January 31, 1871 (LDP); William Hayward (Commissioner of Emigration for the State of Nebraska at London) to Harris, February 18, 1871 (LDP).

[147] See above, p. 359.

with the title of agent general, and sent the two of them to England. In contrast to the relatively small amount paid Edginton for his part-time work, Schaller was to receive $2,500 a year, plus expenses and a commission of one per cent on all lands sold on long credit and one and a quarter per cent on short credit and cash sales, up to the total amount of $4,000.[148] The plan of operations he had worked out with Harris was revealed in his correspondence immediately following his arrival in Great Britain in March.

The new system contemplated the division of the British Isles into districts and the creation of a veritable army of agents, all of whom were to duplicate the work that Edginton had already started.[149] Within a month, Schaller had made a beginning. The London representative for Nebraska, William Hayward, agreed to act as resident agent for that city, Edginton was transferred to Glasgow, and two new men were named for Birmingham and Dublin.[150] Eventually, other district agents, all paid a fixed salary and reporting directly to the Liverpool headquarters, were appointed for Bristol, Leicester, London-derry, Manchester, and Queenstown. In addition to their own busy schedule of proselyting, these men received reports from approximately 1,000 sub-agents within their districts who, on a commission basis, were carrying out on a smaller scale the program followed in the larger cities and ports. Based on these reports, books were kept at Liverpool showing the movements of agents, the number of emigrants leaving for America, and the most likely fields for further emigration.[151] By April, Schaller had organized an emigrant home at Liverpool where persons leaving for America could stay for 25 cents a night, obtain coffee for four cents, a chop for eight cents, and be "thoroughly pro-tected from runners and 'touters.'"[152]

While he was setting up this organization, Schaller was busy with

[148] Memorandum, February 15, 1871 (LDP).

[149] Schaller to Harris, March 30, 1871 (LDP).

[150] Schaller to Harris, April 9, 1871 (LDP).

[151] York Monitor (Nebraska), September 26, 1872 (NSB).

[152] Schaller to the editor of the Omaha Republican, April 25, 1871 (NSB). "What has Nebraska done about Emigrants' Homes?" asked Schaller. "Is Omaha to have one? . . . The most important question I am continually asked [is] 'is there any provision made for our protection?' . . . The B. & M. have established rooms in Burlington and Lincoln. . . . My first home was in Omaha, and I am anxious that that city should not be forgotten." (Ibid.)

a dozen other schemes and activities on behalf of the railroad. Before he had been in England three weeks, he had arranged to put up a boatload of emigrants in Liverpool the night before they sailed for America. In return for this hospitality, they attended a meeting at which Schaller spoke glowingly of the paradise that awaited them in Iowa and Nebraska.[153] The experiment was so successful that he suggested to Touzalin in Burlington that it might be wise to charter a whole ship and send it directly to Baltimore loaded with customers for the B. & M.[154] In the meantime, he continued his travels through the countryside, appointing agents and spreading the Burlington name far and wide.

My next tour [he reported in April, 1871] is South Coast either through Devonshire and Cornwall or round via Scotland to Liverpool, thence taking the interior of Wales, having done the sea coast. We have some really good working agents; men that I am certain will eventually fully repay us. . . .[155]

As time went on, the flood of pamphlets continued, and Schaller even managed to have several of Professor Butler's letters printed in various newspapers;[156] in August, 1871, he told Harris he would like to have testimonials from Englishmen already on railroad lands.[157]

Of a more colorful nature than the company's formal advertising were the special devices for drawing attention to Iowa and Nebraska and to the B. & M. At Derby, for example, Schaller attended a lecture by a Mr. Abington on the "Great West" and, by pre-arrangement, was on hand after the formal speaking to answer questions about ways and means of emigration. "The morning after the lecture," he wrote Harris, "our agent, Mr. Isaac Webster, had no less than 4 or 5 applications." [158] Still another scheme was to supply photographs to a certain C. S. Dawson, who had them converted into paintings and included in what he mellifluously termed his "Sylphorama of America by Sea, River and Railroad." This was a series of 85 views, each covering 250 square feet of canvas, which he exhibited with explanations at evening

[153] Schaller to Harris, March 30, 1871 (LDP).
[154] Schaller to Harris, April 9, 1871 (LDP).
[155] Schaller to Harris, April 29, 1871 (LDP).
[156] *Ibid.*; Schaller to Harris, July 17, 1871 (LDP).
[157] Schaller to Harris, August 16, 1871 (LDP).
[158] Schaller to Harris, August 26, 1871 (LDP).

performances.[159] Dawson did not confine his activities, however, to his unique exhibit. In the spring of 1872, he organized a party of 60 Englishmen for a buffalo hunt in Nebraska the following October. "Buffalo Bill" Cody was hired as a guide. "This," observed the *State Journal*, "is a capital way to make the higher classes of the old country acquainted with the marvellous attractions in Nebraska by those desiring to secure homes in a new and fertile country." [160]

Agricultural fairs offered another opportunity for publicity. Early in 1872, Wilson wrote that samples of Nebraska crops sent over by Harris would be exhibited;[161] a few months later the *Omaha Daily Herald* reported that these exhibits, together with an elk head and horn, had attracted thousands both at Derby and at the opening of Sefton Park by Prince Arthur.[162] Robert W. Furnas, president of the Nebraska State Board of Agriculture, lent his support to this program. In July he urged farmers in the state to coöperate by sending "fine specimens" of soil, oats, corn, barley, rye, potatoes, and fruit to Harris so they could be forwarded to England.[163] When, in November, an Englishman already in Nebraska presented the B. & M with a blooded cow raised on his farm on the Blue River, the land department sent her to Britain for exhibition along with two bales of Nebraska hay. "This is another example," commented the local press, "of the royal way in which this company are advertising Nebraska in the old country." [164]

In contrast to the land department's appeal to the individual in the United States, Schaller and his corps devoted most of their energies to forming colonies who would travel as a unit from the British Isles to Iowa and Nebraska. Their reasons for encouraging this type of immigration were publicly stated:

Nearly all privations and discomforts complained of by settlers in a new country [ran one circular] have arisen from the fact that they have emigrated as individuals, or as isolated families, instead of organized bodies. Let a small community, embracing as many families and individuals previously acquainted as possible, of various trades and professions, and in-

---

[159] C. S. Dawson, Handbill, September 8, 1871 (LDP).
[160] *Nebraska State Journal*, May 27, 1872 (NSB).
[161] Wilson to Harris, February 7, 1872 (LDP); April 22, 1872 (LDP).
[162] *Omaha Daily Herald*, July 9, 1872 (NSB).
[163] Unidentified newspaper, July 24, 1872 (NSB).
[164] *Ibid.*, November 22, 1872 (NSB).

tending to follow various pursuits, emigrate and settle together, then society, mutual help, comfort, security and economy will at once be secured, and anticipated hardships and trials of an emigrant's life will vanish away, and the whole colony, bound together by a community of interest, will rapidly grow in strength and prosperity. . . .[165]

A letter from the central Liverpool office to the district agents in January, 1872, gives a clue to the composition of these groups:

I wish it to be clearly understood [wrote Agent General Wilson] that the Burlington and Missouri River Railroad Cos.' English Agency is for the sale of their lands, and therefore the class we most want is *Farmers* or *Land Buyers*. There is room for agricultural laborers, a few Mechanics, and a few Shopkeepers, but at the same time I must urge upon you not, in my name, to promise employment to anyone as, in a comparatively new country, the facilities to persons dependent upon their labor are not so good as in older States. To Farmers, we offer great things; good climate, excellent soil, and Land for next to nothing — at prices varying from £1 to £3 per acre. . . .[166]

The actual formation of these colonies was left to local or district agents of the towns from which colonists would leave. In the spring of 1871, for example, Ashworth and Parker at Rochdale announced that the next colony for Lincoln, Nebraska, would leave their city on June 28, 1871.[167] Through tickets, they said, could be purchased direct to Lincoln at prices ranging from £11-11/0 to £24-11/5, depending on whether the immigrant traveled by steerage and coach or in cabin class and sleeper. A guide would be furnished to accompany the party from its landing direct to destination, and every care and comfort was promised the travelers "until they are finally settled in their New Home." [168] The next year, Henry Wilson announced that the *Nestorian* would leave Liverpool on March 26, with a large number of "Farmers, Tradesmen, Mechanics, Labourers, etc.," for both Iowa and Nebraska; this time an agent of the B. & M. would accompany the party throughout the journey and "superintend" their settlement.[169] No chances were to be taken of losing such choice customers, and to make matters

---

[165] BMR, Circular, January, 1872 (LDP).

[166] Wilson to district agents, January 1, 1872 (LDP).

[167] BMR, Circular, March? 1871 (LDP).

[168] *Ibid.*

[169] BMR, Circular, January, 1872 (LDP); cf. Circular issued in London by Hayward, November, 1871 (LDP).

doubly sure, each immigrant was given a special letter of introduction to George S. Harris.[170]

Although the bulk of the B. & M.'s foreign colonization work was done in Great Britain during the early 'seventies, other portions of northwestern Europe were by no means neglected. Circulars in Welsh[171] and Bohemian[172] appeared at an early date, and in the spring of 1871, Harris received a letter from one Lycurgus Edgerton, who was living near Tours, France, in regard to advertising in that country.[173] Edgerton had read the B. & M.'s advertisements in various American newspapers and offered his services, on an expense-and-commission basis, as the company's advertising agent in France and Germany. He pointed out particularly that as a result of the Franco-Prussian War, great numbers of families from Alsace and Lorraine wished to emigrate, and

all that is necessary in order to give direction to that emigration *toward any particular district of* the *country,* or *special locality,* is to go among the people and by means of suitable agencies and intermediaries, bring them to their notice, organize colonies and emigrant associations, etc., aid them in making their preparations, . . . etc.[174]

Edgerton was planning to spend several months at this work and to proceed thence into Germany. He declared he was familiar with the West and supplied numerous references, including James F. Joy. Impressed with the proposition, Harris replied in May, sending a package of circulars and maps printed in English and German.[175] Later, the company prepared a special French circular for this project which stated, among other things, that in Iowa and Nebraska the people of Alsace and Lorraine could "escape from the crushing heels of the German Empire's militarism." [176]

In September of the same year, Harris shipped off a batch of English, German, Danish, and Swedish circulars to C. B. Nelson, the agent

[170] BMR, Letter of Introduction, 1871, *et seq.* (LDP).

[171] BMR, Circular, 1871? (LDP).

[172] BMR, Circular, 1871? (LDP).

[173] Lycurgus Edgerton to Harris, April? 1871 (LDP).

[174] *Ibid.*

[175] Penciled notation signed "G.S.H.," May, 1871 (LDP).

[176] BMR, Circular, 1871 (LDP): "échapper des talons écrasants du militarisme de l'Empire Germanique."

NOTICE CONCERNING A COLONY LEAVING ROCHDALE, ENGLAND, FOR B. & M. LANDS, 1871.

for the State of Nebraska at Copenhagen;[177] in the meantime, Joseph E. Osborn opened a regular company agency in Göteborg, Sweden. As it turned out, Osborn's task proved to be not only difficult but unpleasant. The newspapers mainly devoted to emigration did accept his advertising and promised to print articles favoring Nebraska, but he reported that every paper in the country was using fair or unfair means to discourage any exodus from the homeland.

> They recite in the most horrid manner [he explained] the murders and all law breakings from America they can get hold of, but say *never a word* of the good things there. . . .[178]

Public opinion was equally hostile, particularly on the part of the wealthier and educated classes, who deplored the departure of the poorer agricultural laborers. According to Osborn, emigrant and land agents were looked upon as "robbers and scoundrels of the deepest dye," and he frankly admitted he would never have taken his job had he known the reception awaiting him. Nevertheless, he promised to stay at his post and hoped that giving "honest advice" would improve his lot. Meanwhile, he would issue circulars printed in Sweden to supplement the material sent from America.[179]

Through Frederick Hedde, Nebraska's agent in Hamburg, the Burlington found an outlet for its German publicity. A preliminary shipment of pamphlets and maps sent over early in 1871 was rapidly distributed, and in November, Harris sent off 10,000 German circulars, 1,000 Danish, and a supply of colored maps and posters.[180] As in the case of the appeal directed toward the Alsatians, the company showed considerable ingenuity in presenting its arguments for emigration. The Germans, for example, were told that their countrymen were already successful farmers, mechanics, artisans, and teachers in both Iowa and Nebraska, and that they would become increasingly important as landholders because the Americans had "more of a leaning for industrial undertakings and speculation. Thus Americans and Germans live in friendly neighborliness. . . ."[181] As in Sweden, however, the effect

[177] Memorandum signed "G.S.H. . . . Sept. 5/71" on letter from Nelson to Harris, August 6, 1871 (LDP).

[178] Joseph E. Osborn to Harris, October 9, 1871 (LDP).

[179] *Ibid.*

[180] Memorandum attached to letter from Hedde to W. D. Cowles (agent of the B. & M. RRs at New York City), October 31, 1871 (LDP).

[181] BMR, Circular, November, 1871 (LDP): "mehr Neigung für industrielle

of American propaganda was somewhat offset by the newspapers which were controlled by a nobility equally as hostile as the Swedish to the departure of the poorer people. Hedde reported, however, that no government action would be taken, for "Bismarck is smart enough to know that stopping emigration means favoring revolution." [182]

An article by Hedde, published in the *Omaha Daily Herald* late in 1872, added several illuminating sidelights upon his own occupation and the relative activity of western states and railroads in attracting immigrants.[183] Michigan, Iowa, Missouri, Texas, Minnesota, and Oregon, he reported, were all represented by well-paid men; the Michigan agent had been abroad three years, and was spending between $6,000 and $7,000 annually in publishing his "Michigan Guide Board." Hedde, on the other hand, was receiving but $1,200, which forced him to rely almost entirely upon gratuitous editorial comments printed by the more liberally inclined journals. During the year, however, he had received 4,000 pamphlets from the state of Nebraska, 2,000 from the Union Pacific, and 14,000 from the Burlington, all of which he had distributed. Among the railroads, the Northern Pacific, however, was making the most comprehensive campaign in Germany. It had already established two newspapers of its own in Gotha and Frankfort, in addition to its papers in Switzerland and England. This company, commented Hedde, is "sagacious enough to know the importance of using money in the right way." [184] At the same time, he complimented the Burlington on having the only emigrant homes he knew about and urged other states and railways to establish them.

These reports from Europe were not lost upon the state officials of Nebraska. A grand jury investigating the state's immigration office reported in December, 1872, that the B. & M. had spent $500,000 on foreign immigration and the Union Pacific $300,000 during the preceding year. Both companies, it said, had benefited, as well as Nebraska. It recommended that the state continue its own activities with a larger budget.[185]

Unternehmungen und Speculationen hat. Doch leben Amerikaner und Deutsche in freundschaftlichen Verhältnissen. . . ."

[182] Frederick Hedde in *Omaha Daily Herald*, December 4, 1872 (NSB).
[183] *Ibid.*
[184] *Ibid.*
[185] *Omaha Tribune & Republican*, December 19, 1872 (NSB).

V. PUBLIC RELATIONS AND CIVIC DEVELOPMENT, 1871–1873

Between direct advertising, public relations, and civic development as carried on by the Burlington, there was indeed little difference so far as motives were concerned, for all of them were designed to create a prosperous community for the railroad. In method, however, the three forms of activity varied considerably. Direct advertising sought to achieve its object by stimulating the prompt purchase of company lands. Consequently, it appealed exclusively to prospective customers. Public relations work, on the other hand, was more indirect in its operation. By performing some specific service or favor, the railroad endeavored to keep the good will of various people who might become shippers, travelers, land buyers, or merely friends of the system. Civic development was the most subtle procedure of all, for it involved planned projects from which the company might derive no tangible or immediate benefit; its effects on the neighborhood, however, were often more lasting.

One of the most important groups toward which the B. & M. directed its public relations program was that comprising the editors of local newspapers, whose friendship the company diligently cultivated. It was natural that neighboring journalists would, on their own initiative, carry considerable copy on the progress and projects of their railroad, but Harris sought to direct and encourage their efforts by supplying them with favorable items of information from time to time.[186] He accompanied each contribution with a printed notice: "As the matter is one in which we are all materially interested, will you give the notice one or two insertions and oblige." [187] As a rule, the editors did so. Occasionally, the company could offer something substantial in return for such free publicity. In 1872, for example, when two new diners were put into service on the B. & M. in Iowa, the gentlemen of the press from Omaha and Council Bluffs were cordially invited to a meal in the "flying dining palace, St. Charles." There they were welcomed with bourbon and amply nourished upon broiled chicken, broiled ham, Porterhouse steak, rolls, vegetables, relishes, coffee, fruits, champagne, port, and Havana cigars.[188] No wonder that the *Omaha*

---

[186] See below, pp. 372–373.
[187] BMR, Notice to Editors (LDP).
[188] Council Bluffs paper, September 2, 1872 (NSB).

Bee reporters wrote that the " 'favorite route East' will never be forgotten by us!" Incidentally, they not only praised the food but mentioned the politeness of conductors and waiters, the comfort of the "extra springs," and concluded that "travelers would hardly think that they were taking their meals while going at the rate of 25 miles per hour." [189]

The press, however, was by no means dependent on the company for its opinions or news. Aside from serious editorials criticizing various aspects of the company's policy,[190] news items appeared from time to time that quite obviously did not originate with the railroad. In the summer of 1871, for example, the *Saline County Post* amusedly related how some engineers on a handcar caught up with a train bound from Lincoln to Crete, roped the rear car, and rode without exertion to their destination.[191] Another account sounded more like the twentieth century:

> Out on the B. & M. the other day, a couple were married, while the cars were going at the rate of 30 miles per hour. Marital matters and things are becoming of such frequent occurrence on our railways, that we suggest the keeping of train ministers and doctors to meet cases of emergency.[192]

Perhaps such items were not chosen by Harris, but at least they kept the railroad in the public eye.

The local press was not the only object of the railroad's attention. In June, 1871, Butler organized an "Indiana Editorial Excursion" for newspaper men representing 16 towns in that state.[193] Proceeding over the Indianapolis, Bloomington and Western [194] and the C. B. & Q.-B. & M.,[195] the party went direct to Lincoln, Nebraska; free busses took

---

[189] *Omaha Bee*, September 2, 1872 (NSB).

[190] See below, pp. 378–379.

[191] *Saline County Post*, August 18, 1871 (NSB).

[192] *Nebraska Herald*, January 12, 1871 (NSB).

[193] *Saline County Post*, June 30, 1871 (NSB). The editors of the following papers made the trip: *Columbia City Post, Crown Point Register, Elkhart Review, Goshen Democrat, Goshen Times, Kendallville News, Kendallville Standard, LaPorte Argus, Ligonier National Banner, Plymouth Press, Plymouth Republican, Rennselaer Union, Rochester Sentinel, Rochester Spy, South Bend Register, Waterloo Press, Warsaw Northern Indianian, Warsaw Union, Winimac Democrat* (all of Indiana), and the *Plattsmouth Herald*. (*Ibid.*)

[194] Now part of the Big Four (New York Central).

[195] One editor wrote, "I never met a more gentlemanly set of conductors than I

them to hotels where they were "waited upon in the best style, and fed with the beautiful abundance of good things raised from Nebraska's prolific soil."[196] The next morning, Doane and Butler piloted them to the government Land Office, thence to the B. & M., "where they were introduced to those gentlemanly land agents, with Mr. Harris at the head,"[197] and shown maps and plats of the company's western lands. Two days later they were turned over to the Burlington's land agent for York and Fillmore counties and escorted over available portions of the grant. Upon their return to their home towns, the editors naturally gave a glowing account of their outing and included in detail the generous terms offered by the railroad.[198] From the company's viewpoint, the excursion was an excellent investment; Indiana ranked high as a source of B. & M. customers,[199] and it is significant that just a month later, 60 business men, farmers, and mechanics from Indianapolis bought $25,000 worth of lots and lands in and around Lincoln.[200] The local reaction to this excursion, however, was probably of even greater value than the tangible returns from lands sold. During the course of the party's stay in Lincoln, a reception was held in their honor, and one of the local citizens, John S. Bender, took the occasion to propose a toast to the railroad. He pointed out that the regular fare from Chicago to Lincoln and return for 66 people would have been $2,970. This amount, he said, had been donated by the B. & M.

to the editorial party who might ride into Nebraska and advertise more thoroughly her merits to the world . . . a positive argument that railroads possess a soul worthy of cultivation. . . . People should consider what the railroads have done for them. . . . There is a mutual benefit . . . we are tending to an opposition to such corporations that may result more to our detriment than we are inclined at first to suppose. Railroads in a new country cannot be built without liberal aid. There is not the local freight to warrant the expenditure of funds. In the East a railroad is built because the business of the country through which it is to run demands steam transportation. In the West . . . in order that the country may be built. . . . What were the prospects of the South Platte before the Burling-

---

found on the I. B. & W. and the C. B. & Q. and B. & M. railroads." (Unidentified Indiana newspaper, June, 1871, LDP.)

[196] Unidentified Indiana newspaper, June, 1871 (LDP).

[197] Ibid.

[198] Ibid.; another unidentified Indiana newspaper, August, 1872 (LDP).

[199] See below, p. 422.

[200] Ashland Times, August 7, 1871 (NSB).

ton and Missouri and the Midland Pacific began to penetrate her rich prairies? Upon what did Lincoln build her promise of present success if not on the daily arrival of trains? . . . What is the salvation of every ambitious village in Nebraska? The rail. A year ago the wheat in this city without the rail brought 40¢ a bushel. Today with the Iron Horse, the Lancaster Flouring Mills will give $1.10 for every bushel of good wheat they can get. . . . We write thus that a liberal spirit may exist towards the railroads already running and those projected. . . . Legislation crippling railway enterprise is always dangerous to the growth of a people.[201]

Not all excursionists, however, were editors or prospective land customers. On the day that the rails reached Crete, a party that included members of the Congregational Church Association and their friends arrived from Lincoln to look over the site for a denominational college. Acting with commendable energy, they laid the cornerstone of an academy that very day; among those present were George Harris, his wife and daughter.[202] The connection of the railroad with this event was far more than casual and of much greater significance than the particular enterprise in hand, for it illustrated the sort of civic development work carried on by the B. & M.

As early as 1869, a Congregational college for Nebraska was being urged by church leaders in the state, particularly by Frederick Alley, the pastor at Plattsmouth, and Thomas Doane, the engineer in charge of the B. & M. In December, 1870, Doane asked the railroad for 40 or 50 acres of land, and during the winter he and Alley decided that Crete would be the best location. To pave the way for a college, an academy was organized during the spring of 1871, whose articles of incorporation allowed transformation into an institution of higher learning.[203] It was the cornerstone of this academy that was laid on June 12, 1871, by members of the church who had been brought to Crete free of charge on the first train to enter the town.[204] From that time on, Doane never relaxed his efforts. Ten days after the excursion, he offered the Association on behalf of the railroad 80 acres of B. & M. land worth $3,000; at the same time he and his colleagues promised in addition an academy building and lot to cost $5,000, a cash sub-

---

[201] *Nebraska Herald*, July 13, 1871.

[202] *Saline County Post*, June 16, 1871 (NSB).

[203] Willard Scott, "Congregational College History in Nebraska," Nebraska State Historical Society, *Transactions and Reports*, vol. III (1892), p. 248.

[204] See map, p. 283.

scription of $3,000, and announced that the Eastern Land Association would give 50 lots worth $4,000 if the college were authorized.[205] This latter organization was an independent town lot company controlled by B. & M. men.[206] The total value of these various inducements was $15,000, and the *Saline County Post* reported that the railroad was expected to give more.[207] Two weeks later, it added that there were "nine saloons in the place. No school houses yet, no church, but good prospects!"[208] As a matter of fact, the prospects were realized with amazing promptness. On August 25, 1871, the following notice appeared in the newspaper:

> Through the kindness of the B. & M. R. R. Company, the Congregationalists, until further notice, will hold their service in the new Depot Building. Preaching each Sabbath at 10½ o'clock, A.M.[209]

On October 10, the Sunday school was opened with 21 present and Doane busy as its superintendent.[210] Early the next spring, there was another indication of the company's interest. From the East arrived a 500-lb. bell for the Academy, presented "in the interests of a Christian education" by J. W. Brooks, John Murray Forbes, J. N. Denison, and others of Boston.[211]

In April, 1872, the trustees of Crete Academy asked the B. & M. for 600 acres of land, and on May 25, their request was granted on condition that a college recognized by the Congregational Education Promotion Society should remain in Crete for at least ten years and that the churches in Nebraska should raise $30,000 for endowment purposes.[212] News of this gift arrived in Crete along with a tornado which carried buildings "in different and opposite directions" and moved the academy eight feet off its foundations.[213] But Doane was undeterred. At a "College Meeting" a day or two later he was appointed to the committee that would present Crete's plea to the church's association meeting at Omaha.[214] On June 1, it was announced that the

[205] *Saline County Post*, June 23, 1871 (NSB).
[206] *Ibid.*, July 7, 1871 (NSB).
[207] *Ibid.*, June 23, 1871 (NSB).
[208] *Ibid.*, July 7, 1871 (NSB).
[209] *Ibid.*, August 25, 1871 (NSB).
[210] Gregory, *op. cit.*
[211] *Saline County Post*, April 19, 1872 (NSB).
[212] Bullock, *op. cit.*, pp. 216–217; Gregory, *op. cit.*, pp. 181–182.
[213] *Saline County Post*, May 31, 1872 (LDP).
[214] *Ibid.*, May 29, 1872 (LDP). At the same meeting Mrs. Doane helped raise $78 for victims of the tornado. (*Ibid.*)

6

RUSSELL RICHARDSON S.C.

AT CRETE, NEBRASKA.

FROM "VIEWS AND DESCRIPTION OF BURLINGTON AND MISSOURI RIVER RAILROAD LANDS . . ." — 1872.

Eastern Land Association had offered the 50 town lots to the projected college on conditions identical with those attached to the railroad's gift.[215] On June 7, Doane and George Harris appeared before the Omaha meeting and were rewarded when the Congregational Association formally voted to locate the college at Crete. The next month this institution, with Doane as one of the incorporators, was organized and took over the property of the academy; [216] at an early meeting Doane was elected a three-year trustee, put on the executive committee, and made treasurer.[217] Under the circumstances, it was not strange that the new enterprise should be called Doane College.[218]

The man who was thus honored carried the interests of the railroad into other activities as well, for in addition to his duties as engineer and officer of the college, he served as president of the State Bank of Nebraska at Crete.[219] When he finally left for Massachusetts to help build the great Hoosac Tunnel, it was said that he had given the men of the West an example of their own push and energy;[220] at the same time, he had inevitably enhanced the reputation of the B. & M. railroad. It was the activity of men like Doane that prompted an Omaha paper to exclaim late in 1872 that the B. & M. had "introduced to this growing state some of its best citizens, men of means, of character, and of influence." [221]

One type of community development work in which the company participated directly was the encouragement of agriculture. As early as 1871 the railroad was considering the establishment of nurseries along its line, [222] and the next year a contract was let to E. F. Stevens, of Crete, for setting out trees along the 120 miles of road between Lincoln and Lowell. The purpose was to set up effective wind breaks, and to discover what trees were particularly suitable for the territory. In December, 1873, Stevens made his report:

[215] Bullock, *op. cit.*, pp. 216–217.

[216] Gregory, *op. cit.*, p. 182.

[217] *Saline County Post*, August? 1872 (LDP).

[218] *Omaha Herald*, September 6, 1872 (LDP).

[219] *Saline County Post*, May 24, 1872 (NSB).

[220] Morton, *op. cit.*, p. 497.

[221] *York Monitor*, September 26, 1872 (NSB), reprinted from the *Omaha Tribune & Republican*.

[222] *Brownville Advertiser* (Nebraska), August 10, 1871 (NSB). The editor remarked that he had been urging just such a scheme on the Union Pacific for years without success. (*Ibid.*)

Type and Age of Trees	Number Planted	Percentage Still Healthy
Ash, 2-year	20,000	98⅜
Box Elder, 2-year	11,000	92
Honey Locust, set for hedge, 1-year	144,000	not given
Soft Maple, 1-year	17,000	83
Soft Maple, 2-year	60,000	not given
European Larch, 2-year	72,000	82½
Scotch Pines, transplanted and roots pruned	20,000	80
Norway Spruce, transplanted and roots pruned	6,000	80
Norway Spruce, roots pruned	8,000	not given
Cottonwood sprouts	28,000	72
Cottonwood cuttings	82,000	17
White Willow cuttings	92,000	75
Total	560,000	

Thus, more than half a million trees or plants were set out. Because of the great success with the ash, Stevens was given a new contract for the following year to replace failures with this variety.[223]

Meanwhile, the B. & M. continued to forward collections of crop samples to fairs.[224] In 1872, some 600 specimens of Nebraska produce were sent to eastern exhibitions.

> The R. R. Co. doubtless have an eye to business in this matter [accurately remarked the *Beatrice Express*], and while their interests could in no way be more surely promoted than by the exhibitions they are making, . . . they could not have done a better thing for the interests of the whole West. . . .[225]

The next year witnessed a continuation of the same policy; the special car carrying Nebraska fruit to Boston bore the appropriate words "By their fruits ye shall know them." [226] The company's enterprise had an interesting indirect effect locally. Commenting upon the Nebraska State Fair held in the late summer of 1873, the *Beatrice Express* noted that "the only respectable exhibition of cereals, trees, vegetables, etc. was made by the B. & M. Why," inquired the editor, "should not counties use as much foresight as railroad companies in exhibiting their productions?" [227] In the meantime, he urged farmers to send their

[223] *Beatrice Express*, December 18, 1873 (NSB).
[224] See above, p. 364.
[225] *Beatrice Express,* October 17, 1872 (NSB).
[226] *Ibid.*, October 23, 1873.
[227] *Ibid.*, September 11, 1873.

grain samples to George S. Harris. Three months later the same editor noted that the B. & M. had received three diplomas from the American Institute at New York for its display of cereals, apples, and native woods; he concluded that these awards would have considerable influence upon immigration.[228]

In addition to these major undertakings, the Burlington had opportunities to lend its aid in a number of lesser ways. On one occasion, when the settlers at Harvard found themselves without adequate food, the company sent two tons of meal and seven hundredweight of pork, freight free, to be distributed by the local agent and paid for only when circumstances would permit. The local papers regarded this as an act of "unparalleled generosity." [229] About the same time, a railroad coach was left sidetracked at Harvard on Sundays so that the itinerant preacher might hold services in it until the local church was completed.[230]

The importance of keeping on good terms with the local inhabitants was emphasized when a group became discontented with the company. The failure of the B. & M. to build through Camden, Nebraska, for example, was the occasion of a bitter protest on the part of the townspeople. After asserting that they had settled in the country with the full understanding that the line was to be built there "in accordance with the act of Congress donating them half of our national inheritance," [231] those present solemnly resolved:

that the people of the United States looking for a location in Nebraska, are hereby notified that we hold the purchase of said railroad lands to be a dangerous bargain for the purchaser.[232]

It was further resolved that this notice should be printed in the leading Nebraska papers, in at least three in Iowa, and two in Illinois.[233] The actions of the various Burlington subsidiary town companies were also a source of complaint in the public press, and even though these

[228] *Beatrice Express*, January 1, 1874.

[229] *Adams County Gazette*, January 24, 1872 (NSB); *Beatrice Express*, March, 1872 (LDP).

[230] The Reverend J. A. Jones to W. R. Mead in *Cleveland Plain Dealer* (Ohio), 1872 (LDP). The pastor who availed himself of this service wrote that "It is encouraging to labor where there is such a flow of immigration, and such Christian development." (*Ibid.*)

[231] *Blue Valley Record*, August 31, 1871 (LDP).

[232] *Ibid.*

[233] *Ibid.*

companies were actually separated from the land department, the latter suffered for their unpopularity.[234] Likewise, Harris had to contend with whatever adverse feeling was generated by disputes over the traffic department's failure to grant special fares,[235] over taxes,[236] or in regard to any other matter wherein any of the people felt they were shabbily treated.[237]

Perhaps the most revealing expression of public opinion towards the Burlington's work within the community appeared in 1872 in the *Beatrice Express*. Beatrice itself was virtually created by the building of the railroad, a town lot company operated within its limits, and its people were well aware of the monopolistic characteristics of all large corporations. Nevertheless, when the Burlington offered to buy for development 120 acres within the town, the local editor urged that the deal be consummated. His arguments were both shrewd and revealing:

Our Opportunity

In these degenerate days, the growth and prosperity of western towns are dependent almost wholly upon the railroad companies. They, like all the rest of us, are trying to make money. Not only is the location of their lines determined by their pecuniary interest, but a company, like the B. & M., with a great and perfect system of advertising extending throughout the civilized world, can and does build up towns or tear them down, as interest dictates. One place gets a great corporation interested in its welfare, and in a few years it becomes a flourishing city. Another gets the ill-will of some company, and forthwith grass grows in its streets.

These are facts which many towns have learned by experience, and they were never more true than now. It becomes us then to *make the RR Cos. our allies*, by pursuing toward them such a generous policy as will make it possible for them to work for their interest and ours at the same time. We have a fine growing town of good size and prospects, and the B. & M. Company are willing and anxious to obtain such an interest in the place as will justify them in going ahead in their masterly way to build us up. They do not come begging, — it is a fair business transaction, and one of vast consequence to us. They offer a liberal price for what they want — all and more than it is worth. Shall the pennywise policy of one man, or any half-dozen men prevent us from meeting such an offer halfway? Even those

[234] Nebraska, Iowa, and Illinois newspapers, 1871 *et seq.* (NSB), *passim.*

[235] *Omaha Daily Herald*, May 12, 1872 (LDP).

[236] Addison E. Sheldon, *The Semi-Centennial History of Nebraska* (Lincoln, 1904).

[237] Cf. *Lincoln Daily Statesman*, May 25, 1872 (LDP).

interested in the opposite part of the town have no reason to throw a straw in the way, for the benefit to the place as a whole will more than make up for any local effect it may have. There are towns on the north and on the south which they *can* make money by building up, and this they will do if we choose to give them the cold shoulder. It is not too much to say that no more important opportunity ever presented itself to Beatrice. If our citizens do not throw off their lethargy; forget their selfishness; bury their local jealousies, and make a united effort to bring this matter to a favorable issue, they will live to regret it when it is too late.[238]

VI. RESULTS

On Thursday, March 15, 1871, two trainloads totaling 31 cars rumbled westward through Burlington. In four passenger coaches were members of the season's first colony destined for B. & M. lands near Red Oak, Iowa. With them traveled six carloads of horses, eight of cattle, five of household goods, and eight filled with wagons and agricultural tools.[239] Enthusiastically, George Harris told the visiting reporter of the *Burlington Hawk-Eye* that in his 15 years of experience as a land commissioner he had never witnessed such a rush of immigrants.[240] From Liverpool during the spring came news of two colonies on their way to Nebraska;[241] the next year at least four more groups composed of "farmers and other substantial persons possessing some amount of capital" left the same port, most of them planning to buy B. & M. land.[242] One day in March, 1873, the freight agent at Burlington alone checked 15 cars of household goods through the station, "and," added the *Hawk-Eye*, "it wasn't a good day for goods, either. Every day brings more and more of these hardy people seeking homes on the rich soil of Iowa. . . ."[243]

In an apparently endless stream came Middle Westerners moving into cheaper lands further west,[244] Swedes bound to join their fellow-countrymen at Stanton, Iowa,[245] Englishmen whom Professor Butler

---

[238] *Beatrice Express*, May 4, 1872 (NSB).

[239] *Nebraska Herald*, March 30, 1871 (NSB), reprinted from the *Burlington Daily Hawk-Eye*.

[240] *Burlington Daily Hawk-Eye*, March 10, 1871.

[241] *Omaha Republican*, July 2, 1871 (NSB).

[242] *Beatrice Express*, May 23, 1872 (NSB); *Omaha Daily Herald*, June 6, 1872 (NSB).

[243] *Burlington Daily Hawk-Eye*, March 7, 1873.

[244] See table below, p. 422.

[245] *Nebraska Herald*, March 23, 1871 (NSB).

was sure would "make the Great American Desert around Crete, Nebraska rejoice and blossom like the rose," [246] and thousands of others from the United States and Europe. Both at Burlington and at Lincoln, the emigrant houses were continually filled to capacity.[247]

During 1873, the B. & M. in Nebraska recorded the origin of the 2,115 persons who bought company lands in that state. The largest group of 944 came from Nebraska itself, or from the neighboring states of Iowa, Missouri, and Kansas in that order. Because the tally was made to judge the efficiency of the company's advertising, however, anyone who had been in Nebraska over three months was credited to that state.[248] It is probable that of the 708 persons so listed many were comparatively recent arrivals. The old Northwest Territory states furnished the next largest contingent: 621 buyers had moved from Illinois, Wisconsin, Ohio, Indiana, Michigan, and Minnesota. The Middle Atlantic states of New York, Pennsylvania, New Jersey, and Maryland sent 137; Kentucky, West Virginia, and Tennessee accounted for 29, and New England sent 24 persons. Only two settlers came from the South, and one from Colorado. Canada, including New Brunswick, sent 15. Of the 342 Europeans who bought Nebraska company lands, 113 came from Germany, 93 from the United Kingdom, 46 from the Scandinavian countries, 37 from Russia, 31 from Bohemia, 17 from Holland, 3 from Switzerland, and 1 each from France and Iceland.[249]

The tremendous influx into Iowa and Nebraska, of which these immigrants were a part, caused a boom in the B. & M.'s land department. In the three years 1871, 1872, and 1873, the company made 1,308 sales of 101,787.83 acres in Iowa for $1,268,658.13 at an average price per acre of more than $12.00.[250] In contrast, the company's nearest rival, the Rock Island, disposed of slightly more than 50,000 acres at an average figure of about $7.80.[251] Apparently, in boom times, quality

[246] *Saline County Post*, April 22, 1871 (NSB).

[247] *Ibid.*, August 1, 1872 (NSB).

[248] BMN, *Annual Report* for 1876 (MS), p. 57.

[249] BMN, *Annual Report* for 1873 (Chicago, 1873), p. 27. For itemized figures, see table on p. 422.   [250] BMI, Sales Book "A" (LDP).

[251] The Rock Island figures are based on reports from April 1 through March 31. They have been converted to calendar year figures by reckoning sales of the first three months as equal to 20 per cent of the total year's sales. This percentage figure is based on monthly data of emigrant passengers on the Rock Island. For 1870–71 figures see *Poor's Manual for 1878*, p. 727. Thereafter see C. R. I. & P., *Annual Reports* for 1871–72, p. 6; 1872–73, p. 6; 1873–74, p. 7 (Chicago).

IOWA

		Acres	Value	Number of Sales	Average Price	Average Size of Plots
1871 —	Jan.	2,303.66	$ 27,455.76	25		
	Feb.	1,205.82	14,892.11	14		
	Mar.	6,253.21	77,101.65	69		
	Apr.	6,289.89	80,609.84	81		
	May	4,446.96	57,649.70	58		
	June	4,530.32	53,640.20	51		
	July	3,005.20	32,411.66	38		
	Aug.	3,545.99	45,223.98	47		
	Sept.	3,629.19	42,717.13	46		
	Oct.	2,871.83	33,982.55	41		
	Nov.	2,227.48	29,812.36	25		
	Dec.	1,270.98	17,426.96	15		
Gross		41,580.53	$512,923.90	510	$12.34	81.53
Canceled		757.08	7,898.80	8		
Net		40,823.45	$505,025.10	502		
1872 —	Jan.	892.13	$ 10,231.80	16		
	Feb.	960.00	12,040.00	11		
	Mar.	3,403.78	40,464.37	40		
	Apr.	2,739.57	33,364.93	30		
	May	2,089.47	24,931.47	29		
	June	1,758.01	20,312.15	30		
	July	2,068.23	24,243.84	27		
	Aug.	2,578.80	34,783.06	31		
	Sept.	3,674.51	46,611.48	63		
	Oct.	3,545.78	46,548.02	43		
	Nov.	3,109.83	36,951.42	33		
	Dec.	1,924.44	22,335.21	27		
Gross		28,744.55	$352,817.75	380	$12.27	75.64
Canceled		5,120.93	66,328.49	47		
Net		23,623.62	$286,489.26	333		
1873 —	Jan.	711.12	$ 7,997.96	10		
	Feb.	800.00	9,392.00	13		
	Mar.	1,392.32	18,104.67	23		
	Apr.	3,401.76	45,757.76	45		
	May	4,053.70	52,165.49	50		
	June	4,765.58	54,607.96	54		
	July	2,247.78	29,712.04	34		
	Aug.	2,781.06	38,444.80	34		
	Sept.	4,280.39	57,736.95	54		
	Oct.	3,082.66	39,342.82	40		
	Nov.	1,749.10	21,662.75	27		
	Dec.	2,197.28	27,991.28	34		
Gross		31,462.75	$402,916.48	418	$12.81	75.27
Canceled		11,334.72 *	140,624.67 †	123		
Net		20,128.26	$262,291.81	295		

* Includes deduction of 23/100 acre re sale #278.
† Includes net deduction of $1,095.20 for errors re sales #123, 129, 149, 278, 1039, 2472, 2192, 2335.

NEBRASKA

		Acres	Value	Number of Sales	Average Price	Average Size of Plots
1871 —	Jan.	4,431.59	$ 39,952.00	30		
	Feb.	1,720.17	15,802.55	14		
	Mar.	2,638.57	26,096.95	20		
	Apr.	8,488.88	70,967.74	61		
	May	11,253.11	96,892.46	75		
	June	11,371.40	91,562.51	86		
	July	12,935.90	102,123.70	91		
	Aug.	19,583.53	159,106.72	143		
	Sept.	17,461.50	146,031.32	129		
	Oct.	13,987.49	108,559.23	106		
	Nov.	10,339.50	81,239.05	72		
	Dec.	6,545.60	50,758.15	44		
GROSS		120,757.24	$ 989,092.38	871	$8.19	138.64
Canceled		1,791.13	17,977.91	10		
NET		118,966.11	$ 971,114.47	861		
1872 —	Jan.	6,955.52	$ 59,740.67	60		
	Feb.	3,728.64	31,416.28	30		
	Mar.	8,257.18	67,345.33	78		
	Apr.	11,006.37	90,895.54	94		
	May	9,436.34	83,513.97	87		
	June	13,663.77	116,791.82	94		
	July	10,971.05	95,989.24	86		
	Aug.	14,815.57	125,018.36	111		
	Sept.	14,554.95	122,624.09	134		
	Oct.	14,130.43	108,121.11	124		
	Nov.	8,466.94	66,473.15	76		
	Dec.	4,941.38	41,201.95	45		
GROSS		120,928.14	$1,009,131.51	1019	$8.34	118.67
Canceled		6,652.38	73,219.85	42		
NET		114,275.76	$ 935,911.66	977		
1873 —	Jan.	4,998.00	$ 22,424.95	95		
	Feb.	4,555.08	36,514.04	39		
	Mar.	12,422.25	103,449.20	102		
	Apr.	13,048.48	102,111.30	105		
	May	16,822.11	136,184.41	127		
	June	37,081.65	291,949.93	312		
	July	21,066.73	162,286.39	151		
	Aug.	24,251.94	187,461.83	177		
	Sept.	45,883.41	346,415.86	332		
	Oct.	42,700.43	305,347.46	350		
	Nov.	27,827.82	205,591.15	219		
	Dec.	26,046.52	200,283.63	222		
GROSS		276,704.42	$2,100,020.15	2231	$7.59	124.03
Canceled		29,389.09	257,808.92	173		
NET		247,315.33	$1,842,211.23	2058		

and accessibility of land meant more than low price. In Nebraska, 4,121 purchasers bought 518,389.80 acres of B. & M. land for $4,098,-244.04 at an average price of approximately $8 an acre.[252] In the quantity of land sold, the neighboring Union Pacific bettered this showing over the same period; although its receipts totaled but $2,534,019 for an average price per acre of about $4.50,[253] it disposed of 555,782 acres. Here, under roughly similar conditions, price did seem to make a difference.

With amazing regularity, the buying trends that were evident even in 1870 repeated themselves during 1871–73 in the Burlington statistics. In Iowa, the bulk of the sales were of plots of 80 acres or less, while in Nebraska, the average remained close to 140. In both states, early spring and early fall were the favorite seasons for buying.[254] This was to be expected, for March and April were the best months for starting sod crops on unbroken land, and the early fall was the last opportunity to build a shack and become settled before winter set in.[255] The low point in sales came during the middle of winter and was matched by a less marked decline during the summer months. Cancellations, which rarely occurred in 1870, were naturally more frequent as time went on. In Iowa, for the three years 1871–73, inclusive, they amounted to 757.08 acres, 5,120.93 acres, and 11,334.72 acres respectively; in Nebraska over the same period the figures were 1,791.13 acres, 6,652.38 acres, and 29,389.09 acres. In summary, the combined land departments had made 5,026 uncanceled sales and disposed of 565,132.53 acres for $4,803,-043.53.[256] In the meantime, their expenses had amounted to approximately three quarters of a million dollars.[257]

Brooks and Denison, reporting to the stockholders of the B. & M. in Nebraska in January, 1873, did not hesitate to tell why the land department's expenses had been so high for the region west of the Missouri.

As we are making great efforts to attract immigrant settlers, both at home and abroad [they explained], . . . expenses . . . are necessarily large. . . . Yet, if these efforts and expenditures result, as is confidently expected, in bringing on to the line of the road a population sufficient by

[252] BMN, Sales Record No. 1 (LDP). See Statistical Appendix F, below.
[253] Poor's Manual for 1872–73, p. 391; 1873–74, p. 348; 1874–75, p. 399.
[254] See graph, p. 385.   [256] See above, pp. 382–383.
[255] BMR, News Sheet, March? 1872 (LDP).   [257] See below, p. 452.

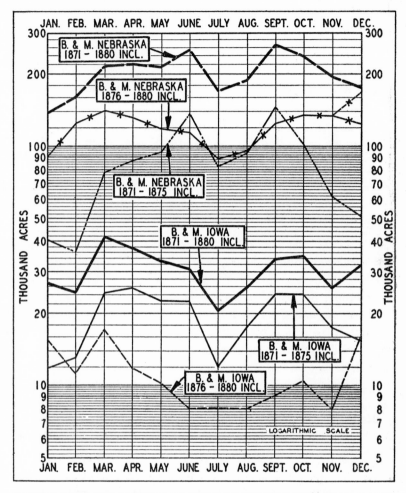

SEASONAL MOVEMENT MEASURED BY AGGREGATE MONTHLY SALES OF GROSS ACRES
BY THE B. & M. RAILROADS IN IOWA AND NEBRASKA FOR THE PERIODS
1871–1875, 1876–1880, AND 1871–1880, INCLUSIVE.

(For underlying statistics see Table 6 in Appendix F)

their business to make the road a success and self-supporting at once, no one will be likely to question the policy of management.[258]

In other words, the B. & M. was a railroad first and a land company second.

In the spring of 1871, the *Burlington Daily Hawk-Eye*, mindful of the vast immigration pouring by its doors, printed a description by one of its correspondents of the transformation in process in western Iowa and eastern Nebraska.

It is wonderful to see the excitement with which emigrants are pushing on along the line of this [B. & M.] road and taking up the land clear to Ft. Kearney and the cars are carrying in colonies whole neighborhoods and church organizations with buildings for dwellings, school houses and churches. . . . The great valley of Nebraska south of the Platte will soon be a blooming garden. Every man can get a farm on ten years credit [from the B. & M.] and can raise enough to pay for it before it is due, as the law supersedes the necessity for fencing, and the land can yet be had at low figures. The railroad is carrying all the comforts and luxuries of the older states into the cheaper, more fertile, and beautiful lands of the West.[259]

According to the *Saline County Post*, by the summer of 1872 the landscape around Crete and Beatrice was "dotted with houses and checquered with new breaking." [260] In December of the same year, the Lowell, Nebraska, newspaper painted a colorful picture of the growth of its own town:

A year ago almost the entire country west of Lincoln was a vast prairie teeming with buffalo, antelope and other game, while Indians hunted unmolested. . . . The frontier is now a word of the past. . . . Lowell is only a few months old, yet already it contains four hotels, one bank, one blacksmith and wagon shop, four general merchandise stores, . . . one hardware and stove store, one lumber yard, one grocery store, one furniture manufactory, one drug and grocery store, one meat market, one livery and feed stable, one physician, seven lawyers and land agents, one newspaper and printing office, and the United States Land Office. . . . Since the above was written, Lowell has been increased by the addition of a drug store, a Jeweler, a barber shop, two physicians and an insurance agency. . . .[261]

Even the more sophisticated *Saline County Post* presented a vivid account of development in its territory:

[258] BMN, Circular to Stockholders, January 22, 1873 (BMN ORB, p. 55).
[259] *Burlington Daily Hawk-Eye*, April 13, 1871.
[260] *Saline County Post*, August 22, 1872 (NSB).
[261] *Lowell Weekly Register* (Nebraska), December 23, 1872 (NSB).

In just two years population has increased probably three-fold, and the acres under cultivation five-fold. The settlers then were mainly scattered along the banks of the rivers and creeks, and in the eastern part of the county, — now the whole prairie is dotted with houses. The dugouts and sod shanties are giving place to comfortable frame dwellings.[262]

Perkins, stopping at Lincoln in the summer of 1873, was astounded at its progress:

The situation is fine, and there are a good many substantial and ornamental buildings for so young a town to have. The Indians were here six years ago — now there are six or seven thousand people, a *University*, . . . a large public school building, . . . and then the State House. . . . People are planting trees and improving things, and in ten years Lincoln will be a very pretty town, and probably a prosperous one.[263]

Meanwhile, the progress of the various colonies on railroad land afforded a measure of the company's colonization activities. The press reports, for example, of the Reverend D. E. Jones' Plymouth Colony in Jefferson County were particularly illuminating.

May 11, 1871: The Reverend D. E. Jones has made arrangements to purchase 40,000 acres from the B. & M. in Jefferson County. He is planning to locate there a colony comprised of "tradesmen and mechanics of all kinds . . . also a number of the best known educationalists in the land." [264]

June 10, 1871: The first ten persons arrived in Plymouth colony.[265]

June 16, 1871: Plymouth colony expects 200 New England families. Land will be sold at from $4 to $7 an acre on ten-year credit at six per cent interest with 20 per cent off for cash.[266]

July 19, 1871: "The Plymouth colony is gaining members. A number of families from Cleveland, Ohio, are going there." [267]

April 27, 1872: The people of Plymouth colony are industrious, of good class, many from New England, and all well-educated. There are already two Sunday Schools with another being formed.[268]

August 17, 1872: Already one-third of the 30,000 [*sic*] acres are sold, usually in lots of 160 acres at $5 to $10 an acre.[269]

[262] *Saline County Post*, August 24, 1873 (LDP).
[263] Perkins to his wife, July 18, 1873 (CNB, ch. x, pp. 18–19).
[264] *Nebraska Herald*, May 11, 1871.
[265] *Beatrice Express*, June 10, 1871.
[266] *Saline County Post*, June 16, 1871 (LDP).
[267] *Beatrice Express*, July 19, 1871.
[268] *Saline County Post*, April 27, 1872 (LDP).
[269] Unidentified newspaper, 1872 (LDP).

August 22, 1872: A few farms have already been commenced and houses built. Portions of other farms have been plowed. In the town, a general store is in operation, a drug store commenced, and foundations laid for a schoolhouse.[270]

September 21, 1872: The new school building 26'x41' "with cupola, side gables and pinnacles on the roof" is completed, cost about $3,000.[271]

In addition to Plymouth Colony, a similar activity was reported from the Mayflower group in York County; from English colonies in Adams, Cass, Clay, and Fillmore counties; from a Michigan colony in Adams County; from a flourishing Methodist group in Fillmore County; from a band of Welshmen in Clay County; and from three Scandinavian colonies in Polk, Saunders, and York counties.[272]

For most of the development along its Nebraska line during the early years of the 'seventies, the B. & M. was undoubtedly responsible, either indirectly through the construction of its line or directly as a result of its land sales and advertising effort. As the directors frankly informed their stockholders in 1873, however, they "ought not to claim the entire credit of the rapid increase in settlement. The homestead and preëmption laws of the United States do their part, — the opening of railroad communication having attracted great numbers into what was before, and would otherwise have remained, almost an entirely unoccupied territory."[273] The Union Pacific likewise contributed to the efforts of its new rival, for its lands in the vicinity of Lowell, for example, were directly on the B. & M. and thus naturally tributary to it.[274] On the other hand, the Burlington's colonization of the North Platte lands brought business to the Union Pacific.

Late in 1871, the *Beatrice Express* pointed to "the steady stream of immigration which has poured through Lincoln and the counties west of that place. It is," declared the editor, "the work of the B. & M. Their interests are identical with those of the people of this county so far as immigration is concerned."[275] From Ashland, a year later, came a letter flatly stating that "no other corporation has done so much for

[270] *Congregationalist* (Boston), August 22, 1872 (LDP).

[271] *Saline County Post*, September 21, 1872 (LDP).

[272] Unidentified newspaper, 1872 (LDP).

[273] BMN, Circular to Stockholders, January 22, 1873 (BMN ORB, p. 55).

[274] This was acknowledged by Touzalin in a memorandum of 1878. See below, p. 434.

[275] *Beatrice Express*, December 16, 1871 (NSB).

the development of this country as the Burlington and Missouri River Railroad." [276] Meanwhile, in an editorial entitled "Our Railroad," the *Beatrice Express* observed:

it only requires a trip on the road to make it appear evident how completely and irrevocably the railroad order of things has taken the place of that under which Beatrice has been existing since it was settled. Who would exchange the new for the old? [277]

These comments and others like them might have been expected from communities that were wholly dependent upon the B. & M. But Omaha, served by more than one railroad, added comments which, even if more moderate in tone, carried the added weight of impartiality.

The B. & M. Railroad [declared the *Omaha Daily Tribune & Republican*] are doing more to invite and induce immigration to our young state than any corporation in the U. S. with, perhaps, the single exception of the Union Pacific Railroad, which traverses more than 400 miles of our state and is, or was, the proprietor of more than 8,000,000 acres of our public domain. . . . We therefore take pleasure in the expression of our entire satisfaction with the course which this great corporation [the B. & M.] has pursued, and is now pursuing, towards the State of Nebraska in the advertisement and sale of its immense land subsidy.[278]

A year later the same paper observed that "the Burlington and Missouri Land Department is, for its size, the most judiciously managed of any railroad of which we have knowledge. . . ." [279] Probably as welcome was the comment that Anna S. Dimock forwarded to the Pittsfield (Massachusetts) *Berkshire County Eagle* under the heading of "Life on the Frontier":

The gentlemen in charge of these [B. & M.] lands [she wrote] . . . are Christian men who personally interest themselves in every project of religious or educational interest, and prove the old saying about soulless corporations to be false in this instance at least. They earnestly desire our new state to win at once a reputation which shall always be a crowning glory to its native lustre. . . .[280]

[276] William Croy in *Beatrice Express*, October 20, 1872 (NSB).

[277] *Beatrice Express*, February 10, 1872 (NSB).

[278] *Omaha Daily Tribune & Republican*, September, 1872 (NSB).

[279] *York Monitor*, September 26, 1872 (NSB), reprinted from the *Omaha Daily Tribune & Republican*.

[280] *Berkshire County Eagle*, 1872 (LDP).

Such opinions must indeed have been gratifying to Harris and his colleagues; furthermore, they represented an asset in good will for the railroad that was of incalculable value. In one respect, however, land department affairs were not entirely satisfactory. As Perkins regretfully reported to Forbes in the fall of 1873, Harris had his strong points, but he was little of a business man.[281] A careful examination of his accounts revealed that out of more than $3,000,000 in gross land sales through August 1, 1873, about $850,000 were so delinquent as to be considered "dead." Most of these, Perkins explained, represented transactions of 1870 and 1871, and

prices were then too high. A certain percentage of sales made under any such system as we are obliged to adopt will always fail. . . . Practically, we sell "options," and those who buy on speculation at such prices as were current in 1870 and 1871 will not pay up. Our terms are now somewhat changed and prices are lower. But it is not encouraging to find that the head of your Land Department had never even checked over his books to see who were delinquent on payments. . . .[282]

This was indeed an unfortunate situation, although it was one that could be and was being remedied. In any event, Harris' shortcomings in this respect were more than offset by his permanent contributions to the Burlington's colonization effort. It had been no easy task to reorganize the ineffective department that he found in 1869. He had, despite his middle age, spent much of his first winter personally inspecting the company's property and working out a comprehensive, uniform sales policy. Otherwise, it would have been impossible to place the company's lands on the market as early as April, 1870. In launching and carrying through the advertising program, Harris displayed energy and ingenuity. Under highly competitive conditions he successfully reached the persons he felt would be the most desirable settlers; when they arrived in B. & M. territory, he worked with them in establishing permanent communities. Most important of all, Harris did more than anyone else, during the critical years between 1869 and 1874, to enhance the company's standing as a good neighbor; only as such could the railroad pretend to be a successful colonizer. When Harris resigned early in 1874 because of frail health, the Burlington lost an able and devoted servant.[283]

[281] Perkins to Forbes, September 8, 1873 (CNB, n.p.).
[282] Ibid.   [283] BMN DRB, p. 64.

CHAPTER XIV

CRISIS AND RECOVERY, 1874–1880

I. THE COMPANY FACES HARD TIMES

In the fall of 1873 a financial panic paralyzed business in the East. Immigration from abroad fell from 459,803 in that year to 313,339 in 1874 and declined at approximately the same rate through 1877. For the last five years of the decade, only half as many immigrants came to the United States as in 1870–75.[1] In Iowa, the state board of immigration was discontinued entirely in September, 1873.[2] As the middle years of the decade rolled by, prosperity seemed a thing of the past, and in the fall of 1877, an exodus from that state to the warmer climate of Kansas and the cheaper lands of Nebraska was well under way.[3] Nebraska, however, fared no better. Although its population rose from 122,993 in 1870 to 230,007 in 1874, there was a gain of but 14,000 the next year and 11,000 in 1876. Homestead entries fell from 6,189 in 1873 to 1,345 in 1877, although the government allowed ex-soldiers or their widows to increase their holdings within railway grant limits to 160 acres.[4]

Meanwhile, Nature contributed her share to the Burlington's difficulties. Although the winter of 1872–73 in Iowa was unusually severe and thus unfavorable for locusts, the insects turned out in full force late in the summer of 1873; in Osceola County it was said that 75 per cent of the population could grow just enough for their own sustenance and for seed, 10 per cent would have enough for bread only, and the remaining 15 per cent would have neither seed nor food.[5] In the following year, Nebraska was visited with the worst scourge of locusts in its entire history. The chief sufferers from this onslaught were those who were depending on their first year's sod crops, and the company was affected not only because its debtors were severely

---

[1] Treasury Department, *Statistical Abstract* (1881), vol. III, p. 136.
[2] See above, p. 359.   [3] Hansen, *loc. cit.*, pp. 185–187.
[4] *Ibid.*, and Donaldson, *op. cit.*, pp. 351–355.
[5] John E. Briggs, "The Grasshopper Plagues in Iowa," *Iowa Journal of History and Politics*, vol. XIII, no. 3 (July, 1915), pp. 349 *et seq.*

hit and its grain business cut, but also because the state was given an unenviable reputation that would require much energy to explain away.[6] Finally, in 1876, Iowa was struck again, but this time the locusts did less damage since more farmers had turned to stock-raising.[7]

Partly as a result of these factors but more because of low agricultural prices, high taxes and interest rates, and a general antagonism against unrestrained corporations, popular discontent in the Middle West reached a peak in the middle 'seventies. Both in Iowa and Nebraska this feeling manifested itself through the organized granges and was directed primarily toward the railroads. In Iowa the Patrons of Husbandry increased the number of their lodges from 1,507 in May, 1873, to 1,999 in September, 1874. Although the organization was not so large in Nebraska, its growth was more rapid, and there were actually more granges in proportion to the agricultural population. Starting with 100 groups in May, 1873, the state had 596 by September, 1874.[8] The result of this agitation was restrictive legislation in both states during 1874 and 1875; at Des Moines the assembly attempted to fix railroad rates and attach heavy penalties for discrimination, while in Nebraska a change in the state constitution permitted the legislature there to take similar steps.[9] Even though the Iowa law was repealed four years later and no action was taken in Nebraska, the B. & M. found that it had to contend with a strong popular sentiment that opposed the railroads as monopolies.

By 1879 the depression was definitely over. National imports leapt from $465,000,000 in 1878 to $760,000,000 in 1880, bank loans exceeded $1,000,000,000 in the latter year, and wheat exports reached the unprecedented value of over $225,000,000. For the first time since 1873, immigration into the country increased during 1879 and by 1880 had gained 250 per cent over the previous year.[10] Despite the ravages of

---

[6] Addison E. Sheldon, *History and Stories of Nebraska* (Chicago, 1914), pp. 183–186; Edna M. Boyle Allen, "A Grasshopper Raid," *Nebraska Pioneer Reminiscences* (Cedar Rapids, Iowa, 1916), pp. 133–134.

[7] Briggs, *loc. cit.*

[8] Solon J. Buck, *The Granger Movement* (Cambridge, 1913), pp. 58–59; W. A. Anderson, "The Granger Movement in the Middle West with Special Reference to Iowa," *Iowa Journal of History and Politics*, vol. XXII (January, 1924), *passim.*

[9] *Ibid.*; cf. Frank H. Dixon, "Railroad Control in Nebraska," *Political Science Quarterly*, vol. XIII, no. 4 (1898), p. 620.

[10] Treasury Department, *Statistical Abstract* (1881), vol. III, p. 136; Hewes and Gannett, *op. cit., passim.*

the chinch bug in Iowa during 1879–80, immigration into the state increased, particularly on the part of foreigners.[11] Nebraska, whose growth had come almost to a standstill during the depression, gained 70,000 people in 1879 and about the same number in 1880; homestead entries rose from the low point of 1,345 in 1877 to 5,648 in 1880.[12]

This, in brief, was the situation in Iowa and Nebraska during the years 1874–80. The general affairs of the Burlington, as well as the colonization program in the two states, were of necessity guided accordingly.

In respect to both Iowa and Nebraska, the successive annual reports of the C. B. & Q. and the B. & M. in Nebraska revealed the rapidly changing conditions of those years. Although earnings in Iowa through 1874 were good,[13] the company was worried over the effects of the new regulatory measures, particularly since the state commissioners had instituted an action against the B. & M. for non-compliance with the prescribed rates and fares.[14] Frequent floods during 1875 required unusually heavy outlays for maintenance,[15] and in 1876 President Robert Harris of the C. B. & Q. commented upon the "great dullness in general business." Nevertheless, crops of that year were good in the company's territory, and a surplus resulted. Only the usual dividend was paid, however; the excess was devoted to a sinking fund for meeting fixed indebtedness and for new construction.[16] In 1877, the United States Supreme Court upheld the right of the Iowa legislature to control freight and passenger rates. Consequently, reported Harris, the company's "moderate success" was due to good crops and "such economy in expenses as we could judiciously practice."[17] Yet, in spite of adverse conditions, the B. & M. of Iowa added many miles of steel rail,[18] second track, and permanent structures during the most difficult years of the decade.[19] "If the West continues in its present career of prosperity," observed Forbes early in 1879, "we shall in the future

[11] Cyrenus Cole, *op. cit.*, ch. lxix.
[12] Donaldson, *op. cit.*, pp. 351–355.
[13] CBQ, *Annual Report* for 1874 (Chicago, 1875), p. 11.
[14] *Ibid.*, pp. 24–25.
[15] CBQ, *Annual Report* for 1875 (Chicago, 1876), p. 21.
[16] CBQ, *Annual Report* for 1876 (Chicago, 1877), p. 16.
[17] CBQ, *Annual Report* for 1877 (Chicago, 1878), pp. 22–24.
[18] *Ibid.*, pp. 15, 18, 19.
[19] *Ibid.*, p. 16.

RAILWAYS IN THE UNITED STATES, 1880.

1880

BOSTON
NEW YORK
PHILADELPHIA
BALTIMORE
WASHINGTON
BUFFALO
CLEVELAND
DETROIT
TOLEDO
CINCINNATI
INDIANAPOLIS
ATLANTA
CHICAGO
NEW ORLEANS
ST. LOUIS
ST. PAUL
DULUTH
OMAHA
LINCOLN
INDIANOLA
SAN ANTONIO
CHEYENNE
DENVER
SALT LAKE CITY
SEATTLE
LOS ANGELES
SAN FRANCISCO

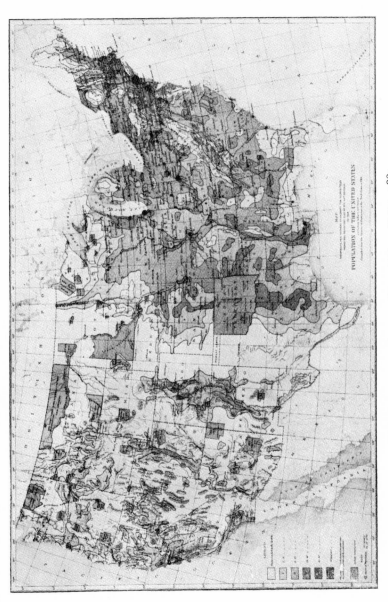

DENSITY OF POPULATION IN THE UNITED STATES, 1880.

need a great many more miles of double track [in Iowa], some other facilities for business, and some additional branches. But," he added conservatively, "we must limit ourselves strictly to the *unquestionable wants* of our Road, and to its means of payment."[20] By the end of 1880, business, already good, was steadily improving.[21]

In Nebraska, the company's position during the middle years of the decade was far more difficult than in Iowa. The widespread failure of crops in 1874 meant that little grain was shipped out of the state and, consequently, few supplies were brought in. One daily freight train sufficed to carry the traffic between Omaha, Plattsmouth, and Crete; west of Crete, service during much of the year was even less frequent. A single passenger train ran over the main line daily, while one mixed train carried all business on the branch between Crete and Beatrice.[22] Perkins revealed the seriousness of the situation in a letter dated January 28, 1875:

I cannot say that beyond a *peradventure* B. & M. R. will get money enough from earnings and lands to pay its interest, altho' I believe it will do so. But if, in 1875 we should have another crop failure like that of '74 we *might* not get enough money this year, and possibly next, to keep us afloat. . . .[23]

In this eventuality, he added, it might be necessary to forego interest payments for a year or two, or mortgage the one-third of the granted lands still unencumbered and keep up the interest. Fundamentally he felt the company's bonds were sound enough, because the soil and climate of the B. & M.'s territory would eventually make farming profitable. "But," he explained, "wheat has been very low in price, and that fact with the failure of corn came upon poor people, the majority of them, who had no surplus. Hence these tears."[24] In Iowa or Illinois, he observed, the same failure would not have been felt. In other words, the problem west of the Missouri River was that of a new community whose single source of wealth had been struck before it had produced a reserve against hard times. The situation was not unlike that in Iowa during the late 'fifties.[25]

[20] CBQ, *Annual Report* for 1878 (Chicago, 1879), p. 18.
[21] CBQ, *Annual Report* for 1880 (Chicago, 1881), pp. 17-19.
[22] BMN, *Annual Report* for 1874 (MS), pp. 1-4.
[23] Perkins to Griswold, January 28, 1875 (CNB, n.p.).
[24] *Ibid.*
[25] See above, chs. iii, v.

The cumulative effect of the drought and grasshoppers of 1874 was even more noticeable in the following year. Gross revenues for the first eight months in Nebraska were $147,879.85 below those of 1873, although receipts increased during the last third of the year.[26] "Freight earnings," the superintendent reported, "were seriously affected by the free transportation of large relief supplies, and the low rates on other freight shipped in aid of the country along the line of the road." [27] Any loss incurred in this way, however, was money well invested. Aside from the obvious assistance to the community in general, it may have had an effect on the state constitutional convention which met during the late spring. "The railroads," Perkins told Forbes, "have done so much for Nebraska during this grasshopper and drought trouble that the feeling is very friendly, especially toward the B. & M. . . ." [28] On September 20, 1875, a daily freight replaced the tri-weekly train on the main line west of Crete; it was a small but significant sign of the better times to come.[29] The next year was marked by the acquisition of the Nebraska Railway; its extension during 1877 toward Seward and York brought a new farming area that was already well-settled and rapidly improving within reach of the company's rails.[30] At the end of 1877, good crops and a revival of immigration marked the end of the depression.[31] Meanwhile, the B. & M.'s relations to the rest of the Burlington system and to its neighboring roads were receiving an increasing amount of attention.

By 1874 it had become apparent that the Union Pacific had no intention of making any interchange of either freight or passenger business with the B. & M. of Nebraska at Kearney. No action was taken by the latter, however, until the summer of 1875 when the board of directors twice formally applied to the president of the transcontinental

---

[26] BMN, *Annual Report* for 1875 (MS), pp. 1–2.

[27] *Ibid.*, p. 7.

[28] Perkins to Forbes, March 16, 1875 (CNB, n.p.).

[29] BMN, *Annual Report* for 1875 (MS), p. 12.

[30] BMN, *Annual Report* for 1877 (MS), p. 8. The Nebraska Railway had been formed by a consolidation of the Brownsville, Fort Kearney and Pacific Rail Road Company, and the Midland Pacific Railway Company. (CBQ, *Corporate History*, p. 344.) These two constituent roads had received grants of land from Nebraska of 19,989.12 and 99,973.08 acres, respectively. All these lands, however, were disposed of before acquisition by the B. & M. (Baldwin to Mitchell, March 18, 1922, LDP.)

[31] BMN, *Annual Report* for 1877 (MS), p. 3.

road for some arrangement. Still, no agreement was forthcoming, and late in the year the B. & M. appealed to Congress for relief.[32] While the matter was pending in Washington, a rumor circulated that Jay Gould, prominent in Union Pacific management, was endeavoring to buy control of the B. & M. Perkins was inclined to believe the story for, as he pointed out to Forbes, B. & M. stock was low, and the road "is the most disagreeable thorn in the side of the U. P. We are . . . trying to force a route via Kearney, and he [Gould] cannot help seeing the danger of our going to Denver some day." Nevertheless, concluded Perkins, "I don't think the C. B. & Q. can afford to lose the B. & M. as a feeder."[33]

As it developed, neither the Burlington's appeal in Washington nor Gould's alleged efforts brought results, and early in 1877, the matter was still deadlocked. Gould now apparently came forward with a new plan, for on March 24, 1877, the directors of the C. B. & Q. voted that in view of the existing relations of their company with the Union Pacific, they would "consider a suspension of all efforts on the part of the B. & M. R. R.R. in Nebraska to get a right to through business via Kearney Junction, as not unfavorable to the interests of our Company."[34] Furthermore, it was voted that the C. B. & Q. would "consent to a lease by the B. & M. R. RR. Co. in Nebr. of its road to the Union Pacific R. R. Co. provided it is conditioned upon the preservation by said lessee, of existing arrangements between the B. & M. R. RR. in Nebr. and our Company."[35] Against both these resolutions Forbes and Griswold constituted a minority of only two, but their influence was sufficient to cause the votes to be reconsidered and laid upon the table.[36] Perkins, who had been elected a vice-president and director of the C. B. & Q. in 1876,[37] was absent from this meeting. His interests, however, were deeply concerned, for although the Nebraska road was technically independent, its stock was largely controlled by directors of the C. B. & Q.[38] Therefore, whatever action they took might well

---

[32] Memorandum by Perkins, 1877 or 1878 (CNB, n.p.).

[33] Perkins to Forbes, December, 1875 (CNB, ch. xi, n.p.).

[34] CBQ DRB, pp. 507–508.

[35] Ibid.

[36] Ibid.

[37] On March 2, 1876 (CBQ DRB, p. 459). Perkins was, of course, already a vice-president and director of the B. & M. in Nebraska.

[38] Memorandum by Perkins, 1902 (CNB, ch. xi, pp. 61–63).

decide the future of the line he and Forbes had so consistently championed.

The spring of 1877 was a critical one in the history of the Burlington system. Following the narrow failure of the C. B. & Q. board to approve a lease of its Nebraska subsidiary to the Union Pacific, Gould made another suggestion in New York City about April 1, this time to representatives not only of his own line and of the two Burlington roads but to certain directors of the Chicago and Northwestern and the Rock Island as well.[39] The essential features of his plan, which soon became known as the "Quintuple Contract," were as follows:

1. The B. & M. in Nebraska should give up its fight in Congress for a pro rata share of business at Kearney Junction;
2. The B. & M. in Nebraska and Union Pacific should make no further extensions, without a mutual understanding, in competitive territory west of the Missouri River until after 1884 and then only on giving a year's notice;
3. Traffic from the B. & M. in Nebraska should be divided into substantially three equal parts between the three pool roads east of the Missouri, namely, the C. B. & Q., the Chicago & Northwestern, and the Rock Island;
4. The B. & M. in Nebraska should have a certain division of through rates;
5. The three pool lines should buy together $1,000,000 in bonds of the B. & M. in Nebraska, and
6. Interest on the B. & M. in Nebraska's debt to the extent of 50 per cent of the earnings of the other lines on B. & M. business should be guaranteed by them.[40]

In a preliminary form, these suggestions were presented to the C. B. & Q. board on April 2, whereupon it was suggested that a committee be appointed to act upon the matter. To this Perkins strenuously objected.[41] Looking at the situation from the C. B. & Q. standpoint, he insisted that it was unfair to divide the business of the B. & M. with the Rock Island and Northwestern; that when the B. & M. in Nebraska was organized and given the Iowa company's grant, it was understood and practically agreed that the Nebraska line should be a feeder to the Iowa line; and that, therefore, while the C. B. & Q. was entitled to share equally in the traffic of a neutral road like the Union Pacific, the Rock Island and Northwestern were

[39] Memorandum by Perkins, 1902 (CNB, ch. xi, pp. 61–63).
[40] Ibid., pp. 69–70.   [41] CBQ DRB, p. 511.

not entitled to an equal share of what was practically an extension of the "Q." Furthermore, from the standpoint of the B. & M. in Nebraska, he felt it was unwise to tie the company's hands against extensions for any length of time.[42]

Perkins, however, was overruled, and the board resolved to appoint a committee to meet with representatives of the other companies, said

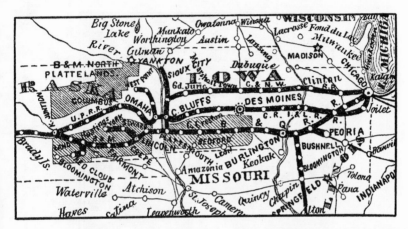

PRINCIPAL COMPETING RAILROADS BETWEEN CHICAGO, OMAHA, AND KEARNEY ABOUT 1878, AND APPROXIMATE AREAS CONTAINING B. & M. LANDS.

committee to have "full power to conclude a business arrangement with those companies, for the mutual benefit of all."[43] The vote in favor of this resolution was unanimous; Forbes and Perkins, however, asked and obtained leave to abstain from voting, not only on the ground of their double relation as directors of both the C. B. & Q. and the B. & M. in Nebraska but also because "of their doubts as to the conference being for the interest of the Company, as a peace measure or otherwise."[44]

Despite a series of meetings and prolonged discussions throughout the spring of 1877,[45] the Quintuple Contract was never signed, for the other roads felt that the B. & M. in Nebraska would receive decidedly the best of the trade.[46] This outcome was of the greatest sig-

[42] Memorandum by Perkins, 1902 (CNB, ch. xi, pp. 61–63).
[43] CBQ DRB, p. 511.
[44] Ibid.
[45] Memorandum by Perkins, 1902 (CNB, ch. xi, pp. 61–63).
[46] Ibid., pp. 69–70.

nificance for the Burlington system, both in the long run and for the immediate future, for within a few months it was apparent to both the C. B. & Q. and B. & M. that their mutual interests lay in extension to Denver. On January 10, 1878, the directors of the latter requested Perkins to furnish them such information as would enable them to judge the desirability of extension down to the Republican Valley.[47]

Interior View of one of the Gorgeous C.. B. & Q. Smoking Cars, Run Only by this Line, for the Exclusive Use of First Class Passengers.

FROM A C. B. & Q. TIMETABLE, 1880.

The results of his report were immediate. On May 8, the directors addressed a circular to their stockholders:

The large and very rapid increase of the population and business of that portion of Nebraska known as the Republican Valley [they said] has created a pressing demand for railroad facilities, and to supply it a company has been incorporated to build a road from Hastings on our road

[47] BMN DRB, p. 153.

into the Valley. It is very important that this road should connect with ours, and that we should secure the large and growing business it will control, and it is also very desirable for our interests that it should be built so as to be most advantageous to the large body of lands that we own in the Valley, in Webster and Franklin Counties, and which would at once be materially advanced in value by the building of such a road through them. To secure these objects, we have arranged for taking a perpetual lease of the new road to be known as the Republican Valley Railroad. . . .[48]

By the fall of 1880, the Republican Valley lines comprised a veritable network in southern Nebraska with a western extension well on the way to Denver.[49]

Meanwhile, relations between the C. B. & Q. and the B. & M. of Nebraska threatened to come into conflict over the exchange of business at Plattsmouth. Even after prolonged negotiation, the views of the two roads in the fall of 1879 were still "too widely separated," as one committee reported, "to give any reasonable ground to expect that an agreement or settlement that would satisfy both parties could be reached." Further discussion, however, revealed that one basic fact was clearly recognized by the members of both committees: the mutual importance of "securing and maintaining entire harmony between the two companies, and the serious danger to the real interests of both of . . . independent and unfriendly action by either of them."[50] Consequently, on September 12, 1879, the two committees simultaneously recommended to their respective directors that "measures should be taken looking to closer relations, and to the possibility of entire consolidation of the interests of the two companies."[51] With this new objective in view, negotiations between the two roads proceeded briskly; during the fall there was indeed more reason than one for haste. "As to consolidation," Perkins wrote Tyson on December 27, "we ought to make it go pretty soon. Gould is determined to keep us out of Denver if he can, and questions are certain to come up in the discussion with him, which the B. & M. and C. B. & Q., if they remain single, may, indeed I fear must, disagree about."[52] Just four days later the directors of the B. & M. accepted the terms of consolidation proposed by the "Q."[53]

[48] BMN DRB, p. 197.
[49] See map, p. 402.
[50] BMN DRB, pp. 263–264.
[51] Ibid.
[52] Perkins to Tyson, December 27, 1879 (CNB, ch. xii, pp. 26–27).
[53] BMN DRB, p. 278.

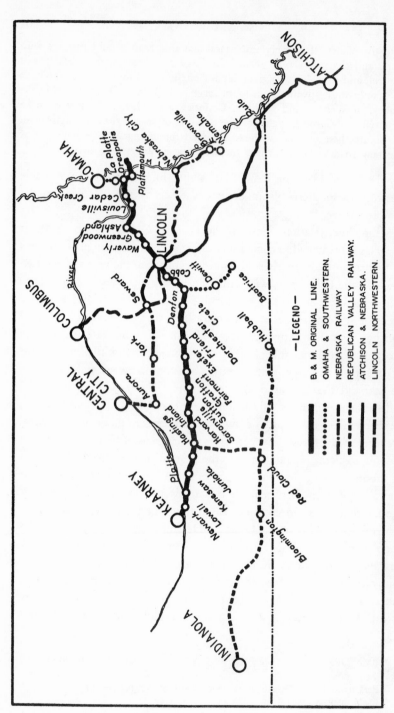

THE B. & M. IN NEBRASKA AND AFFILIATED LINES IN 1886 WHEN THEY BECAME PART OF THE C. B. & Q.

During the early months of 1880, preparations were made for the final merger. In Nebraska, the Atchison and Nebraska as well as the Lincoln and North Western were added to the B. & M.,[54] bringing that company's mileage to over 800 miles.[55] Meanwhile, on May 26, 1880, the directors of the C. B. & Q. separated the offices of vice-president and general manager, formerly both held by Perkins, and gave him, as

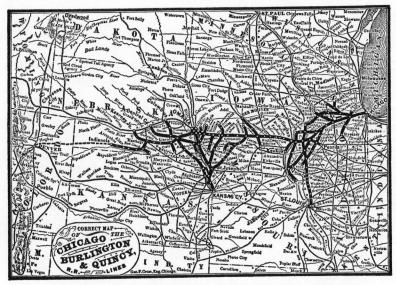

THE CHICAGO, BURLINGTON & QUINCY R.R. CO. IN 1880.

vice-president, authority to appoint with the board's approval two general managers, "one for all roads owned or operated by this company east of the Missouri River," the other for all lines west. T. J. Potter and A. E. Touzalin, respectively, were appointed to the new positions.[56] The stage was now set for the formal consolidation; on July 26, 1880, the property of the Burlington and Missouri River Rail-

[54] CBQ, *Corporate History*, pp. 355, 358.

[55] CBQ, *Annual Report* for 1880 (Chicago, 1881), p. 18. In 1880 the B. & M. acquired the A. & N., which had previously taken over the Burlington and South Western. The latter had originally received 20,000 acres from the State of Nebraska for constructing eight miles of road northwesterly from Rulo. (CBQ, *Corporate History*, p. 353.) Its grant, however, was disposed of before it became part of the Burlington system. (Baldwin to Mitchell, March 18, 1922, LDP.)

[56] CBQ DRB, p. 641.

road in Nebraska was permanently deeded to the Chicago, Burlington & Quincy Railroad Company.[57] The entire road from Chicago to the western counties of Nebraska was now united in name as well as in fact. As in Iowa, however, operations of the land department were carried out under the original corporate title in each state.

While the Burlington was thus attaining its corporate and physical maturity in Nebraska during the years 1874–80, several matters came to the foreground which, while they were not handled directly by the company's land commissioner, had an important bearing on his department. They concerned the old swampland dispute in Iowa, the title to the North Platte lieu lands, the taxability of the unsold portions of the Nebraska grant, and the activities of the various townsite companies.[58]

Although the swampland conflict in Iowa no longer involved a large acreage, its complexity and the uncertainty of its outcome made it unusually troublesome. At the end of 1873, for example, the company required an entire printed page in its report merely to set forth the problem as shown on page 405.[59]

At the end of the next year, the situation as to the lands in dispute was approximately the same,[60] but in December, 1875, the total acreage listed as "lost and to be lost" came to 38,402.14 acres. During the rest of the decade no complete analysis was made available although in 1877 the Iowa Supreme Court awarded 10,000 acres to the company that had been disputed in Mills County. Thus, approximately 25,000 acres was still in dispute as the decade closed. Many of the individual contests arising from this conflict dragged on through the Court during the 'eighties and 'nineties although the majority of them were settled by compromise.[61]

The controversy in Nebraska over the Burlington's title to the North Platte lands was simpler in the issues presented and in its mode of solution, but it was more serious because of the vast acreage involved. In December, 1874, Senator Hitchcock of Nebraska called the attention of United States Attorney-General Williams to Secretary Delano's rul-

[57] CBQ, *Corporate History*, p. 321.
[58] No attempt is made here to describe these matters in detail.
[59] CBQ, *Annual Report* for 1873 (Chicago, 1874), p. 57.
[60] CBQ, *Annual Report* for 1874 (Chicago, 1875), p. 65.
[61] BMN, Swampland Record (LDP).

ing of 1871 which upheld the B. & M.'s claim to the equivalent of ten sections on each side of the road as constructed without lateral limitation. Because of that ruling, the Burlington had obtained, in 1872,

Acres certified		387,352.00	
Acres deeded by Mills Co. in even sections not certified by U. S.		4,934.68	
Approved by U. S., March 4, 1872		520.53	
Total Acres received			392,807.21
Acres sold to December 31, 1872			202,701.72
Net Acres			190,105.49
Less: Acres lost in suit to Fremont Co.		12,562.53	
Acres quit claimed in Mills Co. settlement		8,860.00	
Unadjusted in Mills Co.	8,440		
Of which B&M will probably get	3,480		
Balance supposed to go to Mills Co.		4,960.00	
Deeded to Mills Co. individuals		560.00	
Selected by P. G. Clarke — for services rendered ..		476.23	
Swamp in Page, Montgomery, Taylor, Cass, & Pottawattamie counties		5,680.00	33,098.76
			157,006.73
Claimed by Homesteaders	600		
Preëmptioners	6,000		
Mills Co. Dispute	14,000		20,600.00
Acres clear and unsold			136,406.73

STATUS OF B. & M. LANDS IN IOWA, DECEMBER, 1872.

patents to approximately 1,200,000 acres located more than 20 miles from its tracks.[62]

There is [the Senator wrote] a serious question whether the Company is entitled to this vast body of land — a question which retards the prosperity and hinders the settlement and development of our State. It should be settled promptly and decisively. If it belongs to the Government, it will then be opened for Homestead and Preëmption settlers. If, on the other hand, it belongs to the railroad, the Company will then be able to dispose of and colonize upon it. I deem the matter of sufficient importance to ask that you instruct the United States District Attorney for the District of Nebraska, promptly to commence a suit, the object of which will be to test and definitely settle the rights of said company to said land.[63]

[62] See above, p. 331.
[63] P. W. Hitchcock to George H. Williams, December 8, 1874 (USNA).

At the same time, Hitchcock introduced a measure in the Senate directing the Attorney-General to file a bill to avoid the patents that had already been granted and wrote Secretary Delano requesting him to take parallel action on his own motion.[64] T. M. Marquett, the B. & M.'s attorney, at once sent a letter to Delano:

These proceedings [he explained] have obtained publicity and a doubt has been cast upon the validity of the Company's title by them so that sales are now impracticable. While we have the utmost confidence in your decisions by which these lands were awarded to the Company, we are desirous of bringing the question to a speedy determination. Otherwise, years must elapse before the doubts raised can be set at rest, and the lands [made] saleable.[65]

Therefore, Marquett urged the Secretary to take the action requested by Hitchcock. Four days later, Attorney-General Williams informed Delano that he had instructed the United States attorney for Nebraska to commence a suit to settle definitely the rights of the B. & M. to its lands beyond 20 miles from its track.[66]

The bill thus brought by the federal government in the United States Circuit Court in Nebraska sought avoidance of the railroad's lieu land patents on several grounds. It was asserted

First, that Section 19 of the Act of 1864, making the grant to the B. & M., limited the company to land within 20 miles of its tracks.

Second, that in any event, lands as much as 100 miles from the Burlington's tracks were certainly not "on the line thereof," as required by Section 19.

Third, that only lands lying perpendicular to *each* 20 miles constructed should have been included in patents given as a result of building those particular 20 miles.

Fourth, that the Act of 1864, Section 4, which doubled the Union Pacific's grant as originally made in 1862, did *not* apply to any Union Pacific "branches" such as the B. & M.

Fifth, that even if Section 4 *did* mean that the Burlington [as well as the U. P. and its other "branches"] should have 20 sections per mile, all lands between 10 and 20 miles of *both* Union Pacific and B. & M. [i.e., the so-called "lapped lands"] should have been equally divided between the two roads. Thus, all lands which the B. & M. actually held *beyond* 20 miles, to the extent of what it would have received by a compromise, were illegally held.

[64] Marquett to Delano, December 17, 1874 (USNA).
[65] *Ibid.*
[66] Williams to Delano, December 21, 1874 (USNA).

Sixth, that patents to the B. & M. for approximately 150,000 acres held north of its line in lieu of lands found deficient to the south were void because Section 19 had contemplated that lands should be granted equally on *each* side of the beneficiary road.[67]

Obviously, every argument that could possibly have been urged against the validity of the B. & M.'s patents to its lieu lands was here brought out. In June, 1875, however, Justice Miller handed down a decree dismissing the government's bill. In regard to five of the six points, his decision unequivocally sustained the B. & M.'s position.

First, as to the matter of lateral limits he repeated Hoar's earlier argument that the phraseology of the Act of 1864, considered as a whole, left no doubt but that Congress deliberately omitted lateral limits in the specific case of the B. & M. Furthermore, reasoned the Justice,

it was very well known that the road must run through the most settled part of Nebraska [i.e. between Plattsmouth and Lincoln], and that much of the land along its line was already disposed of, and that within the two years allowed for the definite location of the road, much more of it would be claimed under homestead and preëmption laws. . . .[68]

Finally, the fact that in the Act of 1864 the Union Pacific and all its branches except the B. & M. received bonds was cited as additional evidence of Congress' intention of "equalizing the donations" by omitting lateral limits for the Burlington.

In answer to the government's second contention that lieu lands as much as 100 miles away from the B. & M. were not "on the line thereof," the court replied that the limiting phrase simply meant "parallel with its [the railroad's] course between the two termini." Obviously, all but the few sections directly adjacent to the track were not strictly "on the line thereof," yet most of these were not called in question. It was not possible to set up any arbitrary limit beyond which lands opposite the railroad ceased being "on the line thereof."

The Attorney-General's third argument, that lands had to be taken opposite each 20 miles built, was held by the court to have no foundation in the Act of 1864. In that measure, the railroad had the privilege of selecting its lands as each 20-mile stretch was completed, or

[67] Paraphrase of certified copy of *U. S. v. B. & M. R. R.* in the United States Circuit Court for Nebraska, June, 1875 (USNA); cf. also U. J. Baxter (Acting Commissioner, General Land Office) to Delano, May 8, 1876 (USNA) and *U. S. v. B. & M. R. RR.*, 8 Otto 334 (1878).

[68] *U. S. v. B. & M. R. R.*, 1875 (USNA).

after the entire road was built. The grant, in other words, was in aid of the entire road and not in aid of each 20-mile stretch. Therefore, the company had been justified in filling its quota anywhere within perpendicular lines drawn north and south of its termini.

As to the fourth and fifth points urged by the plaintiff, that the B. & M. should have received but 10 sections per mile, or, if it received 20, that it should have divided the lapped area with the Union Pacific, Justice Miller pointed out that all government departments, ever since 1864, had ruled to the contrary and that patents had been issued and lands sold to private persons on the basis of these rulings. Specifically, the General Land Office had consistently held that all Union Pacific "branches" named in the Act of 1864, including the B. & M. in Nebraska, were entitled to 20 sections per mile; it had likewise held that because the Union Pacific's claim was the older, being based on the original grant of 1862, and because it was limited laterally, that road had prior right to alternate sections within 20 miles of its track. This had forced the B. & M. to seek lieu lands in more remote localities, a procedure authorized by the General Land Office and recognized by the patents issued in 1872. To annul those patents would cause incalculable injustice.

Finally, the government was held correct in asserting that the Act of 1864 contemplated giving the railroad an equal amount of land on both sides of the track. This had not been done. But the plaintiff had not identified which lands north of the B. & M. had been erroneously patented by the General Land Office in place of lands unavailable south of the tracks. Therefore, the court could not void title to approximately 150,000 acres that were not specifically described. Thus, concluded Justice Miller, the government's bill had to be dismissed.[69]

Although this decision, so vital to the B. & M., passed upon every point pertinent to the lieu-land problem, it gave rise to one corollary question on which the company desired further light before placing its North Platte lands on sale. The United States attorney, in his fifth point, had suggested that the Burlington should have received half of the lands falling within 20 miles of its tracks and those of the Union Pacific. Actually, these had been patented to the latter company. They were, however, much nearer to the Burlington and hence far more valuable than the North Platte acreage which the B. & M. had ac-

[69] *U. S. v. B. & M. R. R.*, 1875 (USNA).

cepted in place of them. Thus, when the compromise suggestion was made, the Burlington's attorney appealed to the Secretary of the Interior to institute a separate suit against the Union Pacific to recover for the B. & M. its share of the lapped lands. The Secretary turned the matter over to the General Land Office for counsel, and on May 8, 1876, Acting Commissioner U. J. Baxter replied in a lengthy document. He was convinced, he said, that the intent of Congress in 1864 had been that "both grants should be satisfied and neither defeated wholly or in part by the other," and since the B. & M. was not restricted as to lateral limits, there was a way to satisfy both, as had actually been done. Further, the B. & M. had always acquiesced in this settlement and never, up to that time, questioned the Union Pacific's claim to all of the lapped lands. Therefore, he concluded, "I should regard any construction of said granting statute which would defeat either grant in part by reason of their overlapping as essentially wrong, and I consider the B. & M. River Railroad estopped from its present claim." [70]

Thus, the Acting Commissioner added further weight to the circuit court's decision rejecting the compromise suggestion. In doing so, however, he added another reason for maintaining the B. & M.'s North Platte patents. "The fact that the [lieu] lands actually selected by this [B. & M.] road are remote from its line," he pointed out, "is hardly one to which the government can except, for by its own action under Browning's decision [of 1867], these nearer [lapped] lands were released from withdrawal for the [B. & M.] road, and made subject to settlement and sale." [71] Therefore, the Burlington should at least be confirmed in the possession of the lieu lands it actually held, even if they were not so desirable from a marketing standpoint as the lapped lands might have been.

On May 16, 1876, the Secretary of the Interior, acting on this counsel, formally denied the B. & M.'s application, [72] and for all practical purposes the status of the company's lieu lands was fixed. Although the B. & M. could not claim the lapped lands, its title to the North Platte area was doubly assured, and late in 1876 it placed lands in this region on sale. [73] The final word, however, was not spoken until two years later when the United States Supreme Court passed upon the Attorney-General's appeal from Justice Miller's decision of 1875. As before, the B. & M. was upheld on all points.[74] "The views we entertain," declared Mr. Justice Field, "are so clearly stated in his [Miller's] opinion that we can add but little to what he has said." [75] Such elaboration as there was simply strengthened the findings of the circuit court.

The matter of taxability of unsold portions of the grant fortunately proved a much easier problem to solve, for it lent itself naturally to compromise. On the one hand, county authorities were anxious to obtain some tax revenue from the property held by the company within the limits of their jurisdiction; often this comprised a substantial percentage of the county lands. On the other hand, the railroad felt that high taxes would defeat the purpose of the grant in two ways: by necessitating a higher price on the land and thus retarding colonization, and by diminishing the net return applicable to construction.[76] As the 'seventies wore on, however, settlements were effected in nearly every instance. At the end of 1878 only 17 cases were pending; Touzalin reported that during the year many suits regarding "inside" lands had been satisfactorily adjusted and that about four-fifths of the contests on "outside" lands had been compromised.[77] By 1880, the *Annual Report* stated that the company was "now almost free of litigation." [78]

Nevertheless, despite the generally satisfactory disposition of the tax problem, there were acrimonious exceptions, particularly in the lieu lands. In Boone County, for example, a suit was instituted by the railroad in 1874 against what it felt was illegal taxation.[79] When, in another case decided the next year, the legality of state and county taxation of patented land grants was established,[80] the company obtained temporary injunctions against the Boone County levies and meanwhile sought some basis of compromise. By 1877, nothing had been paid, although the county claimed $60,000 aside from interest and penalties. Such was local indignation that a petition to Congress was

[74] *U. S. v. B. & M. R. RR.*, 8 Otto 334 (1878).
[75] *Ibid.*, p. 334.
[76] Cf. *Boone County v. B. & M. R. RR.*, 139 U.S. 684 (1891).
[77] BMN, *Annual Report* for 1878 (MS), p. 24.
[78] BMN, *Annual Report* for 1880 (MS), p. 11.
[79] Mattison, *op. cit., passim.*
[80] *U. P. R.R. v. McShane*, 22 Wallace 440 (1875).

circulated in the lieu-land counties of Boone, Greeley, Howard, Madison, Platte, Dixon, Cedar, Dakota, Wayne, Sherman, and Valley. In an effort to allay this bitterness, Touzalin called a mass meeting of the people in March, 1878, at Albion. There he was able to explain the railroad's position and make a settlement of the current year's levies; after that date, taxes were duly paid by the purchasers of the company's lands.[81] The taxes of 1873–77, however, remained a recurrent subject of controversy until a suit to recover them was finally dismissed by the United States Supreme Court in 1891.[82]

During the years 1874–80, a number of townsite companies, some of them organized before that period, continued to operate in the Burlington's territory. The South Platte Land Company, for example, devoted its energies to the communities directly on the main line of the B. & M. in Nebraska; at the end of 1876, its statement revealed that it had sold 170½ lots in that year at an average price of $52.51 and 128.81 acres of undivided tracts at an average of $17.89. It listed as still unsold 12,537 lots valued at an average price of $12.35 and slightly more than 10,000 acres in undivided tracts at approximately $12.60 an acre, a total book value of about $280,000.[83] Two years later, with the return of better times and the expansion of its operations, the company's assets were more than $430,000, although the value of its unsold lands had decreased slightly since much of the higher priced property had been sold.[84] As the railroad grew, other similar enterprises were formed. In October, 1877, the *Hamilton County News* reported that a group of C. B. & Q. employees had organized an association to buy 50,000 acres south of the Platte "to obtain a good secure investment for savings." [85] Later on, in the spring of 1880, when the Burlington extended into the Republican River Valley, the Lincoln Land Company was incorporated to develop communities in that region.[86] At the end of its first year, this enterprise reported sales of 259 lots for $14,715.80 and listed its unsold assets as follows: 3,670¼ lots at an average of $9.64 each, $35,378.50; 4,147.41 acres at an average of $13.44 each, $55,750.89.[87]

[81] Mattison, *op. cit., passim.*
[82] *Boone County v. B. & M. R. RR.,* 139 U.S. 684 (1891).
[83] SPL, Statements for 1876 (LDP).
[84] SPL, Statements for 1878 (LDP).
[85] *Hamilton County News* (Hamilton & Aurora, Nebraska), October 5, 1877.
[86] *Ibid.,* April 10, 1880.   [87] LL, Statements for 1880 (LDP).

As before, in both Iowa and Nebraska, the purpose of these companies was to develop communities at fairly regular intervals along the route of the railroad; the sale and colonization of farm lands was handled directly by the company's land department. North of the Platte, however, the situation was different. There the B. & M., being merely in the position of a land owner, was disposed to sell large blocks to individuals or groups. Several companies were formed,[88] and in one case at least, more than 60,000 acres were sold to one group.[89] Nevertheless, in spite of the B. & M.'s willingness to transfer to other companies the task of disposing of its North Platte grant, apparently most of the individual sales there for agricultural purposes were eventually handled through its own land department.[90] Beginning in 1875, the records of the B. & M. in Iowa revealed that the company itself owned certain town lots on its own account. Only 263.06 acres were thus listed, however, and it is probable that this represented excess lands that had originally been bought for sidings, cattle yards, and so forth. The holdings did not increase throughout the decade.[91] Meanwhile, on a similarly small scale, in the fall of 1873, the Nebraska company began to dispose of town lots in Wilber and Firth.[92]

II. LAND DEPARTMENT POLICY AND RESULTS

Early in 1874, when George Harris was forced to resign as land commissioner because of ill health, he was replaced temporarily by Charles E. Perkins.[93] Because of the latter's manifold responsibilities,

---

[88] Such as the Nebraska Land Co. (Articles of Incorporation, January 26, 1878, LDP.) From available records, it is difficult to discover how active this company became, although there is evidence that at one time the B. & M. contemplated transferring the bulk of its North Platte grant to it for $880,000. (NL, Indenture, December 15, 1877, LDP.) The complete history of the Nebraska townsite companies is a subject for further investigation.

[89] Adam Smith bought more than 60,000 acres in Boone County, which he later transferred to the Nebraska Livestock and Improvement Company (Mattison, op. cit.)

[90] There is no way of telling, from the contract ledgers, whether land north of the Platte was bought for the individual purchaser, or by him for some group. It is possible that the voluminous correspondence of the land department, exceeding 600,000 letters might, if completely examined, provide some answer to this problem.

[91] CBQ, *Annual Report* for 1875 (Chicago, 1875), p. 69.

[92] BMN, Town Lot Sales Book (LDP).   [93] BMN DRB, p. 64.

however, the post was soon entrusted to A. E. Touzalin,[94] who had originally been with the B. & M. as general ticket agent and had been responsible for some of the earliest advertising of the company lands.[95] In 1872 and 1873, he served as land commissioner in Kansas for the Atchison, Topeka and Santa Fe Railroad, and was thus fully acquainted with the details of such work.[96] The years that lay ahead of the new manager were to tax his resources to the utmost.[97]

In Iowa, for example, the conflicts with preëmptioners, homesteaders, and swampland claimants still kept several thousand acres out of the market.[98] Meanwhile, in Nebraska, Touzalin had to keep abreast of the lieu-land and tax controversies and advise the company's officers from time to time. His chief duty and responsibility, however, was the sale and colonization of the company's clear lands in both states. In this work, he had the complete coöperation of Charles E. Perkins, particularly in the matter of price and credit policy.

In June, 1874, Perkins addressed a letter to J. M. Walker, president of the C. B. & Q., in respect to Iowa. During the spring, he said, he had had the tracts remaining unsold in Union County thoroughly examined by a competent field man and had reached the conclusion that prices were too high. He asked that the directors, as well as the trustees of the land mortgage, be requested to authorize such reductions as would enable him to dispose of the acres in question.[99] With Walker's approval, both the directors and the trustees gave their consent;[100] by May, 1875, upon Perkins' recommendation, they had au-

[94] Perkins retained the title of land commissioner in Iowa for several years, although the work there was actually handled by Touzalin and his assistants, J. D. McFarland, George Manchester, and Arthur Gorham. (LDP, *passim*.) As vice-president of the B. & M. in Nebraska, Perkins was also Touzalin's superior in that state.

[95] See above, pp. 251–254.

[96] Bradley, *op. cit.*, pp. 111–126; Peter Jansen, *Memoirs of Peter Jansen* (Beatrice, Nebraska, 1921), p. 41. Jansen characterized Touzalin as "a man of strictest integrity and great ability." (Jansen, *op. cit.*, p. 135.)

[97] Discussion of the early years of the Burlington's colonization work has been somewhat detailed in an effort to explain thoroughly the fundamental features of the road's policy. During the succeeding years of the decade, no basic changes took place, although modifications were made in conformity with outside circumstances. The treatment of these years, therefore, is of a more summary nature.

[98] CBQ, *Annual Report* for 1873 (Chicago, 1873), p. 19. See above, p. 405.

[99] Perkins to Walker, June 12, 1874 (BMI ORB, p. 268).

[100] BMI ORB, pp. 266–267.

thorized similar reductions in every Iowa county where the company held lands.[101] As a result, the average price per acre on B. & M. lands in the state declined from $12.81 in 1873 to $12.65 in 1874 and to $11.70 the next year. In Nebraska, prices from the beginning of sales in 1870 had been roughly only two-thirds as high as those in Iowa. Thus, no formal board action was taken in respect to prices there, although the average figure dropped from $7.59 in 1873 to $6.81 in 1874.[102] Apparently, however, this reduction was not the result of a premeditated policy, but rather, as Touzalin explained, because of the sale of a large proportion of cheap lands away from the line of the railroad.[103] Despite the poor crops in Nebraska and the necessity for canceling about six per cent of all sales made because of delinquency in payments, he closed his report for the year there on a note of optimism.

On the whole [he wrote], the result of the year's work . . . is satisfactory. With a more successful agricultural year than 1874, collections would have been better, but they have been sufficiently good to prove . . . that men who have settled on the land desire to stay there, believing Nebraska soil and climate will compare favorably with Illinois and Iowa, and that their farms in ordinary years will yield a good return for labor.[104]

In 1875, the average price for lands in Nebraska actually rose again to $7.29 per acre.[105]

Meanwhile, the credit policy in that state was liberalized. In 1874, the cash discounts and premiums for improvements, which had hitherto been mutually exclusive, were made available at the same time by omitting the requirement that the latter could not be claimed until cultivation had been maintained for four years. The net result was that although the settler was required to improve one-half instead of one-quarter of his holdings, he could, by paying cash at the end of one year, obtain a total reduction from the ten-year price of 30 per cent. If he paid cash at the end of the second or third year and had improved his land in the meanwhile, he was entitled to similar though smaller reductions. Finally, a new inducement was offered by allowing a 20 per cent rebate for cash payment at the end of five years, pro-

---

[101] BMI ORB, pp. 266–329.
[102] See Table 3 in Appendix F.
[103] BMN, *Annual Report* for 1874 (MS), p. 4.
[104] *Ibid.*, p. 6.
[105] See graph, opposite.

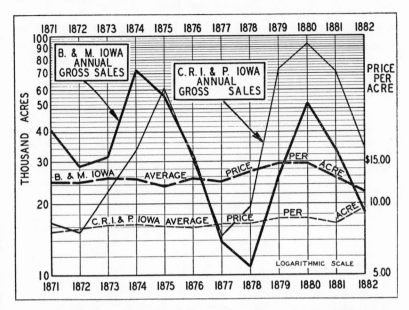

GROSS ACRES SOLD BY THE B. & M. AND BY THE ROCK ISLAND IN IOWA, TOGETHER
WITH THE AVERAGE PRICE PER ACRE, ANNUALLY, 1871–1882.

(For underlying statistics see Tables 1, 3, and 4 in Appendix F)

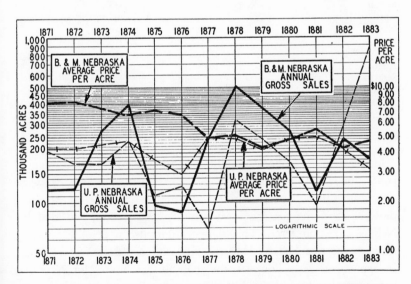

GROSS ACRES SOLD BY THE B. & M. AND BY THE UNION PACIFIC IN NEBRASKA,
TOGETHER WITH THE AVERAGE PRICE PER ACRE, ANNUALLY, 1871–1883.

(For underlying statistics see Tables 2, 3, and 5 in Appendix F)

viding the required improvements had been completed in two.[106] By
1875, and possibly earlier, the original stipulations in all ten-year contracts that a tenth of the land be tilled annually were dropped.[107]

MONTHLY NET ACREAGE SOLD SHOWING

IOWA

	1874	1875	1876
January	1,388.93	3,284.23	2,304.55
February	2,157.50	4,243.82	1,647.17
March	4,424.67	5,634.00	2,329.06
April	3,485.25	6,737.93	2,907.39
May	4,353.05	5,477.41	1,061.32
June	4,953.48	3,801.49	1,076.60
July	1,663.44	1,584.22	899.24
August	2,916.53	1,622.52	901.88
September	7,069.39	2,676.27	1,008.42
October	9,759.76	3,195.37	597.37
November	5,819.79	3,007.75	178.67
December	5,734.90	1,338.22	663.78
TOTAL	53,726.69	42,603.23	15,575.45

NEBRASKA

	1873	1874	1875
January	4,838.00	16,125.04	2,020.96
February	2,795.08	18,237.82	3,011.62
March	11,782.25	37,846.41	3,873.79
April	12,648.41	40,298.59	7,460.31
May	15,192.01	41,330.66	4,992.84
June	36,218.25	59,419.28	6,017.62
July	18,140.33	27,388.29	4,403.55
August	19,652.47	25,925.12	4,151.52
September	41,790.19	30,479.49	7,241.39
October	35,658.59	21,931.98	5,675.28
November	26,547.82	6,098.67	4,385.36
December	22,051.93	4,664.65	741.90
TOTAL	247,315.33	329,746.00	53,976.14

In the light of economic conditions and in view of the company's
policy, the sales figures for Iowa and Nebraska in 1874 and 1875 were
significant. In both states, gross and net sales for 1874 far exceeded
those of 1873, the net for Iowa being 53,726.69 acres, and that for
Nebraska 329,746 acres. This showing indicated a definite time lag
between the financial crash in the East and its effects on the West.
In September, 1874, however, the monthly net figures for Nebraska
began running behind those of the corresponding months of the pre-

---

[106] BMR, Postal with Terms (LDP).
[107] BMN, Ten-Year Contract, dated in MS April 15, 1875 (LDP).

ceding year and continued to do so throughout 1875; the net in that state for 1875 was but 53,976.14 acres, less than one-sixth the previous year's sales. In Iowa, the decline did not begin until June, 1875, and

IMPACT OF PANIC IN IOWA AND NEBRASKA

IOWA

	1877	1878	1879
January	176.42	40.00	49.20
February	160.00	224.33	108.36 [d]
March	636.06	113.00	121.73 [d]
April	536.44	22.99	93.40
May	594.63	412.76	119.92
June	160.00	108.00	200.00 [d]
July	280.00	80.00	80.00
August	328.05	40.00	160.00 [d]
September	14.18	93.93	120.00 [d]
October	400.00	40.00	33.93 [d]
November	236.64	80.00	317.30
December	43.36	43.55	483.25 [d]
TOTAL	3,565.78	1,298.56	567.45 [d]

NEBRASKA

	1876	1877	1878
January	602.07	3,554.49	20,615.88
February	2,524.92	7,817.24	32,680.08
March	6,068.74 [d]	11,815.67	34,947.47
April	2,426.60	4,339.13	47,987.53
May	2,792.83	5,506.49	49,339.60
June	7,891.18 [d]	1,654.55	41,650.39
July	1,219.52 [d]	16,085.82	34,507.12
August	5,797.34	25,093.97 [d]	28,059.24
September	9,157.59	17,095.11	30,680.58
October	5,861.28	29,810.47	26,718.02
November	1,311.19	30,924.92	21,344.73
December	25,648.82 [d]	29,717.21	14,727.45
TOTAL	5,427.92	133,227.13	383,258.09

[d] Deficit.

then it was more gradual. Net sales for that year of 42,603.23 acres represented a drop of approximately 20 per cent from the results of 1874.[108]

Primarily, the decline in Burlington sales was undoubtedly a result of the national depression, and in this connection it was noteworthy that Nebraska was struck more quickly and more sharply than Iowa. It seemed that the effects of hard times, accentuated by the grasshopper plague, were felt sooner in a newer community where there

[108] See tables, above.

were less cash reserves and fewer resources to fall back upon, such as negotiable real estate, savings, and established homesteads where less fortunate members of a family could find work and shelter. In the more established state of Iowa, there was apparently a larger margin of wealth that served to retard the effects of the panic. There were other factors, however, that contributed to the relatively poorer showing in Nebraska. During 1874, when land purchasers there had asked for extensions of time on their installments, their requests had been liberally granted,[109] and cancellations were formally made only when tracts were actually forfeited and resold. This procedure worked well enough while sales were large, but during 1875 the stringency became so acute that the directors decided to write off all contracts that seemed beyond hope.[110] Consequently, in December, sales representing 38,-275.44 acres, about 40 per cent of the year's gross, were canceled. Furthermore, the failure to lower prices in 1875, as opposed to the slight but steady readjustment in Iowa, probably contributed to the poor gross results.

The varying effects of price policy were particularly noticeable in the contrasting results obtained during 1874 and 1875 by the Burlington on the one hand, and by the Rock Island in Iowa and the Union Pacific in Nebraska on the other. As was true throughout the decade, the Rock Island sold its lands, which were less accessible than the Burlington's, at about two-thirds of the latter's price. Despite this differential, the B. & M. made a far stronger showing in 1874. In the next year, however, when cash was hard to find, the Rock Island sales showed their sharpest increase up to that time, while the Burlington's sales fell off. In Nebraska, the Union Pacific suffered from the panic and from crop failures as did the Burlington, but its prices, after rising slightly in 1874, were substantially reduced the next year. Probably as a result of this fact, its gross sales did not decline as rapidly as those of the B. & M. and, in fact, exceeded them in 1875 for the first time since 1872.[111] Thus, although the depression was the chief factor causing the absolute decline in land sales in 1874 and 1875, the high level of Burlington prices, particularly in Nebraska, undoubtedly contributed to the relatively poor showing of the company.

[109] BMN, *Annual Report* for 1874 (MS), pp. 4–5.
[110] BMN, *Annual Report* for 1875 (MS), pp. 4–5.
[111] See graphs on page 415.

Nevertheless, prices remained relatively stable through 1876. In an effort to increase sales, however, and to attract new purchasers, Touzalin announced, on March 29, 1876, an entirely new credit scheme. A six-year payment plan was to be offered in addition to the existing three- and ten-year arrangements. It was to operate like the others: a down payment required when the contract was signed, then two years of interest only at six per cent, followed by four annual installments of the principal.[112] Prices of land under this scheme were to be ten per cent less than ten-year prices, and improvement permiums of seven and a half per cent and fifteen per cent were offered for cultivating one-fourth or one-half of the property, respectively, during the first year and for maintaining such improvements for two years thereafter.[113]

Meanwhile, as a result of the circuit court's decision, the directors of the Nebraska company decided that their title to the more than 1,200,000 acres north of the Platte River was sufficiently clear to permit throwing these lands on the market. Much of this area, however, was relatively inaccessible by rail,[114] so that despite its favorable agricultural prospects, prevailing land prices were much lower than for the region along the B. & M. Thus, the directors authorized Perkins in August and September, 1876, to sell these "outside" lands "for cash prices below those fixed in the schedule, when in his judgment it is policy to do so,[115] or on time, on such terms as he may desire for the interest of the company." [116] Given this discretion, Perkins at once fixed prices at less than half the figures charged south of the Platte. At the same time, credit plans were made available for ten-, nine-, five-, and two-year periods, and no interest was required in any except the last, where a charge of ten per cent was made. In every case, however, part of the principal was demanded when the contract was signed, and a proportion of the balance annually thereafter. These installments were of equal amounts except in the ten-year plan, where the sum required gradually increased to a uniform maximum in the fifth year. Price reductions from the full or ten-year figure for purchasers under the nine-, five-, and two-year plans were 10, 25, and 50 per cent respectively; a discount of one-half was also allowed on cash payments

---

[112] BMR, Circular to Land Agents, March 29, 1876 (LDP).

[113] BMR, Six-Year Contract (LDP).

[114] See map, opposite p. 332.

[115] BMN DRB, p. 112.   [116] BMN DRB, p. 117.

when the contract was signed.[117] No premiums for improvements were offered in the contracts nor stipulations made as to tilling a given area, but in applying for North Platte land under the ten-year scheme, settlers were required to swear that they were not buying for speculative purposes and that it was their intention to use the land for farming or stock raising within two years.[118]

In spite of these measures, the results for 1876 were discouraging. In Iowa, net sales fell nearly two-thirds to 15,575.45 acres, and although the Nebraska gross dropped only about 17 per cent to 76,816.90 acres, there were cancellations of 71,388.98 acres, leaving a negligible net sale for the entire year of but 5,427.92 acres.[119] In the meantime, the Union Pacific reduced its prices still further and was rewarded by an increase in business that was closely parallel to the upturn noted in public land sales in Nebraska for that year. On the other hand, Rock Island sales in Iowa fell off as rapidly as did the Burlington's.[120]

Under the circumstances, on January 5, 1877, the directors of the B. & M. in Nebraska voted, on motion of Mr. Forbes, that "the Vice-President [Perkins] be and he is hereby authorized to dispose of the lands of this company in Nebraska for cash in hand at prices not more than 50 per cent lower than the 10 year prices, and proportionate discount may be made for sales on two and six years credit, the rate of interest on all deferred payments to be six per cent." [121] Less than two weeks later, the directors of the C. B. & Q. took similar action in respect to discounts in Iowa; furthermore, the vice-president and land commissioner were authorized to "reduce prices when and where, in their judgment, it is best to do so, the object being to effect the early sale of the remaining 40,000 acres" in that state.[122] At last the need for a radical revision in prices and terms was recognized. As a result, the terms of sale announced for 1877 were even more liberal and were particularly significant because of the large discounts allowed from ten-year prices to purchasers who were willing to complete their payments sooner. Whereas since 1870 purchasers for cash or on three

[117] BMR, "Iowa and Nebraska Farmer," January, 1876 (LDP); BMN, Circular to Agents, September 28, 1876 (LDP).

[118] BMN, Ten-Year North Platte Contract, 1876 (LDP).

[119] See tables, pp. 424–425.

[120] See graphs, p. 415.

[121] BMN DRB, p. 122.

[122] CBQ DRB, p. 501.

years' time had been entitled to a 20 per cent discount from the ten-year prices, they were now allowed reductions of 45 and 35 per cent, respectively, and buyers under the new six-year plan found their discount increased from 10 to 20 per cent.[123] At the same time, even more drastic cuts were put into effect for "outside lands." Discounts for nine-, five-, two-year, and cash customers rose to 20, 30, 50, and 60 per cent, respectively.[124] These were the greatest concessions ever offered in North Platte territory and coincided in time with the liberal extreme of credit policy south of the river and in Iowa. Although prices in Iowa and for the South Platte region remained fairly stable, the average for Nebraska as a whole dropped from $6.86 to $4.91 per acre in 1877 as a result of selling more than 100,000 acres of "outside lands" at an average of only $2.10.

In Iowa, even these inducements were insufficient to stem the accumulated effects of the depression. Gross sales there fell to a new low of 13,748.69 acres; even the Rock Island, with its considerably lower price scale, experienced an almost identical decline. In Nebraska, however, the combination of better crops, increased immigration, liberal terms, and the availability of the North Platte lands abruptly reversed the downward trend that had begun in 1874. Gross acreage sales were nearly quadrupled, reaching a total of almost 250,000 acres.[125] Meanwhile, the average price of Union Pacific lands jumped from $3 to around $5 per acre; probably as a result that company's sales declined to about 70,000 acres, the lowest figure of the decade. It seemed that, aside from all other factors, the element of price, particularly in a region where much land was still available, was of dominant importance.[126]

During the years 1874 through 1876, the land department in Nebraska continued to keep an account of the origin of its land purchasers. With few changes, they came principally from the same sources listed in 1873: the neighboring states, the old Northwest Territory, New York, Pennsylvania, Massachusetts, and, as to Europe, from Germany, Scandinavia, England, and Russia. The largest and most recent increases were in newcomers from Wisconsin, Ohio, New York, Sweden, and

---

[123] BMR, Circular to Agents, January 1, 1877 (LDP).
[124] BMN, Pamphlet of 1877 (LDP).
[125] See Tables 1–5, inclusive, in Appendix F.
[126] See graphs, p. 415.

	1873	1874	1875	1876
Arkansas	..	..	1	1
Austria	..	..	..	5
Bavaria	..	..	..	1
Belgium	..	..	..	2
Bohemia	31	18	38	49
Canada	14	5	21	19
Colorado	1	1	3	3
Connecticut	2	2	4	8
Dakota	..	..	1	1
Denmark	15	7	..	12
England	59	19	65	75
France	1	..	..	9
Germany	113	12	57	119
Holland	17	4	16	19
Hungary	..	5	5	4
Iceland	1	..	..	..
Idaho	..	1	1	1
Illinois	335	589	962	956
Indiana	57	47	88	101
Iowa	219	157	370	364
Ireland	20	1	1	21
Italy	..	..	1	1
Kansas	4	5	9	6
Kentucky	14	3	13	17
Louisiana	..	2	2	3
Maine	4	3	..	..
Maryland	2	3	4	5
Massachusetts	15	8	20	27
Michigan	42	42	68	59
Minnesota	12	34	39	38
Mississippi	1	..	1	1
Missouri	13	20	32	29
Nebraska	708	1,322	2,115	2,113
New Brunswick	1	..	1	2
New Hampshire	..	..	..	2
New Jersey	6	1	2	6
New York	88	50	111	136
North Carolina	1	2	2	..
Norway	1	..	2	7
Ohio	76	50	100	126
Pennsylvania	41	32	49	70
Prussia	..	22	..	11
Rhode Island	1	..	..	..
Russia	37	85	133	155
Saxony	..	1	1	2
Scotland	14	2	8	10
Sweden	30	5	34	117
Switzerland	3	..	7	7
Tennessee	5	1	4	5
Vermont	2	1	..	1
Virginia	..	..	..	2
Wales	..	..	..	1
West Virginia	10	19	29	33
Wisconsin	99	127	233	230
Wyoming	..	..	1	1
Total	2,115	2,708	4,654	4,993

Russia.[127] Their buying habits, both in Iowa and Nebraska, continued along the lines followed earlier in the decade. In the older state the average purchase ranged between 65 and 76 acres; in Nebraska during the middle years, it remained almost stable around 125 acres.[128]

Throughout this period, the Burlington had increasingly to deal with those who were delinquent in paying for their land. The problem was a difficult one, for the railroad needed shippers and travelers above all else. On the other hand, the amount of arrearage grew alarmingly as the depression deepened. At the end of 1874, for example, a total of $287,386.95 was past due and uncollected in Nebraska alone; [129] two years later the figure was $412,282.59.[130] Faced with such facts as these, the company crystallized its policy. The first step was the collection of information. To some settlers, the land department sent questionnaires with the request for a report on their condition.[131] In other cases, company agents were sent to make a personal call and fill out a prepared blank:

1. What character does the contractor bear in the community?
2. What family has he?
3. Is he living on the land?
4. Has he other lands, and how much?
5. If so, is it improved, and to what extent?
6. What stock and implements has he?
7. Has he other debts and how much?
8. What improvements are on this land? What trees has he planted?
9. What crops has he raised this year?
10. What amount of grain has he on hand now?
11. What stock, hogs, cattle will he have to sell this fall or winter?
12. How much can he pay on account of his indebtedness on the land, and when does he promise it?
13. What does he say about his indebtedness?
14. If it is a bad case, and no probability of the purchaser paying for the land, what will it sell for, and do you know a buyer?
15. Give any additional facts of value, and your opinion of the case.[132]

[127] See table opposite. Figures for 1873 and 1874 are from BMN, *Annual Report* for 1874 (MS), p. 28; those for 1875 are from BMN, *Annual Report* for 1875 (MS), p. 48; those for 1876 from BMN, *Annual Report* for 1876 (MS), p. 57.

[128] See tables, pp. 424–425.

[129] BMN, *Annual Report* for 1874 (MS), p. 5.

[130] BMN, *Annual Report* for 1876 (MS), pp. 28–29.

[131] BMR, Statement of Condition, 1874 (LDP); same, 1875? (LDP); same, September, 1875 (LDP).

[132] BMR, Examiner's Report, 1876? (LDP).

IOWA

		Acres	Value	Number of Sales	Average Price	Average Size of Plots
1874 —	Jan.	3,327.47	$ 44,700.40	44		
	Feb.	4,136.91	60,819.18	49		
	Mar.	6,334.05	85,922.10	81		
	Apr.	4,826.82	60,416.96	61		
	May	5,869.74	81,849.26	77		
	June	6,191.80	75,369.15	62		
	July	2,611.39	30,977.58	38		
	Aug.	6,367.91	82,630.50	80		
	Sept.	9,366.03	118,536.08	123		
	Oct.	10,781.40	134,334.77	141		
	Nov.	6,219.79	69,090.58	89		
	Dec.	7,199.53	81,734.20	112		
GROSS		73,232.84	$926,380.76	957	$12.65	76.52
Cancelled		19,506.15	249,720.20	212		
NET		53,726.69	$676,660.56	745		
1875 —	Jan.	4,732.71	$ 58,941.75	71		
	Feb.	6,066.63	71,777.21	94		
	Mar.	7,104.10	83,982.02	110		
	Apr.	8,387.94	99,574.99	119		
	May	6,177.56	69,616.70	96		
	June	5,439.60	63,741.57	99		
	July	2,104.22	19,864.36	34		
	Aug.	2,379.96	27,767.73	37		
	Sept.	3,276.27	36,451.29	46		
	Oct.	3,915.14	42,101.41	64		
	Nov.	4,338.08	55,664.73	51		
	Dec.	3,118.84	37,647.61	44		
GROSS		57,041.05	$667,131.37	865	$11.70	65.94
Cancelled		14,437.82	179,644.14	157		
NET		42,603.23	$487,487.23	708		
1876 —	Jan.	4,773.96	$ 58,926.41	60		
	Feb.	3,686.17	47,203.50	53		
	Mar.	5,919.92	81,604.19	83		
	Apr.	3,107.39	27,986.38	44		
	May	2,977.19	41,831.69	43		
	June	1,676.60	20,855.22	26		
	July	2,499.24	38,377.56	24		
	Aug.	1,541.88	19,135.16	22		
	Sept.	1,288.42	13,644.72	21		
	Oct.	1,517.37	18,655.81	21		
	Nov.	1,209.77	15,085.18	19		
	Dec.	1,503.78	21,883.40	20		
GROSS		31,701.69	$405,209.22	436	$12.78	72.71
Cancelled		16,126.24	205,587.31	173		
NET		15,575.45	$199,621.91	263		

NEBRASKA

		Acres	Value	Number of Sales	Average Price	Average Size of Plots
1874 —	Jan.	18,561.44	$ 126,912.01	144		
	Feb.	21,455.29	142,656.23	187		
	Mar.	43,650.28	313,702.25	362		
	Apr.	44,049.62	307,794.48	357		
	May	47,998.06	332,873.91	413		
	June	68,018.21	462,437.60	571		
	July	30,870.14	199,367.81	208		
	Aug.	27,605.12	178,835.55	208		
	Sept.	51,970.42	355,914.39	365		
	Oct.	23,406.45	146,070.67	185		
	Nov.	8,440.71	57,971.63	71		
	Dec.	8,235.71	61,592.65	68		
GROSS		394,261.45	$2,686,129.18	3139	$6.81	125.60
Cancelled		64,515.45	552,316.54	445		
NET		329,746.00	$2,133,812.64	2694		
1875 —	Jan.	5,584.61	$ 42,580.00	46		
	Feb.	4,694.91	41,331.74	41		
	Mar.	8,318.56	62,260.32	76		
	Apr.	10,578.73	73,315.93	78		
	May	8,874.45	63,023.49	67		
	June	7,657.62	48,635.34	68		
	July	6,714.72	53,643.47	61		
	Aug.	7,116.85	55,276.38	67		
	Sept.	10,682.87	74,319.11	79		
	Oct.	9,580.51	74,193.49	80		
	Nov.	6,709.90	39,729.40	56		
	Dec.	5,737.85	44,609.74	42		
GROSS		92,251.58	$ 672,918.41	761	$7.29	121.22
Cancelled		38,275.44	344,103.88	293		
NET		53,976.14	$ 328,814.53	468		
1876 —	Jan.	2,602.07	$ 25,654.63	22		
	Feb.	3,883.36	28,045.06	34		
	Mar.	4,716.89	43,573.97	39		
	Apr.	6,916.66	41,817.55	63		
	May	7,280.82	47,047.28	69		
	June	10,400.93	65,565.72	86		
	July	3,236.35	21,039.66	31		
	Aug.	9,147.02	66,522.86	78		
	Sept.	10,732.32	61,075.30	69		
	Oct.	8,222.65	52,485.21	66		
	Nov.	4,153.77	32,033.71	34		
	Dec.	5,524.06	42,086.27	47		
GROSS		76,816.90	$ 526,947.22	638	$6.86	120.40
Cancelled		71,388.98	525,398.45	566		
NET		5,427.92	$ 1,548.77	72		

The order of questions suggests that the company was rather more concerned with the settler's character than with the amount of his negotiable property.

Fortified with the information thus received, the company was in a position to act. Toward non-residents, it took a firm position; a notice was sent to such persons that unless they made their payment within 30 days, the property in question would be placed on the market for resale.[133] To those who were living on and improving their land, however, the B. & M. adopted a liberal attitude. As Touzalin explained in 1877:

> Notwithstanding these large sums overdue, it has been deemed the best course to carry these delinquent contracts, as the lands represented thereby are occupied and improved, and are producing business for the Road. With good crops, the greater portion of the arrearage will be paid. Contracts are watched closely, and collections made when they can be.[134]

A settler, for example, was allowed to post a forfeit guaranteeing payment of interest only on his contract,[135] or some special arrangement was made to suit his individual needs.[136] A squatter on company land, although he had no legal right whatsoever, likewise received lenient treatment providing he was cultivating his tract. For a specific payment, he was authorized to raise crops already planted, although it was stipulated that this accommodation should not interfere with the sale of the property. If the land were sold, however, the farmer would either be given back his payment and reimbursed for his plowing, or, if the crops were already in, he would be allowed to harvest them.[137]

Another problem arising from the depression was the default of taxes on lands bought on long credit. Although all contracts specified that purchasers were responsible for these assessments from the beginning, the obligation was frequently overlooked,[138] and for the convenience of its customers, the road circulated notices of the local tax laws.[139] If the taxes remained unpaid, the company sometimes allowed

---

[133] BMR, Notice to Non-Resident, April 15, 1875 (LDP).

[134] BMN, *Annual Report* for 1876 (MS), pp. 28–29.

[135] BMR, Receipt of Forfeit, 1874? (LDP); BMR, Notice of Forfeit Expiration, 1874? (LDP).

[136] BMN, Contract Ledgers "A" through "G" (LDP), *passim*.

[137] BMR, Permission for Cultivation, 1878? (LDP).

[138] BMR, Request to Pay Taxes, 1875 (LDP).

[139] BMR, Circular of Tax Laws, 1874 (LDP).

the tract to be sold at a tax sale, presumably to one of its own agents, and then informed the delinquent that it was up to him to redeem the property.[140] On other occasions, the B. & M. paid the tax and notified the settler that he had 60 days to make good this disbursement; otherwise his contract would be canceled.[141]

In addition to the various price concessions offered by the Burlington during the depression years, the company granted, on February 1, 1876, a 30 per cent rebate on all "emigrant's movables." Whereas this inducement had been offered for years to purchasers of B. & M. lands,[142] it was now extended to any actual settler who located in a county where the railroad had lands for sale, or to any farmers' clubs who wished to bring in agricultural supplies, livestock, trees, or shrubbery.[143] Meanwhile, seed for the various granges was brought in by the railroad free of charge.[144]

As 1877 drew to a close, the rising tide of immigration and the excellent showing of the land department in Nebraska led Touzalin to adopt more conservative terms for the next year. Also, as he informed his agents, the company's experience with ten-year terms had been a "severe" one; thus, he wished them to encourage buyers to choose the six-year scheme. As an inducement, discounts for cash and three-year sales were reduced to 35 and 32½ per cent, respectively, but the 20 per cent reduction was retained for the six-year plan. At the same time, improvement premiums were liberalized by requiring that only a quarter of the tract need be cultivated within two years and by accepting well-built board fences as permanent buildings that might be substituted for half the required cultivation.[145] To simplify matters, the nine-, five-, and two-year plans in effect north of the Platte were replaced by the ten-, six-, and three-year arrangements prevailing elsewhere in B. & M. territory. Interest would be 3 per cent on ten- and six-year contracts, and 10 per cent, as before, on short credit sales. Discounts from the ten-year prices dropped from their peaks to 25, 35, and

---

[140] BMR, Notice of Tax Sale, January 9, 1875 (LDP).

[141] BMR, Notice of Taxes Paid, January 9, 1875 (LDP); same, January 1, 1876 (LDP).

[142] See above, pp. 335–336.

[143] BMR, Circular of Joint Tariff, February 1, 1876 (LDP).

[144] BMR, Circular on Seed Shipments, February, 1875 (LDP).

[145] BMR, Circular to Agents, December 15, 1877 (LDP); BMR, Six-Year Contract, 1878 (LDP).

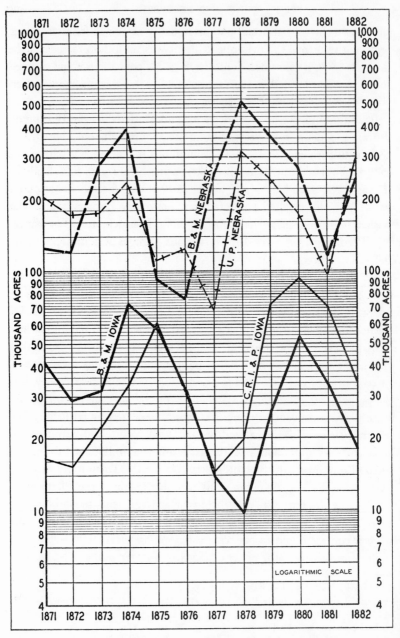

GROSS ACRES SOLD BY THE B. & M. AND BY THE ROCK ISLAND IN IOWA, AND BY
THE B. & M. AND BY THE UNION PACIFIC IN NEBRASKA, ANNUALLY, 1871–1882.

(For underlying statistics see Tables 1, 2, 4, and 5 in Appendix F)

50 per cent for six-year, three-year, and cash terms. The precautions to exclude speculators, however, were retained, and in addition, a limit of 320 acres that could not be exceeded without special permission of the land department was placed on each transaction.[146]

In theory, the B. & M. was thus offering in Iowa and Nebraska four plans of purchase, namely, cash, or over a period of three, six, and ten years. In practice, however, the land department modified these schemes to suit the particular needs of the customer. In 1877 there were no less than 26 different plans in effect in Nebraska; the next year there were 23. A man could arrange to pay for his land over any period from six months to eleven years, and providing he made some down payment as an earnest of his intentions, he could remit his installments of interest and principal according to a wide variety of plans.[147] This flexibility of payment was undoubtedly an added inducement for the prospective settler, or for the delinquent who wished to make a new contract.

During 1878, the effect of price policy was again noticeable in statistics of sales. In Iowa, where B. & M. prices rose to an average of $13.61 an acre, sales continued to fall, though not so fast as the preceding year. On the other hand, the Rock Island increased their sales for the first time in three years. In Nebraska, where both Burlington and Union Pacific prices remained approximately stable, both companies enjoyed a continued upswing in sales. As a matter of fact, the B. & M.'s average price for South Platte lands declined from $6.90 to $5.84, and at this rate 391,930.35 acres were sold. At the same time, 122,167.76 acres north of the Platte brought an average of $2.76 each.[148] The total sales of more than 500,000 acres constituted an all-time record, and even though cancellations likewise reached a peak, net acres sold attained their highest level of the decade. "The tide of emigration," observed Touzalin, "shows no sign of diminution."[149]

Under the circumstances a considerable stiffening of terms and rise in prices might have been expected. On the other hand, as Touzalin pointed out in a memorandum submitted in the late summer of 1878,

[146] BMN, Circular to Agents, 1877 (LDP).

[147] BMN, Contract Ledgers "A" through "G" (LDP), *passim.*

[148] These figures from the manuscript BMN *Annual Report* for 1878 differ to the extent of 1,989.99 acres from the revised and thus more accurate figures in the Sales Books and Journals. For the latter see table on p. 431.

[149] BMN, *Annual Report* for 1878 (MS), p. 9.

IOWA

		Acres	Value	Number of Sales	Average Price	Average Size of Plots
1876 —	Jan.	4,773.96	$ 58,926.41	60		
	Feb.	3,686.17	47,203.50	53		
	Mar.	5,919.92	81,604.19	83		
	Apr.	3,107.39	27,986.38	44		
	May	2,977.19	41,831.69	43		
	June	1,676.60	20,855.22	26		
	July	2,499.24	38,377.56	24		
	Aug.	1,541.88	19,135.16	22		
	Sept.	1,288.42	13,644.72	21		
	Oct.	1,517.37	18,655.81	21		
	Nov.	1,209.77	15,085.18	19		
	Dec.	1,503.78	21,883.40	20		
GROSS		31,701.69	$405,209.22	436	$12.78	72.71
Cancelled		16,126.24	205,587.31	173		
NET		15,575.45	$199,621.91	263		
1877 —	Jan.	1,463.54	$ 21,017.88	22		
	Feb.	640.00	6,710.00	7		
	Mar.	2,202.14	26,931.14	25		
	Apr.	2,304.56	29,219.81	28		
	May	1,057.13	11,504.65	20		
	June	600.00	6,720.00	10		
	July	1,074.36	14,929.26	17		
	Aug.	686.19	5,641.89	12		
	Sept.	705.41	10,904.92	11		
	Oct.	1,440.00	17,512.00	21		
	Nov.	563.72	7,389.76	9		
	Dec.	1,011.64	12,483.38	16		
GROSS		13,748.69	$170,964.69	198	$12.43	69.44
Cancelled		10,182.91	129,585.41	112		
NET		3,565.78	$ 41,379.28	86		
1878 —	Jan.	1,500.17	$ 21,980.83	23		
	Feb.	712.13	8,231.18	13		
	Mar.	1,250.32	18,766.11	18		
	Apr.	1,854.86	27,630.26	20		
	May	1,119.19	13,037.71	12		
	June	833.15	12,458.82	13		
	July	549.65	8,332.30	5		
	Aug.	200.00	2,000.00	5		
	Sept.	973.93	12,214.62	13		
	Oct.	249.20	2,462.80	5		
	Nov.	160.00	1,520.00	3		
	Dec.	305.03	3,464.36	4		
GROSS		9,707.63	$132,098.99	134	$13.61	72.45
Cancelled		8,409.07	113,014.24	101		
NET		1,298.56	$ 19,084.75	33		

NEBRASKA

		Acres	Value	Number of Sales	Average Price	Average Size of Plots
1876 —	Jan.	2,602.07	$ 25,654.63	22		
	Feb.	3,883.36	28,045.06	34		
	Mar.	4,716.89	43,573.97	39		
	Apr.	6,916.66	41,817.55	63		
	May	7,280.82	47,047.28	69		
	June	10,400.93	65,565.72	86		
	July	3,236.35	21,039.66	31		
	Aug.	9,147.02	66,522.86	78		
	Sept.	10,732.32	61,075.30	69		
	Oct.	8,222.65	52,485.21	66		
	Nov.	4,153.77	32,033.71	34		
	Dec.	5,524.06	42,086.27	47		
GROSS		76,816.90	$ 526,947.22	638	$6.86	120.40
Cancelled		71,388.98	525,398.45	566		
NET		5,427.92	$ 1,548.77	72		
1877 —	Jan.	4,034.49	$ 25,620.36	35		
	Feb.	10,446.17	36,213.93	38		
	Mar.	26,265.38	80,821.26	207		
	Apr.	6,376.22	33,904.63	55		
	May	8,125.71	51,133.15	63		
	June	11,731.13	52,500.96	92		
	July	18,422.27	58,787.01	103		
	Aug.	18,373.37	94,597.43	135		
	Sept.	22,115.11	114,832.55	177		
	Oct.	39,210.92	216,695.36	307		
	Nov.	40,443.11	220,272.95	301		
	Dec.	41,194.48	226,246.36	302		
GROSS		246,738.36	$1,211,625.95	1815	$4.91	135.94
Cancelled		113,511.23	866,228.51	937		
NET		133,227.13	$ 345,397.44	878		
1878 —	Jan.	32,350.10	$ 161,365.59	231		
	Feb.	43,375.44	226,933.58	337		
	Mar.	54,969.20	320,467.78	434		
	Apr.	65,356.75	339,931.37	544		
	May	61,861.10	329,739.74	527		
	June	52,617.87	263,572.53	409		
	July	39,617.62	184,011.11	294		
	Aug.	36,749.43	174,561.64	269		
	Sept.	38,707.46	194,732.83	284		
	Oct.	35,084.55	180,720.72	255		
	Nov.	29,916.35	144,274.68	213		
	Dec.	21,502.25	100,213.33	159		
GROSS		512,108.12	$2,620,524.90	3956	$5.12	129.45
Cancelled		128,850.03	913,060.76	1064		
NET		383,258.09	$1,707,464.14	2892		

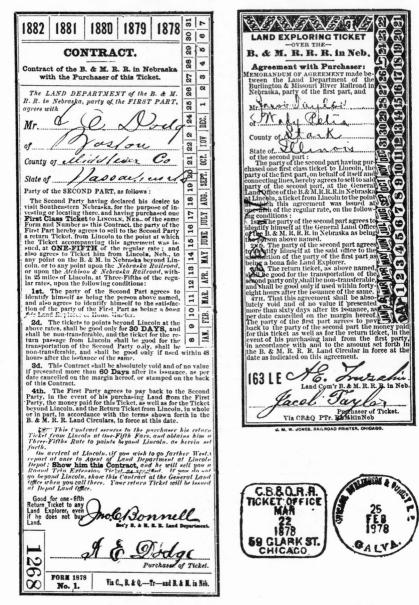

LAND EXPLORING TICKETS ISSUED BY B. & M. IN NEBRASKA, 1878.

changes in prices, changes in our terms of sale, changes in our general operations are as a rule to be avoided unless they are very clearly necessary or desirable. Our business dealings are with an intelligent, shrewd people who calculate quite as closely as we do, and who will not comply with unreasonable demands. . . .[150]

He then proceeded to analyze the factors he thought should be borne in mind in reaching any conclusion as to future policy.

Immigration to the West, he said, was not so large as was popularly supposed. Furthermore, if it were equally divided between all the competing sections of the country proportionate to their vacant territory, the B. & M. in Nebraska would receive less than one-eighth of its actual customers, for although it was questionable whether lands lying further west than 300 miles from the Missouri River were capable of cultivation without irrigation, there were still tens of millions of acres east of that longitude in Dakota, Minnesota, Iowa, Missouri, Arkansas, Texas, Kansas, and Nebraska that were waiting for purchasers. Also, further south such states as Virginia, North Carolina, Tennessee, Georgia, and Alabama were entering the field as competitors. "The B. & M. in Nebraska," he reasoned, "ought not to seek the mere sale of its lands, but *dense settlement* should be aimed at as the true foundation for a broad prosperity in the future." This could be secured only by a continuation of the large immigration such as that in the last twelve months. Notwithstanding the "flourishing appearance" of affairs in Nebraska, the company's enterprise was still "only weak. We need," insisted Touzalin, "double the population, double the wealth, double the cultivated lands and double the manufactures and commercial interests that we have today to be fully prepared for any possible reverses that may arise next year or in any following year." [151]

Thus, to determine the advisability of any further change in prices or terms, it was well to examine in detail the business of the first six months of 1878 in comparison with what others were doing. Of course, if the B. & M. were receiving eight times as much business as an equal distribution of emigration would provide, it could be conceded that the company was doing "reasonably well." Yet if the Burlington were doing as well as any other one section, and selling and settling as

[150] BMN, Memorandum by Touzalin, September?, 1878 (LDP).
[151] *Ibid.*

many or more lands than any other land-grant road in the country, it was all the more reason to "consider well before making any radical change in . . . price, plans or terms." [152]

The two great competitors for western business, said Touzalin, were Nebraska and Kansas, and in point of numbers, each was receiving about the same amount of immigrants, although "the preponderance of wealth and character," he felt, had come to Nebraska. Furthermore, the immigration into Kansas was divided among five land-grant roads, whereas in Nebraska it was divided between two. Of these, the B. & M. was receiving fully two-thirds, and Touzalin believed that "fully one-half of the Union Pacific settlement and land sales for the last year have been on lands lying south of the Platte, and all more or less tributary" to the Burlington. During the first six months of 1878, the B. & M. itself sold 201,654 acres of "inside lands" for $1,328,796, an average of over $6.58 an acre; nearly one-half of these sales were for cash or on short credit. Deducting discounts for improvements, the average figure still remained at $6.13 per acre, thus comparing well with approximately $4.90 obtained by the Union Pacific. Clearly, this was a favorable situation that might not be maintained if prices were raised, at least to any great extent. Furthermore, the company's relation to its South Platte lands was "two-fold, namely as land-owner and as carrier."

If 80 acres of land be taken as an illustration of your interests there [he reasoned], while it may be a fact that by holding that 80 acres for the next three years we can gain 50 cents per annum on the price [per acre] or $1.50 for the three years after deducting taxes, it should be remembered that that same 80 acres put into wheat would yield the road an average of $150 per annum on export and import freights. Hence that which is lost by immediate sale is more than counterbalanced by what we gain in the improvement and development of the land.[153]

Towards the "outside lands," on the other hand, the B. & M. was simply a land-owner. Sales in that region for the first half of 1878 amounted to 108,385 acres for $308,568, or an average of $2.84 per acre, and these included some 20,000 acres sold at an average of 50 cents.

This North Platte country [explained Touzalin] is an exceptional and peculiar one. It has a considerable amount of very poor lands — lands which

[152] BMN, Memorandum by Touzalin, September –, 1878 (LDP).   [153] Ibid.

we cannot expect to be used for agricultural purposes for ten or more years to come; and a good deal of land is scattered throughout this country which will never afford anything but poor grazing for stock. To put it in figures, there is today 300,000 acres of this North Platte land which we should dispose of as rapidly as possible; every dollar invested in taxes will be lost. . . . Leaving out the refuse tracts, we have received about as high a rate upon them as has been obtained by the Kansas Pacific and the Missouri, Kansas and Texas roads upon lands lying within the limits of their respective grants.

In summary, during the first six months of 1878, the B. & M. in Nebraska had sold 310,039 acres, both north and south of the Platte, at an average of $5.21 an acre, and this represented "but a portion of the vast tide of immigration which has poured into our country and is developing its agricultural, commercial and manufacturing interests." Therefore, as Touzalin finally concluded, it was "a great responsibility to take no action at this time towards putting up prices and adopting more conservative terms of sales, but it is perhaps a greater responsibility to make any radical change at this time which may turn away from us the present current of business." [154]

The result of this analysis, duly considered by the directors, was the adoption of a middle course. In 1879, improvement premiums were reduced, and cash discounts from the ten-year prices on six-year, three-year and cash sales were cut 15, 15, and 20 per cent, respectively, below the 1877–78 level. A similar development took place in the North Platte terms.[155] While prices rose gradually in Iowa, they declined to an all-time low average of $4.30 in Nebraska,[156] chiefly because a large sale of poor lands to the Adam Smith Land and Improvement Company north of the Platte brought the average return from "outside lands" down to $1.67 an acre. The next year, as times improved, discounts for the six- and three-year plans were cut another 5 per cent, and that for cash payment, 10 per cent.[157] Prices remained stabilized in Iowa; those in Nebraska recovered slightly to an average of $4.79.

Results for the last two years of the decade reflected both the im-

[154] Ibid.
[155] BMR, Circular to Land Agents, December 15, 1877 (LDP); Circular of North Platte Terms, 1878 (LDP); "Nebraska Statistics," 1879 (LDP).
[156] See graph, p. 415.
[157] BMR, "Nebraska Statistics," 1879 (LDP).

IOWA

		Acres	Value	Number of Sales	Average Price	Average Size of Plots
1878 —	Jan.	1,500.17	$ 21,980.83	23		
	Feb.	712.13	8,231.18	13		
	Mar.	1,250.32	18,766.11	18		
	Apr.	1,854.86	27,630.26	20		
	May	1,119.19	13,037.71	12		
	June	833.15	12,458.82	13		
	July	549.65	8,332.30	5		
	Aug.	200.00	2,000.00	5		
	Sept.	973.93	12,214.62	13		
	Oct.	249.20	2,462.80	5		
	Nov.	160.00	1,520.00	3		
	Dec.	305.03	3,464.36	4		
GROSS		9,707.63	$132,098.99	134	$13.61	72.45
Cancelled		8,409.07	113,014.24	101		
NET		1,298.56	$ 19,084.75	33		
1879 —	Jan.	516.92	$ 6,328.40	9		
	Feb.	1,390.02	19,313.44	22		
	Mar.	2,261.39	34,204.83	34		
	Apr.	1,321.93	20,458.45	16		
	May	2,111.16	30,662.51	26		
	June	1,924.70	26,740.38	21		
	July	1,921.59	29,066.44	21		
	Aug.	910.07	17,248.93	9		
	Sept.	2,769.70	39,796.01	33		
	Oct.	2,900.86	37,455.28	42		
	Nov.	2,593.77	37,917.16	35		
	Dec.	5,517.42	83,905.76	70		
GROSS		26,139.53	$383,097.59	338	$14.66	77.34
Cancelled		26,706.98	376,722.83	301		
NET		567.45 [d]	$ 6,374.76	37		
1880 —	Jan.	6,420.38	$ 95,875.43	81		
	Feb.	4,886.93	69,558.70	60		
	Mar.	5,467.46	78,751.38	73		
	Apr.	3,267.95	48,633.28	33		
	May	2,987.47	46,208.89	39		
	June	3,088.47	46,261.51	40		
	July	2,561.56	36,938.17	34		
	Aug.	4,680.03	67,236.38	65		
	Sept.	3,611.13	52,737.27	50		
	Oct.	4,464.41	61,812.43	64		
	Nov.	3,414.02	47,055.58	50		
	Dec.	7,840.95	121,623.45	109		
GROSS		52,690.76	$772,692.47	698	$14.66	75.49
Cancelled		74,480.55	968,780.81	971		
NET		21,789.79 [d]	$196,088.34 [d]	273 [d]		

[d] Deficit.

NEBRASKA

		Acres	Value	Number of Sales	Average Price	Average Size of Plots
1878 —	Jan.	32,350.10	$ 161,365.59	231		
	Feb.	43,375.44	226,933.58	337		
	Mar.	54,969.20	320,467.78	434		
	Apr.	65,356.75	339,931.37	544		
	May	61,861.10	329,739.74	527		
	June	52,617.87	263,572.53	409		
	July	39,617.62	184,011.11	294		
	Aug.	36,749.43	174,561.64	269		
	Sept.	38,707.46	194,732.83	284		
	Oct.	35,084.55	180,720.72	255		
	Nov.	29,916.35	144,274.68	213		
	Dec.	21,502.25	100,213.33	159		
GROSS		512,108.12	$2,620,524.90	3956	$5.12	129.45
Cancelled		128,850.03	913,060.76	1064		
NET		383,258.09	$1,707,464.14	2892		
1879 —	Jan.	20,391.63	$ 88,025.20	126		
	Feb.	11,465.03	70,429.12	111		
	Mar.	24,156.41	154,289.74	215		
	Apr.	18,795.31	109,019.71	163		
	May	22,360.65	134,476.00	209		
	June	24,326.84	123,779.36	197		
	July	17,628.41	81,762.35	146		
	Aug.	16,651.02	83,733.37	146		
	Sept.	39,252.38	160,625.25	236		
	Oct.	39,103.33	175,553.32	299		
	Nov.	43,166.15	179,518.46	259		
	Dec.	92,134.74	226,299.81	278		
GROSS		369,431.90	$1,587,511.69	2385	$4.30	154.90
Cancelled		87,263.08	701,506.49	740		
NET		282,168.82	$ 886,005.20	1645		
1880 —	Jan.	30,946.55	$ 160,494.35	243		
	Feb.	57,101.72	187,301.44	221		
	Mar.	31,076.36	185,875.75	275		
	Apr.	35,400.18	166,903.77	229		
	May	19,605.70	105,362.37	145		
	June	16,474.53	88,849.95	131		
	July	9,435.92	44,253.55	74		
	Aug.	15,001.65	61,367.21	82		
	Sept.	14,115.66	78,881.59	103		
	Oct.	13,953.25	91,702.90	98		
	Nov.	17,486.32	63,876.34	86		
	Dec.	9,432.23	57,757.38	83		
GROSS		270,030.07	$1,292,626.60	1770	$4.79	152.56
Cancelled		35,839.01	225,116.51	259		
NET		234,191.06	$1,067,510.09	1511		

provement in national conditions and the influence of local factors. Following four years of steady decline, gross sales in Iowa turned sharply upward in 1879 and continued to rise the next year as the new wave of immigration across the Mississippi grew in proportion.[158] Cancellations, however, indicative of an equally large movement out of the state, rose so fast that they exceeded sales in 1879 by 567.45 acres and in 1880 by 21,789.79 acres, although much of this last deficit was a result of writing off "suspended" sales that should have been canceled previously.[159] In Nebraska, gross sales, cancellations, and net sales all dropped gradually; the net for 1879 was 282,168.82 acres and for 1880, 234,191.06 acres.[160] These figures, however, did not imply an unhealthy state of affairs. By the end of 1880, just short of 2,000,000 acres or approximately four-fifths of the B. & M.'s grant had been sold; available lands, particularly the most desirable ones, were becoming scarce. In both Iowa and Nebraska, the trend of the Burlington's gross sales paralleled almost exactly the course of Rock Island and Union Pacific transactions, respectively.[161]

Throughout these years, the earlier policy towards delinquents was continued by both companies.[162] Particularly in Nebraska, such persons were encouraged to make new contracts for a portion of their holdings. This constituted a better arrangement for the company, since it released certain tracts for resale and gave the purchaser a contract he could fulfill.[163]

During the closing years of the decade, no record was kept of the origin of purchasers. The average amounts of land bought, however, were noted; these reflected the different circumstances in the two states. In Iowa, as throughout the decade, tracts averaged between 75 and 80 acres each. In Nebraska the generally larger farms sold north of the Platte raised the average of 125 acres for the middle years to over 150 acres for 1879 and 1880.[164]

---

[158] See tables, pp. 436–437.
[159] BMI, Sales Book "B," MS notation (LDP).
[160] See tables, pp. 436–437.
[161] See graphs, p. 415.
[162] The CB&Q *Annual Report* for 1878 noted that "the policy of considerate dealing with settlers and improvers has been continued. . . ." (Pp. 40–41.)
[163] CBQ, *Annual Report* for 1878 (Chicago, 1879), pp. 40–41; BMN, *Annual Report* for 1877 (MS), pp. 24–26.
[164] See tables, pp. 450–451.

Advertising throughout the period 1874–80 proceeded along the same lines laid down earlier in the decade although some changes were made as the result of the experience of the preceding years. Newspaper advertising continued although the insertions were short and merely told how further information could be obtained.[165] One color-

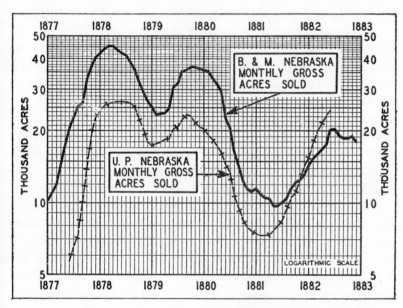

GROSS ACRES SOLD BY B. & M. AND UNION PACIFIC IN NEBRASKA, MONTHLY, 1877–1882, WITH SEASONAL MOVEMENT ELIMINATED.

(For underlying statistics see Table 7 in Appendix F)

ful innovation of 1874 was the offer to certain newspaper editors of a trip over the line for themselves and one friend or member of their families in exchange for publishing an occasional article of general interest to Iowa and Nebraska. So popular did this practice become that in 1875 the railroad printed a form letter repeating the offer.[166]

The principal medium for the company's major advertising, however,

[165] In Ohio, for example, advertisements appeared in papers during February, 1874, in Akron, Cambridge, Canton, Cleveland, Hillsboro, Marietta, Marion, Millersburg, Napoleon, New Philadelphia, St. Clairsville, and Toledo. (LDP.)

[166] BMR, Letter to Editors, January 1, 1875 (LDP).

was the circular which became increasingly elaborate and was illustrated with colored plates.[167] Another striking innovation was the conversion of the hitherto irregular news sheet into a regular monthly publication. It appeared through 1875 and 1876 and, in the latter year, bore the title "Iowa and Nebraska Farmer" in an elaborate masthead.[168] Annual editions appeared in German, Swedish, Norwegian, and Bohemian.[169] In the opening paragraph, the reader was informed that the paper contained "no delusive pictures of paradisiacal farms, nor twisted maps of the United States, but simply leading *facts* in reference to the Land Grants." Essentially the same information was contained as in the earlier sheets, although emphasis was placed on the fact that there was no more good land to be opened in the United States. In 1877 the information carried in the "Farmer" was incorporated into pamphlet form, thus following a practice inaugurated by the Illinois Central, copied by the Hannibal and St. Joseph, and finally bequeathed through Commissioner Harris to the Burlington and Missouri River roads.[170] The bright covers of these pamphlets bore ornate lettering and illustrations depicting a prairie homestead, or, in successive pictures, the evolution of a bleak wilderness to a well-tilled farm. Inside the covers were complete and generally accurate maps of the Iowa and Nebraska grants.[171] The subject matter was similar to that carried in the earlier news sheets and the "Farmer," although there were more testimonials and more complete statistics of crop yields.[172]

---

[167] BMR, Circular of Prices, 1876 (LDP); Handbill of Prices, January 1, 1877 (LDP). Between March 16 and April 22, 1874, circulars were distributed outside of Iowa and Nebraska as follows: Arkansas, 2; Canada, 5; Colorado, 1; Connecticut, 2; Dakota, 1; District of Columbia, 1; Georgia, 1; Illinois, 16; Indiana, 1; Kansas, 1; Kentucky, 1; Maryland, 2; Massachusetts, 6; Michigan, 2; Minnesota, 2; Missouri, 4; Nevada, 1; New York, 7; Ohio, 7; Pennsylvania, 16; Tennessee, 2; Utah, 1; Vermont, 2; West Virginia, 1; Wisconsin, 10.

[168] The Burlington scrapbooks in the Harvard Business School Library (see Bibliography) have every number for 1875 and 1876 except those of August, November, and December, 1875, and of May and December, 1876. It is probable, but not certain, that publication was suspended sometime during the year 1877.

[169] BMR, "Iowa and Nebraska Farmer" (LDP).

[170] Gates, *op. cit.*, ch. x.

[171] The North Platte pamphlets (see fn. 172, below) contained 9x6 inch sectional maps of nine of the northern counties.

[172] The first pamphlet was probably the one issued in February, 1877, entitled "One Million Acres Farming Lands . . . in Iowa and Nebraska" (LDP). This covered both Iowa and the South Platte lands, and was reproduced in German,

Maps were issued with increasing frequency, and after 1875, they appeared for the separate counties of Iowa and Nebraska; company lands still unsold were shaded or marked in red.[173]

As before, the B. & M. relied heavily on "unofficial spokesmen," [174] excursions from various parts of the country,[175] and crop samples to publicize its territory.[176] On July 22, 1875, the *Beatrice Express* noted that one of the company's agents was collecting "agricultural, horticultural, pomological, mineral, botanical, geological, etc." samples of Nebraska products for expositions at Chicago and Cincinnati.[177] The next year, the B. & M. offered to transport free of charge all articles sent from Nebraska for display at the Centennial in Philadelphia.[178] A month later, the *Burlington Weekly Hawk-Eye* observed that the Nebraska state exhibit at the Centennial was largely sustained by the state's railroads, "especially by the B. & M. in Nebraska, which corporation has also wrought no slight work for Iowa." [179] Again at the Nebraska State Fair in the fall of 1880, the Burlington land department was reported to have "an unique and highly attractive display of grains, grasses, timber, vegetables, and various other products." [180]

Swedish, and Danish. A series with slightly varying titles appeared in 1877, 1878, and 1879. Special editions with comparable material appeared for the North Platte region in 1877 and 1878. A pamphlet entitled "Nebraska: Statistics compiled from State Papers," came out in 1879, and combined all information for both North and South Platte regions. (LDP.)

[173] Large wall maps for the various counties of western Iowa were issued throughout the late 'seventies (HBS). The first of the Nebraska county maps appeared in May, 1875, for Lancaster County. There are eleven other varieties in the scrapbooks, some in duplicate, issued for the most part in 1877. A particularly accurate map for all Nebraska was engraved by G. W. and C. B. Colton of New York in 1877. See opposite p. 332.

[174] In 1876 the western editor of a Chicago paper was escorted on an extensive trip over the company's territory, and on his return to Chicago, he issued a long description of the area, and highly praised the company. (*Chicago Commercial Advertiser*, November 23, 1876, LDP.)

[175] BMR, Flier, May, 1875 (LDP); same, June, 1875 (LDP). By 1877 the company was advertising land exploring tickets as better than excursions. They also cost the company a great deal less. (LDP.)

[176] BMR, Slip requesting samples, 1874 (LDP); Letters to Agents, 1874 (LDP).

[177] *Beatrice Express*, July 22, 1875.

[178] *Ibid.*, June 8, 1876.

[179] *Burlington Weekly Hawk-Eye*, July 13, 1876.

[180] *Omaha Daily Herald*, September 21, 1880.

Of more lasting benefit was the continued care and replacement of the 560,000 trees set out between Lincoln and Lowell in 1872 and 1873. These were proving valuable not only as snow breaks but also as an indication of what trees would grow best on the Nebraska plains.[181]

One special advertising effort was directed towards a group of Russian Mennonites which the company heard was bound for the Province of Manitoba. A circular was hastily addressed to these people, describing their avowed destination as a sub-arctic wilderness and contrasting it unfavorably with the fertile paradise of Nebraska.[182] A year later, a Kansas paper reminded the pacifist Mennonites that in Nebraska they would be subject to state military conscription, but within 29 days a B. & M. circular was in the mails declaring that the Nebraska laws had been amended in the interim so as to exclude conscientious objectors who were members of pacifist religious groups.[183]

Meanwhile, the land department's activities continued in the field of public relations and community development. On February 1, 1874, all those who were interested in promoting German immigration into Nebraska met in Governor Furnas' office and organized themselves into a society which promptly issued an eight-page pamphlet, extolling the virtues of the state and explaining the role of the Germans therein. Whether or not the railroad instigated the formation of this society, one entire page of the pamphlet editorially explained the policy and terms offered by the B. & M.; there was no other advertising, direct or indirect, in the publication.[184] Of more lasting importance was the company's introduction of alfalfa seed into the state for commercial uses, and its free distribution for experiment.[185] Governor Furnas complimented the road on this achievement and urged the commissioner

---

[181] BMN, *Annual Report* for 1875 (MS), p. 13. The figure given in this MS source is 460,000, but earlier itemized records indicate that this total should read 560,000.

[182] BMR, Circular to Mennonites, 1876 (LDP). The company coöperated with established counties in forwarding testimonials to relatives in the mother countries. See esp. "Circular Letter from Clay County Russo-Germans," February, 1874 (LDP), and the more elaborate circular "Das Südliche Nebraska," January, 1877 (LDP).

[183] BMR, Circular to Mennonites, February 14, 1877 (LDP).

[184] Anon., "Kurze Beschreibung von Nebraska. . . ." (Omaha? 1874), p. 7.

[185] "California Alfalfa for Nebraska: Distribution of Seed by the Land Department" in unidentified newspaper, 1875 (LDP).

Das südliche Nebraska.

Zeugniß von Prof. Aughey.

Universität von Nebraska.
Naturwissenschaftliche Abtheilung.

Lincoln, Nebraska, den 21ſten Januar 1877.

Mein werther Herr!

Ihrem Wunſche gemäß will ich Ihnen kurz die Thatſachen über Boden und Klima von Nebraska mittheilen.

Drei-Viertheile des Staates ſind von einer loſen Erdlage bedeckt, welche auf vielen Stellen bis 200 Fuß Tiefe hat. Südlich vom Platte-Fluſſe iſt dieſe Erdlage hauptſächlich entwickelt in den Counties von Saline, Fillmore, Clay, Adams, Franklin, Webſter, Nuckolls, Thayer, Jefferſon und York. Dieſe, von vielen amerikaniſchen Geologen „Lacruſtine" bezeichnete Erdlage bildet einen der reichhaltigſten Boden der Welt, und iſt unter anderem merkwürdig wegen ſeiner Gleichförmigkeit und wegen ſeiner gleichviel erzeugenden Fruchtbarkeit, ob vom obern oder untern Theile der Schicht genommen. Der obere Theil der Schicht, für 2 bis 10 Fuß, iſt gewöhnlich ſo mit organiſchen Subſtanzen geſättigt, daß derſelbe dadurch eine dunkle oder ſchwarze Farbe erhält. In dieſem Boden ſind enthalten etwa 10 Prozent Kohlenſäure und Phosphorſäure, beinahe 4 Prozent Eiſenoxid und eine bedeutende Quantität Kieſelerde. Die letztere iſt ſo zerpulvert, daß die einzelnen Theile blos mit dem Mikroskop deutlich zu unterſcheiden ſind. Wegen der Bereitwilligkeit, mit welcher dieſe Erde im cultivirten Zuſtande Feuchtigkeit einzieht, und der bedeutenden Tiefe der Schicht, widerſteht dieſelbe großer Dürre zu einem merkwürdigen Grade. In trockenen Jahreszeiten ſteigt die Feuchtigkeit fortwährend von unten herauf, wie aus einem großen Schwamme. Bei heftigen Regen wird die Feuchtigkeit ſchnell eingezogen. Für die verſchiedenen Getreide und Gräſer, Wurzelgewächſe und Früchte iſt der Boden einer der beſten in der Welt. In Fruchtbarkeit iſt er beinahe unerſchöpflich.

Das Klima von Nebraska iſt in manchen Beziehungen eigenthümlich. Die Luft iſt gewöhnlich trocken, manchmal ſteigt der Thermometer hoch im Sommer und eine beinahe halb-tropiſche Hitze beſteht; doch gewöhnlich erhebt ſich ein kühlendes Lüftchen im Laufe des Tages, wodurch die Hitze gemäßigt wird. In der letzten Hälfte des Monat Mai und im Anfange des Juni giebt es eine Regenzeit von 2 bis 4 Wochen. Da alsdann das Welſchkorn ſchon aufgegangen und die Getreide einen guten Vorſprung haben, wird der Boden genügend durchweicht, ſo daß anhaltende ſtarke Regen nicht nöthig ſind im übrigen Theil des Sommers. Die Herbſte ſind ſprüchwörtlich warm und prachtvoll. Der Winter oft nimmt erſt ſeinen wirklichen Anfang im Januar, jedoch giebt es dann zuweilen heftige Stürme und ſehr kalte Tage. Wegen der trockenen Luft iſt jedoch bedeutende Kälte weniger hart, als unter demſelben Breitengrade weiter öſtlich. Regen im Winter iſt ſehr ſelten, die Näſſe aus der Luft fällt in der Form von Schnee, und ſelten überſteigt der Schneefall des ganzen Winters 6 bis 12 Zoll. Wegen dieſen Eigenthümlichkeiten iſt Nebraska ein ungewöhnlich geſunder Staat. Ihr ergebenſter Samuel Aughey,

Profeſſor der Naturwiſſenſchaften an der Univerſität von Nebraska.

DESCRIPTION OF NEBRASKA SOIL AND CLIMATE IN A GERMAN PAMPHLET ADVERTISING B. & M. LANDS, 1877.

to double his efforts during the following season of 1875.[186] In 1927, alfalfa was Nebraska's leading hay crop in tonnage produced.[187]

The drought and grasshopper plagues of 1874 not only placed a grave responsibility on the railroad, particularly in Nebraska, but also gave it an opportunity to prove tangibly its interest in the community. At the end of that year, the *Burlington Weekly Hawk-Eye* roundly criticized the granges for not helping their starving members west of the Missouri River. It pointed out that the "grasping monopolies . . . , pitiless and avaricious combinations," which had been so "vigorously and unsparingly denounced" by the national grange, had proved far more generous than that organization. Noting that both the B. & M. and Union Pacific in Nebraska had donated $5,000 each for relief, the paper inquired whether the railroads must "take care of their enemies' wounded." [188] Probably the most effective aid offered by the railroad, however, came as a result of Perkins' efforts. In the late summer of 1874, his plan for the Nebraska Relief and Aid Society was approved by Governor Furnas of Nebraska.[189] Among its members were General E. O. C. Ord, E. B. Chandler, Judge Wakeley, Alvin Saunders, and other responsible citizens. The actual organization was undertaken by the *Nebraska City Conservative*, and during its career it distributed more than $250,000 in goods and cash among stricken settlers. "Without that aid," J. Sterling Morton later wrote, "families might have perished, farms been abandoned and the state reverted in part to wilderness. Not one of the Nebraskans who has a recollection of those terrible years and the trials and hardships then entailed can fail to recall the great and generous farsightedness and the judicious management of Mr. Perkins at that time. Under his orders all commodities for the sufferers were carried gratuitously over the B. & M. . . ." [190]

The railroad's policy was carried a step further when Irving, superintendent of the B. & M. in Nebraska, issued an illuminating circular to the public on November 25, 1875. The crop failure of the previous year, he said, had caused most of the stock cattle and hogs

---

[186] Governor Furnas to the B. & M. land commissioner, May 4, 1875 (LDP).

[187] Harold Hedges and F. F. Elliot, "Types of Farming in Nebraska," University of Nebraska, College of Agriculture, *Bulletin No. 244* (Lincoln, 1930), p. 11.

[188] *Burlington Weekly Hawk-Eye*, November 5, 1874.

[189] CNB, ch. x, p. 37.

[190] CNB, n.p.

in the region to be driven out. This, he explained, together with the fact that the many newcomers in the country were without facilities as yet for raising livestock, would deprive the producers of the abundant 1875 corn crop of their best market. Therefore, "desirous of aiding the farmers along its line of road in marketing their corn crop, at remunerative prices, and believing that its prosperity depends on that of the country through which it passes," Irving announced that the B. & M. and the C. B. & Q. would reduce their rates on corn for the first five months of 1876 to a figure little if any above the actual cost of transportation. "The company is led to believe and hopes," concluded the superintendent candidly, "that this measure may enable the farmers to dispose of their crop readily, and that by thus promoting their welfare, it may result in an increased business for the Road in the future." [191] Five years later when another crop failure threatened the farmers in the same state, Perkins was authorized by the directors "if in his judgment it is desirable, to contribute pecuniary assistance to the people in western Nebraska to an amount not exceeding $10,000." [192]

While these activities of the land department were taking place in Iowa and Nebraska, the company's agents in the northeastern United States and Europe were continuing their proselyting. During 1875 and until March, 1876, the domestic agencies steadily grew in number until there were 292 of them, mostly in the states of the old Northwest Territory. During the summer of 1876, however, there was a drastic cut in this number, and by May, 1877, only 32 agents were listed in the "Farmer." [193] From the fragmentary records available, it is probable that foreign advertising continued along the lines marked out by Schaller earlier in the decade but on a more modest scale.[194] In the *Annual Report* of 1875, it was noted that the English agency "which has been a bill of expense and of small value comparatively" had been finally closed out, and the account settled.[195]

The annual expenses of the B. & M. in Nebraska for advertising,

[191] BMN, Circular, November 25, 1875.

[192] CBQ DRB, p. 663.

[193] BMR, "Iowa and Nebraska Farmer" for 1875, 1876, 1877 (LDP), *passim*.

[194] The exact nature and extent of the foreign advertising can be determined only after further investigation in the correspondence of the B. & M. land department records.

[195] BMN, *Annual Report* for 1875 (MS), p. 21.

commissions, and agencies faithfully reflected the activities of the years 1874–80.

Year	Advertising	Local Commissions	Eastern U. S. Agencies
1874[a]	$42,256.42	$44,330.28	[h]
1875[b]	12,190.82	14,356.16	$ 4,523.38
1876[c]	14,971.45	15,986.92	9,465.25
1877[d]	13,398.48	28,027.61	15,023.39
1878[e]	29,156.70	83,165.47	22,000.00
1879[f]	21,806.98	47,674.12	14,590.63
1880[g]	14,851.70	34,661.88	9,784.72

[a] BMN, *Annual Report* for 1874 (MS), p. 24.
[b] BMN, *Annual Report* for 1875 (MS), p. 41.
[c] BMN, *Annual Report* for 1876 (MS), p. 50.
[d] BMN, *Annual Report* for 1877 (MS), p. 41.
[e] BMN, *Annual Report* for 1878 (MS), p. 40.
[f] BMN, *Annual Report* for 1879 (MS), p. 26.
[g] BMN, *Annual Report* for 1880 (MS), p. 30.
[h] Not separately given.

The sharp drop from 1874 to 1875 was particularly significant as was the slow recovery to a peak in 1878. The gradual decline in expenses thereafter reflected the progressive exhaustion of available lands.

For Iowa no separate account was kept of strictly advertising expenses. Total annual costs of selling the lands were recorded, however. These included salaries and office expenses, commissions, fees for land examinations, swampland expenses, advertising, and agencies. As in the case of land sales, expenses reached their lowest levels in 1877 and 1878 and increased in the two following years.

Year	Expenses
1874[a]	$49,952.53
1875[b]	35,665.12
1876[c]	37,089.88
1877[d]	10,848.09
1878[e]	12,970.59
1879[f]	23,953.07
1880[g]	39,411.07

[a] CBQ, *Annual Report* for 1875, p. 68.
[b] CBQ, *Annual Report* for 1875, p. 68.
[c] CBQ, *Annual Report* for 1876, p. 51.
[d] CBQ, *Annual Report* for 1877, p. 50.
[e] CBQ, *Annual Report* for 1878, p. 40.
[f] CBQ, *Annual Report* for 1879, p. 40.
[g] CBQ, *Annual Report* for 1880, p. 30.

III. THE DECADE IN RETROSPECT

Throughout the decade, the price and credit policies of the B. & M. seem to have been dictated by a form of enlightened self-interest. When times were good, the land department asked prices it could easily obtain in an active market, yet there is no evidence that lands were withheld in order to obtain unusually high returns. As the years of depression came on in weary succession, the company shared the common burden of the community for its own future was inextricably bound up with that of its neighbors. Prices and credit facilities were continually adjusted so as to bring land within the reach of the average immigrant, while farmers already settled who could not meet their obligations were treated with considerable patience and forbearance.

In its advertising, the company appears to have acted with vigor and ingenuity. Many of its policies were indeed inherited, or at best initiated in a day of multiple inventions, but the special appeals directed to specific groups, the emigrant houses, and the ingenious schemes of Harris, Butler, and Schaller for commanding public attention showed skill and imagination.

James Samuelson, in his *Useful Information for Intending Emigrants* published at London in 1879, attacked all railroad advertising in general, declaring that crop yields were outrageously exaggerated and that isolated cases of exceptionally good results were described as typical of a whole area.[196] To some extent his criticism applied to the Burlington. The "Iowa and Nebraska Farmer" for September, 1876, reported in an individual testimonial a corn yield of 70 bushels an acre,[197] whereas for 1877 a company pamphlet declared that the average yield in nine counties ranged from 45 to 55 bushels.[198] Whereas this may have been true for these years and for these particular areas, the average Nebraska yield in 1880 when the state stood second in the Union was but 40.1 bushels per acre.[199] These testimonials, of course, appeared under the caption "What Others Can Do You Can Do," and technically this was correct, although liable to misconstruction. On the other hand, an adjoining column carried the warning that "coming west and growing up with the country is no child's play, and the man who seeks to get rich without effort had better stay home."[200] Indeed both Ames and Harris, throughout their tenures of office, often sought to head off unemployed immigrants and consistently advised people not to come unless they had enough capital to get started.[201] Throughout its colonization work, the B. & M. insisted on applying a rigid standard to the persons to whom it sold lands. Speculators, inexperienced farmers, and indigent persons were

[196] James Samuelson, *Useful Information for Intending Emigrants* (London, 1879), p. 25.
[197] BMR, "Iowa and Nebraska Farmer," September, 1876 (LDP).
[198] BMR, Pamphlet of 1878 (LDP), pp. 7–8.
[199] Hewes and Gannett, *op. cit.*, p. 98.
[200] BMR, "Iowa and Nebraska Farmer," September, 1876 (LDP).
[201] See above, pp. 270, 348–349.

not wanted, and the railroad did not hesitate to say so, even when times were hard and sales falling.[202] In summary, the B. & M. seemed to be presenting in its public statements the maximum that could be expected. At the same time, it was made clear that the rewards were only for those who earned them.

In the matter of climate, the road did not risk overstatement. In an article written about the Great Plains, W. B. Hazen of the United States Army stated that

beginning at Omaha, we find for the first two hundred miles, or to Fort Kearney, one of the most beautiful portions of the continent. The Platte and Elkhorn valleys cannot be surpassed in richness by any soil in the world. . . . There is a small quantity of timber, a good rainfall; there has never been a failure of small grains . . . in the twelve years I have known this country.[203]

The region he thus described adjoined the Burlington's territory.

Finally, the management of the land department was particularly shrewd in recognizing that personal contact, public relations, and community welfare work were all part and parcel of successful colonizing. The friendly nod, the ready handshake, and the free meal were all familiar parts of Harris' and Touzalin's equipment. These differed only in degree from the encouragement of agriculture or the founding of a college, for all of them contributed to an atmosphere in which the company could thrive.

The result of these various policies is revealed by the statistics of lands sold in Iowa and Nebraska during the 'seventies. In the older state, from April 1, 1870, to April 1, 1880, the company disposed of 309,949.76 acres net,[204] more than 85 per cent of its granted lands. Its gross sales (net sales plus resales of land that had reverted to the company through cancellations of contracts) totalled 438,881.28 acres at an average price of $12.61. Over the same period the Rock Island made gross sales of 327,984.50 acres at an average price of $8.19.[205] Mean-

[202] BMR, "Iowa and Nebraska Farmer," September, 1876 (LDP), passim.
[203] W. B. Hazen, "The Great Middle Region of the United States and its Limited Space of Arable Lands," North American Review, no. CCXLVI (January, 1875), p. 9.
[204] This figure does not include the 10,728.91 acres sold in 1863–69, inclusive. For all Burlington figures in this paragraph, see table on pp. 450–451 unless otherwise noted.
[205] Chicago, Rock Island & Pacific Railway Company Annual Reports for 1871–72. et seq. (Chicago).

while, the B. & M. in Nebraska sold 1,833,396.58 net acres, representing more than 75 per cent of the company's lands in that state, for an average price of $5.47.[206] Despite its earlier start in 1869 the Union Pacific did not equal this record. By the end of 1880 it had disposed of 1,711,922.07 net acres for an average figure of $4.46,[207] whereas the

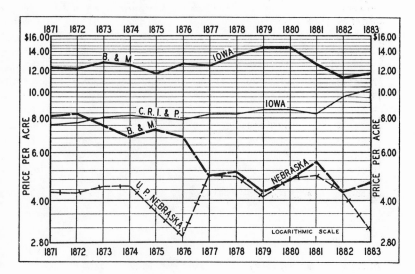

AVERAGE PRICE PER ACRE OF LAND RECEIVED BY THE B. & M. AND BY THE ROCK ISLAND IN IOWA, AND BY THE B. & M. AND BY THE UNION PACIFIC IN NEBRASKA, ANNUALLY, 1871–1883.

(For underlying statistics see Tables 3, 4, and 5 in Appendix F)

Santa Fe, which had replaced the Kansas Pacific as the chief southern competitor, sold 1,016,431 net acres at an average of $5.61 per acre.[208] In both states the B. & M. had received more for its lands than its nearest rivals, and the Nebraska company had outstripped two formidable competitors in the quantity sold.[209] To achieve this result, the

[206] In 1874, 57,446.68 acres were conveyed to William T. Steiger of Washington, D. C., in payment for legal services rendered. (BMN, Final Balance Sheet, January 18, 1906, LDP.)

[207] *Poor's Manual for 1872–73, 1873–74, 1874–75;* thereafter Union Pacific Railroad Company *Annual Reports* (New York).

[208] Atchison, Topeka and Santa Fe Railroad Company *Annual Report* for 1881, p. 39 (Boston, 1882).

[209] From available records it is impossible to tell whether or not part of the 19,004.48 acres received by the Omaha and South Western was included in these

IOWA

	Gross Acres Sold	Gross Value	No. Sales	Avg. Price per Acre	Avg. Size of Plots	Acres Cancelled
1870 *	108,747.25	$ 1,336,177.22	1,154	$12.29	94.24	680.00
1871	41,580.53	512,923.90	510	12.34	81.53	757.08
1872	28,744.55	352,817.75	380	12.27	75.64	5,120.93
1873	31,462.75‡	402,916.48	418	12.81	75.27	11,334.49
1874	73,232.84	926,380.76	957	12.65	76.52	19,506.15
1875	57,041.05	667,131.37	865	11.70	65.94	14,437.82
1876	31,701.69	405,209.22	436	12.78	72.71	16,126.24
1877	13,748.69	170,964.69	198	19.64	69.44	10,182.91
1878	9,707.63	132,098.99	134	13.61	72.45	8,409.07
1879	26,139.53	383,097.59	338	14.66	77.34	26,706.98
1880 †	16,774.77	244,185.51	214	14.56	75.49	15,669.85
TOTAL	438,881.28	$ 5,533,903.48	5,604	$12.61	78.32	128,931.52

NEBRASKA

	Gross Acres Sold	Gross Value	No. Sales	Avg. Price per Acre	Avg. Size of Plots	Acres Cancelled
1870 *	61,623.25	$ 577,281.63	436	$9.37	141.34	240.00
1871	120,757.24	989,092.38	871	8.19	138.64	1,791.13
1872	120,928.14	1,009,131.51	1,019	8.34	118.67	6,652.38
1873	276,704.42	2,100,020.15	2,231	7.59	124.03	29,389.09
1874	394,261.45	2,686,129.18	3,139	6.81	125.60	64,515.45
1875	92,251.58	672,918.41	761	7.29	121.22	38,275.44
1876	76,816.90	526,947.22	638	6.86	120.40	71,388.98
1877	246,738.36	1,211,625.95	1,815	4.91	135.94	113,511.23
1878	512,108.12	2,620,524.90	3,956	5.12	129.45	128,850.03
1879	369,431.90	1,587,511.69	2,385	4.30	154.90	87,263.08
1880 †	119,124.63	533,671.54	739	4.48	161.19	15,472.60
TOTAL	2,390,745.99	$14,514,854.56	17,990	$6.07	132.95	557,349.41

* From April 1.
† Up to April 1.
‡ Includes 23/100 acre erroneously deducted re sale #278.

IOWA

Net Acres Sold	Cumulative Net Acres Sold	Value of Sales Cancelled	Value of Net Sales	Cumulative Value of Net Sales	Cumulative Avg. Price per Acre
108,067.25	118,796.16	$ 7,516.80	$ 1,328,660.42	$ 1,369,172.21	$11.53
40,823.45	159,619.61	7,898.80	505,025.10	1,874,197.31	11.74
23,623.62	183,243.23	66,328.49	286,489.26	2,160,686.57	11.79
20,128.26	203,371.49	140,624.67	262,291.81	2,424,073.58	11.92
53,726.69	257,098.18	249,720.20	676,660.56	3,099,638.94	12.06
42,603.23	299,701.41	179,644.14	487,487.23	3,587,126.17	11.97
15,575.45	315,276.86	205,587.31	199,621.91	3,786,748.08	12.01
3,565.78	318,842.64	129,585.41	41,379.28	3,828,127.36	12.01
1,298.56	320,141.20	113,014.24	19,084.75	3,847,212.11	12.02
567.45[d]	319,573.75	376,722.83	6,374.76	3,853,586.87	12.06
1,104.92	320,678.67	216,060.28	28,125.23	3,881,712.10	12.10
309,949.76		$1,692,703.17	$ 3,841,200.31		

NEBRASKA

Net Acres Sold	Cumulative Net Acres Sold	Value of Sales Cancelled	Value of Net Sales	Cumulative Value of Net Sales	Cumulative Avg. Price per Acre
61,383.25	61,383.25	$ 1,760.00	$ 575,521.63	$ 575,521.63	$ 9.37
118,966.11	180,349.36	17,977.91	971,114.47	1,546,636.10	8.58
114,275.76	294,625.12	73,219.85	935,911.66	2,482,547.76	8.43
247,315.33	541,940.45	257,808.92	1,842,211.23	4,185,818.11	7.94
329,746.00	871,686.45	552,316.54	2,133,812.64	6,319,630.75	7.37
53,976.14	925,662.59	344,103.88	328,814.53	6,648,445.28	7.30
5,427.92	931,090.51	525,398.45	1,548.77	6,649,994.05	7.26
133,227.13	1,064,317.64	866,228.51	345,397.44	6,995,391.49	6.66
383,258.09	1,447,575.73	913,060.76	1,707,464.14	8,702,855.63	6.07
282,168.82	1,729,644.55	701,506.49	886,005.20	9,588,860.83	5.59
103,652.03	1,833,396.58	99,477.21	434,191.33	10,023,052.16	5.47
,833,396.58		$4,352,858.52	$10,161,933.04		

[d] Deficit.

B. & M. spent in Iowa from April 1, 1870, to the end of 1880, $403,039.39. This included the land department salaries, commissions, land appraisals, advertising, and agency costs. Over the same period, the company paid $228,341.89 in taxes.[210] During these years, the B. & M. in Nebraska incurred expenses of $1,835,575.63 and paid taxes of $927,-151.39. Included in the expenses was an item of $318,070.30 for premiums allowed to purchasers on account of permanent improvements on their property.[211]

This showing was indeed creditable as a business transaction, yet an even deeper significance attached to those results of colonization which not only redounded to the company's benefit but contributed to the neighborhood as well. The railroad could not, of course, be credited with every kind of development that took place in southern Iowa or southeastern Nebraska, for much of it was brought about by the general westward movement of the times and the federal land policies, and some was produced by other railroads and colonizing agencies. Nevertheless, a comparison and contrast of the development that took place in Burlington territory with that in other neighboring areas gives evidence that the B. & M. played a vital if not dominant role in the growth of southern Iowa and Nebraska.

By grouping together those counties on or near the two B. & M. lines, the Rock Island, and the Union Pacific, respectively, it is possible to construct four zones of comparable area, topography, and accessibility for which the *Census* provides statistics of population, improved acreage, and area in farms. These zones may then be compared in these respects with each other and the entire state in which they lie. They may also be contrasted with a zone of Mississippi River counties where settlement long preceded that in the railroad areas, and with three zones where development came largely after 1880, namely, the northwestern portion of Iowa, the North Platte granted area of the B. & M. in Nebraska, and certain southwestern counties of Nebraska.[212]

---

figures. It is probable that it was not. Eventually these acres were sold for $65,545.18. See below, p. 477.

[210] These figures are compiled from the separate sources listed as authority for table on p. 446.

[211] BMN, Journal "F" (LDP), pp. 233–234.

[212] The location of these zones is shown on the map opposite. Statistics regarding these zones used in the text or as a basis for the graphs on the following pages will be found in Appendix F, below.

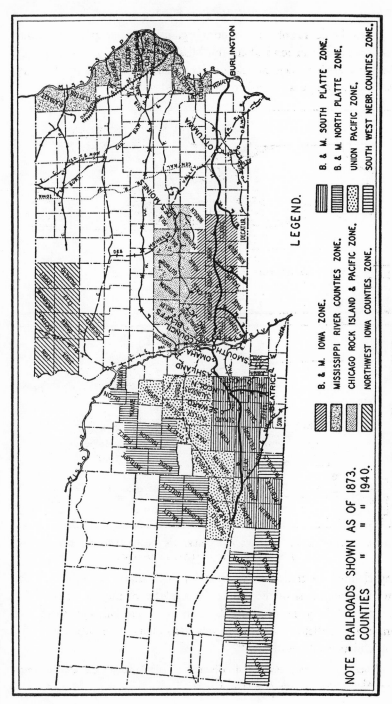

LEGEND.

	B. & M. IOWA ZONE.		B. & M. SOUTH PLATTE ZONE.
	MISSISSIPPI RIVER COUNTIES ZONE.		B. & M. NORTH PLATTE ZONE.
	CHICAGO ROCK ISLAND & PACIFIC ZONE.		UNION PACIFIC ZONE.
	NORTHWEST IOWA COUNTIES ZONE.		SOUTH WEST NEBR. COUNTIES ZONE.

NOTE – RAILROADS SHOWN AS OF 1873.
COUNTIES " " 1940.

LOCATION OF ZONES USED FOR STATISTICAL COMPARISON.

When the decade of the 'seventies began, there were 45 to 90 persons
per square mile in Iowa along the Mississippi in the southern half of
the state. As had been the case on the Atlantic seaboard a half century
earlier, two tongues of settlement stretched westward along the exist-

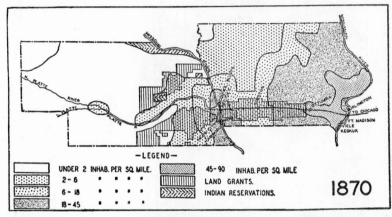

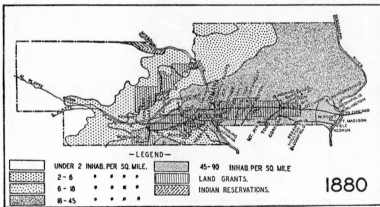

TREND OF POPULATION IN IOWA AND NEBRASKA IN RELATION TO THE B. & M.
LINES AND LAND GRANTS, 1870–1880.

ing channels of trade, in this case the Rock Island and the B. & M.
In Nebraska, most of the people lived in the vicinity of Omaha and
the region along the Missouri River to the south, although there was
an area of settlement extending westward along the Platte River and
the Union Pacific Railway.[213]

[213] See maps above. For the distribution of population in the United States
as a whole, see map following page 394, above.

By 1880, the heavier concentration of people in southeastern Iowa had become dispersed so that all but the northwestern portion of the state contained 18 to 45 inhabitants per square mile; only a small area around Burlington was then more thickly populated. Undoubtedly railroad construction and its attendant colonization were prime factors in this process of distribution. In 1870 slightly more than one-eighth of Iowa's inhabitants lived in the B. & M. and Rock Island zones. A decade later more than one-sixth of the people resided in the two areas, for while the state was gaining 36.1 per cent in population, the Burlington and Rock Island zones grew 97.9 and 95 per cent respectively. These almost identical rates of increase far exceeded those in the older region along the Mississippi and in the relatively isolated counties in the northwestern part of the state.[214]

The shift of population during the 'seventies in Nebraska was even more striking in its relation to the railroads and their colonization work. Once again in 1880 the vanguard of settlement followed the Union Pacific rails, but the heaviest concentration west of Seward and Garrison now lay south of the Platte River and was almost coterminous with the Burlington's South Platte grant. In 1870, there was an average of but 4.3 persons per thousand acres in this region and 4.1 per thousand acres in the Union Pacific zone. A decade later, however, these figures had risen to 29.7 and 22.8 respectively.[215] Whereas each railway zone had embraced approximately one-seventh of all Nebraskans in 1870, by 1880 the U. P. territory held over one-fifth of the state's population and the B. & M. region more than one-quarter. Both railroad zones far outstripped in growth the more inaccessible counties north of the Platte and in the Southwest.[216]

In the railroad and land grant areas of Iowa and Nebraska, therefore, population definitely followed the rails. Newcomers clustered most densely near the actual rights of way and, in the more unsettled regions, formed literal spearheads of civilization along the advancing tracks. Obviously this process was the reverse of that in the East where railroads almost without exception followed old channels of trade and connected already existing centers of population.[217] The western rail-

[214] See Table 9 in Appendix F, below.
[215] *Ibid.*
[216] *Ibid.*
[217] See above, pp. 14–15.

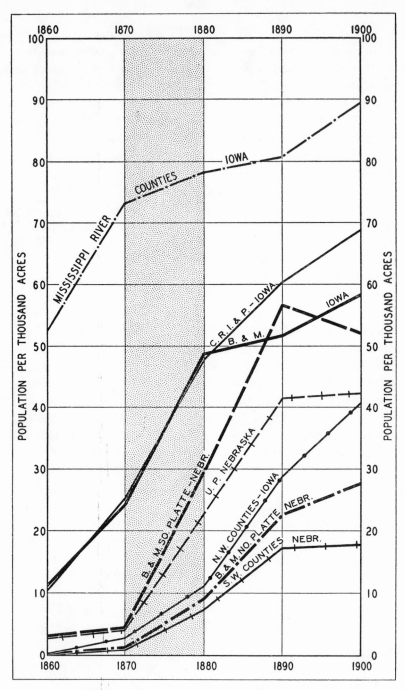

POPULATION PER THOUSAND ACRES FOR SELECTED ZONES IN IOWA AND NEBRASKA, DECENNIALLY, 1860–1900.

(For underlying statistics see Table 9 in Appendix F. Percentage for Nebraska zones in 1860 estimated.)

roads, particularly those with land grants, inevitably played a more intimate role in the founding and development of their respective territories than did the eastern lines. This phenomenon has, of course, been widely recognized as applying in general to the entire region west of the Mississippi; [218] the statistics for Iowa and Nebraska add concrete evidence of its operation in these particular states.

The location of the growing areas of improved acres and new farms in Iowa and Nebraska confirms the influence of the land-grant roads in particular. During the 'seventies, the railroad zones witnessed a far greater development in these respects than did the older established or more inaccessible regions of these states. In Iowa, for example, 17.3 per cent of the state's improved acres lay in either the B. & M. or Rock Island zones in 1880 as compared with 9.7 per cent in 1870. In Nebraska, the percentage of the state's improved acres along the Union Pacific alone rose from 19.5 to 25.1 per cent during the decade, while in the Burlington's South Platte territory the proportion jumped from 13 to 30.4 per cent. The growth and location of acres in farms followed a similar trend.[219] The permanent nature of this development was indicated by the continued growth during the next two decades of all four railroad zones in respect to improved acres and area in farms.[220]

It was natural that observers in the 'seventies should frequently note the day-to-day incidents connected with railroad colonization.[221] It was perhaps more significant, however, that they should grasp the meaning of the colonization process as a whole. In 1879, a Nebraska historian declared:

This corporation [the B. & M.] has adopted and pursued, from the date of its organization, a most liberal and comprehensive policy towards the country through which its lines of road are constructed. To a much larger extent than is usual in railway corporations, it has exhibited a disposition to make its interests and that of the country through which it passes identical. In fact, the history and development of the Burlington and Missouri

---

[218] E.g., Paxson, *op. cit.*, pp. 409, 544–549; Robert E. Riegel, *The Story of The Western Railroads* (New York, 1926), ch. xviii; Schlesinger, *Political and Social Growth of the United States, 1852–1933*, pp. 133–136; Verne S. Sweedlun, *A History of Agriculture in Nebraska, 1870–1930* (MS, Thesis, University of Nebraska, Lincoln, 1940).

[219] See graphs, pp. 458–459.

[220] *Ibid.* By 1900 all zones tended toward an equal level of development in these respects.

[221] See above in this and the preceding chapters.

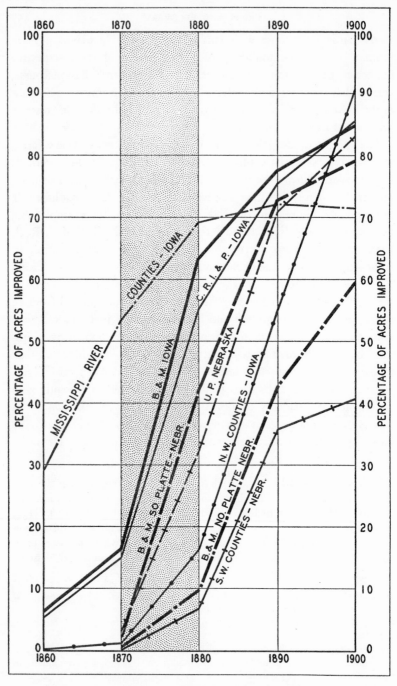

PERCENTAGE OF TOTAL ACRES IMPROVED FOR SELECTED ZONES IN IOWA AND
NEBRASKA, DECENNIALLY, 1860–1900.

(For underlying statistics see Table 10 in Appendix F)

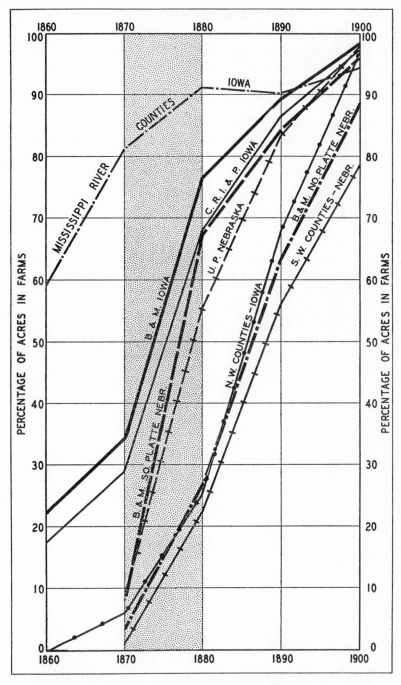

PERCENTAGE OF TOTAL ACRES IN FARMS FOR SELECTED ZONES IN IOWA AND
NEBRASKA, DECENNIALLY, 1860–1900.

(For underlying statistics see Table 11 in Appendix F)

River road is most intimately interwoven with the development and prosperity of the great South Platte country, and the popular voice is that every movement of this corporation has tended toward the material advancement of that beautiful portion of the State occupied by its lines, which has made it one of the most prosperous as well as popular roads in the West. . . .[222]

This was uttered in a decade usually remembered for the granger movement. A more sober estimate appeared in the *Report* for 1880 by the United States Surveyor General of Nebraska to the Secretary of the Interior:

The Burlington & Missouri River Railroad Company, with over 800 miles of road, and the Union Pacific Railroad, with its branches reaching out into the State, have done and are doing much for the development of our resources. By the sale of their lands at low rates and at easy terms, they are adding very materially in the rapid settlement and improvement of the State, which has grown in population from 246,200 in 1875 to 452,542 in 1880, and it is but just to say that its material growth and prosperity has kept pace with the increase of population. . . .[223]

[222] Harrison Johnson, *Johnson's History of Nebraska* (Omaha, 1880). This opinion was repeated in the *History of the State of Nebraska*, edited by the Western Historical Company (Chicago, 1882), p. 205.

[223] Secretary of the Interior, *Report* for 1880, pp. 1004–1005.

CHAPTER XV

CLOSING ACTIVITIES OF THE LAND DEPARTMENT, 1880–1905

I. EXPANSION OF THE BURLINGTON SYSTEM

THE closing activities of the land department took place during the quarter century of the greatest expansion in the nation's railroad facilities. During the 'eighties, the network in the United States grew from 93,262 to 166,703 miles, an increase of over 70,000 miles, equal to 70 per cent of the total built in the preceding half century. By 1905, 217,341 miles of road were in operation in the United States.[1] This tremendous expansion was fully reflected on the Burlington. Between December 31, 1880, and December 31, 1890, its system increased from 2,772[2] to 5,216[3] miles; on June 30, 1905, the company controlled and operated 8,879 miles of road.[4]

The first major accomplishment of the Burlington after 1880 was the completion of the line to Denver, which was put into service on May 29, 1882.[5] Construction of this line not only enabled the company to offer through service between Chicago and Denver under single management but also placed the road in a position to become part of a transcontinental route through Denver. Meanwhile, traffic between the Burlington and the Hannibal and St. Joseph was steadily increasing. Thus, when the latter company seriously considered building its own line into Chicago in 1880, the Burlington began negotiations for its purchase. This was accomplished on June 18, 1883, and the famous Missouri road became an integral part of the Burlington system.[6]

No sooner had the company made this acquisition than its attention was drawn to a new, fast-developing region, the vast timber and spring wheat empire northwest of Chicago. By 1885 the St. Paul,

---

[1] *Poor's Manual for 1906* (New York, 1906), p. v.

[2] CBQ, *Annual Report* for 1880 (Chicago, 1881), p. 12.

[3] CBQ, *Annual Report* for 1890 (Cambridge, 1891), p. 15.

[4] CBQ, *Annual Report* for 1905 (Chicago, 1905), p. 15.

[5] CBQ, *Corporate History*, p. 331.

[6] CBQ, *Annual Report* for 1883 (Cambridge, 1884), p. 17.

Minneapolis and Manitoba Railroad created by James J. Hill had pushed its track northward to a connection with the Canadian Pacific Railroad, and the Northern Pacific had completed its transcontinental line to Puget Sound. Both of these railroads terminated at St. Paul and Minneapolis, with the result that these cities were growing into important market and transfer points. Their trade with Chicago and St. Louis was steadily increasing, and it was apparent that it would grow even more rapidly as lumber from Wisconsin and Minnesota moved southward and as coal from Illinois found its way north. In view of all these factors, the Burlington sponsored an entirely new railroad, named the Chicago, Burlington & Northern, to run northwest from the Illinois lines of the C. B. & Q. to the Mississippi at Savanna and thence up the east bank of the river to St. Paul. A traffic arrangement was concluded between the new road and the "Q," and an agreement was made whereby the latter would gain complete control of its northern extension. Construction proceeded rapidly, and on October 24, 1886, a party of journalists accompanied the officials who "flew" on the first train over the new line from St. Paul to Chicago in eleven hours and ten minutes.[7] A week later the road was open for regular freight and passenger traffic.[8]

While the Chicago–Denver and Chicago–Twin Cities main lines were under construction, numerous branches were built to accommodate the new farms, ranges, mines, and towns in Illinois and between the Mississippi and the Rockies. Among others were: the lines southward to Centralia, Illinois, to tap the coal fields of that region; an alternate main line across southern Nebraska from DeWitt westerly to Sterling, Colorado, and Cheyenne, Wyoming; and finally, a road from York, Nebraska, northwestward to Alliance, thence on to the coal mines at Edgemont, South Dakota, and Newcastle, Wyoming.[9] In 1894, the branch to Alliance and Newcastle was extended to a connection with the Northern Pacific at Billings, and six years later a link was built from Alliance to Brush. This construction enabled the Northern Pacific and Burlington to provide a short route between the Pacific Northwest and such points as Omaha, St. Joseph,

[7] R. C. Overton, *The First Ninety Years: An Historical Sketch of the Burlington Railroad, 1850–1940.* (Chicago, 1940), p. 12.

[8] CBQ, *Annual Report* for 1886 (Cambridge, 1887), p. 20.

[9] See map, inside front and back covers.

Kansas City, St. Louis, and Denver.[10] At the close of the year 1900, the C. B. & Q. operated 7,661 miles.[11]

Meanwhile the Burlington was devoting increasing attention to new

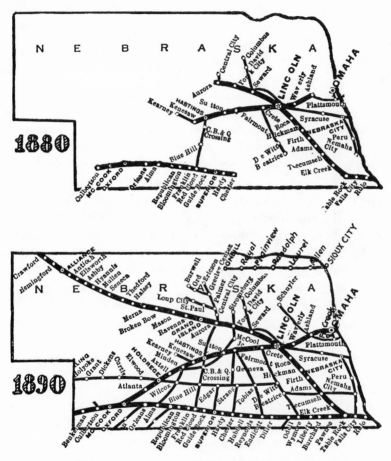

GROWTH OF THE C. B. & Q. IN NEBRASKA, 1880–1890.

technical improvements. Even by 1876, it was apparent that patient research alone could determine which materials were most suitable for the construction of locomotives, cars, bridges, and track, and in that year the C. B. & Q. established a laboratory in Aurora, Illinois. Eight

[10] Overton, *op. cit.*, p. 13; cf. CBQ, *Annual Report* for 1894 (Cambridge, 1895), p. 14.

[11] CBQ, *Annual Report* for 1900 (Cambridge, 1900), p. 18.

years later, a dynamometer car was constructed to obtain additional information for improving the efficiency of locomotives, for determining their proper tonnage rating, and for many other purposes. In 1886 and 1887, on the hill at West Burlington, the company conducted the most exhaustive tests made up to that time in power brakes; there in 1887 George Westinghouse invented the triple valve which perfected the air brake and brought it into universal use to the exclusion of other types of brakes.

Every one of these changes contributed an essential element to the modern railroad. Throughout the years, however, the development of the steam locomotive was the most obvious and popular measure of railroad progress. For the first 30 years, the only type of motive power in general use for freight and passenger service on the Burlington was the American locomotive with a four-wheel pilot truck and two pairs of drivers (∠∞OO). In 1879, however, the first Consolidation engine with eight drivers (∠oOOOO) was inaugurated to take care of the heavier freight trains, and this was followed a dozen years later by the Ten Wheeler (∠∞OOO) designed for the same purpose, while the Mogul, a ∠oOOO type, was developed for handling both freight and passenger trains. At the end of the nineteenth century, two important new engines joined the roster: the fleet Atlantic locomotive, with a ∠∞OOo wheel arrangement, for passenger service, and the Prairie, a ∠oOOOo engine especially adapted for handling freight over the long level stretches of the Burlington. To carry these heavier locomotives, rails were steadily increased in weight and strength.

Although the most striking changes in equipment and service did not come until the twentieth century, some notable advances were made before 1905. In 1888, for example, trains equipped throughout with vestibule cars were running between Chicago and Denver, and between Chicago and the Twin Cities. It took 43 hours, however, to reach Denver from Chicago, and 16 hours to go to St. Paul. By 1900 these schedules had been cut to $27\frac{1}{2}$ and $13\frac{1}{4}$ hours, respectively.

Throughout this period of rapid development, the guiding figure in the Burlington's affairs was Charles E. Perkins, who succeeded John M. Forbes as president in 1881. When he retired in 1901 after a brilliant administration, he was succeeded by George B. Harris, son of the man who had served as land commissioner between 1869 and 1874.

On April 17, 1901, it was announced that the Burlington had come under the control of James J. Hill. There were many reasons on both sides for this serious, far-reaching step. Just before the turn of the century, Hill, who had pushed his Great Northern to the coast in 1893, became heavily interested in the Northern Pacific Railway Company. The chief traffic originating on these two northern lines consisted of grain, livestock, ore, lumber, and some other products from the coast, as well as imports from the Orient. This traffic was eastbound, and much of it, especially lumber, was destined for the treeless corn belt region served by the Burlington. It would be a distinct advantage for the northern lines to have direct access to this market. Furthermore, Hill keenly desired a direct connection between the North and the manufacturing centers and coal fields of Illinois. Such a connection would supply the westbound freight, some of it destined for the Orient, that would prevent cars from returning empty. In addition, the C. B. & Q. served Omaha, St. Joseph, Kansas City, and Chicago, where the packing houses and market for the cattle and sheep of the northwestern ranges were located. At St. Louis and Kansas City, connections were available with lines traversing the southern states, from which came the raw and manufactured cotton required for shipment via the Pacific Northwest to China and Japan. From the standpoint of the Burlington, the new alliance assured a permanent through connection to Puget Sound, a valuable source of traffic interchange, and affiliation with one of the greatest railroad geniuses of America. It also made it unnecessary for the Burlington to build its own line to the Pacific Northwest.[12]

II. SELLING THE LAST OF THE LAND GRANTS

During the period between 1880 and 1905, the Burlington disposed of all its remaining B. & M. land grants, together with 12,841.54 additional acres acquired with the Atchison and Nebraska Railroad in 1880.[13] In Iowa, the final sale took place in 1890, although the last transaction in the larger Nebraska grant was not completed until 1905.

As before 1880, numerous problems arose during this quarter century concerning the company's title to its various lands, particularly in Nebraska. On March 11, 1884, for example, the House of Representatives called for a report of all lands granted the B. & M. in that

[12] Overton, op. cit., pp. 13–14, 32–38.
[13] Baldwin to Mitchell, March 18, 1922 (LDP).

state.[14] This report again raised the questions as to (1) whether the company had not received more total acres in Nebraska than it was entitled to in view of the length of the line between Plattsmouth and Kearney Junction, and (2) whether the railroad could retain the excess of lieu lands north of its track over those to the south.[15] For sixteen years these problems were shunted back and forth between the railroad, the General Land Office, and the Secretary of the Interior. The length of the line that should determine the size of the grant was variously estimated at figures between 180.54 and 190.75 miles.[16] The company consistently held that the controlling length should be 186.11 miles as asserted by Commissioner Drummond in his letter of March 29, 1872. In February, 1901, however, this figure was rejected by Secretary Hitchcock, who ruled that the proper distance was 184.53 miles and that the railroad had therefore received 11,314.23 acres too much.[17] Within a month the company paid the United States in full for this surplus at the regular rate of $1.25 an acre.[18]

The matter of the lieu-land excess north of the railroad had nearly as long a history. In September, 1884, Commissioner McFarland, referring to Justice Miller's decision in 1875, suggested that the acres erroneously patented in this region could and should be specifically identified.[19] On August 22, 1900, however, the Land Office came to the conclusion that the railroad's title to the excess was good.[20] By a departmental letter of March 19, 1901, instructions were sent by the Secretary of the Interior to the Commissioner of the General Land Office that the Burlington and Missouri River Railroads' land grants in both Iowa and Nebraska "have been finally adjusted and closed." [21]

During this closing period of the land department, its affairs were

[14] House of Representatives, *Executive Document No. 118*, 48th Cong., 1st Sess. (1883–1884).

[15] H. M. Teller, Secretary of the Interior, to A. G. McFarland, Commissioner of the General Land Office, July 20, 1885 (USDI).

[16] C. J. Ernst to Baldwin, January 6, 1891 (LDP).

[17] Binger Hermann, Commissioner of the General Land Office, to Baldwin, February 13, 1901 (LDP).

[18] Hermann to E. A. Hitchcock, Secretary of the Interior, March 22, 1901 (LDP).

[19] McFarland to Teller, September 8, 1884 (USDI).

[20] Hermann to Hitchcock, August 22, 1900 (LDP).

[21] Thomas Ryan, Acting Secretary of the Interior, to Hermann, Commissioner of the General Land Office, September 9, 1901 (USDI).

handled by W. W. Baldwin at Burlington and by C. J. Ernst at Omaha; the former marked out the broad policy in both states and supervised matters in Iowa, while the latter took charge of the Nebraska grant.[22] The activity of these men was ably seconded by George W. Holdrege, for many years general manager of the Burlington lines west of the Missouri River.[23] In general, the company's prices and terms remained unchanged so long as a considerable body of lands lay unsold in either state. Thereafter they were adjusted in order to wind up the respective grants as quickly as possible.

In Iowa the price level through 1885 was practically stable near $12 an acre. As the best remaining lands were sold, however, sales declined steadily from 20,245.15 acres in 1881 to 2,887.01 in 1885; as usual, credit transactions outnumbered cash sales by a ratio of six to one. At the end of the latter year, despite the normal rate of cancellations, less than 18,000 acres of the Iowa grant were left unsold. To dispose of this remnant, the company decided to reduce drastically its prices; beginning in 1886, the average figure per acre fell from near $12 to below $7. The result was an abrupt upswing in sales that lasted through the summer of 1888; from then until the final transaction was concluded in 1890, the trend of business was irregular as the last tracts were closed out.

In Nebraska, the decline in sales that had set in after the recovery peak of 1878 continued through 1881, probably for several reasons. Crops of 1880 were poor in the state, and it is possible that the gradual rise of approximately $1.30 in average price per acre between 1879 and 1881 had a deterring effect on new purchasers. From 1881 until the close of business in Nebraska, the number of land sales moved roughly in inverse ratio to price, revealing a more stabilized market condition than had previously existed.[24] Thus, in 1882 a return of prices to the 1879 figure was accompanied by a sharp rise in sales. Conversely, a continued upturn in prices through 1888 was matched by an abrupt drop and practical cessation of sales. Not until average prices fell almost to $7 an acre in 1892 did business pick up.[25] During the course of these fluctuations, which reflected primarily the local ebb and flow

[22] Baldwin and Ernst correspondence (LDP), *passim.*

[23] Dr. Thomas M. Davis of Lincoln, Nebraska, is preparing a biography of Holdrege for publication.

[24] See table 8 in Appendix F, and graph, p. 468.   [25] *Ibid.*

in realty values, the company's policy remained consistent. In 1893, for example, a booklet on Nebraska asserted that

the company does not pretend to sell its lands cheaper than the same grade might be bought from individuals, but it does offer the most advantageous terms, such as no individual could afford or is inclined to give. . . . These lands will continue to advance in the future as they have in the past, but it has always been the policy of the company to dispose of its lands to

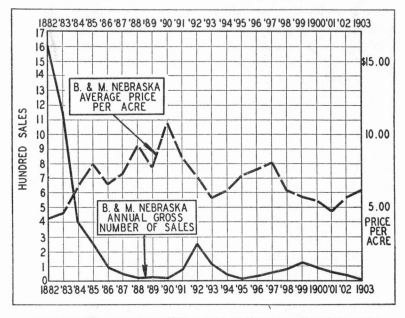

GROSS NUMBER OF SALES BY THE B. & M. IN NEBRASKA, TOGETHER WITH AVERAGE PRICE PER ACRE, ANNUALLY, 1882–1903.

(For underlying statistics see Table 8 in Appendix F)

actual settlers as rapidly as possible, trusting that the increased volume of business given it by them [i.e. the settlers] will be at least as profitable as the gain made by holding the lands. . . .[26]

Elsewhere it was announced that lands priced at less than $5 an acre would be sold on short credit or for cash only, with at least $1 an acre required as a first payment. All other lands were available on six years' credit, with one-sixth of the principal down, interest only at the end of the first year, and the remainder of the principal and interest (at 6 per cent) payable thereafter in five equal installments.

[26] CBQ, *Great Opportunities . . . in . . . Nebraska*, 1893, pp. 30–31.

Sales under this credit plan were to be limited to actual settlers and were therefore restricted to 320 acres each, except by special consent of the company; purchasers were to assume taxes for the current year and thereafter.[27]

As the Nebraska granted lands approached exhaustion, Ernst's functions changed accordingly. "I am confronted with the problem," he wrote in November, 1896, "of trying, if possible, to close out this department within the next five years, and not only sell all of the land, but collect all of the money due thereupon."[28] These objectives he sought first by a further reduction in prices,[29] and second by jogging delinquents when and as good crops enabled farmers to pay up their arrears.[30] In carrying out these two tasks, however, it was Ernst's responsibility to encourage immigration into Nebraska, whether it involved a sale of B. & M. land or not. As he replied to one Swede who inquired about the prospects in the state: "It does not make any difference to us whether you buy railroad or private land. We would like to locate all good Swedish farmers that are willing to come to Nebraska, and are not particularly anxious to sell them our own land if other land will suit them better."[31] In other words, the newcomer was now regarded almost solely as a future shipper and receiver, and but incidentally as a potential purchaser of land.

This shift in emphasis had already been recognized by the company in the gradual transfer of what Ernst described as "the general immigration work" to the passenger traffic department.[32] Indeed, as early as 1882 that department had begun to take over the advertising and community development formerly handled by the land commissioner. In 1882 it issued a pamphlet entitled *The Heart of the Continent: an Historical and Descriptive Treatise for Business Men, Home Seekers and Tourists, of the Advantages, Resources and Scenery of the Great West*.[33] The 64 pages of text in this booklet included descriptive and

[27] *Ibid.*

[28] Ernst to George W. Holdrege (General Manager, Burlington Lines West), November 13, 1896 (LDP).

[29] See graph, p. 468.

[30] Ernst to Holdrege, November 13, 1896 (LDP).

[31] Ernst to C. J. Wastenberg, January 8, 1897 (LDP). Similar language was used by Baldwin; e.g. Baldwin to George Loper, December 1, 1896 (LDP).

[32] Ernst to Prairie Farmer Publishing Company, September 10, 1896 (LDP).

[33] CBQ, Passenger Department, *The Heart of the Continent* (Chicago, 1882) (LDP).

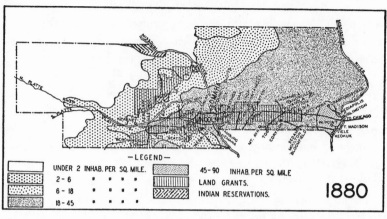

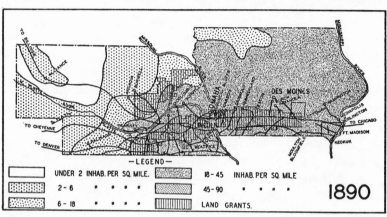

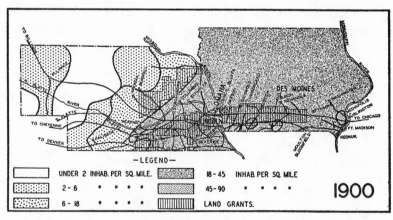

TREND OF POPULATION IN IOWA AND NEBRASKA IN RELATION TO THE B. & M.
LINES AND LAND GRANTS, 1880–1890–1900.

statistical material concerning all the Burlington's territory and were copiously illustrated. The reader was referred to the passenger department for any additional information, including that concerning lands for sale.[34] This department likewise handled the "Homeseeker Excursions" which replaced the old land exploring parties. By 1893 tickets to any part of western Nebraska, eastern Colorado, or northern Wyoming could be bought at a saving of 59 per cent.[35] That year a new booklet on Nebraska expounded the opportunities of that state in particular and devoted more than six pages to the company's lands still available.

By far the most elaborate advertising effort of this period, however, was the *Corn Belt*, a newspaper which made its first appearance at Chicago in December, 1895.[36] It was edited by the passenger department, and in its opening number informed the reader that of its 20,000 copies, 12,000 would be distributed to farmers resident in Illinois, Indiana, Ohio, and Michigan, 4,000 to ticket agents east of the Mississippi River, and 4,000 to Burlington passenger and land agents.[37] In the second number, dated January, 1896, the editor proudly declared that the paper had already achieved "such popularity and . . . so much kindly attention" that it would be increased then and thereafter from 8 to 16 pages; subscription price for the year was fixed at 25 cents. The purpose of the publication, as stated in its columns, was primarily to promote Nebraska, to reveal the opportunities for colonization in that state, and to correct false reports concerning crop conditions in the West.[38] In fulfilling the last object, frequent attention was given to Iowa and Missouri as well as to Nebraska. Titles of the leading articles in the March, 1897, issue, for example, revealed the range of subject matter:

"Nebraska not all for Corn: Raises the finest Celery and Garden Crops that are found in the Best Markets . . . Methods of Celery Growing." (Picture of celery farm)
"New Corn Product Discovered: Pith of the Stalk is Ground and Specially prepared for food for Cattle, Horses and Hogs."
"Iowa's Great Blue Grass Region: Southwestern Part of the State Rivals

[34] *Ibid.*, p. 63.
[35] *New Era* (Wahoo, Nebraska), September 7, 1893.
[36] CBQ, Files of the Colonization Agent, Omaha, Nebraska.
[37] CBQ, *Corn Belt* (December, 1895).
[38] *Ibid.* (January, 1896).

Kentucky's Famous Section in Agricultural Beauty and Richness."
(3 pictures)

"Feeding Thousands of Cattle in Iowa."

"A New Way to Store Water."

"Missouri as a Dairy State: Cheap Corn, Abundant Grass and Good Water
Make it Easy and Highly Profitable for Dairymen."

"Education in Nebraska: Work of the University of Nebraska and Other
Public Places of Learning. High Rank of the Schools." Contains these
sub-headings: "Where Students Come From — Liberal Terms for Tui-
tion — The Men Who Teach — School of Agriculture — Union College
at Lincoln — Lincoln Normal University — Worthington Military Academy — Nebraska Wesleyan University — Cotner University at Bethany"
(Picture of grounds at Lincoln)

"Burlington Route Harvest Excursions"

"Fall Preparation for Sugar Beets"   .

"Profit in Feeding Sheep"

"Gold from Cripple Creek: Output last year Estimated at Ten Millions
of Dollars"

"The Improved Olentangy Incubator"

"The Reliable Hen"

"Irrigation Brings Crops: Advantages of the Method Shown in Morgan
Co. Colo." (Picture of farm)

"The Agricultural Schools"

"How to Make Axle Grease"

"The Secret of Success with Poultry" [39]

In addition to these articles, there were numerous short paragraphs on
freight and passenger service, a sprinkling of testimonials from successful farmers on company lands, and an assortment of agricultural
news items and statistics. Most of the pages contained illustrations.

This paper appeared regularly each month through November, 1902,
and its average circulation for the seven years was approximately 27,000.
In view of this major undertaking by the passenger department, advertising during the late 'nineties by the land department itself was on
a small, rather specialized scale. As Ernst wrote in 1896, the company
had so little good land left to sell that any considerable expenditure for
advertising was not warranted.[40] His efforts in that respect were chiefly
confined to gathering crop samples and arranging for exhibits, notably
at the important Illinois State Fair at Springfield.[41] Occasionally, he

[39] CBQ, *Corn Belt* (March, 1897).

[40] Ernst to Prairie Farmer Publishing Company, September 10, 1896 (LDP).

[41] Ernst to J. Francis, September 1, 1896 (LDP).

also accompanied eastern immigration agents through Nebraska to show them the country.[42]

Even agricultural development was now in the hands of the traffic department. In 1895, experimental farms were set up to test the revolutionary dry farming methods developed by H. W. Campbell of Lincoln. So successful were these experiments that additional demonstrations were soon established on more than 200 farms in Colorado, Wyoming, Nebraska, and Kansas. Farmers set aside certain areas on their farms which were tilled under Mr. Campbell's supervision.[43] The purpose was to demonstrate how moisture could be conserved in the soil so as to afford added protection against drought. And, as the New Era added, "incidentally the company expects returns from its investments in increased and regular crops, necessitating heavy freight and passenger traffic on its network of lines."[44] The results of these experiments were very satisfactory, and in areas where rainfall is limited the principles of Campbell's system are being practiced today.

During the quarter century between 1880 and 1905, the independent townsite companies, notably the Lincoln Land Company, continued their work. Although their property in the granted areas was rapidly sold, they extended their operations into western Nebraska and Wyoming as the system expanded. By doing so, they fulfilled an important function for the Burlington. They were able, as land companies, to obtain property at specified intervals along projected routes at figures much lower than the railroad as such would have had to pay. When the rails were subsequently laid, the townsite companies deeded to the railroad, free of charge, sufficient land for stations and yards. In the course of time, the natural increase of value in their remaining property enabled them to liquidate the original investment.[45]

Late in 1905, just 15 years after the final sale was made in Iowa, the railroad's last tract was paid for in Nebraska. On December 31, the land department of the Burlington closed its books; the task of land-selling

---

[42] Ernst to T. H. Waite, September 7, 1896 (LDP).

[43] New Era, December 24, 1896; Memorandum, J. B. Lamson to the writer, June 23, 1941.

[44] New Era, ibid.

[45] Miscellaneous records of various townsite companies (LDP), passim; Memorandum, Charles E. Perkins, Jr., to the writer, May 9, 1941. The complete story of the nature and function of these companies must await further research.

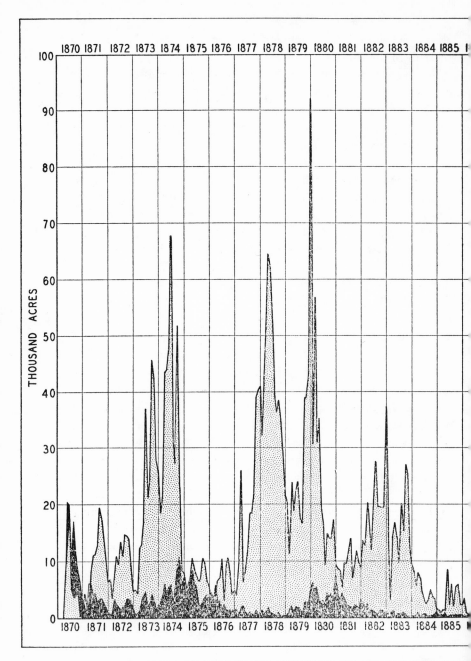

GROSS LAND SALES BY THE BURLINGTON AND MISSOURI RIVER RAILR(

APRIL, 1870, THRO

(For underlying statistics see T

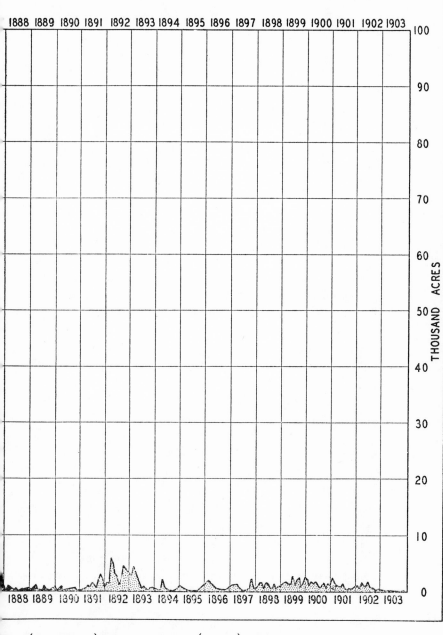

OWA (SOLID BLACK) AND IN NEBRASKA (SHADED), MONTHLY,

:MBER, 1903

d 2 in Appendix F)

that had begun in October, 1863, was finished. The record of those 42 years was indeed impressive.

In Iowa, 359,804.25 acres had been sold for a principal sum of $4,199,657.34 at an average price of $11.67. To achieve this result, the company spent $854,948.08 as follows: [46]

Land Examinations and other preliminary expenses	$122,326.98
Taxes and Tax Expenses	269,674.51
Legal Expenses	33,523.30
Land Department Salaries and Office Expenses	225,461.60
Commissions on Sales, Agency Expenses, and Advertising	185,137.03
Discounts on Prepayment and Exploring Tickets	18,211.95
Town Lot Expenses	612.71
	$854,948.08

These expenses left a return of $3,344,709.26 from the Iowa grant, although a greater sum was probably turned over to the company's treasurer since the above income figures do not indicate the amount received from interest on the long-term payments.[47] Assuming that interest in Iowa bore a relation to principal corresponding to that in Nebraska, the net income from the Iowa grant to the company would approximate $4,436,620.08. When, in 1872, the C. B. & Q. absorbed the B. & M. in Iowa, the construction account for the 444 miles acquired stood at $14,042,188.57.[48] At this rate, construction of the 275 miles of main line from Burlington to East Plattsmouth cost $8,697,301.13, nearly twice the return from the grant.

In Nebraska, the company disposed of 2,365,704.09 acres. This amount included the 50,000 acres received by the B. & M. from the state, but excluded the 19,004.48 acres belonging to the Omaha and South Western and the 12,841.54 acres obtained with the Atchison and Nebraska. For its 2,365,704.09 acres, the B. & M. received $12,402,-837.83 on account of principal, revealing an average price of $5.24 per acre. In addition, the B. & M. received from interest, rent, and forfeited payments $4,318,552.58. Another $9,952.67 came from the handful of town lots at Wilber, Firth, and Sterling, thus bringing the gross income from the Nebraska grants, both federal and state, to a grand

[46] Baldwin to Mitchell, March 18, 1922 (LDP).

[47] Records giving these figures were lost in the fire at the general office building in Chicago on March 15, 1922.

[48] CBQ, *Annual Report* for 1873 (Chicago, 1874), p. 21.

total of $16,731,343.08.[49] Approximately a quarter of this sum had been consumed by taxes and expenses as follows:

Land Examinations and other preliminary expenses ...	$ 164,968.70
Taxes and Tax Expenses	1,229,069.26
Legal Expenses	128,278.66
Land Department Salaries and Office Expenses	558,145.25
Commissions on Sales, Agency Expenses, and Advertising	969,500.35
Discounts allowed on Prepayments and Exploring Tickets	498,627.31
Premiums allowed for Improvements made on lands sold in 'seventies and early 'eighties	566,269.56
	$4,114,859.09

Deduction of these expenses left a surplus of $12,616,483.99 paid between 1870 and 1905 to the assistant treasurer.[50] This sum represented the net return from the B. & M. grants west of the Missouri River and more than covered the actual cost of construction from Plattsmouth to Kearney Junction, which had been approximately $7,000,000. For its 19,004.48 acres, the Omaha and South Western obtained $65,545.18 from the actual settlers who purchased them,[51] and the Atchison and Nebraska received $91,202.61 for its 12,841.54 acres.[52] If the cost of selling this combined acreage amounted to 25 per cent of the gross receipts, the Burlington probably received about $117,000 for this land.

The combined returns from the Iowa and Nebraska grants of the B. & M. were, therefore, approximately $17,000,000. On the other hand, construction of the line from Burlington to Kearney Junction cost approximately $15,500,000. Furthermore, under the terms of both Iowa and Nebraska grants, the Burlington, in common with other land-grant roads, carried United States mail, troops, and property at rates substantially lower than commercial tariffs. Figures are not available showing the total amount withheld from the railroad on this account, but fragmentary evidence provides some indication of the sum. Between July 12, 1876, and October 31, 1916, for example, $2,209,086.82 was withheld for mail transported between Burlington and East Platts-

---

[49] BMN, Final Balance Sheet, January 1, 1906 (LDP), and Baldwin to Mitchell, March 18, 1922 (LDP).

[50] BMN, Final Balance Sheet, January 1, 1906 (LDP).

[51] Memo re O.S.W. grant, n.d. (CR). There is no record of the B. & M. ever having received this money, and no indication as to whether or not it includes interest.

[52] Baldwin to Mitchell, March 18, 1922 (LDP). There is no indication as to whether or not this figure includes interest.

mouth.[53] To this should be added amounts deducted for mail in Nebraska, and for government property and troops in both states; between 1916 and 1940, when the reduced rates were partially abolished, government mail and traffic increased rather than decreased.[54]

In summary, the Burlington received slightly more than enough from the sale of its Iowa and Nebraska B. & M. grants to pay for the construction of its main line from Burlington to Kearney Junction, not including the Plattsmouth Bridge. Over a period of years, because of money withheld by the government in return for making the grants, the company eventually received substantially less than the cost of its line.

For both Iowa and Nebraska, the final balance sheet of the Burlington's land department revealed an extremely successful and well-managed business transaction for all concerned. As had been contemplated by Congress in making the original grants, the receipts from B. & M. lands had proven a decisive "aid in construction" for the line from Burlington to Kearney Junction, and the company emerged from its land-selling enterprise financially sound and still expanding. The government, because of the railroad's construction, had been able to dispose of vast tracts of public domain hitherto inaccessible and had obtained transportation at preferential rates over a new 500-mile route. Finally, and most significant of all, southern Iowa and southeastern Nebraska had been developed into a thriving community of farms and towns.

The *Census* of 1890 and that of 1900 revealed that in Iowa there were particularly heavy concentrations of population in or adjacent to B. & M. territory. Furthermore, by 1890 the Burlington's zone outstripped even the Mississippi counties in percentage of improved lands; the region's development in this respect ran closely parallel to that of the nearby Rock Island territory. In 1900, 98 per cent of the total acres served by the B. & M. and 97 per cent of the acres adjacent to the Rock Island were in farms. This compared with 95 and 96 per cent for the old Mississippi and the new northwestern counties, respectively, and indicated that the granted regions of both railroads continued their

---

[53] Baldwin to Mitchell, March 18, 1922 (LDP).

[54] Transportation Association of America, *loc. cit.*, p. 21.

earlier more rapid development until all but the rare waste lands were put to use.[55]

More illuminating than the absolute increase of population and farms in the Burlington's granted areas was the relative growth in comparison with older established blocs of counties accessible to water transportation and with newer counties whose railroads were not built until the 'eighties. Both in Iowa and Nebraska, the B. & M. zones were far behind the eastern river counties, along the Mississippi and Missouri, respectively, in 1870. In the next decade, however, they advanced more rapidly than any other comparable regions, including those served by rival railroads. The northwestern Iowa and southwestern Nebraska counties, with little or no adequate transportation, lagged far behind. During the 'eighties, the rate of development in Burlington territory slackened, falling behind the newly opened areas but still leading the older established regions. As the turn of the century approached, all county groups with approximately similar climatic and topographical conditions tended towards an equal level of development.[56] In summary, the Burlington's colonization work had its measurably greatest effect on the social and economic development of Iowa and Nebraska during the 'seventies, although its cumulative effect, which cannot be reduced to statistics, was doubtless of even greater significance.

Whether or not it was wise, in the long run, that the great trans-Mississippi West should have been developed as rapidly as it was is still a moot point, but it is an indisputable fact that the nation as a whole and the West in particular demanded such development in the latter part of the nineteenth century.[57]

[55] See graphs, pp. 458–459.
[56] See graphs, p. 456.
[57] Cf. Kirkland, *op. cit.*, p. 391. For a brief statement of the possible relation between the Burlington's colonization work and tenancy in its territory, see Appendix E, below.

CHAPTER XVI

THE RAILROAD AND THE COMMUNITY, 1905–1940

I. CREATING THE MODERN RAILROAD

DURING the twentieth century, the major extension of the C. B. & Q. was accomplished by the acquisition, on December 21, 1908, of over 1,800 miles operated by the Colorado and Southern Railway, and its various subsidiaries, including the Fort Worth and Denver City and the Wichita Valley Lines. This transaction brought to the Burlington system a through line from Cheyenne and Denver southward to Fort Worth, Dallas, Houston, and Galveston and provided by way of Alliance a new short route from the Pacific Northwest to the Gulf. To improve the service with the northern roads, a new line with easy grades was built almost immediately by the C. B. & Q. from Billings via Casper to the northern terminus of the Colorado and Southern at Orin Junction, Wyoming. At the end of 1940, the Burlington system was operating approximately 11,000 miles of road in fourteen states.[1]

During the past generation, however, the Burlington's development has been intensive rather than extensive. Although the railroad plant has actually shrunk in road mileage since 1910, its capacity has been vastly increased by the building of multiple tracks and by the use of better equipment and new techniques.

Prior to 1905, gravel, cinders, burned clay and crushed limestone were the materials used for ballast, but with increasingly heavy power and accelerated train speeds, available ballast of improved quality and reasonable cost was required. Chatts, a waste product from the lead and zinc mines, filled these specifications. Prepared gravel properly crushed and washed also proved satisfactory; these ballasts have been used on all main lines east of the Missouri River. On the main line between Omaha and Denver, slag from gold smelters has been applied, while gravel has been used on other principal main lines in western territory.

Before the end of the last century, the white oak and cedar used for ties were becoming scarce, and since the railroad had to resort to shorter

[1] See maps on both inside covers.

lived timber, it was imperative to develop some form of chemical treatment to provide against rapid decay. Consequently, the company erected its first treating plant at Edgemont, South Dakota, in 1899 and added a second at Galesburg, Illinois; 20 years later treated ties were in use on the entire system. Whereas in 1900 the average life of a tie was 7.3 years, in 1940 it had been prolonged by scientific treatment to over 20 years.

Since 1920, road-bed maintenance as a whole has benefited greatly from the development of the internal combustion engine which has motorized the old hand-car and has been applied to all forms of grading equipment. Meanwhile rails have become heavier and stronger. In 1909, when Open Hearth steel replaced that made by the Bessemer process, maximum weight was 90 pounds per yard; by 1940 that figure had been increased to 131 pounds.

Another important technical improvement has been the installation of automatic signals for the dispatching and safeguarding of trains. Prior to 1903, the manual block system was in universal use on the Burlington, but in that year automatic signals were installed along 23 miles of road; by 1940 some 2,140 miles of principal main lines were so equipped. In addition, Centralized Train Control had been installed on 200 miles of single track line where double tracking would otherwise have been necessary.

Since 1900, the laboratory and the successors of the original dynamometer car have been used in investigating nearly every phase of railroad operation. The laboratory has perfected the treatment of water for boiler use, for example, thus obtaining improved locomotive performance. Recently the Diesel-electric Zephyrs have also participated in tests, first in 1934 and later in connection with disc brakes. These trials have been of vital importance to the progress of high speed operation.

Motive power has kept pace with these developments. After the turn of the century as freight loads grew increasingly heavier, the multiple-wheeled Mallet, Mikado, and Santa Fe ($\angle$oOOOOOo) types were adopted, while the Pacific ($\angle$ooOOOo), the Mountain ($\angle$ooOOOOo), and the Hudson ($\angle$ooOOOoo) were assigned to high-speed conventional passenger service. By 1940 these types had culminated in the efficient Northern ($\angle$ooOOOOoo), capable of handling either heavy freight or passenger trains on very fast schedules. During the last 20 years, improvements incorporated in the most recent types of motive power have doubled the efficiency of the steam locomotive.

The most revolutionary event, however, in the history of Burlington motive power has been the introduction of the Diesel-electric unit. The company's long experience with gas- and oil-electric cars on branch lines had demonstrated the great economy of the internal combustion engine. Thus, when a lightweight Diesel engine was first produced in 1933, and when at the same time lightweight cars became practicable, the Burlington experimented with a complete train for use on the main line. On November 11, 1934, the *Pioneer Zephyr* became the first Diesel-electric streamline train in America to enter regular service. By the end of 1940 a dozen trains of this type were in operation on the system.

Progress in car design has run parallel to that in motive power. As time went on, specialized freight cars were acquired to meet the increasingly diverse needs of agriculture and industry; tank, refrigerated, stock, automobile, grain, coal, and container cars, among others, have made their appearance. Steel has largely replaced wood and a uniform increase has taken place in car capacity. The outstanding advances in passenger equipment have been the advent of the all-steel car about 1910, air-conditioning beginning in the 'thirties, and the more recent introduction of the lightweight stainless steel car.

As a result of these manifold improvements, it has been possible to provide increasingly better service. Between the turn of the century and 1940, for example, freight trains from Denver to Chicago cut their time from 55 to 33 hours. Over the same run, passenger trains reduced their schedule from over 27 to less than 16 hours. Even in 1925 it required 30 hours for freight to reach St. Paul or Omaha from Chicago, and 12 hours or more for passengers to make the same trip. Since then freight trains have cut their time a third, whereas a traveler can reach St. Paul in six hours, and Omaha in less than eight. In addition, traveling and working conditions have never been more safe and comfortable.[2]

The purpose of this vast technical development has been to provide rail transportation that would attract business for the Burlington from the agricultural and industrial communities already established on the system. As before 1905, however, there have been new regions to develop and new techniques to establish in Burlington territory. Thus the company's colonization work has continued, its purposes the same

[2] Overton, *op. cit.*, pp. 14, 32–39.

A CONTRAST IN PIONEERS: STAGE COACH, PRAIRIE SCHOONER, AND PIONEER ZEPHYR AT LINCOLN, NEBRASKA, ON NOVEMBER 11, 1934, THE DAY ON WHICH THIS ZEPHYR BECAME THE FIRST DIESEL-ELECTRIC STREAMLINE TRAIN IN THE UNITED STATES TO ENTER REGULAR SERVICE.

but its methods adapted to the rapidly changing social and economic conditions of modern America.

II. COLONIZATION WORK IN THE TWENTIETH CENTURY

"We are beginning to find that he who buildeth a railroad west of the Mississippi must also find a population and build up business." [3] Thus, in 1859, wrote Charles Russell Lowell. During the busy years between 1863 and 1905 when the company was selling its grants, this principle had been kept firmly in mind. Thus it was natural that when the last of the grant was sold, the Burlington should continue its efforts to colonize the potentially rich acres that were still available in western Nebraska, eastern Colorado, Wyoming, and Montana.

To do so required carrying out a program already familiar. First, the company had to examine the opportunities in lands still available. Second, it had to tell potential customers about them; as Lowell had written long before, "We wish to blow as loud a trumpet as the merit of our position warrants." [4] Finally, having attracted settlers into the area, the railroad could carry on its agricultural development work. The aims of this program were not new; Lowell, Perkins, Harris, Touzalin, Baldwin, and Ernst had all followed them. Changing conditions, however, called for new methods.

Under the original homestead law of 1862, a maximum of only 160 acres could be entered by any one settler. Where the lands were suitable only for grazing, as in parts of western and northern Nebraska, this was too small an amount to be useful. Consequently, in 1904, Congress enacted the Kinkaid Law which made it possible for homesteaders to occupy and claim 640 acres apiece in certain designated regions. In Nebraska, for example, 8,844,757 acres hitherto unclaimed were opened for entry. [5] The Burlington at once saw the opportunity of bringing farmers into this region and in the winter of 1905–06 organized a Homeseekers' Information Bureau under the management of D. Clem Deaver. [6]

Deaver's first step was to go into each land office and locate the plats of available tracts. By diligent inquiry among county offices, he discovered which of these were the best lands for settlement. Within

[3] Lowell to Mason, October 20, 1859 (LDP).   [4] *Ibid.*

[5] Kinkaid Law File, 1904–15 (CBP).

[6] P. S. Eustis to D. Clem Deaver, December 27, 1905 (CBP).

three months he also prepared and distributed no less than 1,500 township plats accompanied by suitable literature to prospective settlers.[7] In June, 1906, Deaver inaugurated his system of Personally Conducted Homeseekers' Excursions into the regions recently made available. These took place on the first and third Tuesdays of each month, a practice, incidentally, which was carried on for more than a decade.[8] In 1907, to explain and popularize these excursions, a farm products exhibit car containing crop samples from the North Platte Valley, the Big Horn Basin, and the Yellowstone River Valley was run over the company's lines in Iowa and eastern Nebraska. For the next four years this car made repeated trips to familiarize farmers with the new opportunities farther west.[9]

This work on the part of the railroad brought a prompt response. In 1914 Deaver's successor, S. B. Howard, reported that the Homeseekers' Information Bureau was receiving yearly about 15,000 inquiries and that in the 12 months just passed, more than 8,000 homestead entries covering over 2,250,000 acres of land had been made in the company's territory.[10]

We have joined with the resident people in parts of Colorado and Nebraska [he added], where lands are wholly in private ownership, in the issuance of folders pointing out the inviting investment and home environment of these particular sections. These are used by the real estate men of the localities and from our office we mail in the neighborhood of 75,000 pieces of advertising under 35,000 separate covers. In caring for our most earnest inquirers aside from the mimeograph letters and the thousands of multigraph letters . . . we write more than 4,500 personal letters. Effective spreading of information about our territory consists in reaching the man who desires it and who is considering a new location.[11]

In 1922, the colonization bureau came under the direction of Val Kuska who has carried the work forward vigorously, particularly in connection with the newly irrigated lands opened for private entry.

We . . . now devote most of our time [wrote Kuska in 1935] in cooperation with the respective localities in our territory in trying to get each community to realize their importance by interesting them in taking a

[7] Deaver to L. W. Wakeley, May 9, 1906 (CBP).
[8] Deaver to Wakeley, May 23, 1906 (CBP).
[9] Special Car File, 1907–11 (CBP).
[10] Howard to Wakeley, July 29, 1914 (CBP).
[11] Howard to Eustis?, December? 1914 (CBP).

moral inventory to see whether or not, in their own minds, opportunities exist. If they find such to be true, then we try to get them to coördinate all their single efforts into one, and start telling the world about their locality. This is done by the issuance of an illustrated folder describing their particular locality; by letter writing to friends in the settlers old home, and by the spoken word and newspaper or other advertising.[12]

A current 28-page folder, for example, describing the North Platte Valley contains 14 articles by specialists in various agricultural fields covering such subjects as climate, irrigation, crop production, dairying, hog raising, soils, poultry and turkey raising, livestock, sugar beets, and industrial development. In addition, there are short sketches of each of the principal towns together with 71 illustrations and two maps. This folder, sponsored by the Associated Chambers of Commerce of the North Platte Valley, provides a veritable handbook of the region.[13]

When, in response to such publicity, a prospective settler calls at the colonization bureau, he is provided with a signed certificate of inquiry stating that the bearer "is in communication with this department and looking for a farm in Burlington territory," and that it is the purpose of the bureau

to keep in touch with him after his removal to our territory to note his progress and learn whether he is satisfied with the business relations he may have with any person or firm selling him land. Any courtesies extended him will be appreciated.

The final brief statement on this certificate might well have been written by Lowell in 1859 for it merely paraphrases in modern terms the fundamental policy that he then set forth:

A well satisfied settler [it reads] is a good asset. A misplaced man is a liability. Our interest does not cease with the location of the settler. We are deeply interested in his success. We have no financial interest in the sale of lands nor any lands to sell. Our sole interest is in the development and general prosperity of the country.[14]

As before 1905, this "interest . . . in the . . . general prosperity of the country" has led the Burlington to do more than simply investi-

---

[12] Val Kuska to J. B. Lamson, October 23, 1935 (CBP).
[13] Associated Chambers of Commerce of the North Platte Valley, "North Platte Valley," n.d. (CBP).
[14] Certificate of Inquiry (CBP).

gate, advertise, and bring settlers into new regions.[15] Particularly in western Nebraska, Wyoming, and eastern Colorado, where soil and climatic conditions require special types of farming, the company has carried out an extensive program of agricultural research and education.[16] Deaver, for example, was in a particularly advantageous position to familiarize himself with the latest developments in dry farming. This information he incorporated in the literature originating in his office.[17] As early as 1904, the Burlington had operated a special seed corn train in Nebraska in collaboration with the state university and the United States Experiment Station. Eight years later, another similar excursion was made, and in 1913, the program was enlarged to include an alfalfa special throughout the states of Iowa and Missouri, a silo train in Colorado, and a dairy train in Nebraska.[18] This last train was sponsored by the Nebraska State Dairymen's Association and by the Agricultural College of the University of Nebraska.[19] When its trip was completed, these organizations wrote the railroad that without the train

it would have been impossible to have taken the information that we did to over 30,000 farmers and homesteaders in . . . the state. We feel it is the unanimous opinion of all connected with the dairy train, and those who witnessed its reception at the many points visited, that it was the most successful promoter of practical information . . . ever heretofore attempted.[20]

Since that day the Burlington has operated more than 25 similar trains through its territory. These have been devoted to the improve-

---

[15] No attempt has been made to describe the extensive program of industrial development which has run parallel to the work of agricultural development and has become an increasingly important phase of the Burlington's activities in the community. Its purpose has been to seek out and publicize industrial opportunities and to encourage the location of new enterprises along the system. Some features of this program have had a close relation to agricultural development such as, for example, the Mineral Resources Map (issued in 1940) which indicates in detail the location of all mineral deposits in states served by the Burlington.

[16] The recent work of the company in this respect has been fully told in O. O. Waggener's *Western Agriculture and the Burlington* (Chicago, 1938).

[17] Dry Farming Files, 1907–10 (CBP).

[18] Special Train Files, 1904–13 (CBP).

[19] Report of Dairy Train, 1913 (CBP).

[20] R. W. McGinnis (president, University of Nebraska, College of Agriculture), *et al.*, to Deaver, October 16, 1913 (CBP).

INTERIOR OF SOIL FERTILITY SPECIAL, 1940.

ment of livestock, seed potatoes, poultry, sugar beets, soil, hogs, hay crops, and farming in general.[21]

In 1924, for example, during the tour of the Nebraska purebred-dairy-sire special, a purebred calf was exchanged for a scrub animal in each of the 31 towns visited. In addition, 71,335 people visited the exhibit train, and fully 20,000 more witnessed the demonstration and heard the lectures that were offered. Approximately 100,000 pieces of literature dealing with dairy and livestock subjects were distributed.[22] A follow-up of this tour two years later, during which 30 of the 31 bulls were inspected, revealed that the animals had made an average gain of 825 pounds in weight. During the two years, these bulls had sired 503 calves, 236 of them heifers. Six of the original purebreds had been exhibited at fairs and won first place, and several were made grand champions. Of more lasting benefit, 52 carloads of cows had been brought into the communities since the operation of the special train, and 59 additional purebred sires had been imported; it was estimated that butterfat production had increased 37½ per cent in the territory.[23]

All attendance records were broken in 1926 by the Nebraska poultry special which was operated in coöperation with the University of Nebraska, the Nebraska Butter & Egg Association, several farm organizations, and poultry feed manufacturers. During 1926 and 1927 it visited 91 towns in Nebraska, 36 in Colorado, 27 in Wyoming, 8 in Kansas, 6 in South Dakota, 4 in Montana, and 3 in New Mexico; approximately 352,754 people passed through the cars. Thousands of bulletins were sent out by the university as a result of requests made on the train.[24]

To consider a recent example, a soil fertility train operated in 1940 in Nebraska, Colorado, Wyoming, and Montana under the auspices of the agricultural colleges of those states and in coöperation with the United States Department of Agriculture.[25] Its purpose was to point the way to more profitable crop production by producing the large yields per acre obtainable on fertile soil. The exhibits were built around results obtained from using manure, legumes, and phosphates at the

[21] Waggener, op. cit., passim.
[22] H. L. Ford to J. B. Lamson, October 29, 1924 (CBP).
[23] Ford to Lamson, October 8, 1926 (CBP).
[24] Waggener, op. cit., p. 39.
[25] Report on Soil Fertility Train, 1940 (CBP).

Scottsbluff, Nebraska, and Huntley, Montana, experiment stations, and from the experience of farmers who were successfully carrying out the practice advocated on the train. Colored movies and lantern slides illustrated the subjects covered by lectures.

*   *   *   *   *

Many years have rolled by since Charles Russell Lowell wrote that he who would build a western railroad must also find a population and build up business. The passage of time has amply demonstrated the fundamental truth of his observation. The colonization work of the Burlington has no ending.

APPENDICES

APPENDIX A

Chronology of events connected with the withdrawal of public lands and the location of the Burlington and Missouri River Railroad in Iowa, 1856–1857

WITHDRAWALS

May 10, 1856 — Telegraphic despatch sent by Commissioner of General Land Office to all Iowa land offices ordering immediate withdrawal of *all* lands from entry within probable limits of railroad grant. Not received at Council Bluffs.

May 15, 1856 — Written confirmation of May 10 orders sent to all Iowa offices. Not received at Council Bluffs.

May 21, 1856 — Effective date of these orders at Chariton.

May 23, 1856 — Effective date of these orders at Council Bluffs.

May 31, 1856 — Withdrawal actually put into effect at Council Bluffs.

June 19, 1856 — Written orders sent by Commissioner of General Land Office to all Iowa offices exempting preëmption entries (only) from withdrawal.

(June 25, 1856 — Effective date of these orders at Chariton?)

(June 27, 1856 — Effective date of these orders at Council Bluffs?)

Sept.–Oct., 1856 — Withdrawal automatically in effect for entries of all kinds opposite actual survey on the ground.

(Oct. 12, 1856 — Written orders sent by Commissioner of General Land Office to all Iowa offices withdrawing lands from preëmption entry?)

(Oct. 18, 1856 — Effective date of these orders at Chariton?)

Oct. 20, 1856 — Effective date of these orders at Council Bluffs.

LOCATION OF ROUTE AND ATTACHMENT OF TITLE TO LANDS

July 25, 1856 — B. & M. Directors adopt map submitted by Engineer.

Aug. 5, 1856 — Governor Grimes certifies filing of this map.

Aug. 20, 1856 — Acting Commissioner of General Land Office acknowledges receipt of this map. Objects to omission of certification that line is "definitely fixed." No additional certificate sent.

Sept. 4, 1856 — Henn, in letter from Chicago, selects lieu lands, all vacant alternate sections between six- and fifteen-mile limits, using July 25 map as basis.

Sept. 10, 1856 — Department of Interior sets this as effective date of Henn's Sept. 4 selections, providing line actually located at that time.

Sept. 29, 1856 — Survey on the ground begins in Council Bluffs district.

Oct. 13, 1856 — Survey completed in Council Bluffs district.

Dec. 19, 1856 — Attorney-General rules date of actual survey on ground determines definite location of route.

Feb. 16, 1857 — Attorney-General rules actual survey on ground sufficient to vest title, but indicates filing of plat "perfects" title.

Mar. 24, 1857 — Officers of B. & M. formally certify map of actual survey.

Mar. 27, 1857 — Secretary of State of Iowa certifies map of actual survey deposited in his office.

Apr. 7, 1857 — General Land Office acknowledges receipt of map of actual survey and certificate of authenticity.

APPENDIX B

Letter of Bernhart Henn describing Iowa and the future of the Burlington and Missouri River Railroad in that state, September 6, 1858

Fairfield, Iowa
September 6, 1858

John G. Read, Esq.
V. P. & Supt. B. & Mo. Riv. R. R.
Burlington, Iowa

Dr. Sir: —

Not having an opportunity to communicate with you verbally and at length concerning the *future* of the Burlington and Missouri River Rail Road, I will take a leisure hour on the eve of my departure East to comply partially with your request, and give you my general views on the subject — leaving it until some future day to give you a *detail* of the statistics which would appear to me as not only a probable but a *certain result*.

Having travelled much for the past eight years, over the principle [sic] Rail Roads in the Northern part of the United States, and naturally taking close observations of the country and its settlement & improvement wherever I go, I feel more free to give my views upon the *general* features of intercommunication between our people and the inland Commerce of the Country, than I do of the detail of Rail Road business, with which opportunity has not been afforded me to post myself.

I propose, therefore, in this communication to treat upon some of the great points which appear to me should be well considered before a Rail Road enterprize [sic] of any magnitude should be undertaken; and then apply these points to the particular road in question — and for the purpose of perspicuity, I will in a measure confine myself, under several heads, to those which are applicable — pro or con.

Iowa and its local position.

By reference to a map which shows the *territory* and *navigable streams* of the Several States and Territories of the United States, unencumbered by the minute annotations of towns, counties, roads, etc. — you get a better general idea of locality than in any other way. Look at such a map and you will at once observe that Southern Iowa and Northern Missouri are as central in location in the United States as the "bulls eye" to a shooting target — that the delta formed by the two great rivers of the World — the Mississippi and the Missouri — has a more prominant [sic] position than any other portion of the map — therefore, *the line* of *inland communication* between the people residing on the Atlantic coast and those on the Pacific coast — other things being equal — must cross this delta — and although there will, no doubt, in time, be many routes of Rail Road across the Continent — some one will be *the great thoroughfare* — it to be determined by *population — quickness of transit — certainty* of *arrivals* and cost of construction — all of which again depend, in a great measure on Climate & Soil — and these, I feel free to say, are not only equal to, but *better* than any other portion of the United States — as both the mortality and produce tables prepared by the Government will show.

So far, *population* as it has flowed West from Plymouth Rock keeps along between the 40th and 43rd parallels — concentrating as it leaves the Eastern States more towards the 41st. *Commerce* on the Atlantic board has for a long time concentrated towards the 41st parallel and the line of the B. & M. R. road is in this very latitude.

In the Settlement of Iowa this was a favorite latitude and the earliest heavy agricultural emigration crossed the Mississippi River at Burlington and roamed to the West of that town — and settlements reached the Missouri River five years sooner than across any other part of the State — and to this cause may be attributed the fact of the better settlement of the *"Second* tiers of counties" than of any other tiers — and this emigration was, no doubt, as is always the case, guided by *Soil* and *Climate*. The *Way* once opened and the Country settled, this became the great Northern emigrating route to Oregon, California, Utah, Nebraska and Kansas, and over it I venture to say, have passed five times the number of teams, during the process of settling those Territories — than passed over any other land route in the United States during the same period of time. And while in one respect it was advantageous to the then people of the State — in this that it gave them prosperous times — a ready sale and high price for their surplus — in another it was very injurious to the state at large — the excitement occasioned by stories of the glittering places in California — the large bounties held out by the Government to men, women & even children who should settle in Oregon — the religious enthusiasm created by the prophesies of Brigam [sic] Young relative to Utah and the later political movements and speculations in Kansas & Nebraska — all took with them thousands and tens of thousands of those who, had they been living *off the thoroughfare* of the emigrant, would now have been citizens of, and producers in, Iowa. I believe it is a conceded fact that the population in Oregon, Utah and Nebraska, each contains a greater number of people from Iowa, than from any other single state. Gen. Lane so informed me concerning Oregon & there is no question as to Nebraska.

While this state of things however has been detrimental to Iowa — it proves that it is the very locality for a profitable Rail Road — for it is a *settled country* and is *already* a *thoroughfare*.

In studying the geography and resources of a country — few persons can

get even a faint idea of what the country is by mere maps or figures —
He must travel over it and see for himself. To illustrate: — I have had
intelligent and prominant [sic] men of Education in the East ask me if
the Mississippi river was Navigable above the Rapids at Davenport! If the
Missouri was Navigable above Council Bluffs! If there was *any timber*
in Iowa! etc. — when the Geography which they committed to memory
during their younger days told them that said Rivers were each about *four
thousand* miles long and their Guide books of the present day told them
how far each town was above the mouth of the river and their newspapers
told them of the arrival of steamers with hundreds of tons of freight at
St. Paul and at Fort Benton. So our own people of Iowa in 1845 showed
their ignorance of what was within our own limits. You will recollect
that Congress proposed to make the 17½th degree of longitude the Western
Boundary of our State — this would run about as far West as the Centre
of Union County — to the "highlands" as they are described in the treaty
of July 15, 1830, dividing the Waters flowing into the Des Moines River
from those flowing into the Missouri River. At that day, so little was
known of the country between those highlands & the Missouri River that
the advocates for accepting the Congressional boundaries met with considerable success, by asserting, *uncontradicted*, that the whole of the country,
was a sandy desert — destitute of timber — and even a year later when
the boundaries of Clarke County were established, and the county named
— Gov. Clarke, for whom it was named, was frequently joked for having
a county named after him which would never have any inhabitants! — but
now we find that the Country West of the "Congressional boundary" in
the Southern part of the State has a more productive soil and is better
watered than any East of it — while Clarke County is one of the best
counties in the State.

Soil and topography

Commencing at Burlington and going westward you will find a rich
black loamy soil as far as Cedar Creek in Jefferson County, peculiarly well
adapted to the production of corn, oats, potatoes, buckwheat, rye, flaxseed
and hay. After you cross Cedar Creek the soil is a little stiffer and across
the Des Moines Valley, it is better adapted to wheat than East of Cedar
Creek — while it produces well every other grain. Leaving the Western
bluffs of the Des Moines River the soil has more sand and lime pebble
mixed with it and the surface is much more undulating, yet not any more
subject to "wash" than the more level land farther East. As you reach
Grand River you find a richer soil than farther East — but all the Country
between the Des Moines and Grand River is, according to my observation,
better adapted to Corn than any other part of the State — the Settlers
always having a *certain* and *large* crop — let the *season* be ever so *wet* or
the *drought* ever so *great*. One remarkable fact might here be stated &
that is, that none of the crops in Southern Iowa ever suffers for the want

of rain in July, August and September, as they do in States where the soil is gravelly. In 1845-'46 — commencing in June of the former year & ending in July of the latter — a space of 13 months, there was not at any one time sufficient rain to wet the surface of the ground one inch in depth — and yet, in those years, we had the best of Corn Crops. But to proceed, after leaving Grand River, you rise to the "Highlands" before referred to, and to the most elevated part of your road — the ground being between four and five hundred feet more elevated than at Burlington. Here there is a marked change in the surface and in the Soil. As you descend towards the Missouri River, the country becomes still more rolling — the streams are narrower and have deeper channels with perpendicular banks — the soil becomes lighter colored more sandy and more pebbly; and yet there is less and less wash until you get to the Missouri Bluffs — where there is none at all. From the "Highlands" to the Missouri — you pass over the Valleys of the two Nodaways and the two Nishnabotonas — four of the most beautiful Valleys in the West — the two latter, especially to use the language of Judge Mason "give you the best idea you can get of Paradise" — the soil being exhuberantly [sic] rich — the country being interspersed with beautiful groves and springs and streams of pure water greeting your eyes on either hand.

One peculiar feature in the topography of the Country and which renders it peculiarly attractive to the husbandman is, that the slope of the Country is wholly to the *Southern East — South* and *South West* — this is occasioned by the flow of the streams South East into the Mississippi and South and South West into the Missouri — thus securing an earlier spring and a later fall than in a country where the exposure of the soil is in a Northerly direction. Another advantage, more particularly beneficial to a rail Road, ensues from the course of these streams and that is — the prairie lands being on the divides and heighth of land between the streams, there will always be good roads leading far into this interior from the Rail Road, on which the farmer can haul his produce, uninterrupted by high water in the Spring — by springs and spouty lands, such as are found in Valleys, and by steep hills such as he would find if the rail road had a North and South direction. Before the settlement of the Country West of the Des Moines River — the hunters living in Missouri, in large numbers made Western Iowa a hunting ground for Deer, Buffalo and Bees, and made long roads up almost every "divide" in that part of the State and they are now the principal roads in the Country and up and down which for distances ranging from 40 to 100 miles the settlers, *at this day*, trade and traffic — and as all of these roads are nearly at right angles with all the Rail Roads, that are projected Westerly through the State, it is a matter of some moment as to which road progresses most rapidly, inasmuch as that road will secure trade of the greatest extent of this country. It is true that it will cost something more for the construction of a road that crosses the streams so nearly at right angles — but when we take into consideration the ease with which

such soil is graded — it can hardly be called a serious matter of consideration in such an enterprize.

Timber

Most of the timber along the whole line of the road is hardwood — Oak
largely predominating. From Burlington to Grand River, there is ample
timber, without the use of coal — beyond Grand River, the timber is found
in *groves* and not in *bodies* of large extent — Sometimes the groves are
on the uplands, but mostly along the Valleys, and along this Western part
of the road there will be a demand for coal for fuel, which will be the
province of the road to supply from the Des Moines Valley — and which
will, eventually afford no small quantity of freightage for trains running
West. In the early settlement of Iowa, as in that of Illinois, there was a
general talk of a "*scarcity* of *timber*," and yet any well informed man will
tell you that there is *more timber* in Iowa, *today*, than there was twenty
years ago — the growth of timber when protected from fires being absolutely greater than the consumption. I have heard farmers who emigrated
from the heavy timbered sections of Indiana and Ohio frequently say that
they would prefer to haul their timber & fuel eight miles and have a
prairie farm than to have a farm to make in the timber. In 1836 — 22
years ago — I travelled from Chicago to Galena — nearly along the line of
the present rail road between those places — and every one of a company
of eleven in number with whom I travelled, gave it as their opinion that
the Country was too destitute of timber ever to be settled — and three
years later — in 1839 — I travelled over the Country between Burlington
and Chicago for half the way — (next to Burlington) near the line of the
C. B. & Q. road in company with a party of five — when a similar conclusion was arrived at in regard to that country — and yet I will venture the
assertion that there is more timber along the Western or more sparsely
timbered half of the Burlington and Mo. Riv road — than there is along
the line of either of the above roads. But timber or no timber — with a
rich soil and plenty of good coal the road can be successfully and cheaply
operated, and can carry timber and fuel to the door of every farmer, as
the two roads before mentioned in Illinois are now doing. It is true that
there is a great scarcity of good tie and bridge timber along the Western
part of the road — and so far the construction of that part of the road will
be more expensive, and so far "calculations" should be made in "counting
the cost." For Bridges, however, pine lumber which is considered the
best — can be had at Burlington & can be transported a long distance with
but little expense to the Company — and such lumber, too, will be in large
demand along the whole length of the road — and be one of the principle [sic] items of freightage as it now is on the C. B. & Q. road in Illinois.

Water

On the Eastern part of the road, extending West as far as the "Highlands" in Union County, there is a scarcity of springs and small living

streams for stock water, which makes it inconvenient to raise cattle, except
in the valleys of the large mining streams — this inconvenience, however,
is partially done away with by the ease with which good wells are made
in all the prairies — the best of water always being found at from 16 to
30 feet in depth — ample at all times for the operation of the road. On
the Western part of the road, the streams are fed with numerous springs
of pure cold water — and as you approach the Missouri increasing in volume
until they obtain a size, at the bluffs on that river, sufficient almost to turn
machinery. The Country along the Western fifty miles of the road is
peculiarly adapted to cattle raising. With a large rich grassy range and a
heavy growth of pea-vine and rush, but little is required to winter stock —
In the Missouri bottoms hundreds of cattle are herded every winter and
keep fat without any feeding whatever, except in the way of salt. I have
known herds wintered in this way, by herdsmen who make it a business —
at a cost of *one dollar* a head to the owner! With the *abundance* of *spring
water*, therefore, and such *fine feed* — the country along the Western part
of your road must become *a great cattle raising region* — as will the country
between the Des Moines River and the "Highlands" become, on account
of the *peculiar adaptation of the soil to corn* and the large quantities of
Mast, a *hog growing region* — thus making a great stock freightage for
the whole length of your road — the cattle all going *East* and the hogs
both *East* and West — the market for the latter being good on the Missouri
river.

Rock

There is, except on the Des Moines River, a scarcity of this article along
the whole line of the road, and in the way of a material for culverts cannot
be had at the ordinary cost. For most purposes, however, brick which can
be made at any point can be used as a substitute — both by the R. R. Co.
and by the Settler. The *finest quality* of rock is found on the Des Moines
River and it will become a considerable article of freitage [sic] for a short
distance each way from that stream.

Coal

Of all the mineral deposits known — none is more beneficial to the
success of a rail road enterprize than beds of coal — and I venture to say
that no road in the United States has a more favorable location than has
the B. & M. Riv. road in this particular. It is first found along the line
about forty miles west of Burlington — but no considerable veins are
worked until you get two miles West of Fairfield — where the road runs
over one of the best beds in the West — as you proceed West, however,
the veins increase in thickness, and a few miles West of Ottumwa, you
strike a five feet vein of what is pronounced *the best coal in the Western
Country*. You continue to pass over coal beds until you approach Chariton
— a distance of say: 120 miles from Burlington — thus running through
a *"coal country"* for a distance of *eighty miles* — affording a *certain* and

constant freightage both East and West — which, when properly developed, will alone *pay the running expenses of the entire road* — besides affording a cheap and convenient fuel for operating the roads and keeping in motion the factories, shops & mills which must grow up and make another class of freightage. When we consider the vast quantity of coal that is already used by steamers on the Mississippi and the numerous factories that have grown up within a few years along its shores — it is impossible to make estimate what will be its demand and consumption at points situated as Burlington is — at the termination of a rail road that penetrates the great coal fields. In two years from this time, with proper encouragement to coal miners and Coal dealers, a business can be built up at that point, which in my opinion, will surprise even the most sanguine expectations of the owners of the road, and will lay the foundation for an emigration into the State along the line of the road that will give a notoriety to the country equal to that of the manufacturing districts of Ohio and Pennsylvania. The Missouri River and her Valley must also be supplied with this *now a necessity* — and a large Western coal trade will spring up *at once* on the completion of the road to that river.

You recollect that the first rail road that was ever constructed in the United States, was for the carriage of this one article to a market — and now the *main revenue* of some half dozen of the roads in Pennsylvania and Maryland is derived from the transportation of this article. It is now the principle article of freight on all the roads and canals penetrating the coal mines of the United States; and must become eventually in this country as in Great Britain — the main spring of commerce and Manufactures.

As to *quality*, the Iowa coal far exceeds that found in Illinois — so much so that about three years ago — before the rail road was operated west of Burlington, our Fairfield teamsters in going to Burlington after goods for the Merchants loaded their wagons with coal for the downward trip, and sold their loads to the Smiths in that city at *35 cents the bushel*, when at the same time the C. B. & Q. rail road was delivering *Illinois Coal* at E. Burlington at *25 cents the bushel!* This *practical* demonstration as to the superiority of Iowa coal has been since that time, fully sustained by the frequently repeated analyses by distinguished geologists and chemists. I myself, predict that the day is not far distant (after the Mississippi is bridged at Burlington as it must soon be to accommodate the great commerce of the country) when Iowa Coal will successfully compete with Illinois coal *in the Chicago market!* thus giving to the C. B. & Q. road a freightage that her owners, a few years ago, would have looked upon with more surprize in possessing than did the *wise men* of 1812 who hooted at the prognostications of John Stevens who ventured the assertion that a carriage could be made "to acquire a greater velocity than could be given by the fleetest horses."

I am not prepared to state at this time what will be the value of this freightage to your road for the coming year, as no preparations have as yet been made for the mining or carrying of it to market — but in one year from now I think it will equal if not exceed that of the freightage on the entire grain and stock grown in Jefferson county. It can be delivered on the cars at from $1.60 to $2.00 per ton, and it will command at from $4 to $7 at Burlington — hence there is now ample margin for a profit — but as the business increases, with the aid of machinery for mining and loading, and with coal cars adapted to the business — the profits to the road will be greater and the price to the consumer *less*. In fact, it would not surprize me if, in five years time, you will find a double track between Burlington and the coal banks indispensible.

Climate

Much has been said pro and con on this question and what I may now say may not be altogether believed by some — yet with a residence of twenty years in Iowa — seven in Burlington and thirteen at this place, I have had no fault to find except in three of those years — and in those three, I might have found the same fault anywhere in West. I allude to the years 1851 — 1856 & 1858 — two of which were *too wet* and *one too* dry for either *crops* or *comfort*. To some the cold dry winds from the prairie in the fall and winter are a subject of disapproval — to others the wet month of May keeps back the burning ardor of the rested tiller of the soil and he cannot plant as soon as did his forefather in Ohio and Indiana — but to me the former objection has less weight than has a wet, slushy winter such as is found further East & south — while the latter is more than counterbalanced by the long and beautiful dry falls that are un-equalled in other parts of The United States. The dry bracing air of winter and the constant prairie breezes of the summer afford to the people of Iowa *a health* such as the inhabitants of a flat country like Indiana and Illinois never possessed — and which must form a great ingredient in the inducement which is held out for emigration to our state. *Winter* emigra-tion, too, must always as heretofore, prevail to a greater extent along your line of road than on either of the roads to the North or South. This is the dividing latitude between *soft* and *hard* or rather *wet* and *dry* snows — the one of which falls at intervals throughout the winter in large quantities — first blocking up the roads — then flooding the country carrying off bridges, tearing up tracks and rendering travel difficult and farming un-pleasant — the other covers the ground for months — drifts along the lanes — fills up the cuts in rail road lines, and not only stops business but adds greatly to the list of yearly losses to which rail roads are subject — During twenty winters I have seen but four when sufficient snow has fallen to make what is generally termed "good sleighing" & during which trains would probably be obstructed. In this particular, therefore, you have a most favored line on which to construct a rail way. While referring to snow allow me to call your attention to the difference between the probable obstructions you will meet with and those which are met elsewhere. In the snow latitudes — all Western prairie roads *which run North and South* meet with constant obstructions *from drifting* which can never be *entirely remedied* but by raising the track on piles. This is owing to the prevailing winds from the West and North West. Witness, for instance the Illinois Central during the Winter of '56 '57. She *seldom* made connections, while the Galena & Chicago & the C. B. & Q. lost but few, except by the succeeding floods which damaged their Culverts and bridges. In the Atlantic States, where the snows come with a strong East wind, there the North and South roads also suffer damage from this cause.

I venture the prediction, therefore, taking all the above causes into consideration that the Burlington & Mo. Riv. road will, when completed, lose less per mile by snows and floods, at least 50 per cent — than any road in Northern Illinois, Wisconsin or even the Hannibal & St. Joseph road in Missouri.

Now as to the *only disadvantage*, occasioned by the want of snow (for the want of it is no inconvenience to farmers in hauling — the wheeling always being good in Winter) and that is it is a serious injury to the crop of *Winter Wheat* — which may be safely set down *as an uncertain crop* in this latitude in Iowa, the dry winters and want of snow causing it to freeze out — so that we do not get a good crop more than once out of four years — take the average.

Capacity of the Country to support a road

I will leave the detail of statistics to prove, what I shall now assert — (my conclusions having been arrived at partly by statistics prepared some three years ago and partly by a general comparison of the country through which the road runs with that through which similar roads are constructed in Illinois and Indiana and which have proved to be *paying roads*) — that no rail road in the United States pays better than will the Burlington and Mo. River road — if economically and properly managed.

Unlike it is in the Eastern States, there is *no waste land* along or on either side of your road. On nearly all the rail roads in the United States — you find the country that is tributary to their support interspersed with Mountains — Marshes — barren knobbs — or perchance when you find a valley road the track may pass through a continuous line of farms — but then the trade of the road for the most part is confined *within the limits of that Valley.* The C. B. & Q. road in Illinois runs through about the same kind of a country as does the B. & M. R. road — with this difference, that the face of the country in Illinois is *too flat* and the prairies are *too large.* While the country along the Illinois road for the width of 20 miles on each side may produce as much per acre as the same width of country along your road — yet I do not think that the crops would be equally as certain — one year with another — as those on your road — Another advantage that your line of road possesses over that of any line in Iowa, Illinois, Wisconsin or Missouri is that the farms will be of *less size* and *more numerous* on each square mile than they are on the lines of the roads before referred to — thus furnishing more freights and more passengers than where the farms are so extensive. Small farms, too, result in *good tillage*, and this again adds to certainty of crop and as a result uniformity of receipts by the Rail Road company. One thought here suggests itself and that is to correct a prevalent error that exists in the minds of Eastern men. They often say: "You have too many towns in the West." Now in this they are mistaken for the very reason that they look at our country from an Eastern stand point — where, on account of the many miles of *waste land*, there can be but comparatively few towns to what we can have in the West where we have no *waste lands*. The truth is that the number of towns along the line of your road is far less in comparison to the number of square miles of tillable lands than you will find along the line of any eastern road — thus showing a large margin for the improvement of receipts in passage money. So, also, is there an equal margin for increase of freightage for your road, by the opening of new farms on the yet uncultivated portion of our prairies. The question naturally arises here as to what portion of the country is owned by non-residents. In answer, I would say that for the first hundred miles, commencing at Burlington, there are but very few non-resident property holders — the number increases, however, as you go west and for the last hundred miles perhaps one fifth of the land is so held. The late monetary crisis, however, has had a very beneficial effect in stopping speculation and further purchases by non-residents and at the same time has induced hundreds to offer the lands heretofore purchased at very low prices — thus holding out inducements to the cultivator to purchase. In five years time, I think that most of the land now held by non residents will have passed into the hands of residents and producers. During the years 1856 & '57 the race for speculation followed in the wake of emigration, and this latter being in the direction of Wisconsin, Minnesota & Kansas, less lands were bought for speculation in Iowa than in either of those states or the Territory of Kansas. The Northern part of Iowa and the Northern part of Illinois have suffered much from non-resident proprietors — yet the summary manner of collecting taxes in Iowa has induced many who owned land here and held it for speculation, to sell out at the earliest day.

The completion of the road to the Missouri River is, to my mind, the great point which your company should strive for, if they wish to secure a large return for their investment. I have no doubts but what it will pay dividends of *ten per cent*, when you reach Ottumwa, for there you will tap the great trade of the Des Moines Valley — which, of itself, will support your road handsomely, without the aid of the way business between Burlington & Ottumwa. In the whole valley of the Mississippi before the introduction of Rail Roads, the natural course of trade is *down the streams* — by water if navigable and by land if not — After the introduction of the iron rail — the course is *across the streams & towards the East.* Thirteen years ago *all* the merchants of Fairfield traded at Keokuk and St. Louis, and they continued so to do until within two years — now all go to Burlington, Chicago or the Eastern cities. So with the Merchants of Agency, Ottumwa, Eddyville, Oskaloosa, Albia, Chariton and all the towns West of here — So with the cattle drovers — hog dealers and wool buyers. Your road has changed that trade town by town as it has approached it, and will continue to so change the trade, until it shall absorb all within say thirty miles of its track — unless headed off by some rival road. As I was about to remark, the trade of the whole Des Moines Valley, from Ft Dodge to Keokuk, a distance of 250 miles has heretofore sought an outlet at Keokuk — not because they had river navigation — for that has been of but little advantage — but because they had one of the best natural "divide" roads in the world, along the whole Eastern side of this valley — a road which, for its distance, has had no equal *for business* in the United States, save the great National Road from Baltimore to Wheeling. To tap this road and this valley then should be *the work of this season*, if you have the welfare of the Rail road at heart; and then, as fast as practicable, you should continue to tap each successive valley that crosses your line until you turn the trade of the Great Missouri herself into an Eastern Channel. As before remarked — the trade always goes *down stream* — the roads in that direction being descending and consequently easier to loaded teams — hence rival roads North of you are the only ones that you need to fear — those South will always draw the trade that is nearer to them than to yours — while such is not the case North, if you *first secure it.*

But to me the enterprize is one of but momentary importance, unless made *a thoroughfare through the State,* for other roads that may be built *through the State,* (if this is not) will attract the travel & emigration — will have the preference of interior shippers and will eventually make yours a road of secondary importance, or a *mere branch* of the C. B. & Q road. If, however, it is pushed through to the Missouri, the trade of three embryo cities of importance on that River — Nebraska City — Omaha & Council Bluffs — will throw their trade into this Channel, and will open up a career of prosperity — second only to such thoroughfares as the N. Y. Central — the Penna. Central & the Balt. & Ohio roads.

Lieut. Warren, of the Topographical Bureau, who has for several years devoted his time in examinations of the Western Country, and particularly that part of it West of the Missouri River, in a late report (Jany 29, 1858) says: "Of all the Valleys of the Rivers running into the Missouri that of the Platte *furnishes the best route for any kind of a road* leading into the interior."

Your road is to run to a point opposite the mouth of this Valley — and when completed to that point, you at once command *the trade of Nebraska Territory.* That appears to me will be the inevitable result.

But I will not longer tire your patience with generalities — predicting only, before I close this communication, that your receipts, before the 1st of

January next (if you reach Agency City by 1st Dec.) will prove to your own satisfaction and to the world, that no road ever built in the West can show a better summing up, per mile, for the first 75 miles of its length than will yours.

As soon as my time will permit, I will give you such statistical information as will show the truth of my predictions, in the meantime, believe me

Yours truly,

BERNHART HENN

APPENDIX C

Source material relating to the formation of a through line between Chicago and the Mississippi River

1. Testimony of James F. Joy, in the case of *Asabel Enigh v. C. B. & Q. R. R. Co.* before the United States District Court for Illinois, November 10, 1860.

I was at the Legislature when the charter of the C. M. Tract RR. Co. was amended in the year 1852, June 19th, and at that session of the legislature I saw the parties who were promoting this enterprise, at Galesburg — Mr. Colton and others — and had an understanding with them, and had their charter so shaped as to authorize them to extend their road to what is now Mendota, to the point where the Chicago and Aurora should intercept the Illinois Central. Mr. Brooks, who was then Superintendent of the Michigan Central Road and myself, had the design to interest the stockholders of the Michigan Central in the Chicago and Aurora and Central Military Tract Roads, and take them up and build them.

Soon after the session of the Legislature at which that charter was amended, and on the eighth day of August, 1852, I went to Galesburg and made a contract with the parties who then controlled the M. T. RR. Co., by which my friends were to have the control of the stock in that road, and the control of the board, that is, a majority of the members of the board, provided I got the stock taken, and we had an arrangement also with the Chicago and Aurora Rail Road by which we should have a majority of the stock of that road, provided they chose to take it. I should have said, that before I went to Galesburg, on the 8th day of August, 1852, having had an understanding at the legislature with Copeland and others, who controlled that road; then immediately after the legislature adjourned I went to New York and to Boston to place the matter before our friends there, and got their subscriptions. The original subscription list I now hold in my hands, dated July 12th, 1852, New York. I took up subscriptions at the same time for the Chicago and Aurora Rail Road, to extend it to Mendota, where it was to connect with the M. T., taking the control of a majority of the stock in both roads. It was after that I went to Galesburg and made a contract above alluded to, which I hold in my hand, which has been in my possession ever since, which subscriptions and arrangements secured the construction of both those roads from Aurora to Galesburg, and the majority of stockholders in both roads being the same parties, and the majority of the boards of both roads being the same parties, the design being to have a road which should be operated continuously by the same Superintendent, and as soon as the respective value of the two stocks should be known, to be consolidated into one company which has been done since. Soon after the contract of the eighth of August, a meeting of the stockholders was held in Galesburg — I think in October — and a board was elected in a manner which had been agreed upon, and of that board Mr. John W. Brooks was made President, that is, of the Military Tract Company. He remained President of that road and of that Company up to about the time of the consolidation of the companies into one. I was made President of the Chicago and Aurora Railroad, and it was by joint effort that the two roads were constructed and brought to completion, the whole being put under contract to Galesburg as rapidly as the same could be made. . . . It may be well to say that the stock of these roads were subsequently enlarged by subscriptions, although they were begun on the subscriptions I had obtained in New York and Boston. It is proper to say, also, that the stock of the Chicago and Aurora was deemed the most valuable, and therefore, subscriptions could be more easily obtained for it than the others. It had, therefore, more money, and furnished mostly the equipment of the two roads; the cars of both, however, running through over both roads, and the roads could hardly be operated without the cars of both running over both roads, and it was designed so to operate from the beginning, and they were operated by the same superintendent until their consolidation, and have been ever since.

2. Colton Manuscript (between 1876 and 1885).

The existence of the Chicago, Burlington & Quincy R. R., as a *Chicago* line of railway, and its consequent importance as a great corporation originated in the fact that certain parties in the village of Knoxville (then County Seat of Knox County) supported by the Directors of the Peoria & Oquawka RR determined to ignore Galesburg in building the Peoria & Oquawka Railroad three miles south of Galesburg: This would have virtually destroyed this town. For self protection the citizens of Galesburg were necessitated to organize a company of their own which took the name of the Central Military Tract RR Company which was to run from Galesburg to the Rock Island R. R. The final results show the proposed measure of the parties inimical to Galesburg, resulted in the greatest benefit of this great rich interior country by forcing into existence a corporation which has expanded into magnificent proportions, as the present Chicago, Burlington & Quincy RR Company, absorbing not only the *Peoria & Oquawka* R.R. but also all the railroad enterprises in the natural territory of the CB&Q, and extending its line out into the then uninhabited regions of the far west.

The Peoria & Oquawka R R Co was incorporated Feb 12. 1849, their line to extend from Peoria to Oquawka. Their charter was amended Feby 10/51 to pass through Farmington (Fulton Co), Knoxvill[e] (Knox Co) and Monmouth (Warren Co.), with the privilege of building a branch, commencing at or west of Monmouth, running thence to the Mississippi river at or *about Shokokon* — which really meant *Burlington!* This charter was amended later by leaving out Farmington. The line between Knoxville and Monmouth was to be so run as to leave Galesburg three miles off of the road, thereby forcing Galesburg & vicinity to do their shipping business at Knoxville five miles east. Galesburg made an effort with the P & O Co. to get their road to pass through Galesburg, & have a station here, offering to subscribe $20.000 stock; a friend & myself met the directors at Knoxville to take the stock between us. We were positively refused any arrangement. Knoxville, at the time controlling the board, gave us to understand they did not need our services. Arguments & patience being exhausted we applied to the Legislature to make Galesburg a *point* on the P & O line: But Knoxville and Monmouth each had a member in the House of Representatives; while our Senator lived south of Knoxville. They all opposed it, unanimously!

The only recourse left us was to act for ourselves, independently. We therefore applied to the Legislature for a Railroad Charter, and, by the assistance and combination of members from other districts obtained, Feby 15 1851, the charter for the "Central Military Tract Rail Road Company."

Prior to this time a general Charter had been granted to the Northern Cross R. R. Co. which was so amended, Feby 1. 1851, as to permit a *branch* to be built, (which subsequently became the main line after slight alteration — & part of the C B & Q). This branch was to commence at "some "point on that road in Adams County, and running thence on the most "eligible, *beneficial, expedient* & practicable route, through the Military "Bounty Tract & terminating at the most convenient & eligible point at or "near the southern termination of the Ill & Mich Canal. *Provided* the S Co. "shall not locate or construct the S branch upon any line east of the *town* "of *Knoxville*"! — Thus they supposed they had Galesburg completely fenced in! Such is a brief statement of events which forced into existence the C.M.T.Co. & subsequently created the CB & Q.

The first company organized under the Central Military Tract RR Charter Made a preliminary survey, but could raise only small local subscriptions; sufficient only for that purpose, as the country was new and sparsely settled with men of small means. It was said by some of the directors that if we would begin work, it would attract attention of capitalists. I opposed that movement, but agreed to call a meeting of stockholders, make our statements and leave it to their vote to decide. The meeting was called and the proposition of commencing operations was fully argued. I opposed beginning work without money, and my position was fully sustained. The stockholders then wished me to express my views, as to what I thought best to do under the circumstances. I told them I thought I would first find the men who had the money, and then, if I could convince such men that our enterprise was a good one, we could get them to furnish the means to build the road.

I will here state that under the original charter of the C. M. T. RR nothing was accomplished, except to organise and make a preliminary survey, which was not finally adopted. It was under the Amended charter, of June 19, 1852, that the road was really begun. The Corporate members of this last Company were Wm. McMurtry, Geo. C Lanphere, Jas. Bunce, Silas Willard, Chauncey S. Colton, Alfred Brown, E. T. Ellet, Edw. Hollister, Amos Ward, Sylvester Blish, Barney M Jackson, Myrtle G. Brace, & Wm Maxwell; mostly put on for local influence; only two or three retained their stock.

In the spring of 1852 all operations & surveying was stopped.

I went to New York, as usual, that Spring, and made an effort to enlist business men there in our enterprise, principally among my old mercantile friends, but soon found that they were not the class of men to build railroads. I went on to Boston and fortunately there met with Mr. Wadsworth of Chicago and Mr. Grimes of Burlington (afterwards Gov of and Senator from Iowa). We were all stopping at the same hotel in Boston. After supper we got together and talked over railroad matters. I remarked that we were each a director in a seperate [sic] railroad, but I thought our interests were identical. Mr. Grimes was a director in "Peoria & Oquawka" RR; Mr. Wadsworth in the "Aurora Branch" R R and I was in the "Central Military Tract" RR. (The "Aurora Branch" was then built 15 miles to Galena Junction, as the station was then called, & connected with what was then the Galena & Chicago R R — now the Chicago & North Western). Neither of the roads was of any value, as they had no valuable connections or outlets. I may here say that I had previously been negotiating with the Chicago & Rock Island R R directors; whose road was then completed from Chicago to Rock Island, to allow us to connect with their road at Sheffield, & thereby have a Chicago outlet. My proposition being that our company should consolidate with the C & R I RR & become a part of their Co. & road. They had refused this, although afterwards Mr. Farnham (of C & R I RR) and Mr. Judd of Chicago came to Galesburg & proposed to build our road under certain conditions, which I refused.

To continue the account of the Boston meeting with Mr. Wadsworth & Mr. Grimes — Mr. Grimes asked what I proposed; I said I considered it feasible to unite & harmonise our three RR enterprises, and by uniting all our influence, we could together built a railroad from *Burlington to Chicago*, via Galesburg: Further that we should endeavor to engage the Michigan Central RR Co., which was composed of wealthy people, in our united project. We could easily show them that such a railroad as ours would be a valuable feeder for their line. If the proposition was favorably received by the M. C. R R people, they could easily carry it through.

I told Grimes & Wadsworth that there was to be an Extra Session of the Illinois Legislature in June (1852) and that I would undertake to get the charter of the "Central Military Tract" R R so altered & amended that the road should run northward to *connect with any railroad leading to Chicago*; Mr. Wadsworth should get the "Aurora Branch" RR charter amended to be extended south so as to *connect* with any road, from the south, *leading to Chicago*. Mr Grimes was pleased with the plan and sanctioned it, & said he would work for that object. Mr Wadsworth heartily approved of the proposition; and promised his hearty support to consummate it. Mr Grimes being connected with the "Peoria & Oquawka" RR Co; and knowing that the construction of such a proposed road would take all the business from Galesburg & west to Chicago, instead of by Peoria, and that a knowledge of his connection with such a scheme would injure him personally, insisted that his name should not be publically connected with the project. For this reason Senator Grimes has never received the credit due to his far sighted vision, in forming a combination, which, in the future, should redound so greatly to the development & welfare of his own State, and to the great State of Illinois whose interests were so intimately connected, and are to day so indissolubly united to Iowa by the consummation of this great railroad enterprise.

The following day Mr. Grimes, according to agreement, returned to New York and made the proposition to John C. Green and Mr. Griswold, stockholders in the Michigan Central RR Co., who received it very favorably and gave Mr. Grimes a letter of introduction to Mr. Brooks of the M. C. RR, at Detroit, in whose judgement Green & Griswold had great confidence. Mr. Brooks thought the enterprise a good one, if we could succeed in getting the two charters amended as we had proposed.

On my return home, a meeting of the C. M. T. Co. was called, and it was agreed that the charter of the Illinois Central R R (excepting the Land Grant) should be taken as a model for our amended Charter. I contended that the most important feature in our Charter should be *absolute self control* as to rates & fares, for our company, *free from all subsequent legislation*. We were unanimous on this point. I was chosen to go to Springfield to secure the passage of such a charter. We had strong opposition in securing any amendments as to change of line, from all connected with the Peoria & Oquawka R R Co., while many influential members opposed strongly the idea of granting a charter which should be beyond their control, by future legislation, in regard to *establishing rates & fares!* This is a matter I wish to have understood for all time to come. viz That the subject of fixing *rates and fares*, was made a square open issue in the Legislature, in obtaining this foundation Charter, of the CB&Q RRd. I told the members & committee that we could not raise money to build a railroad upon the uncertainties of future legislation on the subject of fares & rates! I told them that, under the old style of charters, we could not build a road, but under the principle of *no future legislation*, we *could*; & that it was a question of a road or no road. Upon this plain distinct understanding we secured the grant of a charter subject to no legislative control.

For the first time I met Mr. J. F. Joy, at Springfield. I asked his opinion, as a railroad man, as to the Charter. He pronounced it good & gave it as his opinion that it could not be altered without our consent.

I asked Mr. Joy's opinion in regard to our road as an outlet for the Michigan Central RR. He said there was one thing in the way which was a great obstacle; which was that the Northern Cross RR Co. was authorized to construct a road to the mouth of the Illinois & Michigan Canal, and not further east than Knoxville, which was only five miles from Galesburg. The *two* roads cannot be built he said. He added, what do you propose to do about that? I said, when I return home, I will go to Quincy and arrange with the "Northern Cross" people to terminate their road at Galesburg, and get them to surrender the right to build any farther than that point. He said that if I could accomplish that, our road could be built. I was intimately acquainted with Mr. N. Bushnel the President of the Northern Cross RR Co., and several of their directors, and felt quite confident that I could induce them to accede to these two important points.

Mr. Joy then agreed that, if I could succeed in my negotiations with the Northern Cross Co., that he would undertake to raise the money; and would afterwards visit Galesburg & make more definite arrangements. I called our board together and they voted me full powers to close a contract with "Northern Cross" Co. I went to Quincy and succeeded in consummating the arrangement.

Mr. J. F. Joy came to Galesburg with his eastern stock subscription for the Central Military Tract R R, conditioned for payment upon a requirement of us to raise a local subscription along the line of the road, between Galesburg and Mendota, of three hundred thousand dollars. It can hardly be understood, at this day, what an undertaking it was then to secure such an amount of railroad stock subscription along 80 miles of sparsely settled country, at a time when farmers & business men alike were scarcely able to carry their own business; & to meet their personal obligations: Besides there was a general distrust & lack of knowledge in regard to railroad enterprises. The state had attempted to build railroads, & had failed in all, except securing a large state debt. In the face of these embarrassments, our board of directors voted to undertake raising the $300.000. local stock. After several months of strenuous effort, during which time the country had been thoroughly canvassed, we still were $50.000 short of the amount required to be raised. Messrs Joy & Brooks came to Galesburg, at this time. They said the eastern subscriptions could not be held unless the remaining $50.000 was subscribed here, and that although they personally would use their influence to help us out, but they couldn't promise as to the result. They said that if the remaining $50.000 was subscribed, the eastern subscription would be paid, and the road would be built. I consulted with my friend Silas Willard, and we thought it too much to risk, after all we had done to bring the enterprise to this point. We two therefore concluded to subscribe the $50.000, although neither of us could afford to embarrass our business by such an amount at that time. I will here say that Mr. Willard was almost the only man I relied on in the whole undertaking. He was a man of good judgment & great energy, and never discouraged by failure. He has been dead many years.

The Central Military Tract R.R, after above subscriptions were secured, came under the management of the new organization, with Mr. Brooks as the President.

When the three roads (the C.M.T. RR the P & O R R and the N.C.R R) were located, with Galesburg as the diverging point, the question of depot grounds, right of way &c had to be settled. I was a trustee, also member of the Executive Committee & financial agent of Knox College, whose property was largely in real estate in Galesburg. I advised the College Trustees to donate to the Railroads all the lands required for depot purposes; and also to give them free right of way through all their lands in and around the town. My suggestion was adopted by the board of trustees, and deeds ordered for all such proposed grants, free to the railroads. The Northern Cross R R Co. subsequently desired a tract of land which they could control independently, which they valued at $6000. & which they wished to purchase of the College: when the deeds were executed, they wished to pay for it in their *stock*. This was acceded to. When that R R was closed out, under C B & Q RR mortgage, the N. C. stock was of course *worthless*. But no one ever complained. We were determined to have a rail-road. You ask how the CMT RR came to be sold to the C. B & Q RR Co. I answer It was *never sold*, but *consolidated* with the Aurora road. This Aurora road had had four names, viz, first "Aurora Branch RR" — 2ᵈ. "Chicago & Aurora RR" — 3ᵈ "Chicago & Southwestern RR" & finally by a special act of the Legislature the name was changed to the "Chicago Burlington & Quincy Rail Road Co. before, but in view of the consolidation with the Central Military Tract RR. The latter road dropped its distinctive name at the time of consolidation, and the whole line was afterwards known as the C B & Q RRᵈ.

Now the programme was carried out, which was made in Boston between Mr. Grimes, Mr. Wadsworth & myself; except the connection of the Peoria & Oquawka RR with the Central Military Tract RR *at Galesburg.*

There was a directors meeting of C. M. T. R R Co. called at Galesburg, at which Mr. Joy & Mr. Brooks were present. I had previously advised Mr. Grimes and Genl. A. C. Harding (of the Peoria & Oquawka Co) of this meeting of our Co., and they called a meeting of the P. & O directors at Monmouth for the same day, to be in session, in the *afternoon.* Our meeting was held in the *forenoon.* I will here say that, at this time, the Burlington & Monmouth people had come to own a majority of the "Peoria & Oquawka RR" stock, and they were favorable to making Galesburg a point on their road, although strongly opposed by the Peoria and Knoxville influence.

After the meeting of the C M T RR directors was over, (mentioned on page 14) I told Mr. Brooks & Mr. Joy of the meeting to be held at Monmouth, in the afternoon, by the P & O directors. They had never entertained a very favorable opinion of the "Peoria & Oquawka" road, although very favorable to the Quincy road (Northern Cross). They, at first, were disinclined to going to Monmouth. I told them, in my opinion, the Burlington Road would in time be the most valuable road; and that I predicted, that in time the Burlington road would go through to the Missouri River. After considerable hesitation and argument Messrs Joy & Brooks consented to go to Monmouth. At that meeting the Peoria & Oquawka R R Co. directors proposed to Brooks & Joy that if they would take fifty of their $1000. Bonds and pay par for them, in cash, their co. would make the connection at Galesburg. The proposition was accepted. This last arrangement fulfilled, in every particular, the Boston programme, as per agreement between Grimes Wadsworth & myself at the out start of the whole enterprise.

Now both companies — the C. M. T. RR and the Peoria & Oquawka RR, — went to work building their respective roads. But when the P & O reached Kirkwood (then called Young America) eight miles west of Monmouth, they had exhausted all their money and credit, and stopped work. They then asked our company to help them again, which was at first refused. But we had $50.000 already in the concern, which was worth nothing unless the road could be helped to connect with the "Central Military Tract RR." Soon after our Board met and authorized our President to advance money, at his discretion, to make this connection: which was done; but when it was made there was a debt created amounting to $583.000. as was afterwards proved up in court, against the P & O. Co. There was no way to collect the debt except to buy the road; but there arose another difficulty, as both roads had agreed with General Harding & his associates, that if they would push the road to Peoria, they should have the first lien on that part of the road. They finished the road but in doing so became badly embarrassed, and proposed to sell their claim to the C. M. T. RR Co. Our Co. was willing to trade, but when the propositions, from both sides, were presented, they were $50.000 apart, and negotiations were broken off, as both declared they had made their best offer. Then a railroad war was waged hotly for some time. The P & O folks cut their rates to ruinous figures, while our Co. were compelled to adopt like rates, to meet them, as both cos. run to Burlington. The business was all done at a loss, for sometime. Finally Gen Harding came to Galesburg to see me; & after hearing his statements, I suggested that the difference ($50.000) should be divided. He declared he could not, as he was losing money on his original proposition to our co. I said, if you can secure this last compromise, I propose, you are rich, but as you are you are broke; and even if you have made a fair offer you had better lose the whole $50.000 than run the road longer at a loss. After a long conference General Harding finally yielded the point, and agreed to accept my proposition, if the Boston people would sanction it. I told him I felt confident they would, although I could promise nothing positively. I advised Gen[1]. Harding to go to Boston personally, as

I was soon going there myself on business, & should talk with our directors on the subject. The Gen[1]. wished me particularly to see Mr. Forbes as he considered him to be the leading man in the co. When I reached Boston Mr. Forbes was out of town. I talked with the other directors, but they did not seem to realize our position, with a strong probability of some other company buying Hardings interest & becoming permanent & strong competitors for our business. On my way west I had some business at Northampton. I met Mr. Forbes on the train, on my return to Springfield. We talked over the P. & O. negotiation. Mr. Forbes said he had made that co. a good offer, and was unwilling to recede from his position. I told him that both roads were running at a loss, and that the small matter of $25.000 could be made up in a few days earnings at fair rates; besides I was confident a short delay, even, would hazard our chances of getting control of that road, & if we lost it now we would get a permanent competitor. I was convinced it was now or never. Mr. Forbes would give me no encouragement. After dinner at Springfield, I went to the train to go west, and Mr. Forbes was to go to Boston. As I was stepping on the cars, Mr. Forbes called to me & said I have been considering that matter and think your arguments have weight, & should be heeded. I will do it. I replied General Harding will be in Boston in two or three days and you can close a bargain with him, I am confident. The result was Harding did go to Boston, and the contract was concluded, and we never had reason to regret the transaction. In the light of subsequent events, this was, in all human probability, the last opportunity for securing control of the P. & O road, & the turning point in the history of the C B & Q RR, as to its future great development; — especially as to its western interests, beyond the Mississippi & the Missouri; all of which unfolded in time as a natural sequence.

After having secured Hardings interest in the Peoria & Oquawka RR, the way was then open to buy the whole road; which was afterwards accomplished. This is the reason why the Peoria people have always been opposed to our Company. They intended, & fully expected, the road to be connected & controlled by the RR Co east of the Illinois River, and thus make a line westward to & through Iowa — and eastward to New York: — Thus making a great Trunk line between New York and the Missouri river, with Peoria as the central point. If their scheme had succeeded the C B & Q RR might have been a very good local road, but never a great institution.

A stockholder in the P & O told me very plainly, after the Harding contract was known, that we had stolen their road.

Now, in regard to the "Northern Cross RR" & how we came to get control of that road, I will briefly state a few facts.

The Northern Cross RR Co had borrowed in Europe $1.200.000.; securing the same by first mortgage bonds on their road (our Quincy branch). This amount was supposed to be sufficient to complete their road. But after the million two hundred thousand dollars was expended, it was estimated that it would require a million dollars in addition to complete the road. The Company again sent an agent to Europe, supposing they could easily get the additional million, by asking for it! They were informed that the money could not be raised on second Mortgage Bonds, unless *our company* would endorse the Bonds. Our Board held a meeting to consider the matter and concluded to authorize the President to endorse the "Northern Cross" 2^d Mortgage Bonds. The N. C. RR Co obtained the million dollars and with it were enabled to complete their road to Galesburg, although in a very poor condition. The N. C. Co. were unable to meet their interest. If I remember aright, our company made one payment of interest on the Bonds. At this juncture Mr. Joy advised our Board not to pay interest or principal on these bonds of the "Northern Cross" Co., as that Co had not done according to contract. The Bondholders of the "Northern Cross RR Co" were notified of the determination of our Co. — After considerable delay the bondholders concluded to accept the situation, and the final arrangement, as I remember it, was that our company gave for the 1st Mortgage 8% bonds on the N. C. RR, our bonds running 30 years at 4% interest; — and for the N. C. RR 2^d Mortgage bonds (1000.000$) we gave an equal amount of our Bonds payable in 16 equal annual payments, *without* interest. The Northern Cross RR was then closed out under the Mortgages and our Company bid it in.

The foregoing is the history of the different transactions connected with the origin & consummation of the enterprise, resulting in the Chicago, Burlington & Quincy Railroad's trunk lines in Illinois.

I will add a few words, giving the reasons why the C B & Q RR has proved such a great success, and has assumed its present mammoth proportions & enviable position. In the first place its lines cover the finest agricultural districts of the west — indeed of the world. This is a great natural advantage which is not to be ignored. But the same fact holds true in the case of the Northern Cross and the Peoria & Oquawka under their old management — & more recently of the Rockford R. I. & St Louis RR! Our road & its branches have as a rule reached out through new districts sparsely settled & made the country as the lines advanced & in this have had an apparent disadvantage at the outstart; but the good judgement used in locating such new lines has told in time. With all the advantages & disadvantages attending our efforts, the success, in my opinion, has been dependent upon the character of the men who directed the great enterprise. I cannot forbear saying of my old associates in the Board of Directors of the C B & Q RR, with whom I was intimately connected for nearly quarter of a century, that they were, without exception, men of broad, comprehensive minds — many of whom were possessed of the highest order of financial sagacity & executive ability. The management of the C B & Q from the first has been characterized by energetic enterprise, and honest business principles. The credit of the company has never been shadowed by a doubt. It has never contracted any local indebtedness, as many other western roads have done to their great disadvantage; therefore the co. could always command material, supplies & labor at the lowest market price. The road has been most fortunate, from the beginning, in being well & ably officered, by men who have conducted it [manuscript illegible] with as much pride & interest as if they were its owners. No road can boast of such a corps of men, from the lowest to the highest grade, as the C B & Q RR. The road has, from the first, stood high as a well & honestly built road, with excellent machinery & rolling stock, which has been kept in such good condition as to insure safety & recommend the C B & Q as *the* safe route for travel, & sure line for general traffic. Such has always been its best advertisement.

I must refer again to the Board of Directors and say that I believe one great secret of their success, in the management of the C B & Q, was in the fact of the unanimity of their councils. A majority vote in our board included every Director: When we could not all see alike on a subject under consideration, it was laid over for further information, and finally so amended or changed as to command the united support of the board; in such union there was immense strength.

C S COLTON

To C. E. Perkins Esq.
Vice Pres^t. & Genl. Mngr
C B & Q RR

3. Letter of James F. Joy to *The Galesburg Republican Register* [1]

To the Editor of *The Republican Register*,
Detroit, Mich., Aug. 15, 1885.

I observe in the *Republican Register* a sketch of the life of the late Chauncey S. Colton, referring to events which took place now more than thirty years ago in connection with the railroads which have done so much to make Galesburg the flourishing and beautiful city it now is, at which time I made his acquaintance and with whom for many years I was intimately associated. The events took place not quite as the sketch relates them, but were equally to the credit of Mr. Colton.

It was in the year 1852 that I first met him and some other gentlemen from Galesburg at Springfield where they were endeavoring to procure an amendment to the charter of the Central Military Tract Railroad Company. I was there for the purpose of procuring an amendment to the charter of what was then the Aurora Branch Railroad Company. This latter was a short road extending thirteen miles from what was then termed the Galena Junction to Aurora. The Michigan Central Railroad had then just been completed or was nearly completed to Chicago. It was seeking connections with the country west of Chicago. The Illinois Central Railroad was then in process of construction through the prairie where Mendota now is from Cairo to Dubuque. The object of the amendment of the Aurora Branch charter was to enable that little company to extend its road

[1] The letter was printed on Aug. 18, 1885.

to Mendota to connect with the Illinois Central there and furnish an avenue for the business of a large distance of its long line to and from Chicago, and also furnish business for the Michigan Central Railroad Company whose stockholders were interested in the Illinois Central as well as the owners at that time of the Aurora Branch mainly if not entirely [sic]. The object of Mr. Colton was to have the charter of the Central Military Tract amended in several particulars to put it in better shape, and when I first saw his plan was to connect it with the Rock Island Railroad at some point specified, I think in Henry County, and the amendment was so prepared that the connection could only be formed with that road. He explained to me his object which was connection with Chicago, and the Rock Island was the nearest road at that time with which the connection could be made by many miles. I stated to him our plans and stated that the road to Mendota would be immediately built and advised him and his friends to have the Military Tract charter so amended as to enable it to connect with any railroad extending to the city of Chicago. On looking over the map and line of the proposed road from Aurora to Mendota, he made up his mind, that that line would furnish for the Military Tract Road the best line to Chicago, and changed the form of the amendment so as to leave the northern end of the proposed road open to form any other connection. He was anxious to secure some connection with Chicago at the earliest possible time. I said to him that I believed the men interested in the Michigan Central Company would take an interest in the Military Tract Company and help build the road. I agreed also if he secured his amendment in the shape advised that I would go directly to Boston and New York and make the effort to induce them to do it. He agreed on his part that the charter should not be disposed of in any form to the Rock Island Company until I should have returned from Boston and come to Galesburg. The amendments of both charters were passed in the form agreed upon and I went immediately to Boston and New York and the desired aid was secured upon condition that Galesburg and the country along the line should contribute a certain amount. That amount I do not now remember with certainty but think it was $200,000, but possibly it might have been $300,000 though I think not. The $200,000 was a very large amount to be raised there at that time.

On my visit to Galesburg at that time the late J. W. Brooks, then president of the Michigan Central Company, accompanied me. The proportion to be raised at Galesburg was a very large proportion of the whole. At a meeting of all the people there where all who were able subscribed liberally, including Mr. Colton and Mr. Willard, and after all possible effort, there were $50,000 lacking of the amount. The meeting adjourned without having accomplished the object. It was then when we had almost lost hope, that Messrs. Colton and Willard subscribed the additional sum of $25,000 each. This was a very large sum and to Mr. Brooks and myself an astonishing subscription. It obviated all difficulty and the line of roads from

Chicago to Galesburg which has since expanded into the great Chicago, Burlington and Quincy Railroad system was secured. The work began at once and was prosecuted to completion as fast as possible. On our way back from Galesburg to Peoria on our way to Chicago we met the then treasurer of the Rock Island going to Galesburg to subscribe stock and make an arrangement to contract in behalf of that company for the charter of the Central Military Tract Railroad. So near did the Chicago, Burlington and Quincy miss of becoming a part of the Chicago, Rock Island and Pacific and all of its great country becoming tributary to that road. That company is a very prosperous one, one of the most valuable in the country, but what would it have been if it had acquired the command of the country which has made the C. B. & Q., perhaps, the most prosperous company in the world, in addition to that which the Rock Island now controls. From that time to about two years since I have been always in relations with Mr. Colton, for many years intimate an[d] close, and have all the time known him well. He was a sagacious, honest, public-spirited, good and noble man. The brief funeral discourse of the Rev. Mr. Williston is an admirable and true description of the man and his character.

At the time the Military Tract Road was laid out there was yet a considerable amount of government land along its line. Between Princeton and Galesburg there was scarcely any settlement. The country had been settled on each side of it from the middle portion between the Illinois and Mississippi and through which the line of the Military Tract road was laid was almost wholly uncultivated though settlements on either side were not far away. At Mendota there was hardly a house. Princeton was a small hamlet. Galesburg still smaller. In all the intervening country there were but few farms. How changed that rich and populous country covered with beautiful farms now and with many towns and villages from what it was then.

JAMES F. JOY.

APPENDIX D

Extracts from letters of Charles E. Perkins to his wife, Edith Forbes Perkins, August 7–19, 1866, describing his trip with James F. Joy from Burlington to Omaha, thence to St. Joseph, Kansas City, Leavenworth, Quincy, and Galesburg, and back to Burlington [1]

[1]

Library, [Burlington] 10 1/2 P.M.
Tuesday
Aug. 7, '66

Late this afternoon came a dispatch from Mr. Joy, saying he would be here in the morning to start overland — so after tea Emerson and I drove down to lay in a supply of whisky and quinine to take along. . . .

We shall leave here tomorrow at 9 A. M. or at 5 in the evening — I don't yet know which. At Chillicothe, the next station beyond Ott'a, we shall take to horse power. We are to have a covered wagon, with curtains to roll up all around, and a model darkey to drive — one who knows how to take care of horses and men too. Thursday we shall be at Chariton; Friday expect to drive to Osceola, in Clarke Co.; Saturday, Afton, Union Co.; Sunday, Quincy, Adams Co.; Monday, Red Oak, Montgomery Co.; Tuesday, Glenwood, Mills Co. Thence we have not decided yet whether to go to St. Jo, 100 miles south of Glenwood, or to the R. R. which runs west from Clinton (on the Mississippi), which is completed to within about 100 miles of the Missouri and is 50 miles north of Glenwood.

Get a map of Iowa and trace our progress. I shall write to you as often as possible as we go along — if only a line to drop in some wayside Post Office. I shall take my little gun and powder and shoot eno' to knock over an occasional supper.

There will be much of interest in the country and I expect to enjoy the trip. The weather is pleasant, nights cool and roads in good order. Mr. Joy is a pleasant travelling companion and full of information of all kinds. . . .

*　　　*　　　*　　　*

[1] These letters are from Chapter VII of the unpublished manuscript "Letters of Charles E. Perkins," a collection of letters edited by Mrs. Edward Cunningham, of Boston, daughter of C. E. Perkins. They are reproduced here with her kind permission.

[2]

Osceola
Thursday, Aug. 9, '66

Arrived here at 7 this morning. It is now 10 — we have had a meeting and start at 6 tomorrow — have driven today 55 miles. Expect to make Quincy tomorrow night. Hotelkeeper is looking over my shoulder — don't know whether he can read or not. . . .

Weather is fine, roads good, and I am perfectly well. We shall, I hope, get to the Missouri by Saturday night, and we mean to go out on the Pacific Road as far as it is completed. . . . People here are not very enterprising on the R. R. question.

*   *   *   *

[3]

Quincy, Adams Co.
Aug. 10, '66

Arrived here, dear Edie, at 10 o'c'k this evening and have just had supper and are waiting for Mrs. Shepard to prepare beds. . . .

We left Osceola at 7 this morning — had rather a poor night there — beds were not clean. We drove 25 miles to Afton to dinner and since dinner have come 37 miles, making 62 miles for the day. Twelve miles from here, about six this evening, one of our horses gave out and lay down flat in the road! We had nothing to do but to hunt up a farmer and hire him to put his horses into our buggy and bring us along. Our darkey followed, riding our well horse and leading the tired one.

Tomorrow we are going to Glenwood, in Mills County, 60 miles hence. Being doubtful about our team, I have just been round with the man Shepard to the house of "Jim Miles" to hire Jim's team for tomorrow. Jim and his family had retired, but the front door being open, old Shepard walked in, and I, standing at the door, bargained with Jim, who was in bed, for his team!

During the day's journey today I have wasted some ammunition and succeeded in bagging two prairie fowl — Mr. Joy says they were too young to fly away, but that is slander.

The country we have come thro' today is the highest part of the State, in this latitude at least. Afton, Union County, where we dined, is the tip-top. It is a beautiful rolling country, with here and there a patch of timber, but mostly prairie. Most of the prairie is just as the Indians left it — very little of the country west of Osceola is cultivated. What people there are here *waiting*, and have been for 10 years, for the Railroad. . . .

*   *   *   *

[4]

Glenwood
Saturday, Aug. 11, '66

Arrived here late last night and am to leave in a few minutes for Plattsmouth, where we hope to find a boat on the Missouri River for Omaha.
We shall go 150 miles west on the Pacific R. R. and shall then go down
the river by boat to Kansas City. Down there we shall go west on the other
Pacific R. R. for 100 miles or so.

Yesterday we had no adventures — saw very few chickens and shot only
one. For breakfast yesterday, at Shepard's in Quincy, we had my chickens
of the day before's sport.

Weather is getting a little too warm for perfect comfort, but we are
enjoying the trip very much. The country is beautiful.

Wagon is here.

                    *   *   *   *

[5]

Omaha
Nebraska Territory
Aug. 13, '66

I wrote a hasty line yesterday morning as we were leaving Glenwood.
We arrived here last evening at 6, after a drive of 30 miles and a rest of
two or three hours for dinner. We left Glenwood in a light open wagon
drawn by two black ponies, and with the most remarkable specimen of a
man to drive us that I ever fell in with. He was sixty years old perhaps,
and the father of the man of whom we hired the team. You will be surprised to hear who he was, so reduced as to be driving us about the
country — and worse than that, he told us he had kept two billiard tables
for the public and sold whisky by the glass. This man was the son of
General C———, of Virginia, a distinguished man in the Revolutionary
War and aide to General Washington. His mother was an English Lady,
sister of the Duchess of ———. He had been brought up in the midst of
great wealth, was educated at Eton and a graduate of Oxford! He had
lived for some years in Paris and spoke French well eno' to satisfy us that
he told the truth. He was clearly a man of learning, for he talked of ancient
history and the old philosophers as if he knew all about them. He told us
he was ruined some years ago by the failure of an Englishman, Sir ———.
The circumstances of that failure I know but little about. Sir ——— was
sent to Botany Bay, and our friend came out to Iowa with his two sons to
begin life over again. . . . The old gentleman is a great talker, has some
very sound opinions about things, and gave us a good day's entertainment.

We crossed the Missouri at 10 A. M. to get to Plattsmouth. There we
staid until 2 P. M. The town lies in the hills, is a place of 12 or 15 hundred people, with half a dozen brick buildings in it, the rest wooden. At
2 we started up the river for Omaha. Four miles north of Plattsmouth is

the Platte River, emptying into the Missouri, and we must cross it to get to Omaha. Our experience in getting over would make a good subject for a picture. The river was higher than ordinary and in order to reach the point from which the ferryboat ran it was necessary that we sh'd drive for some distance over what in the dry season is a sand flat, but which is now covered with three feet of water, running six or eight miles an hour. In we drove, expecting every moment that something would give way and we should be washed down the Missouri and thence probably to the ocean! At last, however, we reached the ferryboat, and before attempting to drive onto it, which was a hard pull up of 3 feet or more, we stopped to rest. This was a bad move. The wagon began to settle in the sandy bottom, and when the ferryboat man took the horses' heads to lead them onto the boat they broke both whiffletrees and walked aboard, leaving us ten feet off in the wagon. It was evidently an occurrence not extraordinary to the ferryman. Without delay he waded into the water and told Mr. Joy to get onto his back! Mr. J., after some hesitation, complied and was carried to the boat, and so one by one the rest of us were saved!!

You have never seen a western ferry and don't understand perhaps how the boat is propelled across the stream by the force of the current. A wire rope is stretched from one side to the other of the river, fastened securely on both sides to posts ten or twenty feet high. To this wire rope the ferryboat is secured by ropes which are attached to a wheel that runs on the wire. By pulling one end of the ropes attached to the wheel on the wire the current of the stream is made to strike the side of the boat obliquely, and as the boat can't go down stream, being secured by ropes to the wire, it must go across. The engineering is bad at the crossing of the Platte, and the affair worked so badly that the ferryman had to wade in the water (the Platte River is very shallow) up to his armpits and push us by main strength for some distance. We were half an hour in getting over.

On this side we found a wagon, and helping ourselves to the whiffletrees, came on to Omaha. We ascertained that the wagon from wh. we took the whiffletrees belonged to the Western Stage Co., and our driver was instructed to see that they were returned to the Stage Company here today. . . .

We are laid up here for we can't tell how long. We find that trains on the Pacific Road run only at night for passengers, so the object of the visit to Omaha is defeated. We are now waiting for a boat to go down the river to St. Joseph and Kansas City — shall probably get off tonight or tomorrow morning.

The weather still continues fine. We are at the Herndon House — the Barrett of Omaha — just about the same kind of establishment as that disgrace to Burlington is, but the best the town affords.

Last evening we went to the Episcopal Church. This morning have been looking about the town. Business seems to be lively, many new houses going up, etc. Omaha is nearly as large a place as Burlington, I judge.

I am going after a while to see the shops of the Pacific Railroad. I am
sorry not to go out on the Road a little way, but there would be no object
in going at night. So far the trip has been a very satisfactory one, and I
have learned a good many things I didn't know before about the country
thro' wh. our Road is projected. It would not be in all respects a comfortable trip for you, tho' not as hard as it might be, and I would like
some day to come with you part way at least. There is something to learn
by it and a beautiful farming country to look at, tho' most of it is yet a
stranger to the plough. Some of the taverns are dirty — that is the most
unpleasant feature of it — but you *can* get along, and you are not so silly
about such things as most women are. I saw a woman at breakfast this
morning who made a point of wiping her knife and fork on the tablecloth
before she used them, and who pushed the dishes of meat, etc., which were
brought to her as far away as she could from herself. I couldn't help
laughing at her. The food was not of the best but it is weak and silly to
act so. . . .

*   *   *   *

[6]

Tied to a tree on the bank of the Missouri
Steamship "Colorado"
Aug. 14, '66
9 1/2 P.M.

We are tied up for the night, dear Edie, and before turning into my
bunk I will give an account of myself since I wrote yesterday. I am sitting
in the cabin of the "Colorado." Mr. Joy is reading a swamp-land agreement near by. Outside it is blowing, and now and then I hear the noise
of the darkey deck hands who are bringing wood on board by the light of
a torch wh. is planted in the ground on the river bank. The Missouri
River is so full of sand bars and the channel is so uncertain and changeable
that it is not safe to run boats after dark — so we tie up and wait for
daylight. I have been watching the darkeys load wood for an hour or so.
We are not near any houses, but tied up on woods.

All day yesterday was spent at Omaha, waiting. I went over the R. R.
shops with Sam B. Read, the Supt. — otherwise did nothing but walk
about. In the afternoon the "Colorado" arrived, and the hotelkeeper took
us down to engage our stateroom in an elegant two-horse hack. This morning we came on board at 9 but didn't leave Omaha landing until 12. . . .
At Plattsmouth, King, my land man, came on board, quite unexpected by
me. He came 40 miles with us, to Nebraska City — we are now tied up
a little below there. The distance from Omaha to St. Joseph (where we
land) is 100 miles by land and 200 by water, the river winding about so.
I wish you were here — you would like this part of the trip. The boat
is clean and new and the table is very fair.

*   *   *   *

[7]

St. Joseph, Mo.
Aug. 15, '66

We arrived on the "Colorado" at 6 this evening, and after getting tea at the Pacific House, where I now am, walked a mile or so to the H. & St. Jo R. R. telegraph office for Mr. Joy to send a dispatch. I have been loafing about looking at the town, wh. is quite a flourishing one and has more of a city air than anything I have seen west of the Mississippi River. The Pacific House is a large one and appears to do a good business — but I am grieved to say is a little Barretty. We are to leave here at 2 in the morning for Leavenworth.

Last night I had a tolerable sleep on the banks of the Missouri. We began to move at daylight this morning, but owing to frequent stops to take on a man or a bag of corn, were all day getting here. The Missouri River is not an interesting one to sail on.

I must turn in and get some sleep — we shall have to get up by 1 o'c'k.

*   *   *   *

[8]

Leavenworth, Kan.
Thursday, 5 P.M.
Aug. 16, '66

We arrived here at six this morning, and have been on the go ever since. There are two or three R. R. projects, one in this State and one in Missouri near by, which the people out here are anxious for our people in Boston to aid in. Mr. Joy is here to see how the land lays, so as soon as we arrived this morning he was seized upon. At breakfast I was introduced to two gents from Lawrence, in this State (one of the R. R. projects is near Lawrence). One of these chaps, now a leading citizen of Lawrence, was formerly a clergyman in Boston. As soon as breakfast was over the leading men of Leavenworth came in — amongst them ex-Gov. Carney, a rich man and one of the leading men in the State, and a Mr Smith, who, I believe, has made a great deal of money on Government contracts. They brought their carriages — quite elegant turnouts — and took us to drive to see the town and to look at some proposed places for building bridges over the Missouri — Leavenworth, you will find (if you look on the map!), is on the Missouri River. It is a Government station — was originally Fort Leavenworth. We drove to the fort, which is no fort at all but a collection of Government warehouses, barracks and officers' residences, very nicely laid out and maintained. The Government has about six thousand acres of land adjoining Leavenworth. On it are their warehouses from which all the frontier posts and forts in this entire western country are supplied.

*   *   *   *

[9]

Kansas City
Friday, 1 A. M.
Aug. 17, '66

I am just about going to bed — was interrupted this afternoon by Contractor Smith, who took me to drive in his buggy, with a little bay mare that had made 2:32 — had a fine drive and got back to the hotel just in time to take the omnibus for the Kansas City cars at 7 o'c'k. We arrived here at 9 and found a lot of R. R. men ready to "talk," and they have just got thro', after midnight, and have gone home.

Tomorrow we go out on the Pacific Road, starting at 7. Mr. Joy will stop at Lawrence. . . .

I am sleepy and must turn in. Last night we were called up at 1 and I got no more sleep. I have lots more to write about this country and sat down after we arrived this evening to do it, but Mr. Joy sent down for me to come up and hear the talk.

Kansas City and Leavenworth both want our people, that is, the H. & St. Jo R. R., to help them with a connection. The H. & St. Jo can't do but one — and the question is which one. The people of the two towns hate one another bitterly and it is amusing to hear them talk. I think Kansas City is the point, and I am satisfied the H. & St. Jo, or Mr. Joy rather, will so decide. This P. M. at Leavenworth the two leading men came to me to see if I could give them any light as to what Mr. Joy would decide. I hadn't been here then, and I told them I didn't think Mr. J.'s mind was made up and had no idea what he w'd determine.

I forgot to say that in the course of our drive at L. this A. M. we stopped at Gov. Carney's house, a large and handsomely-furnished one, and had champagne.

*   *   *   *

[10]

Burlington
Sunday noon
Aug. 19, '66

Home again at last . . . and a file of letters from you. I arrived last night at 12 o'c'k or after from Galesburg. . . .

The last letter I wrote was from Kansas City. . . . On Friday I went over the Pacific Road and back that night to Leavenworth — thence over H. & St. Jo Road to Quincy. There I left Mr. Joy and came on to Galesburg — too late for the regular train, so I telegraphed to the Asst. Supt. at Galesburg to have a special ready for me. . . .

To complete my account of our journeyings I must go back to Kansas City and tell you about my doings on Friday. I got up early and went out with a Mr. Hayward, formerly Supt. of the H. & St. Jo R. R., to look at the town. It is in Missouri, just on the Kansas border and at the elbow which the Missouri River makes there — vide map. The town is built on the bluffs on the river bank, and it must have been a man of courage who located it. To make streets and build houses the people have had to cut into the hills. Streets are, many of them, bounded on each side by perpendicular clay walls *50 feet high* — about as high as J. M. F.'s house (!) — and many of the stores and houses are set into the hills, so that on three sides the bank is perhaps ten feet higher than a three-story house. All the windows but front ones look out on clay walls. The new parts of the town are up on top, but still on very rough ground.

At 7 we left Kansas City and at Wyandotte got breakfast. There we took the Pacific R. R., which is bound for California and which runs along the Kansas River and the Smoky Hill Fork and the Big Sandy to Denver City, the heart of the Pike's Peak gold regions. That is, it *is* to run there. At present it is in running order only 104 miles — to Wamego on the Kansas. The entire distance from Wyandotte to Denver is 540 miles. At Lawrence, 32 miles out, Mr. Joy got off, being urged by some R. R. men. He asked me to stop also, but I preferred to keep on. Lawrence is on the Kansas River, and was the scene of that terrible massacre by Quantrell and his Rebel band on August 22, 1863. The Rebels entered the town that night, unexpected, unthought of by the people there, and before people were fairly awake the town was in flames and the men and boys all being murdered. Mr. Joy saw there a man who told him he saw his two sons shot in the street. He saw a house where six young married men were taken and shot in the yard in the presence of their wives. There is scarcely a man there who hasn't some tale of horror to tell. The Rebels killed that night 173 of the leading and best men in the town, and burnt every building in the main street but one. And notwithstanding all this, only 3 years ago, that town of Lawrence is today perhaps the most flourishing and enterprising town in the whole West. It has about 10,000 inhabitants and the main street is, Mr. Joy told me, the best built street in any western town outside of St. Louis and Chicago.

Kansas was mainly settled by Massachusetts people, and it makes one proud of his blood to see what a state they are building up. The valley of the Kansas River is very broad and beautiful and the richest agricultural land in the West. . . .

At Wamego we stopped 40 minutes, and got dinner in a shanty near the railroad. On the way back we picked up Mr. Joy at Lawrence and came on to Leavenworth (from Lawrence there is a railroad to Kansas City and one to Leavenworth) and thence directly on over the H. & St. Jo Railroad.

The trip has been a very interesting one and a very profitable one to me. As a result of it, Mr. Joy will recommend another 50 miles of Road at once for us, and if he can make arrangements with the Pacific R. R. for a bridge over the Missouri, so as to give us a connection with that Road, he will recommend that we go right through. But this is only for you to know.

There are two Pacific Roads, remember. The one we are to connect with is not the one I went over in Kansas, but is in Nebraska Territory, and is the one we went to Omaha to see, but failed to go over.

*   *   *   *

APPENDIX E

Tenancy in Iowa and Nebraska, 1880–1900

RECENTLY, much attention has been devoted to the growth of tenancy in the Middle West during the latter part of the nineteenth century.[1] Statistics reveal that in Iowa the percentage of tenant operated farms in neither Burlington nor Rock Island zones appreciably exceeded the state average, and fell far below that of the northwest counties.

Zone	1880 Per cent Tenancy	1890 Per cent Tenancy	1900 Per cent Tenancy*
B. & M.	27	29	36
C. R. I. & P.	25	31	37
Northwest Counties	23	32	44
Whole State	25	28	35

* *Census* of 1880–1900

In Nebraska, although the percentage of tenancy in the North Platte and Union Pacific regions was very similar to that for the state as a whole, the South Platte area revealed a substantially higher rate, particularly in 1900.

Whether, or to what extent, the various rates of tenancy in the Burling-

Zone	1880 Per cent Tenancy	1890 Per cent Tenancy	1900 Per cent Tenancy*
South Platte	20	31	47
North Platte	7	27	35
Union Pacific	15	27	37
Whole State	18	25	37

* *Census* of 1880–1900

ton zones of Iowa and Nebraska resulted from the company's colonization methods is difficult to determine; there were many factors, such as public land policy [2] and local economic conditions [3] which may have been responsible for the varying situation. The correlation, if any, between railroad colonization and tenancy will have to be ascertained by further research.

[1] Cf. Louise O. Bercaw and Helen E. Hennefrund, "Farm Tenancy in the United States, 1925–1935: A Beginning of a Bibliography," No. 59 in *Agricultural Economics Bibliography* (Washington, 1935); Paul W. Gates, "Land Policy and Tenancy in the Prairie States" in *The Journal of Economic History* (May, 1941), pp. 60–82.

[2] Gates, *loc. cit.*, p. 82.

[3] Buck, *op. cit.*, ch. vii.

APPENDIX F: STATISTICS

TABLE 1

GROSS LAND SALES BY THE BURLINGTON AND MISSOURI RIVER RAILROAD (IOWA), MONTHLY, 1870–1890

(Basis for Graphs on pages 415, 428, and 474–475.)

Unit: 1000 Acres

Year	Jan.	Feb.	Mar.	Apr.	May	June	July	Aug.	Sept.	Oct.	Nov.	Dec.	Total
1870	0	0	0	9.6	20.6	20.0	11.8	17.1	10.9	8.5	6.5	3.7	108.7
1871	2.3	1.2	6.3	6.3	4.4	4.5	3.0	3.5	3.6	2.9	2.2	1.3	41.5
1872	.9	1.0	3.4	2.7	2.1	1.8	2.1	2.6	3.7	3.5	3.1	1.9	28.8
1873	.7	.8	1.4	3.4	4.1	4.8	2.2	2.8	4.3	3.1	1.7	2.2	31.5
1874	3.3	4.1	6.3	4.8	5.9	6.2	2.6	6.4	9.4	10.8	6.2	7.2	73.2
1875	4.7	6.1	7.1	8.4	6.2	5.4	2.1	2.4	3.3	3.9	4.3	3.1	57.0
1876	4.8	3.7	5.9	3.1	3.0	1.7	2.5	1.5	1.3	1.5	1.2	1.5	31.7
1877	1.5	.6	2.2	2.3	1.1	.6	1.1	.7	.7	1.4	.6	1.0	13.8
1878	1.5	.7	1.3	1.9	1.1	.8	.5	.2	1.0	.2	.2	.3	9.7
1879	.5	1.4	2.3	1.3	2.1	1.9	1.9	.9	2.8	2.9	2.6	5.5	26.1
1880	6.4	4.9	5.5	3.3	3.0	3.1	2.6	4.7	3.6	4.5	3.4	7.8	52.8
1881	4.0	3.3	4.6	3.5	2.3	2.1	2.0	1.5	2.6	2.3	1.8	3.4	33.4
1882	2.9	1.7	2.6	1.5	1.6	1.3	.80	.63	1.29	1.81	1.17	.76	18.06
1883	.80	.50	1.26	.79	.64	.75	.41	1.05	.68	.08	.36	.32	7.64
1884	.24	.56	1.04	.28	.35	.61	.66	.29	.32	.21	.75	1.12	6.43
1885	.40	.78	.32	.94	.12	.31	.48	.36	.55	.51	.56	.55	5.88
1886	.04	.20	.52	.11	.03	.46	.20	.96	.28	1.50	1.70	3.16	9.16
1887	.56	.36	.14	.40	.16	.32	.28	.12	.51	.31	3.07	1.14	7.37
1888	.22	1.19	.92	.26	.24	.62	.04	.08	.08	.36	.17	.40	4.58
1889	.32	.83	1.12	.22	.20	.09	.01	.04	.08	.12	.11	1.29	4.43
1890	.08	.44	.94	0	0	0	0	0	0	0	0	0	1.46

Source: BMI, Sales Book (LDP).

TABLE 2
GROSS LAND SALES BY THE BURLINGTON AND MISSOURI RIVER RAILROAD IN NEBRASKA, MONTHLY, 1870–1903

(Basis for Graphs on pages 415, 428, and 474–475.)

Unit: 1000 Acres

Year	Jan.	Feb.	Mar.	Apr.	May	June	July	Aug.	Sept.	Oct.	Nov.	Dec.	Total
1870	0	0	0	9.7	14.1	18.5	5.3	3.8	4.0	5.3	.5	.5	61.7
1871	4.4	1.7	2.6	8.5	11.3	11.4	12.9	19.6	17.5	14.0	10.3	6.5	120.7
1872	7.0	3.7	8.3	11.0	9.4	13.7	11.0	14.8	14.6	14.1	8.5	4.9	121.0
1873	5.0	4.6	12.4	13.0	16.8	37.1	21.1	24.3	45.9	42.7	27.8	26.0	276.7
1874	18.6	21.5	43.7	44.0	48.0	68.0	30.9	27.6	52.0	23.4	8.4	8.2	394.3
1875	5.6	4.7	8.3	10.6	8.9	7.7	6.7	7.1	10.7	9.6	6.7	5.7	92.3
1876	2.6	3.9	4.7	6.9	7.3	10.4	3.2	9.1	10.7	8.2	4.2	5.5	76.7
1877	4.0	10.4	26.3	6.4	8.1	11.7	18.4	18.4	22.1	39.2	40.4	41.2	246.6
1878	32.4	43.4	55.0	65.4	61.9	52.6	39.6	36.7	38.7	35.1	29.9	21.5	512.2
1879	20.4	11.5	24.2	18.8	22.4	24.3	17.6	16.7	39.3	39.1	43.2	92.1	369.6
1880	30.9	57.1	31.1	35.4	19.6	16.5	9.4	15.0	14.1	14.0	17.5	9.4	270.0
1881	8.9	8.6	5.5	9.8	9.6	12.1	14.0	7.2	9.9	11.9	9.9	8.8	116.2
1882	13.9	12.9	20.3	16.5	12.0	22.3	27.8	19.5	19.7	19.5	19.4	37.4	241.2
1883	13.6	3.4	14.3	17.0	14.3	9.6	20.1	15.5	27.3	25.5	12.7	9.4	182.7
1884	8.3	5.8	8.3	7.0	4.6	3.2	2.4	3.2	5.0	3.9	3.6	1.7	57.0
1885	1.5	.8	1.5	1.5	8.6	2.3	6.0	2.2	5.8	6.0	2.4	2.2	40.8
1886	3.5	.9	.5	1.4	.9	2.0	1.3	1.0	1.4	1.0	.6	.4	14.9
1887	.5	1.0	.2	.2	.7	.9	.6	.2	1.2	.5	1.0	.2	7.2
1888	.3	.2	.3	.5	.3	.4	:	.1	.4	.3	.4	.5	3.7
1889	.1	:	.4	.4	.2	.2	1.0	.3	:	.1	.6	.1	3.4

TABLE 2 (continued)

Year	Jan.	Feb.	Mar.	Apr.	May	June	July	Aug.	Sept.	Oct.	Nov.	Dec.	Total
1890	.2	.2	:	.4	.2	.2	:	:	:	.6	.1	.1	2.0
1891	:	:	.5	1.0	.8	1.7	1.0	.6	2.2	3.1	2.6	.7	14.2
1892	1.7	1.5	6.3	5.0	3.3	2.6	1.1	2.0	4.7	4.4	3.9	3.5	40.0
1893	2.9	4.6	3.4	2.2	1.1	.7	1.0	.5	.2	.7	.8	:	18.1
1894	.4	.2	.2	2.3	.8	:	.2	:	.1	.4	.5	1.0	6.1
1895	:	.7	:	.2	.2	:	:	:	.2	:	:	:	1.3
1896	:	2.1	:	:	:	.5	:	:	.3	.2	.6	1.0	4.7
1897	1.2	:	1.6	.9	.4	.2	:	.3	.5	2.2	.5	.7	8.5
1898	.9	1.6	1.7	.6	1.6	1.4	.6	.5	1.5	.6	1.0	1.0	13.0
1899	1.5	1.7	1.9	1.3	1.3	2.8	1.1	2.3	2.7	.8	1.6	2.8	21.8
1900	2.2	1.1	1.8	1.4	1.9	1.3	.6	1.1	1.8	.7	1.4	1.3	16.6
1901	2.7	1.4	1.1	.9	.9	1.8	.5	.3	.6	.5	.6	1.0	12.3
1902	1.1	.5	1.8	.1	1.3	1.9	.8	.8	.6	.2	.5	:	9.6
1903	:	:	.1	.2	:	:	:	:	.03	:	:	.2	.53

Source: BMN, Sales Books and Journals (LDP).

TABLE 3

AVERAGE PRICE PER ACRE OF B. & M. LANDS IN IOWA AND NEBRASKA,
ANNUALLY, 1871–1883

(Basis for Graphs on pages 415 and 449.)

Year	B. & M. of Iowa	B. & M. in Nebraska
1871	$12.34	$8.19
1872	12.27	8.34
1873	12.81	7.59
1874	12.65	6.81
1875	11.70	7.29
1876	12.78	6.86
1877	12.43	4.91
1878	13.61	5.12
1879	14.66	4.30
1880	14.66	4.79
1881	12.74	5.58
1882	11.23	4.25
1883	11.85	4.63

Source: BMR, Sales Books and Journals (LDP).

TABLE 4

GROSS LAND SALES BY THE CHICAGO, ROCK ISLAND & PACIFIC RAILWAY AND
AVERAGE PRICE PER ACRE OF LANDS SOLD, ANNUALLY, 1871–1883

(Basis for Graphs on pages 415, 428, and 449.)

Year ending March 31	Acres Sold	Value	Average Price per Acre	Acres Sold Calendar Year *
1871	28,022	$213,575	$7.63	16,775
1872	13,964	107,693	7.75	15,267
1873	15,592	126,779	8.10	22,748
1874	24,538	200,152	8.20	33,537
1875	35,787	287,032	8.00	61,062
1876	67,380	532,961	7.90	30,702
1877	21,532	178,596	8.29	14,675
1878	12,961	108,663	8.30	19,670
1879	21,348	183,455	8.59	73,758
1880	86,860	747,691	8.60	92,934
1881	94,453	781,261	8.27	70,153
1882	64,078	617,935	9.64	34,660
1883	27,307	278,513	10.19	15,742
1884	12,851	123,795	9.63	

* Computed from years ending March 31 by reckoning sales of the first three months as equal to 20 percent of the total year's sales. This percentage figure is based on monthly data of emigrant passengers on the C. R. I. & P. Railway.

Source: Chicago, Rock Island & Pacific Railway Company *Annual Reports*.

TABLE 5

Gross Land Sales by the Union Pacific Railroad and Average Price per Acre of Lands Sold, Annually, 1871–1883
(Basis for Graphs on pages 415, 428, and 449.)

Year	Acres Sold	Value	Average Price per Acre
1871	206,590	$ 795,558	$4.29
1872	172,108	755,431	4.26
1873	177,084	983,030	4.52
1874	236,230	1,099,467	4.65
1875	111,050	404,462	3.66
1876	125,905	375,541	2.98
1877	69,016	343,768	4.98
1878	318,903	1,557,082	4.88
1879	243,337	1,007,856	4.14
1880	176,202	850,089	4.82
1881	96,060	474,343	4.94
1882	292,159	1,250,364	4.28
1883	867,871	2,701,115	3.11

Sources: *Poor's Manual for 1872–73, 1873–74, 1874–75*; thereafter Union Pacific Railroad Company *Annual Reports.*

TABLE 6

Seasonal Movement Measured by Aggregate Monthly Sales of Gross Acres by the B. & M. Railroads in Iowa and Nebraska for the Periods 1871–1875, 1876–1880, and 1871–1880, Inclusive

(Basis for Graph on page 385.)

Unit: 1000 Acres

Periods	Jan.	Feb.	Mar.	Apr.	May	June	July	Aug.	Sept.	Oct.	Nov.	Dec.
IOWA												
1871–1875	11.9	13.2	24.5	25.6	22.7	22.7	12.0	17.7	24.3	24.2	17.5	15.7
1876–1880	14.7	11.3	17.2	11.9	10.3	8.1	8.6	8.0	9.4	10.5	8.0	16.1
1871–1880	26.6	24.5	41.7	37.5	33.0	30.8	20.6	25.7	33.7	34.7	25.5	31.8
NEBRASKA												
1871–1875	40.6	36.2	75.3	87.1	94.4	137.9	82.6	93.4	140.7	103.8	61.7	51.3
1876–1880	90.3	126.3	141.3	132.9	119.3	115.5	88.2	95.9	124.9	135.6	135.2	169.7* (126.5)
1871–1880	130.9	162.5	216.6	220.0	213.7	253.4	170.8	189.3	265.6	239.4	196.9	221.0* (177.8)

* Total increased contraseasonally by sale of 92,100 acres in December, 1879. The bulk of this represented purchases by one buyer in the North Platte region. (BMN Contract Ledger "G.") Assuming that normal December sales had equalled November sales (43,200 acres), results would have been as indicated by the second, smaller figure in parentheses.

Source: BMR, Sales Books and Journals (LDP).

TABLE 7
Gross Acres Sold by B. & M. and Union Pacific in Nebraska, Monthly, 1877–1882, with Seasonal Movement Eliminated
(Twelve Months' Moving Average)
(Basis for Graph on page 439.)

Unit: 1000 Acres

B. & M. IN NEBRASKA

Year	Beginning 15th Jan.	Feb.	Mar.	Apr.	May	June	July	Aug.	Sept.	Oct.	Nov.	Dec.
1877	10.3	11.0	12.0	14.6	17.6	20.5	22.9	25.7	28.1	33.0	37.5	40.9
1878	42.6	44.2	45.5	45.2	44.3	42.7	41.7	39.0	36.5	32.6	29.3	26.9
1879	25.1	23.4	23.5	23.8	24.9	30.8	31.7	35.5	36.1	37.4	37.2	36.6
1880	35.9	35.7	33.6	31.5	29.4	22.5	20.7	16.6	14.5	12.4	11.5	11.2
1881	11.5	10.9	10.5	10.4	9.7	9.7	10.1	10.5	11.7	12.3	12.5	13.3
1882	14.5	15.5	16.3	16.9	17.7	20.1	20.1	19.3	18.8	18.8	19.0	18.0

UNION PACIFIC

Year	Jan.	Feb.	Mar.	Apr.	May	June	July	Aug.	Sept.	Oct.	Nov.	Dec.
1877						5.7	6.5	7.3	9.9	13.9	18.7	22.7
1878	24.4	25.4	26.0	26.3	26.5	26.6	26.4	26.3	25.1	22.8	20.3	18.1
1879	17.4	17.7	17.9	18.4	18.6	20.3	20.9	22.3	23.5	23.0	21.8	20.8
1880	20.4	19.3	18.4	17.3	16.5	14.7	13.6	11.8	9.5	8.6	7.9	7.7
1881	7.5	7.3	7.4	7.4	7.7	8.0	8.4	9.6	10.6	11.0	12.6	14.3
1882	15.5	17.9	19.9	21.6	23.1	24.4	0	0	0	0	0	0

Source: BMN, Journals (LDP) and Union Pacific R.R. Co., *Annual Reports*.

TABLE 8

Gross Number of Sales by the B. & M. in Nebraska, together with Average Price per Acre, Annually, 1882–1903

(Basis for Graph on page 468.)

Year	No. of Sales	Avg. Annual Price	Year	No. of Sales	Avg. Annual Price
1822	1,614	$ 4.25	1893	113	$5.63
1883	1,146	4.63	1894	40	6.06
1884	398	6.35	1895	10	7.19
1885	256	7.91	1896	27	7.55
1886	99	6.55	1897	60	8.09
1887	51	7.32	1898	84	6.12
1888	26	9.28	1899	127	5.68
1889	28	7.70	1900	96	5.40
1890	19	10.79	1901	60	4.73
1891	83	8.39	1902	51	5.89
1892	256	7.14	1903	4	6.14

Source: BMN, Journals (LDP).

NOTE CONCERNING ZONES FOR STATISTICAL COMPARISON

Aggregate figures for the zones referred to in the text, in Graphs on pages 456, 458, and 459, and in Tables 9, 10, and 11, have been derived from census statistics of the following counties or parts of counties. For location of these counties, see map on page 453.

Zone	Counties or Parts of Counties
B. & M., Iowa	Adair (½), Adams (1), Cass (½), Clarke (1), Decatur (½), Fremont (½), Madison (¼), Mills (1), Montgomery (1), Page (½), Pottawattamie (¼), Ringgold (½), Taylor (½), Union (1).
C. R. I. & P., Iowa	Adair (½), Audubon (1), Cass (½), Dallas (1), Guthrie (1), Harrison (½), Madison (½), Polk (½), Pottawattamie (¾), Shelby (1), Warren (½).
Mississippi River Counties, Iowa	Allamakee (1), Clayton (1), Clinton (1), Dubuque (1), Jackson (1), Louisa (1), Muscatine (1), Scott (1).
Northwest Counties, Iowa	Cherokee (1), Clay (1), Dickinson (1), Emmet (1), Lyon (1), O'Brien (1), Osceola (1), Palo Alto (1), Sioux (1).
B. & M., South Platte, Nebraska	Adams (½), Clay (1), Fillmore (1), Franklin (1), Gage (½), Jefferson (½), Kearney (½), Lancaster (1), Saline (1), Seward (1), Webster (1), York (1).
B. & M., North Platte, Nebraska	Antelope (½), Boone (1), Dakota (½), Dixon (½), Greeley (1), Howard (1), Madison (1), Pierce (½), Platte (½), Sherman (1), Valley (1), Wayne (1).
Union Pacific, Nebraska	Adams (½), Buffalo (1), Butler (1), Colfax (1), Cuming (1), Dodge (1), Hall (1), Hamilton (1), Kearney (½), Merrick (1), Platte (½), Polk (1), Saunders (1).
Southwest Counties, Nebraska	Dundy (1), Frontier (1), Furnas (1), Gosper (1), Harlan (1), Hayes (1), Hitchcock (1), Johnson (1), Nuckolls (1).

TABLE 9

Total Population and Population per Thousand Acres for Selected Zones in Iowa and Nebraska, Decennially, 1860-1900

(Basis for Graph on page 456.)

Zone	1860	1870	1880	1890	1900	Total 1000 Acres
IOWA						
B. & M.	31,426	69,328	137,174	145,744	164,760	2,824
Pop. per 1000 Acres	11.1	24.5	48.6	51.6	58.3	
C. R. I. & P.	31,030	74,551	145,401	181,048	205,983	3,004
Pop. per 1000 Acres	10.3	24.8	48.4	60.3	68.6	
Mississippi River Counties	154,333	215,748	229,728	237,999	263,627	2,944
Pop. per 1000 Acres	52.4	73.3	78.0	80.8	89.5	
Northwest Counties	545	9,119	33,836	88,572	124,468	3,055
Pop. per 1000 Acres	.2	2.98	11.1	29.0	40.7	
Entire State	674,913	1,194,020	1,624,615	1,912,297	2,231,853	
% Increase over Preceding Decade		76.9	36.1	17.7	16.7	
NEBRASKA						
South Platte	*	17,010	116,749	223,425	205,855	3,935
Pop. per 1000 Acres		4.3	29.7	56.8	52.3	
North Platte	*	4,033	31,836	78,396	95,629	3,468
Pop. per 1000 Acres		1.2	9.2	22.6	27.6	
Union Pacific	*	17,499	96,891	175,755	179,695	4,244
Pop. per 1000 Acres		4.1	22.8	41.4	42.3	
Southwest Counties	*	3,437	28,098	66,825	68,987	3,877
Pop. per 1000 Acres		.9	7.2	17.2	17.8	
Entire State	28,841	122,993	452,402	1,062,656	1,066,300	
% Increase over Preceding Decade		326.5	267.8	134.9	.3	

* Unavailable.

Source: United States *Census*.

TABLE 10

TOTAL IMPROVED ACRES AND PERCENTAGE OF TOTAL ACRES IMPROVED FOR SELECTED
ZONES IN IOWA AND NEBRASKA, DECENNIALLY, 1860–1900

(Basis for Graph on page 458.)

Unit: 1000 Acres

Zone	1860	1870	1880	1890	1900	Total 1000 Acres
IOWA						
B. & M.						
1000 Acres Improved	175	467	1,788	2,194	2,401	2,824
% of Total 1000 Acres ..	6.2	16.5	63.3	77.7	85.0	
C. R. I. & P.						
1000 Acres Improved	158	450	1,656	2,268	2,570	3,004
% of Total 1000 Acres ..	5.3	15.0	55.1	75.5	85.6	
Mississippi River Counties						
1000 Acres Improved	855	1,574	2,039	2,121	2,111	2,944
% of Total 1000 Acres ..	29.0	53.5	69.3	72.1	71.7	
Northwest Counties						
1000 Acres Improved	1.23	36.6	500	1,684	2,760	3,055
% of Total 1000 Acres ..	0.04	1.2	16.4	55.1	90.3	
NEBRASKA						
South Platte						
1000 Acres Improved	*	84.2	1,673	2,865	3,126	3,935
% of Total 1000 Acres ..		2.1	42.5	72.8	79.4	
North Platte						
1000 Acres Improved	*	16	342	1,484	2,078	3,468
% of Total 1000 Acres ..		0.5	9.9	42.8	59.9	
Union Pacific						
1000 Acres Improved	*	126.2	1,380	3,011	3,530	4,244
% of Total 1000 Acres ..		3.0	32.5	70.9	83.2	
Southwest Counties						
1000 Acres Improved	*	11	272.6	1,391	1,582	3,877
% of Total 1000 Acres ..		0.3	7.0	35.9	40.8	

* Unavailable.
Source: United States *Census*.

TABLE 11

(Basis for Graph on page 459.)

Unit: 1000 Acres

Zone	1860	1870	1880	1890	1900	Total 1000 Acres
IOWA						
B. & M.						
1000 Acres in Farms	624	969	2,162	2,524	2,777	2,824
% of Total 1000 Acres ..	22.1	34.3	76.6	89.4	98.3	
C. R. I. & P.						
1000 Acres in Farms	524	871	2,044	2,605	2,926	3,004
% of Total 1000 Acres ..	17.4	29.0	68.0	86.7	97.4	
Mississippi River Counties						
1000 Acres in Farms	1,746	2,393	2,685	2,659	2,808	2,944
% of Total 1000 Acres ..	59.3	81.3	91.2	90.3	95.4	
Northwest Counties						
1000 Acres in Farms	6.8	186	777	2,084	2,945	3,055
% of Total 1000 Acres ..	0.22	6.1	25.4	68.2	96.4	
NEBRASKA						
South Platte						
1000 Acres in Farms	*	334	2,653	3,315	3,781	3,935
% of Total 1000 Acres ..		8.5	67.4	84.2	96.1	
North Platte						
1000 Acres in Farms	*	122	932	2,204	3,072	3,468
% of Total 1000 Acres ..		3.5	26.9	63.6	88.6	
Union Pacific						
1000 Acres in Farms	*	391	2,358	3,543	4,164	4,244
% of Total 1000 Acres ..		9.2	55.6	83.5	98.1	
Southwest Counties						
1000 Acres in Farms	*	39	874	2,181	3,059	3,877
% of Total 1000 Acres ..		1.0	22.5	56.3	78.9	

* Unavailable.

Source: United States *Census*.

BIBLIOGRAPHY

BIBLIOGRAPHY

SOURCES

I. COLLECTIONS

(a) Land Department Records of the Burlington and Missouri River Railroads and of the Hannibal and St. Joseph Railroad

The chief source for this history is the voluminous collection of Land Department records now deposited in the Baker Library of the Harvard Graduate School of Business Administration in Boston. These records, over six tons in bulk, were originally scattered in Chicago, Burlington, Omaha, Lincoln and St. Joseph, but with the consent and coöperation of the Chicago, Burlington & Quincy Railroad, and with the additional aid of a grant from the Baker Library, they were concentrated in Boston in 1936. Unusually complete, they include, among other things, all contract, sales and plat books for both Iowa and Nebraska, from which has been drawn a full statistical abstract of the disposal of the grant. The Land Department correspondence, both incoming and outgoing from 1852–1906, reveals the development and changes in company policy, and, of equal importance, the living conditions, ideas and aspirations of the people of western Iowa, eastern Nebraska and northern Missouri. Additional sources of information are the miscellaneous record books containing digests of law cases, special projects and office procedure. Also an integral part of this collection are the scrapbooks containing Land Department circulars and extensive newspaper clippings.

(b) Corporate and Historical Records of the Chicago, Burlington & Quincy Railroad

The greater part of these records is located in the Secretary's Office of the company at 547 West Jackson Boulevard, Chicago. They include the manuscript minutes of directors meetings and reports of all constituent Burlington companies. In the historical files are such items as time cards, photographs, clippings, miscellaneous record books and relics. The Department of Industry and Agriculture possesses considerable historical and current material concerning its community development work. The General Office of Lines West, at Tenth and Farnam Streets, Omaha, Nebraska, also has a smaller amount of general material. In the Colonization Bureau at Omaha are extensive records of the various agricultural experiments sponsored by the railroad. The most complete file of the *Corn Belt* is also located there. Additional agricultural records are in the Agricultural Agent's office in Denver, Colorado. Photographs of the system are scattered at various points along the line.

(c) The Cunningham Collection of Letters to and from Charles E. Perkins

These letters and memoranda, covering the period 1859–1907, are in the possession of Mrs. Edward Cunningham of Boston, daughter of Charles E.

Perkins. As a preliminary to their publication under the title "Letters of Charles E. Perkins," they have been sorted and edited by Mrs. Cunningham, and in this form were lent by her to the writer for use in this book. The material fills some 20 loose-leaf notebooks and eight bound typescript volumes.

II. OFFICIAL DOCUMENTS, FEDERAL AND STATE

United States, Bureau of Corporations, *Report on the Lumber Industry*, 1911.

—— *Census Reports*, 1830–1930.

—— Commissioner of the General Land Office, *Annual Reports*, 1851–1897.

—— —— *Circular*, November 21, 1850.

—— *Compendium of the Tenth Census*, 1883.

—— *Congressional Globe*, 31st–38th Congress, 1849–1865.

—— Department of Interior, "Indian Land Cessions in the United States," prepared by Charles C. Royce, *Eighteenth Annual Report of the Bureau of American Ethnology*, 1896–1897, pt. 2.

—— General Land Office, *Receivers' Accounts*, 1856 et seq.

—— *Statement showing land grants made by Congress*, 1908.

—— *House Document*, 48th Congress, 1883–1885.

—— *Opinions of the Attorney-General*, VIII, IX, 1856–1858.

—— Secretary of the Interior, *Report* for 1880.

—— *Senate Documents*, 34th, 42nd, and 50th Congress, 1855–1889.

—— *Statutes-at-Large*, IX–XVI, 1845–1871.

—— Supreme Court, *Boone County v. B. & M. R. RR. Co.*, 139 U. S. 684 (1891).

—— —— *Railroad Company v. Fremont County*, 9 Wallace 89 (1869).

—— —— *Railway Company v. McShane*, 22 Wallace 444 (1875).

—— —— *U. S. v. B. & M. R. RR.*, in U. S. Circuit Court for Nebraska (1875).

—— —— *U. S. v. B. & M. R. RR.*, 8 Otto 334 (1878).

—— Treasury Department, *Statistical Abstract*, I, III, 1879, 1881.

Illinois, *Laws*, 1835–1836.

Iowa, *Acts*, 1853–1858.

—— Board of Railroad Commissioners, *Annual Reports* for 1878, 1879, and 1880, Des Moines.

—— *Census for 1880*, Des Moines, 1883.

—— Register of the State Land Office, *Annual Reports* for 1861 and 1863, Des Moines.

III. OFFICIAL DOCUMENTS, CORPORATION

Atchison, Topeka and Santa Fe Railroad, *Annual Report*, 1881.

Burlington and Missouri River Railroad (Iowa), *Annual Reports*, 1855 *et seq.*

Burlington and Missouri River Railroad in Nebraska, *Annual Reports*, 1873 *et seq.*

Burlington and Missouri River Railroads, Circulars to Stockholders and the Public.

Chicago Board of Trade, *Annual Report*, 1865.

Chicago, Burlington & Quincy Railroad (and predecessors), *Annual Reports*, 1854 *et seq.*

—— *Corporate History*, prepared by W. W. Baldwin, Chicago, 1921.

—— *Documentary History*, 3 vols., prepared by W. W. Baldwin, Chicago, 1928–1929.

Chicago, Rock Island & Pacific Railway (and predecessors), *Annual Reports*, 1853 *et seq.*

Hannibal and St. Joseph Railroad, *Annual Reports*, 1854 *et seq.*

—— Talcott, Edward B., *Report upon the Hannibal and St. Joseph Railroad . . . and the Land*, Boston, 1854.

Michigan Central Railroad, *Annual Reports*, 1852 *et seq.*

Michigan Southern and Northern Indiana Railroad, *Annual Report*, 1853.

Union Pacific Railroad, *Annual Reports*, 1874 *et seq.*

IV. CORRESPONDENCE, SPEECHES, DIARIES, AND REMINISCENCES

Allen, Edna M. Boyle, "A Grasshopper Raid," *Nebraska Pioneer Reminiscences*, Cedar Rapids, Iowa, 1916.

Brady, Lorenzo D., *Lorenzo D. Brady, His History Written by Himself*, MS, Chicago? 1877?

Hughes, Sarah Forbes, *Letters and Recollections of John Murray Forbes*, Boston, 1899, 2 vols.

Jansen, Peter, *Memoirs of Peter Jansen*, Beatrice, Nebraska, 1921.

Joy, James F., "James F. Joy tells how he went into the Railroad Business," Michigan Pioneer and Historical Society, *Historical Collections* (1894), XXII, reprinted from *Detroit Free Press*, May 1, 1892.

Nisbeth, Hugo, "Iowa of the Early Seventies As Seen by a Swedish Traveller" (translated by Roy W. Swanson), *Iowa Journal of History and Politics* (October, 1929), XXVII.

V. NEWSPAPERS

Aurora Beacon, Aurora, Illinois, 1850.
Beatrice Express, 1871–1877.
Burlington Daily Gazette, 1879–1884.

Burlington Daily Hawk-Eye, 1864–1885.

Burlington Daily Telegraph, 1851–1873.

Burlington . Weekly .Hawk-Eye, 1857–1890.

Burlington Weekly Telegraph, 1852–1855.

Chicago Daily Democrat, 1850.

Chicago Daily Journal, 1848–1850.

Chicago Tribune, 1868.

Daily Gazette, Burlington, Iowa, 1870–1871.

Daily Gazette & Argus, Burlington, Iowa, 1868–1869.

Eddyville Free Press, Eddyville, Iowa, 1854–1855.

Fairfield Ledger, Fairfield, Iowa, 1854–1855.

Fremont Herald, Fremont, Nebraska, 1880–1885.

Hamilton County News, Hamilton & Aurora, Nebraska, 1877–1880.

Iowa Capital Reporter, Iowa City, Iowa, 1854–1855.

Iowa Sentinel, Fairfield, Iowa, 1854–1857.

Iowa State Gazette, Burlington, Iowa, 1852.

Iowa Weekly Observer, Mt. Pleasant, Iowa, 1854–1855.

Monmouth Atlas, Monmouth, Illinois, 1854–1856.

Nebraska Advertiser, Brownsville, Nebraska, 1857–1860.

Nebraska Herald, Plattsmouth, Nebraska, 1865–1872.

New Era, Wahoo, Nebraska, 1890–1896.

New York Tribune, 1870–1872.

Omaha Daily Herald, 1880–1901.

Rural New Yorker, 1871.

Saline County Post, Crete, Nebraska, 1871–1873.

Wapello Intelligence, Ottumwa, Iowa, 1855.

Weekly Hawk-Eye & Telegraph, Burlington, Iowa, 1855–1857.

VI. MISCELLANEOUS GUIDES AND PAMPHLETS ISSUED BY LAND COMPANIES,
"EMIGRATION AGENTS," AND PROFESSIONAL WRITERS
OF GAZETTEERS AND GUIDES

Associated Chamber of Commerce of the North Platte Valley, "North Platte Valley," n.p., n.d.

Aughey, Samuel, *Sketches of the Physical Geography and Geology of Nebraska*, Omaha, 1880.

Bemis and Bowers, *The Outlook for Nebraska*, Omaha, 1879.

Bradlaugh, Charles, *Hints to Immigrants*, London, 1878.

Curley, Edwin A., *Nebraska, Its Advantages, Resources, and Drawbacks*, New York, 1875.

Merrill, Samuel, "Iowa in 1868," *Annals of Iowa* (November, 1868), first series, VII.

Noteware, J. H., *The State of Nebraska*, Omaha, 1873.

Parker, Nathan H., *The Iowa Handbook for 1856*, Boston, 1856.

Samuelson, James, *Useful Information for Intending Emigrants*, London, 1879.

Young, Edward, *Special Report on Immigration Accompanying Information for Immigrants*, Philadelphia, 1871.

VII. ADVERTISING LITERATURE ISSUED BY RAILROADS

Burlington and Missouri River Railroad (Iowa), *Southern Iowa Land & Railroad Gazette*, April, 1869.

Burlington and Missouri River Railroads, *Iowa and Nebraska Farmer*, 1875–1877.

—— "Nebraska, Its Characteristics and Prospects," prepared by J. D. Butler, n.p., 1873.

—— "Nebraska: Statistics compiled from State Papers," n.p., 1879.

—— *News Sheet*, 1870 *et seq.*

—— "One Million Acres Farming Lands . . . in Iowa and Nebraska," n.p., 1877–1879.

—— *Views and Description of Burlington and Missouri River Railroad Lands. . . .* Omaha? 1872.

Chicago, Burlington & Quincy Railroad, *Corn Belt*, December, 1895–November, 1902.

—— *Great Opportunities for Farmers, Business Men and Investors in Nebraska, Northwestern Kansas and Eastern Colorado*, Omaha, 1893.

—— *The Heart of the Continent*, Chicago, 1882.

Chicago, Rock Island & Pacific Railroad, "Description of Six Hundred Thousand Acres of Choice Iowa Farming Lands," Davenport, 1871.

Hannibal and St. Joseph Railroad, *The Hannibal and St. Joseph Railroad Company Have Received . . . over 600,000 Acres . . .* , Hannibal, 1859, 1860.

Union Pacific Railroad, *Guide to the Union Pacific Railroad Lines*, Omaha, 1870.

The pamphlets and papers listed above include only the major publications. There were many minor items, usually issued for special purposes. Most of them are included in the Land Department records in the Baker Library.

GUIDE TO THE LOCATION OF SOURCE MATERIAL

(Unpublished and Published)

(a) Baker Library, Harvard Graduate School of Business Administration, Boston, Massachusetts

In addition to the unpublished material of the Burlington and Missouri River and Hannibal and St. Joseph Railroads listed above, there are many annual railroad reports, not only of the Chicago, Burlington & Quincy

Railroad and its constituent companies, but also of the early competing lines such as the Lake Shore and Michigan Southern, the Chicago and Rock Island, the Union Pacific, and many others. With these reports are land-grant pamphlets, engineering surveys, assorted circulars to stockholders and the public, and many early guidebooks to the West for immigrants.

(b) Harvard College Library, Cambridge, Massachusetts

Particularly useful for its complete collection of government documents and reports. Also contains Colton Manuscript (see Appendix C).

(c) Boston Public Library, Boston, Massachusetts

Railroad reports and circulars, in some cases supplementing the material in Baker Library.

(d) Brown University Library, Providence, Rhode Island

Railroad reports and pamphlets.

(e) New York Public Library, New York, N. Y.

Railroad reports and pamphlets.

(f) Engineering Societies Library, New York, N. Y.

Railroad reports and pamphlets.

(g) Columbia University Library, New York, N. Y.

Railroad reports and pamphlets.

(h) Library of the Bureau of Railway Economics, Washington, D. C.

Extensive railroad material.

(i) United States General Land Office, Washington, D. C.

Original correspondence between the Land Office and the Hannibal and St. Joseph and Burlington and Missouri River Railroads; Receivers' Accounts showing quarterly receipts at land offices in Iowa and Nebraska; maps, plats, and patents of all Burlington land grants.

(j) United States National Archives, Washington, D. C.

Miscellaneous correspondence and documents relating to the Burlington grant.

(k) Burton Historical Collection, Detroit Public Library, Detroit, Michigan

Reports and articles pertaining to the railroad activities of James F. Joy, particularly in connection with the Michigan Central Railroad, the Chicago and Aurora Railroad, the Central Military Tract Railroad, and the Chicago, Burlington & Quincy Railroad.

(l) University of Michigan, Transportation Library

Railroad reports and pamphlets.

(m) Chicago, Burlington & Quincy Railroad Company Archives, Chicago, Illinois

(n) Chicago Public Library, Chicago, Illinois

Railroad reports and pamphlets.

(o) Warren County Library, Monmouth, Illinois
Valuable file of early Illinois newspapers along the line of the Burlington.

(p) Minnesota Historical Society Library, St. Paul, Minnesota
Particularly valuable for its files of Minnesota newspapers.

(q) Burlington Public Library, Burlington, Iowa
Newspaper files relating to the early development of Burlington and of the railroad.

(r) Iowa Historical Society Library, Des Moines, Iowa
Extensive files of Iowa newspapers.

(s) Omaha Public Library, Omaha, Nebraska
Pamphlets on Nebraska, and a large file of Omaha newspapers.

(t) Nebraska State Historical Society Library, Lincoln, Nebraska
Fourteen scrapbooks of newspaper clippings referring to the Burlington, 1870–1873, are located in the University of Nebraska Library. Also, in the basement of the Capitol is the largest existing collection of Nebraska newspapers, many of them indexed according to subject. Numerous articles on the Burlington and Missouri River Railroads have been listed.

(u) University of Nebraska Library
Railroad pamphlets, also several unpublished theses on various phases of the Burlington.

(v) Files of the *State Journal*, Lincoln, Nebraska

(w) Dominion Archives, Ottawa, Canada
The Baring Manuscripts which are valuable for information on John Murray Forbes.

SECONDARY WORKS

I. BIOGRAPHY

Aldrich, Charles, "Comment By the Editor," *Annals of Iowa* (April, 1896), third series, II.

Bobbé, Dorothea, *De Witt Clinton*, New York, 1933.

Brainerd, John M., "Charles Aldrich," *Annals of Iowa* (January, 1909), third series, VIII.

Briggs, John Ely, "Comment By the Editor," *Palimpsest* (October, 1935), XVI.

Brigham, Johnson, "James Harlan," *Iowa Biographical Series* (Iowa City, 1913).

Cunningham, Edith Perkins, *Owls Nest*, Boston, 1907.

Dictionary of American Biography, edited by Allen Johnson and Dumas Malone, New York, 1928–1936, 20 vols.

Emerson, Edward W., *Life and Letters of Charles Russell Lowell*, Boston, 1907.

Hedge, Thomas, *Charles Elliott Perkins*, Boston? 1931.

Nevins, Allan, *Grover Cleveland*, New York, 1932.

Pearson, Henry Greenleaf, *An American Railroad Builder, John Murray Forbes*, Boston, 1911.

Remey, J. T., "William F. Coolbaugh," *Annals of Iowa* (July, 1906), third series, VII.

Salter, William, *Life of James W. Grimes*, New York, 1876.

Stiles, Edward H., "David Rorer," *Annals of Iowa* (July, 1907), third series, VIII.

Wright, Judge, "The Yewall Portrait of Charles Mason," *Annals of Iowa* (July–October, 1895), third series, II.

II. LOCAL HISTORIES

Aldrich, Charles, "The County Judge System," *Annals of Iowa* (April, 1911), third series, X.

Anonymous, "E. F. Stephens Actively Engages in Orchard Work as He Nears 84," *Idaho Statesman* (January 1, 1928), II.

Antrobus, Augustine M., *History of Des Moines County, Iowa*, Chicago, 1915.

Battle, Charles S., *Centennial Historical and Biographical Record of Aurora, Illinois for 100 Years, and of the C. B. & Q. R.R. for 86 Years*, Aurora? 1937?

Bentley, Arthur F., "The Conditions of the Western Farmer as Illustrated by the Economic History of a Nebraska Township," *Johns Hopkins University Studies* (Baltimore, 1893), XI.

Boggess, Arthur Clinton, "The Settlement of Illinois, 1778–1830," Chicago Historical Society, *Collections* (Chicago, 1908), V.

Boyd, G. D. R., "Sketches of History and Incidents connected with the Settlement of Wapello County, from 1843 to 1859, inclusive," *Annals of Iowa* (July, 1868), first series, VI.

Bradford, H. E., and Spidel, H. A., *Nebraska, Its Geography and Agriculture*, New York, 1931.

Brown, George L., "History of Butler County," Nebraska State Historical Society, *Transactions and Reports* (1892), IV.

Bullock, Motier A., *Congregational Nebraska*, Lincoln, 1905.

Carlson, Carl Frederick, *Aurora, Illinois: A Study in Sequent Land Use*, Chicago, 1940.

Chapman, Charles & Co., *History of Knox County, Illinois*, Chicago, 1878.

Child, A. L., "History of Cass County," Nebraska State Historical Society, *Transactions and Reports* (1887), II.

Cole, Cyrenus, *A History of the People of Iowa*, Cedar Rapids, 1921.

—— *Iowa Through the Years*, Iowa City, 1940.

Federal Writers, *Iowa*, New York, 1938.

—— *Nebraska*, New York, 1939.

Frazee, George, "An Iowa Fugitive Slave Case," *Annals of Iowa* (April, 1903), third series, VI.

Gregory, Annadora Foss, *The History of Crete, Nebraska, 1870–88* (MS Thesis), Lincoln, 1932.

Gue, Benjamin F., *History of Iowa*, New York, 1903, 4 vols.

Hebard, Alfred, "Recollections of Early Territorial Days," *Annals of Iowa* (July–October, 1895), third series, II.

Hedges, Harold, and Elliot, F. F., "Types of Farming in Nebraska," University of Nebraska, College of Agriculture, *Bulletin No. 244* (Lincoln, 1930).

Herriott, F. I., "The Transfusion of Political Ideas and Institutions in Iowa," *Annals of Iowa* (April, 1903), third series, VI.

Hollingshead, August deB., *Trends in Community Development; A Study in Ecological and Institutional Processes in 34 Southeastern Nebraska Communities, 1854–1934* (MS Thesis), Lincoln, 1935.

Hunter, Capt. W. A., "History of Mahaska County," *Annals of Iowa* (April, 1869), first series, VII.

Johnson, Harrison, *Johnson's History of Nebraska*, Omaha, 1880.

Johnston, David M., "Nebraska in the Fifties," Nebraska State Historical Society, *Publications* (1919), XIX.

Louis, John J., "Shelby County, A Sociological Study," *Iowa Journal of History and Politics* (January, 1904), II.

Merk, Frederick, *Economic History of Wisconsin during the Civil War Decade*, Madison, 1916.

Merritt, W. W., *A History of the County of Montgomery*, Red Oak, Iowa, 1906.

Morton, J. Sterling, *Illustrated History of Nebraska*, Lincoln, 1905–1906, 2 vols.

Negus, Charles, "The Early History of Iowa," *Annals of Iowa* (July, 1867), first series, V.

Patterson, Robert Foster, *Plattsmouth, Nebraska 1853–1900* (MS Thesis), Lincoln, 1932.

Pierce, B. L., *History of Chicago*, New York, 1937, vol. I.

Scott, Willard, "Congregational College History in Nebraska," Nebraska State Historical Society, *Transactions and Reports* (1892), III.

Seeley, H. H., and Parrish, L. W., *History and Civil Government of Iowa*, Chicago, 1897.

Sheldon, Addison E., *Histories and Stories of Nebraska*, Chicago, 1914.

—— "Land Systems and Land Policies in Nebraska," Nebraska State Historical Society, *Publications* (1936), XXII.

—— *The Semi-Centennial History of Nebraska*, Lincoln, 1904.

Sweedlun, Verne S., *A History of Agriculture in Nebraska, 1870–1930* (MS Thesis), Lincoln, 1940.

Western Historical Company, *History of the State of Nebraska*, Chicago, 1882.

White, Charles A., "The Early Homes and Homemakers of Iowa," *Annals of Iowa* (October, 1899), third series, IV.

—— "Some Characteristic Features in the Early and Present History of Southeastern Iowa," *Annals of Iowa* (April, 1867).

Wilbur, C. D., *The Great Valleys and Prairies of Nebraska and the Northwest*, Omaha, 1881.

III. MIGRATION, IMMIGRATION, AND IMMIGRANTS

Abbott, Edith, *Historical Aspects of the Immigration Problem*, Chicago, 1926.

Alexis, Joseph, "Swedes in Nebraska," Nebraska State Historical Society, *Publications* (1919), XIX.

Anderson, Helen Marie, *The Influence of Railway Advertising upon the Settlement of Nebraska* (MS Thesis), Lincoln, 1926.

Blegen, Theodore C., "The Competition of the Northwestern States for Immigrants," *Wisconsin Magazine of History* (September, 1919), III.

Buchanan, J. R., "Great Railroad Migration into Northern Nebraska," Nebraska State Historical Society, *Proceedings and Collections* (1907), XV.

Clark, D. E., "The Westward Movement in the Upper Mississippi Valley during the Fifties," Mississippi Valley Historical Association, *Proceedings* (1913–1914), VII.

Flom, George T., "The Coming of the Norwegians to Iowa," *Iowa Journal of History and Politics* (July, 1905), III.

—— "The Danish Contingent in the Population of Early Iowa," *Iowa Journal of History and Politics* (April, 1906), IV.

—— "The Early Swedish Immigration to Iowa," *Iowa Journal of History and Politics* (October, 1905), III.

Gates, Paul W., *The Illinois Central Railroad and Its Colonization Work*, Cambridge, 1934.

Goodwin, Cardinal, "The American Occup:.tion of Iowa, 1833 to 1860," *Iowa Journal of History and Politics* (January, 1919), XVII.

Ham, M. M., "The First White Man in Iowa," *Annals of Iowa* (April, 1896), third series, II.

Hansen, Marcus L., *The Atlantic Migration, 1607–1860*, Cambridge, 1940.

—— "Official Encouragement of Immigration to Iowa," *Iowa Journal of History and Politics* (April, 1921), XIX.

Hedges, James B., *Building the Canadian West; the Land and Colonization Work of the Canadian Pacific Railway*, New York, 1939.

—— "The Colonization Work of the Northern Pacific Railroad," *Mississippi Valley Historical Review* (December, 1926), XIII.

—— *The Federal Railway Land Subsidy Policy of Canada*, Cambridge, 1934.

—— "Promotion of Immigration to the Pacific Northwest by the Railroads," *Mississippi Valley Historical Review* (September, 1928), XV.

Hrbkova, Sarka B., "Bohemians in Nebraska," Nebraska State Historical Society, *Publications* (1919), XIX.

Jerome, Harry, *Migration and Business Cycles*, New York, 1926.

Johnson, Willis Fletcher, *America's Foreign Relations*, New York, 1916.

Lynch, W. O., "Colonization of Kansas, 1854–1860," Mississippi Valley Historical Association, *Proceedings* (1916–1918), IX.

Schmidt, Theodore, *The Mennonites of Nebraska* (MS Thesis), Lincoln, 1933.

Woolworth, J. M., "The Philosophy of Emigration," Nebraska State Historical Society, *Transactions and Reports* (1880), I.

IV. TRANSPORTATION

Adams, Charles Francis, *Chapters of Erie*, Boston, 1871.

Ager, J. H., "Nebraska Politics and Nebraska Railroads," Nebraska State Historical Society, *Proceedings and Collections* (1907), XV.

Baker, George W., *The Formation of the New England Railroad Systems*, Cambridge, 1937.

Baldwin, W. W., "Mail Pay on the Burlington," Chicago, 1922?

—— "Some Features in the History of the Burlington Road," Albia, Iowa, 1901, reprinted in *Burlington Gazette*, March 24, 1906.

—— "The Making of the Burlington," Chicago, July 2, 1920, reprinted from *Professional Engineer's Magazine* (1920?).

Bradley, Glenn D., *The Story of the Santa Fe*, Boston, 1920.

Calkins, Earnest Elmo, "Genesis of a Railroad," reprinted from Illinois State Historical Society, *Transactions for the Year 1935* (1935?).

Chicago and Northwestern Railway, "Historical Background of the Chicago and Northwestern Railway" (MS Chicago, 1936?).

Corliss, Carlton J., *Trails to Rails: A Story of Transportation Progress in Illinois*, Chicago, 1934.

Dey, Peter A., "Railroad Legislation in Iowa," *Iowa Historical Record* (October, 1893), IX.

Dixon, Frank H., "Railroad Control in Nebraska," *Political Science Quarterly* (1898), XIII.

—— *State Railroad Control — With a History of Its Development in Iowa*, New York, 1896.

Ellis, David Maldwyn, *The Forfeiture of Railroad Land Grants* (MS Thesis), Ithaca, New York, 1939.

Gates, Paul W., "The Railroads of Missouri, 1850–1870," *Missouri Historical Review* (January, 1932), XXVI.

Haney, Lewis H., *A Congressional History of Railroads in the United States, 1850–1887*, Madison, 1908, 1910, 2 vols.

Hargrave, Frank F., *A Pioneer Indiana Railroad: The Origin and Development of the Monon*, Indianapolis, 1932.

Hebard, Alfred, "The Original Survey of the C. B. & Q. RR. Line," *Annals of Iowa* (October, 1903), third series, VI.

Hedges, James B., *Henry Villard and the Railways of the Northwest*, New Haven, 1930.

Hungerford, Edward, *The Story of the Baltimore & Ohio Railroad, 1827–1927*, New York, 1928, 2 vols.

"Iowa and Its Railroads," *New York Tribune*, November 15, 1877, reprinted in *Iowa Journal of History and Politics* (1905), III.

Irwin, Leonard B., *Pacific Railways and Nationalism in the Canadian-American Northwest, 1845–1873*, Philadelphia, 1939.

Jones, Virginia B., *The Influence of the Railroads on Nebraska State Politics* (MS Thesis), Lincoln, 1927.

Larrabee, William, *The Railroad Question*, Chicago, 1893.

Laut, Agnes C., *The Romance of the Rails*, New York, 1929.

MacGill, Caroline, *A History of Transportation in the United States before 1860*, Washington, 1917.

Mattison, Ray Harold, *Burlington Railroad Land Grant and the Tax Controversy in Boone County* (MS Thesis), Lincoln, 1936.

Nevins, F. J., *Seventy Years of Service*, Chicago, 1922.

Newton, A. W., "Aurora Branch Railroad Company: First Depot and Its Successors" (MS, Chicago, 1940).

—— "Chronology of Events Leading up to the Advent of Eastern Capital into the Aurora Branch Railroad. . . ." (MS, Chicago, May, 1939).

—— *Early History of the Chicago, Burlington & Quincy in Illinois*, MS, Chicago, 1939.

Overton, R. C., *The First Ninety Years: An Historical Sketch of the Burlington Railroad, 1850–1940*, Chicago, 1940.

Paxson, Frederick L., "The Pacific Railroads and the Disappearance of the Frontier in America," American Historical Society, *Publications* (1907), I.

Petersen, William J., "The Burlington Comes," *Palimpsest* (November, 1933), XIV.

Poor, Henry V., *Manual of the Railroads of the United States*, New York, 1870–1940.

Putnam, James W., "The Illinois and Michigan Canal: A Study in Economic History," Chicago Historical Society, *Collections* (Chicago, 1918), X.

Railway & Locomotive Historical Society, *Locomotives of the Chicago, Burlington & Quincy Railroad, 1855–1904*, Boston, 1937, pt. 2.

Riegel, Robert E., *The Story of the Western Railroads*, New York, 1926.

Sharp, Mildred J., "The Mississippi and Missouri Railroad," *Palimpsest* (January, 1922), III.

Smalley, Eugene V., *History of the Northern Pacific Railroad*, New York, 1883.

Stevens, Frank Walker, *The Beginnings of the New York Central Railroad*, New York, 1926.

Thompson, Slason, *A Short History of American Railways*, Chicago, 1925.

Transportation Association of America, "A National Transportation Program" (Chicago, 1938), supplement no. 2.

Vernon, Edward, *American Railroad Manual for the United States and the Dominion*, New York, 1873.

Waggener, O. O., *Western Agriculture and the Burlington*, Chicago, 1938.

Wakeley, L. W., *Summary of the Geographical Development of the Chicago, Burlington & Quincy Railroad in the Territory between Lake Michigan and the Rocky Mountains; a Reference to the Character of its Traffic, its Influence and Service as a Transportation System within this Territory and a Comparison of its Gross Earnings as between those of 1854 and those of 1901 and of 1915* (MS Thesis), Lincoln, 1916.

Wilson, Ben Hur, "Burlington Westward," *Palimpsest* (November, 1935), XVI.

—— "From Planks to Rails," *Palimpsest* (November, 1935), XVI.

—— "Planked from Burlington," *Palimpsest* (November, 1935), XVI.

V. MISCELLANEOUS

Aldrich, Charles, "The Repeal of the Granger Law in Iowa," *Iowa Journal of History and Politics* (April, 1905), III.

Anderson, W. A., "The Granger Movement in the Middle West with Special Reference to Iowa," *Iowa Journal of History and Politics* (January, 1924), XXII.

Bercaw, Louise O., and Hennefrund, Helen E., "Farm Tenancy in the United States, 1925–1935; A Beginning of a Bibliography," *Agricultural Economics Bibliography* (Washington, 1935), no. 59.

Bogart, E. L., *Economic History of the United States*, New York, 1922.

—— and Thompson, C. M., *Readings in the Economic History of the United States*, New York, 1929.

Branch, Edward Douglas, *Westward: The Romance of the American Frontier*, New York, 1930.

Briggs, John Ely, "The Grasshopper Plagues in Iowa," *Iowa Journal of History and Politics* (July, 1915), XIII.

Buck, Solon J., *The Agrarian Crusade*, New Haven, 1920.

—— *The Granger Movement*, Cambridge, 1913.

Clark, D. E., *The West in American History*, New York, 1937.

Cole, Arthur C., *The Irrepressible Conflict*, New York, 1934.

Donaldson, Thomas C., *The Public Domain*, Washington, 1884.

Dunn, Arthur W., *An Analysis of the Social Structure of a Western Town*, Chicago, 1896.

Faulkner, Harold Underwood, *American Political and Social History*, New York, 1937.

Fite, Emerson D., *Social and Industrial Conditions in the North during the Civil War*, New York, 1910.

Gates, Paul W., "Land Policy and Tenancy in the Prairie States," *The Journal of Economic History* (May, 1941).

Gras, Norman Scott Brien, *A History of Agriculture in Europe and America*, New York, 1925.

Hacker, Louis M., and Kendrick, Benjamin B., *The United States Since 1865*, New York, 1939.

Hart, A. B., "Disposition of our Public Lands," *Quarterly Journal of Economics* (1887), I.

Hazen, W. B., "The Great Middle Region of the United States and its Limited Space of Arable Lands," *North American Review* (January, 1875), CCXLVI.

Hewes, F. W., and Gannett, Henry, *Scribner's Statistical Atlas for 1880*, New York, 1883.

Hibbard, Benjamin H., *A History of the Public Land Policies*, New York, 1924.

Hockett, Homer C., *Political and Social Growth of the American People, 1492–1852*, New York, 1935.

Kirkland, Edward C., *History of American Economic Life*, New York, 1934, 1939.

Lippincott, Isaac, *Economic Development of the United States*, New York, 1933.

—— and Tucker, H. R., *Economic and Social History of the United States*, New York, 1927.

McMaster, J. B., *History of the People of the United States*, New York, 1883–1913, vols. V, VI.

Messages and Papers of the Presidents, New York, 1897, vol. VI.

Milton, George F., *The Eve of Conflict*, Boston, 1934.

Nevins, Allan, *Emergence of Modern America*, New York, 1927.

Ogg, Frederick Austin, *Economic Development of Modern Europe*, New York, 1920.

Paxson, Frederick L., *History of the American Frontier, 1763–1893*, Boston, 1924.

Quiett, Glenn Chesney, *They Built the West*, New York, 1934.

Riegel, Robert E., *America Moves West*, New York, 1930.

Royce, Charles C., "Indian Land Cessions in the United States," *Eighteenth Annual Report of the Bureau of American Ethnology* (Washington, 1899).

Sanborn, John Bell, *Congressional Grants of Land in Aid of Railways*, Madison, 1899.

Schlesinger, Arthur Meier, *Political and Social Growth of the United States, 1852–1933*, New York, 1935.

—— *The Rise of the City, 1878–1898*, New York, 1933.

Sheldon, Addison E., "Land Systems and Land Policies in Nebraska," Nebraska State Historical Society, *Publications* (1936), XXII.

Smith, Theodore Clarke, *Parties and Slavery*, New York, 1906.

Stephenson, George M., *The Political History of the Public Lands*, Boston, 1917.

Stevens, W. E., *The Northwest Fur Trade, 1763–1800*, University of Illinois, 1928.

Turner, Frederick J., *The Frontier in American History*, New York, 1910.

Wertenbaker, T. J., *Virginia Under the Stuarts*, Princeton, 1914.

INDEX

INDEX